Listed below is the name of God, as He is known in 46 languages

Anglo-Saxon	God	Hebrem	
Arabic	Allah	(Eleah)	Jehovah
Armenian	Teuti	Hindustani	Khuda
Assyrian	Eleah	Hindi	Brahma
Chaldaic	Eiliah	Icelandic	Gud
Chinese	Prussa	Italian	Dio
Creatan	Thios	Japanese	Goezer
Danish	Gud	Lapp	Jubinal
Dorian	Ilos	Latin	Deus
Dutch	God	Lithuanian	Diewas
Egyptian		Low Latin	Diex
(old)	Teut	Mahrati	Deva
English	God	Malay	Alla
Erse (Irish)	Dia	Egyptian	Teun
Finnish	Jumala	Norwegian	Gud
Flemish	God	Old Norse	Tiwar
French	Dieu	Persian	Khoda
Gaelic	Diu	Polish	Bog
German	Gott	Portuguese	Deos
German (old)	Diet	Punjabi	Deva
German (high)	Got	Sanskirt	Deva
Gothic	Guth	Spanish	Dios
Greek	Theos	Swedish	Gud
		Tatar	Magatai
		Turkish	Allah

The word GOD is said to be derived from the initials of the three Hebrew words Gomer, Oz and Dabar, meaning Beauty, Strength and Wisdom, as follows:

Gomer—Beauty

Oz—Strength

Dabar—Wisdom

The letters of the Greek alphabet corresponding to our letters G. O . D. are Gamma, Omicron and Delta, which are ALL perfect Masonic symbols. The "G" or Gamma is a Square, a Right Angle symbolizing Justice and Mercy. The "O" or Omicron is a circle, symbolizing the Infinity of God. It has no beginning or ending, while the "D" or Delta is an equilateral triangle symbolizing the Wisdom, Power and Harmony of God.

THE HEBREW IMPACT ON
WESTERN CIVILIZATION

THE HEBREW IMPACT ON WESTERN CIVILIZATION

Edited by DAGOBERT D. RUNES

PHILOSOPHICAL LIBRARY
New York

Printed in the United States of America

To the sainted memory of the six million children of Israel who were put to the axe by the German nation because they were of the same blood as Jesus Christ.

Preface

THE HEBREW IMPACT ON WESTERN CIVILIZATION

THIS BOOK is a book of propaganda. It has the mission to bring intelligence about the work and the life of the Hebrews pro paganis. The pagans for whom this volume is intended are the many, many people in whose midst the Hebrews have lived for thousands of years. The Jews had to learn the ways of their harborers in order to live, but seldom did the princes and the people of the West give more than a passing glance to their strange Asiatic guests.

For almost eighteen hundred years—with few and brief exceptions—the Jews of the Western World were confined in high walled corrals, the gates to which were rarely opened and then only by the kings, knights and crusaders who combined the infernal spectacle of slaughtered, defenseless Jewish men and women with their instinct for robbery, together with a remarkably recurrent Christian theology of vengeance on the descendants of those who allegedly had executed the son of God.

During these many hundreds of years of their ghetto life, the mind of Israel and the art of Israel and the courage of Israel were pining away in a captive's existence, chained to frustration by intolerant and bigoted nations. The Great Show of the world was closed to them. On rare occasions only was it possible for some—and few—to break out and to storm into the whirl of events.

Then, two hundred years ago, there rose the American rebellion against a king and his disciples, and the jubilant Dare, so vehemently sparked in America, flamed up in France and from there spread over most of the Western World. The same spirit that drove tyranny from American soil and corruption from France, the same spirit smashed the ghetto walls of Europe and set the Jew free.

THE HEBREW IMPACT ON WESTERN CIVILIZATION

It is actually with the American and French revolutions that the real life and influence of the Israelites in the Western World begins.

If what the Jews have done for Europe and America in these few hundred years appears gigantic, the statement of it here is no exaggeration, as the scholar can quickly discover, and it is not overstressed, I am sure, by any of the contributors, of whom some are Jews and some are not. It is rather related purposefully so that those who disapprove of an act or person of a Jew may balance such acts and persons against the magnitude of Jewish Drama on the other scale.

It is with the Christians among whom Jews reside as it is with the human heart: they are rarely aware of the Jew unless he hurts them. His silent and constant work for their welfare—one would almost think it doesn't exist.

And still, their every church is a monument to the Jew Jeshu ben Joseph and his Apostles:—Saul, whom they named Paul; and Shimon, whom they named Peter; and Levi, whom they named Matthew; and so on. It is true—if it is—that many of those who knew Jeshu (whom we call, after the Greek, Jesus), did not take him for the Messiah (in Greek: Christos) but many of them did, and they all, as well as Miriam (Mary), (and her sons whom she bore after Jeshu) were Jews. The whole ancient church of Christendom is Jewish in origin, Jewish in concept (Messiah) and Jewish in followship; and if there were many who wished his death, there were many who wished his life to be unending.

When Christianity made its great reforms in the 16th and 17th centuries, it opened the pages of the Old Testament and drank from the Hebrew fountain of wisdom. The Hebrew testament was the light and the guide by which not only the Puritans but also the other great armies of pioneers and settlers worked, lived and governed. In the later years our greatest statesmen and reformers, men like Thomas Jefferson, Benjamin Rush, Abraham Lincoln,—they held the Hebrew Testament to be the Truth forever.

THE HEBREW IMPACT ON WESTERN CIVILIZATION

The Western World has pulled some sordid jokes on the Jew. For almost two thousand years they stopped him from owning land, and then they accused him of refusing to work it; they stopped him from bearing arms, and then they called him a coward; they kept him from their schools and laughed at his ignorance; they kept him from public office and the right to vote, and then they called him subversive and disloyal; they stopped him from engaging in anything but small trade, and then they referred to him sneeringly as an unmitigated tradesman; and some of the grand lords in the manors of the Medieval Ages used the Jews to administer their loan business, and then they called them usurers.

This book will show to those who wish to learn that the Jew is a diligent farmer, an heroic soldier, a loyal servant of his people and an ardent scholar.

Many of the facts quoted in this book may startle even the well-read. How many people know, for instance, that half of the German Nobel Prize winners were men of Jewish descent? Six hundred thousand Jews of pre-war Germany produced as many Nobel Prize winners as sixty million Germans, the *Herrenvolk* that showed its gratitude to the men who so tremendously helped in their growth by massacring the Jewish people of Europe. Six million souls in six years! A million Jews a year were hunted down by German nationals in every corner of Europe, dragged to the executioners, choked to death in sealed trains or gassed in torture chambers and burned in huge bread ovens. This is how one Christian nation repaid its debt to the people of Israel. And of the millions of the Teutonic malefactors, the axemen as well as their millions of helpers and their multi-millions of Jew-denouncers and Hitler-heilers, all but an ugly few are alive and kicking the same bloody boots in goose-step.

Perhaps it would be better to forget the Hitler monstrosities. The Western World is somewhat embarrassed about its indifference towards Teutonic inhumanity. Perhaps we Jews would like to forget too. Forget the joyful victory marches in every town and hamlet of Germany when their last Jew was safely squeezed into the awaiting freight car, to die of asphyxiation with the other hundred members of his tribe, men, women and infants, living for minutes and minutes without a breath of air, body after body collapsing, so closely packed that the dead would hang against the shoulders and backs of those still living, and at the point of destination, hours away, the whole sordid mess of human cadavers would be shovelled into huge stoves by their German tormentors.

We would like to forget those things. We would like to forget the cultured German officers who so carefully lined up three children in a row that they might kill them with one bullet instead of three . . . we would like to forget the German scientists who vivisected our mothers and sisters and daughters in cannibalistic fashion . . . we would like to forget the group of German scholars that succeeded in making soap out of Jewish body fat, and later sold it to the Jews at exorbitant prices, for burial purposes. . . . We would like to forget those things, but the Germans don't forget. They haven't forgotten the glory and the strut of their Jew-killing heydays, even though they go to church on Sundays, and to the Salzburg festivals and the Passion play in Oberammergau. And though by all candid reportage they may have some doubts as to Hitler's political craftsmanship, there is no doubt today in their black hearts, after all has been shown and told, that they enjoyed this spirit of Jew-killing and regret nothing more than that it stopped.

And the Christian nations of the Western World speak to these Teutons as if they were humans! Some even join them in their festivals and their cultural activities, which are typical German intermezzos between wars and assassinations. . . .

Perhaps the world needs to know more about the Jews.

Perhaps they ought to know that were it not for Jewish discoverers in medicine, millions of their children and people

[x]

might have perished. Perhaps this book will help to show that in these two thousand years of unwanted neighborness the Jew has contributed a goodly share for the betterment of this, our society, for which thanks were few on the record, and humiliations many.

This book will show only some of the Jewish contributions to Western culture. Space did not permit its dwelling upon many other aspects which must be left missing from this volume. But there is enough, I feel, to demonstrate our case— that the Jews have done their share and more than their share in building the culture of the West. They have given of their heritage a full measure, and given it diligently—to science and literature, statesmanship and art. How the Christian world has repaid them—I leave that evaluation to the reader. I hope my contributors have succeeded in showing the Hebrews to the Western World in their true light, in their deeds. And by their deeds you shall judge them.

D. D. R.

Table of Contents

THE HEBREW IMPACT ON WESTERN CIVILIZATION

Contributors

L. L. BERNARD
Professor of Sociology, Pennsylvania State College.

HUGO BIEBER
Author of The Struggle for Tradition.

VERGILIUS FERM
Editor, Encyclopedia of Religion.

SOLOMON R. KAGAN
Author of Jewish Contribution to Medicine in America.

MAURICE J. KARPF
Formerly Director, Jewish School of Social Work.

ABRAHAM I. KATSH
Professor of Education, New York University.

RUDOLF KAYSER
Member of Faculty, Hunter College, New York.

KURT F. LEIDECKER
Professor of Philosophy, Mary Washington College of the University of Virginia.

CURTIS LUBINSKI
Distinguished author and theatre critic.

PAUL NETTL
Professor of Musicology, Indiana University.

A. A. ROBACK
Author of Jewish Influence in Modern Thought.

CECIL ROTH
Eminent Historian and Biographer.

KARL SCHWARZ
Formerly Director, Museum of Fine Arts, Tel Aviv.

WALTER SORELL
Distinguished playwright and essayist.

RICHARD VAN DYCK
Author and journalist.

MARTIN L. WOLF
Co-author, Encyclopedia of Criminology.

WILLIAM B. ZIFF
Special Consultant to the Economic Warfare Division of the U. S. Department of Justice during World War II; author of The Coming Battle of Germany.

Contributors

I. L. BERNARD
    Professor of Sociology, Pennsylvania State College

HUGO BIEBER
    Author, *The Struggle for Freedom*

VENIAMIN TEGAL
    Editor, *Encyclopedia of Religion*

SOLOMON R. KAGAN
    Author of *Jewish Contribution to Medicine in America*

MAURICE J. KARPF
    Formerly Director, Jewish School of Social Work

ABRAHAM E. KATSH
    Professor of Education, New York University

RUDOLF KAYSER
    Member of Faculty, Hunter College, New York

KURT F. LEIDECKER
    Professor of Philosophy, Mary Washington College of the University of Virginia

CURTIS LORENSKI
    Distinguished author and theatre critic

PAUL NITZE
    Professor of Philosophy, Indiana University

A. A. ROMER
    Author of *Jewish Influence in Modern Thought*

CECIL ROTH
    Eminent historian and biographer

KARL SCHWARZ
    Formerly Director, Museum of Fine Arts, Tel Aviv

WALTER SORRELL
    Dramatist, biographer and essayist

RICHARD VAN DYCK
    Author and journalist

MARTIN L. WOLF
    Compiler, *Encyclopedia of Criminology*

WILLIAM R. ZIFF
    Special contributor to the *Encyclopaedia Britannica*; Author of *The U. S. Aggressor*, *Two Worlds*, *The Gentlemen Talk of Peace*, and *The Rape of Palestine*; in World War II, editor of *The Coming Battle of Germany*

Hebraic Foundations of American Democracy

By ABRAHAM I. KATSH

Introduction

EVEN a most cursory study of early American life reveals the vast influence on it of the Scriptures and the Hebrew language. The New World as an extension of the Old absorbed much from its cultural roots. The importance of the Bible in day-to-day living in Europe was transferred with appropriate changes to the new soil. The earliest settlers were men who carried their Bibles both in their hearts and hands.

The Scriptures which have come down to us today in Hebrew have importance in half a dozen fields. Their historical significance is too obvious to need expansion here. The far-reaching effect of Biblical law and lore is sometimes amazing. Consider for instance, the number of uses to which the Ten Commandments have been put. Much in many Occidental and Near Eastern philosophies stems from the Bible. Whole non-Jewish theologies of today derive their authenticity from, and have their roots in the Old Testament.

The influence of the Scriptures on literature is all-embracing. Writers in all ages and in all places have drawn on it both as a source of material and as a model for style. The simplicity, brevity, and clarity of the Old Testament in the original Hebrew is a monument to the men who compiled it. Consider for a moment the question of vocabulary. Shakespeare, thought by many to be the finest poet of the English language, employed approximately 20,000 different words. Milton to realize his epics required 10,000. But the vast panorama of Biblical thought and emotion is conveyed in little more than 6,000!

Unfortunately, this point gives rise to one of the prime difficulties in dealing with the Scriptures. The style and flavor of biblical language is, in essence, untranslatable. Indeed one might go so far as to say that in another language some phrases are virtually unintelligible. What meaning has this quotation to the reader who has no knowledge of Hebrew as we find it in the English translation? "And thou shalt call me Ishi, and shalt call me no more Baali." (Hosea ii, 16)

Time, repeated translations from one language to another, actual misinterpretation of words, misunderstandings, all have played their part in contributing to the confusion. For example: The first part of verse two in the Song of Deborah (Jud. 5, 2), has been rendered by many scholars in the following ways: ". . . when men let grow their hair in Israel,"[1] "Because the leaders took the lead in Israel."[2] "When the people willingly offered themselves."[3] There is little standardization of meaning here; little agreement on the actual equivalents for the Hebrew words.

Numerous other examples can be cited. The same English word "ark" is used to denote the craft in which Noah sailed-out the flood and the receptacle that held the Five Books of Moses. The terms are wholly different in Hebrew. The phrase "voice of the turtle" has in recent years become increasingly popular. Much of the bewilderment that arises from the anomaly of the voice of a mute animal could have been forestalled had the phrase been rendered "voice of the turtle-dove," a more accurate reading of the Hebrew. Moses is often depicted with horns, notably in Michelangelo's masterpiece, because the Hebrew word, *qrn*, used to describe Moses can be translated either "ray of light" or "horn." The ancient writer was obviously pointing out a ray of light about the great leader's head, not a horn.

W. L. Roy wrote "The Bible can never be understood, unless through the medium of the language in which it was originally written, and the spirit by which it was dictated . . . Hebrew is so pregnant and rich in sense that no translation can do it justice."[4] Careful examination of what has been done to scriptural text in translation bears this out.

The value of Hebrew to Christian and Jewish scholars alike has been well documented. Luther, in speaking of the 45th psalm, said: "I am acquainted with a sufficiency of Hebrew to be able to combat all my enemies, the knowledge of which, though small, I prize above millions of gold." Roger Bacon, always an advocate of precise and pure thought, on more than one occasion expressed his zeal for the language. With extraordinary acumen for his times he felt that all translations of the Bible had become hopelessly corrupt. The Puritans and the Quakers to whom we owe so much that is basic to our concept of democracy both highly cherished the Old Testament and Hebrew as a language. For the inspiration and buttressing of their religious and political views they drew freely on this great source.

Throughout all the history of the United States the story has been much the same. Time and time again men have returned to the spirit of the Hebrews. Much of the contribution of England to the colonies was in terms of this spirit. Indeed, in the Occident at any rate, wherever men read they are almost certain to be touched in some degree by it. To vivify this the writer in the coming pages presents in some measure the contributions of the Hebraic spirit to the English-speaking peoples as a whole and to America in particular. For convenience this study has been divided into the following subdivisions: (a) The Influence of the Bible, (b) Early Popularity of the Hebrew Language, (c) Influence of the Judaic Spirit, (d) Legislation, (e) Polity, and (f) The Literature of England and America.

Both the language and the message of the Bible are very much alive even today. Both—one through the other—are equally potential as forces that may well help to restore some order to our age of chaos. And perhaps, as never before in world history, has there been such a need for order.

FOOTNOTES

1 *Holy Scriptures*, Jewish Publication Society.

2 J. A. Bewer, *The Literature of the Old Testament in its Historical Development*.

3 E. S. Bates, *The Bible as Literature*.

4 W. L. Roy, *A Complete Hebrew and English Dictionary*, pages 736-7.

A.—THE INFLUENCE OF THE BIBLE

ALTHOUGH the influence of Jewish culture on Western civilization is generally recognized by scholars, the majority of people are unaware of any such contributions. Of course, this influence was not wholly one-sided. As the Jews exerted considerable influence on non-Jewish elements, so they too were influenced by others.

In the modern world the most exemplary link between Judaism and Western civilization is the Bible. Specifically the Jews were concerned with the Old Testament; the Histories, Laws and Psalms, the words of the Prophets, all of which they created out of their own experiences.[1] In its pages are found the whole duty of man, the constant outcry of the prophets for peace, the elevation of man to the height of his potentialities.

Despite our current emphasis on science and our ability to "disprove" certain bald statements in the Bible, its precepts remain as valid today as they have ever been. Matthew Arnold, the classic minded author of *Dover Beach,* in speaking of this point said; "To the Bible men will return; and why? Because they cannot do without it. Because happiness is our being's end and aim, and happiness belongs to the righteous, and righteousness is revealed in the Bible."[2] Philo is quoted as saying that: "The laws of Greek legislators are continually subject to change; the laws of Moses alone remain steady, unmoved, unshaken, stamped as it were with the seal of nature herself, from the day when they were written to the present day, and will so remain for all time as long as the world endures. Not only the Jews but all other people who care for righteousness adopt them . . . Let all men follow this code and the age of universal peace will come about, the kingdom of God on earth will be established."[3]

The Bible has been put to every conceivable use. It has been translated with varying success (but always with remarkable devotion) into upward of one thousand languages. One can readily go along with Norman Bentwich when he says: "The Bible is the one book which appears to have the capacity of eternal self-adjustment."[4] It can not be regarded merely as the dead record of an ancient people. Rather should we think of it as a living literary possession of the modern world. Time and time again the moral feelings of men have been deepened, strengthened, and one might go so far as to say even created by the Hebrew prophets. Into this account of the welding of a relatively weak federation of tribes into a homogeneous and dynamic entity is the whole story of the fashioning of man from his feeble beginnings to vast civilizations. Here are the materials with which man toughened the fibre of his character, emancipated himself from the bondage of idolatry and nothingness to moral triumph and spiritual excellence.

Despite the almost constant ill-treatment suffered by the Jews in most of their contacts, their culture left permanent marks wherever it touched. Beginning with their initial exilic period, the original Babylonian captivity, when they were for the first time forcibly exposed to undesirable influences, through the period of the early Samaritans, Ethiopian Africa, Babylonian and Persian Asia and down to their wanderings in Christian and Moslem Europe, the Old Testament has been carried by the Jews. Their conception of morality, godliness, and ethics left its mark quietly but firmly. As they moved they carried their particular usage of the Scriptures with them and so not only transplanted it to ever new and fertile soil, but also strengthened their own ideas about monotheism, morality, and ethics.

During the Dark Ages, when all cultures slept, the Jews by nature and instinct observant and restless, kept alive what little knowledge was vouchsafed to them and constantly expanded theirs. The era abounds in names that would do honor to any people; Gabirol, Halevi, Maimonides, Rabbi Gershom, Eldad the Danite, and the inveterate traveler, Benjamin of Tudela, to name but a few. But this is not the place to treat the accomplishments of individual men no matter how worthy they might have been. How can one summarize the importance and consequences of the work of men like Saadia Gaon, Jona Marinus or Abraham Ibn Ezra. Utilizing their brilliant command of languages, they laid the foundation for much of the subsequent Biblical criticism that has been so important a part of the work of Christian scholars.

Indeed, during all of the Middle Ages, Hebrew scholarship flourished among enlightened Latin Christians. As early as the thirteenth century disputations between Hebrew and Christian scholars arose concerning the exact meanings of the Hebrew text of the Old Testament. The result of the first great public hearing was what has been called "a vast bonfire of Hebrew books,"[5] a phenomenon not unknown in more recent times.

But to others, Hebrew writings and Hebrew as a language was something to be treated with respect and diligence. Robert Grosseteste, bishop of Lincoln and teacher of Roger Bacon, was a pioneer in this field. Bacon himself repeatedly stated that a knowledge of Hebrew was necessary for proper comprehension of science, theology, and philosophy. Bacon went so far in this belief to work on a Hebrew grammar. He was a Franciscan friar and so characteristic was his attitude of the order as a whole that "when in a thirteenth or fourteenth century manuscript we find any evidence of Hebrew knowledge we may suspect a Franciscan origin."[6]

There was considerable activity during the Middle Ages in the translation of the Bible from Hebrew into other languages. Several attempts were made from Hebrew to Latin; one of them a rare example of interlinear technique. Some fragments have been found of an Italian version based on the

Hebrew. But by far the most interesting are those in Castilian. A number of people—all of them Christian—worked on them. One such example had an interesting history. "When the Jews were expelled from Spain at the end of the fifteenth century they took with them to the Eastern Mediterranean the language of the country of their birth . . . These people needed a Bible and it was first printed for them in Ferrara in 1553."[7]

The transition out of the Dark Ages was in great part due to the scholarship of the Moorish Arabs, "and they were solely indebted to the Jews who interpreted Greek literature to them."[8] The work, the debt, the perseverance was extraordinary. Schleiden sums it up as follows: ". . . we find that during the intellectually dark and slothful Middle Ages, the Jews were the preservers of agriculture, of all large industries, the cultivation of silk, dyeing and weaving works. It was they who carried on an international trade which was and ever will be necessary for the well-being of all nations. (They) left no branch of science or learning untouched, ever searching and developing, and at the end of the Middle Ages handing over the results of their long and arduous labors to the nations who were only then commencing to wake up."[9]

As world attitude changed, the Jews were treated accordingly. As the Middle Ages gave way to the Renaissance, they were able to assume a new position in the emerging world with little effort. The Age of Enlightenment still found them adhering to the old truths. Industrialization affected them as a people almost not at all. Great individuals rose from their ranks as they always had in the past. Now we have emerged into the Atomic Age, and here, too, is valid the basic contribution of the Jews to civilization. As man has pushed back the horizons of learning, he has sought to apply the principles which for over 2000 years have guided him.

Expression and explanation of this opinion is found in every literature but in none more profoundly than the English.

Were one to eliminate from English literature whatever it owes to the Bible and Hebraic writings, the remainder would be "barely recognizable."[10] The extent and influence of English literature is almost inestimable. It is the direct expression of a people that have spread out from their small island to every corner of the world carrying their particular institutions and beliefs. Where the English have gone they have taken their literature. As a result ". . . could the Bible be erased from the consciousness of those peoples, it would forfeit wellnigh half of its influence over the world."[11]

But the English language has been repaid for this service ". . . by an elevation, a picturesqueness, and an affluence of beautiful sentiments which confers . . . a great advantage over those which, whether from national incompatibility, or the impediments created by sinister interests have been more or less debarred from this treasury of grandeur."[12]

All modern literatures have borrowed unsparingly from the Scriptures and subsequent Hebrew literature and commentaries. But in the case of English literature there has been so thorough an assimilation that the Hebrew Patriarchs and Prophets often seem to have been rendered into people born on English soil.

Let us begin to narrow down the scope of our observations to matters of more immediate concern to the subject at hand, the Puritans. These stern and devoted self-styled saints had a great deal to do with the establishment of much that can be called "typically American." What influenced them, therefore, can be said to have influenced America. Prime among their source books was the Old Testament. Living as they did in the wilderness, the Puritans found there not only history and morality but also a far-reaching theology. To them, the Book was not a mere narrative of days gone by but a Scripture-in-life, meeting their daily needs and aspirations.

Think what we will about their narrowness and bigotry, there is probably nothing more valuable, memorable, weighty or even commendable about the Puritans than their religion and in that they were almost solely influenced by the Old Testament. "The whole Old Testament is vital and commanding with examples of the Puritan spirit. . . . They with their more virile temper, their experience of hardship, and their secluded homes in the wilderness, saw in the ancient Testament not history only, theology, or praise, but the glory of man reflecting and celebrating the glory of God. It was a Scripture in life which smote and stirred their strong emotion. Not merely as to Deborah under the palm-tree, or to Ezekiel by the river of Chebar, was the majesty of the Eternal manifest to them. The whole Hebrew economy bore its radiance, and declared its effect; an economy stern, sublime, working for freedom because binding to God; training men to be careless of the world with its lusts, that they might be champions for the kingdom unseen. This was the lambent cloud of glory which filled all Puritan temples when the ancient Scriptures were opened within them."[13]

The Puritans found the whole of their religion in the Bible. Ecclesiastical rules and traditions played only a minor part. (This last can be used in direct refutation of the generally accepted idea that the Puritans established a theocracy.) A chief guide for the actions was the Old Testament. To them it contained ". . . the only and the perfect Rule of Faith."[14] It is interesting in this connection to quote the following: "God declares it to be a sinne for the godly to leave the worship of God for the wickednesse of those that come unto it. We know that the sinne of the sonnes of Ely was so great, that men abhorred the offerings of the Lord: but in so doing it is said, that the Lord's people did transgresse, even unto a cry. Surely, this truth will not easily bee outfaced; yet some of them to avoid it say, that no marvell if morall wickednesse did not pollute the Jewish worship, because God required only ceremoniall cleannesse then. But how false this is, appears by God's Covenant with *Abraham* where God requires *Sincerity;* by the morall law which was God's *covenant:* by God's requiring then, truth in the *inward part;* by his injoyning sacrifices for morall transgressions as well as ceremoniall: by his signifying of pollution by morall uncleanesses: and by threatening of morall sinnes, and *abhorring all ceremoniall* service when men sinned morally against God."[15]

The idea of covenant between God and man warrants investigation for a moment. This subtle agreement capable of so many and such diverse interpretation is first mentioned in Genesis. There are numerous other references. The Puritans time and time again drew on it, referred to it, worked it into their dealings both religious and secular. The first major Pilgrim document, the so-called Mayflower Compact, employs the word. "We whose names are underwritten . . . having undertaken . . . a voyage to plant ye first colonie in ye Northerne parts of Virginia, doe by these presents solemnly & mutually in ye presence of God, and one of another, covenant & combine our selves together into a civill body politick . . ."[16]

They felt that their Church was in actuality a continuation of the covenant between God and the Jews. This theme was hammered out from every pulpit. John Stevens in a church in New Marlborough, Massachusetts, said: *"The Christian Church* so called, *is only a continuation and extension of the Jewish church."*[17] With unconscious and unexpected humor William Brattle drove this home with: "The covenant of grace is the very same now that it was under the Mosaical dispensation. The administration differs but the covenant is the same."

The Puritans built up a body of law about the covenant, interpreted previously existing laws in terms of it, and derived a great deal of their power from it. As Thomas Jefferson Wertenbaker says: "But whatever its origins the covenant gave to each congregation an independence which would have been impossible had it been constituted by any superior human authority. It made of it, in the words of Ames and Cotton and other Puritan leaders, a Church responsible not to bishops or assemblies or kings, but to God Himself."[18]

This idea certainly stemmed from a very palpable relationship with the Old Testament. It should not be assumed from this, however, that the Puritans were the only sect to find refuge in the New World who drew inspiration from the doctrine of the covenant. The dour and hard-hitting Scotch Presbyterians who came in such large numbers between 1730 and 1770, settling in the upland areas some hundred miles inland from the coastal developments, held firmly to their own ideas about the meaning of the covenant. Theirs was an austere life following the principle of John Knox. To them the Bible was law. "They were brought up on the Old Testament, and in the doctrine of government by covenant."[19]

Morality, not ceremony, was the vital teaching here. The accent was always placed on moral conduct rather than on ritual alone. "Three-fourths of human life are conduct. Hebrew Scriptures deal pre-eminently with conduct. Their influence, at any rate on the English-speaking portion of our Western civilization, is three times as important as the influence of the Greeks."[20] It would appear from this that one might say that the civilization of Great Britain was influenced by Hebrew Scriptures and by Greek philosophy at a proportion of three to one respectively. John Cowper Powys feels that the Bible is to us what Homer was to the Greeks; that the words of the Bible have become a magic touch that ". . . throws across the passing details of each individual life the undying beauty of the life of humanity."[21]

It would be easily possible to trace Hebraic influences in the life of the Puritans before they came to these shores. One brief instance will suffice. When Scrooby Congregation left Leyden in Holland for a new land they fasted. "It then became necessary to decide who should go, that such might prepare themselves. 'They had . . . a sollemne meeting and a day of humiliation to seeke ye Lords for his direction: and their pastor tooke his texte, I Sam. XXIII: 3, 4. "And David's men said unto him, see we . . . etc." From which texte he taught many things aptly, and befitting the present occasion and condition, strengthening them against their fears and perplexities, and incouraging them in their resolution.' "[22]

Once in America such procedure was retained. "In the beginning of 1620 they kept a solemn day of prayer, when Mr. Robinson delivered a discourse from I Sam. XXIII: 3, 4 in which he endeavored to remove their doubts, and confirm their resolution."[23] Even as late as 1744 Massachusetts held a day of fasting and prayer when England passed the Intolerance Acts. We find that President Adams called a day of fasting during the Napoleonic Wars. The link with the Old Testament-inspired preparation in Holland was direct and evident.

Time after time the Puritans outrightly identified themselves with the Israelites as they toiled and wandered in the wilderness. Consider this brief poem from a life of Roger Williams.

> "Like Israel's host, to exile driven,
> Across the floods the Pilgrim fled;
> Their hands bore up the ark of Heaven,
> And Heaven their trusting footsteps led,
> Till on these savage shores they trod,
> And won the wilderness for God."[24]

When the Pilgrims reached America, a bitterly persecuted people, they drew sharp parallels between themselves and the Jews. They drew constantly on the Bible and their own experience to renew the similarities. Its philosophy soon came to permeate their very beings. Like Israel of old, the Pilgrims were able to regard themselves as the elect of God and throughout the Revolutionary War visualized themselves as fighting against their enemies who were to them Philistines or Amalekites.

Not unlike the recitation by the Jews of the Haggadah on Passover night, they too recited: "Ought not, and may not the children of these fathers rightly say, our fathers were Englishmen, which came over this great ocean, and were ready to perish in this wilderness; but they cried unto the Lord; and he heard their voice, and looked on their adversity; Let them therefore praise the Lord, because he is good and his mercy endureth for ever; yea, let them who have been the redeemed of the Lord, shew how he hath delivered them from the hand of the oppressor, when they wandered in the desert wilderness out of the way, and found no city to dwell in; both hungry and thirsty, their soul was overwhelmed in them. Let them there confess before the Lord his loving kindness, and his wonderful works before the children of men."[25]

It was from the days of the Puritans that the Psalms rooted themselves permanently in the affection of most English-speaking people. They considered the Psalms which they sang while going into battle, as the deepest expression of their noblest ideals, a source of encouragement and inspiration. They used them constantly in a literal translation in public worship. When Isaac Watts' version of the Psalms reached the Colonies they were at once widespread hearings. This was doubtless due to the affection in which their originals were held. "The introduction of these Psalms . . . provoked considerable controversy, but they were soon in general use everywhere."[26]

The first book printed in America was the *Bay Psalm Book*. Its title page reads: "THE WHOLE BOOKE OF PSALMES Faithfully TRANSLATED into ENGLISH Metre. Whereunto is prefixed a discourse declaring not only the lawfulness, but also the necessity of the heavenly Ordinance of singing Scripture Psalmes in the Churches of God. . . . Imprinted 1640."[27]

How closely the Puritans identified themselves with the Israelites is hard to over-emphasize. This identification becomes manifest when we realize that they actually thought of themselves as a new Israel, fighting in a land of wickedness and paganism to exterminate those who were on the side of Satan. The Puritans' lot became the lot of Israel. If Egypt had been to Israel a "land of bondage," so was England to the Puritans. Like the Israelites they commemorated, in the Scriptural text, their plight. On the title page of the first edition of

"New England's Memorial" appears the biblical text: ". . . and thou shalt remember all the way which the Lord thy God led thee this forty years in the wilderness."[28]

In searching the Scriptures for a text relevant to their own particular needs the Puritans soon discovered the general similarity between themselves and the ancient Israelites. They firmly believed that the Hebrew prophets spoke to them as directly as they had spoken to the Hebrews. The life of the Israelites as related in the Bible served as a mirror, according to the ministers of the time, in which they could see reflected their own activities. "From the beginning of the enterprise the leaders were conscious of a similarity between New England and the Jews: 'Let *Israel* be the evidence of the *Doctrine,* and our glass to view our Faces in', said the ministers, while the irreverent Peter Folger threw the idea into satirical verse,

New-England they are like the Jews,
As like, as like can be."[29]

Not only was it possible to draw parallels between narrative actualities but in fundamental doctrine the Puritans returned to the Israelites. In this they differed most sharply from the majority of the older Christian theologies. To the Puritans the outstanding moral of the Old Testament was that a nation as well as an individual could be in covenant with God, and therefore a nation could be constrained by its own assent to obey the laws of God. "If wee keep this covenant," Winthrop assured his people, "wee shall finde that the God of Israell is among us, but if wee deal falsely with our God . . . wee be consumed out of the good land wither wee are goeing."[30]

The Bible was in all instances and for all occasions the ultimate source of knowledge and precedent. They believed in it utterly and with a kind of rigorous literal-mindedness. They regarded it only in terms of the unchangeable. "That the Bible is the inspired word of God rested for the Puritans upon absolute conviction."[31] It was the measure for everything. This Miller and Johnson have sharply summarized in these typical words: "When both sides agree that these are the words of God, and the question of faith is concerning the meaning of the words, nothing is an article of faith, or a part of religion, but can be proved by reason to be the sense and intention of God. Reason is never to be pretended against the clear sense of scripture, because by reason it is that we came to preceive that to be the clear sense of the Scripture . . . We do not test the Bible by nature, but nature by the Bible."[32]

Failure to abide by the strict interpretation of the Old Testament was punishable with whipping. "If any 'Christian, so called,' spoke contemptuously of the Scripture, or of the holy penmen thereof, they were to be punished by fine or whipping. Laws were also passed punishing those who violated the Sabbath. . . . One of the most prominent traits was a conscientious adherence to what they believed were the teachings of the Sacred Scriptures. To them the authority of God was most supreme. Believing as they did that the Bible was his revealed will, they made that their exclusive guide in matters of faith and practice. Creeds, characters and customs were all tried by this unfailing test, and all was rejected which, in their opinion, did not stand this ordeal. Laws and regulations adopted by them, which, at the present day, are stigmatized as singularities, were, in many instances, the legitimate fruits of their strict adherence to the teaching of the Bible."[33]

If Israel had its Pharaoh, so had the Puritans one in the person of King James I. The Atlantic Ocean was to them the Red Sea. America was the new Canaan and Washington and Adams, their Moses and Joshua.

These analogies should not in any way seem strange coming from a people who so constantly drew the Old Testament into their lives. This reference to politics in no way equals in intensity the official acts of the colony of Connecticut. "The Mosaic Law was adopted in the Connecticut Code of 1650; while half the statutes in the Code of 1655 for the colony of New Haven contain references to the Old Testament, and only three percent to the New."[34]

Comparisons with Moses and Joshua for Puritan leaders were very common. For example, in Cotton Mather's *Magnalia Christi Americana* we find the following paragraph in regard to John Winthrop of the Massachusetts colony: "Accordingly when the *noble design* of carrying a colony of *chosen people* into an *American* wilderness, was by *some* eminent persons undertaken, *this* eminent person was, by the consent of all, *chosen* for the *Moses,* who must be the leader of so great an undertaking; and indeed nothing but a Mosaic spirit could have carried him through the *temptations* to which either his *farewell* to his *own land,* or his *travel* in a *strange land,* must needs expose a gentleman of his education."[35]

In Davis' book is recorded the saying on the tomb of John Cotton:

"But let his mourning flock be comforted,
Though Moses be, yet Joshua is not dead;
I mean renowned Norton; worthy he
Successor to our Moses is to be,
O happy Israel in America,
In such a Moses, such a Joshua."[36]

John Norton was herein called a Joshua and, in his turn, when Norton died, an elegy was written by Thomas Shepard:

". . . Oh that mine eyes a fountain were of tears!
I'd day and night in mourning spend my years.
My father! father! Israel's chariots thou,
And horseman wert! Sons of the prophets now."[37]

William Bradford too was often called Joshua. When after his death, Thomas Prince was chosen governor of New Plymouth, it was said of him: "At such a time and when the condition of this colony was such as hath been declared, God was pleased to mind it, even in its low estate, and when he had taken unto himself not only our Moses, but many of the elders and worthies of our Israel, he hath not hitherto left us without a Joshua, to lead us in the remaining of our Pilgrimage."[38]

In the use of invective the Puritans frequently employed Biblical expressions and allusions. The famed heretic, Anne Hutchinson, was to them a "Wretched Jezebel." A coachman driving recklessly was often called "Jehu." While they uttered with contempt the names of the unpraiseworthy characters of the Old Testament, they cherished the names of those they exalted and perpetuated them by naming their offspring after them. Thus the names Daniel, Jonathan, Esther, Enoch, Ezra, Rachel and many others were constantly used among them while there was a conspicuous absence of names commemorating the Christian saints. In short, "They discarded the old English names and those of the saints and confined themselves to names taken from the Scriptures, especially from the Old Testament."[39]

Names of colonies, cities and settlements were likewise chosen from Hebraic Scripture. The names Salem (peace), Bethlehem (house of bread), and others will bear witness. The name Nahumkeik, given, according to Cotton Mather, to a plantation settlement in 1628 was not, as is generally believed, of Indian but rather of Hebrew origin. The name, argues Mather, is composed of two Hebrew words: Nahum (comfort, or console) and Keik (Heq—a haven). "And our *English* not only found in it an *Haven of Comfort,* but happened also to put an *Hebrew name* upon it; for they called it *Salem,* for the *peace* which they had and hoped in it; and *so it was called* unto this day."[40]

Mather was preoccupied with Hebrew to an extraordinary degree. Words and phrases in the language are interlaced into everything he wrote. In the First Book of *Antiquities* the Introduction begins with the Hebrew words *'Im yirzeh ha-Shem*; chapter six starts with the words *ba'ale nefesh,* and in the Sixth Book the title begins with the Hebrew words meaning *liber memorabilium.* In the second volume of the *Magnalia* appears the following: "The Jews tell us of *kilyah* or a *scare-crow* upon the top of the *temple,* which kept off the fowls from defiling it. . . . The same practice was used for candidates for admission to the church—only defilers of the temple were kept out."[41] In speaking of the first ministry when they left England, Mather refers to them as *Hasidim Rishonim* (our first good men).[42] As to the conduct of the magistracy, he states that it was according to Jewish wishes *Beáhavah Veyir'ah, cum mansuetudine ac Timore.*[43]

The Puritans bent the Book to serve their own peculiar needs—often in almost arbitrary fashions. Often they resorted to a primitivism contradictory to the very spirit of the second Isaiah. "For this it is they and not Hebraism that must bear the blame. But their errors in this respect must not be allowed to obscure the positive advantages they obtained from their familiarity with the Scriptures. The legacy of Judaism was to them a real inspiration, and they have handed it on to their posterity in an intensity of religious devotion and a passion of moral fervor for which the whole world is still in their debt."[44]

FOOTNOTES

[1] James Henry Breasted, *Ancient Times*, page 335.
[2] Matthew Arnold: *Literature and Dogma*, page 308.
[3] Norman Bentwich: *Philo-Judaeus*, page 106.
[4] *Ibid.*, page 104.
[5] Edwyn R. Bevan and Charles Singer, *The Legacy of Israel*, page 295.
[6] *Ibid.*, page 301.
[7] *Ibid.*, page 310.
[8] M. I. Schleiden: *The Importance of the Jews for the Preservation and Revival of Learning during the Middle Ages*, page 54.
[9] *Ibid.*, page 55.
[10] Cecil Roth, *The Jewish Contribution to Civilization*, page 16.
[11] Richard Garnett, *English Literature, an Illustrative Record*, Vol. I, page 204.
[12] *Ibid.*, page 204.
[13] R. S. Storrs, *The Puritan Spirit*, pages 52-3.
[14] *The Second Part of a Reply to the Vindication of the Subscribing Ministers by a Committee of the Non-Subscribing Ministers*, page 12.
[15] Robert Abbot, *A Trial of Our Church-Forsakers*, pages 127-8.
[16] *Bradford's History "Of Plimoth Plantation"*, page 110.
[17] *Sermons on Important Subjects collected from a number of ministers, in some of the northern states of America*, page 62.
[18] Thomas Jefferson Wertenbaker, *The Puritan Oligarchy*, page 59.
[19] Frederick Jackson Turner, *The Frontier in American History*, page 103.
[20] John Cowper Powys, *Enjoyment of Literature*, Introduction.
[21] *Ibid.*, page 12.

22 W. De Loss Love, Jr., *The Fast and Thanksgiving Days*, pages 61-2.
23 Belknap, *American Biography*, Vol. II, page 171.
24 Romeo Elton, *Life of Roger Williams*, page 2.
25 John Davis, *New England's Memorial*, page 36.
26 P. Marion Simms, *The Bible in America*, page 52.
27 *Ibid.*, page 111.
28 Davis, *op. cit.*, title page.
29 Perry Miller, *The New England Mind*, page 475.
30 *Ibid.*, page 477.
31 *Ibid.*, page 20.
32 Perry Miller and Thomas H. Johnson, *The Puritans*, pages 49, 54.
33 Joseph Banvard, *Plymouth and the Pilgrims*, pages 204, 231-2.
34 Paul Masserman and Max Baker, *The Jews Come to America*, page 69.
35 Cotton Mather, *Magnalia Christi Americana*, Vol. I, pages 109-10.
36 Davis, *op. cit.*, page 255.
37 *Ibid.*, page 301.
38 *Ibid.*, page 272.
39 C. E. Whiting, *Studies in English Puritanism from the Restoration to the Revelation 1660-1688*, page 445.
40 Mather, *op. cit.*, Vol. I, page 63. The influence of Judaic culture went far beyond the bounds of technical scholarship and professional training for theologians. One has only to look at some of the names of the towns of the United States: Salem, Canaan, Zion, Hebron, Bethlehem, Sharon, Palestine, Jaffe, Goshen, Beth-el, Carmel, Eden, Jordan, Jericho, Rehoboth, Pisgah, Nimrod, Shiloh, Gilead, to see that the intellectual and spiritual geography of the founders of the colony was derived as much from Hebrew culture as from their immediate experience in the Old World or the New. A. I. Katsh, *Hebrew in American Higher Education*, pages 61-65.
41 *Ibid.*, Vol. II, page 244.
42 *Ibid.*, Vol. I, page 213.
43 *Ibid.*, page 130.
44 Bevan and Singer, *op. cit.*, page 431.

B.—EARLY POPULARITY OF THE HEBREW LANGUAGE

One can easily deduce from the wealth of material in the foregoing discussion that since Hebrew names, proverbs, excerpts and interjections, to say nothing of the generalized use of Hebrew thought, played so great a role in American Colonial life, the Hebrew language itself had to occupy a correspondingly prominent position in Colonial education. The study of Hebrew long ranked high in popularity among the clergy of New England. Cotton Mather records in the second volume of the *Magnalia Christi* that at the second session of the Synod of the Elders and Messengers of the churches an article was drawn up to provide for the study of the Old Testament in the original Hebrew, ". . . the native language of the people of the God of Old."[1]

Early American education was tightly linked with religious studies. Indeed, the main purpose for most early institutions of higher education was the provision of the requisite number of clergy. Most of them were in the service of a specific denomination and most, at any rate in New England, drew their inspiration from Puritan sources. Hebrew, therefore, played its part.

"Not only was Hebrew considered the foundation for an exact understanding of the Old Testament, but it was then as later thought to be the mother of languages; a knowledge of it therefore was believed to advance learning in the best sense."[2] An early president of King's College which later became Columbia University said: "As soon as a lad has learned to speak and read English well, it is much the best to begin a learned education with Hebrew . . . the mother of all languages and Eloquence."[3] Many of the leading citizens of the age were distinguished Hebrew scholars. Among them John Eliot, Isaac Addington, Ethan Allen, both Mathers, father and son, William Bradford, Charles Chauncey, Joseph Green, John Dunster and Samuel Sewall can be cited as particular examples.

One must remember that, as has been pointed out, the first book published in the Colonies was the so-called *Bay Psalm Book,* a rendering of the Psalms into English from the original Hebrew by Richard Mather, John Elliot and Thomas Welde. This joint labor was later submitted to President Dunster of Harvard who drawing on his own extensive knowledge of the language revised and polished the translations.

Little wonder that in such an intellectual climate, Harvard, the first American institute of higher learning, established in 1636 and endowed by John Harvard in 1639, followed the English cultural tradition so deeply rooted in the Bible, and included the language of the Bible as an essential course in its curriculum on a level with Latin and Greek. Many generations of students at Harvard devoted one day each week for three years to the study of Hebrew and allied tongues. In addition to the texts in grammar and syntax, the books of the Old Testament were the principal study material used.

The College regarded Hebrew as a key to the textual study of the Bible. It had been founded on principles of Scriptural influence. In all matters of administration, the leaders ". . . were agreed in declaring the Scriptures, as the *direction* of all. . . . It is *not* the opinion of *men,* but the *Scripture* which must decide the controversy."[4]

Samuel Eliot Morison has this to say about the historical basis of this insistence on the study of Hebrew. "Authorities on the history of education have too readily assumed that colonial students were forced to study Hebrew and Greek simply in order to read the Bible. As regards Hebrew, that may well have been the real reason, though the *good* one assigned in an early commencement thesis was that Hebrew is the mother of languages. This theory that Hebrew was the archetype of all western tongues, was common in the Renaissance; the great English Hebraist, John Selden, among others, believed it. A smattering of that language was then supposed to be a classical education in England; Sir Humphrey Gilbert had it on the program for his proposed academy for young gentlemen of the court and even in the late eighteenth century, President Samuel Johnson of Columbia declared that Hebrew was part of a 'gentleman's education.' Wilhelm Schickard, professor at the University of Tübingen, prepared especially for his pupils a Hebrew text with the attractive title (in Latin) 'The Hebrew Sun-dial, or advice as to how the elements of that Holy language may be sufficiently apprehended by College students in a space of 24 hours.' "⁵

Further historical evidence comes directly from Mather. "The reader knows that in every town among Jews, there was a *school*, whereat children were taught the reading of the *law*; and if there were any town destitute of a *school*, the men of place did stand excommunicate, until one were erected: besides and beyond which they had *midrashoth*, or *divinity-schools*, in which they expounded the law to their disciples. Whether the churches of *New-England* have been duly careful or not about *their* other *schools*, they have not been altogether careless about their *midrashoth*; and it is well for them that they have not."⁶

Freshmen at Harvard began with Hebrew. The first textbook was Wilhelm Schickard's *Horologium Hebraeum* (Hebrew Sun-dial) mentioned above by Morison. Several other formal texts for grammar were used. One of these was the Martinius of Navarre grammar; another a general grammar by Christian Ravis. John Harvard's initial contribution of books to the college library included several commentaries on the Old Testament. There still remain twelve Bibles from the year 1651 which contain inscriptions by their original owners. Time and time again interest in the language manifests itself in baccalaureate theses. Some subjects covered at one time or another include: *"Aleph* with the function of a point has the sound of all vowels," "By contracting their sentences the Hebrews enlarge their meaning," "Points received on both sides of a letter remove *sheva*," "*Benoni* (the participle) takes the place of the present, which is wanting in Hebrew."[7]

A custom inaugurated at Harvard in 1655, and continued for many years, called for the mention by all students except Freshmen, of a verse from the Hebrew original of the Old Testament into Greek, as a part of morning prayer. In 1735 the college sponsored publication of a Hebrew grammar prepared by Judah Monis, a converted Jew. Monis, a colorful character of Portuguese Marano extraction, was the first full-time Hebrew instructor in any American college. Though he was converted to Christianity through the efforts of Increase Mather, all through his life he was referred to as "Rabbi".

In 1782 the first concessions concerning the study of Hebrew were made in the Harvard curriculum. At that time students were formally allowed to substitute French for Hebrew provided they obtained special permission. For over a century and a half, until 1817, the commencement exercises at the college included a Hebrew oration which during the early years was concerned solely with questions of syntax and grammar but which later was extended to broader and more varied topics.

Yale, established in 1701, followed the same tradition. Its seal at the very outset depicted an open Bible with a Hebrew inscription spread across its pages, *Urim Vetumim*. But feeling as they did that Hebrew was the province of advanced students, the founders "In charity to their successors who might be less familiar with the language of scholars . . . happily added a translation in the vernacular: *Lux et Veritas*".[8] From the very beginning Hebrew was a required subject.

Ezra Stiles, who surely ranks as one of the most learned men ever to hold a college presidency, was during his entire lifetime an ardent Hebraist and philo-semite. He set the standards during his day, making the knowledge of Hebrew an integral part of a scholar's liberal education and a requisite for a minister. When elected president of Yale and Professor of Ecclesiastical History, he voluntarily took upon himself the teaching of Semitics. In his diary Stiles records: "From my first accession to the Presidency 1777-1790, I have obliged all the Freshmen to study Hebrew. . . . This year I have determined to instruct only those who offer themselves voluntarily and that at Subsecivis Horis only with omitting any of the three daily classical Recitations to their Tutor. Accordingly of 39 Freshmen, 22 have asked for instruction in Hebrew, and these accordingly I teach. IV.P.M. Mondays, Wednesdays, and Fridays. I have besides several of the other classes at other times."[9] Stiles "drilled his pupils especially in one of the Psalms which he thought 'would be the first we should hear in Heaven.' He would have been ashamed if any graduate of Yale should be entirely ignorant of the holy language when he got to heaven!"[10]

In 1781 the commencement address at the University was delivered by Stiles in Hebrew. He based his remarks on a verse from Ezra (VII, 10). "For Ezra had prepared his heart to seek the law of the Lord, and to do it, and to teach in Israel statutes and judgments." He went on to evaluate the study of Hebrew and referred to it as ". . . a glorious language which throws more light on the Old Testament than all the Commentators." Throughout his life Stiles persisted in his enthusiasm for the language. For him it was indispensable for a properly balanced liberal education.

The popularity of Hebrew at Yale continued for many years and towards the end of the 19th century Professor William Rainey Harper's students were said to have filled the largest of the lecture halls. Harper, a colorful personality, was a brilliant Hebraist. As one of the founders and later first president of the University of Chicago, Harper made the study of Hebrew a national fad, establishing summer courses, institutes, and correspondence courses. It is said that he had so much mail in connection with his instructional activities that the salary of the local postmaster had to be raised.[11]

Samuel Johnson, the first president of King's College, now Columbia, gave expression to the sentiments of intellectuals of his time when he referred to Hebrew as "being essential to a Gentleman's education." Johnson was the most scholarly American of his time and with Jonathan Edwards, another student of Hebrew, he "takes rank as one of the two really powerful and constructive American philosophers of the 18th century." Johnson had a passionate love for Hebrew and demanded a knowledge of it from all King's College tutors. He studied Hebrew in his early years, at the Guilford Grammar School in Connecticut and later taught his children and his grandchildren the rudiments of the language. He also wrote *An English and Hebrew Grammar, Being the First Short Rudiments of Those Two Languages Taught Together, to Which is Added a Synopsis of all the Parts of Learning*. A son of a successor to Johnson, Clement Clarke Moore, who graduated from King's College in 1798 at the head of his class, composed a *Compendious Lexicon of the Hebrew Language* in two volumes, a work which is presumed to be the first of its kind in this country. In his middle years he taught Hebrew and Greek to students of the General Theological Seminary, established by the Protestant Episcopal Church through his efforts. In 1859 the Seminary established the Clement Clarke Moore professorship of Hebrew. It is interesting and a little ironical to note that Moore is now known almost exclusively as the author of the ever popular *A Visit from St. Nicholas*.

King's College and the Philadelphia Academy, now the University of Pennsylvania, were exceptions to the usual pattern of the early colleges which served as theological seminaries. The curriculum of the Philadelphia Academy, on the instance of Benjamin Franklin, was not limited exclusively to the classics, but was broadened to include many other subjects such as applied mathematics, science, natural history, international law and modern languages. Yet one of the seven professorships in the institution in 1782 was in Hebrew and Oriental languages. In 1792, a combined professorship of Hebrew, Oriental languages and German was established. About a century later, in 1885, the noted Jewish scholar, Dr. Morris Jastrow, Jr., was at the head of the Semitics Department. Dr. Jastrow also distinguished himself as the University librarian.

Dartmouth, organized before the outbreak of the Revolution, as an institution to train missionaries to evangelize the Indians also followed the Hebraic tradition of the older American Colleges. Professor John Smith, who was appointed to the chair of Oriental languages as a very young man, prepared a treatise on Hebrew grammar in his junior year, in 1772. In 1803, he published a grammar for the use of his students. Hebrew was said to be as familiar to him as his native tongue. Professor Benjamin Hale, who was professor of medicine at Dartmouth in 1827, also held "recitations in Hebrew," for two years "not perhaps" as he put it "much to the profit of my classes but because I happen to be fresher in that study than any college officer."

The pattern set by the early institutions was followed by the colleges in America until about the Civil War. In addition to Harvard, Yale, King's College, the Philadelphia Academy, other great institutions of higher learning founded in the eighteenth century, including William and Mary in Virginia, Rutgers and Princeton in New Jersey, and Brown University in Rhode Island, were conducted with a religious or classical motif, and regarded Hebrew as a major subject in the course of study. It is of interest to note that Harvard, Yale, King's College, the Philadelphia Academy, Brown, Princeton and Johns Hopkins are among the schools which have been teaching Hebrew without interruption since their inception.

It has been said to fully understand a poet one must dwell in his homeland. But in actuality this is only a secondary qualification. A primary one is the poet's language. For it is through his language that one finds the expressive spirit of his thought and creativity. As has been pointed out, one can not fully appreciate the Hebrew Scriptures in any translation —even the best. This attitude in the Puritans was perhaps best exemplified in William Bradford's attempts to master

Hebrew. "The French tongue he (Bradford) could also manage; the Latin and the Greek he had mastered but the Hebrew he most of all studied, because, he said, he would see, with his own eyes, the ancient Oracles of God in their native beauty."[12] This spirit died hard in American colleges—if indeed it ever actually did. The revival of interest in Hebrew in widely divergent universities in recent years would argue that it did not.[13]

Though we have thus far concentrated our observations on American colleges it should not be assumed that it was only the institutions of higher learning which were interested in Hebrew. Not only in colleges but in lower schools as well was Hebrew offered as a language. Miller and Johnson point out that it was taught at the Boston Latin School in the seventeenth century. In an act dated 1695 providing for the establishment and building of a free school in St. Andrew's parish, a clause was inserted which read; "Along with instructions in reading, writing, Latin, Greek . . . arithmetic . . . the scholars were to receive instruction in Hebrew."[14]

John Davenport, himself a Hebraist and a colleague of John Cotton, "was directly instrumental in introducing the study of Hebrew in the first public school of New Haven, an action which was in part inspired by a bequest in the will of Governor Hopkins; according to the records of the colony, the instructor was appointed June 28, 1660."[15] It was this early and continuing interest in the language that enabled most colleges to require their freshmen to study it. Some basic work had been done before their arrival at the higher level.

This avid study of the language brought forth many first rate scholars of Hebrew. Increase Cotton knew the language well enough to deliver discourses in it. As has been pointed out many times, his son, Cotton, was much interested in the language and wrote a relatively scholarly dissertation on Hebrew punctuation. John Udall translated Peter Marinius' Hebrew Grammar and compiled a Hebrew dictionary, *The Key of the Holy Tongue*. At the first Harvard commencement an oration was delivered on the topic "Hebrew Analysis, Grammaticall, Logicall and Rhetoricall of the Psalms."

It might be interesting at this point to list the rules and precepts at the College as they were listed in this discourse.

> "*The fifth day reads Hebrew, and the East-
> erne Tongues*
> *Grammar* to the first yeare houre the 8th
> To the 2d. *Chaldee* at the 9th houre,
> To the 3d. *Syriack* at the 10th houre,
> Afternoone
> The first practice in the Bible at the 2d. houre
> The 2d. in *Ezra* and *Daniel* at the 3d. houre"[16]

At commencement questions were asked of the students by the examiners who ". . . did heare their Exercises; which were . . . and Hebrew Analysis grammaticall, Logicall and Rhetoricall of the Psalms. . . ." The questions asked concerning Hebrew were: "Haebrea est Linguarum Mater," "Consonates et vocales Haebreorum sunt coaetaneae," and "Punctationes chatephatae syllabam proprie non efficiunt."[17]

There were many other serious students of the language. The work and influence of Ezra Stiles have already been noted. John Dunster was called upon to work on the *Bay Psalm Book*. Others have been mentioned.

The position of Hebrew in the Puritan world can perhaps best be understood from their concern with the *Bay Psalm Book*. The book, an original translation of the Psalms from the Hebrew text into English, was the first printed in the Colonies. Copies are now reckoned among the rarest treasures of Americana and as such bring tremendous prices. The purpose of the publication was to replace the Sternhold and Hopkins version then in popular use. This rough rendering of the Psalms frequently sacrificed literal translation for the sake of poetic effect. The inaccurate reading of the text troubled Puritan conscience and this was to be rectified with the publication of the *Bay Psalm Book*.

In a similar spirit, Cotton Mather wrote: "But of all the more than twice seven versions, which I have seen it must be affirmed, that they *leave out* a vast heap of those rich things, which the Holy Spirit of God speaks in the original Hebrew; and that they *put in* as large an Heap of poor things which are entirely their own. . . . I am therefore strongly of the opinion, that the *Poesie* of the Ancient Hebrews, knew no *Measure*, but that of the unknown Music, wherein it was to be accomodated. Our Psalms in the Hebrew, are not so much *metrical* as *musical*."[18]

While the Puritans regarded the Old Testament as the supreme authority they did so on the basis of the original Hebrew rather than the Latin Vulgate. From this stems their reverence for Hebrew as the holy language. God spoke to them much as he did to the ancient Hebrews. As was natural He spoke the ancient tongue. They adopted not only their version of the spirit of the Old Testament but the letter of it as well. The most famous of grammar school texts was *The New England Primer,* better known as Milk for Babes which was based largely on Biblical narratives. (Seven million copies of this remarkable book were published before 1840 alone!) The alphabet was taught by means of verses. From "A—in Adam's fall we sinned," to "Z—Zaccheus, he did climb a tree, His Lord to see."[19]

There was a sufficiently widespread interest and knowledge of Hebrew in the Colonies at the time of the Revolution to allow for the circulation of a story that ". . . certain members of Congress proposed that the use of English be formally prohibited in the United States, and Hebrew substituted for it."[20] Whether or not there is any basis of fact in this story has never actually been determined but that is relatively of little moment. The important thing is that the people of the time thought it logical enough to circulate.

The instances that have been previously mentioned indicate the prominent place of Hebrew in the early academic life of this country and the esteem in which it was held by the pioneers in American collegiate education, religious thought, and general scholarship. The decline in the study of Hebrew in American institutions of higher learning may be attributed to many and varying factors. Almost immediately after the Revolutionary war, following the growing tradition of separating church and governing bodies, education in general was shifted from religious to a political basis. It was now regarded as essential to liberty and the preservation of the state; and higher education, too, began to reckon with this broader aim, rather than merely with the training of ministers. Moreover, the rapid and extensive growth of the natural sciences impelled the universities to broaden their curricula to meet the growing demand for professional, technical, and scientific courses. The older colleges, now endowed by men of wealth, expanded their facilities and established schools of engineering and law, medicine and science.

The new tendency was reflected in the utilitarian educational philosophy advocating the application of knowledge to everyday affairs, and derogating the value of the study of the classics for mental discipline, or of learning for its own sake. Education, according to this doctrine, was to provide for a useful and happy life. In this pragmatic view Hebrew and the classics played a very minor part.

The colleges which greatly increased in number during the 19th century, and the state universities established during that period followed the new mode and did not provide for Semitic departments; they did offer courses in Bible, but these were given in the English translation as a part of English literature, rather than as sacred text, as formerly. A knowledge of Hebrew was, of course, not considered essential for either teacher or student in this type of course.

A number of American universities during the 19th century transferred their early function of training for the ministry, with its attendant courses in classics and Hebrew, to theological departments or schools. In most instances, universities assigned their courses in Hebrew to the Semitic or Oriental language departments which were associated with their graduate divisions, thus restricting these studies to a more limited number of students. The poor methods of teaching based on the traditional way of conjugating the verb *Qatal, Qatalti* were enough to "kill" interest in any language, and this contributed further to its decline. The secularization of the universities and colleges also resulted in a departure from the custom of appointing clergymen to the presidencies of universities—a practice which had strengthened the religious tone of the institutions and created an atmosphere favorable towards Hebrew. As we have seen, many of the presidents were themselves Hebrew scholars and had also served as instructors in the courses.

The content of the Hebraic studies was meager and with the diminution in enrollment, the universities permitted the Semitic departments to lapse, particularly in those schools where the original endowment for the chair was depleted. Because of the lack of financial support, several institutions such as New York University in 1923, Cornell University in 1938, Buffalo University in 1940, and Wilson College in 1941 discontinued their Hebrew and Semitics departments with the death or retirement of the individual professor in charge.

In the case of New York University this situation has since changed. A course in Modern Hebrew was introduced by the writer in 1934 in the Division of General Education on an experimental basis. Three years later, in 1937, this course was incorporated, by Dean E. George Payne, into the accredited curriculum of the School of Education of the University. Success of this course led to the introduction of additional courses and in 1944 the first Chair of Modern Hebrew Culture and Education in an American institution of higher learning was established. The department of Modern Hebrew Culture and Education now sponsors two curricula, one in the language proper and one in general Hebrew culture. It thus enables students to pursue a course of study leading to the baccalaureate, masters and doctoral degrees majoring in Hebrew, Jewish culture or Jewish education.

This pioneering work was a source of inspiration to other colleges and universities. In the last few years seventeen institutions of higher learning in the country introduced in their curricula departments in Modern Hebrew as well as courses in Hebrew culture as a living dynamic civilization. There are also 199 colleges and universities which teach Hebrew as a Semitic tongue. Harvard and Columbia have had endowed chairs in Jewish philosophy and in Jewish history for some time.[21]

FOOTNOTES

[1] Mather, *op. cit.*, Vol. II, page 183.

[2] Miller and Johnson, *op. cit.*, page 698.

[3] Anita Liebman Lebeson, *The Pilgrim People,* ms.

[4] Mather, *op. cit.*, Vol. II, page 53.

[5] Samuel Eliot Morison, *Puritan Pronoas,* pages 41-2.

[6] Mather, *op. cit.*, Vol. II, page 7.

[7] Samuel Eliot Morison, *Harvard in the 19th Century,* page 205.

[8] Charles Seymour: From an address delivered in New Haven, Conn. February 13, 1949.

[9] Lee Friedman, *Rabbi Haim Isaac Carigal,* pages 36-7.

[10] Seymour, *op. cit.*

[11] Abraham I. Katsh, *The Teaching of Hebrew in American Universities,* page 577.

[12] Davis, *op. cit.*, page 270.

[13] Abraham I. Katsh, *The Study of Hebrew Language, Literature and Culture in American Institutions of Higher Learning.* Some of the material used in this section is based upon pages 1-13 of the book.

[14] *Publications of the American Jewish Historical Society,* Vol. V, page 56.

[15] L. I. Newman, *Jewish Influence on Christian Reform Movements,* page 636.

[16] *New England's First Fruits with Divers other Special Matters concerning that Country,* pages 29-35.

[17] *Ibid.,* pages 29-35.

[18] Miller and Johnson, *op. cit.*, pages 678-80.

[19] *The New England Primer,* pages 10-14.

[20] H. L. Mencken, *The American Language,* page 79; Supplement I, page 138.

[21] A. I. Katsh, *op. cit.*, pages 40-58.

C.—INFLUENCE OF THE JUDAIC SPIRIT

"The priceless jewel of Hebrew religious development, a pure ethical idealism of the prophets, was not lost to the religious experience of Israel, but was rather preserved for her and for all ages and all races through the ritual legalism of the priests. The world's richest treasures of religious and moral truth are the gifts and fruitage of Jewish ethical idealism."[1] Such is the opinion of one scholar on the far-reaching influence of the spirit epitomized in the Old Testament.

Relating it more specifically to American life we find that mastery of Hebrew only served to intensify the Puritan roots in Jewish ethical idealism. By knowing the language they were more easily able to acquire the spirit and meaning of the Old Testament. This particular idealism as they chose to interpret and use it, not only dominated their theology but reached over into the patterns of everyday life. It helped them to discipline their minds. It fortified their will. It confirmed in divine terms the principles for which they stood. And these were the factors which enabled them to survive. Perhaps as much as any more practical factor, their belief in their divinely inspired mission enabled the Puritans to triumph over the difficulties which had defeated preceding colonists. It gave them a hardihood and a tenacity of purpose, a will and courage which were sorely needed to withstand the rigors of life in the wilderness that was America during the early years of the seventeenth century.

Life in general was modeled as much on the Hebraic pattern as was possible for them under the circumstances. When occasion for a holiday arose, they drew their inspiration from Jewish models. The first Thanksgiving celebration in 1621 was not a joyous holiday but rather an imitation of a Jewish fast day. It was a purely religious service with the emphasis on fasting rather than on feasting as has become the custom in more recent years. "Let us, we beseech you (all you that love Zion) your prayers, and helpe in heaven and earth for the furtherance of this great and glorious worke in our hands; great works need many hands, many prayers, many tears."[2]

In their commonwealth there was, according to the historian Fiske, "the same ethical impulse which animates the glowing pages of the prophets and which has given to the history and literature of Israel their commanding influence in the world."[3] The foreword to the 1656 revision of the Pilgrim code carries this idea forward with this comment: "It was the great privilege of Israel of old and soe was acknowledged by them, Nehemiah the 9th and 10th that God gave them right judgments and true Lawes. They are for the mayne so exemplary, being grounded on principles of moral equitie as that all Christians especially ought alwaies to have an eye thereunto in the framing of their politique constitutions. We can safely say both for ourselves and for them that we have had an eye principally unto the aforesaid platforme in the framing of this small body of Lawes."[4]

An interesting parallel can be noted here. The government of the Puritan colonies was not, strictly speaking, in the hands of the ministers. In this sense they never actively achieved a theocracy. There is little doubt, however, that they aimed at one. Laws and regulations were determined for them. The "saints" were merely given the privilege of confirming them. For this they drew again on the numerous examples of such procedure in the Old Testament. They were more concerned with the religious ideals involved than with any concept of political or even social democracy. And Millar Burrows has said of the Hebrew ideal that it "was not democracy but theocracy. The days when 'there was no king in Israel,' when 'every man did that which was good in his own eyes,' were regarded in retrospect, not as a time of hateful anarchy, but as a time when God ruled his people directly."[5] The Puritans looked for this situation again in the new Canaan of America.

"Now Puritanism was, in essence, the rebirth of the Hebrew spirit in the Christian conscience. It was the Hebrew religious genius come to life to wage battle for God and soul-freedom, once more to impress upon the world the sovereignty of God and the holiness of life. . . . The most drastic reforms which Puritanism introduced in the church polity, when it broke away from the Anglican episcopacy, lay in the decentralization of the Church, the abolition of the hierarchy, and the bridging of the gap between the minister and the laity. In all of these directions, Puritanism paralleled or unconsciously followed Jewish precedent. Every Synagogue was an independent entity; formal ranking and grading of the rabbinate was unknown; and the rabbi, like the Puritan elder—the order should be reversed—laid no claim to supernaturalism in any form. Learning, piety, interpretation of God's will as revealed in the Law—a source open to all—these were the essential qualifications for spiritual authority in Judaism as in the Puritan Churches. In both institutions, the religious head was chosen by the people."[6]

This is a rather striking similarity. Despite the fact that President Neuman sees in it a model for all religious leadership, both the Jews and Protestants have often been criticized for it. Actually, it allowed participation on the part of church members in matters both of dogma and church government. Herein lay the crux of the objections. Yet, in more than one fundamental have the Puritans, consciously or unconsciously, followed the Jewish ethical tradition of idealism. Like the Jews, the Puritans began observance of the Sabbath at sundown of the previous day; and would not, within the full twenty-four hours of the day, shave, have their rooms swept, beds made, dishes washed, any cooking done, or perform work of any kind.

There is a good deal of evidence on many of these points. Whiting states quite flatly: "The Puritans treated it (Sunday) as the Jewish sabbath; no work was to be done, no amusements to be indulged in, it was a day of prayer and worship."[7]

Gregory gives us this picture of the Puritan Sabbath. "From sunset on Saturday until Sunday night they would not shave, have rooms swept, nor beds made, have food prepared, nor cooking utensils and tableware washed."[8] There is more than a superficial resemblance here to the traditional Hebraic observation of the Sabbath. Indeed, were it not for the difference in the day (the Jews observing Saturday rather than Sunday) one might be tempted to call the imitation exact.

Again, as in the orthodox Jewish Synagogue, in the Puritan Churches, the sexes were separated. John Cotton on a Sabbath day would not even study for a sermon for fear of "wearisome labour to invention or memory."[9] Banvard states: "The peculiarities of some of the forms of legislation were occasioned by their imitation of ancient Jewish customs. Thus, in New Haven the members of the constituent committee were called the 'seven pillars hewn out of the house of Wisdom,' and Rhode Island performed for one or two years a 'Jewish masquerade.' Their language was quaint, because interlarded with the phraseology of Scripture. They disapproved of wigs, veils, and long hair. They were equally opposed to immodest and extravagant apparel because both were alike at variance with the simplicity and purity inculcated by the Bible. They were precise in their manners, because, as one of them said, they had 'a precise God to deal with.' They repudiated crosses and beads, surplices and prayerbooks. To their minds, these were too intimately allied to Rome. They denied the superiority of the bishops over other orders of ordained ministers. With them all the ministry occupied the same official privileges and powers. They maintained that the Church was independent of the ministry; that every church possessed the right of electing its own pastor; that no power outside of themselves, whether king or archbishop, had any right to impose upon them a minister, contrary to their wishes. In ecclesiastical and civil government they were republicans—the majority ruled."[10]

There is a decided turning away here from the complicated

hierarchy which the Church had become and a resurgence of the vastly more independent spirit which marked the ancient Israelites. Though the power of the ministry remained tremendous in civil affairs (this point making of the Puritans republicans but not democrats) the people had a say in the choice of their ministers. The spirit of exhortation had returned to religion and the voices of the prophets were heard again calling for the correction of sins in government as well as in religion. In all of this the Bible served as the model.

In fine, the state, civil laws, the Sabbath, the general rules of conduct and behavior, justice and equity, both in act and in thought ("They rejected trial by jury, that being no part of the Mosaic law."[11]) had to derive their sanction from the Old Testament in which the Puritans believed "God had revealed for all time in its entirety all true religion, a revelation absolute and final."[12] As a consequence of this repeated and devoted use of the Bible, this highly conscious emulation of Biblical models, this infiltration of the general spirit of Hebraism, it is safe to say with Simms that: "The American people owe more to the ancient Hebrews than to any ancient people. More than to either the Greeks or the Romans, because to the Hebrews we owe our ethical and spiritual ideals."[13]

FOOTNOTES

1 Frank H. Ridgley, *Jewish Ethical Idealism*, page 88.
2 *New England's First Fruits*, op. cit., page 21.
3 Abraham I. Katsh, *Biblical and Hebraic Mortar in American Structure*, page 9.
4 Newman, *op. cit.*, page 638.
5 *Science, Philosophy and Religion*: Second Symposium, page 400.
6 A. A. Neuman, *Relation of The Hebrew Scriptures to American Institutions*, pages 6, 12.
7 Whiting, *op. cit.*, page 442.
8 J. Gregory, *Puritanism in The Old and in The New World*, page 318.
9 Mather, *op. cit.*, Vol. I, page 253.
10 Joseph Banvard, *op. cit.*, pages 318-26.
11 J. Gregory, *op. cit.*, page 293.
12 James Ernst, *Roger Williams*, page 89.
13 Simms, *op. cit.*, page 222.

D.—LEGISLATION

We have previously considered the importance of the Hebraic elements in the Mayflower Compact. This document was by no means, however, the sole instance of such an instrument. The covenant of the Salem colonists is replete with a spirit that directly reflects the Old Testament. It reads in part: "We covenant with the Lord and with one another, and doe bynd our selves in the presence of God, to walk together in all his waies, according as he is pleased to reveale himself unto us in his Blessed word of truth."[1] There are echoes here of the prophetic and legislative portions of the Hebrew Scriptures. A similar spirit prevailed among the colonists at New Haven when, in 1639, they assembled at a general meeting to discuss the setting up of a civil government that would be in accordance with the wishes and uses of God.

In a sense one might say that this meeting marked the inception of the peculiar type of legislation that the English colonists fostered in America. The general form of the meeting was something they evolved for themselves, but in drawing up their legislation they followed closely the models of Hebraic law. The set-up of the legislators was also based on a Hebraic pattern. "When the great God of heaven had carried his *peculiar* people into a *wilderness* the theocracy wherein he became . . . the Lord of Host, unto them and the four squadrons of the *army,* was most eminently displayed in his enacting of their *laws,* His directing of their *wars,* and his electing and inspiring of their *judges.* In some resemblance hereunto, when *four* colonies of Christians had marched like so many *hosts* . . . into an American *wilderness,* there were several instances wherein that *army* of *confessors* was under a *theocracy;* for their *laws* were still enacted, and their *wars* were still directed by the voice of God, as far as they understood it, speaking from the *oracle* of the *scriptures.*"[2]

[39]

To comprehend better the attitude of the colonists one must study the individual attitudes of their leaders and the cumulative effect of their general concern with the Scriptures. These men were all highly revered and honored. Their influence extended to every facet of life in the colonies. They were successful in leaving their imprint on business, politics, theology, morals, and in the case of Roger Williams, the actual extension of the settlements to new and untried areas. It naturally follows that those things which were of concern to men like Williams, William Bradford, John Davenport, were of concern to the whole colony. These leaders leaned heavily upon the Scriptures in practically all their undertakings. "John Davenport came to New England 'resolved . . . to drive things . . . as near to the precept and pattern of Scripture as they could be driven.' "[3] And Hugh Peter, in his public letter of 1646, requested to ". . . keep a window open to more light and truth."[4]

An interesting parallel was drawn by John Davenport from biblical narrative in a letter to Alexander Leighton. He wrote: "How much better would it beseeme us to combine together in an holy league against the common Adversary, according to Joab's agreement with Abishai, if the Aramites be stronger than I, thou shalt helpe me, and if the children of Ammon be too strong for thee Ile come and succor thee, then thus to resemble those servants of Saul and David, under the command of Abner and Joab, each of which caught his fellow by the head, and thrust his sword into his fellowes side so they fell downe together?"[5]

Roger Williams, who in many of his speeches suggests an Old Testament prophet, in his *Queries to Parliament* in 1643 remarked: "Yea, one Scripture in the mouth of a mechanic before any decree of the whole council . . ." is expected to be ". . . a far greater light than yet shines."[6]

To return for a moment to the widespread influence of John Davenport, it is worthwhile revealing that, when at the

Restoration of 1660, Major Generals Goffe and Whalley and Colonel Dixwell fled to the colonies and were pursued from New York, they found a refuge in the Massachusetts and Connecticut colonies. To insure the safety of the refugees Davenport undertook to preach publicly from a text appropriate to his sentiments in the matter. "Take counsel, execute judgment, make thy shadow as the night in the midst of the noon day; hide the outcasts, betray not him that wandereth. Let mine outcasts dwell with thee; Moab, be thou a covert to them from the face of the spoiler." (Isaiah XVI, 3-4) The sermon had its desired effect.

At the first assembly of the colonists in New Haven in June of 1639, Davenport asked whether the ". . . . Scriptures do hold forth a perfect rule for the direction and government of all men in all duties which they are to perform to God and men as well as in the government of families and commonwealth as in matters of the church?"[7] No one even bothered to debate the point with him. The thesis was irrefutable. Upon further questions of like import it was voted unanimously that the word of God as revealed in the Bible was to be the only rule to be observed in executing the duties of government in the plantation.

Before selecting any officials, the several Biblical verses dealing with the council of elders established by Moses were read. These verses ranged through Exodus, Deuteronomy, and first Corinthians. The high standards of justice and equity, the care with which the elders were to be selected—but not forced upon the people—were rehearsed in order to serve as a pattern for their own actions. In matters of crime and the administration of justice a prisoner was always reminded that: "He that hideth his sin shall not prosper, but he that confesseth and forsaketh his sins shall find mercy." (Proverbs XXVIII, 13)

It was a fundamental thesis, not subject to dispute or refutation, that ". . . the judicial law of God given by Moses and expounded in other parts of the Scripture, so far as it is a hedge and a fence to the moral law and neither ceremonial nor typical nor had any reference to Canaan, has an everlasting equity in it and should be the rule of the proceedings."[8] This spirit is clearly evident in all of the legislation of 1639 and in the subsequent law reinforcements in 1642 and again in 1644.

The Massachusetts settlers, headed by Cotton, in 1684 also based their administration on the Scriptures. "The government might be considered as a theocracy, wherein the Lord was judge, law-giver, and king; that the laws of Israel might be adopted so far as they were considered God's people in a covenant with him; that none but persons of approved piety and eminent abilities should be chosen rulers; that the clergy should be consulted in all matters of religion; and that the magistrates should have a superintending and coercive power over the Churches."[9]

In Massachusetts, as in New Haven before it was formally joined to Connecticut, English Common Law was largely neglected and textual rulings from the Old Testament substituted for it. Some of the resentment the Puritans felt towards English Law undoubtedly was the result of their extremely unpleasant experiences with it before they sailed for the New World. But by far their more significant regard grew from their long established concept of a direct covenant with God. For more than ten years the administration of justice in Massachusetts during the Confederacy of the four colonies (Massachusetts, New Haven, Connecticut, and Plymouth; Rhode Island having been excluded for its radical and separatist views) ". . . . was without the security of either a system of statutes, or of any recognition of the authority of the Common Law. The law dispensed by the Magistrates was no other than equity, as its principles and rules existed in their own reason and conscience, instructed by Scriptures."[10]

In a great many of the laws framed by all of the New

England colonies there was constant reference to the Bible. "The choice of magistrates, legislation, the rights of inheritance, and all matters of that kind were to be decided according to the rules of Holy Scripture."[11] Ever since the bold and shocking work of men like Robert Browne, the Puritans had declared the sanction of the Mosaic legislation for their own regulatory laws. While still in England they had rejected the authority of both the established church and the magistrates. Their authoritative statute book was the Pentateuch and directly from this was drawn the first formal code of laws framed at the request of the General Court of Massachusetts.

"When, in 1646, the General Court found it necessary to convoke a public assembly of the elders they did so protesting, however, that 'their lawful power *by the word of God* to assemble the churches or their messengers upon occasion of counsel' is not to be questioned, and therefore the said assembly of elders, after having 'discussed, disputed and cleared up *by the word of God* such questions of church government and discipline . . . as they shall think needful and meet,' is to report to the General Court, 'to the end that the same being found *agreeable to the word of God,*' it may receive from the said General Court such approbation as is meet. . . . Not only the church synod is to judge what is 'agreeable to the holy Scriptures' but the civil government takes it as its own duty to make sure that the resolutions of the synod are really in accordance with the Scriptures and only then to give their approbation."[12]

In 1641, a Body of Liberties was framed. In a proposed draft consisting of forty-eight laws, forty-six of them were drawn from the Old Testament, and only two from the New Testament. In 1648 a new code, based on the previous one was adopted and published. This code, though never formally adopted in a legal sense, was considered by the legislative body as the general standard. The virtual unity of the source of these laws led Gregory to say with understandable exaggeration: "For their sumptuary laws and regulations the Puritans of New England pleaded the sanction of the Mosaic legislation. The Bible was their statute book, the law of Moses their fountain of authority. The first code of laws drawn up at the request of the general court of Massachusetts was taken entirely from the Old Testament."[13]

An interesting test case is cited by James Truslow Adams wherein the court was divided in a complicated dispute concerning the ownership of a cow.[14] A question of precedence was raised. Was it possible for a small number of judges to hamper lawfully the decision of a large number of deputies? Winthrop wrote a treatise on the subject claiming that: ". . . were the magistrates forbidden to veto the action of the deputies, the colony would not be a democracy, and *there was no such government in Israel*."[15]

It was not only occasionally or incidentally that the Mosaic rulings played an important role in Northern Colonial legislation. They were used as supreme authority when any occasion arose that required the citation of a precedent. They were a source of power which, not only no one would dare to question or refute, but which were willingly and reverentially accepted as supreme authority. There was no question of the imposition of an outside code of laws but rather a willingness to abide by these Biblical rulings. In them, the colonists felt, was to be found democracy as they understood it. Thus from these halting beginnings did Hebraic law and legislation extend and prevail in the colonies. Eventually they found a place in the more unified laws of the separate colonies, and, still later, in the system of constitutional law that governs today.

FOOTNOTES

[1] Ezra Hoyt Byington, *The Puritan as a Colonist and Reformer,* page 81.
[2] Mather, *op. cit.,* Vol. I, page 131.
[3] John Wingate Thornton, *The Historical Relation of New England to the English Commonwealth,* page 38.
[4] *Ibid.,* page 38.

HEBRAIC FOUNDATIONS OF AMERICAN DEMOCRACY

5 I. M. Calder, *Letters of John Davenport*, page 24.

6 Thornton, *op. cit.*, page 38.

7 Ernst von Dobschutz, *The Influence of Bible on Civilization*, page 153.

8 *Ibid.*, page 156.

9 Hannah Adams, *An Abridgement of the History of New England*, pages 21-2.

10 John Gorham Palfrey, *The History of New England*, page 279.

11 Gregory, *op. cit.*, page 292.

12 Dobschutz, *op. cit.*, pages 158-9.

13 Gregory, *op. cit.*, page 324.

14 James Truslow Adams, *The Founding of New England*, pages 208-11.

15 *Harvard Classics*, Vol. 43, page 90.

E.—POLITY

The full import of the Hebraic influence on early American life and its subsequent passage down the years to the present can only be grasped in all its completeness if one examines the statistical data compiled from the various codes of the New England Colonies. To use as an example the code of 1655 which was drawn up in New Haven: there were in it 79 statutes of government. Of these 50% contained Biblical references; 47% from the Old Testament and the remaining 3% from the Christian Gospels. In essence, any body of legislation derives from the underlying body of polity* which motivates it. One might say that formal law is the outgrowth of polity. And in the particular case of the United States (though the example could be applied to other countries) there is an outstanding parallel between the basic idea of the Old Testament and the law of the land as exemplified in the Constitution.

"The government of the United States . . . is based upon a . . . unique principle. The Declaration of Independence, endorsed and enforced by the Constitution, states that governments are not laws unto themselves, that they can not create right, that they are accountable to a Higher Power. It asserts that governments exist to 'secure these rights'—the 'unalienable rights' with which men 'are endowed by their Creator.' It recognizes 'the laws of nature and nature's God' as a Higher Law binding on all governments. . . . The Declaration of Independence thus affirms the duty of the government to uphold the Right and rights as ordained by Divine Law. And it declares that the citizen is obligated in obedience first to the Divine Law, and that he should defend it against the encroachment of even his government."[1]

*Polity (according to Webster), the form, constitution, system, or fundamental principles of government of any political body or other organization; the recognized principles on which any institution is based.

[46]

As we have seen the "Divine Law" and the "Higher Law" which so much concerned the men who framed both the Constitution and the Declaration of Independence was in effect the restoration of the ancient God of the Hebrews. The use of the phrase "laws of nature and nature's God", of course represented the preoccupation during the latter half of the sixteenth and the early part of the seventeenth centuries with the concept of God, Nature and Reason. "The sermons of the century are filled with it—proving the existence and goodness of God from the intelligence which the delicately adjusted mechanism of Nature everywhere exhibited."[2]

Thus it can be seen that there runs through the deeper meaning and higher purpose of our two prime instruments of government a constant regard for principles and theocratic ideas based largely on protracted study of the Old Testament. Though the actual words of the Scriptural text were not used, the spirit was present in a marked manner. Henry M. Field, a distinguished Christian clergyman, summed the matter up as follows: "Perhaps it does not often occur to readers of the Old Testament that there is much likeness between the Hebrew Commonwealth and the American republic. . . . At the bottom there is one radical principle that divides a republic from a monarchy or an aristocracy, and that is the natural equality of men . . . which is as fully recognized in the laws of Moses as in the Declaration of Independence. Indeed, the principle is carried further in the Hebrew Commonwealth than in ours, for there was not only equality before the law, but the laws aimed to produce equality of conditions in one point, and that is a vital one; the tenure of the land, of which even the poorest could not be deprived, so that in this respect the Hebrew Commonwealth approached more nearly to pure democracy."[3]

As we have had occasion to mention before the government of New England was as near an approach to a theocracy as the world had witnessed since the ancient Jewish state. Great diversity of opinion has persisted in all attempts to determine the exact form of government in Massachusetts. Wertenbaker sums the matter up as follows: "When the historian seeks a name for the Massachusetts type of State he encounters difficulties. The use of the word 'theocracy' has been criticized. In a theocracy, it is argued, the clergy are rulers, whereas in Massachusetts the ministers, even though they had a deciding voice in picking the electorate, did not themselves hold civil office. The word 'commonwealth' is also open to objection, since it is defined as 'a State especially viewed as a body in which the people have a voice' or as 'a State in which the sovereignty is vested in the people,' or 'a government chosen directly by the people,' and none of these definitions fits the society established in Massachusetts."[4]

To the early English settlers on the Northern reaches of the American Continent worship was not merely a passion but a final objective in itself. "It had been as unusual for a right New England man to live without an able ministry as for a smith to work his iron without a fire."[5] In the original conception of the Puritan's Bible State one of the cornerstones was to be an attempt to introduce into the theocracy of New England the minute control and punctiliousness of the laws which had governed the ancient Jewish theocracy in its wandering in the wilderness between Egypt and old Canaan. To the Puritans, their period of uncertainty, of trial, of violent conflict with the elements and the savage inhabitants of the land was in every way comparable to the trials of the Israelites in the desert.

Stemming directly from this identification with Israel was one of the main objections raised to the idea of a king. From the very beginning, the Puritans abhorred the idea of kingship. To them he was the embodiment of the forces of Satan working against their new Canaan. The clergy very early took up this idea and constantly hammered away at it. All throughout the seventeenth century struggles between Massachusetts and the throne over the all-important charter for the Colony, the ministry called out against the king. Moses had been extremely reluctant to allow any monarchic considerations to enter the government of Israel and the modern Israel would follow his example! Samuel had nothing but ill-will when called upon by the elders to establish a monarchy. The prophets of New England would follow his tastes. Long after the clergy had lost its power, after devastating inroads had been made into the government by the elite, the Congregational ministers kept up the battle. There was no king but God! They had so completely assimilated the Old Testament idea that, though virtually without effect and out of touch with the world of eighteenth century realities, they still opposed a concept they felt out of keeping with the Scriptures.

Though the ideas had come originally from the pulpit, the masses of people in New England turned willingly to the Old Testament for their political ideas and governmental procedures. They found there what was for them full justification for their antagonism to any idea of absolutism, to the principle of divine right. Samuel's distaste for monarchy was often the starting point for the clergy in advocating the separation of the colonies from England. Jonathan Mayhew, a leading clergyman and often referred to as the father of true civil and religious liberty in America, in a sermon delivered in Boston on May 23, 1766 on the repeal of the Stamp Act declared: "God gave Israel a king (or an absolute monarch) in his anger, because they had not sense and virtue enough to like a free commonwealth, and to have himself for their king— where the spirit of the Lord is there is liberty—and if any miserable people on the continent or the isles of Europe be driven in their extremity to seek a safe retreat from slavery in some far distant clime O let them find one in America."[6] With these ideas in mind, Mayhew fought not to table the idea of a pure democracy.

It became clear that Moses' warning and Samuel's admonition against monarchy played a considerable part in actuating the polity of the Colonies at the crossroads of their life during the third quarter of the eighteenth century. Hebraic idealism had inspired many of the practical considerations which spurred the patriots to challenge monarchy in a decisive way and to offer their blood in the Revolutionary War. Monarchy was termed by Jonathan Mayhew "unbiblical and unHebraic." And so it was for the clergy. To the masses it had become more succinctly "unAmerican."

Of striking interest is the draft for the seal of the new United States which was drawn up by Franklin and Jefferson. It showed Pharaoh, with a crown on his head and a sword in his hand, sitting in an open chariot and passing through the divided waters of the Red Sea in pursuit of the fleeing Israelites. Moses, beams of light protruding about his head, stands on the shore extending his hand over the sea and causing it to overwhelm Pharaoh and his men. Underneath was the motto: "Resistance to tyrants is obedience to God."[7] The general plan and spirit of this draft by two of the fathers of our democracy convey unquestionably the weight of Hebraism in their thinking.

The Puritans viewed their stand as a fight in the name and cause of God against mere human tyranny, for the vindication of the rights of man against despotism. This idea was often expressed by the preachers of the Gospel who, as we have seen, had no small part in stirring up and keeping alive the reaction that culminated in the break with England. W. E. H. Lecky wrote: "It is at least an historical fact that in the great majority of instances the early Protestant defenders of civil liberty derived their political principles chiefly from the Old Testament."[8]

Basing their work on the general idea behind Lecky's statement quoted above, many scholars have felt that this led certain Puritan leaders to be tolerant towards the Jews. Investigation does not bear this out for the vast majority but in connection with radical visionaries like Roger Williams it often does. For instance the following statement from Williams: "I humbly conceive it to be the duty of the civil magistrates to break down that superstitious wall of separation (as to civil things) between the Gentiles and Jews, and freely without their asking to make way for their free and peaceable habitation among us. . . . For who knows that but many of the Jewish religion may be clear and free from scandalous offences in their life, and also from disobedience to the civil laws of the State."9

Williams' biographer carries this idea forward. "Actuated by the lofty idealism of Williams and the significant Jewish interest in things biblical of the first settlers, Rhode Island paved the way for the recognition of the rights of the Jewish people in all American colonies."10

But to return to a more general consideration of polity. Once the concept of democracy as a form of government had gained practicing adherents, it was a natural and inevitable step that the laws governing the democracy be drawn from the source most familiar and revered. The Old Testament was, of course, one such inspiration. The government the founding fathers evolved was one based on practical experience. It was not at the outset (with the exception of New England) ". . . the conscious creation of far-seeing statesmanship but of adventurous, hard-working, home-loving men and women of the middle and lower classes of society of the British Isles and of Europe who were endowed with extraordinary initiative, tenacity of purpose, and resourcefulness in meeting as individuals the problems of frontier life." The Bible had become an integral part of that frontier. Its precepts and intentions had seeped deeply into the lives of the people. Its influence, as we have seen, was present in a dozen fields. It was, in short, part of American thinking.

"As a political *modus vivendi* . . . democracy presupposes a moral basis and background. Democracy is moral before it is political. That people may rule, there must prevail among the people justice and righteousness and a passion for liberty for oneself and one's brothers. Without these virtues a people, even when living under a democracy in form, will find itself living under tyrannous masters in fact."12

[51]

THE HEBREW IMPACT ON WESTERN CIVILIZATION

This philosophical statement is a double tribute to the early settlers of New England and to the English pioneers in the interior regions. Firstly, by their lives they proved that they possessed the prerequisite love of liberty for true democratic government and were, therefore, like Israel in its oppression, free within slavery. Secondly, the Puritans upon entering America were like Israel under Joshua at the River Jordan, fully prepared for an ideal theocracy. It is everlastingly to the credit of the men and women of early America that, as they came to realize that the exacting principles of a theocracy were not feasible in their infinitely practical world, they were able to supplant the rigid code of one with the more liberal laws of the other, always retaining the moral forces which motivated their initial move. The thesis in both polities came from the same source, the Old Testament.

FOOTNOTES

1 Dan Gilbert, *The Biblical Basis of the Constitution*, pages 77-8.

2 Carl Becker, *The Declaration of Independence*, pages 77-8.

3 Quoted in Masserman and Baker, *op. cit.*, page 108.

4 Wertenbaker, *op. cit.*, pages vii-viii.

5 Gregory, *op. cit.*, page 317.

6 Oscar S. Strauss, *The Origin of The Republican Form of Government*, pages 119-20.

7 *Ibid.*, page 140.

8 W. E. H. Lecky, *Rationalism in Europe*, Vol. II, pages 281-3. In connection with Lecky it is, perhaps, in place to note that the phrase "Hebraic mortar cemented the foundations of American Democracy" quoted by so many scholars and attributed to Lecky, is not to be found in any of his writings.

9 Ernst, *op. cit.*, page 350.

10 *Ibid.*, page 351.

11 Lawrence Henry Gipson, *The British Empire Before the American Revolution*, Vol. I, page 32.

12 Louis Witt, *Judaism and Democracy*, page 7.

F.—THE LITERATURE OF ENGLAND AND AMERICA

We have discussed the influence of Hebrew both directly and indirectly on the morality, legislative procedure and contents, and general polity of early American life. We shall now turn to the position of Hebrew in English and American literature.

In England, as in America, the Bible has long been recognized as the best selling book. Its popularity is an accepted fact. Perhaps more than any other book, it is constantly read and reread. Some people have, by virtue of their frequently repeated readings, committed whole chapters, even books, to memory in the exact phraseology. Until well into the nineteenth century and the spread of mass-produced cheap books, the Bible was frequently the only book that was owned in many homes. It was well-thumbed and finger-stained. It was the record of living and dying, of marriages and divorces. It was passed on from father to son, as much a part of the physical inheritance as the spiritual. And this reverence for the book was by no means confined to one class. All men knew it. All men were exposed to it. Through direct personal contact in addition to the more formal efforts of the clergy, familiarity grew. In this way, the English language and through it English literature acquired so many phrases and idioms grounded in or directly quoted from the Bible.

In his book *Mithridates* (1555), Conrad Gesner indicated that when Hebrew, as an Oriental language, joined Greek and Latin, linguists began to observe it with peculiar interest. Among the scholars of the time it was an irrefutable hypothesis that since the Old Testament was written in Hebrew, that tongue must have been the earliest of mankind; that by philological analysis Hebrew was the mother language from which all other living languages sprang, "... a theory which has found adherents down to Gesenius in recent times."[1]

Modern philological research has forced the abandonment of this idea in favor of a more general and inclusive picture. There is no doubt, however, that Hebrew is an extremely ancient tongue, one of the very oldest in the Semitic group, and the only one to have maintained an active position. Its influence on the languages spoken near it started extremely early in its development. As far back as the second millennium B.C., several Hebrew words are found in the letters of Tel El Amarna in Egypt. The exact position of Hebrew in the development of the Semitic languages has never been determined. Many scholars have accepted Hebrew as the most ancient. More recently, it has been suggested that Arabic preceded Hebrew. Others give precedence to either Aramaic or Assyrian. One thing is fairly well agreed upon: that the present Semitic languages are all dialects of one common ancient language.

But these fine points are of concern more to the philologist than the social historian. In any event, for purposes of this study, it may flatly be stated that Hebrew is the oldest of the ancient Semitic languages to exert a continuing influence on modern languages. This is equally true of Hebrew literature. This projected, long-range influence has reached our present English and American literature primarily through the agency of the Scriptures. Biblical precepts, injunctions, nobility of thought, and matchless eloquence are the source of much that is great in English and American literature.

If one wishes to study English literature from its beginnings there is little doubt that an intimate acquaintance with the Bible is an excellent preparation. Caedmon, who is often referred to as the father of English poetry, won early fame for his paraphrases of Biblical tales. The Anglo-Saxon Chronicle of King Alfred the Great was modeled on the Hebrew Chronicles and was prefaced with a copy of the Decalogue and other verses of the Mosaic law. The works of Shakespeare—a unique treasure to fall so early in the history of a national literature—are replete with references to Biblical characters with direct quotations from the Bible. (There are, for instance, eight different cases in which Shakespeare uses the story of Cain and Abel.) Shakespeare's England, despite repeated endeavors to exclude the Jews, was in many ways influenced by Hebraic thought. The Talmud had seeped deeply enough into the general culture to provide writers like Shakespeare with inspiration on many occasions.[2]

Moving on to classical poetry, the case can best be exemplified in the work of John Milton. Speaking of Milton's three great narratives, Whiting says: ". . . Milton was much more successful with the Old Testament story than with the new. *Paradise Lost* is an infinitely greater work than *Paradise Regained* and *Samson Agonistes* is so great because blind, captive Samson is, in one sense, none other than blind John Milton, who had been so great, and had fallen so low."[3] The Bible was, in a sense, the basis for most of the major work of Milton. He studied Hebrew at an early age (probably while still in grammar school) and made it a part of him. He was able to paraphrase in a highly poetic manner many of the Psalms. He referred to "the great task-master," "Babylonian woe," "cherubim and seraphim," "the sons of morning and fountain of light." There is hardly a place in his writing where a Biblical spirit and Biblical diction do not shine through.

At a later date, though Biblical influence is not lacking in the poetry of Shelley, Keats and Tennyson, it is perhaps Robert Browning who best epitomizes late Hebraic learning of any considerable extent. Browning's "intellectual subtlety, the metaphysical minuteness of his argument, his fondness for parenthesis, the way in which he pursued the absolute while he loaded it into a host of relatives and conceived the universal through a multitude of particulars, the love he had for remote and unexpected analogies, the craft with which his intellect persuaded him that he could insert into his poems thoughts illustrating legends and twisted knots of reasoning which a fine artistic sense would have omitted were all Jewish as the Talmud."[4] His acknowledgment of his Hebraism is found in his own words. Speaking of his use of Hebrew phrases in the body of poems like *Jochanan Hakkadosh* he said: "The Hebrew quotations are put in for a purpose: as a direct acknowledgment that certain doctrines may be found in the Old Book which the Concoctus of Novel Schemes of Morals put forth as discoveries of their own. I have put those into English characters with the proper pronunciation that you may see they go properly into English verse."[5] The stern moralizing of *Rabbi Ben Ezra* is too well known to require repetition at this point.

In the field of prose, Thomas Hardy might serve as an example. His plots are motivated by the Bible; his characters bear Old Testament names. There is a conscious imitation of the beautifully idiomatic prose of the Bible. In *Far From the Madding Crowd,* the characters plainly speak the speech of the Scriptures. In *Jude the Obscure,* Bath Sheba speaks the ironic words of Hebrew vengeance, "burning for burning," "wound for wound," "strife for strife." In *The Mayor of Casterbridge* the characters are strikingly similar to Biblical narrative.

"All our English literature is saturated with its (the Bible's) imagery; reference and echo are everywhere. It underlies the pomp of Milton, the vigor of Johnson, the limpid flow of Wordsworth, the rhythms of Ruskin, the eloquence of Macaulay, the severe, swift ease of Arnold, the roll of Hooker and Browne, the perfect periods of Dryden, the rugged fire of Carlyle, the companionability of Emerson, the clarity and repose of DeQuincey, the chastity of Whittier, the music of Tennyson, the conviction of Browning, Bacon, Jeremy Taylor, Charles Wesley, Southey, Newman, Webster, Froude, and so many, many more answer the trenchant mastery, the polychromatic vividness, the purged and exalted, the liquid and pellucid style of the book that bred them."[6]

When we turn to American literature the same picture is repeated. In the earliest native efforts scriptural influence and evidence is obvious. The one truly creative center of the early colonies was New England. Here the austerity of Puritan belief ruled out self-expression in any but divine channels. Painting and music they regarded as either frivolous or actually the work of the devil. Most of the very early writers like Roger Williams, Nathaniel Ward, John Cotton, and Thomas Morton must still be regarded as English rather than American writers.

With the growth of the first native-born into productive maturity the all consuming subject became religion. (The concern of their elders for matters of government strangely disappeared for a while or, at best, became subservient to the interests of God.) Even in their diaries everything was related to their faith. Samuel Sewall's *Diary* is replete with Old Testament references. By using and extending the story of Joseph and his brethren he wrote in *The Selling of Joseph* what "... was probably the first published attack on slavery in America."[7] The use Cotton Mather made of the Bible has been too often mentioned in these pages to require detailed repetition at this point. Wigglesworth, Edwards, John Hull, all wrote with an eye to the Scriptures.

Their books were circulated widely. When in June of 1774 dissatisfaction with the rule of the British Parliament had spread through the colonies and Virginia was in a turmoil, it was decided to call for a day of fasting and prayer to protest the closing of the Boston harbor. The leadership of New England in such matters was acknowledged as Thomas Jefferson was sent "... rummaging for precedents and Puritan forms."[8] These he found and promptly expressed with a fury suggestive of Jeremiah. The purpose of the fast day, he explained, "... was devoutly to implore the divine interposition in behalf of an injured and oppressed people."[9]

It must be pointed out in reference to Jefferson that when Benjamin Franklin first told him of the slogan "Resistance to tyrants is obedience to God," it was then ascribed to one of the regicides of Charles I. It is, of course, a quotation from the Book of Maccabees. Jefferson at once adopted it as his own motto and later in 1776 urged that it be used on the great seal of the newly proclaimed United States.

As time passed and the stresses of the Revolution relaxed literature (as all of life) took a more secular turn. But for many the Bible still pointed the way. Leon Spitz, with justifiable pride if slight exaggeration, calls Bryant the ". . . first of America's great poets," and goes on to say that he ". . . has shown the way to the Bible."[10] His ideas were basic, simple, the common knowledge of all. In a deeper sense, however, he reverted to the past. "His metaphysics was predominantly that of the Old Testament: God is the Creator and His works and His purposes are good."[11]

In the conflict over slavery that tore the Union apart for so long, the Bible was used by both sides to bolster arguments. Theodore Weld in 1837 published *The Bible Against Slavery* in which he used Old Testament texts extensively to prove the evils of the South's "peculiar institution." This was answered by a host of articles and pamphlets originating with the slaveholders proving the validity of slavery with Scriptural texts. The climax of this verbal battle was probably *Domestic Slavery Considered as a Scriptural Institution,* published in 1845, an exchange between Richard Fuller, a prominent clergyman from South Carolina, and Francis Wayland, then president of Brown University. Both men predicated their arguments on the Word of God as they felt it had been revealed in the Bible.

One of the most literate converts to the cause of the Abolitionists was John Greenleaf Whittier. Through all of Whittier's impassioned anti-slavery poetry burns a fierce light of Biblical inspiration. Spitz says flatly: "Whittier may justly be crowned The American Bible Poet."[12] His Puritan ancestry is clearly marked in much that he wrote. Though he abandoned the faith of his fathers for Quakerism, he took with him the stern New England regard for the validity of Scriptural text. Take away from Lincoln's Gettysburg address the biblically flavored words and phrases, writes Auerbach, "and much of the solemn music has died out forever from this inspiring Battle Hymn of consecration to the Republic." Numerous biblical phrases and words from the Hebrew language have become an integral part of our daily speech and vernacular.[13] "We simply cannot estimate the effect of the Biblical influence on English—in style, imagery, and narrative technique, in moral and even political concepts. What, for instance, would have given so persuasive expression to the egalitarian ideas of Cromwell's followers if they had not been able to present them in a guise of a reversion to the simple, healthy ideals of the ancient agricultural commonwealth in Palestine? Even the idiom of characteristic Hebrew expressions, shining through the King James translation, has repeatedly affected English stylists. A recent example is Pearl Buck, who perhaps unconsciously has recourse to Biblical style in trying to convey alien culture of quite a different kind, namely, the Chinese. Many speakers, pamphleteers, orators and moral allegorists have made use of the technique of balanced metaphor, so characteristic of the Hebrew poetic books like the Psalms, without being aware of its origin."[14]

This detailed enumeration of works and authors could easily be brought step by step down to the present. But certainly enough has been presented to make clear the point that, in the development of the literature of America, the Bible in general and the Old Testament in particular has been a constant and potent force. In all stages of our development, in periods of peace and times of troubles our authors have turned to the Scriptures for inspiration and guidance. Many of our ideas of government, of morality, many of our turns of speech, many of our customs have their origins in the Bible. It loomed large in the life of the early New England settlers. It is an active force to-day. One of the most persistent and sensational best-selling books of recent years is the work of a rabbi, Joshua Loth Liebman. Dr. Liebman, drawing heavily on his experience as a teacher and clergyman, brought together the ancient world of the Bible and the modern era of psychology and psychoanalysis. The unbroken continuity of interest in this great flowering of Hebraic genius made this synthesis inevitable.

FOOTNOTES

1 H. Thomas Rack, *A History of Classical Philology*, page 398. See also Lynn Thorndike, *University Records and Life in the Middle Ages*, pages 297-8.

2 Haim Shechter, *The Influence of Talmudic and Midrastic Literature on Shakespeare* in "Areshet" (Hehers) pages 394-399.

3 Whiting, *op. cit.*, page 442.

4 S. A. Brooke, *The Poetry of Robert Browning*.

5 Judith Berlin Lieberman, *Robert Browning and Hebraism*, page 85.

6 Henry Kendall Booth, *The Background of The Bible*, page 260. See also David Daiches, "The Influence of the Bible on English Literature", pages 1114-1132, *The Jews, Their History, Culture and Religion*, Vol. III, edited by Louis Finkelstein.

7 Bernard Smith, *The Democratic Spirit*, page 15.

8 Dumas Malone, *Jefferson the Virginian*, page 172.

9 *Ibid.*, page 172.

10 Leon Spitz, *The Bible, Jews, and Judaism in American Poetry*, page 6.

11 *The Cambridge History of American Literature*, Vol. I, page 266.

12 Spitz, *op. cit.*, page 6.

13 Katsh, *Hebrew in American Higher Education*, pages 54-61.

14 Margaret Schlauch, "General Values of Study of Hebrew", pages 7-8. *Proceedings of the Hebrew Panel*, (Mimeograph), edited by A. I. Katsh. Much of the material used in this study is based on the author's *Hebrew in American Higher Education*, pages 4-18; 26-54.

BIBLIOGRAPHY

BEVAN, EDWYN R. and SINGER, CHARLES, *The Legacy of Israel.*

BEWER, J. A., *The Literature of the Old Testament in Its Historical Development.*

DAVIS, JOHN, *New England's Memorial.*

ELTON, ROMEO, *Life of Roger Williams.*

GREGORY, J., *Puritanism in the Old and in the New World.*

KATSH, A., *The Study of Hebrew Language, Literature and Culture in American Institutions of Higher Learning.*

LECKY, W. E. H., *Rationalism in Europe.* Vol. II.

MALONE, DUMAS, *Jefferson the Virginian.*

RACK, H. THOMAS, *A History of Classical Philology.*

RIDGLEY, FRANK, *Jewish Ethical Idealism.*

SCHLEIDEN, M. I., *The Importance of the Jews for the Preservation and Revival of Learning during the Middle Ages.*

SIMMS, P. MARION, *The Bible in America.*

STORRS, R. S., *The Puritan Spirit.*

THORNTON, JOHN WINGATE, *The Historical Relation of New England to the English Commonwealth.*

WERTENBAKER, THOMAS JEFFERSON, *The Puritan Oligarchy.*

Jewish Sociologists and Political Scientists

By L. L. BERNARD

I. ANCIENT TIMES. One would scarcely expect to find sociology or political science in the modern sense among the ancient Hebrews. But they, like the ancient Greeks, and even earlier than the Greeks, were discussing fundamental problems of society which we would now consider under the category of these two social sciences.

In ancient times the great social problem was how to secure justice for all men in society. The Egyptians, the Mesopotamians, the Chinese, the Hebrews, and the Greeks were all trying to solve this problem. The Hebrews, Egyptians and Mesopotamians sought the solution to the problem of human rights and welfare, as H. Frankfort and his associates have pointed out,[1] through conformity to the will and dispensation of their gods. The heavenly or divine order was set up, according to these authors, in the form of an idealized and perfected mundane system. The Greek poet Hesiod in the eighth century before the Christian era expressed a similar idea when he stated that men had created the gods in their own image. This rather roundabout effort to enlist divine authority on the side of human welfare was doubtless a somewhat Freudian device of these ancient peoples to achieve in a practical way the ideals which their leading thinkers—the Hebrew prophets, for example—had wishfully set forth as the commandments of God. These ancient thinkers—the analogs of our modern sociologists—did not possess the prestige to bring their own ideas to popular fruition. So they turned to God as their helper and, through Abraham and Jacob, made a reciprocal agreement with him[2] and later drew up a code called the Mosaic Code[3]

[63]

by which they sought to institute a social order which would realize their social idealism.

The Chinese and Greek social philosophers sought to achieve through reason or metaphysical philosophy and the operation of Natural Law much the same sort of just social order that the Hebrews aimed at through divine agency. Confucius, equally with Socrates and Plato, stated his aim as justice. Plato opens *The Republic* with this stated purpose. The whole history of the Hebrew prophets is one of an unremitting struggle against oppression by the powerful, against corrupt social ideas and theories and for rational and functional thinking as opposed to superstition and partisan propaganda. History does not record a more determined effort of any class of men in the service of honest thinking and right action than that of the Hebrew prophets and of the rabbis who followed in their tradition, even up to and including the work of the late Rabbi Stephen Wise.

Louis Wallis, in his various works on the backgrounds of Hebrew social and ethical theory and practice,[4] has traced the origins, development, and motives for this thinking and action with a wealth of details which our limited space denies to us; but it is an inspiring and interesting story. The exposure of the Hebrews to the attacks of many peoples because they were located on the great Asian-African highway between the two richest agricultural and trade regions of the ancient world —the Euphrates and Nile valleys—and the difficulty which they experienced in maintaining intact their ethical and social idealism were perhaps the chief causes of their close dependence upon supernatural aid for the realization of their idealized social system. From the same sources probably sprang their intense conviction that they were the people peculiarly chosen as the agents of God to carry out the teachings which they believed had been received from God.

The social and ethical teachings of the ancient Hebrews are themselves so voluminous that they cannot even be summarized in this brief chapter. Fortunately they are so well known to Jews, Christians and others that this is not necessary. But it is possible to call to the attention of the reader some of those social emphases of the Hebrews which have been most influential in later times. The Hebrew proverbs are perhaps the richest of all sources of proverbial wisdom. Elmslie has given us a systematic summary of their teachings.[5] Their richness as a depository of life wisdom is striking. Before men wrote essays and treatises, they compressed their practical perceptions of the meanings of life in these capsule forms. As Elmslie shows, they taught, among other things, that the experience of the past must not be ignored, neither must apparently small things be neglected; out of conflict of interests and wits comes insight, constant and concentrated effort brings desired results, the most important source of human wisdom is the attentive study of the ways of men, while the study of nature conduces to material success in the productive pursuits. This last emphasis is the proverbial fruit of an agricultural and grazing people. The emphasis upon the study of mankind relates to the needs of commerce and politics.

Ecclesiasticus or the Book of Ben Sirach represents a definitive step from the proverb toward the sociological treatise. When the intellectuals first began to write essays they made them up primarily by putting together groups of similar proverbs arranged under a single theme. *Ecclesiasticus* is such a grouping of proverbs for the most part and its theme is desirable individual and social behavior. It treats man in his personal, familial and wider social relationships with strong emphasis upon the political. The sociological importance of this work has not been adequately recognized. Professor Joseph Jastrow of the University of Pennsylvania paid high tribute to it,[6] but more as a philosopher than as sociologist. It ranks along with the *Analects* of Confucius and *The Republic* of Plato, with which it was fairly contemporaneous, as a serious attempt to indicate to men the most acceptable and convenient forms of behavior to bring about the realization of social and personal ideals. It is in this treatise that Hebrew social thought marks the transition from a theological to a secular sanction and comes to rely more upon social action in conformity with reason than upon revelation and the direct intervention of divine will. If the tone of the book is highly pessimistic, as Dr. Jastrow has said, what else could be expected of a keen observer like the son of Sirach viewing so many failures of men both in rationality and in action?

But like the other Wisdom literature of the Hebrews, *Ecclesiasticus* offers abundant good counsel and illustrates the penalties for failure to act wisely. The virtues and the vices are emphasized. Model family life, the good wife, obedience to parents, discipline of children, the treatment of servants, the conduct of servants and of neighbors, the duties of justice and of benevolence toward others, the conduct of the poor and the wealthy, the duty of wise and seemly conduct are among the teachings of both the *Proverbs* and *Ecclesiasticus*. The importance of custom and tradition is insisted upon, as was natural in an age when scientific method and guidance were not yet out of their swaddling clothes. The emphasis in the old Hebrew literature upon introspective examination of motives and thought is remarkably strong, however; a fact which indicates the beginning of an appeal away from mere custom and tradition to more rational standards of conduct.

The writer knows of no other ancient society in which this introspective tendency to self-examination was so strong. It was encouraged, even demanded, especially by the Hebrew prophets. Approximately 800 years B.C. Amos staged one of the most remarkable realistic dramas in human history, when he hurried from tiny Tekoa, past Jerusalem, over to Bethel, all in one day, to defy a king and a high priest with the message that not the magic of customary sacrifice but justice and righteousness are what the Lord requires of men. His words are memorable: "I hate, I despise your feast days, and I will not smell in your solemn assemblies. Though ye offer me burnt offerings and your meat offerings, I will not accept them; neither will I regard the peace offerings of your fat beasts. Take thou away from me the noises of thy songs; for I will not hear the melody of thy viols. But let judgment run down as waters, and righteousness as a mighty stream." Essentially the same protest against formalism and the same plea for functional behavior was made by another Jew eight hundred years later. Because his plea was rejected in an age ripe for social control through introspective adherence to the teachings of current experience rather than to outworn tradition and custom, this last of the ancient Hebrew prophets became the founder of a Jewish sect which outgrew the mother religion itself.

Many pages might well be filled with an account of later social ideas and forms of social organization which the Jews developed after they had established a stable political life as a nation. Increasing social complexity necessarily called for a correspondingly complex economic life and for rules and regulations governing it. Family life developed its characteristic problems, discussed in part in the writings of Hosea and Isaiah. The prophecies of Jeremiah constitute the materials for a treatise on economic and political justice. Isaiah makes profound comments on the mores and their disintegration under the pressure of foreign influences. A new jurisprudence was developing to take care of the growing complexity of social relations in the Jewish commonwealth following the political expansion of Solomon and the cultural inroads of the Hellenic conquests in the fourth century B.C. These and other matters of an early sociological import, for which space is lacking here, are treated by many Jewish and non-Jewish writers, two of which may be mentioned especially because of their wide appeal. These are Alfred Bertholet[7] and Louis Wallis.[8] Dr. Hertzler has also emphasized the intense social idealism of the ancient Hebrew prophets in his works on the history of utopian thought and ancient social theory.[9]

II. MEDIAEVAL JEWISH SOCIAL THOUGHT. In this period Moses Ben Maimonides (1135-1204) stands out as the representative figure in Jewish social philosophy. Like many other Jews of the Middle Ages who were born in Spain, he had profited from both the Jewish and the Arabic learning, which was at that time more advanced than the Christian. Forced to take up his residence in Egypt, Maimonides finally became religious head of the Jews in that region. He was a noted physician, but even more distinguished as a philosopher of religion and of society. In the latter capacity he endeavored to harmonize the Jewish Torah and the Aristotelian social philosophy. He developed a classification of the virtues and the vices, wrote on the duties of man, reinterpreted the Mosaic law in terms of hygiene and social obligations, and attempted to intellectualize the whole of the Talmudic and scriptural traditions. The religious and ethical interpretations which he arrived at were generally adopted by the Jews—only the more orthodox rejecting some of them—for several centuries. His rationalizations of Hebrew scriptural and Talmudic teachings profoundly influenced Spinoza and Moses Mendelssohn, who in turn set the pattern for modern Jewish cosmopolitan social thought.

Maimonides preceded Albertus Magnus, Thomas Aquinas and other transitional Christian social thinkers of the thirteenth century who held many similar theories about philosophy, religion and social relations and duties. His harmonization of Aristotle and the Bible preceded that of St. Thomas and, like the latter, he expanded the concept of revelation of social and religious duties to cover subsequent and gentile developments of the same sort. He also sought to reconcile Judaism and philosophic truth much as St. Thomas later proposed a reconciliation of Catholicism with pagan philosophy. Like Spinoza later, he intellectualized the concept of God and taught that theoretical knowledge is the best approach to an understanding of the works and will of God. He also dealt with the problem of miracles, explaining some rationally and others as the product of phantasy. He was surprisingly modern and his ideas are still accepted in many fields by modern Jews.

Both Jean Bodin and Leibniz are supposed to have been indebted to him, but his influence upon Spinoza is of most significance from the standpoint of this chapter.

III. SPINOZA MAKES THE TRANSITION TO MODERN TIMES. Baruch Spinoza (1632-77) may be taken as representative of early modern social philosophy, partly because of his pre-eminence in that field regardless of cultural, national, or religious antecedents. Born and reared in Holland of Jewish-Moorish descent at a time when Holland had close contacts with the rest of the world, it was easy for him to assimilate the cosmopolitan culture of the West without being narrowed by either Jewish or Christian extreme sectarianism. As a consequence, in his *Tractatus Theologico-Politicus* (1670) he argued most effectively against church dominance of the state and theocratic censorship of opinion in Holland, thus proving himself a useful supporter of the liberal political policies of the statesman, Jan de Witt. In this same work he proved himself to be a forerunner of modern higher biblical criticism and treated religion as a social process which tended through education to become universalized social and ethical idealism. His point of view was essentially that of the ancient prophets modernized and fertilized by an international ethics extended to all mankind.

In political and social philosophy Spinoza sought to abandon mere scholastic speculation and to base his conclusions on a realistic analysis of social processes as they are in order that they may be controlled and directed by a feasible social idealism. For example, he was one of the earliest advocates of a democratic social order, such as was beginning to take form in Holland at that time. The instruments of this democracy he conceived as a passion for justice, education in the facts of social life, and the power of contract residing in the people. The social contract had, in his opinion, a double aspect. First, the people, desiring to escape from the natural rule of force into a rationally controlled society, had organized governments by means of implied and actual contracts among themselves to obey the authorities which they established. But, in the second place, they sought to protect themselves against tyranny and injustice by making a contract with the rulers in whose hands they placed this government to rule justly. The political constitution, whether written or implied, was the embodiment of both these contracts. If the people broke their contract with one another to obey the authority they had set up, social and political chaos resulted and they returned to a natural condition of rule by force, from which they might extricate themselves only by another contract or constitutional sanction arising from their own action. If, on the other hand, the ruler to whom the government had been intrusted broke his implied or actual contract with the people, they might depose him by revolution (force) or by the election of a substitute where the constitution provided for this procedure. Thus, through the increasing development of personality (not by its subjection to external domination) and its socialization, mankind were learning to become masters of their collective destiny by means of the growth of a realistic democracy. Spinoza rejected all absolute authoritarianism, whether divine or human, and made the solution of individual and social problems depend upon the growth of an intellectualized, moralized and socialized personality which sought union and understanding with all other like personalities.

Spinoza, despite his relatively short life, was the most dynamic social and political intellectual force before the eighteenth century. He not only profoundly influenced the social and political thought of Montesquieu, Rousseau, and other leaders of the eighteenth century French enlightenment, but also Lessing, Fichte, Schelling and Hegel in Germany. In the United States, the social and political ideas of Jefferson and his associates are traceable largely to Spinoza either directly or indirectly. His influence upon British social and political thinking was perhaps only slightly less evident.

JEWISH SOCIOLOGISTS AND POLITICAL SCIENTISTS

IV. MODERN JEWISH SOCIAL CRITICISM. A number of circumstances have conspired to interest Jewish intellectuals in the field of sociology. Modern Jews, in spite of their intense devotion to their own traditional culture, are for the most part highly cosmopolitan. Sociology, as a study of social inter-relations, invites the attention of the cosmopolitan intellectual, and many of the ablest Jewish intellects have responded. The traditional interest of the Jews in social justice, from the time of the prophets to the present, is close of kin to the pre-occupation of the sociologist with the aims and methods of social interaction and organization. The fact that Jews have often been exploited and persecuted in most societies has had the effect of either intensifying their concern for the conditions of social justice or has driven them into a habit of withdrawal into the interior life and a preoccupation with self-expression through the various forms of art or into those forms of economic self defense and the control of power which we call business and politics. The cosmopolitan scholar is thus naturally propelled in the direction of sociology. Denied participation in politics in many countries and mistrusted in the teaching of contemporary social science subjects and forced to consider the question of his racial status, he formerly concerned himself largely with primitive social relations, or anthropology and ethnology, or at most with the highly abstract aspect of sociology and political science. There was no barrier against him in economics and philosophy, and in these fields he has been highly active since the Middle Ages.

Jewish efforts at social philosophy in the nineteenth century took largely the form of an intellectual protest against a social order in which the Jew was not a major participant. The names of Karl Marx, Friedrich Engels, Feuerbach, Ferdinand Lassalle immediately suggest themselves in this connection.

It is characteristic of this protest that it was not made in the interest of the Jew alone; it was couched in terms of all mankind. Perhaps the cosmopolitanism of the enlightened Jew had made it possible for him to sympathize more deeply with mankind in general than was possible for those who held to particularistic creeds and social and political dogmas, such as Nordicism, the "white man's burden," and religious bigotry of all sorts. To be sure, the Jews themselves had their own examples of narrowness incapable of this enlightened cosmopolitan outlook. Many non-Jews also not only had the cosmopolitan spirit and universal sympathies in equal measure, but they also shared in the Jew's traditional passion for justice and civic righteousness which was such a remarkable characteristic of the old Hebrew prophets.

It is not possible here to review the intellectual work of all of the Jewish critics of the social order who drove their pens in behalf of a more equitable social and political system. We must select examples to speak for the rest. Ludwig Andreas Feuerbach (1804-72) is reputed to have been of mixed Jewish and German ancestry. He, as a worthy successor of Spinoza in many ways, laid the foundations for the philosophic social revolt from the smug notions of social conformity which followed the era of the Holy Alliance in Europe. His first revolt was against the speculative neoscholasticism of Hegel. He demanded that human need and human nature should be the measure of all things social, not the assumed and unproved assumptions of social order of the speculative idealists. In his *Wesen des Christenthums* (1841) he redefined religion in terms of human moral aspirations in place of the old traditional doctrines based on a theory of revelation. The similarity of this view to that of Spinoza is unmistakable and its divergence from Hegelian theology is obvious. In many respects, including his adoption of the sensationalistic psychology of Hobbes, Locke, Hume and Condillac, he approached close to modern behaviorism. In large measure his point of view was adopted by the German social biologists, such as Buchner and Vogt, and by the recent German philosophers Dilthey and Heidegger and by the great French sociologist Durkheim. In his enthusiasm for a theory of environmental causation to replace the old dogmas of mystical influences he fell into the oversimplified error of supposing that the character of men could be remade by the food they ate.

Karl Marx, perhaps the most outstanding critic of the dominant bourgeois social system of the nineteenth century, objected to this crude materialism, while at the same time accepting Feuerbach's environmentalism in general. Marx was better versed in the mechanics of indirect psychological conditioning and placed the emphasis for character integration upon psycho-social rather than bio-social processes. Marx' interpretation of social dynamics had in large measure captured the imagination of the more responsible social critics in the fields of politics, economics, sociology and ethics, by the end of this century.

Marx (1818-83), like the Count Saint-Simon, built his interpretation of society upon the dynamics of the industrial revolution, but, unlike Saint-Simon, he opposed the political and social leadership of the captains of industry. Rejecting the autonomous theories of social evolution implicit in the old Natural Law doctrines which had been perpetuated in the current Christian theology and the eighteenth century and Hegelian philosophy, he joined Feuerbach in the search for dynamic causes of social change in the actual environmental conditions of living. But he much less than Feuerbach found these causes in what people eat and much more in what they do in the process of getting their food, clothing and shelter. Like Spinoza, he became a champion of democracy, but unlike Spinoza he sought as a publicist to arouse the people to the assertion of their civil rights. With Friedrich Engels in 1848 he published *The Communist Manifesto,* calling upon the masses to rise and throw off their economic chains. His maturer theories of society were late in life elaborated in his large and abstruse work *Das Kapital.* Starting as a non-violent revolutionist, he ended life as a major social theorist more or less sympathetic with violent revolution, if such became necessary in order to change the social system which he believed to be frankly predatory upon the masses. Engels finished the incomplete second and third volumes of *Das Kapital* after Marx' death.

On the theoretical side Marx set up the doctrine of surplus value as the chief element in capitalistic exploitation. According to this theory, the ruling classes no longer employed military force primarily as a means to plundering the people. Instead, they used their control over employment and working conditions under the bourgeois capitalistic system for this purpose, paying only a bare subsistence wage to the worker while they appropriated all surplus values in the productive process. While this has often been denied by capitalistic sympathizers it seems to have been amply illustrated as far as the consumer-worker is concerned by the upward swing in prices and industrial income following the second World War. He further taught that the strategic disadvantage of the worker in industry prevented him from obtaining a fairer share of the earnings by bargaining methods and drove him to revolutionary procedures as a means of establishing his economic and social rights. This revolution might be peacefully consummated by parliamentary procedures if the people prepared themselves for political action by mastering the materialistic interpretation of history and by organizing politically for the final event. It was his belief that the aggressions of the capitalist class would eventually destroy the middle class and take over all their sources of income by a process of capitalistic absorption of industry—another process which some non-socialistic critics of the present trend say is now occurring through capitalistic inroads upon small business —and leave only two classes confronting each other, the capitalist ruling class and the proletarians. If the proletarians are alert their overwhelming numbers will allow them to expropriate legally the wealth of the capitalist class and absorb their industry through state ownership. But if the capitalist class should resist expropriation by means of a kept army and political trickery and bribery, violent political revolution would become necessary somewhat after the manner in which the bourgeois class took over control from the landed noble classes in the French revolution. In this event the proletariat would claim their rights from the bourgeoisie by violent political revolution as the bourgeoisie had demanded theirs from the noble and clerical classes.

With minor exceptions this social philosophy is now generally accepted by the so-called "labor movement" in most modern countries, typically in Europe, and by the more definitely leftist movements everywhere. The present British government is endeavoring to accomplish the ends here indicated by means of a peaceful parliamentary revolution. In Russia, Lenin and his immediate followers adopted the methods of violent revolution because of the strenuous opposition of the ruling class. The fascist movement in Europe and the imperialistic upsurge in Japan were interpreted by the pro-Marxians as attempts to back up a counter-revolution against proletarian parliamentary revolutions in various countries by means of military dictatorships. Many now hold that the present Communist regime in Russia and her satellite countries is no longer a proletarian movement based on Marxist social and political theory, but a camouflaged imperialistic effort to dominate the world in the interest of a new ruling class.

V. JEWISH SOCIOLOGISTS AND POLITICAL SCIENTISTS PROPER. The Comtean positivism of the middle third of the nineteenth century made a strong appeal to Jewish social and political philosophers of a cosmopolitan outlook. In the first place it discarded the old mystical theology as a religion and substituted human sympathy or humanism as a guiding principle of moral values. It also emphasized a sensationalist psychology and the environmental factors as the determinants of individual and social behavior, two points of view which, as we have seen, were directly in line with the thinking of the most outstanding Jewish social philosophers. Jewish social scientists were also strong believers in the Comtist contention that man's social problems must be solved through the application of empirical and experimental science, including social science, rather than through mystical and metaphysical speculation. The Jews who have become sociologists and political scientists or practical administrators in recent times were not cloistered men, but were men of practical affairs well informed on what was going on in the world. Marx was a journalist, Engels a successful business man, Lassalle a practical politician, Ricardo a banker, Disraeli a member of parliament who prophesied in 1847 that the growth of daily newspapers would foster such an intelligent public opinion that the public press would ultimately replace parliament in making decisions with regard to public policy. Men of this type were strongly hospitable to the scientific investigation of public phenomena.

Perhaps the greatest of the Jewish sociologists and, after Comte, the greatest of French sociologists—Emile Durkheim (1858-1917)—was himself a neo-positivist, a follower of Comte. An almost equally distinguished German Jewish sociologist—Georg Simmel (1858-1918)—was likewise in large measure a disciple of Comtist positivism. These two modern sociologists will occupy our attention immediately, before we pass on to other Jewish sociologists prominent on the stage of European and American sociology and political science.

Durkheim, more than any one else, may be regarded as the sociological continuator of the scientific method of Auguste Comte. To this method he added new sources of data, partly inspired by his early contact with Fustel de Coulanges, the great institutional historian, and Alfred Espinas, the profound student of animal societies, as well as his own extensive researches into ethnology and social organization. He anticipated the anthropologists of the Boas school in his decision that specific societies must be studied before society in general can be understood. He did distinguished work in several fields of sociological investigation. He was the first to examine in detail the social and psychological effects of the division of labor in society which had been hinted at by Plato. His *De la Division de Travail Social* (1893) is still the outstanding authority in that field. This division of labor having come about with the increased complexity and multiplication of functions in society necessarily resulted in a vast differentiation of individual functions and consequently of individual traits, thus producing a hitherto unknown multiplication of personality traits. This fact is responsible for the richness of modern individuality while at the same time it prohibits the development of an equally marked social individualism. Like Spencer, he perceived that individual differentiation goes along with increasing social integration, but on a complementary rather than an identity of personality traits basis. Men must work cooperatively or perish in conflict when they cease to perform the same supplementary tasks. This increasing integration of society he called *solidarité*, which became the symbol of a new school of sociology in France. Solidarity is both mechanical or compulsory (and therefore dependent upon outside pressures, as in dictatorships) and organic. The organic solidarity is the product of mutuality of interests and leaves people free to pursue their own strictly personal interests but admonishes them to join forces where there is mutual interdependence, as in a modern democracy.

Durkheim applied these principles of solidarity to his study of institutions, which study he held must be completely objective in order to avoid distortion of scientific judgment through personal bias. Thus was emphasized the principle of relativity of moral and social practices according to time, place and circumstances. There could be no uniform rule for domestic, religious, political, economic or other institutional conduct in all parts of the world or at all periods of social evolution, nor even in all parts of a single modern society. Men might follow cults of their choice, accept different ideologies, or practice different family folkways at will, short of interfering with the essential cooperative unity or solidarity of society. This was the essence of modern democracy in its truly responsible sense, and in it was to be found that flexibility of social forms and practices which render mutual adjustment more rational and social evolution more facile and functional.

From this point of view it followed that the most effective social control resides in the mores rather than in political authority, because the mores grow directly out of a collective appreciation—however dimly perceived—of collective needs and are less subject to class domination than are political parties. Of course Durkheim wrote before modern means of communication had made mass control through propaganda as prevalent as it now is. He might, however, have argued in rebuttal that this propaganda may much more easily sway immediate decisions than create mores and that such propaganda pertains more to governing bodies—political, economic, cultist, or otherwise—than to the mores. Out of this conception of the dominance of the mores grew his doctrine of collective representations, which is ordinarily held to be the most characteristic contribution of Durkheim to social and political theory. Like W. G. Sumner, the American sociologist, he held that these collective representations or convictions are the true compulsory forces in society and account for the great solidarity of institutions, cults, creeds, ideologies, and folkways. The collective representations or mores (group convictions) may stem from tradition, from interest, rumor, or science, but they become effective and compulsory through the interaction and interstimulation of individual minds in society. They hold men together in common causes and they are the mothers of institutions.

Durkheim applied his theory of collective representations to the analysis of religious institutions in particular. His conclusions were recorded in *Les Formes Elementaires de la Vie Religieuse* (1912). He held that religion is a social product, a complex of collective representations, carrying a heavy moral imperative or commission from the mores, obedience to which is the sanction common to all religions however much they may differ in their morenic content. This is true of religions at all levels of social development. In the most primitive religions the morenic content takes on a mystical sanction which is referred to as mana, a totem, a spirit, or a god, from which the morenic sanction is supposed to be derived. In modern religions the morenic sanction tends to be recognized as a collective representation arising from collective interaction and thinking and thus loses its mystical complexion. This idea of Durkheim caused him to be accused of making God over into a collective representation. The kinship of his theory of religion to that of Comte, as well as to that of Spinoza, is sufficiently obvious. But despite his emphasis upon the element of moral sanction in religion he scarcely went as far as Comte's religion of humanity in setting up a purely humanistic ideal. He demanded something more than human consensus for a valid religion, and this was the sanction of reason with a sociological basis, the thing Comte also sought to bring about through the instrumentality of his priests of positivism. To Durkheim religion, like all other institutions, was a constantly growing thing—past, present and future—finding its validation at all stages of its development in human needs.

This point of view brings us to Durkheim's theory of knowledge, which also is definitely sociological and is closely allied with his theory of collective representations. With Locke he held that all ideas, all knowledge is acquired. How, then, is it built up in human experience? As a sociologist, he does not enter into the details of the conditioning of symbolic responses. He takes the mechanics of conditioning for granted and starts with the frame of intellectual reference built up gradually phylogenetically and ontogenetically through social interaction and interstimulation and response into collective representations. One symbol or group of symbols having been established as a result of common experiences and accepted by the group as a communication device, others are assimilated to these and a body of ideas and values becomes authoritative or the test of all other ideas and values, until and unless it is overthrown by new experience and interpretation. As these ideas and values become numerous and complex, they are of necessity classified and analyzed. Thus all knowledge and value standards partake essentially of the nature of collective representations and are essentially relative to place, time and circumstances. They are never to be assumed to be absolute and free from error by the intelligent man; but faith in their dependability is the securest anchorage of the ordinary man. New types of experience, observation, or experimentation in any area of knowledge or values may upset the existing frame of reference and compel the revision of accepted fact not only in the field where the new knowledge originated, but ultimately in all fields. This principle might be illustrated by the influence of Einstein's theory of relativity upon physical science or by the impact of modern biology upon the older theories of genetics and even upon traditional religious notions.

Finally, we may consider the implications of Durkheim's sociological theories for political theory and policy. He is usually regarded as leaning toward conservative systems of social control. Undoubtedly his sociology of solidarity, dependent upon his analysis of the social division of labor and the consequent need for some sort of social integration to offset the increasing differentiation of individual types, drove him in the direction of an emphasis upon law and order. This emphasis may have been derived in part from Comte, who made these two words, "law" and "order," the symbols of his social system. Both men have been identified in some measure with pre-fascistic theory. In the present writer's opinion, Durkheim was not essentially concerned with political institutions or with the legal and political means by which the necessary solidarity of society was to be integrated out of differential individual types and personalities. He was convinced that the old integrating forces, such as the kingroup, the neighborhood, cult and guild, had so disintegrated that they could no longer perform the task. New integrative forces must be found. Perhaps trade unions, professional associations, ideologies, might do something in this direction. If the state, despite its tendency to utilize artificial mechanical controls, could do more, so much the better; but his real hope was in a broader understanding of the nature of society and the mutuality of interests. Hence he hoped more from education and a science of solidarity or sociology than from anything else. He wished, as was indicated above, to keep the way open for social revision through the differentiation of personality and interests, but without falling into social anarchy. His democracy therefore rested on science, not license. He believed that a social science properly encouraged and exercised could solve these problems of social solidarity and still keep the individual free from intellectual and emotional servitude. The problem was to find the devotees of social science.

This problem was partly solved by the large number of disciples that attached themselves to Durkheim. No other sociologist has had as large a following. Both Jewish and non-Jewish scholars came to his lectures at the universities of Bordeaux and Paris and collaborated with him and wrote under his guidance and inspiration in *L'Année Sociologique,* which he established in 1896 and continued to publish until the eve of the first World War, when culture went into a necessary decline in France. The most devoted of his followers was perhaps Marcel Mauss, a kinsman, who led in the perpetuation of the Durkheim school after the latter's death. Others of his disciples were Georges Davy, Paul Fauconnet, Henri Hubert, Maurice Halbwachs, Celestin Bougle, Charles Blondel, George Dumas, Lucien Levy-Bruhl, Henri Wallon, and, indeed, many more. These men have themselves been very productive in sociology and in the field of collective behavior, where the theory of collective representations has had marked influence upon them. Some, like Levy-Bruhl, Hubert and Mauss, have worked mainly in the field of ethnic behavior and primitive thought. Fauconnet, who succeeded to Durkheim's Sorbonne professorship, Halbwachs, also of the Sorbonne, and R. Aron, have been concerned with methodology and with statistics. Bougle likewise was much interested in methodology and collective behavior. Durkheim gave a strong impetus to the study of the sociology of law, particularly through Davy, A. Moret, A. Bayet, Jean Ray, E. Levy, Georges Gurvitch, Rene Maunier, and others. In the sociology of art his influence has extended through G. H. Luquet and Charles Lalo especially. In the field of the folkways and mores should be added the distinguished names of J. Sion, R. Dion, Maunier, and A. van Gennep. Durkheim's influence on the anthropogeographers, historians, and ethnologists was exerted in so many directions that it is not possible to list even the leading cases. Francois Simiand's work in the sociology of economic behavior, similar to the American institutional economics, is also outstanding. Altogether it may be said that Durkheim did much to transform, not only sociology, but all the social sciences and even psychology in France since 1900.

Not all of the Jewish sociologists of France belonged to the Durkheim school with its filiation of ideas and attitudes running back through Spinoza, Maimonides and the Hebrew prophets. A notable exception was Rene Worms (1869-1926), the brilliant founder of the International Sociological Institute and of its organ, the *Revue International de Sociologie.* Worms emphasized more especially the biological and individual psychological aspects of society, while Durkheim was concerned more with collective behavior. Worms was also a psychological organicist, somewhat after the manner of Spencer and Lilienfeld. In his fifty-seven years he was incessantly active in organization and promotion. He wrote several sociological works, the most notable of which were *Organisme et Société* (1896), *Les Principes Biologiques de l'Evolution Sociale* (1910) and *Philosophie des Sciences Sociales.* When he died the secretaryship of the International Institute passed into the hands of G. L. Duprat of Geneva and the editorship of the *Revue* passed into those of Gaston Richard and later into the care of M. Lasbax. The *Revue* is now published in Madrid as the *Revista Internacional de Sociologia*.

Max Nordau (1849-1923), although born in Hungary, lived so long in France that he may be regarded almost as a French sociologist because of three of his books which had a wide circulation and were much discussed in their day—*The Conventional Lies of Our Civilization* (1884), *Degeneration* (1895), and *The Interpretation of History* (1910). He also wrote *Morals and the Evolution of Man* (1922). He was an associate of Herzl and an ardent Zionist. The present generation can scarcely realize his prestige in the last decade of the nineteenth century. Although primarily an anthropologist and folk-lorist, Solomon Reinach (1858-1932), a French professor and student of religion, produced books of great interest to sociologists. *Cultes, Mythes et Religions* (5 vols., 1905-23) and *Orpheus* (1924) are still of great value for cultural sociology. His *Short History of Christianity* (1922) was a more specialized study of the same character. Reinach, who was a loyal Jew, illustrates well the liberal and cosmopolitan character of Jewish scholarship in the social sciences. He applied the principles of criticism equally to his own and other traditional religions.

Mention should also be made of Jean Finot (Finklestein) among French Jewish sociologists. Born in Warsaw in 1856 he was forced to emigrate at the age of thirty and spent the rest of his life in Paris, where he died in 1922. He was editor of the *Revue des Revues* and *Revue Mondiale* and author of *Race Prejudicé* (1905) and *Problème et Prejuge des Sexes* (1900), both of which circulated widely in France and abroad. His last important book was *Saints Initiés et Possedés Modernes* (1918).

Georg Simmel (1858-1918) exercised a somewhat similar, but less marked, influence over the development of German sociology to that of Durkheim over French sociology. Born in the same year, the lives of these two men paralleled each other in many ways. They were both positivists or followers of Comte in a general way. Both were much concerned with basic methodological problems, and each took the lead in developing sociology in his own country. The American sociologist, Albion W. Small, regarded Simmel as the leading German sociologist in his day and translated and published in the *American Journal of Sociology* many chapters of his works. Both Simmel and Durkheim were among the collaborating editors of this review.

While Durkheim entered sociology through pedagogy and ethnological-cultural studies, Simmel came to the field through philosophy. There were no separate chairs in sociology in Germany, and philosophy was the only academic door open to sociology in that country. Simmel was evidently drawn to sociology, although he had no professorship in it, for the same reason pointed out above which made the subject attractive to Jews. His Jewish background also doubtless determined his approach to the field as it did in the case of Durkheim. The latter was much concerned with the sanctions of the beliefs which men hold and he found them in collective representations. Simmel was more interested in the directions and forms which human relationships assume. He early took this field of interrelational forms and social processes for his own as a sociologist. Being a cosmopolitan Jew he must have recognized the problem of maintaining his own individuality in a predominantly gentile world. Consequently throughout his career he insisted upon the fact that society is not made up of identical individuals, nor does it achieve cooperative unity through mechanical coercion, but rather through mutual adaptation and cooperation. Because he did not approach social dynamics through the analysis or differentiation of functions, as did Durkheim, he did not make so much of the processes by which personalities are individualized in our complex society. He merely insisted (in his *Lebensanschauung*) upon the fact that people are different and that they achieve cooperative behavior and social unity through working out a modus vivendi. This point of view has also been strongly emphasized in this country by F. H. Allport in opposition to the "social mind" theories of Tarde, Le Bon, McDougall, Giddings and the suggestion social psychologists.

Simmel's sociology early became known as formal sociology, which meant sociology of the forms of collective behavior rather than the study of authoritarian behavior. By analysis of collective behavior he was able to detect the processes of interstimulation going on within the mass behavior and to isolate the leading forms of communication and interaction. Among these forms of intercourse were dominance, subjection, convention, contract, competition, conflict, gratitude, conservatism, ordination, prestige, fashion, conformity, and the like. This isolation of the social interaction processes threw so much light on collective behavior by breaking it up into its constituent parts, so that it could be seen from many points of view and in perspective instead of as a single blur too confused to be easily understood, that Simmel had many followers and imitators. He wrote a book on fashion and conformity (*Philosophie der Mode,* 1905) and thereby gave an impetus to a form of sociological analysis which is still in full swing. He devoted much attention to domination and social control. He points out that even the modern political state cannot dominate effectively through force, but must employ symbolic controls if it seeks the most active conformity. He analyzed domination into three major types: domination (1) by a single individual, (2) by groups of persons acting together, and (3) by an objective or impersonal principle. The last of the three grows in importance with the development of improved means of communication and more effective means of symbolization. It becomes the great instrument of ideologies, fashion, propaganda. It is not surprising therefore that social psychology in this country has continued the analysis of the processes of domination and subordination and applied the analysis to the interpretation of modern methods of social control, especially in connection with salesmanship, proselytising, the propagation of ideologies, the direction of public opinion and the like.

In the opinion of Simmel the field of general sociology consisted of the application of these principles of interaction patterns to the specific institutions of society. Understanding the mechanics and processes of the social institutions was to comprehend sociology in its general aspects. Being a philosopher by profession, he spoke of another aspect of sociology —philosophical sociology—which he regarded as a sort of methodology. Its field was the determination and validation of sociological concepts, largely on the subjective side. This was the angle from which he approached sociology. Practically the only points at which he touched political theory were when he dealt with political interaction patterns and with the phenomena of money. He wrote a *Philosophie des Geldes,* but he was more concerned in this treatise with the free response patterns in financial relations than with governmental controls over the money market. The main political implication of his theory of money is the aid which the modern money economy has brought indirectly to the support of democracy. In the early stages of society money was merely a commodity like any other, except that it was more readily employable in barter and market exchanges. In our day money is no longer primarily a commodity, but is a symbol of economic values. It is not so much to be grubbed from the earth as it is to be obtained by intellectual manipulation and planning. When commerce and finance replaced agriculture as the dominant economy, intellect became supreme over muscle power. Merit in this higher sense might now rule and class status was replaced by individual ability as the key to power. This made for greater democracy and helped to abolish slavery even more than skilled artisanship did. But the avenue through which this new democracy was made effective was economic before it was political.

Simmel did not have as many or as devoted disciples as did Durkheim. But Leopold von Wiese, Ferdinand Toennies, Max

Weber, Max Graf zu Solms, and Ludwig Stein in Germany owed much to him and in this country Albion W. Small, R. E. Park and Nicholas J. Spykman were in some measure his disciples.

Germany has had its full share of distinguished Jewish sociologists. Among them may be mentioned Franz Oppenheimer, born in 1864, and trained at first as a physician. In the course of time his interest in the social studies, particularly in economics and sociology, became dominant and he was made a professor in the University of Frankfurt. Driven out of Germany when Hitler came to power, he taught in Paris, Jerusalem, and Los Angeles, where he died in 1943. It is interesting to note that his starting point in sociology is the struggle for justice. Justice is obtainable only through an understanding of social processes and laws. He was influenced early in his career by the theories of Karl Marx and Gumplowicz. His book *The State* traces political evolution back to exploitation of the masses by bands of armed leaders who became the great landholding nobles and kings who organized their power politically and economically and reduced the workers to serfdom. This was not a theory calculated to recommend him to Hitler and the Nazis. Oppenheimer was also much interested in social reform, holding that the use of social theory is in its application to the solution of social problems.

A group of important younger German Jewish sociologists were also driven out of their native land after 1933. Among these, Karl Mannheim, who was born in Budapest in 1893 and was professor at Frankfurt until 1933, was especially active in developing the newer discipline of the sociology of knowledge. His early works were philosophic essays in this field and included *Strukturanalyse der Erkenntnistheorie* (1922), *Zum Problem einer Klassification der Wissenschaften* (1922), *Beitrage sur Theorie der Weltanschauungsinterpretation* (1922), *Historismus* (1924), *Das Problem einer Soziologie der Wissens* (1925). His *Ideology and Utopia* (1936; German edition 1929) has had an almost universal circulation. *Man and Society in the Age of Reconstruction* (1940; German edition 1935) was an attempt to account for the existing disturbed condition of society and to indicate some remedies. After being forced to leave Germany he was added to the sociology staff in the University of London, where he remained until his untimely death in 1948.

Albert Salamon was another Hitler casualty among German Jewish sociologists. After taking refuge in France for some time he migrated to the United States and has been connected with the New School for Social Research in New York City since 1935. In Germany he was editor of *Die Gesellschaft* and taught at the University of Cologne until 1933. Gottfried Solomon (born in Frankfurt 1892) was assistant professor in the University of Frankfurt 1924-1933. Having to leave Germany in the last named year, he was attached to the Sorbonne in Paris until 1940. He has been at the New School for Social Research in New York since 1943. He was a pupil of Simmel and Franz Oppenheimer and was editor of the *Jahrbuch für Soziologie*. His main interest was in political sociology, as is shown by his *Allgemeine Staatslehre* (1930) and *Politik als Wissenschaft* (1930). Edward Husserl (1859-1938), although a philosopher by training and predilection, had much influence on German sociology through his theories of phenomenology. His influence on A. Vierkandt[10] was especially marked.

The dean of Austrian sociologists—Ludwig Gumplowicz (1838-1909)—was a Polish Jew. His influence on Oppenheimer has already been noted. He was perhaps the most outstanding representative of the conflict school of sociologists. Living in the polyglot Austrian Empire, he was an intimate observer of the conflict of classes, nationalities and races. His theory of social conflict was summed up largely in *Der Rassenkampf*, which enjoyed a wide circulation in the French and English translations as well as in the original German. His *Outlines of Sociology* (Philadelphia, 1899) was also based largely on the theory of social conflict. The social conflict point of view necessarily induced in Gumplowicz a strong interest in political theory. He believed the state arose out of the exploitation of the agricultural masses by the armed hunters and robbers and that this exploitation has continued to the present day, although its employment of force has been replaced or supplemented in part by political intrigue and propaganda. He published an important series of works dealing with this theory of the state and with modern political problems. Among these are *Soziologie und Politik* and *Die Soziologische Staatsidee* (1902), *Geschichte der Staatstheorien* (1905) and *Das Allgemeine Staatsrecht* (1907), which summarized such earlier studies in political sociology as *Philosophisches Staatsrecht* (1877), *Das Oesterreichische Staatsrecht* (1891), and *Rechtstaat und Socialismus* (1881). He greatly influenced the American sociologist Lester F. Ward, who visited him repeatedly on his European tours.

Another Austrian Jewish sociologist of note was Ludwig Stein (1859-1930), a rabbi and philosopher. Stein was much more cosmopolitan than Gumplowicz. Although born in Hungary, he was educated in Holland and Germany and taught at the University of Berne. He was active in journalism and in public affairs generally and was employed at one time as a diplomatic mediator between the German and British governments. He published works dealing with the social question (1897), the organic method in sociology (1898), social optimism (1905), the beginnings of human culture (1906), philosophical tendencies of the present (1908), introduction to sociology (1921), and *Evolution and Optimism* (1926). This last book was a reply to Oswald Spengler's *Decline of the West*. He spent the year 1923-1924 in the United States lecturing before various universities. Barnes says that Stein conceived the three main tasks of sociology to be "(1) the investigation of the history of social institutions; (2) the tracing of the development of social theories; and

(3) the formulation of rules and ideals to guide the social development of the future."[11]

Stein depended largely on Gumplowicz's theory of the origin of the state and private property. He believed that the greatest step in the exploitation of the masses was taken with the establishment of private property in land. He schematized the stages of the development of social and political authority in terms of the rule of (1) the elders, (2) the sacred leaders, (3) the priestly class, (4) royalty, (5) the public military, (6) legal administrators, (7) school authorities, and (8) scientific rules of conduct. He thought the best guarantee of civic freedom was to be found in the further socialization of the law. On the whole, he believed that the state should assume a large number of functions, both for social welfare and in the conduct of economic affairs. He emphasized the need to bring political and juristic institutions, says Barnes, up to a par with social evolution in other aspects, since both law and government now lag behind in the stream of cultural progress. He was a strong believer in internationalism.

VII. OTHER EUROPEAN COUNTRIES. Cesare Lombroso (1835-1909) was the most outstanding of the Italian Jewish sociologists. His first academic interest was in Roman history, which seems to intrigue almost all Italian scholars. Having been trained in medicine and receiving an appointment as superintendent of an asylum, he developed concern with pathology which characterized his future studies. He produced an ecological study, a *Medical Geography of Italy,* in 1865. But already in 1864 he had published *Genio e Follia. L'Uomo Dilinquente* followed in 1876. He also wrote on prostitution, normal and abnormal types of women, and in the eighteen-nineties appeared his great work on the criminal. He is known as the founder of the positive or scientific school of criminology, which had so much prestige around the turn of the century and produced Enrico Ferri, his disciple. Many of his biological theories are now discounted, but as a pioneer his work was remarkable. As a Zionist he developed political interests, but he was not particularly active in public matters outside of penal reform. He resented anti-semitic criticisms and sought at one time to establish the existence of physical stigmata in these critics.

More of an economist than a sociologist, Achille Loria (1857-1936) nevertheless had strong sociological and political interests. He taught successively at the Universities of Siena, Padua and Turin—at the last after 1903—and was made a senator in 1919 despite the fact that he was an outspoken advocate of the Marxist materialistic interpretation of history. He was also editor of an economic and political journal. He applied the Marxist theories of history and economics in a number of works, including *Analisi della Proprietà Capitalista* (1889). His *Verso la Giustizia Sociale* (*Toward Social Justice,* 1920) reveals him in the traditional role of the Hebrew prophet-reformer. He published a work on Karl Marx in 1924.

Pessach Liebman Hersch was born in Lithuania in 1882. He attended the University of Warsaw, but was driven out of Poland because of his liberal views. He took his doctorate at the University of Geneva and later became a professor there. Although primarily a statistician, he has written extensively in the field of Jewish sociology. Among these writings are *Die Kooperative Bevegung* (1911), *Le Juif Errant d'Aujourdhui* (1913), *La Mortalité chez les Neutres au Temps de Guerre* (1915), *L'Inégalité devant la Mort d'après les Statistiques de la Ville de Paris* (1920), *La Mortalité causée par la Guerre mondiale* (1925), *International Emigration of the Jews* (1931), *Fabrecherishkeit fun Iden un Nit-Iden in Polen* (1937), *Le Juif Delinquant* (1938).

England, although manifesting no obvious prejudice toward Jewish social scientists, has only one outstanding Jewish sociologist to her credit—Morris Ginsberg, born in 1889. His early teaching at the University of London was in philosophy. But, as one of the ablest students and disciples of L. T. Hobhouse, he succeeded to the Martin White professorship in sociology upon the death of Hobhouse in 1929. He collaborated with Hobhouse in the first effort to introduce statistical measurements into anthropological theory, *The Material Culture and Social Institutions of the Simpler Peoples* (1930), and with John A. Hobson he published a life of Hobhouse in 1934. He has not been particularly prolific in sociological theory. His *Psychology of Society* (1921) owed much to Graham Wallace. His *Studies in Sociology* (1932) deals effectively with special problems. He published a popular work on *Sociology* in 1934. He was instrumental in providing a teaching refuge at the University of London for an abler sociologist, Karl Mannheim, when the latter was driven out of Germany in 1933.

England has a somewhat better showing with respect to political science. Harold Laski, born in 1893, taught at first in McGill and Harvard Universities, but returned to England in his early thirties to teach political science in the University of London. He has been a prolific writer of good books in his chosen field. Interested at first in formal political controls, he published *The Problem of Sovereignty* in 1917 and then *Authority in the Modern State* in 1919. His *Grammar of Politics* appeared in 1925. Other books followed rapidly, showing his increasing interest in popular political behavior: *Communism* (1927), *Liberty in the Modern State* (1930), *Democracy in Crisis* (1933), *The State in Theory and Practice* (1935), *The Rise of European Liberalism* (1936), *Where Do We Go From Here?* (1940). More recently he has written extensively about American institutions, partly for the American public, but also to make clear the nature of our political institutions to the British, whose destiny has become so closely interlaced with our own. *The American Presidency* appeared in 1941 and, in 1948, a large and ambitious work entitled *The American Democracy*. Laski, like most other Jewish social scientists, is a liberal in the typical prophetic tradition of his people. For some time he served as secretary of the British socialist Labor party. He writes extensively for the press in England and the United States and has lectured widely in both countries on international and domestic problems. He has suffered some opposition from conservative governmental agencies, having been fined heavily in England because of reputed misquotation of Winston Churchill and having lecture engagements cancelled in California. He died in 1950.

VIII. THE UNITED STATES. In the United States, within the present generation, Jews have been increasingly identified with both sociology and political science. They first entered the field of politics through journalism and local political leadership. They did not become extensively associated with academic service in these two fields before the nineteen-thirties. Bernard Moses was head of the department of political and social science at the University of California before the end of the nineteenth century. He was succeeded there by one of his students, Jessica Peixotto, who taught courses in the field of applied sociology and economics. Isidor Loeb taught political science at the University of Missouri and Washington University for nearly fifty years and was a dean in each institution successively. Professor Ernst Freund was long a leading authority on social legislation and administrative law at the University of Chicago in the first third of the twentieth century. Jacob H. Hollander (1871-1940), long a professor of economics in Johns Hopkins University, dipped into the field of sociology as a side line in two of his books, *The Abolition of Poverty* (1914) and *Want and Plenty* (1932). Since these works constitute the major part of his literary output, it may perhaps be inferred that his interest was really more in sociology than in economics. But Jews generally found their best opportunities for work in political and sociological science in connection with public and private social agencies, in editorial and publicity efforts, rather than in teaching.

Walter Lippmann, born 1889, entered journalism after leaving Harvard and served for several years as an editor of *The*

New Republic. He brought out his first book, *A Preface to Politics* (1913), at the age of twenty-four. Other books dealing with politics and social problems followed fast: *Drift and Mastery* (1914), *The Stakes of Diplomacy* (1915), *The Political Scene* (1919), *Liberty and the News* (1920), *Public Opinion* (1922), still a standard work; *The Phantom Public* (1925), *American Inquisitors* (1928), *A Preface to Morals* (1929), *The Method of Freedom* (1934), *The Good Society* (1937), *War and Peace* (1940). Many other books on current political and social problems filled in the spaces between the works listed here. As a syndicated columnist Lippmann has exercised a wide and profound influence—progressively more conservative as he grew older—over American public opinion. He is credited with originating the term "cold war." A companion editor on the *New Republic* staff was Walter E. Weyel, who gave most of his attention to social and economic problems. But he also produced three works in the field of popular democracy before his death in the nineteen-twenties. These were *American World Policies* (1917), *The End of the War* (1918), which made some pertinent suggestions for future democratic policy, and *The New Democracy,* which pointed out possible democratic trends after the war.

Another influential political writer, publicist rather than academic theorist, is Louis Fischer, born in Philadelphia in 1876. In his capacity as war correspondent—notably in the late civil war in Spain—and as a roving correspondent, he has made many challenging interpretations of international affairs. His early book, *Oil Imperialism* (1926), attempted to get at a fundamental economico-political force in international relations. *Machines and Men in Russia* (1932) had a similar bearing upon Russian domestic affairs. *The War in Spain* (1937) was an impassioned appeal, richly documented from current history, to the so-called democracies to support democracy in Spain. But the appeal went unheeded as far as the so-called democratic governments were concerned. *Men and Politics* (1941) is more in the manner of Walter Lippmann. More recently he has written penetratingly on Russia, India, and Gandhi. He left an editorship on the *Nation* because he said that periodical had developed a pro-Russian "line."

Combining the work of a publicist as a side line with teaching (first at the University of Chicago and later at Williams College), Frederick L. Schuman (born 1904) has been outstanding for his liberal views in politics and for his tolerant interpretation of Russian policy. His first book was *American Foreign Policy Toward Russia* (1928). From the first he concentrated on international politics, publishing *War and Diplomacy in the French Republic*, 1931; *International Politics*, 1933; *Conduct of German Foreign Affairs*, 1934; *The Nazi Dictatorship*, 1935; *Germany Since 1918*, 1937; *Europe On The Eve*, 1939; *Night Over Europe*, 1941; *Design for Power* (with George Brodsky), 1942; and *Soviet Politics*, 1946. He has also been active in the public press and forums and in professional magazines.

Morris Ernst (born in Alabama, 1888), a New York lawyer interested in civil liberties, probably ranks next after Walter Lippmann as a political publicist in the field of individual freedom. His *Ultimate Power* (1937) was a defense of democracy in general. *Too Big* (1940) dealt with modern business, while *The Censor Marches On* (1940) discussed the tendency to strangle democracy. *The Fight Against Freedom* (1946) continued the theme, and *The People Know Best* (1949) points out a possible means of restoration of popular rights. Max Lerner (1902) is a more recent and perhaps a somewhat more leftist commentator on the undemocratic trends of the times. His *Ideas Are Weapons* (1939) emphasizes the uses of propaganda. *Ideas for the Ice Age* (1941) voices a note of pessimism not uncommon among lovers of democracy. *It Is Later Than You Think* (1943) continues this note and carries an invocation. *The Mind and Faith of Justice Holmes* (1943) calls to witness the work of a great legal democrat, while his *Public Journal* (1945) recapitulates some of the political events of the war having significance for democracy. Lerner left teaching at Williams College for an editorship on *PM* early in the war. After *PM* folded up he joined the staff of Brandeis University.

Other Jewish political publicists and commentators deserving notice include Harold Lavine (1915), who produced the exciting *Fifth Column in America* in 1940, and, with James Wechsler, published *War Propaganda in the United States* in the same year. Marcus Eli Ravage, who was born in Rumania in 1884, wrote *The Malady of Europe* (1923), but was best known for his *An American in the Making* (1917). Several Jewish immigrants have described the interesting process of adaptation to the new world. Mary Antin's *The Promised Land* (1912) was the most popular of these. *They Who Knock at Our Gates* (1914) was a less personal account of the immigrants by the same author. Isaac A. Hourwich's *Immigration and Labor* (1912) was a defense of immigration on economic grounds. Lilliam D. Wald's *House on Henry Street* (1915) and *Windows on Henry Street* (1934) were graphic pictures of the immigrant adjustment process. Reuben Fink (1889) wrote *America and Palestine* (1944) and Zera Silver Fink (1902) produced *The Classical Republicans* (1945). Horace M. Kallen wrote along the same line in *Zionism and World Politics* (1921).

The more systematic writers on public opinion have also been at work. For example, Paul Felix Lazersfeld (1915), of the Columbia University faculty, has written extensively on the means of communication and public opinion. Among his books are *Radio and the Printed Page* (1940), *The People Look at Radio* (1946), *Radio Listening in the United States* (1948). His *The People's Choice* (1948) deals with opinion polls and the 1948 political campaign. A. A. Roback (1890) has dealt more generally with communication in *Jewish Influence on Modern Thought* (1929) and *Personality, the Crux of Social Intercourse* (1931). Edward L. Bernays (1891), a public relations counsel with a strong theoretical interest, has carried his work into the academic field of social psychology in two books on propaganda: *Crystallizing Public Opinion* (1924) and *Propaganda* (1928).

Jews have entered sociology in the United States so recently that most of those who have become distinguished in the field (1) have worked in the applied aspects, frequently as government or institutional experts, and (2) were born abroad, especially in Germany, where their opportunities for this sort of training were perhaps better than elsewhere. Maurice Fishberg (1872-1934) is an example. Born in Russia, trained in medicine, and for long head of the Montefiore Hospital in New York, he developed a strong secondary interest in anthropology, which probably would have been his primary concern had leisure or profession permitted. His book, *The Jews —A Study in Race and Environment* (1911), was long the standard sociological work in this field. He emphasized the influence of environment upon both the culture and the biological traits of the Jews. The *Universal Jewish Encyclopaedia* says that he demonstrated "the heterogeneous racial elements entering into the Jews of modern times."

Bruno Lasker, born in Germany in 1880, came to the United States by way of England, where he did social work from 1904 to 1914. In this country he held editorial positions on *The Survey* (1915-23) and *The Inquiry* (1923-32). Since 1932 he has been educational and research secretary of the Institute of Pacific Relations. He also served for a time as secretary of the Commission on Race Relations. Three of his sociological works are *Race Attitudes in Children* (1929)—an attempt to illustrate the environmental origins of prejudice; *Jewish Experiences in America* (1930); and *Filipino Immigration* (1931). He has been interested in housing, unemployment, and race relations primarily. Louis Israel Dublin, the statistician for the Metropolitan Life Insurance Company and the source of much of its better health education and propaganda, was born in Lithuania in 1882. He had teaching experience at Yale from 1917 to 1923 and was President of the American Statistical Association in 1924 and President of the Population

Association of America in 1935-36. His sociological works are *Population Problems in the United States and Canada* (1926); *Health and Wealth* (1928); *The Money Value of a Man* (with A. J. Latka, 1930); and *To Be Or Not to Be* (1933), a study of suicide with B. Brinzel. He has also collaborated with other writers in works on social insurance.

Jacob Lestschinsky (born in the Ukraine, 1876) made a Jewish community study in Russia in 1904 and an investigation of Russian Jewish workers in 1907. From 1923 to 1935 he was editor of *Bleter far Yidishe Demografie, Statistik un Ekonomik.* He was a Zionist and active politically in Jewish world affairs. He became international correspondent of *Der Idisher Arbeiter* in 1906 and wrote *Marx i Kautsky o Yevreiskom Voprosie* (1907), *Dos Idishe Folk in Tzifrn* (1922), *Di Yidishe Vanderung* (1927), *Tzvishn Leben un Toit* (1930), *Di Ekonomische Lage fun Yidn in Poiln* (1931), *Das wirtschaftliche Schicksal des Deutschen Judentums* (1932), *Der Yidisher Ekonomisher Churban noch der Welt Milchom* (1934), and *Dos sovietsche Yudentum* (1941). Julius Friedrich Hecker, also born in Russia (1881), gave his attention more closely to the field of sociological ideas. His important book on *Russian Sociology* (1915) was followed by *Religion and Communism* in 1933 and by *Religion and a Changing Civilization* in 1935. Dr. Max Weinreich, research director of the Yiddish Scientific Institute of New York, was co-editor of the *Yivo Bleter* of that Institute from 1931 to 1940 and editor since that time. Besides directing and editing the research of the Institute, he has published a number of sociological works of his own, among which are *Der Veg tsu undzer Yugnt* (1935), which describes the aim and methods of youth research; *The Classification of Jewish Immigrants* (1945); and *Hitler's Professors: The Part of Scholarship in Germany's Crimes against the Jewish People* (1946).

Horace M. Kallen was born in Germany in 1882, but was educated in the United States. Teaching first at Clark College and the University of Wisconsin, he later transferred to the

New School for Social Research in order to be more closely in touch with Zionism and other Jewish activities. He is a keen observer and critic of social institutions. Among his books are *Zionism and World Policy,* which is an argument for world peace; *Individualism;* and *Culture and Democracy in the United States.* Julius Drachsler (1889-1927) was born in Czechoslovakia but received his college education in the United States. He taught sociology in the College of the City of New York and engaged actively in such programs for social welfare as social insurance, industrial relations and inter-racial contacts. He wrote two influential books: *Democracy and Assimilation* (1920) and *Intermarriage in New York City* in 1921.

Another Czechoslovakian by birth who now teaches in the United States is Hans Kelsen, born in Prague in 1881. His field is political sociology and political science. He became a professor of law at the University of Vienna in 1919 but transferred to the University of Cologne in 1930. Being expelled from Germany in 1933, although baptized as a Christian, he was associated with the Institute of International Law at Geneva until 1936, when he became a professor at the University of Prague. After the Hitler invasion of Czechoslovakia he came to the United States and taught at the University of California. He has written mainly in the field of political science: *Hauptprobleme der Staatsrechtslehre* (1911); *Vom Wesen und Wert der Demokratie* (1920); *Sozialismus und Staat* (1923); *Allgemeine Rechtslehre* (1925); *Der soziologische und der juristiche Staatsbegriff* (1928); *Theorie Generale du Droit International* (1932); *The Legal Process and International Order* (1934); and *Reine Rechtslehre* (1934).

Max Radin (1880-1950, Germany) also a professor of law at the University of California, has written extensively in the field of the social relations of law. His first book, however, was *Jews Among the Greeks and Romans* (1916). His *Life of the People in Biblical Times* appeared in 1929. His preoccupation with the historical perspective was further indicated in a

Handbook of Roman Law (1927) and *The Trial of Jesus of Nazareth* (1931). His *Lawful Pursuit of Gain* (1931) entered the fields of economics and sociology, while *The Law as Logic and Experience* (1940) dealt with legal philosophy. *The Day of Reckoning* (1943) discussed the problem of the disposal of Nazis after the war. Jerome N. Frank (1889), lawyer and federal judge, has contributed one of the best sociological interpretations of legal institutions in *Law and the Modern Mind* (1930). More particularly concerned with government and the problems of democracy are his *If Men Were Angels* (1942) and *Fate and Freedom* (1945).

Of the many younger Jews who have been productive in the borderlands of sociology, Louis Berman (1893) may be mentioned for his application of sociology to endocrinology in *Glands Regulating Personality* (1921) and *Food and Character* (1932). Abraham Epstein, born in Russia in 1892, but educated in the United States, did his first book on *The Negro Migrant in Pittsburgh* (1918). But his major work has been on the margin between economics and sociology. He wrote *Facing Old Age* in 1922, *The Challenge of the Aged* in 1928, and *Insecurity* in 1933. Clayton James Ettinger (1881) brought out *The Problem of Crime* in 1932. Frank Tannenbaum, born in Austria in 1893, but educated at Columbia University, where he also took his Ph.D. and is now a member of the faculty, may be regarded as the most outstanding of the Jewish applied sociologists in the United States. He has worked and published in several fields. He began with *The Labor Movement* in 1921. Then he turned to the field of criminology and penology with *Wall Shadows* (1922), *Osborne of Sing Sing* (1933), and *Crime and the Community* (1938). He has spent considerable time in Latin America, and especially in Puerto Rico and Mexico, where he has made surveys, including one on rural education for the Mexican government. He published *The Mexican Agrarian Revolution* in 1928 and *Whither Latin America* in 1934. His *Darker Phases of the South* appeared in 1924 and his *Peace by Revolution* in 1933. *Slave and*

Citizen: *The Negro in the Americas* was published in 1947. He has combined journalism with academic sociology. Louis Wirth, who teaches sociology at the University of Chicago, was born in Germany. His chief interests are in the city (his *The Ghetto* appeared in 1928) and in the sociology of communication. He was president of the American Sociological Society in 1947.

Bernhard Joseph Stern (1894), the editor of *Science and Society*, has also covered a wide range of sociological subjects. His first interest was in the social aspects of medicine. He published *Social Factors in Medical Progress* in 1927 and *Sociology and Medical Progress* in 1941. He edited *Young Ward's Diary* in 1935 and has written and edited material on L. H. Morgan, Lester F. Ward, E. A. Ross and A. W. Small. In 1938 he entered the field of the family with a work on that subject and in 1942 published with Alain Locke a work on social contact processes called *When People Meet*. He teaches at Columbia University. Harriet Rosenthal Mowrer (1899) first published *Domestic Discord,* a research work, with her husband E. R. Mowrer, in 1928. In 1935 she published independently a work on *Personality Adjustment and Domestic Discord*. These studies were based on her research as a social worker in Chicago. Pauline Vislick Young of the University of Southern California, also trained in social work and sociology, made a study of immigrant adjustment in *The Pilgrims of Russian Town* (1932). Her later work has been mainly in the field of research and methodology, in which she has published three standard works, *Interviewing in Social Work* (1935), *Scientific Social Surveys and Research* (1935), and *Social Treatment in Probation and Delinquency* (1937). For a while, prior to the second World War, she and her husband, Erle F. Young, published a social work magazine.

Jewish anthropologists in the United States have frequently produced work in sociology and political science. Robert H. Lowie, professor of anthropology at the University of California, was born in Vienna in 1883. He has specialized in the sociological aspects of anthropology. Among his works in this field are *The Social Life of the Crow Indians* (1912), *Societies of the Crow Indians* (1913), *Age Societies of the Plains Indians* (1916), *Culture and Ethnology* (1917), *Myths and Traditions of the Crow Indians* (1918), *Primitive Society* (1920), *Primitive Religion* (1924), *Origin of the State* (1927), *Are We Civilized?* (1929), and *The German People* (1945). Paul Radin has produced *Social Anthropology* and *Primitive Man as Philosopher*. Melville J. Herskovits (1895) has leaned heavily toward the sociological side of anthropology. His *The Cattle Complex in East Africa* (1926) has a sociological theme. *The American Negro* (1928) was basically sociological. *Life in a Haitian Valley* (1937) and *Trinidad Village* (with Frances Herskovits, 1947) were sociological studies of backward and primitive communities. *Acculturation* (1938) is an essay in social adaptation. *The Economic Life of Primitive Peoples* (1940) and *Man and His Work* (1948) are works on social anthropology. *The Myth of the Negro Past* (1941) is a study in folk psychology. In the field of folklore, Benjamin Albert Botkin (1901) has interpreted regional and class beliefs and traditions in terms of their social setting. His *Treasury of American Folklore* (1944) was a survey of the whole field. *Lay My Burden Down* (1945) was based on Negro remembrances of slavery. The *Treasury of New England Folklore* (1947) is a regional study.

Jewish scholars entered the field of sociological theory relatively late and are only now coming into prominence. Fay Berger Karpf (1891) surveyed the field of *American Social Psychology* in 1932. Maurice H. Krout, after publishing a work on the psychology of personality, brought out *The Psychology of Children's Lies* in 1932 and *Autistic Gestures* in 1935. His major work on *Introduction to Social Psychology* was published in 1942. Harry Alpert has interpreted the theories of Durkheim in his *Emile Durkheim and His Sociology* (1939). Samuel Chugerman has done the same service for Lester F. Ward in his *Lester Frank Ward, the American*

Aristotle (1939). Horace M. Kallen has written on *Art and Freedom* (1942) and *The Liberal Spirit* (1948). There are now many young Jewish instructors in political science and sociology teaching in American universities, some of whom will doubtless require further notice in years to come.

In general summary it may be said that the history and traditional culture of Jews have predisposed them toward political science and sociology in those countries which have admitted them to activity in these subjects. This brief sketch, which has not afforded space for the mention of all the important contributions of Jews to these two fields, has nevertheless shown clearly that their contributions to them have been noteworthy. It has also shown that their contributions have almost always been on the side of democracy and public welfare.

FOOTNOTES

[1] *The Intellectual Adventures of Ancient Man,* University of Chicago Press, 1946.

[2] Genesis, 12:7.

[3] Leviticus.

[4] *A Sociological Study of the Bible* (Chicago, 1912); *God and the Social Process* (Chicago, 1935); *The Bible Is Human* (New York, 1942).

[5] W. A. L. Elmslie, *Studies in Life from Jewish Proverbs,* James Clarke, London, N. D.

[6] *The Gentle Cynic.*

[7] *A History of Hebrew Civilization* (Geo. Harrap and Co., London, 1926).

[8] *God and the Social Process* (University of Chicago Press, 1935).

[9] J. Hertzler, *History of Utopian Thought* (1923) and *The Social Thought of Ancient Civilization* (New York: McGraw-Hill, 1930).

[10] Theodore Abel, *Systematic Sociology in Germany* (New York, 1929).

[11] *Introduction to the History of Sociology,* University of Chicago Press, 1948.

BIBLIOGRAPHY

ABEL, THEODORE FRED, *Systematic Sociology in Germany*. Columbia University Press, 1929.

BARNES, HARRY ELMER, *Historical Sociology*. New York: Philosophical Library, 1948.

BARNES, HARRY ELMER, *Introduction to the History of Sociology*. University of Chicago Press, 1948.

BARNES, HARRY ELMER, *Sociology and Political Theory*. New York: Knopf, 1924.

BARNES, HARRY ELMER and BECKER, HOWARD, *Contemporary Social Theory*. New York: Appleton-Century-Crofts, 1940.

BARNES, HARRY ELMER and BECKER, HOWARD, *Social Thought from Lore to Science*, 2 vols. Boston: D. C. Heath and Co., 1938.

BERTHOLET, ALFRED, *A History of Hebrew Civilization*. London: Harrap, 1926.

DURANT, WILL, *The Story of Philosophy*. New York: Simon and Schuster, 1920.

Encyclopaedia of the Social Sciences. New York: Macmillan, 1930.

Encyclopedia Universal Ilustrada. Bilbao, Spain: Espasa-Calpe.

GURVITCH, GEORGES and MOORE, WILBERT E., *Twentieth Century Sociology*. New York: Philosophical Library, 1945.

ROUCEK, JOSEPH S., *Twentieth Century Political Thought*. New York: Philosophical Library, 1946.

ROUCEK, JOSEPH S., *Slavonic Encyclopaedia*. New York: Philosophical Library, 1949.

SOROKIN, PITIRIM, *Contemporary Sociological Theory*. New York: Harper, 1928.

SPYKMAN, NICHOLAS J., *The Social Theory of Georg Simmel*. University of Chicago Press, 1925.

Universal Jewish Encyclopaedia. New York: 1939.

Who's Who in America. Chicago: A. N. Marquis and Co., 1948-49.

Who's Who in American Jewry. New York: National News Association.

Jews in Public Office

By HUGO BIEBER

THE appointment of a Jew to a public office is often regarded with apprehension even by those who usually recognize and exalt Jewish contributions to modern civilization on scientific, artistic, economic or philanthropic fields. Some people, ready to protest against persecution of Jews, are still inclined to think that nearly two thousand years of stateless existence and deprivation of civil rights made the Jew unfit for the management of public affairs, even if he has the best intention to serve the common weal. Others, equally opposed to oppressive anti-Semitism, dislike political activities of Jews because they conclude from their knowledge of Jewish history that these activities are bound to favor radicalism and revolution. Both of these arguments, however, are wrecked on undeniable facts which prove that Jews, in many epochs and particularly in modern times, have been instrumental to the construction, preservation, and peaceful progress of the communal and national institutions of the peoples among whom they live.

It is true that the remembrance of centuries of oppression and the awareness of subsisting discriminations induced numerous Jews to concentrate their energies upon the struggle against privileges and restrictions of every kind. Consequently, there was a relatively great number of Jews among parties that combated oppressive governments or even tried to overthrow reactionary regimes by revolutionary action. Every nation, striving for liberty and democracy, has experienced situations that urgently called for men to defend the cause of justice and progress in popular meetings, in press and parliament, or to lead mass movements for the improvement of social and economic conditions. In many countries Jews have been outstanding among the champions of reform who met these requirements. However, the conspicuous part Jews have taken in producing political changes often misdirected the understanding of the scope of Jewish participation in public life. It was not only as tribunes of the people but also as government's agents that Jews promoted general welfare. They deserved well of the countries wherever they lived, not only by voicing and supporting popular demands but by their sense of obligation to the state, by securing the continuity of cultural work, by consolidating the fundamentals and framework of humanitarian civilization.

From the Early Middle Ages to the Era of the Great Revolutions

Jews actively contributed to the rudimentary formation of the states which became the essential parts of modern Europe. After the decline of ancient Graeco-Roman civilization, the Christian rulers of the early Middle Ages very often had to resort to Jews in order to solidify their government by establishing and maintaining the elements of administration. This happened in spite of the perpetual protests of the Church against the appointment of Jews to high office. While in Islamic countries Jews, apart from very rare and short interruptions, continued to serve as viziers, governors, army and navy officers, without being impeded by the Mohammedan clergy, the Christian Church was not prepared to tolerate a Jew in a position of authority. From the fourth to the twelfth century, church councils and synods, popes, bishops, and influential preachers and writers persisted in urging the Christian princes of Europe to refrain from using Jewish officials. It took such a long time before the Church became able to establish the exclusion of Jews from public office as a rule because neither the secular nor the ecclesiastical princes could miss Jewish assistance in managing their governmental business, and even thereafter the rule was not without exceptions.

Until the death of Alexander III in 1181, the popes themselves frequently employed Jews as financial directors of their household, and the ultra-Catholic kings of Spain relied on Jewish ministers of finance until the late fifteenth century. For the Jews whose legal status, up to the ninth century, was that of citizens of the Roman empire, had preserved the knowledge of administrative methods of that defunct state while, for long periods only very few members of the Christian clergy were capable of competing with them in this field.

After the Church had become able to educate enough Christians to replace all Jewish officials, Jews continued to act in positions of semi-official character, or some of them carried on their private business in a way that served as substitute for a public office. In the later Middle Ages, money lending had become the principal calling of the Jews who, neither in biblical times nor in the early diaspora, had been interested in financial operations. They were by no means the only money lenders in Christian Europe during the Middle Ages. The Church, although stigmatizing money lending as usury, gave financial loans without renouncing gain, and Christian merchants, originally coming from Lombardy and Cahors, France, always were sharp competitors of the Jewish money lenders. The latter, however, having acquired methods of trading which were superior to those of the Lombards, rendered by far greater services as well to the economic development of Northern Europe in general as to the governments in particular. They granted credits not only to private merchants and craftsmen but also to guilds, city councils, feudal lords and kings. Emperors Rudolf of Hapsburg and Louis of Bavaria owed the maintenance of their power to the financial aid on the part of Jewish money lenders. Many other kings appealed to Jewish financiers in order to conduct war. German, French and English townships borrowed money from Jews for the fortification of their palaces. In England, during the reign of King Stephen alone, 1,115 castles were built with the financial aid of the Jews. The conquest of Ireland was financed by the

Jew Josce of Gloucester. Another Jew, Aaron of Lincoln, advanced money for the erection of the abbey of St. Albans and nine monasteries, besides substantial loans given by him to the archbishop of Canterbury, the earl of Leicester, the cities of Southampton and Winchester. In this way, numerous Jewish money lenders became in fact treasurers, financial councillors or commissioners of kings and towns, although they did not bear the title.

Regular collection of taxes, always of major importance for the support of a political system, was highly difficult, if not impossible in the Middle Ages when barter economy was predominant, and the governments lacked officials who were acquainted with the methods of both orderly taxation and gathering revenues in a systematic way. The rulers, wishing to obtain their feudal dues in coin, therefore had to resort to private businessmen who advanced the amount equal to the presumed revenues, and operated the collection of taxes, in particular the conversion from the gathered fruits of the soil into money, in their own way. Jews were the first to prove ability in farming and collecting taxes, and thereby to enable the monarchs to utilize public revenues which otherwise would have been unavailable. The Merovingian kings of France, the Angevins of England, the rulers in Christian and Islamic Spain, most of the ecclesiastical and secular princes in Germany, and above all, the kings of Hungary and Poland, farmed out their revenues to Jewish financiers, until their Christian bureaucracy learned to replace the Jews. The first monarchs to refrain from appointing Jewish tax collectors were the kings of France, where, however, farming of taxes subsisted until the revolution of 1789. Emperors Rudolph II and Ferdinand II highly esteemed the services of the Jewish tax receiver Jacob Bassevi, the first Austrian Jew to be ennobled in 1622. Bassevi was closely associated with the famous generalissimo Albrecht von Wallenstein, and financed the latter's campaigns. Tsar Peter the Great who made the first attempts to modernize the administration of Russia, also employed several Jewish tax collectors. Farming and collecting of taxes was in fact a public office, and at the same time a private enterprise, full of risks, and very unpopular. But for a long period of European history it was indispensable for the adjustment of a backward economy to the needs of the new states of Europe.

Of at least equal importance were the services Jews rendered to the formation of the modern states of Europe by managing coinage. Up to the end of the eighteenth century, most of the governments in Europe were incapable of administering the mint on their own responsibility. They were aware of their lack of resources and experience, and were afraid of the risks which the minting business involved. These risks were taken by Jewish jewellers and dealers in precious metals who were well acquainted with the vicissitudes of the market, and able to provide supply of gold, silver and copper at the cheapest rate. In 555 the Jew Priscus coined money for the Merovingian king. During the eleventh and twelfth centuries, Jewish minters were known in England, Italy, Germany, Hungary and Poland. Their number rather increased. They particularly acted, until the end of the eighteenth century, in the service of the emperors of the house of Hapsburg and the dynasty of the Hohenzollern in Prussia, although most of these rulers would have liked to employ non-Jewish minters.

In the era of absolutism which lasted from the end of the Thirty Years' War until the French Revolution, almost every prince in Europe, from the Carpathian Mountains to the Rhine Valley, from the Baltic to the Adriatic coast, used to have a "Court Jew", also called "Court Agent" or "Head Factor". Although absolutism soon degenerated, and then more and more lagged behind its time, in its early stage it was conceived and practiced as a constructive force, bound to restore the countries which were devastated by the Thirty Years' War and many other struggles. In their endeavor to improve the situation of their subjects, the absolute rulers were efficiently aided by the Court Jews. The Court Jew was as well the general manager of the prince's private fortune and household as a commissioner whose duty was to promote the commerce and industry of the country, to supply the army with victuals and munition, and frequently to negotiate treaties with foreign powers. For half a century, Samuel Oppenheimer and Samson Wertheimer supported the house of Hapsburg in its wars against France and Turkey. Berend Lehmann served the elector of Hanover, the duke of Brunswick, and especially August the Strong of Saxony who owed his accession to the throne of Poland to Lehmann's diplomatic and financial help. Many Court Jews acquired great wealth but some of them lost all their money, while serving the ambitious aims of their sovereigns. So did Aaron Israel, the Court Jew of the Great Elector of Brandenburg. The most unfortunate was Joseph Süss Oppenheimer (Jud Süss) who became the almighty state minister of Wuerttemberg, but was sacrificed by his duke to the jealousy of the noblemen and the hate of the mob, and hanged, although no accusation could be proved true in his trial. One of the latest Court Jews was Mayer Amschel Rothschild, the founder of a dynasty of modern bankers. He was the devoted agent of the elector of Hesse-Cassel.

Because of their ability to maintain relationship with their coreligionists in their wide dispersion, Jews, during the Middle Ages, possessed a knowledge of the languages and customs of foreign peoples that was very rarely to be found among Christians. For that reason, Christian rulers often made use of the Jews as diplomats. In 797, Charlemagne sent the Jew Isaac, together with two Christian officials, as ambassador to Caliph Haroun al Rashid. Isaac who alone survived the dangerous mission, returned in 802 to Charlemagne's residence where he delivered the Caliph's reply and gifts. The practice of using Jewish merchants or physicians as ambassadors, especially to non-Christian rulers, lasted from the early Middle Ages to the era of absolutism. On the other hand, Hasdai Ibn Shaprit, diplomatic adviser of the Caliph of Cordova, established friendly relations with the Holy Roman Empire and Byzantium. Jews became, occasionally and permanently, diplomatic representatives of the counts of Provence, the dukes of Austria, the kings of Castile and Aragon. In the fifteenth century, Isaac Abravanel negotiated diplomatic agreements in the service of the kings of Portugal, Spain, Naples and the Doge of Venice. Salomon Natan Azkenazi was sometimes ambassador of the Sultan to Venice but also served that republic as well as the king of Spain, and helped, in 1572, Henri of Anjou to be elected king of Poland. Sampayo Diego Teixeira and his son Manuel, both Marranos who returned openly to Judaism, represented Sweden at Hamburg in the later seventeenth century. Among other Marranos who were noted diplomats, François Schonenberg was outstanding. For nearly forty years he was in the diplomatic service of Holland, and when William of Orange, Stadtholder of that country, became king William III of England, also of Britain. As Dutch and British minister to Madrid, Schonenberg successfully counteracted the efforts of the French party at the Spanish court, although the latter were eager to denounce his Jewish origin. It was Schonenberg who advised the British government to seize Gibraltar, just as the Jew Simon de Casseres had advised Oliver Cromwell to capture the island of Jamaica in 1655.

All these services have been rendered by Jews to peoples who denied them equality of rights, more than once even the right to exist, and to rulers most of whom treated them arbitrarily, made use of their talents for reasons of mere egoism, always ready to confiscate their fortune or even to kill them or to let them be killed by the mob when they were no more wanted. Against princely disgrace almost every Jew was defenseless, and frequently the favor of even the most powerful ruler could not safeguard the life of the Jew who was exposed to the fury of fanaticism. However precarious the situation of Jewish money lenders, minters, tax collectors and the Court Jews remained, they showed and developed talents which enabled later generations of Jews to serve the general good in more favorable circumstances.

The Rise of Democracy

The American Declaration of Independence, by enunciating the principles of human equality, made the decisive break in the doctrine and practice, which, as James Madison, later the fourth president of the United States, said, "degrade from the equal rank of citizens all those whose opinions in religion do not bend to the legislative authority". The constitution of the United States refrained from any discriminatory law against the Jews. Complete separation of Church and State was established. The First Amendment to the Constitution provided that "Congress shall make no law respecting the establishment of religion or prohibiting the free exercise thereof". Although several States of the Union were rather slow in rising to the spirit of the Federal Constitution and the First Amendment, Jews immediately began to hold public offices in Federal and State governments as well as in local bodies.

The principle of human equality was introduced into European law by the Declaration of the Rights of Man and Citizen pronounced by the French National Assembly on August 27, 1789. It was realized, as far as the Jews of France were concerned, by granting them citizenship in 1791; however, the last remnants of former discrimination were not extinguished before, in 1846, the "Jewish oath" was abolished. In England, granting of equality to the Jews made slow progress from the early eighteenth century to the year 1866, when professing Jews were admitted to the House of Lords and the House of Commons. In Central Europe, the administration frequently undid what the constitution granted to the Jews in the later nineteenth century. During the short interval between the collapse of the monarchies and the accession of, or the conquest by, Hitler, Jews held important offices. In the Scandinavian countries and in Italy, Jews enjoyed full equality of rights. Italian Jews were oppressed only during the years between Mussolini's subjection to Hitler in 1938 and his fall in 1943. While France, under German domination, from 1940 to 1944

[112]

had to imitate Hitler's Jews' laws, French Jews were among the principal political advisers of general Charles de Gaulle as well as among the leaders of the French resistance movement. The more the democratic ideas spread over Europe, the more obstinately the Tsars of Russia refused to grant civil rights to their Jewish subjects. Consequently Russian Jews did join not only the liberal opposition, among whose outstanding leaders were some Jews, but also the Bolshevist party.

Wherever the principle of human equality became dominant, its victory changed both the scope and character of the public services done by Jews. During the pre-revolutionary eras, Jews, functioning as, or instead of, officials, had been dependent on the grace or egoistic considerations of arbitrary despots. Now, they had to rely on the confidence and esteem of their fellow-citizens. Whether appointed by superior officials or elected by the people, their way of working always was to be controlled, approved or criticized by the public. The fact that Jewish officials held their position for long times or were re-elected more than once, proves their ability to stand the test of competence, integrity and devotion to their country.

UNITED STATES. Beginning as an uprising for "the rights of Englishmen", the American Revolution soon proceeded to the defense of human "unalienable" rights without distinction of religion and origin. Such a development which led to the recognition of the Jews as full-fledged citizens, endowed with the same unalienable rights, was caused not only by a political philosophy but also by the experience that the American Jews had proved to be ardent patriots, devoted to the cause of the revolution, and ready to sacrifice fortune and life for the defense of the country. Among those who were most deeply impressed by this experience, were George Washington, high commander in the war and first president of the United States, and John Adams, Thomas Jefferson and James Madison, his successors in the presidency, and equally eyewitnesses of the services rendered by Jews to the victory of the young republic.

In the revolutionary war, George Washington had three Jewish aides-de-camp, namely Manuel Noah, David Salisbury Franks, and Isaac Franks. Benjamin Nones who later commanded a "Hebrew Legion of four hundred men", was also a member of Washington's staff. In a non-official position, Haym Salomon enabled Washington to keep his army effective, assisted the Department of Finance of the Continental Congress, promoted the Franco-American alliance, and negotiated political and financial agreements with Holland and Spain. In 1784, David Salisbury Franks was appointed vice-consul at Marseille, the first Jew to serve the United States as a diplomat. In 1785, Franks went to Morocco, and succeeded in negotiating a treaty between his country and the sultan.

Thomas Jefferson, the third president of the United States, an intimate friend of David Franks and commodore Uriah P. Levy who distinguished himself in the war against England of 1812, and at the time of his death was the highest ranking naval officer in the service of the United States, appointed Ruben Etting, a Jewish veteran of the War of Independence, United States Marshal for Maryland. In the war of 1812, Etting was a member of the committee of defense for the city of Philadelphia.

President James Madison, called the "father of the Constitution of the United States", appointed many Jews to office, among them John Hays as collector for the Indian Territory, Joel Hart consul at Leith, Scotland, and Mordecai Manuel Noah consul general at Tunis. Hays, descending from a widely ramified Jewish family, of which many members had participated in the War of Independence, was a pioneer Illinois settler and Indian trader, sheriff of St. Clair County, and later, for many years, Indian agent at Fort Wayne, Ind. Another member of the Hays family, Jacob Hays, was, in 1798, appointed a city marshal at New York City, and from 1802 to 1840, he was re-appointed chief of police (then called high constable) by every mayor of the city. In this quality, Hays became of world-wide fame for his efficiency. The criminologists of two continents exalted him as "terror to evildoers". Joel Hart, a physician by profession, had been a charter member of the Medical Society of the County of New York. He knew England well, and served as a diplomat from 1817 to 1832. Mordecai Manuel Noah, son of Manuel Noah, was, as consul at Tunis, highly successful in liberating American sailors who had been captured by Algerian and Tunisian pirates, and in making the United States respected in the Mediterranean. Afterwards, Noah served as sheriff, judge and surveyor of the port of New York, and as a major in the New York militia.

The more the political and economic relations between the United States and the rest of the world became important and complicated, the greater became the number of Jews in its diplomatic service. August Belmont, American chargé d'affaires in The Hague from 1853 to 1857, went, after the outbreak of the Civil War, to Europe, to defend the financial interests of the Union. President Abraham Lincoln and his cabinet considered Belmont's successes "invaluable". It was also Belmont who raised and equipped the first German-born regiment which was sent from New York to the front. Benjamin Franklin Peixotto was sent, in 1870, by president Grant to Bucharest to normalize the strained relations between the United States and Roumania. After five years of activities which highly satisfied both the United States government and Carol I of Roumania, Peixotto was, from 1876 to 1885, United States consul general at Lyon, France. Oscar Solomon Straus was appointed, in 1887, Envoy Extraordinary and Minister Plenipotentiary to Turkey by president Grover Cleveland. Straus arranged so that sixty American schools which had been closed by the Turkish government six years before his arrival, were reopened, and that the sale of Christian religious literature was permitted in Turkey. He also secured for American scientific expeditions the right to make excavations. In 1889, Straus was succeeded for three years by another Jew, Solomon Hirsch, a former state senator from Oregon, but in 1897, after the Armenian massacres had roused indignation in America, and many missionaries had become the victims of fanaticism, president William McKinley appealed to Straus, calling him "the only man in the United States who could save the situation", to resume his post in Constantinople, in order to support the persecuted people and to safeguard the moral, political and economic interests of America. After completing this commission, Straus became, in 1906, the first Jewish cabinet member in the United States, since president Theodore Roosevelt appointed him Secretary of the Department of Commerce and Labor. Roosevelt's successor, William H. Taft, intended to maintain Straus in his cabinet, but the outbreak of the Turkish revolution and the ensuing disorders which caused again persecutions of Christian minorities, urgently demanded Straus' return to Constantinople. More than three hundred American organizations were benefited by Straus' intervention which resulted not only in easing the general situation but also in securing new rights for all foreign religious and humanitarian institutions in the Turkish empire.

Lewis Einstein began his diplomatic career as third secretary at the American embassy in Paris in 1903. In 1906 he was a member of the American commission at the Algeciras Conference where the first Franco-German Morocco conflict was settled. He advanced as a member of the American legations in Constantinople and Peking and was, from 1911 to 1913, Envoy Extraordinary and Minister Plenipotentiary to Costa Rica. After the outbreak of World War I, the state department sent him as special agent to Constantinople and Sofia, Bulgaria, where he also took care of British interests. After the war, Einstein was the first minister to Czechoslovakia.

After beginning as consul at Patras, Greece, Edward Isaac Nathan served in the same capacity for seven years, from 1909 to 1916, at Mersina, Turkey, a very difficult, even dangerous position, since that place was the scene of fierce atrocities. After Turkey entered the war of 1914 on the side of the Central European powers, Nathan courageously and efficiently protected those British and French nationals who had not been able to leave Turkey at that time. From 1917 to 1937 Nathan was consul in Vigo, Spain, Palermo, Italy, Santiago, Cuba, and finally consul general at Monterrey, Mexico.

For three eventful years, Henry Morgenthau Sr. was United States ambassador to Turkey. During most of that time, from 1914 to 1916, Morgenthau's duties were not limited to the regular diplomatic service but also included the protection of British, French, Russian, Belgian, and Serbian nationals. Great as they were, these achievements were surpassed by the solution of one of the most formidable problems known in history, namely the interchange of Greek and Turkish population which took place under Morgenthau's chairmanship of the Refugee Settlement Commission of the League of Nations. This great cross migration of around 700,000 Greeks and 400,000 Turks, organized under the leadership of Morgenthau, terminated not only a terrible war between the two nations but also their mutual hostility which had lasted for many centuries.

As ambassador to Turkey, Morgenthau was succeeded by his coreligionist Abram I. Elkus who previously had been special United States attorney to prosecute bankruptcy frauds, and afterwards chairman of the New York State Reconstruction Committee. In 1920, Elkus was designated a commissioner to settle the dispute between Sweden and Finland concerning the Aland Islands.

During World War I, the State Department was rather well informed about the situation in the belligerent countries by Ira Nelson Morris who, after successfully discharging a special diplomatic mission to Italy, was United States minister to Sweden from 1914 to 1923, and afterwards distinguished himself on missions to Turkey, Germany and Mexico. After the war, Joseph Saul Kornfeld, noted rabbi and scholar, made use of his Oriental studies while serving as Envoy Extraordinary and Minister Plenipotentiary to Persia from 1921 to 1924. In 1928 and the following year, David I. Kaufman,

United States minister to Bolivia, was instrumental in removing a grave danger to peace in the Western hemisphere by settling the conflict between Bolivia and Paraguay. Thereupon he became minister to Siam. Harry Frank Guggenheim, who had participated in World War I as a naval aviator, and after the war had been an outstanding promotor of American aeronautics, discharged his diplomatic mission to Cuba, from 1929 to 1933, during which the island was gravely afflicted by political disorder and economic depression, with great ability and tact, so that not only presidents Hoover and Franklin D. Roosevelt were highly satisfied with his achievements but also the government of Cuba. A decoration was awarded him "to recognize and reward outstanding merit in the diplomatic order and eminent service rendered to Cuba and to humanity." Guggenheim frequently represented the United States on international commissions, and continued to promote American aeronautics and public welfare in New York City. As ambassador to France, Jesse Isidor Straus kept president Roosevelt and Secretary of State Cordell Hull informed about the danger of a second world war, and protected the material interests of American citizens from 1933 until the year of his death, 1936. Excellent work done by Laurence A. Steinhardt as minister to Sweden and at the Eighth Pan-American Conference, induced president Franklin D. Roosevelt to entrust him with a mission which demanded extreme caution and energy, tact and presence of mind, by sending Steinhardt as ambassador to the Soviet Union in 1939. When Steinhardt arrived at Moscow, the conclusion of the non-aggression pact between Soviet Russia and Nazi Germany had caused great anxiety which was even aggravated after the Russian armies invaded Poland and attacked Finland. While expressing frankly America's disapproval of these measures, Steinhardt always proved to be able to do it in a way that did not endanger the delicate relations between his country and Russia, and to bring more and more members of the Russian government to a better understanding of the American point of view. When, in June 1941, Hitler invaded Russia, and the Soviet government became ready to co-operate with the Allies, president Roosevelt thought that Steinhardt's skill should be used in Ankara where the German ambassador Franz von Papen attempted, by means of economic pressure, military threats and various intrigues, to draw Turkey into the orbit of the Axis powers. Although, for a while, military setbacks of the British favored Papen's projects, ambassador Steinhardt succeeded well in counteracting all German practices and keeping Turkey neutral until the Allied victories in all theatres of war made the Turkish statesmen adamant against German seduction. He died in 1950.

After Oscar Solomon Straus, only one Jew has entered the cabinet of an American president. It was Henry Morgenthau Jr. who previously had won great fame because of his successes in promoting American food production during and after World War I. In 1934, president Roosevelt appointed Morgenthau Secretary of the Treasury whose rank in the cabinet is inferior only to that of the Secretary of State, and held him in office as long as he lived. Until Roosevelt's death, the president's confidence in his Secretary of Treasury, and Morgenthau's devotion to his chief never slackened nor wavered. Morgenthau's activities were so closely connected with those of president Roosevelt that for a long time it will be impossible to define the influence Morgenthau exercised upon Roosevelt's policy, or the president's ascendancy over the Treasury. Neither can Roosevelt's leadership be characterized adequately without mentioning the part Morgenthau took in the president's general policy, nor is it fair to overlook the directive rules given by Roosevelt to his Secretary of Treasury if the latter's achievements are to be described. Certainly, Morgenthau, both as Roosevelt's follower and as an administrator of finance, met with violent opposition. But even his embittered adversaries could not deny his technical skill and his sense of duty, his patriotism and his zeal for social justice.

To harmonize law and social justice, to imbue jurisdiction with the spirit of social responsibility was the earnest and untiring endeavor of the three Jews who became associate justices of the Supreme Court of the United States: Louis Dembitz Brandeis, Benjamin Nathan Cardozo, and Felix Frankfurter. These eminent jurists, although of different temper, combined thorough knowledge of the law with a philosophical conception of its fundamentals and its function, and with vivid interest in daily life as well as in the political, social and economic progress of the American nation. Devoted to the form of American government and the constitutional guarantees of liberty which they refused to sacrifice to the niceties of procedure they used their juridical learning and acuteness to adapt the constitution to a changing civilization, and, in this way, contributed a new chapter not only in the legal history but in the development of moral standards in America.

The number of Jewish federal judges and of Jews who served as State Supreme Court Judges is so great that even the prominent ones cannot be mentioned here, except judge Samuel Irving Rosenman who was Franklin D. Roosevelt's legal counsel when the latter was governor of New York, and the president's principal adviser on national issues. Before Jerome N. Frank was appointed judge of the Federal Court of Appeals he had served as general counsel of the Agricultural Adjustment Administration, as special counsel of the Reconstruction Finance Corporation and the Public Works Administration, and as a member of the Security and Exchange Commission. David Eli Lilienthal, a lawyer by profession, became, in 1931, a member of the Wisconsin Public Works Commission, and, in 1935, chairman of the Tennessee Valley Authority, the gigantic enterprise of the federal government in the public utility field. Recognizing Lilienthal's outstanding merits, president Harry S. Truman appointed him chairman of the Atomic Energy Commission of the United States, an office of greatest consequence for the security of America and the peace of the whole world. Herbert Feis, noted economist, had been appointed economic adviser to the State Department under the Hoover administration. Under Roosevelt's presidentship Feis became adviser on international economic affairs and was instrumental in the State Department's negotiations of trade agreements, in particular with the Latin American countries. Ardently devoted to the cause of Pan-Americanism, and dealing with its problems as a learned historian and experienced statesman, Leo Stanton Rowe was instrumental in laying the basis for the governmental policy in Porto Rico, after the United States had occupied the island, and represented the United States, at several Pan-American Conferences. In 1919, Rowe was appointed chief of the Latin American division in the State Department, and in the following year he became director general of the Pan-American Union of which twenty-one American republics were members. In this capacity, Rowe was generally recognized as an inspiring mediator who loyally and efficiently did his utmost to promote intellectual, political and economic co-operation between all the American republics.

Repeatedly in times of national emergency Bernard Baruch was summoned by the government of the United States to do extraordinary work that none other could do. During two world wars and both domestic and international crises, Baruch became a great figure in American history, ready to vanish into private life when normalcy returned. In 1916, president Woodrow Wilson appointed Baruch a member of the advisory commission of the Council of National Defense, and subsequently entrusted him with the direction of all industrial activities in the United States. It was mainly due to Baruch's talents of organization and his quick and thorough understanding of the necessities of war-time production that the effort of the United States astonished its Allies, surprised the enemy, and accelerated victory. President Franklin D. Roosevelt often consulted Baruch about "measures that a stricken nation in the midst of a stricken world may require", as he said in his inaugural address. Again, when the United States entered the Second World War, Baruch devoted his energy to the co-ordination of all efforts to equip the army and to supply the Allies. After the war, Baruch took a leading part in elaborating a system of international control in the use of atomic energy.

From Wilson to Truman, all presidents of the United States, whether Republicans or Democrats, highly esteemed the participation of Eugene Meyer in governmental work. Woodrow Wilson used Meyer, in 1917, as adviser on non-ferrous metals, and it was due to Meyer's experience and care that the government saved several millions in this field. Then Meyer was appointed by Wilson assistant to the Secretary of War on aircraft production, and in this capacity Meyer urged and obtained a thorough reorganization of that department. Thereafter Wilson entrusted him with the management of the War Finance Corporation whose function was to provide enterprises essential to the conduct of war with capital. In this position Meyer was retained by Wilson's Republican successors Harding and Coolidge until the corporation was dissolved in 1925. Two years later, president Coolidge entrusted Meyer with the reorganization of the Federal Farm Loan Board, and, in 1930, president Hoover appointed him governor of the Federal Reserve Board. Because Meyer did not agree with Franklin D. Roosevelt's economic policy, he did not serve under Roosevelt's administration in peace-time. But in 1941, the president appointed Meyer a member of the National Defense Mediation Board. In 1946, president Truman made Meyer president of the International Bank for Reconstruction and Development.

By far greater than the number of American Jews who were appointed to office by the government is that of those who were elected by the people. Jews were elected and re-elected, often for decades, mayors, aldermen and city councilors and congressmen, state and federal senators, judges of municipal, county, district and state courts, justices of peace, sheriffs, postmasters, fire commissioners, city and state attorneys, commissioners of police and public utilities, members and chairmen of boards of education, trade, commerce, charities and corrections, mediation, members and presidents of bar associations and in all the states and Territories of the Union from Alabama to Alaska, from California to Rhode Island. Three Jews, namely Julius Fleischman, Frederick S. Spiegel and Murray Seasongood, were successively elected mayors of Cincinnati, Ohio; Albert Strasburger, Henry E. Faber and M. M. Moses were mayors of Montgomery, Alabama; David Solis Cohen, Philip Wasserman and Bernard Goldsmith were mayors of Portland, Oregon. Benjamin Stedman was elected mayor in San Francisco, Albert Elkus and Bernard V. Steinman in Sacramento, California, Louis P. Aloe in St. Louis, Martin Behrman in New Orleans, Michael Seligson in Galveston, Texas, George Goldman in Kansas City, S. Campner in New Haven, Connecticut, Meyer Charles Ellenstein in Newark, New Jersey, and Baily Gatzert in Seattle, Washington, not to mention the great number of Jews elected mayors in smaller towns. The highest office Jews obtained in popular elections was that of governor. In 1801, David Emanuel, of Jewish birth but a convert to Presbyterianism, became governor of Georgia, after having been president of the State Senate. The first professing Jew to be elected governor was Michael Hahn in Louisiana, 1864. In 1870, brigadier-general Edward S. Solomon, famous hero of the Civil War, was appointed governor of the territory that later became the State of Washington, by president Ulysses S. Grant. Moses Alexander who, as mayor of Chillicothe, Missouri, had saved the town from bankruptcy, and then became popular as mayor of Boise, Idaho, was elected governor of Idaho for two terms. Simon Bamberger became the first non-Mormon governor of Utah. Julius I. Meier, the son of an Oregon pioneer, had promoted agriculture, industry and aviation in Oregon, actively contributed to the development of the state's highway system, and, during World War I, served as northwest director of the Council of National Defense before he was elected governor of Oregon. He effected important administrative and social reforms, and was praised as the best governor the state of Oregon ever had. Arthur Seligman, former mayor of Santa Fe, was elected governor of New Mexico and re-elected. He died, while in office. Henry Horner began his public career as probate judge, and was re-elected four times. During the two terms of his gubernatorial office in Illinois he successfully combated corruption, and fought for social reform. Herbert Henry Lehman, during World War I, an aide of Franklin Delano Roosevelt, who was Assistant Secretary of the Navy, and later a colonel on the General Staff, was elected lieutenant governor in 1928, and in 1932 governor of the state of New York. Re-elected three times Lehman held his office for ten years. His great experience in finance enabled him to overcome enormous budgetary difficulties, and at the same time to lower public utility rates. Always a self-denying philanthropist, Lehman, while in office, promoted public welfare and supported institutions to help the needy. Occasionally he restored law and order with courage and energy. After the end of his governorship Lehman was appointed by president Roosevelt director of Relief and Rehabilitation, whereupon he became the first director of the United Nations Relief and Rehabilitation Administration (UNRRA). For outstanding merits as first director of the Federal Division of Territories and Island Possessions, Ernest Gruening was rewarded with the appointment as governor of Alaska in 1929, and continued to hold office for ten years. He did very much to develop Alaska economically, and sincerely endeavored to harmonize the often antagonistic interests of the various groups of inhabitants. Moreover, the first to recognize the necessity that the United States should acquire Alaska, until 1867 a part of the Russian empire, was Lewis Gerstle, a Jewish pioneer settler in California who was interested in trade with Alaska. By the intermediacy of senator Cole, Gerstle suggested to Secretary of State Seward the purchase of the territory whose importance to the defense of the United States became evident during and after the last war.

FRANCE. After the French National Assembly had granted equality of rights to the Jews it took several decades before a larger number of Jews was admitted to public office. One of the rare exceptions was Abraham Furtado who became vice-mayor of the city of Bordeaux after the fall of Robespierre. Until the revolution of 1830, professing Jews, serving in the armies of the First Republic and Napoleon I, could become commissioned officers, and retained their commission in peace-time, but the government, particularly that of Napoleon, remained reluctant to give a Jew a post in the administration. Under the regime of Louis Philippe several Jews entered parliament, among them Michel Goudchaux who also was mayor of a borough (*arrondissement*) of Paris and councillor general of the Seine department. The revolution of 1848 opened to Goudchaux and his coreligionist Isaac Adolphe Crémieux the way to the cabinet of the Second French Republic. Goudchaux, who was elected vice-president of the Constituent Assembly, became minister of finance, and Crémieux minister of justice. It was due to Crémieux that slavery in the French colonies was abolished, trial by jury re-established, and no more political offenders, until 1940, could be sentenced to death in France. Emperor Napoleon III appointed Achille Fould minister of finance. Although personally devoted to the emperor, Fould resigned more than once when he disapproved of Napoleon's policy, but was recalled again and again, because of his efficiency. Immediately after the collapse of Napoleon's empire in the war of 1870, Crémieux entered the government of national defense, led by Léon Gambetta, as minister of justice, and took also an active part in the organization of armed resistance to the German invaders. In 1875, Crémieux was made a senator for life-time. When Gambetta became president of the council of ministers in 1881, he appointed Joseph Reinach head of his office (chef de cabinet), in France a post of greatest influence and importance. Reinach became one of the leading defenders of the republican form of government in France, operating as well behind the scene during more than one ministerial crisis as in the first line of the parliamentarian and journalistic battle-front. In the cabinets led by Gambetta and Jules Ferry, David Raynal was minister of public works, and, in 1893, minister of the interior. In 1897 he was elected senator and president of the commission for the improvement of the French merchant marine.

Under the regime of the Third French Republic which lasted from 1871 to 1940, many Jews were elected deputies and senators most of whom had previously been mayors or other municipal officers, and retained their local posts while sitting in parliament. In France where the administration is highly, and in many regards too rigidly centralized, one of the main functions of a deputy or senator is to defend the legitimate local interests of their electors against the bureaucracy which is concentrated in Paris. On the other hand, as members of the various parliamentary commissions, they have to take care of the common interests of the whole country, and, as a consequence of the frequent ministerial changes which are a French peculiarity. A large part, if not the majority of the deputies and senators have been, for a shorter or longer time, ministers or under-secretaries, in which capacity they could not risk to favor local claims at the expense of national interests, without being exposed to violent criticism, even on the part of their own party. The fact that a great deal of Jewish deputies and senators were re-elected until their death or old age, proves their ability to harmonize their care of local and national wants. Thus the French merchant marine owed its high development before World War II to ministers Jacques Stern and Léon Meyer. The latter, for many years mayor of Le Havre, made his city a center of maritime trade whose new constructions were admired in the whole world.

When Georges Clemenceau, in a highly critical stage of the war, formed his cabinet, he called in three Jews, namely Louis

L. Klotz, Georges Mandel and Edouard Ignace. Klotz, for thirty years a deputy, had to perform the difficult task of rearranging French finances at a time when war expenses surpassed every experience and expectation. Ignace, undersecretary in the ministry of war, ruthlessly broke down all persons and red-tapism that impeded vigorous warfare. Mandel, Clemenceau's chef de cabinet, prosecuted defeatists and frustrated traitors with extreme energy and acuteness. He often astonished the Allied chiefs of intelligence service by his intimate knowledge of enemy agents and their tricks, and sometimes he even terrified the "Tiger" by accusing and convicting of treason persons who had enjoyed Clemenceau's confidence. After the war, Mandel was untiring in counter-acting all attempts to lull suspicion against German nationalism, and therefore became unpopular, but retained his seat in the Chamber of Deputies from 1919 to 1924, and from 1928 to 1940, without being supported by, or adhering to, any party. When Hitler came to power, Mandel demanded strong resistance to German claims, denounced Germany's secret armaments, and urged France to strengthen her armed forces. This policy of Mandel's was violently opposed by a coalition of French fascists and pacifists. In 1935, Mandel was appointed postmaster general, and considerably improved the services administered by him. From 1938 to 1940, Mandel, as minister of colonies, succeeded in raising rapidly the economic standard in French Africa, and in improving the military readiness of the colonies. In May 1940, when France already was collapsing, Mandel was made minister of the Interior. But the government had hesitated too long to entrust him with the removal of traitors. When Mandel entered his new office his highest subordinates already had deserted it. Nevertheless, Mandel, in the council of ministers, advocated transfer of the government to Africa in order to continue the war. His constant valor has been recognized by Winston Churchill, but was bitterly combatted by marshal Pétain, general Weygand and

Pierre Laval. Finally Mandel was imprisoned, and, after four years of detention, murdered by order of Hitler.

For nearly two decades, Léon Blum was a staunch adversary of Mandel until the common distress brought them nearer to each other, especially when both of them were prisoners in the concentration camp of Buchenwald. At the age of twenty-three, Blum was appointed member of the Conseil d'État, in many regards a French analogon to the Supreme Court of the United States. The prospects of his career were brilliant but he sacrificed them to his sympathy with the French working class and his devotion to socialism. As leader of the French Socialist party, Blum advocated reconciliation between France and Germany, general disarmament, and nationalization of key industries, while constantly facing the hate of nationalists and capitalists. His attitude toward Germany changed after Hitler invaded Austria and threatened Czechoslovakia. In 1936, the victory of the Popular Front made Blum chief of the French cabinet. In this capacity, he accomplished many reforms whose necessity could not be denied even by his political adversaries, but in many regards he became rather moderate, and sincerely endeavored to govern as a representative of the whole nation, and not as a party leader. Nevertheless, his best intentions could not soften his enemies. After the collapse of France Blum was among the first to be imprisoned by the Pétain government, and later he was handed over to the Germans. Surviving heroically nearly five years of prison and concentration camp, Blum, after his return to France was generally respected as a martyr, and proved to be a wise statesman whose principal aim was to restore France and to put an end to discord among Frenchmen.

The reconstruction of France after World War II was, in spite of many hindrances, promoted by Jules Moch, minister of the Interior in several cabinets, and Pierre Mendès-France who, for many years had been the youngest French deputy and the youngest lawyer in Paris. Mendès-France had been imprisoned by the Vichy government but, in 1941, succeeded in escaping and joined general De Gaulle in England. After the liberation of France, De Gaulle made him a member of his cabinet in which capacity Mendès-France laid the first fundamentals to a revival of economic activities in his country.

French Jews also served their country as prefects (governor of a *département*), sub-prefects, judges, members of the Institut de France and the French Academies, educators, librarians, archivists, chiefs of division in various ministries, inspectors of finance and technical services. Eugene Dreyfus was, from 1925 to 1934, president of the First Court of Appeals of France, and then, until his death, presiding justice of the French Supreme Court. Charles Lyon-Caën, one of the most prominent jurists of his time, was, in 1893, elected permanent secretary of the French Academy, and, in this capacity, its representative at national and international meetings. He also was a member, or president of the disciplinary courts of the ministries of justice, finance, marine and colonies. It was only in the diplomatic service that French Jews did not advance to higher positions.

BRITISH EMPIRE. When the first professing Jews were admitted to the British parliament, Benjamin Disraeli, baptized at the age of thirteen, had already become a great figure in the House of Commons, a leader of the Tories, and a member of the cabinet. Disraeli, who later received the title of earl of Beaconsfield, is generally considered one of the greatest statesmen of the nineteenth century. Despite his conversion, Disraeli always expressed pride in his Jewish origin, and extolled the spiritual values of Judaism which he regarded as the source of his own creative faculties as well as of Christian civilization. The first professing Jew to enter a British cabinet was Sir George Jessel, eminent jurist, who was made Solicitor-General by William E. Gladstone in 1871, and became master of the rolls in 1873. His son, lord Herbert Morton Jessel, was member of the House of Commons from 1896 to 1906, and from 1910 to 1918, in 1924 he entered the House of Lords, after distinguishing himself in the Indian army, and, during

World War I, was promoted to colonel. While Jessel was a liberal, the second Jewish member of the British government was appointed by the conservative lord Salisbury in 1885. It was Henry de Worms, later Lord Pirbright, parliamentary secretary to the Board of Trade, and, from 1888 to 1892, under-secretary for the colonies, the first Jew to become a member of the Privy Council. The most brilliant career was that of Rufus Daniel Isaacs, a highly reputed lawyer who, in 1904, entered parliament, was appointed, in 1910, Solicitor-General, and within a short time Attorney-General by the liberal Prime Minister Herbert Asquith. In 1913 he became Lord Chief Justice of England, during World War I served as a special envoy to the United States, and, from 1921 to 1926 was viceroy of India. After his return to England, he was created Marquess of Reading and, shortly before his death, honored with the dignity of Lord Warden of the Cinque-Ports. Herbert Louis Samuel entered parliament in 1902, was appointed, in 1905, under-secretary to the Home Office, in 1909, chancellor of the Duchy of Lancaster, and in 1919 postmaster-general. In 1920, Samuel became the first British High Commissioner to Palestine. In 1937, king George VI made him viscount. Like his father, Samuel Montagu, first Lord Swaythling and his brother, Louis, the second Lord Swaythling, Edwin Samuel Montagu was an outstanding member of the House of Commons before he entered the government. From 1910 to 1914, he was under-secretary of state for India; during the First World War, he was financial secretary to the Treasury, chancellor of the Duchy of Lancaster, minister of munitions, and secretary of state for India. In 1922, Montagu retired into private life because he disagreed with the policy of Lloyd George, then prime minister. Louis Infield began his governmental career as assistant secretary to the Ministry of Health. Then he served in the ministry of blockade, was director of Rationing and Distribution in the ministry of Food, and after the war a British Delegate and Inter-Allied Commissioner to supervise the execution of the Spa protocol. Sir Albert Stern, after distinguishing himself at the front in 1914, was appointed secretary to the Landship Committee of the British Admiralty in 1915, director of the Tank Supply Department in the ministry of Munitions in 1916, and Commissioner of Mechanical Warfare in 1917. His great merits and experience in the construction of armored cars induced Neville Chamberlain and Winston Churchill to re-appoint Stern as an expert of tanks in 1939 and 1941. Philip Sassoon was instrumental in the development of British aeronautics as under-secretary of state for Air, from 1924 to 1929, and from 1931 to 1937. He also promoted aviation while not in office. Leslie Hore-Belisha had fought for nearly four years at the front in the first World War, and was promoted major, before he was elected to the House of Commons in 1923. In 1931, he was appointed Parliamentary secretary to the Board of Trade, in 1932, financial secretary to the Treasury, in 1934 Minister of Transports, and in 1937 Secretary of State for War. He did much to democratize the British army officers corps and to modernize the equipment of the army. It was due to his foresight and energy that compulsory military service was introduced into England before the outbreak of the second World War. Several Jewish members are serving in the British Labor Government that is still in office.

Jews also took a leading part in the public life of the dominions and colonies of the British Empire and Commonwealth. It was Matthew Nathan who, by virtue of his unique experience and his capacity of attending the interests of both the British government and the native populations, contributed greatly to the modernization of the structure of the British Empire and its administrative departments. In 1880, Nathan, at the age of eighteen, entered the Royal Engineers, distinguished himself in the Sudan expedition and the Lushai expedition, and, promoted lieutenant-colonel, was appointed, in 1895, secretary to the Colonial Defense Committee. Joseph Chamberlain, secretary of colonies, greatly impressed by Nathan's ideas and performances, made him, in 1898, governor of Sierra Leone, and in 1900 governor of the Gold Coast. A year later, Nathan's report to the British government, dealing with the problem of governing the natives and laying out a broad view on their mental peculiarities, initiated a new era in the history of the British colonial service, although, however, the vast majority of British officials were reluctant to adopt Nathan's conclusions. Recognized as one of the most efficient colonial administrators, Nathan became governor of Hong Kong in 1903, and, in 1907, of Natal. After Natal, in 1909, was incorporated into the Union of South Africa, Nathan was appointed secretary to the Post Office; in 1914, permanent under-secretary to the government of Ireland, and then minister of pensions in Lloyd George's cabinet. From 1920-1925, Nathan was governor of Queensland. Thereafter, Nathan was elected chairman of several committees for the reform of civil service and dealing with colonial questions.

Sir Sidney Solomon Abrahams also served in various areas of the British Empire. In 1922, he became attorney-general of Zanzibar, in 1925 he obtained the same office in Uganda, and in the Gold Coast in 1928. In 1933, he was appointed chief justice of Uganda; in 1933 he held the same office in Tanganyika, and in 1936 in Ceylon. Previously he had served in Bagdad and Basra. Simeon Jacobs was attorney-general of British Kaffraria, solicitor-general of the Cape, and attorney-general and member of the cabinet of the Cape colony. Leopold Greenberg was judge-president of the Transvaal, and Philip Millin justice of the South African Supreme Court.

In Australia, Sir Julius Vogel was twice prime minister of New Zealand, and subsequently agent-general for New Zealand in London. Sir Julian Emanuel Salomons was solicitor-general and a member of the cabinet of New South Wales, thereafter vice-president of the cabinet and agent-general for New South Wales in London. For the last years of his life (1903-1909) he was honored with the post of standing counsel to the goverment of the commonwealth of Australia. Sir Isaac Alfred Isaacs became, in 1893, solicitor-general, and in

1893 attorney-general of Victoria. In 1906 he was appointed justice of the High Court, and in 1927 chief justice of Australia. From 1931 to 1936 he was governor-general of Australia. Sir Saul Samuel was minister of finance, postmaster-general, and later on agent-general for New South Wales. In Canada, David Arnold Croll was the only Jew to become a cabinet member as minister of Labor and Public Welfare from 1934 to 1937. Croll was also elected mayor of Windsor, Ontario, and distinguished himself in the Second World War.

Apart from viceroy Rufus Isaacs, a remarkably great number of Jews held office in the administration of British India. After serving, since 1832, in the Bombay administration, Henry Edward Goldsmid became, in 1847, private secretary of the governor of Bombay; in 1848, financial secretary of the government, and in 1854 chief secretary. He introduced a new system of taxation which satisfied both the government and the native population. His Jewish successor Sir Barrow Ellis also left a good memory in the mind of the people of India. So did Sir Albert Michael Green, Sir Robert Nathan, Charles Nissim and E. F. Oppenheim all of whom showed understanding of, and sympathy with, the native population while at the same time they were eager and able to enhance the prestige of the British government. Until the end of British administration in India, Sir Abraham Jeremy Raisman held high posts, being respected by all parties.

Everywhere in the British Empire and Commonwealth, Jews were active in local self-government. David Salomons was the first Jew to be elected Lord-Mayor of the city of London in 1855. He was followed by Benjamin Phillips in 1865, Henry Aaron Isaacs in 1889, George Fandell-Philips in 1897, Marcus Samuel, Lord Bearsted, in 1902, and Frank Joseph Pollitzer in 1942. Louis S. Cohen was mayor of Liverpool, and Hyman Morris mayor of Leeds. Benjamin Benjamin was elected, and unanimously re-elected, mayor of Melbourne. Edward Cohen was also mayor of Melbourne, and E. N. Marks of Sydney. Arthur Myers, A. P. Philip, Henry Isaacs and Ernest Davis were mayors of Auckland, New Zealand; M. J. Harris and Sir Harry Grauman were elected mayors of Johannesburg; Louis Gradner was elected twice, and Hyman Liberman three times mayor of Cape Town; Ivan Solomon was mayor of Pretoria, South Africa.

ITALY. In the struggle for Italy's independence and unity, Isacco Artom served as a soldier and diplomat. He was closely associated with Count Cavour, the leading statesman and real founder of the kingdom of Italy. In 1862, Artom served in the Italian legation at Paris, and in 1867 he became minister to Denmark. From 1876 until his death, Artom, as under-secretary of state, was dominant in the Foreign Office of Italy. His nephew, Ernesto Artom, also served in the Foreign Office and represented Italy at important conferences. He took a leading part in the diplomatic preparation of the Libyan expedition and in the elaboration of Italy's demands at the Peace Conference of Paris in 1919.

One of the greatest statesmen, and certainly the most universally respected statesman, modern Italy ever had, Luigi Luzzatti served for more than fifty years his country as under-secretary of state, minister and prime minister. A powerful orator and a conscientious scholar, a lofty idealist and a sober expert of finance, Luzzatti promoted Italy's commerce and agriculture, and reduced the deficit of the Treasury. He used his influence for the improvement of the relations between Italy and France, and, during World War I, appointed Commissioner of Relief, did what the limited means of Italy allowed, for the organization of help to the needy population. Other Jews, like Elia and Emilio Morpurgo, Lodovico Mortara, Angelo Pavia and Leone Romarin, ministers or secretaries of state, rendered also memorable service to Italy; in particular Carlo Schanzer, from 1901 to 1905 director general of the civil administration of the Italian ministry of Interior, in 1906 postmaster-general, in 1919 minister of finance, and in 1922, in the last pre-fascist cabinet, minister of foreign affairs. Jews of national and international renown were members of the Consulta (Chamber of Deputies) and the Senate. Ernesto Nathan was mayor of Rome for several terms, and Enrico Salem mayor of Trieste.

In Denmark Edvard Cohen Brandes was minister of finance for about ten years. In Holland, Tobias M. Asser, Michael H. Godefroij and M. E. van Raalte were ministers of state, and several other Jews were members of provincial governments. In Belgium Paul Hymans, whose father Salomon Louis Hymans was a deputy and the author of the Belgian national anthem, was minister to Great Britain, minister of foreign affairs and justice for more than twenty years. At the beginning of his career attacked by anti-Semites, he was later on considered Belgium's leading statesman who successfully represented his country at the Peace Conference in Paris and many other international conferences. Camille Gutt, for many years minister of finance, escaped to England after the Germans invaded Belgium in 1940, and acted there as a member of the Belgian government in exile. Paul May was minister to the United States.

Several Jews held office in Germany and Austria-Hungary or the latter's successor states. Under the imperial regimes they had to abandon Judaism. After these countries had become republics, Jewish statesmen and officials were still hampered by anti-Semitic prejudices and attacks or they had not time enough to stabilize their work before Hitler put an end to their activities.

Soviet Russia is no democracy in the Western sense of the word. The persecutions of Jews, tolerated and even favored by the Tsars, exasperated a part of the Russian Jews so intensively that they joined the Bolshevist party. The vast majority of the Jews of Russia, however, were bitterly opposed to the Soviet system. The great Jewish labor organizations combated the Bolshevists until they were dissolved. Many Jewish intellectuals were killed or exiled. Maxim M. Winawer, the leader of the Jewish opposition against Tsarism, was even minister of foreign affairs under the anti-Bolshevist government of General Wrangel. The number of Jewish dignitaries in Soviet Russia was always relatively small, and decreased considerably after Stalin's accession. Yakov M. Sverdlov who passed away in 1919, was called by Lenin "the first man in the socialist republic." Lev D. Trotzky who became Stalin's bitter enemy, organized the Red Army. Lazar M. Kaganovich did military work during the civil war, directed the industrialization of Soviet Russia, and became vice-president of the Council of Commissars of the People and deputy to the Supreme Council. After Russia was attacked by the Germans in 1941, Kaganovich took an important part in the organization of the army and in planning the strategy which defeated Germany on its Eastern Front. Maxim M. Litvinov was for many years leader of the foreign office. Adolf Joffe was ambassador to Germany, Japan and China. Ivan Maisky was ambassador to Great Britain and Konstantin Umansky ambassador to the United States.

The Jews of Palestine will stand the test of their ability to construct the democratic state of Israel.

Apart from the Jewish officials in Soviet Russia most of whom abandoned Judaism, the great majority of Jews in public office, mentioned in this selective survey, have also been active in Jewish communal work. There was, and is, no contradiction between their allegiance to the non-Jewish country where they live, and their loyalty to Judaism.

BIBLIOGRAPHY

ABRAHAMS, ISRAEL, *Jewish Life in the Middle Ages.* 2nd ed. London: 1932.

BARON, SALO W., *The Social and Economic History of the Jews.* New York: 1937.

GRAETZ, HEINRICH, *History of the Jews.* Philadelphia: 1927.

GRAYZEL, SOLOMON, *A History of the Jews.* Philadelphia: 1947.

HERRMAN, LOUIS, *A History of the Jews in South Africa.* Johannesburg: 1935.

HYAMSON, ALBERT M., *A History of the Jews in England.* 2nd ed London: 1928.

JACOBS, JOSEPH, *Israel among the Nations.* New York: 1934.

LEVINGER, LEE JOSEPH, *History of the Jews in the United States.* 1931.

PARKES, JAMES, *The Jew in the Medieval Community.* London: 1938.

ROTH, CECIL, *History of the Marranos.* London: 1932.

ROTH, CECIL, *A History of the Jews in England.* Philadelphia: 1941.

ROTH, CECIL, *The Jewish Contribution to Civilization.* London: 1938.

WIERNIK, PETER, *History of the Jews in America.* 2nd ed. New York: 1931.

WOLF, SIMON, *The American Jew as Patriot, Soldier and Citizen.* Philadelphia: 1895.

Jewish Social Service and Its Impact Upon Western Civilization

By MAURICE J. KARPF, PH. D

THE JEWISH CONCEPTION OF CHARITY
FROM THE CODE OF MAIMONIDES (13TH CENTURY)*

1. The following are eight degrees of charity work arranged in a descending order. The noblest form is to strengthen the hand of an Israelite in need, to give him a gift as a loan, or to join him in partnership, or to find him work, that he may not become a public charge and beggar.

2. The next highest form—is to give in such a way that the giver should not know the recipient and the recipient should not know the donor. Contribution to a charity fund is a clear analogy, but one should not contribute to a fund unless he knows that the official in charge is trustworthy and knows how to manage it.

3. A lower form is when the donor knows the recipient but the latter does not know the former.

4. A still lower form is when the recipient knows the donor but the latter does not know to whom he gives.

5. A still lower form is to give before being asked.

6. The next lower form is to give after being asked but in a sufficiently large amount.

7. The seventh lowest form is to give even what is insufficient but with a pleasant countenance.

8. The eighth and lowest degree of charity is to give grudgingly after being asked.

* Adopted from the Laws of the Hebrews, Relating to the Poor and The Stranger, from the Mishnah-Hatara of the Rabbi Maimonides, Translated by James W. Peppercorne, pp. 45-71. Cf. *The Shulhan Arukh*, translated by Louis Feinburg, pp. 247-259.

THE ENGLISH CONCEPTION OF CHARITY
FROM THE POOR LAW (16TH CENTURY)

The Poor Law, adopted in England in the middle of the 16th Century, punished wanderers and vagabonds by branding them with the letter "V", assigned them as slaves to those who would claim them, fed them with "bread and water and refuse meat", branded them with the letter "S" on the cheek and enslaved them for life if they escaped during the first year, and put them to death as felons if they escaped again.**

Jewish Attitudes Toward Charity

THE two quotations at the head of this chapter, typify the difference in approach and philosophy which has characterized the point of view and procedure of Jewish and non-Jewish philanthropy from time immemorial, and in some respects still holds true today. The Jew was always extremely concerned about his less fortunate fellow man and gave thought how to alleviate his suffering in the most humane manner. Due to the genius of the Jew, this became not merely an individual matter, a question of individual predilection, but one of group concern and responsibility. The Jewish group seemed to recognize that its welfare as a people was involved in the proper care of the sick, the poor, the widow, the orphan, the stranger, etc., and must not be left merely to chance or the conscience of the individual. Accordingly, the sages and thinkers, the formulators of Jewish folkways, sought to set down, in concrete and permanent form, the best practices of their day and these became, in their turn, the guides for future generations.

It would lead us too far afield to inquire into the social conditions in early Hebrew society that gave rise to the needs

** Taken from Clarke, John J., *Social Administration Including the Poor Laws*, Isaac Pitman and Sons, London, 1922, p. 24.

for these formulations, or the practices on which they were based. It will have to be sufficient for our present purpose, to inquire into the nature of these practices and their formulations, the institutions that were created to give them practical expressions, the means which the early Hebrew teachers and leaders devised to perpetuate these practices, the extent to which they held sway in western communal life, and what influence they exercised on the non-Jewish communities. These questions we shall try to inquire into in the pages following.

Until comparatively recent times, the Jew lived almost entirely by the teachings in the Bible. For him the Bible was more than a holy book. It was a guide to his daily life. In many significant ways the Bible, or rather the five Books of Moses, the Pentateuch, and the other Wisdom literature of the ancient Hebrews, still exercise a powerful influence on social and individual behavior. And it may be safely said that whenever the Jewish group deviates from the early and traditional teachings, some are sure to protest.

This is especially true with respect to the practice of charity. In fact organized Jewish social work is frequently criticized in the Jewish press on the ground that in its methods and procedures "it is not Jewish." Jewish social workers often meet with resentment and antagonism from their clients and other members of the community on the same ground. The charge is made that traditional practices have been abandoned, and mechanical, heartless procedures have been substituted which have nothing Jewish in them. Demands are sometimes voiced for a return to so-called Jewish practices of charity.

These criticisms and demands are based on a highly emotional and subjective reaction against what is termed the cold, calculating and unemotional consideration which the modern social worker, influenced by the non-Jewish environment, presumably gives his client. There is supposed to be "too much questioning," "too much investigation," "too much planning," "too much delay," "too much red tape," "too little feeling," etc. "This is not the way of Jewish charity," say the critics.

Precept and example are cited to illustrate how charity was practiced in Jewish communities of old and Biblical and Talmudic passages are occasionally quoted to prove how far modern Jewish charity has strayed from the paths of "the Fathers" and how foreign current practices of charity are to those who were schooled in the ways prescribed by Jewish law.[1]

Limitations of space do not permit exhaustive treatment of Jewish law relating to charity. All that can be done here is to cite a few basic concepts from the Bible, by way of illustration, because, as already indicated, these biblical concepts helped determine and shape the attitudes of the Jewish people throughout the ages on this problem.

The Bible was one of the means of transmitting the Jewish social heritage regarding the care of the poor. There can be little doubt that its precepts gave and still give direction to the institutions, agencies and practices, which have grown up in the Jewish community. However, it should be made clear that although the Bible is the major source of sanctions for Jewish charitable practices it is by no means the only source. The Apocrypha, the Talmud, the Codifications, the Responsa, etc., are also important in this connection. But the Bible is the earliest source that we have and contains a great deal of material illustrative of traditional Jewish attitudes on man's responsibility toward his less fortunate fellow-man. The Talmud presents the developments which took place in the post Biblical period. The Codifications, especially those of Maimonides (13th Century) and Joseph Karo (17th Century) are particularly important because they became the codes of ethics by which Jews were governed in their individual and group relations during the last six or seven centuries. Less important, only because they are less generally known, are the Apocrypha and Responsa.

I. *Biblical Concepts of Charity*

If one were to cull all the passages in the Bible referring to the poor, the widow, the orphan, the stranger, etc., and were to group them, several concepts would appear which would clearly indicate what their place is in the Jewish community. In fact it would be possible to construct a syllogism of the Biblical admonitions which would go somewhat as follows: God is the creator of all things, i.e., all wealth comes from God; God is the father of all men, i.e., all men are brothers; therefore, all men are entitled to a share of God's wealth.[2] Accordingly, there are admonitions and direct commandments for sharing one's wealth with the poor. More than that, the poor stand under God's special protection, so that kindness and considerateness of the poor is rewarded and inconsiderateness of the poor is punished by God; and the ideal man is one who, in addition to other virtues, possesses also that of sympathy for the suffering of his fellow-man.

The concept that God is the Creator of everything, appears in the very first verse of the Bible, Genesis, (1-1):

In the beginning God created the heaven and the earth.

Naturally, anything that God created belongs to Him and He has the right to dispose of it as He sees fit. Indeed, the Bible so conceives it and it is made clear that man's possessions are held only by the Grace of God and only temporarily, for we are told in Leviticus (XXV-23):

And the land shall not be sold in perpetuity; for the land is Mine; for ye are strangers and settlers with me.

And in Chronicles, I (XXIX-12):

Both riches and honor come of Thee, and Thou rulest over all; and in Thy hand is power and might; and in Thy hand it is to make great, and to give strength unto all.

Later on in the same chapter, the Chronicler goes on saying, (XXIX-14):

. . . For all things come of Thee, *and of Thine own have we given Thee.*

The Prophet Haggai, speaking in the name of the Lord, says, (II-8):

Mine is the silver, and Mine is the gold, saith the
Lord of Hosts.

And the Psalmist has it, (XXIV-1, 2) that:

1. The earth is the Lord's, and the fullness thereof;
   the world, and they that dwell therein.
2. For He hath founded it upon the seas, and established it upon the floods.

The Prophet Samuel admonishes his hearers, (1 Sam. II-7,
8):

7. The Lord maketh poor, and maketh rich;
   He bringeth low, He also lifteth up.
8. He raiseth up the poor out of the dust,
   He lifteth up the needy from the dung-hill,
   To make them sit with princes,
   And inherit the throne of glory;
   For the pillars of the earth are the Lord's,
   And He hath set the world upon them.

The concepts that God is the father of all men, and that all
men are brothers appear frequently in the different books of
the Bible. We are told in Deuteronomy, (XIV-1):

Ye are the children of the Lord your God.

And in Proverbs, (XXII-2):

The rich and the poor meet together—the Lord is
the Maker of them all.

When the Prophet Malachi cries out against the iniquitous
practices of his time and against the unfair dealing which is
the rule, he asks, (II-10):

Have we not all one Father? Hath not one God created us? Why do we deal treacherously every man
against his brother, profaning the covenant of our
fathers?

And in Job we are again reminded that God created all
men and that therefore fair and humane dealing is necessary,
for one is answerable for his acts with regard to his fellow-
man to God. He asks, (XXXI-13-15):

13. If I did despise the cause of my manservant, or
    of my maid-servant, when they contended with
    me—
14. What then shall I do when God riseth up? And
    when he remembereth, what shall I answer him?
15. Did not He that made me in the womb make
    him? And did not One fashion us in the womb?

Since God is the father of all, it follows that all men are
brothers. This is not only a conclusion in logic, but is actually
impressed upon us by the frequent use in the Bible of the concept "brother" as applicable not alone to the off-spring of the
same physical father, but also to all Israelites. Thus we find
in Leviticus, (XXV-25):

If thy brother be waxen poor, and sell some of his
possessions, then shall his kinsman that is next unto
him come, and shall redeem that which his brother
hath sold.

Again in the same chapter, (XXV-39):
And if thy brother be waxen poor, with thee, and sell
himself unto thee, thou shalt not make him to serve
as a bondservant.

The Deuteronomist tells us, (XV-7):
If there be among you a needy man, one of thy
brethren, within any of thy gates, in thy land which
the Lord thy God giveth thee, thou shalt not harden
thy heart, nor shut thy hand from thy needy brother.

If it be true, as suggested, that the early Hebrews looked
upon the world and all its material goods as belonging to
God, and that they considered God the creator of all men,
with its logical corollary that all men are brothers, is it not to
be expected that they would hold the view that all men are
entitled to a share of their father's possessions? This is precisely what we find. There are numerous passages in the Bible
which are direct commands for sharing with the poor. These
are scattered in the Pentateuch and in the Prophets as well as

in the Wisdom Literature. Reference is frequently made to Biblical admonitions regarding the Sabbatical period, the corners of the field and the gleanings; that each of these has a special purpose and is especially designed for the poor and the stranger. We are told in Exodus, (XXIII-10, 11):

10. And six years thou shalt sow thy land, and gather in the increase thereof;

11. But the seventh year thou shalt let it rest and lie fallow, that the poor of thy people may eat; and what they leave the beast of the field shall eat. In like manner thou shalt deal with thy vineyard, and with thy olive-yard.

Again, in Leviticus, (XIX-9, 10):

9. And when ye reap the harvest of your land, thou shalt not wholly reap the corner of thy field, neither shalt thou gather the gleaning of thy harvest.

10. And thou shalt not glean thy vineyard, neither shalt thou gather the fallen fruit of thy vineyard; thou shalt leave them for the poor and for the stranger; I am the Lord your God.[3]

Deuteronomy is replete with various commands with regard to the care of the needy, the widow, the orphan and the stranger. Thus we are told, (XV17, 11):

7. If there be among you a needy man, one of thy brethren, within any of thy gates, in thy land which the Lord giveth thee, thou shalt not harden thy heart, nor shut thy hand from thy needy brother.

8. But thou shalt surely open thy hand unto him, and shalt *surely lend him sufficient for his need* in that which he wanteth.

9. Beware that there be not a base thought in thy heart, saying: The seventh year, the year of release is at hand; and thine eye be evil against thy needy brother, and thou give him naught; *and*

> *he cry unto the Lord against thee, and it be sin in thee.*
>
> 10. Thou shalt surely *give him*, and thy heart shall not be grieved when thou givest unto him; because that for this thing the Lord thy God will bless thee in all thy work, and in all that thou puttest thy hand unto.
>
> 11. *For the poor shall never cease out of the land*; therefore I command thee, saying: Thou shalt surely open thy hand unto thy poor and needy brother, in thy land.

There are three rather important notions in these passages. The first is that we are commanded here to "lend" and that, "sufficient for his need." While it may not be wise to be too literal in the interpretation of these passages, there does seem to be a new notion of sufficiency for one's need. This comes to mean, later, in accordance with one's previous standard of living.

Another interesting notion is the concept of duty, or justice, or reward, which appears in verse 10. According to this verse "it is because of this (helping the poor) that the Lord will bless thee in all thy work, and in all that thou puttest thy hand unto." A third important item is the prophecy that "the poor shall never cease out of the land." Whatever we may think of this passage as signifying a rather narrow and perhaps limited social vision as judged by present-day hopes and aspirations, it does indicate that the economically maladjusted are viewed as a definite and integral part of the whole social structure and therefore thought must be given to their problems and methods must be devised for their alleviation.

The widow and the orphan are given special consideration in the Bible. We are commanded, (Exodus XXII-21): "Ye shall not afflict any widow or fatherless child." It is no doubt because of the numerous references to the widow and orphan that the Jewish communities throughout the ages have been especially solicitous for their welfare. Even today, when every other appeal for funds falls on deaf ears an appeal for widows and orphans will bring forth a generous response.

The relation of man to man, rich to poor, master to servant, as conceived in the Bible, is perhaps best illustrated in Deuteronomy, (XVI-11, 14):

> 11. And thou shalt rejoice before the Lord thy God, thou, and thy son, and thy daughter, and thy man-servant, and thy maid-servant, and the Levite that is within thy gates, and the stranger, and the fatherless, and the widow, that are in the midst of thee, in the place which the Lord thy God shall choose to cause his name to dwell there.
>
> 14. And thou shalt rejoice in thy feast, thou, and thy son, and thy daughter, and thy man-servant, and thy maid-servant, and the Levite, and the stranger, and the fatherless, and the widow, that are within thy gates.

Here may be said to be the origin of an age-old practice among Jews that no feast is considered complete unless provision is made for the poor to share in it. The Medieval and later European Jewish communities developed the practice of inviting the poor to sit at the feast tables of weddings and other occasions for rejoicing, and where this was not possible, to arrange special banquets for the poor. To be sure these were usually held away from the main banquet hall. But the poor were never forgotten and they participated in the feasts and showered their blessings upon the festivities and the occasion.

Reference has already been made to the comments regarding the corners of the fields and the gleanings, as found in Leviticus, (XIX-9, 10). They appear again, although in a somewhat different form in Deuteronomy, (XXIV-19-21):

> 19. When thou reapest thy harvest in thy field, and hast forgot a sheaf in the field, thou shalt not go back to fetch it; it shall be for the stranger, for

the fatherless, and for the widow, that the Lord thy God may bless thee in all the work of thy hands.

20. When thou beatest thine olive tree, thou shalt not go over the boughs again; it shall be for the stranger, for the fatherless, and for the widow.

21. When thou gatherest the grapes of thy vineyard, thou shalt not glean it after thee; it shall be for the stranger, for the fatherless, and for the widow.

A very interesting and complete statement of motive for aiding one's less fortunate fellows as conceived by the Deuteronomist appears in Chapter XXVI. In the first portion of this chapter appear the reasons for the commandments. Later (8-9), the thought is developed that the offerings of the first fruit are brought to the priest as a thank offering because:

8. The Lord brought us forth out of Egypt with a mighty hand, and with an outstretched arm, and with great terribleness, and with signs, and with wonders.

9. And he hath brought us into this place, and hath given us this land, a land flowing with milk and honey.

Toward the end of the chapter, it becomes clear that what belongs to the Levite, the stranger, the widow and the orphan is sacred to God and that the Hebrew may not rest until he has carried out the commandments to the letter. It is only after he has completed his tithing and has given the tithes to whom they belong, that he can be at ease and offer up a prayer. But even then he prays not for himself or his children but for the welfare of his people and his land. We are commanded, (12-15):

12. When thou hast made an end of tithing all the tithe of thine increase in the third year, which is the year of tithing, and hast given it unto the Levite, to the stranger, to the fatherless, and to

the widow, that they may eat within thy gates
and be satisfied.

13. Then thou shalt say before the Lord thy God:
"I have put away the hallowed things out of my
house, and also have given them unto the Levite,
and unto the stranger, to the fatherless, and to
the widow, according to all thy commandments
which thou hast commanded me; I have not
transgressed any of Thy commandments, neither
have I forgotten them.

14. I have not eaten thereof in my mourning, neither
have I put away thereof, being unclean, nor
given thereof for the dead; I have hearkened to
the voice of the Lord my God, I have done according to all that Thou hast commanded me.

15. Look forth from Thy holy habitation, from
heaven, and bless Thy people Israel, and the
land which Thou hast given us, as Thou didst
swear unto our fathers, a land flowing with milk
and honey.

We get a glimpse into the interpretation which the Prophets
placed on these practices with particular reference to the sacrifices, and the prophetic conception of man's duty to man in
the famous 58th chapter of Isaiah. He tells his hearers (4-7):

4. Behold, ye fast for strife and contention, and to
smite with the fist of wickedness; Ye fast not this
day so as to make your voice to be heard on high.

5. Is such the fast that I have chosen? The day for a
man to afflict his soul? Is it to bow down his
head as a bulrush, and to spread sackcloth and
ashes under him? Wilt thou call this a fast, and
an acceptable day to the Lord?

6. Is not this the fast that I have chosen? To loose
the fetters of wickedness, To undo the bands of
the yoke, And to let the oppressed go free, And
that ye break every yoke?

7. Is it not to deal thy bread to the hungry, And thou bring the poor that are cast out to thy house? When thou seest the naked, that thou cover him, And that thou hide not thyself from thine own flesh?

It is hardly necessary to point out that this is one of the loftiest conceptions of man's relation to God and man, to be found anywhere.

These and other commandments would alone justify the conclusion that early tradition among the Hebrews considered God the protector of the poor. But there are many passages in all books of the Bible indicating that God *is* the protector of the poor.

We are told in Exodus, (XXII-25, 26):

25. If thou at all take thy neighbor's garment to pledge, thou shalt restore it unto him by that the sun goeth down;

26. For that is his only covering, it is his garment for his skin; wherein shall he sleep? And it shall come to pass, when he crieth unto Me, that I will hear; for I am gracious.

And in Deuteronomy, (X-17-19):

17. The Lord your God, He is God of Gods, and Lord of Lords, the great God, the mighty, and the awful, who regardeth not persons, nor taketh reward.

18. He doth execute justice for the fatherless and widow, and loveth the stranger, in giving him food and raiment.

19. Love ye therefore the stranger; for ye were strangers in the land of Egypt.

Note here the concept of justice to the widow and love for the stranger. The same conception of God as the protector of the poor appears again in a later chapter of Deuteronomy. After the specific requests are made for attention to the poor

[151]

and the needy, the passage ends with "lest he cry against thee unto the Lord, and it be sin in thee," (XXIV-10-15):

10. When thou dost lend thy neighbor any manner of loan, thou shalt not go into his house to fetch his pledge.

11. Thou shalt stand without, and the man to whom thou dost lend shall bring forth the pledge without unto thee.

12. And if he be a poor man, thou shalt not sleep with his pledge.

13. Thou shalt surely restore to him the pledge when the sun goeth down, that he may sleep in his garment, and bless thee; and it shall be righteousness unto thee before the Lord thy God.

14. Thou shalt not oppress a hired servant that is poor and needy, whether he be of thy brethren or of thy strangers that are in thy land within thy gates.

15. In the same day thou shalt give him his hire, neither shall the sun go down upon it; for he is poor, and setteth his heart upon it; lest he cry against thee unto the Lord, and it be sin in thee.

And Job tells us, (XXXVI-6):

He preserveth not the life of the wicked; but giveth the poor their right.

There are numerous passages in the Bible throwing a flood of light on the question of how the early Hebrews regarded charity. The quotations given below illustrate the role played by the concept of reward, punishment and the ethical relations between man and man as practiced by the ideal person. Thus we are told in Deuteronomy (XIV-28-29), in connection with tithing, that:

28. At the end of every three years, even in the same year, thou shalt bring forth all the tithe of thine increase, and shalt lay it up within thy gates,

29. And the Levite, because he hath no portion nor

inheritance with thee, and the stranger and the fatherless, and the widow, that all within thy gates, shall come, and shall eat and be satisfied; that the Lord thy God may bless thee in all the work of thy hand which thou doest.

Isaiah's lofty conception of man's relation to man and the Deity, has already been referred to. After enumerating what God expects from man, in the way of caring for the oppressed and the poor, as we have seen, he outlines the rewards to be derived from righteous living. (LVIII-8-12):

8. Then shall thy light break forth as the morning, and thy healing shall spring forth speedily; and thy righteousness shall go before thee, the glory of the Lord shall be thy reward.

9. Then shalt thou call, and the Lord will answer; thou shalt cry, and He will say: "Here I am." If thou take away from the midst of thee the yoke, the putting forth of the finger, and speaking wickedness;

10. And if thou draw out thy soul to the hungry, and satisfy the afflicted soul; then shall thy light rise in darkness, and thy gloom be as the noonday;

11. And the Lord will guide thee continually, and satisfy thy soul in drought, and make strong thy bones; and thou shalt be like a watered garden, and like a spring of water, whose waters fail not.

12. And they that shall be of thee shall build the old waste places, thou shalt raise up the foundations of many generations; and thou shalt be called the repairer of the breach, the restorer of paths to dwell in.

In like manner, Ezekiel speaking in the name of the Lord and admonishing Israel says, (XVIII-4-9):

[153]

4. Behold, all souls are Mine; as the soul of the father, so also the soul of the son is Mine; the soul that sinneth, it shall die.

5. But if a man be just, and do that which is lawful and right,

6. And hath not eaten upon the mountains, neither hath lifted up his eyes to the idols of the house of Israel, neither hath defiled his neighbor's wife, neither hath come near to a woman in her impurity;

7. And hath not wronged any, but hath restored his pledge for a debt, hath taken nought by robbery, hath given his bread to the hungry, and hath covered the naked with a garment;

8. He that hath not given forth upon interest, neither hath taken any increase, that hath withdrawn his hand from iniquity, hath executed true justice between man and man;

9. Hath walked in My statutes, and hath kept Mine ordinances, to deal truly; he is just, he shall surely live, saith the Lord God.

Here the care of the needy is included among the first and foremost virtues for which life is vouchsafed. We are told in Proverbs, (XIX-17):

He that is gracious unto the poor lendeth unto the Lord, And his good deed will He repay unto him.

Just as kindness to the poor is a special virtue and is subject to reward so is neglect of the poor a special transgression and is punished by God. The Deuteronomist warns us, (XV-9):

Beware that there be not a base thought in thy heart, saying: "The seventh year, the year of release, is at hand"; and thine eye be evil against thy needy brother, and thou give him nought; and he cry unto the Lord against thee, and it be sin in thee.

Ezekiel says that among the vices of Sodom disregard of the poor was included, (XVI-49):

> Behold, this was the iniquity of thy sister Sodom: pride, fulness of bread, and careless ease was in her and in her daughters; neither did she strengthen the hand of the poor and needy.

We learn in the Psalms that God punishes those who seek to injure the poor, (XXXVII-14-15):

> 14. The wicked have drawn out the sword, and have bent their bow; To cast down the poor and needy, To slay such as are upright in the way:
>
> 15. Their sword shall enter into their own heart, And their bows shall be broken.

But it is in Job that we get the fullest account of the results of neglecting the poor. One of Job's three friends who came to console him, enumerates a series of dreadful punishments for oppression and neglect of the poor, (XX-12-19:)

> 12. Though wickedness be sweet in his mouth, though he hide it under his tongue;
>
> 13. Though he spare it, and will not let it go, but keep it still within his mouth;
>
> 14. Yet his food in his bowels is turned, it is the gall of asps within him.
>
> 15. He hath swallowed down riches, and he shall vomit them up again; God shall cast them out of his belly.
>
> 16. He shall suck the poison of asps; the viper's tongue shall slay him.
>
> 17. He shall not look upon the rivers, the flowing streams of honey and curd.
>
> 18. That which he laboured for shall he give back, and shall not swallow it down; according to the substance that he hath gotten, he shall not rejoice.

19. For he hath oppressed and forsaken the poor; he hath violently taken away a house, and he shall not build it up.

The author of Job in considering man's relation to God apparently finds its basis in his relation to man with particular reference to the poor. In a passage which almost equals the 58th Chapter of Isaiah, another of Job's friends asks, (XXII-3-11):

3. Is it any advantage to the Almighty that thou art righteous? Or is it gain to him, that thou makest thy ways blameless?

4. Is it for thy fear in Him that He reproveth thee, that He entereth with thee into judgment?

5. Is not thy wickedness great? And are not thine iniquities without end?

6. For thou hast taken pledges of thy brother for nought, and stripped the naked of their clothing.

7. Thou hast not given water to the weary to drink, and thou hast withholden bread from the hungry.

8. And as a mighty man, who hath the earth, and as a man of rank, who dwelleth in it,

9. Thou hast sent widows away empty, and the arms of the fatherless have been broken.

10. Therefore snares are round about thee, and sudden dread affrighteth thee,

11. Or darkness, that thou canst not see, and abundance of waters cover thee.

In another instance Job cries out in protest against existing conditions; against oppression of the poor, against the neglect of the needy and finds fault with the Almighty for condoning it. He asks, (XXIV-1-13):

1. Why are times not laid up by the Almighty? And why do not they that know Him see His days?

2. There are [those] that remove the landmarks; they violently take away flocks, and feed them.

3. They drive away the ass of the fatherless, they take the widow's ox for a pledge.

4. They turn the needy out of the way; the poor of the earth hide themselves together.

5. Behold, as wild asses in the wilderness they go forth to their work, seeking diligently for food; the desert yieldeth them bread for their children.

6. They cut his provender in the field; and they despoil the vineyard of the wicked.

7. They lie all night naked without clothing, and have no covering in the cold.

8. They are wet with the showers of the mountains, and embrace the rock for want of a shelter.

9. There are [those] that pluck the fatherless from the breast, and take a pledge of the poor.

10. So that they go about naked without clothing, and being hungry they carry the sheaves;

11. They make oil within the rows of these men; they tread their winepresses, and suffer thirst.

12. From out of the populous city men groan, and the soul of the wounded crieth out; yet God imputeth it not for unseemliness.

13. These are of them that rebel against the light; they know not the ways thereof, nor abide in the paths thereof.

In protesting his own innocence and complaining that he has not deserved the punishment meted out to him, he says, (XXXI-16-23):

16. If I have withheld aught that the poor desired, or have caused the eyes of the widow to fail;

17. Or have eaten my morsel myself alone, and the fatherless hath not eaten thereof—

18. Nay, from my youth he grew up with me as with a father, and I have been her guide from my mother's womb.

19. If I have seen any wanderer in want of clothing, or that the needy had no covering:

20. If his loins have not blessed me, and if he were not warmed with the fleece of my sheep:

21. If I have lifted up my hand against the fatherless, because I saw my help in the gate;

22. Then let my shoulder fall from the shoulder-blade, and mine arm be broken from the bone.

23. For calamity from God was a terror to me, and by reason of his Majesty I could do nothing.

Finally, when Job's young friend enumerates the powers and virtues of the Lord and how just He is in punishing those who transgress His commandments without regard to persons, he says, (XXXIV-26-28):

26. He striketh them as wicked men in the open sight of others;

27. Because they turned aside from following Him and would not have regard to any of His ways;

28. So that they cause the cry of the poor to come unto Him, and He heareth the cry of the afflicted.

The Proverbs are frequently most telling because of the short, pithy sayings which contain so much thought. Consider, for instance, this passage (XIV-31):

He that oppresseth the poor blasphemeth his Maker; but he that is gracious unto the needy honoureth Him.

Not only oppression of the poor is blasphemy but even mocking the poor is likewise blasphemy and will be punished for we are told that, (XVII-5):

Whoso mocketh the poor blasphemeth his Maker; and he that is glad at calamity shall not be unpunished.

And again, (XXII-16):

> One may oppress the poor, yet will their gain in-
> crease; one may give to the rich, yet will want come.

In picturing the ideal man or woman attention to the poor
was always a very important item. Isaiah, in describing what
he calls a "vile person" and in enumerating his shortcomings
and transgressions, makes a good deal of the failure to provide for the hungry and the thirsty, and the oppression of the
poor, (XXXII-5-7):

> 5. The vile person shall be no more called liberal,
>   nor the churl said to be noble.
>
> 6. For the vile person will speak villany, and his
>   heart will work iniquity, to practice ungodliness,
>   and to utter wickedness against the Lord, to make
>   empty the soul of the hungry, and to cause the
>   drink of the thirsty to fail.
>
> 7. The instruments also of the churl are evil; he de-
>   viseth wicked devices to destroy the poor with
>   lying words, and the needy when he speaketh
>   right.

According to the Psalmist, he who is to be exalted and honored is the one who is interested in and has compassion for
the needy, (CXII-9):

> He hath scattered abroad, he hath given to the needy;
> his righteousness endureth for ever; his horn shall
> be exalted in honour.

Job in bemoaning his fate and reminiscing on his past glory
and the honor which was his, describes himself as one who
was blessed wherever he went, most respected among men,
and of great influence because he had gone in the way of the
Lord and took care of the poor, (XXIX-7-17):

> 7. When I went forth to the gate unto the city,
>   when I prepared my seat in the broad place,
>
> 8. The young men saw me and hid themselves, and
>   the aged rose up and stood;

9. The princes refrained talking, and laid their hand on their mouth;

10. The voice of the nobles was hushed, and their tongue cleaved to the roof of their mouth.

11. For when the ear heard me, then it blessed me, and when the eye saw me, it gave witness unto me;

12. Because I delivered the poor that cried, the fatherless also that had none to help him.

13. The blessing of him that was ready to perish came upon me; and I caused the widow's heart to sing for joy.

14. I put on righteousness, and it clothed itself with me; my justice was as a robe and a diadem.

15. I was eyes to the blind, and feet was I to the lame.

16. I was a father to the needy; and the cause of him that I knew not I searched out.

17. And I broke the jaws of the unrighteous, and plucked the prey out of his teeth.

But not only upon men is the duty of taking care of the poor incumbent, and not only are men to be honored for taking care of the poor, but women, too, are charged with this responsibility. In describing the ideal housewife and in enumerating her virtues we are told (Proverbs, XXXI-20) that she is one who:

stretcheth out her hand to the poor; yea, she reacheth forth her hands to the needy.

The foregoing passages and many others not included here,[34] leave no doubt as to the place which the poor, the widow, the orphan, in fact all needy persons occupy in Jewish living. But not only to the poor of his own people did the Hebrew have a special obligation. The stranger, too, was to receive consideration. There are many admonitions like the following:

And a stranger shalt thou not oppress; for ye know the heart of a stranger, seeing ye were strangers in the land of Egypt. (Ex. XXII-9).

The stranger that sojourneth with you shall be unto you as the home-born among you, and thou shalt love him as thyself; for ye were strangers in the land of Egypt: I am the Lord your God. (Lev. XIX-34). And if a stranger who is a settler with thee be waxen rich, and thy brother be waxen poor beside him, and sell himself unto the stranger who is a settler with thee, or to the offshoot of a stranger's family, after that he is sold he may be redeemed; one of his brethren may redeem him; or his uncle, or his uncle's son, may redeem him, or any that is nigh of kin unto him or his family may redeem him; or if he be waxen rich, he may redeem himself. (Lev. XXV-47-49).
And if a stranger shall sojourn among you, and will keep the passover unto the Lord: according to the statute of the passover, and according to the ordinance thereof, so shall he do; ye shall have one statute, both for the stranger, and for him that is born in the land. (Num. IX-14).

Thou shalt not pervert the justice due to the stranger, or to the fatherless; nor take the widow's raiment to pledge. But thou shalt remember that thou wast a bondsman in Egypt, and the Lord thy God redeemed thee thence; therefore I command thee to do this thing. (Deut. XXIV-17-18).

It may be worthwhile to point out that these admonitions, commandments and precepts were not dead letters. The orthodox Jew lived by them. The Bible, especially the Pentateuch, was read constantly at home and in the Synagogue. Every Jew read it through at least once a year and most read it many times during the year. They studied it carefully, including the commentaries. Jewish children studied every word of it so that many memorized it. The same is true of the Prophets. The Psalms were recited daily. Besides all these there were many books in Hebrew and the vernacular which dealt with the rewards of charity and the punishments for failing to give to charity. The *Talmud*, and the *Shulhan Aruch* (Codifications) were constantly studied by every religious and observing Jew, and they, too, give an important place to charity.

II. *Jewish Charitable Practices in Post Biblical Times*

Such was the traditional and religious background for charity among the Jews. The Biblical sanctions outlined in some detail in the above quotations, because of their important influence, were formalized in concrete applications in the post-Biblical and Talmudic period. The concept of charity was broadened to one of social justice and righteousness. In fact, the Hebrew word, *Zedakah*, meaning charity, originally meant righteousness.[3b]

To give charity, to protect the poor, the widow, the orphan and the stranger, came to be looked upon not only as an essential act of elementary social justice, but as something which benefited the group as well as the immediate beneficiaries, i. e., the donor as well as the recipient.

The benefits to the recipient were, of course, obvious and needed comparatively little interpretation. The advantages to the donor were more difficult to envisage, hence the elaborate interpretations and at times far-fetched accounts of the intercessive powers which charity was supposed to have with the Creator. All of them, at least by implication, take the injustice of poverty for granted and count it as a great virtue in the donor that by his act of charity or "loving kindness" he mitigates somewhat the disadvantages of poverty thus, in part, righting a wrong to the disadvantaged and easing his complaint against the Almighty. He, in turn, will reward the donor with long life, health, happiness, and by diverting calamity from individuals and groups and even averting death. The Hebrew chant, "charity averts death" may still be heard at funerals of the orthodox Jew and the blessings heaped upon those who give charity by the recipients are only limited by their vocabulary and imagination.

To the orthodox Jew charity was not an abstract notion; it was a way of life. Children were taught to give from the time they could handle coins. There was a practice in most orthodox homes for the young children to place a coin in the Charity Box Friday evenings before the blessing of the candles, ushering in the Sabbath, and again on Saturday night at the *Havdallah* service, signifying the end of the Sabbath. Every event in the Jewish home, whether of joy or sorrow, every celebration, required some form of alms-giving. Little wonder then that the "charity habit" became second nature to the Jew. He was born and bred to it, and it became part of his daily activity.

It was in this way, through these teachings and practices, that Jews came to look upon charity as one of the cardinal virtues to be cultivated by all who would live in accordance with Biblical teaching as interpreted and amplified by the scholars and sages of later days. This they did in their individual and group practices which have become imbedded in the social consciousness of the Jewish people reaching down to our own day.

The institutionalization of charity among the Jews during the Middle Ages was due to two important factors. First the persecutions, expulsions and wanderings imposed upon the Jews by their Christian neighbors created hordes of penniless wandering individuals and families—the "displaced persons" of a former day, who had to have help if they were to survive. But it was not only the wanderers who needed financial and other types of assistance for survival. Many of the older residents of the ghettos, limited as they were to a few pursuits with the many restrictions against land ownership, tilling of

[163]

the soil, and most of the occupations controlled by the guilds, were forced to resort to charity to maintain themselves. This required some concrete organizational forms for collecting and administering charitable funds. At first there were two such funds: the general Fund *Kuppah* and the soup-kitchen fund, *Tamhui*. Later seven well organized funds became the general practice and each community established them. Indeed, no community was considered a good community to settle in by the observing Jew, unless it had adequate charitable funds. These Funds in the main were: feeding the hungry; clothing the naked; burying the dead and comforting the mourners; care of the sick; redemption of captives and slaves; providing dowries for poor maidens and free loans; educating the fatherless and sheltering the homeless. Each of these funds had its own ramifications and became a basic and accepted form of Jewish benevolence which held sway until modern times.

The place which charity and benevolence occupied in Jewish life had its counterpart in the prestige which those who were charged or charged themselves with the care of the poor, had in the Jewish community. From the earliest period of organized Jewish life it was considered a great honor to be selected as an "overseer" of the poor and only the most respected and trustworthy individuals were chosen. Indeed, the son of such an "overseer" could marry into a priestly family without examination into his antecedents, an honor to which none but descendants of the priesthood could aspire. This, too, has come down to us as a tradition which is still observed in principle as well as in practice. For although the priesthood is no more as such, and no particular prestige attaches to their descendants, only the leaders of the Jewish community are entrusted with the responsibility and funds for charitable purposes. Engaging in philanthropic activities is still frequently the easiest and quickest way to acquire community leadership and prestige.

III. *Influence of Jewish Conceptions of Charity*

It is almost impossible to tell with any degree of certainty what influence the Jewish concepts and practices of charity had upon their neighbors. We know that the teachings of Jesus and his Disciples in the New Testament regarding charity closely parallel those in the Old Testament. Since these teachings constituted the basic philosophy of the early Church Fathers, we can be certain that the early church practices were based upon the Hebrew concepts. We know also that throughout the ages, various Christian leaders and church scholars spoke and wrote in complimentary fashion about Jewish charitable practices. Thus, to cite only a few examples, the Emperor Julian (4th Cent. A. D.) in ordering the creation of inns in cities, could not conceal his admiration of the Jews because they had no beggars in their midst even as he could not refrain from characterizing the Jews as "the enemies of the Gods."

Writing many centuries later (1675) on "The Present State of The Jews in Barbary," Lancelot Addison describes in some detail the charitable practices of the Jews at the time and the relative superiority of the Jewish way of taking care of the poor over that of "either the Moore or Christian." He says:

> "Those who have observed that the Jews have no beggars, seem not well informed of the manner of their alms, and their way of providing for the poor. Whom 'tis true we may not reckon among *Beggars*, as that word usually implies a seeking Relief from house to house. For though the *Jews* in *Barbary* there is great store of needy persons, yet they are supplied after a manner which much conceals (as to men of other Religions) their Poverty. For the Wealthier take care to provide for them, and very much magnifie their Religion upon this very score, that they live under its profession in a more mutual Charity of Alms than either the *Moore* or *Christian*; both

which (with great insulting) I have heard them up-braiding with their common Beggars."

Addison then proceeds to describe in great detail the methods employed by the Jews for collecting and distributing charity and makes a special point of the fact that "it cannot be denied, but that the *Jews'* manner of Relieving their Poor is Regular and Commendable. For first they suffer them not to take Alms of any man who is of a different Religion from their own; and this inspection of them and their wants, is consigned to no meaner persons than their chief *masters* . . ."[4]

Another writer in dealing with the *History of English Philanthropy*, has a good deal to say about the influence of Jewish philanthropy on the development of English philanthropy. He describes the problems of the Jewish returnees to England, in the time of the Commonwealth, after an absence of almost 350 years, and the speed with which they adjusted themselves and developed their own institutions. He goes on to say that:

"In the first instance these foreign immigrants were dependent on English hospitality, but they quickly began to organize their own charities for their own poor. Their efforts, which attracted the attention and received the support of native philanthropists, exercised in their turn a reciprocal influence through the stimulus they gave to the imitative faculty, and established the first model of one special form of hospital which was to play a considerable part in the social economy of the poor."

The hospital he refers to is the British Lying-In which was organized in 1749 and which "followed and imitated the Jewish provision for women in child-birth," (the Jewish Lying-In Hospital, established in 1747).[5]

Finally, Beatrice Potter, later to become the famous Beatrice Webb, the wife and co-worker of Sidney Webb, in a chapter in Charles Booth's epochal study of the *Life and Labour of the People in London*, on "*The Jewish Community of London*",[6] describes the organization, growth and activities of the

Jewish community of London. Its provisions for charity receive special attention and emphasis. She is at great pains to defend the "Jewish Board of Guardians," the over-all Jewish organization of London, against the charge leveled against it in an article in *The Spectator* (April 22, 1887) that it is creating a great deal of pauperization among the Jews in London with its methods of charitable assistance.

She points out that of the 3,313 cases dealt with in 1887 only 268 were known to the Board prior to 1886 and adds, "If we remember the many thousands of cases treated during the Board's existence, we can hardly, in the face of these statistics, describe those relieved by the Jewish Board of Guardians as belonging to the chronically parasitic class of paupers."

She goes on to say: "If we mean by the word pauper, a person supported by state provision, there are no paupers within the Jewish Community, except a few isolated individuals chargeable to the English parochial authorities." She concludes with the statement: "While all groundwork for the charges of pauperization is absent, we have conclusive evidence that either from the character of those who take, or from the method of those who give, Jewish charity does not tend to the demoralization of individual recipients."

This is high praise indeed from the foremost student and authority of English poor relief. For Beatrice Potter, or Mrs. Webb, or Lady Passfield, was probably one of the greatest single influences in the development and modification of the English Poor Law of the present century. It may go without saying that her criticism of the English Poor Law and her efforts at their modification and reform were in part at least influenced by her admiration and approval of the constructive and humane methods which the Jewish community of London and other Jewish communities developed for caring for their poor.

Similar developments could be traced in Germany, France, Poland and Russia where there were substantial Jewish populations and well organized Jewish community structures, if space permitted.[7] But it was in the United States of America that Jewish philanthropy in its modern connotation of social service had its greatest growth, and it will be with its examination and discussion that the remainder of this essay will deal. For here the Jewish population increased from approximately 3,000 in 1818 to more than 4,500,000 in 1950, or 1500%.[8] This means that the Jewish population of the United States is the largest of any country. In fact, it constitutes almost half the Jewish population of the entire world.

In addition to being the largest, the Jewish population in the United States is also the wealthiest and is mainly concentrated in the larger cities. This fact of the urbanization of the Jewish people together with the relative newness of the population, most of it having come through immigration, required large and comprehensive social service programs for meeting the problems which customarily arise in an urban setting and accompany the adjustment efforts of an immigrant population.

An important influence in Jewish philanthropic effort in the U. S. A. during the first half of the 20th Century was the heavy responsibility American Jewry was forced to assume in the alleviation of suffering, the rehabilitation of Jewish communities in other countries, and the reconstruction of Palestine, as a result of the two world wars and their aftermath. These efforts required the raising of unprecedented sums of money and necessitated the creation of instrumentalities which, in themselves, made for an earlier maturation of American Jewish communities than might otherwise have been the case. This maturity made it possible for American Jewish philanthropy to play an important role in influencing general philanthropy in the U. S. A.

But it should not be assumed even for a moment that the lines of influence are either in one direction or are so clearly visible as to be easily traced out. Nothing could be further from the truth. In fact no one could say with any degree of certainty that the general social services did not exercise a greater influence on the Jewish social services than vice-versa.

Indeed, in some phases such as family welfare and what is known as the case work fields, that is quite clearly the case. On the other hand, in some fields such as fund-raising for social service, it is just as clear that the line of influence went in the opposite direction. In most instances, however, Jewish and general social service exercise an interinfluence which it is almost impossible to untangle.

Before proceeding to discuss the individual fields and their relation to each other, it seems important to sound a word of caution to the unwary reader, i. e., that in addition to the indistinguishability of the lines of influence and the uncertainty and insecurity which must, at best, characterize this type of discussion, there is also the question of the relative importance of initiating a desirable or beneficial social effort on the one hand, and making possible its best development on the other. Who shall say who is the greater social benefactor, the person who becomes cognizant of a social need or problem and suggests or agitates for its solution, or the person or group that creates the social situation which makes the discovery of the problem and its solution possible? And who shall say who is deserving the greater credit, he who suggests the first steps in a solution of a social problem or he who makes possible the solution on the highest level? It is important to recognize and constantly bear in mind, especially in connection with social effort, that the question of credit for initiating a social good is relatively unimportant, and that those who frequently make the most significant contributions are usually the ones who seek and receive the least credit.

Another difficulty in determining who influenced whom and to what degree lies in the fact that unlike the isolation of the Jews in the ghetto where they were obliged to live by themselves with very little contact with the outside world, Jews in the United States have been and are in an ever increasing degree, part and parcel of the American scene. They participate with their fellow Americans of other faiths in the stream of intellectual and social life and make their contributions to it as individuals and as a group without anyone stopping to think of these contributions as coming from Jews. Jewish social workers and Jewish philanthropists participate in non-Jewish philanthropic and social service efforts and make their contributions to them, directly and indirectly. They thus come to influence general social welfare efforts and are, in turn, influenced by them. It would, therefore, be unsafe and unwise to be too dogmatic about debits and credits in this respect.

Nevertheless, some priorities may be discerned and we shall turn our attention to them.

Mention has already been made of Jewish family welfare work having been influenced by the general field. This is due mainly to the fact that the technical progress in that field stemmed from the fields of social science and psychiatry. But Jewish family welfare work made its contribution to the general field in several important respects. First was the element of standards of financial assistance. Records kept by the Russell Sage Foundation of New York City, over a period of 25 years of the work of the most important family welfare societies in the country make it clear that the Jewish agencies support their families on a much higher standard than do the non-Jewish agencies. Similarly, the Jewish agencies are much more ready to supplement the financial assistance granted by the governmental agencies than are the non-Jewish private agencies.

All of this is in line with the Biblical admonition, mentioned earlier in this Chapter, to give to the poor, and that sufficient for his need, which was interpreted in Talmudic times to mean that a poor man should be supported in accordance with his previous standard of living. The sages taught and it was so recorded in the Codifications of Karo and Maimonides, that if a poor man was accustomed to ride upon a horse with a servant running before him, it is incumbent upon the Jewish community to supply him with a horse and a servant. While Jewish agencies do not observe this admonition to the letter they do try to adhere to it in spirit by enabling the poor to live on a decent standard so that the family and particularly the children may retain their self-respect, which is frequently a most important factor in their rehabilitation.

Jewish family agencies also aim to make it possible for the children of their families to secure a good education, and where native ability and capacity warrant it, to obtain professional training, thus strengthening the inner resources of the family and enabling them to achieve an independent status at the earliest possible date.

Perhaps the most constructive type of work undertaken by these societies is to set their families up in business. In many instances several thousand dollars will be invested by the organization in purchasing or establishing a business for one of its families where illness or some other misfortune makes it impossible for the bread-winner to engage in his previous occupation and where a study of the family situation indicates that the family will be able to manage the business. Here again, current practice is in line with Jewish tradition, for it will be recalled that the highest type of charity in Maimonides' eight degrees of charitable giving, is that which sets the poor person up in business and makes him independent.[9]

The non-Jewish agencies are aware of these standards and efforts of the Jewish organizations and some have striven to reach them. But thus far few, if any, have achieved this goal. However, it is safe to say that the standards of the Jewish societies are a constant reminder of the inadequacies of general relief standards and have served as an inspiration and stimulation to them to go and do likewise.[10]

In the care of dependent children, a similar situation prevails. Here, too, Jewish child care institutions maintain their children on a higher level, offer them better education and professional preparation for life than do the non-Jewish institutions. The Jewish organizations also have higher standards in selecting foster parents and usually pay them at a higher rate than do others.

The practice of boarding out dependent children in homes instead of keeping them in large orphans homes, by whatever name these institutions may be known, had its greatest development since 1909 when President Theodore Roosevelt called a conference of social workers and prominent lay persons to consider what is the best type of care for dependent children. This conference was a landmark in child care efforts in the United States and many Jewish child care specialists were in prominence and took a leading part in its preparation and deliberations. One of the important conclusions or findings of the Conference was that the best place for rearing children is their natural home and where no such home exists or can be re-established, every effort should be made to simulate it or reproduce a situation which would give the child the warmth, affection and love of a natural home.

This principle influenced child care in important ways. It made the large congregate institution for children, where hundreds and some times thousands of children were crowded together, appear like a monstrosity, and sounded its death knell. The cottage plan type of institution and boarding out or foster home care gradually took its place. It was fortunate that Jewish child care institutions had been experimenting with both types of care and were therefore in a position to make their thought and experience on these substitutes available to the Conference—as indeed they have been doing since then, so that in some ways the Jewish agencies were the laboratories for experimentation and progress in this field.

Perhaps the most important area of contribution in the social service field which Jews have been able to make was that of central fund raising and distribution. Here too, the contribution was direct and indirect, by precept and example, and by what one might term social osmosis. This was made possible by the development of the Jewish federations of charities.

The Federation movement had its beginning at the close of

the nineteenth century. It came about because of the duplication of appeals for charitable donations in the Jewish community occasioned by the multiplicity of organizations created for aiding the newly arrived immigrants who began coming to the United States as a result of the persecutions and restrictions instituted by the Czarist government in Russia, in 1881. First Boston, in 1895, then Cincinnati in 1896, created central communal funds. This meant one fund-raising effort a year which aimed to collect sufficient funds of all recognized agencies (usually members of the Fund or Federation) to meet their needs for the entire year. This movement took hold, spread to other communities, and became the established practice for raising and distributing charitable funds in the Jewish community.

At first these Federations were purely fiscal in their method and approach. But as their work developed it became clear that in order to distribute their funds wisely and equitably among their beneficiary agencies they would have to know how well each organization is functioning; whether there was a need for the type of services it was prepared to render; whether there was duplication of efforts by the various agencies; whether economies could not be introduced and practiced; whether there were needs in the community which were not met; which organization was best equipped to meet those needs or whether a new organization would have to be created; etc. All this meant that the Federation had to become, as indeed it later became, a planning, coordinating and controlling agency. In the twenty or twenty-five years which followed, every Jewish community in the country of any importance organized a federation of Jewish charities.

Curiously, although the federation movement is commonly assumed to have originated with the Jews, it really began with the non-Jews in Denver, ten or fifteen years earlier. But the Denver experiment led nowhere, for the central fund there was not a conspicuous success and no one wanted to imitate it. It was only after Cleveland organized a community chest in 1913, under the leadership of a Jew who knew about the philosophy, principles of operation and success of the federation movement in the Jewish community, that the community chest movement caught fire so that today practically every community of any considerable size has a community chest.

It should be noted that in addition to the success of the Jewish Federation, there was another very important factor which influenced the growth and development of the community chest movement, namely, the First World War.

The period of 1914 to 1919 was one of tremendous expansion and growth of the community chest movement in the United States. The public became aware of needs and problems and began to think in financial terms on an unprecedented scale. The war itself, after the U. S. entered it in 1917, brought problems to the various communities and made them conscious of the need for their solution as never before. Among these was the problem of caring for the men in the armed services in a civilian atmosphere where they could relax and be free from the military discipline during their recreational and social activities. Seven service organizations were united in their fund raising efforts for this purpose. War Chests were created in many communities which were to meet the needs of the civilian philanthropic as well as the war service organizations. What more natural, then, that the experience of federations and community chests should be drawn on for guidance and inspiration?

These War Chests included, in many instances, the Jewish Federations and the Community Chests. The experienced leadership of the Jewish federations was utilized in planning and conducting campaigns which included the entire community. With this leadership and under the impact of patriotic fervor, large sums were raised which made the Chest idea popular and the movement made great strides.

After the close of the First World War, Jewish overseas needs were so great that heretofore undreamt of sums had to be raised. The war and its aftermath in the United States and overseas made Jewish community leaders think in terms of national needs as never before. The Welfare Fund movement came into being as a result of this new awareness of greater and greater need and responsibility. These funds, although created originally largely for overseas needs, became increasingly more inclusive, so that eventually they supported all Jewish needs whether local, national or overseas. Campaigns and fund raising in the Jewish community took on the aspect of big business and communities and individual donors vied with each other in the amounts raised, the standard of giving, and the number of contributors covered in proportion to the Jewish population.

Here again the non-Jewish community was a direct and indirect beneficiary of Jewish imagination, initiative, enterprise and generosity. The lessons which Jewish campaign leaders and managers learned in welfare-fund campaigns were transmitted to the general community through the participation of Jewish leaders in the general campaigns. The standards of giving developed by Jewish contributors were frequently used as goals in the non-Jewish campaigns with the inevitable result that the general standard of giving was raised.

It must be added, however, that neither as individuals nor as communities did the non-Jews attain the Jewish standards of giving. It is a common and frequent occurrence that the Jews, who rarely exceed 10% of the total population in any one city, raise much more for their welfare fund needs than does the community chest in the same community. The same is true nationally. The Jews who constitute less than 4% of the total population undertake campaigns for their Welfare Funds which exceed the totals raised by all the Community Chests in the country and they contribute to the Chests in addition to supporting their own Welfare Funds so generously.

It is only fair to add that the high standards of Jewish giving have not always been a source of credit to Jewish generosity. The large sums raised by the Welfare Funds amounting to many hundreds of millions of dollars and the campaign propaganda have created the false impression in the minds of many non-Jews that the Jews as a class or group, are enormously wealthy which brings them the envy and jealousy of many of their neighbors. Also, their contributions to the community chest are compared with their contributions to the Welfare Funds and since there is a necessary differential in these contributions due to the extent of need and the fact that only Jews, by and large, contribute to the welfare funds, they are criticized for giving so much less to the Community Chests. On the other hand, where Jewish donors and workers set a high standard for the Community Chest, they are frequently criticized for these high standards. It would almost seem as if the old anti-Semitic maxim: *"Tut nichts, der Jude vird verbrandt,"* holds in this instance too.

But on the whole no one would deny that Jewish philanthropy has made a first rate contribution to general social welfare through Jewish participation and leadership in fund raising by the general community.

There are numerous other areas in which Jewish philanthropy has made important contributions and which can only be mentioned here. Thus, in the treatment of tuberculosis and the care of the tuberculous patient, Jewish initiative has frequently pointed the way to progress. The Jewish hospitals, local and national, in Denver, Los Angeles, and elsewhere, have been models of what such institutions should be. They have been important factors in the advances which have been made toward stamping out this scourge both by their advanced therapy and the research they have conducted. In the creation and maintenance of a sheltered workshop for the rehabilitation of the tuberculous, they have not only helped many patients reestablish themselves but have pointed the way toward one of the most constructive methods of solving the problem of financial independence for the victims of tuberculosis, which the general community has not yet caught up with.

Jewish social service has covered a wide variety of activities and made its contribution to all of them. Perhaps no problem

[176]

attracted so great a continuing interest and activity as immigration and immigrant adjustment. Jews believe passionately in the open-door policy and have fought continuously to keep the United States a haven for the downtrodden and persecuted. They believe in a liberal immigration policy not only because this was the great American tradition but because they are convinced that it was free immigration that brought the inexhaustible and precious human resources to these shores that made this country the greatest on earth. In this fight against a restrictionist movement and policy they were among the leaders and are largely responsible for whatever freedom of immigration has been maintained in the United States including the recent legislation in favor of displaced persons. It is safe to say that but for the initiative and organizing genius of Jewish organizations, the restrictionists in the United States Congress would have had their way even to a greater extent.

But it was not only in keeping the doors open to immigrants that Jewish social service made an important contribution. Perhaps an even greater service was rendered by its pioneering efforts toward the solution of the problem of adjusting the immigrant and aiding him to establish himself in his new home and learn what America is and what it stands for. Jewish organizations have helped also in distributing the new arrivals so that they would not all settle in the port cities. This required a close and well integrated relation between various cities, agreements as to responsibility for non-residents, and a recognition of the right of the individual to seek his own adjustment and betterment. This gave rise to an agreement between cities early in the present century, known as the "Transportation Rules", which was later adopted with restrictive modifications, by general social service agencies and still later incorporated into state laws as residence requirements for financial assistance.

The need for adjusting Jewish immigrants and distributing them more evenly throughout the United States led to the creation of various experiments which were later adopted and conducted on a larger scale. Among these should be mentioned the efforts of the Jewish Agricultural Society, established with funds from the Baron de Hirsch Fund, for aiding Jews to go on the land and become farmers. This organization helped its protege farmers develop various types of cooperatives for buying and selling as well as a credit cooperative which engaged in banking and credit extension on a mutually helpful basis. This organization also helped initiate a program of subsistence homesteading long before such homesteading was thought of by other private organizations or by the American government during the New Deal of the Roosevelt administration.

Jewish organizations also played a leading part in the fight for civil rights and against discrimination of all sorts. In their efforts to help Jews adjust vocationally and educationally, Jewish organizations met discriminations on all sides. They realized that this evil can be fought and won only on a nonsectarian basis and that discrimination of any kind, whether social, educational, vocational, economic or political, or whether practiced against white or colored, Jew or Catholic or Seventh-Day Adventist, is an evil and must be fought by all right thinking men. For strategic reasons, Jewish organizations frequently stay in the background in this fight. But they are ever ready to use their resources to help maintain the democratic tradition and to do battle against bigotry wherever it rears its ugly head.

This admittedly incomplete review of the contributions of Jewish philanthropy to general social welfare has thus far dealt with the programs and activities of movements and organizations. Very little has been said as yet about the role of the individual worker and philanthropist who influenced the field in which he labored. Nothing like a complete treatment is possible here. But a few outstanding examples may serve to illustrate the far-reaching influence of Jewish philanthropists and social workers.

JEWISH SOCIAL SERVICE AND ITS IMPACT

It was a Jewish philanthropist, Nathan Strauss, who educated this country and the world to the importance of pasteurization of milk and by devoting his entire fortune to this enterprise, was perhaps one of the greatest single factors in reducing infant mortality the world has known. This he accomplished against tremendous opposition by the vested interests in the milk industry.

Another Jewish philanthropist, Julius Rosenwald, raised the standard of giving to charitable purposes in his own community and the country to unprecedented levels by matching his contributions with those of others, thus stimulating them to give more and more. He was especially interested in the welfare of the colored people. By his munificent contributions to their educational institutions he helped create facilities for leader training which they would otherwise not have had, and called attention to the discrimination practiced against the colored people in educational institutions.

Rosenwald made another outstanding contribution through his espousal of a type of liquidating foundation. His idea, in brief, was that each generation should meet its own needs and that foundations should be set up to last only 25 or 30 years and should spend their capital as well as income. He set up the Rosenwald Foundation on that basis. There is still considerable controversy about the social soundness of his idea. But it made people think about foundations, their programs, their influence, etc., as few ideas about foundations have.

There are numerous other foundations set up by Jews for social service purposes which made and are making important contributions to social welfare, e. g., the Baruch Foundation for Physio Therapy, the Columbia Foundation, The Hofheimer Foundation, the Fels Foundation, The Fuld Foundation, The Guggenheim Foundation, the Lasker Foundation, The Lavenberg Foundation, The Littauer Foundation, The Rosenberg Foundation, The New York Foundation, The Warburg Foundation, to mention only a few of the more important ones.

Former Governor and now Senator Herbert H. Lehman of New York rendered an outstanding service to local, national and international social welfare when he was Governor of the State of New York and Director General of the United Nations Relief and Rehabilitation Administration. His life-long association with Jewish philanthropy in its local, national and international phases undoubtedly played a most important role in supplying the standards and ideals which he employed in the legislation he sponsored as Governor, and which he and his associates, many of whom were Jewish social workers, used in the administration of UNRRA. In this way Jewish social service made a most important contribution to western civilization although less directly.

There are too many Jewish social workers who made important contributions to social welfare for any considerable number to be included in this necessarily abbreviated discussion. Here, too, a few names will serve to illustrate the nature and diversity of their interests and activities.

Lillian Wald of Henry St. Settlement fame was responsible for the introduction of school nurses and, more important, for the creation of the Visiting Nurses Association, a movement which spread throughout the United States and other countries. In this work she was greatly aided by two famous Jewish philanthropists, Jacob H. Schiff and his son-in-law, Felix M. Warburg.

Judge Julian W. Mack, an intimate friend of Julius Rosenwald and Jewish social workers, was responsible for the creation of the Juvenile Court system. Jacob Billikopf was among the prime movers for the creation of the Mother's or Widow's Pension movement which has been adopted by every state; Dr. I. M. Rubinow was among the leaders in the movement for social security; Abraham Epstein was one of the chief architects of old age pensions; Ludwig B. Bernstein was one of the creators and leaders of the cottage plan institution for dependent children; Boris D. Bogen, while European Director of the Jewish Joint Distribution Committee, was instrumental, although indirectly, in the development of standards, by the Hoover Commission, for feeding the starving children of Europe after the first World War; David M. Bressler and Morris D. Waldman were jointly responsible for initiating and developing a program for immigrant distribution and settlement through their work in the Industrial Removal Office, in the early part of this century, again helped by the two leading Jewish philanthropists of their respective generations, already mentioned, Jacob H. Schiff and Felix M. Warburg; Maurice J. Karpf, while head of the graduate School for Jewish Social Work, the first strictly graduate school for social workers, greatly influenced the training of social workers through the high standards of the Jewish school, the emphasis upon a scientific and cultural background for social workers and the development of a uniform graduate curriculum for schools of social work, during his Presidency of the American Association of Schools and Social Work.

Candor and a decent respect for historical accuracy seem to require that it be recorded, in connection with the last paragraph, that Jewish social workers were not always wise or farsighted in recognizing their opportunities for pioneering in social service or in encouraging such pioneering when engaged in by their colleagues. As an illustration may be cited the attempt to develop the scientific and more especially, the cultural aspects of Jewish social work which could have been one of the most outstanding contributions of Jewish social work but which was fought and deprecated by highly placed Jewish social workers. Perhaps it is part of the so-called self-hatred, desire for assimilation, or the fear of being different and unique which characterizes many Jews, or it may be a neophobia or plain professional jealousy, which is true of almost all professional groups and professionals, that was responsible for the opposition to the Graduate School for Jewish Social Work which aimed to foster and develop both these approaches to social work. At any rate, the School which achieved outstanding academic success and distinction could not achieve the undivided support of Jewish social workers. Previous efforts at providing training for Jewish social work similarly failed to obtain their support although here, too, they could have led in pioneering in the field of education for social work. Now that the general field of social work is turning to the social sciences for light on the problems facing it and for an interpretation of the role which one's cultural background plays in human behavior, Jewish social workers, too, are beginning to recognize these viewpoints.[11] But instead of being the leaders they have become the followers if not the laggards in a most important aspect of social service.

Another illustration of the failure of Jewish social workers to recognize an opportunity for a distinctive service to Jewish and general philanthropy, was the alacrity with which they turned over their clientele to the public agencies during the depression. In their eagerness to take advantage of the availability of public funds they lost sight of the distinctiveness of Jewish social work in point of view, method, and approach. The voices which were raised in opposition were as voices in the wilderness, unheard and unheeded. Here, too, the result was that not only have they failed to lead where they could have been in the vanguard with great credit and distinction, but their willingness to compromise with the high standards which characterized Jewish social work in the past, and their accepting federal and state funds for the relief of their clients on a level which did not insure their rehabilitative potentialities, took from them one of their strongest appeals to, and claims upon, the interest and generosity of the Jewish community.[12]

However, important as these and other negative elements in the picture may be, such as, for instance, their failure to establish or even encourage a truly scientific program on Jewish life,[13] the balance sheet is overwhelmingly in favor of the boon which Jewish social work and workers have been to general philanthropy. In fact, the foregoing list of positive and substantial contributions could be extended almost indefinitely. But enough has been said to indicate the wide variety of contacts, the catholicity of interest and the important and compelling role which Jewish social service has played directly and indirectly in its impact upon western civilization.

FOOTNOTES

[1] See Silver, Harold, *Attitudes of East European Jews Toward Organized Charity*, The Graduate School for Jewish Social Work, 1935, pp. 109-146, and his *The Russian Jew Looks at Charity*, Jewish Social Service Quarterly, Vol. IV, pp. 129-144.

[2] Cf. Schechter, S., *Studies in Judaism*, Third Series, The Jewish Publication Society of America, 1924, pp. 238-249. Also, Kohler, K., *Historical Development of Jewish Charities, Hebrew Union College and Other Essays*, pp. 56-61; 229-252; 274-275, and his article on "Charity," *The Jewish Encyclopedia*, Vol. 3, pp. 667-671.

[3] Cf. Deut. XXIV, 19-21.

[3a] Cf. "Toward a Source-Book of Jewish Philanthropic Origins—Biblical Excerpts on Benevolence," by Maurice J. Karpf, *The Jewish Social Service Quarterly*, Dec., 1936, pp. 287-303.

[3b] For an outline of the concepts regarding Charity contained in the *Talmud*, see "Toward a Source-Book of Jewish Philanthropic Origins—Talmudic Period," by Maurice J. Karpf, *The Jewish Social Service Quarterly*, June 1936, pp. 396-410.

[4] Addison, Lancelot, *The Present State of the Jews in Barbary*, London, 1675, pp. 213-216.

[5] Gray, B. Kirkman, *A History of English Philanthropy*, pp. 154-157.

[6] Booth, Charles, *Life and Labour of the People in London*, Ch. IV, Vol. 3, Macmillan, London, 1902, pp. 166-174.

[7] See Roth, Cecil, *Jewish Contribution to Civilization*, Macmillan & Co., 1938, pp. 287-315.

[8] See Karpf, Maurice J., *Jewish Community Organization in the U. S. A.* Bloch Pub. Co., New York, p. 8.

[9] Karpf, Maurice J., *op. cit.*, pp. 70-71. See also his *"A Social Audit of a Social Service Agency"*, The Jewish Social Service Bureau, Chicago, pp. 109-125.

[10] See Bruno, Frank J., "A Romance of Family Case Work, A Review of *A Social Audit*", by Maurice J. Karpf, *The Survey*, Vol. LV, No. 2, Oct. 15, 1925, pp. 87-89.

[11] For a statement on the School's position on this matter see the last available *Catalogue of the Graduate School for Jewish Social Work*, 1938-1940, pp. 13-15. Also, "The Need and Problems of Training for Jewish Communal Work" by Maurice J. Karpf, *Proceedings*, The National Conference of Jewish Social Welfare, 1940, and "Cultural Factors in Social Work Education Today". Address delivered at the 3rd Annual meeting of the Amer. Assn. of Schools of Soc. Wk., Jan. 22-25, 1950, by Dr. Florence Kluckholm.

[12] See "Wanted—A Return to Basic Values" by M. J. Karpf—*The Social Service Quarterly*, Vol. VIII, No. 2, Dec. 1931, and "The Status of Case Work

in The Jewish Community" by Maurice J. Karpf, *Ibid.*, Vol. XVII, No. 1, Sept. 1940.

13 On the importance of research see: *Symposium on Research, The Annual,* Pub. of the Yiddish Scientific Inst., New York. Vol. IV, 1949. Also Karpf, Maurice J., Jewish Community Org., *op. cit.*, pp. 152-168 and references in Bibliography, pp. 201-2.

BIBLIOGRAPHY

ABRAHAM, ISRAEL, *Jewish Life in the Middle Ages.* London: Edward Goldston, 1932.

AMERICAN JEWISH COMMITTEE. See Annual and Special Reports dealing with immigration and Civic protection.

AMERICAN JEWISH CONGRESS. See the Congress Bulletin.

AMERICAN JEWISH JOINT DISTRIBUTION COMMITTEE. See its various reports.

BARON, SALO W., *A Social and Religious History of the Jews,* Vol. I, pp. 119 ff.; pp. 281 ff.; Vol. II, pp. 86-117; pp. 387 ff.; pp. 432 ff.

BOGEN, BORIS D., *Jewish Philanthropy.* New York: Macmillan, 1917.

BRUNO, FRANK J., *A Romance of Family Case Work.* A Review of a Social Audit by Maurice J. Karpf, The Survey, Vol. LV, No. 2, Oct. 15, 1925, pp. 87-89. This is especially pertinent as an appreciation by a leading non-Jewish social worker of Jewish social work.

CRONBACH, ABRAHAM, *The Me'il Zedakah,* Hebrew Union College Annual, Vol. XI, 1936, pp. 503-567.

DAVIDSON, GABRIEL, *The Jew in Agriculture in the United States,* American Jewish Year Book, Vol. 37, 1935-36, pp. 99-134. This is an interesting and informative statement of what a Jewish organization is doing to help people go to and stay on the land.

EPSTEIN, MORDECAI, *Aspects of Jewish Life and Thought,* Chapter on Jewish Charity. New York: 1922.

FLUEGEL, MAURICE, *The Humanity, Benevolence, and Charity Legislation of the Pentateuch and the Talmud.* Baltimore: 1908.

FREUND, MICHAEL, *The Community Chest and Its Influence on the Jewish Community,* The Jewish Social Service Quarterly, Vol. VII, No. 2, Dec. 1930, pp. 30-37; *ibid.*, No. 4, June 1931, pp. 27-32.

FRISCH, EPHRAIM, *An Historical Survey of Jewish Philanthropy*. New York: 1924.

HEXTER, MAURICE B., "Evolutionary Tendencies in the Federation Movement," *Proceedings,* National Conf. Jewish Social Service, 1926, pp. 9-29.

HYMAN, J. C., *Twenty-five Years of American Aid to Jews Overseas,* in the American Jewish Year Book, Vol. 41.

KAPLAN, MORDECAI M., *Judaism as a Civilization,* Chaps. 21, 27, 30. New York: Macmillan, 1934.

KARPF, MAURICE J., *Jewish Community Organization in the United States.* New York: Bloch Pub. Co., 1938. Contains chapters on various phases of social welfare and an extensive bibliography.

——, *Progress and Problems in Social Work Education during the Depression,* President's Report to American Association of Schools of Social Work, Jewish Social Service Quarterly, Vol. X, No. 4, June 1934, pp. 257-262.

——, *The Scientific Basis of Social Work.* New York: Columbia University Press, 1931.

——, *Toward a Source Book of Jewish Philanthropic Origins,* Jewish Social Service Quarterly, Vol. XII, No. 3, March 1936, pp. 324-336; *ibid.,* No. 4, June 1936, pp. 396-410; *ibid.,* Vol. XIII, No. 2, Dec. 1936, pp. 297-303.

——, *The Fourth International Conference of Jewish Social Work,* Jewish Social Service Quarterly, Vol. XXV, No. 2, Dec. 1948.

LURIE, HARRY L., *Jewish Social Welfare in the United States,* in The American Jewish Year Book, Vol. 47.

SCHECHTER, SOLOMON, *Studies in Judaism* (Third Series), Section on Jewish Philanthropy. Philadelphia: 1924.

WALDMAN, MORRIS D., *The Galveston Movement,* The Jewish Social Service Quarterly, Vol. IV, No. 3, March 1928, pp. 197-206. This is an interesting account of an effort to distribute Jewish immigrants into the interior of the United States.

The Jew in Modern Science

By A. A. ROBACK

FOREWORD

The treatment of the various parts in this chapter which I have been commissioned to do is by no means exhaustive even in regard to mathematics, although from the reader's angle it may seem as if too much has been made of this science, while chemistry has been almost cramped.

My object has been to approach each subject not in a uniform manner but in accordance with its significance and destiny. Mathematics has been surveyed more in detail in order to show what (space permitting) might be done with the other disciplines. Were this method extended even to the physical and natural sciences alone, nothing short of a few volumes would be required to carry the idea through. The unevenness, which, no doubt, will be recognized by the trained eye, is, therefore, advised. The author said to himself "Let me show how at least one of the sciences should be covered." As to the others, each has its own story to tell, but we cannot do the same for all, since my own assignment is but one of many; and a single volume is to encompass all the contributions. Besides, physics lends itself to subject-treatment, while mathematics is more the product of individuals. Physics forms almost a drama centering around the discoveries of electricity, relativity, and nuclear fission, with its political angles. Chemistry, if surveyed on the same scale as mathematics, would need hundreds of pages, hence only the highlights have been flashed.

Some of the minor sciences, if sciences could be designated as such, have been glossed over—again, as the newspapers would explain "for technical reasons". Perhaps "mechanical reasons" would be less ambiguous here.

In spite of the strenuous efforts to obtain certain dates, I found the various reference works inadequate. Particularly is this true in regard to dates of deaths. There is no dearth of Jewish encyclopedias, yet *the* Jewish encyclopedia is still to be compiled. The omission of important names in science is altogether too frequent. It is sad to reflect that the Jews, who deserve a national biographical dictionary at least as much as any other people, have none, although Salomon Wininger's *Grosse jüdische National-Biographie* has been of some value, its many hundreds of errors and omissions notwithstanding. Furthermore, this work has been out of date for many years.

Even the general reference works are unsatisfactory. The wars have been instrumental in reducing to a minimum all international coöperation in the compilation of data on scholars and scientists, and the various biographical dictionaries tend to stress either politicians and public men or their own intellectual celebrities.

The academic lexicons and other reference works have fallen into neglect and it is no longer possible to verify simple biographical facts as in pre-war years.

I have tried to verify the Jewish lineage of scientists in every possible way, and if a slip has been made in this direction at rare intervals, let us remember that the number of unidentified Jewish scientists, and therefore not included here, would surely more than make up for the exaggeration.

THE JEW IN MODERN SCIENCE

INTRODUCTION

THE world at large, and this is true even of educated circles, is still prone to think of Jews in terms of old clothes or manufacturing, or as money lenders, peddlers, storekeepers, and on the highest level, as professionals, either as clever physicians or shrewd lawyers. The clothing industry and the movie industry represent to many a "well-informed" person the empire of the Jew.

Indeed, perhaps the foremost historian of science of our day once admitted to me—or was it a boast?—that he never considered the origin of a scientist, and that it was a revelation to learn that this mathematician or that physicist was Jewish; yet he was well aware that Galileo was an Italian, that Copernicus was a Pole, that Huyghens was Dutch, and that Vesalius would have been classified today as a Belgian. In other words the attitude is: let us forget nationality—when the famous man is a Jew. If the Jew should happen to be a financier, then he is euphemistically referred to as an international banker or broker.

When liberal scientists are gently rebuked for this inconsistency, they—that has at least been my experience—merely laugh mischievously or are mildly amused. There are anti-Semitic scientists who are more genealogically minded; and once they are successful in uncovering the Jewish skeleton in the scientific closet, the man is paged in the *semi-Kürschner Lexikon,* a sort of academic laundry bag for such unfortunates as have been contaminated by owning a non-Aryan grandfather or grandmother, and therefore must be kept apart until the stain is washed or stamped out after generations of dilution with pure "Aryan" blood, if there is any such article in civilized countries.

The name Albert Einstein has done much to focus attention on the possibility that a Jew might be a great scientist; for even the newspaper reader has heard the name and has associated it with the most seen and least known of peoples. Perhaps a few other names have since been singled out as those of Jewish scientists, but, in general, the ignorance of even the upper classes in this regard is appalling and requires some stimulant in the first place, and perhaps a sedative afterwards. . . .

Every time someone writes about the Jewish contribution to science, there is a reaction to it of an ambivalent nature. It seems as if the writer is boasting or attempting to show off the Jews. Frequently a non-Jew is assigned to the task of singing the Jew's praises. Ada Sterling's *The Jew and Civilization* has been motivated by such scruples; and every intelligent Jew knows what a farrago of truth and fiction that book is— a miscarriage of the plan to disseminate information about the Jews.

The usual attitude toward a biographical collection of Jewish celebrities is to ask: What purpose does it serve? Suppose we know that the Jews have contributed their quota and more to the world's culture, what benefit will accrue to anyone? Should we not be content in the awareness that the Jews are constantly furthering science without bothering about comparisons, statistics, etc.?

The famous Emile Meyerson once attempted to persuade me that as Jews we should do no stock-taking of this sort, that we are doing our share in advancing the cause of progress; and that should be sufficiently gratifying. My answer was that if all nations were willing to refrain from recording the exploits of their individuals as national achievements, I should of course, subscribe to his view but since (as in the matter of disarmament, where every country is anxious to have the others disarm while making her own military programme more and more elaborate) every national group is doing its utmost to claim as many distinguished men and women as its own, there is no reason why the Jews should relinquish their privilege and cede their notables to other nationalities.

There is, however, a more cogent argument for the research in question. Unless we took the trouble to bring together all the Jewish philosophers, scientists, literary men, artists, philanthropists, etc., under one rubric we should never learn just how we stand in this regard. For all we know, we might be extremely backward in the domain of science or art, particularly as the masses still believe that Jews are shrewd businessmen, financiers, money lenders, and nothing more. Every ignoramus of a Hitler, every brigand of a Goebbels and every mountebank of a Streicher might come forward with the challenge, as indeed these sorry specimens of humanity did, to show our intellectual credentials. If no bookkeeping is done, there can be no records to present, and as time goes on, the problem becomes more and more complicated. Even today it is by no means easy to establish the Jewish descent of some of the most renowned scientists of their generation, e.g., the great astronomer, Herschel.

The case is somewhat similar to the hue and cry raised against the teaching of Greek and Latin. If these subjects are not taught on the ground that they are not practical and that the students forget all they learn about these languages, it must yet be urged that certain authorities will be needed to interpret the cultures of the Greeks and Romans, that translators will always be in demand for the rendering of the best of these cultures into other tongues, and should the study of Greek and Latin be discontinued in the advanced schools and colleges, where are we to obtain our experts and authorities, our translators and interpreters? Similarly, unless we make an effort to collect all the data about Jewish leaders in every walk of life, we shall be groping and floundering, and the libels of anti-Semitic writers will seem even to the educated close to the truth.

As a matter of fact, the belittling of Jewish achievement in the sphere of the abstract and theoretical is of frequent occurrence in the writings of Jew-baiters from Apion down to the Nazi race investigators of 1933. Has not Voltaire repeated parrot-like Apion's charge that the Jews have never invented or discovered anything? And has not the British renegade, Houston Stewart Chamberlain, who became a lackey of the last Emperor of Germany, ruminated the same chaff without bothering to examine the issue fairly?

Compilers of Jewish biographical data and historical writers often make the mistake of citing the activities of Jews during the Mediaeval period, or dwelling on a relatively insignificant fact, to the exclusion of contemporary achievements. While we are all interested in the fact that Levi ben Gerson's *Jacob's Staff* which he invented in 1325, was used by Columbus in the discovery of America, it is a good deal more consequential to turn to the illustrious scientific productions of our own generation. To be sure, individuals like Levi ben Gerson deserve even greater credit than the Michelsons and Lippmanns who had at their disposal the finest laboratories and observatories and moved in an academic atmosphere, yet it is not the man we are judging but his results.

At a time, when the Jews were to be counted not in the millions, but in the thousands and when over half of them scarcely lived, but merely existed in a cage-like ghetto, we could hardly have expected them to produce Newtons and Galileos, but since the nineteenth century with the comparative emancipation of the Jews a change has been wrought in their cultural status; and scientists of Jewish parentage were remaking the world.

It would take reams and reams of paper to set down the accomplishments of Jews in every branch of science. There are the mental sciences, the social sciences, the medical sciences, and the physical sciences, with mathematics forming a sort of foundation for the whole structure. In every group and in every single branch we find Jews pre-eminent. If Voltaire's perverse remark that "all their thoughts are about money" were true, so many Jews of ability would not turn to such an unprofitable pursuit as science, but instead would enter business. Thousands and thousands of Jews have worshipped at the shrine of science, in many cases enduring privation and taunts, for the sole reason that they were idealists and wished to help humanity and realize their own powers.

In Jewish reference works our subject has been handled frequently but with varied success, never on such a large scale, as in the present volume, although possibly more comprehensively as to names. One might list a few thousand names of Jews engaged in science either as contributors after a fashion or as teachers, or as research workers, but the weighing of values is a requisite if the compendium is to be an adequate and reliable summary.

BASIC PROBLEMS

At the very outset, we are confronted with the questions: when does modern science begin? What is to be subsumed under science? To what extent, if any, should the sons of converts or demi-Jews be included?

It is not the purpose of the author to pack the scientific pantheon. At the same time, we cannot afford to ignore some significant facts in our investigation.

There are numerous other queries which crop up, and which will at least be adverted to even if the answers can at most be tentative or hypothetical. Matters such as the predilection of the Jews for some particular branches or phases of science, or the possible physiological substratum of special endowments, may also be reasonably tackled; but first of all, there is the question of the growth of Jewish achievement in science within the past century or so—a growth which has been steadily increasing until it has reached a stage of the phenomenal.

Writers of considerable vogue have often contrasted the Jews and the Greeks as to scientific prowess. I shall not allude to Houston Stewart Chamberlain in whose *Foundations of the Nineteenth Century,* the Greeks are unfavorably compared with—of all people—the Persians, and are even rated an "ignorant people". Carlyle, however, and Buckle, who show a supreme contempt for the attainments of the Jews, should have known better, and Voltaire had he lived in the twentieth century could not have brought himself, prejudiced as he was, to write *"Les juifs n'ont jamais rien inventé",* adding that all their thoughts were about money—a beautiful example of the projection mechanism operating in the great petty Frenchman.

It is true, nevertheless, that in antiquity the Jews did not cultivate scientific pursuits. Their tradition was along different lines. They were intent upon laying the foundations of justice, humanitarianism, world peace, and spiritual values rather than discovering laws of nature. The desert was not likely to bring into being academies and lyceums.

It is during the diaspora, and, nevertheless, in connection with the *Torah,* that numbers and measurements, the stellar bodies, and bodily organs and functions begin to take on a special coloring for the students of the law of God and man. Science in the Talmud is, of course, only observational and fragmentary, but as one of my collaborators will doubtless prove, in this symposium, it is unjustified to suppose that ancient Jewish thought was entirely devoid of scientific tendencies.

The mediaeval period is not within my scope either. Suffice it then to say that where there was so little accomplished in general, the Jews, who were constantly living in mortal fear, lest they be banned or burned, enjoying a breathing spell now and then between one crusade and another, now perishing by the sword of the Crusaders, and now by the fire and fury of the Moslems, could hardly be expected to busy themselves with evolving scientific principles. The Talmudic tradition absorbed what little time was left in respite after the harrowing experiences of pillage and exile, let alone ghetto restrictions reminiscent of conditions under the Nazis, at their worst. The least facilities were missing; for when the Talmud would be burned periodically, what availability was there of books along general lines for the denizens of the compounds in which the Jews were forced to live?

Notwithstanding, luminaries like Ibn-Gabirol, Ibn-Ezra, Maimonides, Gersonides, and others did arise who conquered adversity and carved out a niche for themselves in the secular hall of fame. When we compare their wretched existence with the secure, leisurely, and comfortable lives of the scholastic monks, we can only marvel at the works they have wrought.

As we approach the Renaissance or the Revival of Learning (disregarding the pronunciamento of T. S. Eliot and his cohorts to the effect that there was no such Revival, in other words that the Dark Ages were just flooded with light) Jewish scholars and savants begin to emerge more distinctively in some countries, where they had been able to achieve a modicum of ease—Spain, Portugal, and Italy. It was not long, however, before the Holy (Sic) Inquisition swooped down upon the "infidels"; or else some Prince or Duke would make short shrift of his Jewish subjects, and either a painful double life had to be led or an equally painful baptism had to be submitted to, or as in the case of a genius like Abarbanel, a forced march out of the country had to be undertaken.

Under such conditions, inhibitions would set in, the daily tension would cramp every impulse, and worse still, all the brilliant work of crypto-Jews such as Pedro Nuñes, whose treatise on the Sphere (Lisbon 1537) was rated "one of the scientific glories of Portugal" and Joseph Vecinho, who was, besides court physician, a scientific consultant in the court of King Manoel, particularly in the field of navigation, which was so important for Portugal at the time of Columbus, would redound to the credit of the Portuguese alone. Vecinho's grandchildren, in the following century, taking up residence in Italy, practiced Judaism openly.

Of a perhaps greater calibre was Vecinho's teacher, Abraham Zacuto, an astronomer who taught at the University of Salamanca, but after the wicked edict of 1492, fled to Portugal, whence, five years later, he was compelled to make his escape again to North Africa, unless he became an apostate. Zacuto is well remembered because of his conference with Columbus, who used his nautical tables, thanks to which the great discoverer not only was able to reach further than his destination, but dumbfounded the natives by "wishing" on them an eclipse, as predicted on the basis of the tables, and saving the day for himself and his little band of adventurers. Zacuto's astrolabe was of great assistance to another explorer, Vasco da Gama who was on the most friendly terms with this early Jewish scientist.

It is one of the most tragic ironies that the countries which profited most from Jewish genius were the very ones to treat the Jews cruelly and to "kill the goose that laid the golden eggs". Germany might have easily won the war, if the scientists she had practically exiled had, in consequence, not been giving invaluable aid to the Allies. We shall see later the part they played in the atomic drama.

As we draw closer to the era of Emancipation, the interest of the Jews in matters scientific increases, but for the most part, it is in the forensic studies of the rabbis that we find some raw ore; for what grains these masters in Jewish lore could have gleaned through autodidactic channels would hardly have contained more than textbook material which may have been pioneer work centuries previously. The celebrated gaon of Wilno, Elijah, managed to set down a number of reflections on astronomy (upon which the Talmudic masters would have come by way of their preoccupations with the calendar, new moon, computations in regard to the holidays) geometry, trigonometry and algebra, but in spite of his fabled mental powers, there appears to be nothing of the originality characteristic of those who have made mathematics their life work.

I

WHICH SCIENCES ARE FAVORITES WITH THE JEWS?

The question as to Jewish preference for any one science will be answered variously by different writers. If the Jews are only a religious group and represent no biological or anthropological entity, but adopt the tradition and adjust themselves to the facilities of the country in which they happen to reside, then *cadit quaestio*. Indeed, environmentalists and specificists, will probably deny that there are special national endowments or even proclivities. According to them, the individual might be conditioned in youth or even childhood in divers ways, and as a nation or any other group consists of individuals, certain traditions might prevail in a certain country, due to the founding of a school, or the attraction of noted teachers, or special encouragement by a government through stipends, or the particular needs of a given territory (agricultural or maritime, or military requirements) in which case the Jews, who, aside from Israel, are cast in the same environmental mould as the rest of a given country, would naturally be expected to follow the general trend. Nor are Jews supposed to have any scientific traditions of their own.

This, curiously enough for environmentalists, materialists, and mechanists is a deductive approach—from the general environment to individual output. The empirical method would be to view the individual cases of each group for the various sciences so that we might establish what uniformity or deviations there are.

It is true, is it not, that some sciences, whatever the reasons therefor, have been more steadfastly cultivated in some countries rather than in others. Do the Jews fall in line in every instance; do they turn the scales and actually dominate that field, or do they stand off and evince a different leaning? Any scientific worker who is both ethnically alert and *au courant* with the facts must have been able to observe certain

[197]

tendencies in one direction or another; and I think it may safely be concluded that the Jews of the past century have excelled in two general fields of science which are disparate and yet in a sense they complement each other, *viz.*, mathematics and medicine. Mathematics is the most fundamental and most speculative of sciences (unless philosophy is accorded the honorific of *scientia scientarum*) while medicine is perhaps the most practical science, since there is not a soul, or perhaps, better, body, which does not enlist its services at one time or another; and therefore it may be called the most urgent in life, even if mathematics should prove just as necessary in shaping the conditions of living.

Mathematics, as the most abstract of sciences, and healing, as the most concrete, make a good combination in which the head and the heart arrive at their highest functions; and although medicine was even many centuries ago bringing emoluments to its practitioners, and particularly influence, although to Jewish physicians, occasionally, as in the case of Lopez, Queen Elizabeth's personal friend and counsellor, it had brought cruel death following torture, the prime impulse was doubtless to allay suffering. Perhaps medicine, until modern days, could scarcely be considered as anything more than an art based on experimental common sense and intuition rather than on experimental procedures.

Why should mathematics have had such a great appeal for the Jews, assuming, of course, that they have distinguished themselves in this science more than in others? Furthermore, in mathematics, are there specific branches for which the Jews have a special penchant? This may be posed with every other large field of science. It would be possible even to institute an investigation on the relative strength in a given science on the part of Jews in various countries, e. g., France, Germany, England, Russia. Many are the factors to be considered in such a piece of research—opportunities, the proportion of the Jewish population, tradition, and quality of the members of the group. It has been often remarked that each country has the Jews she deserves. Is the obverse of this proposition worth looking into, *viz.*, that Jewish merit is commensurate with the people among whom they sojourn? Certainly what has happened in Germany would tend to disprove such a generalization. If anything, it may be concluded emphatically that wherever and whenever the Jews have rendered conspicuous service to the culture of the country, as in Spain, Portugal, and Germany, they have been made the scapegoat up to the point of extermination.

In spite of the Nazi infamy toward the Jewish scientists every close observer of German intellectual life for the past fifty years is impelled to descant with admiration on the subject of Jewish intellectual activities in Germany.

"Take away the Jews—and Germany is destitute"—is the way ex-Ambassador Gerard has expressed it in his *Four Years in Germany.*

First of all it might have been the great Frenchman, Ernest Renan, who, in his *Recollections of Infancy and Youth,* gave expression to this fact in the following passage "Germany, after devoting herself entirely to military life, would have had no talent left if it were not for the Jews, to whom she has been so ungrateful".

Renan wrote his appreciation in 1883, while ex-Ambassador Gerard, who certainly knew all the ins and outs of Germany, had occasion to remark, thirty-five years later: "Germany boasts of her *Kultur,* her learning, that she is pre-eminent in philosophy, literature and art. But that is not true. It is not they—but the Jews. Take away the Jews from all branches of her culture and Germany is destitute".

Renan's opinion was seconded by an equally famous man, though in a different field of endeavor. In 1884, Sir William Osler wrote: "Should another Moses arise and preach a Semitic exodus from Germany, and should he prevail, they would leave the land impoverished far more than was ancient Egypt by the loss of the jewels of gold and jewels of silver, of which the people were spoiled. . . . There is not a profession which would not suffer the serious loss of many of its most brilliant ornaments, and in none more so than in our own." (i. e. medicine)[1]

How prophetic the passage from Sir William Osler sounds today. Little did that illustrious physician realize in 1884—just about 65 years ago—that the hypothetical event would come true, but not because another Moses preached a Semitic exodus! Certainly the most bizarre mind could not for a moment have imagined that a band of hoodlums would create an exodus or wreak the destruction of their precious ornaments in the most truculent manner conceivable.

One thing which has been puzzling me is this: with all the millions of Jews killed off and still more millions forced to assimilate in every respect, largely through conversion to Christianity, the comparatively small number left by far exceeds its quota in practically every sphere of civilization. The ancient Greek legend of the phoenix seems to be applicable to the Jews rather than to the Greeks.

It is not in a spirit of pride or ethnocentricity that this matter has been brought up, but rather in a scientific vein. It is a problem like any other problem to be solved outside the bounds of emotion, just as the genius of the ancient Greeks during the fourth century B. C. has yet to be explained. The facts cry for justice, but the cry is a *vox clamantis in deserto.* Yet another matter suggests itself: is there a national equation with the Jews, dispersed as they are, as in the case of other peoples, as has been argued by the present author,[2] or is all science strictly universal, the Jewish contribution partaking of this general attribute? If the Jews do offer a separate slant, then, is there a common denominator which can be detected as applying to the scattered groups in different lands through the generations?

The following pages can but allude to the possibilities. Regrettably, the whole field of collective psychology has been allowed to lie fallow, while mechanistic doctrines bolstered alike by behaviorist in psychology, materialist in the historical and philosophical framework and environmentalist in the sociological sphere, have cluttered up the approach with complicated terms and oversimplified theories which, when exploded, take refuge in other theories, equally oversimplified and equally fantastic. In many instances these allies will shut their eyes to the hard facts often because they are not inclined to discern the particulars. They will first treat the Jews as an ethnically mixed group, and therefore nondescript or at least undifferentiated from the dominant group, and in consequence will asseverate that there is nothing to look into except the assumed ecological processes, conditionings, adjustments, acculturations, etc. In large part, the scientific smugness, if not priggishness, is due to the ignorance of origins. If as Pasteur has so pointedly remarked: "in the sphere of observation, chance will favor the prepared mind", then how much more necessary is it to be prepared at least by keeping one's mind open to the facts that almost stare us in the face?

It is these facts which I have tried to collect for decades, so that the chain could be forged out of the links, and when a German, Frenchman, or American would ask me why I bother accumulating such insignificant data, I ask him in return whether such data on Germans, Frenchmen, or Americans are more significant, and if so, why, except that in the one case it is a political majority and in the other it is a political minority. What is it, then, but a fascistic method in science? During the Hitler regime we were all shocked to find Nobel Prize men, scientists of world renown accommodating their scientific temper to the raving doctrines of an ignoramus and his cohorts, which goes to show that although science is objective, scientists who have made wonderful discoveries, laboratory champions are not necessarily champions of truth and justice, that a certain dissociation holds in some whose intellectual endowments and character traits are not in harmony *ab initio*.

And yet the procedure of such studies as have been suggested does not require elaborate techniques. No interferometers, no cyclotrons need be constructed for such purposes. First, the enumeration of outstanding contributions by those of Jewish antecedents is essential, which means that the investigators must be familiar with ethnic origins; and then comparison with non-Jewish productions, both quantitatively and qualitatively, is apt to establish the preliminary results, which must be checked against methodological fallacies.

The present work, a sequel to others of a similar nature, is the first step in this direction; and it is toward that end we begin with Jewish achievement in mathematics.

II

MATHEMATICS

In our survey, it is meet perhaps to begin with mathematics, not only because Jews have enriched it so considerably even in the Middle Ages when, aside from the treatises written in Hebrew, according to the authoritative testimony of Ibn Ezra, the modern notation referred to as Arabic numerals was brought to Moslem dominions from India by a Jewish scholar, while another, Ibn Daud, later relayed the information from Moslem soil to Christendom via Spain.

It will scarcely serve any useful purpose to make an inventory of the individual works treating of mathematics during the past four centuries covering the period of my present assignment. We are primarily interested in the highlights, the pioneers, the spearheads of a new movement or trend in science. While it is true that given the same opportunities many an obscure writer in Hebrew might have been a director of a university institute or a laboratory instead of turning out an autodidactic lucubration which has gone over the ground of others, nevertheless, in our realistic world, we must reckon with the accomplished and universally recognized facts —all the more so as space is restricted, and the subject is so extensive that comprehensiveness is out of the question.

What is particularly enlightening is the upswing of Jewish

scientific achievement in our own century; and despite the Nazi attempts to undermine its progress, Jewish research and discovery has been in the ascendant for the past fifteen years.

There are many names which become stereotyped because of the accumulated weight of their mention in compendium after compendium, while those of worthier bearers, contemporaries of ours, have not had the chance of being bruited around. Another handicap is the difficulty, almost impossibility, of a compiler of data in so many different fields doing justice to the various representatives as to their relative merit, so that for the most part the same amount of space is allotted to each. To some extent this defect will be noticeable here too, but at least a conscious effort will be made to ameliorate, if not remedy, the situation.

There are other snags too, *e. g.,* the paucity of genealogical data and sometimes even the attempt to conceal the Jewish origin of some scientists. One of the foremost French mathematicians of the seventeenth century, Ozanam, has been repeatedly spoken of as of Jewish descent, and probably the greatest mathematician Russia has produced, Lobatchevsky, a co-discoverer of non-Euclidean space, was also alleged to have been born into a Jewish family.

There is nothing doubtful about Carl Gustav Jacobi (1804-1851) who in his short life has packed in a century of original thought along different lines of mathematical theory: Homogeneous functions, spatial functions, calculus of variations, elliptic functions and, not least, the theory of numbers.

Leo Koenigsberger's large volume on Jacobi gives us a full-size and many-sided picture of the man who, although not as great as Gauss or Euler, was much gentler than the former, who reminds one of a dictator, and more influential than the latter. Had he lived longer (he died at the age of 46) he might have approximated them in mathematical stature.

Jacobi's works were published in 7 volumes by the Prussian Academy of Science after his death. The editor, K. W. Borchardt, one of Jacobi's most brilliant students and a mathematician of note and also Jewish, did not live to complete his task, which was carried out by the famous Weierstrass. His message to the widow of Jacobi on publication of the set was a high tribute to her husband, whose qualities of the heart endeared him to all his students, first at Koenigsberg and later in Berlin, which thanks to him had begun to compete with Goettingen as a mathematical centre. There is, in addition to the large biography and monographs on his mathematical labors, a little book entitled *C. G. J. Jacobi als Politiker,* which describes some interesting episodes at the Prussian Academy in connection with his liberalism.

Transfinite Numbers

A second mathematical giant of the nineteenth century, more concentrated and more influential, although not at so many points, was Georg Cantor[3] (born in St. Petersburg, in 1845 and died at Halle in 1918) who may be looked upon as the man who established the mathematics of infinity, thus bringing into the science not only a new dimension but a new mode of thinking. The great mathematician, Gauss, had, by his authoritative decree, once and for all, as it seemed to his contemporaries and the succeeding generation of mathematicians, given the *congé* to the concept of infinity in mathematics except as a mere limit, not as a thing allowing of definite relations (Adolf Fraenkel *Einleitung in die Mengenlehre,* p. 1), half a century before. It was left to Georg Cantor not only to dispute this doctrine, but actually to supplant it in favor of a decidedly broader view which represents transfinite numbers on an equal footing with the finite. Euclid's axiom, 'The whole is greater than its part', with which we are all familiar, must be further qualified in the light of the new mathematical system and thus becomes only an axiom applicable to finite collections only, not an absolute and universal one.

Cantor, like his younger and more famous contemporary in mathematical physics, Albert Einstein, was obliged to contend against a host of great minds until his voice was heard. In the '80's of the last century, after dealing with the negative views regarding the possibility of infinite numbers set forth by philosophers from the time of Aristotle, Cantor put his finger on the weak spot and declared 'All so-called proofs of the impossibility of actually infinite numbers are, as may be shown in every particular case and also on general grounds, false in that they begin by attributing to the numbers in question all the properties of finite numbers, whereas the infinite numbers, if they are to be thinkable in any form, must constitute quite a new kind of number as opposed to the finite numbers, and the nature of this new kind of number is dependent on the nature of things and is an object of investigation'.[4] This observation was the first step to the establishment of a mathematics of classes, aggregates or types, and to the conception that in the realm of number we are dealing with types of order, and that every class or aggregate is a 'totality of definite elements which can be bound up into a whole by means of law'.

What two other celebrated Jews, viz., Lazarus and Steinthal, have accomplished in psychology by their pleading that the mental properties of a group of people are not to be confused with the characteristics of the individuals who go to make up the group—Cantor has accomplished in mathematics, and it is not an idle compliment when Bertrand Russell, acknowledged as the foremost mathematical philosopher of our time, says in the introduction of his *Principles of Mathematics*—the work on which his reputation rests—'In mathematics my chief obligations, as is indeed evident, are to Georg Cantor and Professor Peano'.

Hebrew Symbols in Higher Mathematics

While a student, I once had occasion to look into a ponderous and highly technical work of Bertrand Russell (*Princi-*

ples of Mathematics), probably the clearest philosophical mind of our generation; and was struck by a very familiar symbol. At first I thought that the resemblance between the particular symbol and the first letter in the Hebrew alphabet was but a coincidence. But no, a moment's scrutiny convinced me that the character was identical with the first letter of the Hebrew alphabet.

The next question was: Did Russell first introduce the aleph into mathematics, or was there a Jewish hand in it? Naturally the latter hypothesis seemed more reasonable, though we know that often Jewish scientists will go out of their way to conceal their ethnic origin, and might likely draw on a Sanskrit or Chinese source, when in need of a new symbol, in preference to a Hebrew one. In this instance, however, the reasonable turned out to be the likely explanation; for it was actually Georg Cantor who introduced the *aleph* into his special brand of mathematics, the mathematics of infinity; and, curiously enough, in the *Annuario del Circolo Matematico di Palermo*, a biographical handbook for mathematicians, the *aleph* placed, in agate type, before the name of some of the members, denoted that they were—not Jews, but distinguished enough to be incorporated as life members.

Whether this introduction could be considered an intrusion by Judaeophobes, or whether the Nazis and their ilk looked upon this as a Jewish conspiracy in the abstract region of mathematics, the *aleph* is here to stay. Let us now see what the *aleph* represents in mathematics.

Cantor makes this symbol designate a class of transfinite numbers, the smallest of which would be denoted by *aleph*-zero and would consist of the totality of finite cardinal numbers. The series may be drawn up endlessly by placing at the bottom right of the aleph various symbols, first of all, in Arabic numerals, then in Greek, such as *nu* and *omega*—and even then the series of classes is not exhausted.

But Cantor was not the only mathematician to make use of Hebrew characters. Another shining light in this respect was James Joseph Sylvester, about whom more will be said later in various connections.

In his remarkable treatment of what he called syzygetic relations, he introduces Hebrew letters from *aleph* to *Kaph* to designate the references to his articles or sections in that paper. It is scarcely a coincidence that two mathematicians of Jewish descent have reverted to the alphabet of their ethnic group in order to express their needs in symbols.

The other symbol which may be regarded as a Hebrew character is a sort of inverted C, but which a Jew would easily recognize as a *kaph,* though it is hardly likely that Peano, who has introduced the symbol into mathematics, had taken it from that source. Originally, of course, the Roman C was merely an inversion of the Phoenician letter, which, in Hebrew, is called *kaph.* But it is noteworthy that in mathematics, this symbol stands for 'implies', and the *kaph* is the most suitable letter to designate the relation of implication; for it is used in the sense of 'like' very frequently.

But why stop at symbols, alone, from the Hebrew, when we can pick up a volume edited by one of England's most illustrious astronomers, of Halley-comet fame, and find many words, *i.e.*, technical terms in Hebrew? For it was Edmond Halley who translated into Latin the *Spherics* by Menelaus of Alexandria from a Hebrew version of an Arabic translation, made perhaps from a Syriac rendering of an imperfect Greek original Ms. Costard, in his preface, published after Halley's death, tells us also of the version of Isaac ben Khunain; and Max Krause's edition of the *Spherics* preserves that translation,[5a] while Halley's was based on that of Jacob ben Makhir, the Provençal grandson of the famous translator of Maimonides, Samuel Ibn-Tibbon. It was around 1273 that ben Makhir completed his version. Thus we see that Hebrew figured in England as late as the eighteenth century, and unlike Arabic which was acquired comparatively late in life, Hebrew was, with Halley, a subject he had taken up at Oxford in his teens; for at the age of 22, this genius had already been elected a Fellow of the Royal Society.

Some of the illustrious names associated with both mathematics and physics, like that of Heinrich Hertz, will appear in their more familiar realm, viz. physics, while others will be referred to under astronomy or engineering. For the time being, we shall endeavor to stick closely to the sphere of mathematics, following a politico-geographical plan, for the most part; and since modern mathematics was mainly cultivated in Germany, we shall start with that country, as, indeed, we have already made the first approach with Jacobi and Cantor. In some cases, the mathematicians were born in Russia or Poland but have received their training and laurels in Germany.

GERMANY

One of the great losses to science was the early death, at the age of 29, of F. G. M. Eisenstein (1823-1854) who, according to the greatest of all modern mathematicians, Gauss, as expressed in a letter to Alexander Von Humboldt, "belongs to those talents who are born but once in a century". To what extent he was esteemed by the *princeps* of mathematics is evidenced by the fact that Gauss edited and published Eisenstein's collected writings, chiefly on algebra and the theory of numbers, in 1848.

J. G. Rosenhain (1816-1887), professor at Koenigsberg, established the *Abelian* and *theta* functions toward which another Jewish mathematician, Jacobi, had given the first impetus.

Leopold Kronecker (1823-1891) elder brother of the physiologist, Hugo Kronecker, taught, at the University of Berlin, algebra and the theory of numbers receiving his chief attention. The Russian Academy of Science published his collected works. Kronecker was the champion of natural numbers—the integer was to him a sort of god-arithmeticist. For this reason he took unkindly to Georg Cantor's revolution in constructing a world of transfinite numbers.

His successor, in a sense, was Immanuel Lazarus Fuchs (1833-1902) who became Rektor of the University of Berlin for a period. The theory of linear differential equations is largely associated with his name.

Leo Koenigsberger (1837-1922) whose work lay in the treatment of elliptical functions and differential equations was a pupil of Jacobi and his ardent admirer. The science of mechanics also took his attention, and his voluminous biography of Helmholtz showed that he had broader interests than many mathematicians. His large biography of Jacobi has already been alluded to.

One of the earliest to establish the theory of invariants, which was developed by another Jew, Sylvester, proves to be Siegfried Heinrich Aronhold (1819-1884) who demonstrated the existence of invariants S and T, of the ternary cubic, while Paul Gordan (1837-1912) who was Professor at Erlangen "showed with the aid of symbolic methods that the number of distinct forms for a binary quantic is finite".

Hermann Schapiro's life (1840-1898) could be read as a novel. Here was a young Lithuanian Jew who, after serving as a rabbi, chanced to look into a work on mathematics. Immediately the urge to study overwhelmed him. He first went to Odessa, and after much hardship managed to reach and study in Berlin, whence he was compelled to return to Odessa, but again set out for Germany, studying at Heidelberg and receiving his Ph.D. at the age of 40. As a *Privatdocent* at Heidelberg, he could not support himself and his family, so he took to repairing watches. His work in co-functions and algebraic iterations was only a portion of the planned project, but it was sufficient to prove his worth as a mathematician. Meanwhile, however, he became interested in problems of Jewish nationalism and Zionism, became the patron of Jewish students from Russia and subsequently the promoter of an idea, which, three years after his death, became known as the Jewish National Fund to provide for the purchase of land in Palestine. The new flourishing Hebrew University was also his brain child, absurd though it seemed in his day. His great mathematical gifts were, in a sense, dissipated on propaganda; and yet his dream came true, although he did not live to see it.

Jacob Rosanes (1842-1922) was equally grounded in algebra and geometry. This Galician-born Jew, of an old Sephardic family, even became the Rektor of the University of Berlin, and before that he was made Privy Councillor.

Alexander Brill (born 1842), who was professor for many years at Tübingen, is often mentioned in histories of mathematics.

Eugen Netto (1846-1919) who, after teaching at Strassburg and Berlin, became full professor at Giessen, was well-known for his studies on substitutions and combinations.

Adolf Hurwitz (1859-1919) ranked high in the theory of functions and especially elliptical functions. His work in this sphere was revised and enlarged by R. Courant, while the Technical College at Zürich published his collected papers in 1932-1933.

Friedrich Schur (1856-1941) working on finite transformation series, has not neglected his analytic geometry, and ranks as a mathematician of considerable eminence. While he hailed from Prussian Poland (the lively town of Krotoschin) his more original namesake, Isai Schur, was born in Mohilev, Russia (1875) and became full professor in Berlin, in 1920, after publishing some remarkable work on the theory of aggregates, integral equations, and functions. He was the last Jewish professor in the University to be ousted under the Nazis. Subsequently, he taught at the Hebrew University in Jerusalem, dying in Tel-Aviv in 1941. At the time of his death, he was working on a book which was to revolutionize the science.

Ludwig Schlesinger (1864-1933) although born in Hungary

and for a time teaching in Budapest, published altogether in German, largely in the field of linear differential equations and automorphous functions.

Hermann Minkowski (1864-1909) while not possessing the originality of a Jacobi or Cantor, was held in great esteem at such seats of learning as Bonn, Koenigsberg and Goettingen, where he died in the prime of life. Minkowski's formulae, as we shall have occasion to mention later, were helpful to Albert Einstein in the formulation of his epoch-making theory. Minkowski, who was born in Russia, but left in order to study in Germany when he was in his teens, specialized in the theory of numbers.

The theory of numbers was, together with the theory of functions and aggregate series, the chief interest, aside from art and music, of Alfred Pringsheim (1850-1941) the father-in-law of Thomas Mann.

Felix Haussdorff (Paul Mongré) (1868-) was professor at Bonn, and was one of the first to recognize the scope of Cantor's work by basing his own theory of dimension on it.[5]

Edmund G. H. Landau (1877-1938) who was professor at the University of Goettingen, left German soil in 1934 and took up the duties which were offered him years earlier at the Hebrew University, where he had previously helped establish a mathematical institute.

Leon Lichtenstein (1878-1933) was more versatile than most mathematicians, specializing along the lines of astronomical mathematics. He was spared the humiliation of dismissal by dying before Hitler came into power.

Felix Bernstein (1878-) who was Professor at Goettingen assisted his former teacher, Georg Cantor, by supplying the important principle of equivalence, which smoothed the path of the aggregate theory.

We can point to the contributions of Max Noether of Erlangen (1844-1921) on singularities of curves, Rudolf Lipschitz (1832-1903) of Bonn and Ferdinand Joachimsthal (1818-1861) at Halle and Breslau, Louis Saalschütz (1835-

1905) of Koenigsberg, Paul Epstein (1871-   ) who was professor at Strassburg and brought out a compendium of higher mathematics; Meyer Hamburger of the Technical Institute in Charlottenburg, and scores of others who have made a mark in mathematics, but then it would require ten times as much space as is at our disposal.

Only those who are conversant with Jewish biography will appreciate to what extent German mathematics is in large part Jewish mathematics, even if the mathematicians themselves renounced their faith and became converts to Christianity. Any history of mathematics—and the most comprehensive historian of mathematics is, again, a Jew, viz., Moritz Cantor, who has taken about 4000 pages to tell the story—will show how the progress of new mathematical movements depended on the Jews. So inextricably intertwined are the Jewish names with each other, as well as with the general group, that if the former were eliminated, the gaps in mathematical advancement would seriously affect the science.

Here is reproduced part of a page in Cajori's *History of Mathematics* with the names of the Jewish mathematicians capitalized (by myself). Germany, France, and England are represented in this passage, but in the final analysis, most of those mentioned are Jewish.

In the *American Journal of Mathematics* are memoirs on binary and ternary quantics, elaborated partly with the aid of F. FRANKLIN, now professor at the Johns Hopkins University. At Oxford, SYLVESTER has opened up a new subject, the theory of reciprocants, treating of the functions of a dependent variable y and the functions of its differential coefficients in regard to x, which remain unaltered by the interchange of x and y. This theory is more general than one on differential invariants by HALPHEN (1878), and has been developed further by J. Hammond of Oxford, McMahon of Woolwich, A. R. Forsyth of Cambridge, and others. SYLVESTER playfully lays claim to the appellation of the mathematical Adam, for the many names he has introduced into mathematics. Thus the invariant, discriminant, Hessian, Jacobian, are his.

The great theory of invariants, developed in England mainly by Cayley and SYLVESTER, came to be studied earnestly in Germany, France, and Italy. One of the earliest in the field was SIEGFRIED HEINRICH ARONHOLD (1819-1884), who demonstrated the existence of invariants, S and T, of the ternary cubic. Hermite discovered evectants and the theorem of reciprocity named after him. PAUL GORDAN showed, with the aid of symbolic methods, that the number of distinct forms for a binary quantic is finite."[6]

It is true that at times Jewish encyclopedias and reference works erroneously include a few names of non-Jews, like Felix Klein, Hilbert, or Hermann Weyl, but probably many more of Jewish descent are not known to be such.

I have a faint suspicion that the famous Ludwig Otto Hesse (1811-1874) was of Jewish origin. The clues? It took some time before he was given a professorship, and in this connection, J. J. Sylvester, himself the victim of prejudice or bigotry, as we shall see later, in one of his many original papers, viz., "On a Theory of Syzygetic Relations" while speaking of the Hessian curve, pauses to interpolate, amidst the intricate reasoning, a temperamental aside which reminds us of a prophetic outburst in these words: "named after Dr. Otto Hesse of Koenigsberg (the worthy pupil of his illustrious master)[7] but who, to the scandal of the mathematical world, remains still without a chair in the University he adorns with his presence and his name". My third clue is the fact that Moritz Cantor wrote the obituary article on Hesse in both a technical journal and also the dictionary of German biography, and he mentions there only one other obituary in a mathematical journal—written by Hamburger. Naturally these may all be coincidences, but such coincidences are worth looking into.

Among the more recent mathematicians who have attained fame are Richard Courant (born in Poland 1888) who after serving as professor at Goettingen and director of the Institute for Mathematics and Mechanics in that place, left Germany in 1933, and after a year at Cambridge University, arrived in New York to head the department at New York University; Richard von Mises, one of the foremost authorities on the theory of probability, aeronautics and the applications of mathematics to physics. On the termination of the First World War, in which he served as a pilot and plane designer, he was dismissed, as a German, from the University of Strassburg; while under the Nazi regime, he was forced to leave under the Aryan clause. After teaching in Turkey for some time, he received a call to Harvard where he is professor in the graduate School of Engineering. Besides his philosophical diversions, von Mises happens to be an authority on Rilke too, having published much on the German poet.

Philipp Frank, who originally was in the general field of mathematics, is now identified with physics where he will appear later in this discussion; Alfred Rosenblatt, formerly of the University of Cracow, later taught in the University of Peru, Lima, dying there in 1947.

Adolf Fraenkel, Director of the Einstein Institute of Mathematics at the Hebrew University; F. W. D. Levi, formerly of Leipzig and recently teaching at the University of Calcutta, are others of some distinction.

Let us take note of the fact that many mathematicians have distinguished themselves primarily in allied fields like astronomy (Schwarzschild) mechanics or physics (Heinrich Hertz) (Arthur Moritz Schoenflies, who was a protégé, or perhaps aide, of Nernst). These will be discussed in their proper sphere.

ENGLAND

England has not been productive of great mathematicians; and, of course, there were few Jews who distinguished themselves in this field as compared with German or Italian Jews, but there is hardly a mathematician in England, after Newton, who could compare in stature with James Joseph Sylvester (1814-1897) the son of Abraham Joseph (the name Sylvester was adopted by James later in deference to an older brother, living in the United States), unless it is Sylvester's collaborator and friend, Arthur Cayley. Sylvester, as irony would have it, one of the most original and influential mathematicians of his day in England, did not receive his bachelor's degree from Cambridge University until long after he had been a professor in several universities—and only for the reason that he was a professing Jew. Besides collaborating with Arthur Cayley in the establishment of the theory of invariants, he covered a vast amount of mathematical territory, such as reciprocants, the theory of forms, matrices and Hamiltonian numbers. In addition, he invented a few geometrical devices, among them, the plagiograph, which reproduces similar figures but turned at an angle to the original. The Royal Society in England struck a medal in his honor commemorating his great service to mathematics, and one of the first recipients of the Sylvester medal was Georg Cantor, who received it in 1904 for his original work in aggregates.

The Cambridge University Press has brought out four huge volumes containing Sylvester's collected writings, under the editorship of Prof. Baker. Sylvester was the sage among mathematicians. Many of his witty remarks appear in a book called *Mathematical Memorabilia*. His verse writing was a hobby which shows his well-rounded personality. In appearance, he resembled a genial rabbi of the old generation, with the polish of an English lord.

The anecdotes told about him would fill a volume. I remember reading once that when he was teaching at Johns Hopkins University, he was invited to dinner at the home of a colleague. Since it began to pour as the mathematician was ready to depart, the hostess insisted that he spend the evening there. Somewhat reluctantly, Sylvester accepted the invitation, but a few minutes later, the household missed him. When he returned he was asked where he had been during the period, and to their astonishment, it turned out that Sylvester had gone out in the rain for his pajamas.

At Johns Hopkins, Sylvester trained a number of students who subsequently became leaders in the discipline. We shall have occasion to refer to him again in connection with the founding of the chief mathematical journal in the United States, when he taught in Baltimore.

Although Benjamin Gomperz (1779-1865) was a mathematician of a different sort, and might be mentioned perhaps more appropriately under another rubric, as an astronomer, he was in fact a pioneer in vital statistics, having worked out the tables of mortuary resistance to the extent that the whole actuary system may be said to date from him.

Selig Brodetsky (1888-   ) formerly professor of applied mathematics at Leeds, and now Chancellor of the Hebrew University in Jerusalem, is prominent in the mathematical phase of aerodynamics, although his leadership in the Zionist movement and other Jewish activities, as well as general professional organizations, has sidetracked him considerably. In his student days in Cambridge he distinguished himself by his attaining the senior wranglership.

Louis Joel Mordell (1888-   ) is professor of pure mathematics at Manchester University.

H. Levy (1889-   ) head of the mathematical department at the Imperial College of Science in London has written prolifically on various subjects but differential equations and the theory of probability have been his mainstay. Like Brodetsky, he takes an interest in Jewish affairs, but is leftist in orientation otherwise.

ITALY

Coming to Italy, we have in the person of Luigi Cremona (1830-1903) who was director of the school of engineering in Rome, and even at one time minister of education, a geometrician of unusual acumen, especially in the synthetic sphere. Cremona's textbook on projective geometry has been translated into many languages and his treatises on graphical calculus and reciprocal figures have also had a wide vogue in academic circles. We shall return to Cremona in another section, since he stood high in another sphere of activity too. At present suffice it to record that he stands out as one of the great geometricians of his generation, and Italy is truly proud of him.

Italy has been especially fortunate in its Jewish mathematicians who, it has been said, constitute 80% of its more conspicuous representatives. Although Volterra was also a physicist and an aeronautic engineer and inventor, his chief contribution lay in his studies on permutable functions and integro-differential functions, which brought him fame throughout the world. He was, however, disposed to make theory the all-in-all, and we find him now revising and modifying theories of elasticity, and now laying the foundations for a mathematics of the social and biological sciences; but from one angle, his character interests us even more, for he was brave enough to refuse taking the Fascist oath in 1931, and thus was dismissed by Mussolini from the University of Rome where he served as professor of mathematical physics for 31 years.

Guido Ascoli (1843-1890) was equally versed in algebra and geometry, and his chair was at the Milan Technical Institute where he has done some important work.

Salvatore Pincherle (1853-1930) whose chief work lies in developing the field of analytic functions was professor at Bologna University where he presided in 1928, at the International Congress of Mathematics.

Corrado Segre (1863-   ) Professor at Turin, was a devoted pupil of Cremona, whose geometrical contributions he brought up to date with researches of his own.

Among the world's foremost authorities on calculus and probability was Guido Castelnuovo (1865-1947) late professor of analytic geometry at the University of Rome. It is my recollection that Castelnuovo was one of the bitterest opponents of Mussolini's Fascism.

Another brilliant name in the annals of Italian mathematics is that of Tullio Levi-Civita (1873-1942). That this beacon should have been given the congé by Mussolini (in consequence of Nazi pressure to enforce the Nuremberg laws in Italy, too) only to find a haven in the Vatican is one of the ironies of science and progress. His work on absolute differential calculus was at the basis of Einstein's relativity theory, and his three volumes on rational mechanics, as well as his *Fondamenti di Meccanica Relativistica,* were hailed as monumental. While he was a member of the Pontifical Academy of Science (Volterra was the only other Jewish member) he was also on the academic board of the Hebrew University at Jerusalem.

One of the most prolific mathematical textbook writers is Giulio Vivanti (1859-   ) who, according to my Italian informant, was listed as a Jew under the fascist restrictions. Vivanti, trained as an engineer, held a chair in mathematics at the University of Messina, then at Padua and Milan, carrying on in several different fields: calculus of variations, theory of analytic functions, infinitesimal calculus, and theory of transformations. Some of his works were translated into French and German. His name appears in the 1948 edition of the Italian *Chi è.*

Federigo Enriques (1871-1942) was known in circles of philosophy largely because of the journal *Scientia* which he founded in 1909; but it was as a geometrician that the mathematical world hailed him when his three volumes on advanced geometry appeared. Enriques worked in several sectors, algebraic functions and mechanics too, but he was not content to stay in the technical field. His highly speculative mind led him beyond to the foundations of all science, to methodology and the theory of knowledge; and his deductions touched upon the theory of relativity. Prior to the Nazi war, he served as the head of the Italian Institute of Mathematics and the Italian Institute for the History of Science.

A geometrician of a high order was Gino Loria (1862-   ) who received gold medals for his ingenious research from the Academy of Madrid and the French Institute. His "side line" was the history of mathematics.

One who might have risen to the heights of a Volterra or a Levi-Civita was the brilliant mathematician, Eugenio Elia Levi (1883-1917) professor of infinitesimal calculus at the University of Genoa, had he not been killed in his 34th year during the First World War; Levi's papers were many and on diverse problems. His brother Beppo Levi (1875-   ) formerly professor at Bologna (theory of functions) is now teaching in Rosario, Argentina.

Equally noted as a geometrician is Beniamino Segre who, after teaching at Rome and Bologna for many years, was removed by the general edict of Mussolini and left for England. His *Non-Singular Cubic Surfaces* was published at Oxford.

For a country which, prior to the Nazi War, harbored only from forty to fifty thousand Jews, Italy might be said to have fared quite well by her Semitic minority, although during the Nazi bond, or better perhaps, under Nazi bondage, she has not done so well by them.

Among the younger Italian mathematicians of prominence is Alessandro Terracini of a Jewish family which has produced a number of notables like the leftist leader and publicist and the scholar in comparative literature (all brothers). Terracini, who has been professor at the University of Turin, is a specialist in analytic geometry (in the tradition of the illustrious Cremona).

FRANCE

In France, mathematics has had a glorious following, but as is well-known, the arts and humanistic subjects have been far better cultivated; and as the saying goes *Wie es sich christelt so jüdelt sich es* is true here. In Italy, we found the Jews outstripping the Italians. In France, the Jewish mathematicians take their place, more in keeping with our expectations.

Georges-Henri Halphen (1844-1889) although not one of the more original minds, and never divorcing himself from his military interests (as an artillery captain in the Franco-Prussian War of 1870, he was decorated) succeeded in becoming one of the most influential mathematicians in Europe and was even a member of the French Academy of Science, in addition to winning honors for his mathematical articles from German learned societies as well. Making allowance for his brief life, he has certainly made a mark for himself.

Probably one of the most recognized mathematicians in France is Jacques Hadamard (1865-   ) who eventually became professor of mathematics at the University of Paris, but lectured in the United States during the Nazi upheavals in Europe. When we consider that this man who looked like an East European rabbi with an expression of tragedy, perhaps the reflection of his feelings during the persecution of his brother-in-law Alfred Dreyfus, had discovered and formulated important theorems in regard to determinants, upon which is based the modern treatment of integral functions, it is no wonder that the University of Goettingen, the citadel of mathematics, bestowed an honorary degree on him. The general theory of functions, calculus of variation, and the field which Georg Cantor had opened up, viz. infinite series, were also his favorite "pastimes". Hadamard took time off nevertheless to devote his energies to Jewish causes.

Some of the lesser known figures are Paul Emile Appell (1855-1930) who was at one time President of the French Mathematical Society, Isaac Auguste Blum (1812-1877) Eugène Cahen (1865-   ) while André Weil (1906-   ) who was professor at the University of Strassburg and is now teaching at the University of Chicago, promises to take his place with Halphen and Hadamard. His work on topological groups and his *Foundations of Algebraic Geometry* have won recognition in mathematical circles throughout the world.

Among the younger mathematicians attached to French universities, mainly as professors, are S. Mandelbrojt (originally from Poland), J. Frenkel, Paul Lévy, Jacques Lévy-Bruhl and H. Lewy.

UNITED STATES

It is noteworthy that in the United States, there is hardly a university of some standing which does not count at least one Jewish professor of mathematics or even head of the department. Thus at Columbia there are Edward Kasner and Joseph F. Ritt; in Princeton we find the noted topologist, Solomon Lefschetz and also Solomon Bochner, formerly lecturer at Munich; at Harvard, O. Zarisky and Richard von Mises are teaching in different schools; Yale has its N. Jacobson, and Columbia, besides Kasner, counts S. Eilenberg. Hans Lewy and A. Seidenberg are at the University of California. At the University of Chicago, we have I. Kaplansky and the algebraist, A. A. Albert as professors. J. S. Cohen is at the University of Pennsylvania. P. Erdös teaches at Syracuse University; Otto Szasz is a well-known mathematician at the University of Cincinnati; Hans Samelson at the University of Michigan, while at Brown University, which has a strong mathematical department, there are with J. D. Tamarkin, deceased, W. Prager, M. H. Heins and H. Federer; at the Massachusetts Institute of Technology, there are several Jewish mathematicians like Norbert Wiener, Withold Hurewicz, who taught in Holland, before coming to this country, both well-known in their respective specialties; N. Levinson, I. S. Cohen, S. D. Zeldin and others; Johns Hopkins has had a Jewish tradition beginning with the celebrated James Joseph Sylvester, who was succeeded by Fabian Franklin, while at present, we find Abraham Cohen, Aurel Wintner, and Leonard M. Blumenthal carrying on the work; Jacob D. Tamarkin was at the time of his death professor at Brown University; at Cornell, Wallie Abraham Hurwitz has made an enviable reputation for himself nor should we forget M. Kac at Cornell; the late Emmy Noether, who has been mentioned earlier was associated with Bryn Mawr; at the University of North Carolina, A. T. Brauer occupies a prominent place; J. B. Rosenbach, a successful text-book writer, is professor at Carnegie Institute of Technology, and at Duke, Leonard Carlitz occupies the chair in mathematics; at the University of Pennsylvania, Isaac J. Schwatt has served as professor for many years until his retirement, and is I believe succeeded by J. A. Shohat; at the University of Minnesota we find S. E. Warschawski; Louis L. Silverman is head of the department at Dartmouth, and Henry Blumberg is professor at Ohio State University; while at Antioch College, Max Astrachan is head of the department; at Texas University, Hyman J. Ettlinger is professor; and at Oklahoma University, we find Nathan A. Court in the same capacity; R. J. Levit holds a like position at the University of Georgia.

Furthermore there are Benjamin A. Bernstein at the University of California, L. W. Cohen at Kentucky, Jekutiel Ginsburg at Yeshivah College, Tobias Dantzig at Maryland University, M. G. Gaga at Nebraska University; Arthur Rosenthal, formerly of Munich and Heidelberg, is now head of the department at Purdue University; B. Z. Linfield at the University of Virginia; M. Salkover is at the University of Cincinnati; H. L. Slobin at the University of New Hampshire; E. F. S. Weinberg, head of the department at Rollins College; M. Marden is at the University of Wisconsin (in Milwaukee) and at least a score of others who are professors of mathematics in American universities.

In Canadian universities, Jewish mathematicians are not as plentiful but L. Infeld at the University of Toronto and I. Halperin at Queens, in Kingston have made a reputation beyond the Canadian border. Leopold Infeld, in fact, has a place in the section on mathematical physics as a collaborator of Einstein.

Thanks to the exodus from Germany, Central and South America now have their quota of eminent Jewish mathematicians, which means that they nilly-willy are the disseminators of the Science throughout the Western hemisphere, but such countries as Egypt, Turkey, India, and Japan have also benefited to some extent by the Brown Plague. Thus the dictum "One man's meat is another man's poison" may here be adapted to read "the Brown beast's poison becomes the normal man's meat", or the stones which the Nazi masons have rejected have become a magnificent edifice detracting from the erstwhile grandeur which was German mathematics.

RUSSIA AND THE REST OF EUROPE

In Russia, even during the Czarist regime, a few Jews succeeded in attaining prominence in mathematics, naturally paying the price of their credal affiliations. In Soviet Russia, it was not necessary to become baptized in order to advance professionally or professorially, hence some of the foremost mathematicians in USSR are of Jewish parentage. We do not hear much about them because of linguistic as well as political barriers, but the names of Sergey Bernshteyn, who is professor at Leningrad, P. S. Uryssohn, who is professor at Moscow University, Landau, Frenkel, P. B. Frumkin, E. A. Vainrib, G. B. Spivak, G. Y. Liubarsky and Y. L. Rabinovitch are not the only ones of Jewish origin that are outstanding in this field. In the branch known as topology, L. Lusternik (reported to have been killed during the Nazi War) and L. Shnirelman have been regarded as original exponents.

Poland has been, or should have been indebted to the efforts of Samuel Dikstein, Natanson, both of Warsaw and both editors of journals; H. D. Steinhaus, who was the Dean of the mathematical Faculty, at the University of Lwów, and the late Alfred Rosenblatt who taught at Cracow before he emigrated to Lima, Peru, before the German occupation.

Even Roumania numbered a few well-known mathematicians, like David Emanuel and Valcovici, Professors at Bucharest; and in Hungary, Julius König and R. Eötvös, as well as Izidor Fröhlich were editors of mathematical journals. At the present time, Leopold Feier is recognized internationally as a mathematician of considerable achievement.

Several Jews in Holland made distinct contributions to the science, particularly Lobato and Teixeira de Mattos, the latter of a distinguished Portuguese family that settled in Holland after the ban against Jews in their native country. Latterly, the names of D. Van Danzig and Hans Freudenthal (Utrecht) have loomed up on the mathematical horizon.

It would take altogether too much space to set forth the attainments of Jewish mathematicians in Czechoslovakia, in Jugoslavia, and one or two other countries in Europe, but the work of Harald Bohr in Denmark deserves special mention.

Harald Bohr (1887-   ) younger brother of the more famous Niels Bohr, like him, is a professor at the University of Copenhagen, and has been more popular as a football champion in Denmark than as a mathematician; nevertheless his contributions to harmonic analysis and the Fourier series ("Analytic almost Periodic Functions") have placed him among the foremost of modern mathematicians. Harald Bohr maintains some contact with the Hebrew University.

JEWS AS FOUNDERS AND EDITORS OF MATHEMATICAL PERIODICALS*

It is really difficult to know where to begin in enumerating the most important mathematical periodicals which were edited by Jews. The *Journal für die reine und angewandte Mathematik* was for a long time edited by K. W. Borchardt. J. L. Fuchs was editor and, at a later period, Moritz Cantor was co-editor of the *Zeitschrift für Mathematik und Physik*. The latter also founded the *Abhandlungen zur Geschichte der mathematischen Wissenschaften*, was co-editor, from 1859 to 1900, of the *Zeitschrift für Mathematik und Physik,* and was among the founders of the *Jahresbericht der deutschen Mathematiker-*

*The present tense is used, in order to simplify matters. Naturally all the editing of German periodicals by Jews has been in the past . . .

Vereinigung, which later came in the hands of L. Bieberbach, a non-Jew with a vengeance! Otto Blumenthal and G. Faber. Einstein is co-director of the *Mathematische Annalen,* which is edited by Otto Blumenthal. L. Lichtenstein, who originally came from Poland, not only edits the *Jahrbuch über die Fortschritte der Mathematik* but also the *Mathematische Zeitschrift,* of which I. Schur was co-editor. H. Hahn is co-editor of the *Monatshefte für Mathematik und Physik.* Hermann Blumenberg edits the *Allgemeine Vermessungs-Nachrichten,* and von Mises (whose mark of nobility is not disproof of his Jewishness) directs the *Zeitschrift für angewandte Mathematik und Mechanik.* F. Riesz is an editor of the *Acta Mathematica Universitatis Francisco Josephinae,* and Julius Schuster is director of the *Archiv für Geschichte der Mathematik der Naturwissenschaften und der Technik.*

The versatile Ludwig Grossmann founded both the *Mathematisch-physikalische Zeitschrift* and *Die Controle,* an economic review. (See Wininger's *Grosse Jüdische National-Biographie*). On the other hand, Felix Klein, one of the founders of the *Mathematische Annalen,* although apparently regarded as a Jew by the *Jewish Encyclopedia,* was, I am assured indirectly by his Jewish colleagues in Goettingen, of non-Semitic stock.

In Italy, where the most distinguished mathematicians have recently been Jews (V. Volterra, T. Levi-Civita, C. Segre, Gino Loria, and F. Enriques, all in the line of the illustrious Luigi Cremona, the *ne plus ultra* geometrician of his day) the *Annali di Mathematica* has the second and third of the group for editors; the fourth, Gino Loria, is director of the *Bollettino di Bibliografia e Storia delle Scienze Mathematiche;* while the *Periodico di Mathematiche* is being co-directed by Enriques.

Poland, the majority of whose mathematicians are Jews, has to thank Samuel Dikstein for a number of mathematical periodicals and other serials, inaugurated by this versatile and energetic scientist. Not only has he founded, together with Wladyslaw Natanson, the *Prace Matematyczno-Fizyczne,* but has further established the *Wiadomosci Matematyczno-Fizyca,* not to mention his part in editing the large Polish general encyclopedia, *Wielka Encyklopedja Powszechna,* and other publications. It is rumored, too, that Waclaw Sierpinski, co-editor of the *Fundamenta Mathematicae,* is partly Jewish. In Lwów, the *Studia Mathematica* between 1929-1939, until Poland was invaded, had as its editors Stefan Banach and Hugo Steinhaus.

In Hungary, there are very few outstanding mathematicians who are not Jews, the most illustrious of them being Julius König who, together with R. Eötvös, founded the *Mathematische und naturwissenschaftliche Berichte aus Ungarn.* Another mathematician of note is Izidor Fröhlich, a member of the Hungarian Academy, who edits the *Mathematikai es Termeszettudomanyi Ertesitö* ("Mathematical and Physical Index").

In Copenhagen, Harald Bohr, the younger brother of Niels Bohr, (q. v. in the sections on "Physics" and "The Jews and the Nobel Prize"), is co-editor of *Matematisk Tidsskrift.*

France has comparatively fewer Jewish mathematicians than other countries of like culture, and I know of only one Jewish founder of a mathematical periodical in France, and that is Isaac Auguste Blum, who directed the *Bulletin Polytechnique,* from 1844 till his death in 1877, and edited his daily (?) journal *La Science,* which was devoted mainly to mathematics. Yet Paul Levy, as president of the French Mathematical Society, would naturally *ex officio* take a hand in the *Bulletin de la Société Mathématique de France.*

In Holland, two or three Jews, but particularly Teixeira de Mattos (from Portugal) have been prominent in connection with publications like the *Révue Semestrielle des Publications Mathématiques,* but so far as I could discover, they were not officially known as editors.

In America, J. J. Sylvester founded the *American Journal of Mathematics* in 1878 which was, I believe, the first mathematical periodical of any importance to be published in this country, while the lesser B. F. Finkel (who, judging by the name, is of Semitic descent), was the organizer, in 1894, of the *American Mathematical Monthly*. E. Kasner is an editor of the *Transactions of the American Mathematical Society;* A. Dresden is co-editor of the *Bulletin of the American Mathematical Society,* W. A. Hurwitz was editor of the *American Mathematical Monthly,* 1919-1922, and of the *Bulletin of the American Mathematical Society,* 1921-1924; while Abraham Cohen is an editor of the *American Journal of Mathematics;* R. Brauer is editor of the *American Journal of Mathematics* and Nathan Jacobson is one of the editors of the *Bulletin of the American Mathematical Society,* while at Duke, Leonard Carlitz edits the *Duke Mathematical Journal.* The *Transactions of the American Mathematical Society* are edited by Antoni Zygmund and S. Lefschetz edits the *Annals of Mathematics.* W. Prager is managing editor of the *Quarterly of Applied Mathematics* and J. Ginsburg founded the quarterly *Scripta Mathematica.*

Naturally if we were to include associate editors, the list would be much longer. Thus, we see how the Jews in America have carried on the traditional activity in this branch of science. Here, at any rate, they have advanced beyond the mark of their British brethren. Certainly the list is far from exhaustive, but we must proceed to other fields.

Considering the mathematical strength of the Jews, it is small wonder that the *Scripta Mathematica et Physica* (volume I) of the Hebrew University and Library of Jerusalem (edited by Albert Einstein) shows an excellence which has probably never been paralleled; for here are brought together a galaxy of men, each of whose writings would do honor to any publication; and the fact that perhaps none of them has written his paper originally in Hebrew does not invalidate the national status of the volume, especially as each of the papers appears in Hebrew translation. The collection of *Scripta* is a unique phenomenon because of the international canopy which overspreads a group of scientists with a like national subconsciousness, dormant though it may have been for a generation.

Jews and the Internationality of Mathematics

We have come to the end of this section, and if there is still the question open to what extent modern mathematics has been influenced by Jewish investigators, the reason can only be that so many factors are apt to becloud the issue, personal, philosophical or psychological bias being not the least.

Aside from the original work of men like Jacobi, Georg Cantor, Kronecker, Cremona, Volterra, Levi-Civita and a score of others, there is to be recorded their international *élan* in welding the science, their vision, their disinclination to keep it within national or local bounds.

Cantor was particularly active in separating the German mathematicians from the general group of naturalists and physicists, and became chairman of the first convention which finally took place in 1890. But that was not sufficient. Cantor still felt that the German conclave was too narrow. He wanted mathematics to be *free* from the shackles of any foregone conclusions or clique, and had formulated plans of a far-reaching nature, but they were in advance of the time. It was only in 1897 that the first International Congress of Mathematics took place in Zürich; and it is interesting as well as instructive to note who the mathematicians were that ranged themselves with Cantor, who could perceive the value of his theories, despite the fact that little was being made of them in the "halls of the mighty". We find here the names of Hurwitz, Minkowski and Hadamard.[8] In other words, Jews in France as well as in Germany sensed the significance of the transfinite series. One might almost say that although Kronecker was the marring exception, the concept of the infinite, which Spinoza had made the foundation of his philosophy, was the guiding star or pillar of fire for Jewish mathematicians. Not only the men mentioned but others are to be included in the taking of sides. Felix Bernstein supplied an important proof which smoothed Cantor's path. Schoenflies, Haussdorff and others, too, soon took up the cudgels, and although there were many non-Jews too who ranged themselves with Cantor, while Julius König, a Jew took it upon himself to refute Cantor at one of the Congresses, which drew the latter's ire to such a pitch that he wittily exclaimed that it was not the King that he suspected so much as the Minister (i. e., Kronecker's minister) there is some indication, at least, that Jewish mathematicians were on the alert to see the originality of Cantor's work in the possibilities especially that the system opened up. Certainly they were not considering Cantor's origin, even if that were at all known to them. It was their progressiveness that drew them close to him.

Philosophy of Mathematics

A list of illustrious names may be drawn up here of Jewish philosophers who dealt with this realm—Otto Liebmann's important paper on the "Philosophical Value of Mathematical Natural Science" made some stir about 25 years ago. Hermann Cohen's little book on the *Principle of Infinitesimal Methods* was apparently avidly read by William James, to judge from his notations and underscorings, and was reviewed by G. Cantor, but it had been recognized also in general as a penetrating study. Gaston Samuel Milhaud who taught mathematics at Montpellier, in several works, considered most painstakingly the foundations of mathematics, while his countryman Léon Brunschvicg treated the étapes of mathematical philosophy in his masterly way. It is scarcely known that Edmund Husserl, the founder of the most important philosophical school of the past generation—phenomenalism—made his debut as a lecturer in Halle with a dissertation "on the concept of Number", and one of his early works was entitled *Die Philosophie der Arithmetik.*

Among the leading symbolic logicians in America are Ernest Nagel, Professor at Columbia, Alfred Tarski, formerly of the University of Warsaw, and now at the University of California, and Henry Sheffer, Professor at Harvard.

Probably the chief mathematical philosopher today is Hans Reichenbach (1891-   ) who was Professor at the University of Berlin, but with the accession of Hitler in 1933, left for Turkey where he taught at Istanbul until 1938, when he received a call from the University of California at Los Angeles. He has written extensively in German on topics such as probability, natural philosophy, the space-time relationship, and relativity. In English there appeared several volumes, among which *Experience and Prediction* is the best known.

III

ASTRONOMY AND METEOROLOGY

Astronomy is associated with mathematics on the one hand, and with mechanics or dynamics, on the other. It is not quite as abstract as the former and not as concrete as the latter. For mathematical research, only paper and pencil are required. To observe the stellar bodies more than a bright night is needed. Astronomy was relatively late in developing for lack of telescopes and other paraphernalia. Perhaps that is one reason why Jews could not have been among the pioneers of the science, but it does not fully explain why the number of celebrated mathematicians by far exceeds the number of distinguished astronomers among the Jews.

Astronomy, as a matter of fact, because of the very remoteness of its objects and their romantic associations attracted scores of rabbis and Jewish scholars, so that a few hundred might be listed of those who dabbled in astronomy, but in the first place, they were too deeply rooted in Talmudical studies to specialize even to the extent of acquiring the propaedeutics of methodology; and then, too, their training along mathematico-physical lines was limited, with the result that at most they could turn out popular presentations in Hebrew or scattered speculations which showed an interest in the subject. Of these, Davis Gans and Joseph Delmedigo were the most outstanding, largely because of their friendship and correspondence with the pioneers.

In general, however, it is small wonder that Jewish astronomers were sooner recognized than Jewish mathematicians. Astronomy was bound up with the needs of Jewish religion, inasmuch as problems of the calendar, as Neugebauer, the foremost historian of ancient mathematics and astronomy contends, directed the first steps in astronomy. It was not only the calendar as such; such matters as the start and close of the Sabbath and festivals or the blessing of the new moon prodded some of the learned Jews centuries ago to become preoccupied with the stars and the moon.

At the present time, Millas Vallicrosa, of the University of Barcelona (a non-Jew) is preparing an edition of Abraham Ibn Ezra's astronomical treatise which he believes was originally written in Latin, in 1154. Prof. Millas Vallicrosa has already written two articles on this remarkable work by a man who was a great poet, a philosopher, a Biblical commentator of acute powers, and a globe trotter who even visited England, at a time when travel was beset by all sorts of hazards; and wherever he set foot, he seemed to be at home, making his influence felt, in learned circles.

In the current issue of *Isis* (February 1949) the eminent mediaevalist, Lynn Thorndike, in an article entitled "More Abrahamismus" writes, "It seems strange that an author whose astrological treatises later so popular in Latin translation, who travelled in Christian Europe and was in close relation with Christian scholars, and himself put forth astronomical works in Latin should have had to wait for over a century for the Latin translation of his numerous astrological tracts".

The distinguished writer apparently does not know of Ibn Ezra's epigram in Hebrew, about his fate, to the effect that if he were to begin selling candles, the sun would shine forever, and if he were to deal in shrouds no one would die. Ibn Ezra was the vagabond genius. Had he settled somewhere and specialized in astronomy, his lot might have been different.

Of the older Jewish astronomers, men like Isaac Ibn Said and Abraham Zacuto became well-known, the latter even teaching at the University of Salamanca. His part in the discovery of America has already been dwelt on in the Introduction, where such names as Joseph Vecinho and Pedro Nuñes, "the glory of Portugal", have also been mentioned.

It cannot be said that the Jews have produced a Copernicus, a Kepler, a Newton, or a Tycho Brahe; and although some apologists, in their zeal, will seize on the fact that both Tycho Brahe and Kepler corresponded with David Gans, or that Galileo knew a Marrano poet, it is not till the advent of William Herschel that the Jewish contribution takes on a gigantic proportion. But how could it be otherwise? The Jews were secluded in their ghetto. The Talmud was their mental fare. The universities were closed to them. Observatories, even the most primitive, were non-existent for them. They could indeed be star-gazers, but it required more to become an astronomer.

William Herschel (1738-1822), the young musician who came from Hanover, Germany, and settled in England as a part-time organist, while studying astronomy, achieved the impossible except for a genius such as he was, and became the greatest astronomer of his century. Together with his sister he charted the sky, discovered planets, constructed his own telescope on a large scale, and in a practical way, it may be said that no astronomer, not even the great pioneers who gave a new turn to science, compared with him.

Of him, Brodetsky writes "There can be no doubt that William Herschel was of Jewish origin. Whether we have any right to claim him as in any way belonging to us is a different matter. His connection with the Jewish people or anything that can be called Jewish was absolutely zero."[9]

The truth of the matter is that we do not consult the words or the acts of the scientists, in this regard, but take cognizance of their origin. Once we are aware that Herschel's parents were both Jewish, we have every right to claim him as our own, for without his heredity, all the telescopes in the world and all the royal favors which were lavished on him would not have made of him an acceptable astronomer.

If we were to drop every Jewish scientist who left his people, or who took no interest in their weal and woe, then we should make a sorry showing in the intellectual sphere. That scientists, devoting their life in quest of truth, should deny their heritage, when faced with the dilemma of pursuing an academic career or turning their back on their ancestors, is a telling commentary. In some cases, even when it was not necessary to forswear their antecedents, the snobbish attitude still prevailed. The *reductio ad absurdum* of this perverseness was evinced in the lawsuit of Karl Landsteiner, a Nobel Prize man, against the publishers of a Jewish *Who's Who*, wherein a great scientist revealed himself a small man, and unbelievably naïve; for the *cause célèbre* only served to advertise the very fact which he was anxious to conceal.

In general, scientists claim to be international, but their achievement redounds to the credit of their native or adopted country, but why should their racial origin be totally ignored?

If a Herschel ("a young deer") ruled in modern astronomy, a "bear" played a prominent part, on a smaller scale; for Wilhelm Beer (1797-1850), brother of the famous composer Meyerbeer, after service in the army and success in commercial pursuits, devoted himself entirely to observing the course of the stars in a privately built and equipped observatory. Together with another astronomer he charted the moon so carefully that the joint work received the Lalland prize from the French Academy. He may be regarded as the selenograph, *par excellence,* but his observations of Mars were also well received. For a businessman and banker to have become an astronomer of note and to have ended his days as a member of the Upper House in Prussia was an achievement which academic astronomers cannot boast of.

Another Jew made a thorough study of the moon. This time it was the Viennese, Maurice Loewy (1833-1907) who arrived in Paris while quite a young man and succeeded in becoming the Director of the Paris Observatory as well as a member of the *Académie des Sciences*. If Loewy had done nothing else than to invent the bi-partite telescope, which has been such a boon to astronomers, because while one half is fixed, the other rotates and can be so adjusted as to catch a beam of light from the stellar body, he would have deserved great recognition, but the instrument called the equatorial conde, which he devised in collaboration with Puiseux, aside from his observations and cataloguing of numerous asteroids, brought him in the forefront of nineteenth-century astronomers.

Painting and astronomy are scarcely related, yet H. Goldschmidt (1802-1866) like Beer, gave up his previous vocation and turned astronomer, discovering many of the minor asteroids and planets. Goldschmidt was awarded the Lalland prize of the Académie des Sciences in Paris and also the Gold Medal of the Astronomical Society in London.

In Russia, Ilia S. Abelman (1866-1898) might have shed lustre upon Russian astronomy, if he were given the opportunity such as his confrères had had in Engand or France. He was not quite 32 when he died, yet his texts and articles have become well known.

We know little about the Jewish astronomers in U.S.S.R., but occasionally a news item in connection with awards reveals a Jewish name. Thus in March, 1950, Grigory Sheyn was the recipient of 200,000 rubles for discovering the heavy isotopes of carbon in the atmosphere of a number of stars. Sheyn is the Director of the Crimean Astro-Physical Observatory.

In Poland, the versatile Khayim Zelik Slonimsky, famous as the editor of *Hatsefirah* (Hebrew Weekly) was, in addition, a mathematician and amateur astronomer, who nevertheless was highly regarded by scientists of his day.

In England, in addition to the renowned Herschel, mention must be made of Sir Arthur Schuster, who, although primarily a physicist, as we shall see later, directed several solar expeditions, particularly the Eclipse expedition to Siam in 1875, and Lord Burnham *i.e.*, *Edward Lawson* (*né* Levy) who, outside of his newspaper ventures, devoted much time in observatories.

France has had its native Jewish astronomers like Armand Lambert, who has distinguished himself through numerous researches.

Italy, with its Azeglio Bemporad in Catania, and Vittorio Boccara, who was the director of the meteorological observatory at Leghorn, and others, reminds us only faintly of its Jewish stronghold in mathematics.

As usual, however, it is in Germany that Jewish names appear most frequently in connection with astronomy, even though in order to reach their goal, they have severed their ties with their people. Karl Schwarzschild (1873-1916) stands out as one of the foremost mathematicians and astronomers of the past generation, and one whose researches on space and gravitation helped greatly to intrench Einstein's theory of relativity. Fritz Cohn (1866-1922), who was director of the Astronomical Institute in Berlin, Berthold Cohn (1870-1930) who taught many years at Strassburg, Eugen Goldstein of the Babelsberg Observatory and Friedrich S. Archenhold, whose devices in photographing celestial bodies brought him considerable attention, as well as Adolf Marcuse, who had undertaken expeditions for the purpose of astronomical observations in various countries, are among the leading names, although they by no means exhaust the list of able astronomers in Germany.

We can scarcely omit, e. g. a man like E. W. Freundlich (1885-   ) who was Director of the Potsdam Einstein Institute until 1933, when he took up a similar post in Istanbul,

Turkey. In 1937, he returned to Europe and settled in Prague. We have yet to discover what has become of him since. His chief work was an examination of the law of gravitation and a thoroughgoing survey of the relativity theory.

Geodesy and meteorology, which are closely related to astronomy, claim such men as Robert Rubensen, the chief meteorologist at the University of Upsala, in Sweden; V. Boccara at Leghorn, and perhaps the foremost of them all, Georg Lachmann of the Meteorological Institute in Berlin. A geodetist of a high order was Moritz Low (1841-1900) of the Prussian Geodetic Institute in Berlin.

The great contribution of Albert A. Michelson to astrophysics both by the construction of the giant interferometer and his measurement of the velocity of light should not be omitted from a survey like this, although his work will be taken up in its proper sphere, viz., experimental physics.

We have not nearly so many Jewish astronomers in the United States as mathematicians, which is understandable because there are comparatively few astronomers altogether, but even proportionately the Jews have not measured up to their usual stature.

Frank Schlesinger (1871-1943), who served, in turn, as director of the Allegheny and Yale University Observatories, is the most distinguished name we can find in the United States among Jewish astronomers. Not only was he President of the American Astronomical Society but headed, at one time, the International Astronomical Union. Among his awards were the Valz prize of the French Académie des Sciences and the Gold Medal of the Royal Astronomical Society. He was also an officer of the French Legion of Honor. Paul S. Epstein, born in Poland and trained in Russia, where he taught for some time, is professor of physics at the California Institute of Technology but his study of the composition of the moon entitles him to a place with the astronomers. One of the very few women astronomers is Sophia H. Levy of the University of California, where she is professor of theoretical astronomy.

Finally mention must be made of Louis Berman's discovery at the Lick Observatory of new types of stars.

IV

PHYSICS

The farther we get from the abstract and semi-abstract, the fewer Jews we find in the scientific realm prior to about a century ago. Not only the Jew-baiter but the sympathetic observer would conclude that the Jews in physics "are far to seek"; and naturally we would expect the usual apologetic tone of Jewish publicists in explaining the deficiency. But time has shown that there was no deficiency. Like the human child who takes longer to develop than the animal, the Jew needed centuries to mature along these lines, and once he was emancipated and could take part in the general growth of experimental procedure, he could more than hold his own, and, as we shall see later, the two greatest epics in modern physics, the establishment of the theory of relativity and the rise of nuclear physics, including the construction of the atom bomb were largely the work of Jewish physicists.

Development of Electricity

Prior to relativity, the most fruitful field was electricity; and it is here that we find a demi-Jewish pioneer in the person of Heinrich Hertz[10], whose genius was cut short at the age of 37, but in that space of life he succeeded in supplying the experimental proof of Maxwell's electro-magnetic theory, which was the first step toward the development of wireless telegraphy as well as radio, establishing once and for all the identity of light and electro-magnetic waves, a feat which won for him the admiration of men like Helmholtz, who wrote a preface to his collected works (published posthumously) and Lord Kelvin, who wrote the *Foreword* to the English translation of Hertz's chief work, while Sir Oliver Lodge delivered

[237]

the Memorial Lecture in honor of the man who, in an unwitting contest, if that is not just a tale, had scored first in a
series of experiments which Lodge was conducting, unbeknown
to Hertz. Hertz's production and measurement of the electro-
magnetic waves has led to the development of radar, and
had far-reaching consequences in various directions. Thus the
Englishman, Faraday, the Scotsman, Maxwell, and the German half-Jew, Hertz, the Italians Galvani and Volta, the
Swede Oersted, the Frenchman, Ampère, each had his share
in the progress of electrical science during the early days of
its history.

Hertz in his youth was also a student of languages. He
could recite Homer in Greek, and had even taken up Arabic
and Sanskrit, but his side-stepping Hebrew is symptomatic
for a man who may have owed his mental gifts to the people
which was identified with Hebrew.

A man who is not so well known as Hertz, but who also
gave great impetus to the then nascent field of electricity,
even before Hertz took to it, was Peter Theophil Riess (1805-
1883) who was primarily an experimentalist, and his work
on induction and friction became classical. To his great credit
it must be said that he steadfastly refused to change his religion
in order to be elected to the Prussian Academy of Science.
Eventually, on his induction into this august and learned society, the great Alexander von Humboldt remarked on this
occasion that the "event was the first step of atonement for
the twenty-five-year-old injustice which the Prussian Jews
had to endure".

Just as Hertz was the father of the radio through his
electrical discoveries, so another Jew could be called the
father of the telephone, for it was Phillip Reis who also
contributed significantly to the advance of electricity by managing, in 1863, to translate melodies into electrical waves
which afterwards were given out in tones again. Had he then
been able to use the direct instead of only the alternating
current, the human voice, which was reproduced too nasally

for the purpose, would have had that quality required for transmission at a distance. Nevertheless it was Reis's principle which later became the basis of the telephone.

Eugen Goldstein (1850-1930), who looked like a good-humored rabbi, was also a pioneer in the field, principally in connection with the deflection and reflection of cathode rays, but his prologue part in the atom drama will be adverted to in the section on the atom. The fact that the celebrated Helmholtz was his sponsor and that Goldstein was the physicist at the Berlin Observatory should place him at once as a major scientist.

Emil Warburg (1846-1931), the father of the Nobel Prize laureate Otto Warburg, as head of the Charlottenburg Physico-Technical Institute, which was a Department of the University of Berlin, engaged in miscellaneous researches, such as the kinetic theory of gases and galvanic polarization; but electricity, again, was the nucleus—which led him to examine electric currents in gases and the process of electrolysis. His textbook in experimental physics passed into more than 25 editions, and his monograph on the thermal unit is still considered a standard work.

Leo Graetz (1856-1942), the son of the famous historian, Heinrich Graetz, is known for his many contributions in various fields, but particularly for having devised the bridge connection of rectifiers (*Graetz-Schaltung*) and his method of converting alternating into direct currents. On a lower level, his incandescent *Grätzin* light has kept his name before the public. Of his German work on electricity and its applications, about 25 editions have appeared in various languages, and his textbook on physics is highly regarded throughout the world.

Speaking of Graetz, our mind turns to another son of a famous Jew, Daniel Khvolson, the orientalist in St. Petersburg, who despite his conversion was a warm friend of his people. His son, Orest D. Khvolson, was one of the leading physicists in Russia, and it is strange that none of the half-dozen Jewish encyclopedias mention him.

Of about the same period was the Italian physicist, Moise Ascoli (1857-1921) professor at Rome. Magnetism in relation to electricity occupied his chief attention, in addition to the problems of elasticity of certain metals, especially iron.

Electrical charge through gases was the study of Arthur Schuster (1851-1934), although spectroscopy, terrestrial magnetism, and meteorology were his stamping grounds also. In general, Sir Arthur was an organizer of extraordinary ability, as was his father, a Frankfort banker, and his brothers. The name Arthur Schuster has already come up in our section on astronomy; and in England, he was held in great esteem because of his educational promotion.

One of the foremost authorities on electricity was Max Abraham (1875-1922) Professor of physics at the University of Munich. His book on the subject became a standard work having been translated into English, French, and other languages. Radiation was a specialty of his too and even the foundations of geometry were grist to his mill, probably at the time he taught at Milan.

In discussing electricity, one could also find a niche for the Nobel Prize man, Henri Moissan, if only for his spectacular electric furnace and his more theoretical inquiries into the nature of electricity, but his real place is in chemistry. Moissan is not generally known to have been Jewish or half-Jewish, but we have this information on the authority of Sir Arthur Schuster, who should be a reliable source in this connection.

But if Moissan was not a full-blooded Jew, his compatriot, Gabriel Lippmann (1842-1919) equally famous and also a Nobel Prize man, may be added to our galaxy. Lippmann was professor of mathematical physics at the Sorbonne, and later became a member of the Académie des Sciences. He was a pioneer in the then new field of electrocapillarity, although the Nobel Prize was awarded him in 1908 for his devising the process of color photography, which would imply, of course, that he was an authority on optics. His courses at the Sorbonne were among the most popular in that Institution, and his textbooks on thermodynamics and light were standard works in France for a long time.

Among electrical engineers (although engineering in all its departments will have to be treated in a separate chapter) there was probably none greater than Charles Proteus Steinmetz (1865-1923) who for all his denials, on the assumption that the Jews were a religious sect, must be added to the minority which has given so much to the majority. Steinmetz, who, in addition to his tasks as chief consulting engineer of the General Electric Company, where he found himself nicknamed the "Electrical Wizard", served as professor of electrophysics at Union University in Schenectady was just about to be deported when he arrived in the United States, in 1889, on the ground of his deformity.

An engineer and specialist along the same lines or, rather, high voltage electricity, is Reinhold Ruedenberg (1883-   ) who until the Nazi regime had been Professor at the Technological Institute in Berlin—Charlottenburg, and at present is head of the Department of Electrical Engineering at Harvard University. Ruedenberg, who is the son-in-law of the famous mathematician, Minkowski, has invented the electronic microscope and has written a number of works on applied electricity.

Felix Ehrenhaft (1879-   ) also belongs to the inventive physicists, although many of his projects seemed altogether too fantastic to his colleagues. In fact I was persuaded to delete the paragraph or two on him in this survey; and only after reflecting on the fact that he could not have risen to a professorship in the University of Vienna if he were not a physicist of high merit, did I decide to give him his place here.

Ehrenhaft was an experimentalist primarily, and his researches on the Brownian movements in the molecules of gases, as well as on the transportation of micro-particles through light, were carried on in the University of Vienna years ago. After the annexation of Austria, Ehrenhaft came to the United States, where he began to elaborate some spectacular projects which caused many of his colleagues to suspect that he was exaggerating his potentialities, but there is no denying that he did devise some very useful laboratory apparatus. It is probably due to the scornful attitude of his colleagues here that he returned to Vienna in 1947.

James Franck (1882-   ) will receive his proper place in the section on atomic physics, but he could well be discussed under several different rubrics. One of the foremost experimentalists of our time, he was the youngest Nobel Prize Laureate in the sciences, at any rate, and became Professor at the University of Berlin at the age of 36.

His chief work was done at the University of Goettingen, where he worked with Gustav Hertz on phenomena caused by collisions between the electron and the atom. For a time he was guest professor at the University of Copenhagen, then accepted a call to Johns Hopkins and finally joining the department of chemistry.

In Italy, Alessandro Artom (1867-1927) made a great contribution toward the development of telegraphy by using circular or elliptically polarized waves, thus preventing the possibility of interception—a matter of tremendous military importance. He also was the inventor of various electrical devices, among them an instrument to locate direction in the air. His investigation of the electrical properties of the diamond and other substances added to his fame in the early part of the present century.

Quantum and Mathematical Physics

In Max Bernhard Weinstein (born 1852) the modern theory of thermodynamics had an exponent of great scope. In his four large volumes (1901-1908) on the subject, he treated kinetics of gases and thermodynamics, as well as electrolysis and magnetism, electrochemistry and thermo-electricity on a comprehensive scale, but his writings on relativity and mathematical physics give him high rank in this field too. Mathematical physics always slants toward philosophical problems, and Weinstein concerned himself with such too, when he taught at the University of Berlin.

Paul Ehrenfest (1880-1933) though born in Vienna settled in Holland where he succeeded H. A. Lorentz, one of the founders of quantum physics at the University of Leyden, to which he and his wife contributed their modest part. Because of his special interests, he might be placed in the circle of Planck, Debye, and Einstein, for whom theoretical physics was the all-absorbing study.

Philipp Franck (1884-   ) who succeeded Albert Einstein at the German University in Prague has been mentioned casually in the section on mathematics, but as a theoretical physicist, verging on philosophy, he has published several works, dealing principally with the question of mechanism and idealism in modern physics. He is at present on the Faculty of Harvard University.

The most important name in theoretical physics today is probably that of Max Born (1882-   ) who, after his dismissal from the faculty of Goettingen in 1933 for the crime of being Jewish, lectured at Cambridge University and is now Professor of Natural Philosophy at the University of Edinburgh.

The dynamics of matter, in particular crystals, the atom, the quantum theory, as well as optics have all received his attention; and he is one of the most brilliant exponents of the relativity theory, so that we shall be obliged to revert to him presently. A productive writer, his many books and articles have received world-wide recognition, passing through several editions.

L. S. Ornstein (1880-1941) Professor of physics and Rektor at one time of the University of Groningen, was a productive author in several departments of physics, including ray measurement, opalescence, crystal magnetism, barometric variations, probability, optics, heat, and entropy. The Institute of Physics of the Hebrew University of Jerusalem owes much to his assistance, and the esteem in which he was held in Holland may be gathered from the virtual demonstration which his funeral in German-occupied Holland during the Nazi War was turned into.

RUSSIA

In Russia there are quite a number of Jewish physicists who have distinguished themselves, but owing to space restrictions, only three of the score or more will be dealt with. The German-trained Leonid I. Mandelshtam (1879-   ) who after teaching at various Russian institutions became Professor of physics at the University of Moscow, is one of the trio. Optics, the dissemination of light, and the radio were his territory. Abraham F. Joffe (1880-   ) is probably the most outstanding applied physicist in USSR and one who organized the scientific institutes in Russia, becoming President of the All-Russian Association of Physicists shortly after the Revolution. An assistant of Roentgen in Munich, he made radiology his central subject of research, but he did not limit himself to any one field. Of a lesser calibre than his American namesake was Vladimir A. Michelson, professor of physics and meteorology at the Agricultural Institute in Moscow about half a century ago.

Relativity

It is very seldom that the world turns a corner in scientific progress, but when it does happen, there is a sequel of events which comes about, stupendous in scope. The Jews were not, for reasons already set forth, privileged to take a hand in such turns until recent years, but the last two turns which came almost on the heels of one another might have had to wait decades, if not a whole century, were those scientists, or their parents, to have been "selected" by the Nazi Stormtrooper Commanders as material for their new crematories.

Of all the great revolutions in thought that have been thrust upon an unwilling world in the last few centuries, that of relativity seems to have had the most far-reaching effect in intellectual circles. Whatever might be thought of the special theories of relativity, the general doctrine is here to stay. The literature on the subject constitutes a library of many thousands of volumes and articles. There is scarcely a branch of science which has not been affected to some extent by this remarkable innovation, and yet its importance does not lie in its being an innovation but in being proven a fact. Its truth has been demonstrated more than once, and all its traducers put together have not been able to dislodge it from its scientific throne.

It is common knowledge that the man whose name is most intimately associated with the theory of relativity is a Jew of unmistakable Semitic origin and avowedly nationalistic tendencies. Albert Einstein has already taken his place with Galileo, Kepler, Copernicus, and Newton in the forefront of scientific achievement. But it is not generally known that the doctrine of relativity has been reared, so to speak, on a Jewish foundation. It was not Einstein alone who evolved this cosmic theory. He had his predecessors in physics and mathematics, as well as his collaborators, and it may be of significance that the most prominent among them are Jews.

Einstein was only 26 at the time his original paper on the photo-electric effect was published in 1905, but already the hint of Planck's quantum theory had become a gigantic idea with Einstein.

Perhaps the starting-point in the development of the relativity theory was the result of an experiment made possible through the ingenuity, if not genius, of another Jew, also an Albert. It was Albert Abraham Michelson, a German-born Jew, making his domicile in America, who constructed the giant interferometer which was the essential medium in the famous Michelson-Morley experiment. There were, to be sure, other experiments undertaken to ascertain whether there was an ether drift with the earth's motion or not, and possibly Michelson's rather negative result was one of several bits of evidence which were instrumental in overturning the Newtonian system; but it seems as if Einstein was more impressed by the amazing technique of the Michelson-Morley experiment, in 1887, which, by the way, was the earliest, as well as the most accurate, of all these tests.

"Discussion provoked by the negative result of the Michelson-Morley experiment was to result in the theory of relativity. It was typical of Einstein that he regarded this failure to detect motion of the ether past the earth as evidence that no such motion existed. It is also true that the world had to wait for an Einstein to hit on such a simple explanation. The ether had too firm a hold on scientific minds."[11]

Let us not, however, lose sight of Michelson's stature, when viewing a Titan like Einstein. The following evaluation by a former professor of physics at New York University is of significance here.

"Albert A. Michelson stands preëminent among American physicists. No man in any field has worked longer or more conscientiously for the attainment of his ideal. No scientist has ever left his lifework in more complete form. No physicist has ever made more exact measurements, or shown more skill in the design and manipulation of scientific apparatus. No man has been a greater inspiration to younger men. He was the first American recipient of the Nobel Prize in physics, and for a number of years the only other physicists to receive this award in America have been associates or students of his. Those who have known him best have been loudest in his praise."[12]

It is not my purpose to enter into the intricacies of the relativity theory, even were I to flatter myself in supposing that I belong to the proverbial few who are thoroughly conversant with it. It is only as an historian, approaching his subject from a certain angle, namely, the socio-psychological angle, that I am eager to bring up the matter in this brief survey.

It will be sufficient here to quote, from one of the leading physicists in England, Arthur Schuster, also a Jew, a passage written in 1908, and printed in 1911, to show how skeptical the scientific world was about Einstein's theory, until Eddington, in a spectacular expedition (1913) confirmed Einstein's assertion in regard to the curvature of space (1913); and Millikan had completed experiments in 1916 which favored the acceptance of Einstein's equation as to the light quantum, or photon.

Schuster, alluding to Einstein's "imagined law" 'the principle of relativity' has the following to say of it, in 1911.

"The theory appears to have an extraordinary power of fascinating mathematicians, and it will certainly take its place in any critical examination of our scientific beliefs; but we must not let the simplicity of the assumption underlying the principle hide the very slender experimental basis on which it rests at present, and more especially not lose sight of the fact, that it goes much beyond what is proved by Michelson's experiment. In that experiment, the source of light and the mirrors which reflected the light were all connected together by rigid bodies, and their distances depended therefore on the intensity of molecular forces. Einstein's generalisation assumes that the result of the experiment would still be the same, if performed in a free space with the source of light and mirrors discontinued from each other but endowed with a common velocity. This is a considerable and, perhaps, not quite justifiable generalisation."[13]

[247]

If Einstein has taken his cue from a Jew on the physical side, he has turned to another Jew on the mathematical side. The name of the distinguished mathematician in Italy, Levi-Civita, is, for obvious reasons, less well-known than that of Michelson, but it was this Italian Jew who practically created the branch of mathematics called tensor calculus, which enables us to analyze manifolds of any number of dimensions. The doctrine of relativity contains so many aspects that threads must be seen connecting it with a variety of scientific branches.

It is a pity that those who consider Lorentz a Jew are mistaken about his origin, for it was this Leyden mathematical physicist who served as the forerunner of Einstein, in that he supplied the famous "transformation" formula for turning one set of co-ordinates (say, at rest in a vacuum) into another set (in motion with a given velocity).

Lorentz has so often been represented to me as Jewish by his students, and looks so much like his great compatriot, Jozef Israëls, that at one time there was no doubt in my mind that he belonged to Einstein's people. Even Weyl, the chief exponent of relativity after Einstein, supposed that Lorentz was a Jew, but to make sure, I took the liberty of addressing the question, which at times is rather delicate, to the man himself, and his reply was an explicit denial that he was of Jewish descent. Lorentz's "foreignness", in this regard, somewhat lessens the solidarity of the Semitic builders of the relativity conception, but Lorentz, I understand, from some of his students, was so modest as to give Einstein all the credit for the discovery, and he even referred to the transformation formula as the Einstein equation.

If, however, Lorentz could not be added to the list of Jewish scientists who might be regarded as the midwives of the relativity principle, at least one other brilliant Jewish name can be added to our record—that of Minkowski. It was he who supplied the notation for the great symphony which Einstein conceived. According to Hermann Weyl (*Space-Time-Matter*, English translation of the fourth German edition, page 173), "The adequate mathematical foundation of Einstein's discovery was first given by Minkowski. . . . To him we are indebted for the idea of a four-dimensional world geometry, on which we based our arguments from the outset."

As Yourgrau tells us,

> "The fusion of time and space in one unitary concept was already suggested by Einstein's former teacher, Minkowski, who made the following statement: 'Henceforth, space by itself and time by itself are doomed to fade away into mere shadows and only a kind of union of the two will preserve an independent reality."[14]

In America, the chief exponent of the relativity theory, until recent years, has been L. Silberstein, (1872-1948) formerly of the University of Rome. His *Theory of Relativity* was published in several editions. Many years ago, Silberstein, who has been with the Eastman Kodak Company in Rochester, was invited to give a series of lectures on relativity by the University of Toronto, which at the time undertook the publication of the course. He gave similar courses at the University of Chicago and Cornell University, when the subject was still in the controversial stage. In L. Infeld, the University of Toronto has now another noted specialist in the field of relativity, who has worked for a time, together with Einstein at the Institute for Advanced Study, in Princeton.

Max Born's felicitous exposition, which has passed through several editions in German, appeared in an English translation, as early as 1922, under the title of *Einstein's Theory of Relativity*. The author, a leading Jewish physicist, taught at the University of Goettingen, until Hitler came to power, but has found a haven in England since, lecturing at Oxford.

We must not forget that the theory of relativity also provoked a great deal of discussion in the academic philosophical world, and here, again, we find that those who showed a mastery of the subject and made a deep impression on workers in that field by their penetrating analysis of the concepts are Bergson and Cassirer. There have been, of course, many other writers who dealt with the philosophical phase of this universal doctrine, but the works of the French Jew and the German Jew tower above the rest. More recently, another Franco-Jewish philosopher, Emile Meyerson, has published a vigorous discussion of the relativity theory that created a good deal of comment. At the present time, Hans Reichenbach, of the University of California, who has already been discussed as a mathematical philosopher (page 230), may be regarded as one of the leading philosophers of physics, especially the theory of relativity.

Weyl himself, who ranks as the leading authority on relativity next to Einstein, and whose original investigations on the subject have been universally recognized, has also been taken for a Jew in many quarters, perhaps because his name sounds Jewish. Again I thought it best to have the fact on record, and Professor Weyl[15] was kind enough to advise me in writing that he was not of Jewish origin.

No wonder the late Alfred Korzybski, known perhaps better as a leader in the general semantics movement, but also a deep student of the implications of relativity, has written me years ago that whenever he finds it necessary to peruse a book in connection with his investigations, he almost always finds it to be the product of a Jewish author, which fact, he goes on to say, discloses not only Polish but also Jewish elements in his results.*

The best biography of Albert Einstein, before Philipp Frank's appeared, was written by Alexander Moszkowski, and

*This is what the late Alfred Korzybski (a titled newcomer to this country, at the time, but one who soon made his name count rather than vice versa) wrote me in 1926: "Many thanks for . . . the reprints. I enjoy them greatly. For Buddha's sake, is Cassirer also a Jew? If this is the case, I begin to worry rather seriously. It is not even difficult to explain. In my whole work, of course, I select my favorite authors not by noses but by the intrinsic character of the work. It happens this way that in my whole work whenever I pick a writer as very fundamental for my purposes he happens to be a Jew. This coincidence is rather more than a coincidence, but at present, of course, I do

even if it bears the earmarks of a Boswellian attitude, it is none the less fascinating. Apropos of our fundamental point of view, there is a striking sentence in this biography, which goes to show that, even in his early youth, Einstein was influenced by a Jewish work. "A new world was opened for him," Moszkowski tells us, "when he made the acquaintance of A. Bernstein's comprehensive popular books on scientific subjects."[16] This same Aaron Bernstein, who wrote *Vogele der Maggid* and other Jewish novels, also apparently wrote the first letter of relativity in Einstein's plastic mind.

CONCLUSIONS AND REFLECTIONS

I fear that some readers who are altogether sold on the slogan that "science knows of no nationality"—until, naturally, their own country's scientists are under discussion—will frown upon the idea of casting the principle of relativity in a Jewish mould. They will explain the Jewish associations in the development of this conception as due to sheer chance, or they will, after the fashion of a Jewish professor of philosophy, dismiss the matter impatiently with the remark: "What have the Jews to do with relativity? If they are interested in the theory, it is because they are always active in every new movement." This is an attitude which reminds us somewhat of the profound declaration that "not Homer wrote the *Iliad* but another man by the name of Homer."

If Michelson, Minkowski, Levi-Civita, and other Jews all had a hand with Einstein in the establishment of the great principle, only as a result of chance or coincidence, then the line between a coincidence and a miracle almost vanishes. In self-defense for broaching this delicate subject, I may call at-

not understand what, and how, and why. Your articles throw some light on the question. What worries me (rather seriously) is the fact that my whole work carries not only Polish marks but also definitely Jewish marks, *both* of which will not make my work popular." In another letter, Korzybski tells me that my enlightening him on Weyl's non-Jewish origin affords him a cue as to why he found Weyl so disturbing as a proponent of relativity. He can see now that at heart Weyl was an absolutist who finds it not easy to break away from his old moorings.

tention to the fact that the issue between the House of Israel and the principle of relativity has already been picturesquely and good-humoredly brought up by a non-Jew. Perhaps this revelation will relieve my burden.

In *The Scientific Monthly* of July, 1926, Dr. Paul R. Heyl, of the National Bureau of Standards of the United States, vividly describes a number of experiments that were conducted to disprove the Einstein theory. He himself, in fact, confesses that his own crystal weighing experiments were "indeed undertaken by the experimenter in a spirit of definite skepticism regarding Einstein's theory, which appeared (to one who had learned his physics before the discovery of the X-rays) rather too bizarre and fantastic." But the negative result of the work places the experimenter very much in the same position as that in which Balak, the king of the Moabites, found himself on a certain occasion. It requires a little self-effacement for the author to liken himself in this connection to Balak, although the analogy, to be complete, should have contained the name of Balaam instead of that of Balak.

Here, Dr. Heyl reproduces effectively the well-known story of Balak and Balaam ben Peor (which, after thousands of years, still finds its way into the average Jew's daily idiom), and therewith ends this stimulating article.

> The land of Moab had been invaded by the host of Israel, as the sands of the sea in number. A battle was impending and Balak was none too certain of the outcome. He felt that he needed moral support and ghostly counsel, and he sent messengers to Balaam, the soothsayer, saying: 'Come, curse me Jacob; come, defy me Israel!'
>
> It was a professional call, and Balaam came. Balak was glad to see him. He gave him presents; he showed him much honor; he took him up to a high place where he might see the host of Israel en-

camped on the plain below, and he waited impatiently for the soothsayer to speak.

And Balaam spoke the words which the Lord put into his mouth; but Balak looked at him aghast, and said: 'What is this? I called thee to curse mine enemies, and lo! thou hast blessed them altogether!'

This biblical allusion makes an excellent peroration, but that is not where the matter rests for us. We must go on further in our search. As psychologists, have we not a right to ask whether or not the gap between Newton and Einstein bespeaks the gulf between the gentile and the Jew? Our search may be fruitless, but the question nevertheless suggests itself. Newton's mind could not conceive a space that was not absolute. Einstein was ready to deny even to time an absolute character, so that when Lorentz suggested that the only way to reconcile the negative results of the Michelson-Morley experiment was to posit an artificial time side by side with a real time, Einstein was quick to perceive that *both times were real but relative to the observer*. Both he and Minkowski gave the most emphatic expression to the principle that space and time together go to make up a single continuum.

What, then, characterizes Einstein's type of thought? We know it was a bold step to take in the first place. While others were seeking to explain the experimental results with as little damage as possible to the existing conception of physics, Einstein dared to change the whole point of view, and on the basis of his speculation, built up a new system. It was no less an illustrious mathematician than the late Henri Poincaré who spoke enthusiastically about the originality of Einstein's mind and the thoroughgoingness with which he followed his trend of thought to its ultimate conclusion.

I do not wish to claim that none but a Jew could have formulated the principle of relativity in its definite form. That were perilously near committing the fallacy of *post hoc ergo propter hoc,* or in a broader view, it would simply be a case of faulty generalization. But it is, I think, justifiable to hold that Einstein, being a Jew, might have found it easier to cut himself loose from the absolutistic moorings of physical concepts than his Gentile colleagues.

The Jewish mind, it would seem from a survey of Jewish thought, is less susceptible to dogma, to rigid conventional discipline than, let us say, was the Greek mind. The latter always aimed at definition; and what is definition but setting a limit to a concept, laying down laws? In Jewish philosophy, from Philo to Spinoza, we find the dictum, *Omnis determinatio est negatio*—"Every determination is a negation," playing a prominent part. The Jews were not scholastic in the real sense of the term. Some of the mediaeval Jewish philosophers were, of course, influenced in their method by their non-Jewish contemporaries, but where in Maimonides, Ibn-Gabirol, Crescas and Gersonides do we find the absolutistic method pursued by St. Thomas Aquinas, the prince of Roman Catholic philosophers?

The Jews, possibly because of their constitutional make-up, steered clear of the Scylla of absolutism and the Charybdis of nihilism (Gorgias in Greece and the Hindus in general). Even the most pessimistic of Jewish thinkers, Ecclesiastes, is, as the Semitic scholar, Morris Jastrow, called him, a "gentle cynic," probably comparable in this respect with the great half-Jew, Montaigne. Out of such soil, relativity can very well be expected as a product.

It is my belief that a theory, principle, or even law, *must be in us first before we can discover it in nature.* Millions of people may have the same facts before them without seeing the unity to which they point. Is it not possible, then, that certain cultural groups are prone to make certain discoveries rather than others? Evolution as a theory may have been cultivated by German and French biologists and naturalists, but it was through Englishmen (Darwin, Wallace, Spencer, Huxley) that the evidence reached its crystallized form.

Similarly, the principle of conservation of energy was rather a German discovery (Robert Mayer), although in England and in France, scientists worked along these lines.

We are all trained to see and interpret natural phenomena in much the same way, but there is always a *personal equation*; and it is my contention that the personal equation contains an unknown *national* quantity, which sets the world athinking.

In the development of the relativity theory, it is perhaps significant that the Jewish stamp is found at almost every turn. Were Einstein, alone of all Jewry, responsible for the vast physical transformation, the connection between relativity and the Jews could be regarded as wholly fortuitous, but where the names of Michelson, Levi-Civita, Minkowski, Born, Schwarzschild,[17] and Silberstein are all associated, in a more or less intimate way, with Einstein's achievement, one begins to feel that the "Elders of Zion" have unwittingly conspired to explain the world's most baffling phenomena, and apparently have met with success.

On the eve of 1950, the world's press reported a pronouncement which, coming from Albert Einstein, in his 71st year, has interested the many millions of people who even have no notion of relativity. Einstein's new "generalized theory of gravitation", as he calls it, is an overall conception that would dovetail the relativity theory and the quantum theory, which hitherto led a sort of independent existence, even though both have been accepted by physicists the world over. To verify this theory experimentally will be far more difficult than was the proof of the relativity theory by astronomers, nearly forty years ago, but it is more than likely that the four equations which constitute the core of Einstein's new world-view, an expansion of his earlier one, will lead to something epoch-making, just as his transformation equation has figured in nuclear fission and its either beatific or catastrophic sequels, as history in the shape of political leaders' motives will decide.

V

THE ATOM AND RELEASE OF ENERGY

If the principle of relativity has developed into a cosmic drama, then its dénouement became fraught with something of a terrible nature, although it also contains, aside from adding to the store of knowledge and wisdom, potentially the greatest blessing for mankind. We thus are reminded of the Biblical injunction "And I have given you both life and death; and ye shall choose life."

The most remarkable thing about this possible universal boon or global calamity is that the tiniest thing imaginable could be the source of such a tragedy. Common sense would regard as absurd beyond words a view that a particle of matter invisible even through the most powerful microscope could wreak such destruction; and that such force could inhere in an intangible, imponderable, and invisible particle is a theoretical marvel. What would Democritus and Leucippus have said if told that their atom would, two thousand years hence, be in a position of filling a whole world with dread anxiety, and the scientists who explored it, even with anguish, if not bitter remorse?

We are, however, in this quasi-prologue anticipating too much. The experimental study of the atom began quietly enough in the English laboratories, although excitement grew as the phenomena showed up perplexities, and then pointed to solutions which, in their turn, brought forth new problems.

How far back might we go to examine the history of the atom as fashioned by apparatus and the inception of the new sub-science of electronics? Shall we start with William Crookes whose experiment with electricity passing through a vacuum gave us the first hint of the later spectra, which he called the cathode? Or should we accord the first honor to the great

Cambridge physicist J. J. Thomson, who actually discovered the electron, which meant that the atom must have dropped it. The atom indivisible really consisted of much more minute particles, but the nucleus was still a perfect mystery.

It was, however, an Australian, who taught at McGill (my alma mater) in Montreal, and eventually settling in England —Ernest Rutherford—who succeeded, not without the help of a colleague's device in another connection, in making the greatest metamorphosis in nature—something that went farther than the dream of the mediaeval alchemist to transmute ordinary metals into gold, viz., breaking up the nucleus of an atom, something which was by its very nature, as the name implied, supposed to be indivisible.

In 1919, Rutherford made it plain that not only can the atom change its constitution, which was indeed happening often, even accidentally, but that the very core of the atom could be smashed. Rutherford, too, was the first to give us an insight into the nucleus of the atom; and within the last two decades or so, nuclear physics i. e., the department of physics which deals with the tiny nucleus of that invisible atom has become the most important study, it would seem, in all science, and something upon which rests the fate of the world.[18] A lay person who for the first time hears the name "nuclear physics" is prone to associate it with vast areas, whereas in reality so far as space goes, it deals with a millionth of a pinpoint, really next to nothing. Such is the great lesson which present-day results have brought to the world. Adapting a New Testament dictum, one might say in this regard, "For the great will become tiny and the tiny will become great." The atom, with its nucleus and electrons, neutrons and protons, positrons and deuterons has become a sun for us. The atom now has the status of a large world populated with billions of particles of several different kinds.

In the interim, between Rutherford's exposition of the atomic nucleus, through a model he devised, and the next big advance, activity in the many laboratories throughout Europe

[257]

and America was not lagging, and one discovery would lead to another, would become another brick in the great edifice of science, even if *via* such an infinitesimal what-not as an atom, or even its nucleus. But it was Niels Bohr's publication, in 1913, of an article explaining the structure of the atom which soon disclosed a new luminary in physics. Bohr is now considered the foremost authority on the atom, and it was in his laboratory at Copenhagen where most of the work had been done that eventuated in the perfecting of the atom bomb in the United States. Several of the most important nuclear physicists took their apprenticeship in the Bohr laboratory, and his presence in the United States during the War on special invitation would go to show his prowess in this particular branch of physics.

Niels Bohr was born in Copenhagen, Denmark in 1885, the son of a Christian father (named also Christian) and a Jewish mother (Ellen Adler). When only 35, he became Director of the Institute for Theoretical Physics at the University of Copenhagen. Later he lectured in many foreign universities, principally in England. In 1922, he was awarded the Nobel Prize for his pioneer work on the atom in relation to the release of energy. It was well that he succeeded in escaping from Nazi-occupied Denmark in a small boat in 1943; for had the Nazis laid hands on him, the atom bomb might have been *their* weapon.

> It often happens that a scientific hypothesis seems completely absurd and yet leads to significant conclusions. Such was the case with Bohr's assumptions regarding electronic orbits. He assumed that an electron might move around in an orbit of fixed size for a considerable time without radiating energy or falling in toward the nucleus. Luckily he did not have to explain this departure from current belief, but merely wondered what would happen if such were the case.[19]

It is characteristic of Bohr, as it was of his peer, Einstein, that he was not afraid to frame theories of a radical nature, theories which were soon to be validated, and indeed it was Einstein's photoelectric equation, formulated in 1905, but not verified until Millikan, in 1916, by actually making use of it, made exact measurements of Planck's elementary quantum of energy, which assisted Bohr in his inferences and experiments. While theoretical physics has often been belittled and, in Germany, the Nazis would refer to it as *Judenphysik*, in contrast to experimental physics, it is remarkable how the intuitions of such men as Einstein, Bohr, and others transcended the received conclusions based on the then researches. Einstein, in particular, turned out to be a sort of prophet-scientist, whose deductions and computations unerringly forecasted results obtained after years of laborious experimentation. Actually the first adumbration of the atomic bomb is to be found in Einstein's special theory of relativity.

If Enrico Fermi, who had to make a speedy exit from Italy, not so much because of his own Semitic antecedents as for the reason that his wife is of Jewish origin, made urgent representations when in this country to survey the military exploitation of the atomic nucleus, it was because of what he had seen going on at the Bohr laboratory; and the reason for the feverish activity in Copenhagen was the arrival there of Lise Meitner and her nephew, O. R. Frisch. Dr. Meitner was working in the Kaiser Wilhelm Institute in Berlin, together with O. Hahn and Strassmann on the neutron bombardment of the uranium atom, which, when broken up, disclosed some mysterious barium.

At this moment, the Gestapo stuck its long nose into the work, having itself discovered that Dr. Meitner was a racially diluted person. Suddenly cut loose from all that was near and dear to her, she found herself on a train Copenhagen-bound. The mystery of the barium persisted in her tortured mind, and to ease her mental pain, she wove a masterful piece of mathematics around the experiment. She already knew the exact amount of energy released by the few uranium atoms that *did* explode and she wanted a mathematical justification for the result. . . .

Dr. Meitner's pencil flew through abstruse mathematical formulae. Yes, the energy that would be released by such disunion, or splitting, was the exact equivalent of that measured by the uranium explosion in Berlin, when barium was discovered in the bombardment chamber.[20]

In the Smyth Report on the Development of Methods of Using Atomic Energy for Military Purposes, which the United States Government issued, there is the following significant paragraph "The announcement of the hypothesis of fission and its experimental confirmation took place in January 1939. . . . There was immediate interest in the possible military use of the large amounts of energy released in fission. At that time American-born nuclear physicists were so unaccustomed to the idea of using their science for military purposes that they hardly realized what needed to be done. Consequently the early efforts both at restricting publication and at getting government support were stimulated largely by a small group of foreign-born physicists centering on L. Szilard and including E. Wigner, E. Teller, V. F. Weisskopf and E. Fermi."[21]

It was G. Breit who proposed the formation of a censorship committee to control publication in all American publications, and it was he who served as the chairman of the subcommittee which dealt with uranium fission—the first of the many subcommittees that were to take up the gigantic task.

To what extent Jewish ingenuity and zeal shaped the atomic bomb, just after O. Hahn and F. Strassmann in Berlin discovered the isotope of barium on bombardment of uranium by neutrons, may be gathered from another passage in the same report.

THE JEW IN MODERN SCIENCE

On January 16, 1939, Niels Bohr of Copenhagen, Denmark, arrived in this country to spend several months in Princeton, N. J., and was particularly anxious to discuss some abstract problems with A. Einstein. (Four years later, Bohr was to escape from Nazi-occupied Denmark in a small boat.) Just before Bohr left Denmark two of his colleagues, O. R. Frisch and L. Meitner (both refugees from Germany), had told him their guess that the absorption of a neutron by a uranium nucleus sometimes caused that nucleus to split into approximately equal parts with the release of enormous quantities of energy, a process that soon began to be called nuclear 'fission'.[22]

Refugees they were all four, and what kind of refugees? Jews who were candidates for the Maidanek or Auschwitz crematories.

The conference between Fermi and the Navy Department which Pegram of Columbia University arranged was the first attempt made to contact the Government, but it was not until Einstein, in conference with Szilard and Wigner (all three Jews), sent a personal letter, through A. Sachs, a non-scientist, to the late President that the War Department began to take this matter seriously, although there apparently was not a great deal of faith evinced in the project. Meeting after meeting was held, committee after committee was organized, and only the fear that the Germans would appear on the scene first with their diabolical weapons led to the grants which enabled the carrying on of collective research and made possible the coördination of results which culminated in the construction of the Los Alamos Laboratory in New Mexico, with its seven distinct divisions. Among the heads here we find G. B. Kistiakowsky of the Explosive Division, R. F. Bacher of the Bomb Physics Division, while J. Robert Oppenheimer was the Director to whom all the chiefs were to report their findings. Niels Bohr, arriving from Denmark, served in the capacity of an adviser. According to the official War Department report "He is to be credited with achieving the implementation of atomic energy for military purposes." The man who was charged with the actual assembly core was R. F. Bacher, Professor of physics at Cornell. When the assembly of an important section was delayed because of the tight wedging of an insertion, Dr. Bacher assured the anxious group of scientists watching over each process that this would work itself out in minutes, and so it did. It was P. H. Abelson who submitted, in September of 1940, a 17-page memorandum on the possibility of separating the isotopes of uranium by thermal diffusion. The suggestion was accepted, and under Abelson's direction at the Naval Research Laboratory, work was begun on thermal diffusion.

It is not necessary to go into further details on the atom bomb. The awesome event in Los Alamos is now common knowledge to all who read the newspapers of that period. In the Laboratory there worked many young Jewish scientists in addition to those already mentioned, e. g., Frank Oppenheimer, brother of Robert, K. Cohen, M. Benedict Weinberg, and Finkelstein, while the British group arrived here during the winter of 1941-1942. "At that time the British were planning a diffusion separation plant themselves so that the discussion with F. Simon, R. Peierls and others were particularly valuable." (From the Smyth report). H. Halban had visited this country in 1942, to tell about his 165 liters of heavy water. It would appear that the three names mentioned are Jewish, but this is in the form of a conjecture.

It was principally K. Cohen, of Columbia, who had developed the theory for the single units and for the series of cascade units that would be necessary.

It is certainly not fortuitous that of the chief workers on the atom smashing, and particularly in the military applications, over a score were Jews, that Einstein was probably the first to recognize the tremendous import of the release of energy, and that his simple equation in connection with the Planck constant, which was questioned by the majority of physicists until Millikan supplied the experimental evidence, was the first step toward the ushering in of a new era, that Bohr, Meitner, Frisch, Oppenheimer, Rabi, Goudsmit, Breit, Wigner, Cohen, and a dozen others engaged in this stupendous task were Jews. Robert Oppenheimer is chairman of the Atomic Energy Commission's Advisory Council, and at the same time Director of the Institute for Advanced Study, an institution, incidentally established with the funds of the late philanthropist, Louis Bamberger, and his sister Mrs. Fuld. It is at this Institute in Princeton that Albert Einstein found a haven, when he shook the German dust off his shoes.

Of the 26 sponsors of the *Bulletin of the Atomic Scientists* 11 are Jews, and these include four Nobel Prize laureates. One may, as is often done, refer to some as refugees or immigrants. The fact remains that they are Jews, whether immigrants or not. Nor does it mean that the Jewish physicists are bent on fashioning destructive implements. It must be borne in mind that the release of energy from the smashing of the atomic nucleus is not necessarily in itself lethal and need not serve a deleterious purpose. The forces may be harnessed in such a way as to bring about the greatest comforts at the least possible expense. Medicine, too, has already profited by the result of the scientists whom we call nuclear physicists.

It is true, however, that in 1941, when Hitler and his hordes were about to strangle Europe and America, there was nothing so imperious in the world as a weapon to stem their advance, particularly as the rockets which the Germans were working on, and the atom bomb too, were becoming real dangers. Had the Nazis not banished the Jewish scientists, then even if they were not engaged on the atom projects, it is very doubtful whether the United States could have forestalled the havoc created by the German scientists' diabolic inventions. Whether it was destiny or a quip of fate, or just the folly of madmen who planned their own destruction, it was thanks to the Jews that the antidote against the dreadful pest was found, even if the Nazis did not get the medicine after all. Its value, however, is unmitigated, and "forearmed is forewarned" just as much as "forewarned is forearmed", and *"foreatomed"* is the best security in a topsy-turvy world, at least until an iron-clad pact is possible.

Dramatis Personae *of the atom performance*

Before this section is concluded, it would be in order to become acquainted, so to speak, with the Jewish heroes of the atomic drama, which, for the first time has convinced the war chiefs that science can accomplish in a minute what all the combined forces cannot achieve in years—a drama which has no parallel in all history.

The following names are mostly of those scientists who have played an important role in the preparation of the material and the devising of the processes, but some of the Jewish sponsors and members of the Advisory Council on Atomic Energy have already been referred to in other connections. Only a few lines have to suffice for each of the men, although pages have been devoted in some of the national publications to several of them.

The order of the names is not significant, nor is there any attempt made to evaluate the work of each. Their status as professors in the best American universities, their awards, including the Nobel Prize, should be sufficient for us to perceive their merit, whether we have ever had a course in physics or not.

Isidore Isaac Rabi, who was one of the youngest Nobel Prize laureates (1944) at the age of 46, is head of the Department of Physics at Columbia University, and Chairman of the National Research Council. A member and fellow of many learned societies and recipient of numerous awards, he has devoted most of his time to the study of the spin and electrical, as well as magnetic, properties of the atom. The director of one of the most important laboratories at Harvard told me that Rabi's achievement is so complicated, so ramified, that even in his seminars with advanced students, he finds it difficult to give an adequate exposition of it.

Samuel Abraham Goudsmit (1902-   ) now at the Brookhaven National Laboratory (a Gompers on his mother's side) received his intensive training at Leyden, Holland, and arrived in this country in 1927, joining the Faculty of the University of Michigan. In 1941, he was visiting professor at Harvard. In 1944-1945 he was chief of the Scientific Intelligence Mission to Europe, receiving the Medal of Freedom in recognition of his services. Together with G. E. Uhlenbeck, he discovered the so-called "spin" of the electron in 1925. His collaborations on the structure of line spectra and on atomic energy states were fundamental in building up the practical possibilities of the atom.

Edward Teller, of the University of Chicago, born in Hungary, and trained in the best laboratories in Germany, leaving soon after the Nazis got into the saddle during the second World War, has been engaged in nuclear physics research, and took part in the collective experimentation on the atom bomb.

Another Hungarian-born physicist who had a part in the fission super-drama and the consequent release of energy, culminating in the preparation of the atom bomb, was Eugene Paul Wigner, whose mother was Elizabeth Einhorn. Coming to the United States in 1930, he taught mathematical physics at various universities, and though theoretical rather than experimental physics has been his domain, he was among the first to confer with Albert Einstein on the momentous question of using the information at hand for military purposes.

Still another Hungarian Jewish physicist who has been of the greatest service at the time when the civilized world was fighting for a chance to live is Leo Szilard. Together with Enrico Fermi, Bohr's brilliant student, he devised the chain reaction system composed of uranium and graphite without which the atom bomb could not have been effective. Gaining his specialized experience in Berlin, London, and Oxford, he is now Professor at the University of Chicago.

The organization of the uranium fission project was practically in the hands of Gregory Breit, who was born in Russia in 1899, and after studying at Harvard and Leyden, he specialized in terrestrial magnetism. During the War, he acted as either chairman, adviser, or coördinator of various committees connected with the development of atomic energy. His name is mentioned frequently in the Smyth report.

Julian S. Schwinger, one of the youngest of the atom scientists, who took his doctorate at Columbia and, scarcely 30, is full professor of physics at Harvard University, has made the scattering of neutrons his chief study.

Victor F. Weisskopf, who is professor at the Massachusetts Institute of Technology, had received his doctorate at Goettingen, and soon began to engage in investigations along the line of spectroscopy, radiation, and nuclear physics.

Another Professor at the same institute, probably the greatest of its kind in the world, Jerrold Reinach Zacharias, is on the Board of Sponsors of the Atomic Scientists. His researches on molecular rays happen to tie up closely with the development of the most formidable weapon known to man.

A Laboratory Hero and Martyr

Nor was the work on the atom without its martyrs. We do not know how many of the nuclear scientists will have in subsequent years shown the effects of their proximity to the dangerous material in the laboratory, but the death of Dr. Louis Slotin, of Winnipeg, Canada, is decidedly and directly the result of a heroic attempt made to save the lives of seven or more scientists engaged in preparing the piles for the chain reaction, in the Los Alamos Laboratory, which in this case was precipitated violently. Let us quote from *Time* part of the story: "Perhaps Dr. Slotin was watching the warning instruments more carefully than his fellows; perhaps he saw the bluish glow. At any rate, he realized that the chain reaction had spurted to high intensity. The room was being swept with deadly radiation. He leaped forward, put his body between his colleagues and the radiating mass, scattered its materials. The chain reaction halted immediately.

"Then Dr. Slotin was taken to the hospital where, nine days later, he died of the peculiar and imperfectly understood burns produced by radiation. Seven co-workers, less seriously injured, hoped to recover."

The letter to his parents from Major General Groves, praising Dr. Slotin's "Keen mind, technical skill, and heroic action" and telling of the high esteem and admiration he was held in by all of his colleagues and associates is an adequate characterization. Furthermore The Newspaper Guild of New York dedicated a Page One Award to "the memory of the late Dr. Louis Slotin, who willingly laid down his life to save fellow workers from certain death during experiments at the Los Alamos atomic research project.

"Louis Slotin knew that he had only about a week to live but decided to make the best possible use of this short time. He called his secretary and began dictating, handing over to humanity the heritage of his short but fruitful life.

"More and more he felt the approach of death and the gradual weakening of his body. His hands which were most directly exposed to the influence of the dreadful rays had to be packed in ice to soothe the terrible pain. His hair turned brittle. But relentlessly he continued to dictate. His body finally gave way to the impact of the force which his brain had helped to create.

"His parents who spent the last few days of his life at his bedside reported that even in the dreams of his agony he was thinking of his duty only. 'Why couldn't I finish my work?' was the cry that he repeated again and again between the moans of his last few painful hours. Until his death he kept his wartime activities secret from his parents.

"In honor of the late scientist, his friends and fellow workers in the Los Alamos laboratory, established a memorial fund to care for two refugee children in special rest centres under the Foster Parents Plan."[23]

I understand that the top nuclear physicist in Russia is Capittsa, who on a visit to the USSR after he had made his residence in England was not permitted to leave. His name occurs frequently as the hydrogen bomb is looming larger and larger in our turbulent discussions.

Custodians of Atomic Energy

If J. Robert Oppenheimer is Chairman of the Advisory Council of the Atomic Energy Commission, then another Jew, David Lilienthal is practically the custodian, the man who is responsible to the Government for the scientists. His appointment and the incidents revolving around it, the opposition by reactionary senators, have constituted an interesting episode in American history, disclosing the parallelogram of forces in American political life. To the credit of the United States, it must be said that all the red herrings brought in by the prejudiced and narrow-minded gentlemen, even to the extent of wishing to make capital out of the fact that Lilienthal's parents were born in Czechoslovakia, which *today* is a satellite of the USSR, although at the time of their birth it was under the heels of Austria—all this puerile sophistry was of no avail, and Lilienthal, in an inspired apologia, which was really the vigorous expression of an American credo worthy of Jefferson or Lincoln, carried the day and his appointment as Chairman of the Atomic Energy Commission was a triumph for the principle of democracy.

Later, in consequence of the spying cases which came before the courts, another attempt was made to force the resignation of Lilienthal, or his dismissal. Promises and threats were made by politicians who had some power in the Investigating Committee. It transpired that a fraction of an ounce of uranium was not accounted for, and that a student with Communist leanings had been awarded a fellowship in nuclear physics. Lilienthal, in spite of his more difficult position under the circumstances, managed to pull through. When toward the end of 1949, he ultimately resigned his post, President Truman prevailed upon him to stay in office until February 1950, because, as it transpired, there is no one in the United States who could replace this extraordinarily efficient and conscientious public servant especially at a time when the hydrogen bomb is under way.[24]

If Lilienthal may be called the custodian of atomic energy in the United States, then Bernard Baruch, the "elder statesman" as he has been admiringly known in government circles for decades, may be considered to be the chief executive, in this connection, in dealing with the world at large, for he represents the United States in the United Nations Commission; and his policy has heretofore been the deciding factor as to what extent the information should be released or kept a secret.

Thus we have in Lilienthal and Baruch the controls of atomic energy; and that is perhaps as it should be; for their judiciousness, efficiency, and experience have long been established by enlightened public opinion and more than one President of the United States. The responsibility with which they are invested is perhaps greater than has devolved upon the shoulders of anyone else since the War, but it is possibly another symbol of destiny that atomic energy, the most salutary and at the same time the most dangerous instrument known, the *very core of nature,* should be, in large part, the handiwork of Jews and also in charge of Jewish guardians; for we cannot imagine any ethnic group which would approach the colossal problems—virtually the question of being or not being, not in relation to a single individual, but as it affects *mankind as a whole*—with the prophetic vision peculiar to this ethnic group.

The man who evinced most concern about the outcome, as we know from his fervent appeals in national monthlies and the press, was no other than Albert Einstein himself, who had more to do with evolving the weapon than anyone else; and if there is a concerted effort made by the atomic scientists to take the control out of the hands of the military authorities, and set up an international policy banning the use of such an infernal weapon especially in its infernal hydrogen shape, we may be certain that the Jewish members of the group have exerted considerable influence in this direction. Both Oppenheimer and Rabi have discussed the seriousness of the situation in a frank tone.

One of the number, Norbert Wiener, whose field is mathematics, has even gone so far as to state in print that he would not lend his assistance to bolster up the war machine. Had German scientists abided by such a principle, there might not have broken out even the First World War, and certainly the murderous experiments on innocent victims would not have been carried out. Certainly the Maidanek and Auschwitz gigantic furnaces would not have smoked from the burning of human flesh, after the scientific asphyxiation of human beings, whose only crime was to have been born in a Jewish family.

In fine, the closing reflection is that there is a line of continuity from Isaiah to Einstein, and that the ominous atom, with its global catastrophe in store, can be turned to benign uses, if justice and righteousness be our guide. This prophetic strain appears to inhere in most of the Jewish scientists engaged in eliciting the secrets out of nature. Scientists under the aegis of Nazidom would experience no compunction in making out of the world a shambles, so long as their own party or group or *Herrenvolk* survives and rules with superbrute force.

VI

THE JEW IN CHEMISTRY

Chemistry is a comparatively young science, not even two hundred years old, and it is only within the last 125 years that the remarkable discoveries began in the rather primitive laboratories in France, Germany, England and Italy. Since then, largely because of its practical and industrial possibilities, it has advanced by leaps and bounds.

Prior to about 1850, we do not find Jews prominent in this branch of science, although occasionally a Jewish convert, like N. W. Fischer, born in 1782, manages to become a professor in a German university (Breslau). Fischer was one of the first experimenters to have established the laws of sublimation and vapor-tension.

The first Jew who distinguished himself in chemistry, to the point of winning the Nobel Prize was Adolph von Baeyer (1835-1917). True, only his mother was Jewish, scion of the wealthy and cultured Itzig (Hitzig) family, but the cross-inheritance theory (son after mother and daughter after father) would allow us to include him in our survey without the decided reserve shown in the Heinrich Hertz case. Von Baeyer was one of the pioneers of organic chemistry having discovered eosin, a boon in medicine, and many aniline dyes, including artificial indigo. His seminars and laboratory in Munich became a sort of Mecca for ambitious students throughout Germany, and even other countries.

About the same time, industrial chemistry received its great impetus, and largely through Jews. Adolf Frank (1834-1916) made a careful study of the nature of potash, and established the potash industry in Germany through his own large factory. The manufacture of bromide, ammonia, and the chlorides owes much to him too.

[271]

The notorious I. G. Farben Company, which played such a sorry part in Hitler's day, would never have been so powerful were it not for the efforts of Jews like Heinrich Caro (1834-1910) who practically started the dye industry in Germany, and much later Richard Willstätter (1872-1943), Nobel Prize winner, who, for all his extraordinary labors on behalf of his country in raising the German dye industry to an enviable position, for all his invaluable discoveries in the field of biochemistry, resigned his post at the University of Munich in protest against the Nazi dismissals of Jewish professors. Prior to that, when told that he would be retained because of his unusual services, his characteristic reply was "Of genius there is no dearth; but character is a rare article", and he clung to his decision.

Another Nobel Prize laureate who came to grief during the same dreadful period in history was Fritz Haber, the very man who, by ingeniously deriving the very much needed ammonia from the nitrogen in the atmosphere and hydrogen, made it possible for Germany to carry on during the first World War. Haber, a convert to Christianity, was only a lieutenant, although famous already as a chemist, and when he wished to make his discovery known to the desperate German general staff, in 1917, the problem presented itself how that Jewish bedraggled lieutenant could enter the presence of the august high command without contaminating it. During the early part of the Hitler regime, Haber, who had also made some studies on poisonous gases, which the Germans were about to use, went into voluntary exile, and died of a broken heart. It took the courage and high standing of Max Planck, who was the venerable head of the Prussian Academy of Science, to pronounce the eulogy on a mental giant who abandoned his own people, working for the Germans, with all his might and zeal, only to be cast aside as so much refuse.

Victor Meyer (1848-1897) at the age of 19 became Bunsen's assistant, and at 23 became Professor at the Stuttgart

Polytechnicum. After advancing to other institutions, he settled at Heidelberg as the successor of his famous master, Bunsen. In 1897, in a fit of despondency, he died by his own hand. Meyer was one of the pillars of organic chemistry. His investigations of vapor densities, which were carried out by means of an apparatus he himself invented, his extension of our knowledge in regard to iodine; more especially, his establishment of the new field, stereochemistry, were all of vast importance in the young science. Indeed his work was so fruitful whether he dealt with derivatives of benzene, or the principle of isomerism, or the aromatic maines, or the constitution of camphor, that he was a sort of Midas, whose very touch turned out derivatives and substitutes. His imagination and intuition were such as were found in scientists of the highest order. His discovery of theophene compound in impure benzene belonged to such original flashes, and had he lived his natural years, he doubtless would have joined the illustrious array of Jewish Nobel Prize men.

Matthias E. O. Liebreich (1839-1908) Director of the Pharmacological Institute in Berlin, served as a seaman before taking up the study of chemistry, and eventually medicine, rising to the privy councillorship in medicine, which, in Germany, meant a great deal. His discoveries ranged from anaesthetic drugs to lanolin, a paste from sheep's wool, and the mercury treatment of syphilis. His contributions to chemical therapy were immense. Medicine is obligated to him for the phaneroscopic method in treating lupus, the effect of cantharides on pathological capillaries and many other studies. Between 1895 and 1900, he published three volumes of an encyclopedia of therapy, and his book on boracic acid (1903) is still regarded as valuable. Among the many researches he had tackled successfully are the use of strychnine as an antidote to chloral hydrate cresol, formaldehyde and methyl violet. Furthermore, he established the presence of protagon in the brain. He was also the first to differentiate between neurin and cholin.

It is interesting to note that the Jews made such rapid strides in chemistry that C. Liebermann (1842-1914), who was professor at the Berlin Technical Institute, served, for a time, as President of the German Chemical Society. He was best known for his investigations of naphthalene alkaloids and the synthesis of alizarin from anthracene.

Of the various fields of chemistry, organic, inorganic, analytical, industrial, and physiological chemistry, there is no doubt that the Jews have contributed most to organic and industrial chemistry, with biochemistry a close third. At the present time, biochemistry is taking the lead.

We have seen that Victor Meyer was one of the founders of organic chemistry, but another Meyer, Lothar, was a bold explorer in the field of biochemistry. According to P. Blackman, himself a chemist, "Lothar Meyer was one of the originators and founders of biological chemistry, and by his wonderful investigations and marvellous presentation of the results on the absorption by defibrinated blood of oxygen, nitrogen, and carbon dioxide, and of the action of carbon monoxide on blood, together with other work in biochemistry, was the first to place the chemistry of the gases of the blood upon a firm and sound experimental basis; and not only did he carry out a vast amount of work independently, but he also advised, directed and collaborated with others in kindred researches, all of which produced results of the utmost value and importance in this branch of chemistry."[25]

It is surprising that the Meyers and Mayers, not a common Jewish surname, had at least a dozen representatives in chemistry, not to mention the philosopher, Emile Meyerson, who was an industrial chemist before devoting himself to philosophy. R. J. Meyer specialized in inorganic chemistry, at the University of Berlin, while K. F. Meyer, a biochemist, who has significantly added to our knowledge about anaerobic bacteria, is another distingushed namesake.

Eduard Lippmann (1842-1919) an organic chemist of distinction, occupied the chair of chemistry at the University of Vienna, and the preparation of quinine homologues is associated with his name.

As regards physical chemistry, James Franck, the Nobel Prize man, who has been mentioned in the section on physics, O. W. Sackur one of the former deans at the Dahlem Kaiser Wilhelm Institute (Berlin University), Kazimir Fajans (1887-) sometime head of the Physio-Chemical Institute at Munich, whose discovery of the element brevium has been hailed at the time, F. Paneth noted for his work on radio-activity, Alfred Byk, who was professor of physical chemistry in Berlin, and Lassar Cohn (1858-1922) who was professor at the University of Koenigsberg, and a popular writer (*Chemistry in Everyday Life*) as well as a researcher—are sufficient proof that this phase has not been neglected.

It would be possible to compile a book about the contributions of Jewish chemists in Germany alone, but only a few of the shining lights can be presented in the space at our disposal; and certainly one of these is Otto Wallach (1847-1931) a former Director of the Clinical Institute at Goettingen and Nobel Prize laureate, in 1910, for his work on alicyclic compounds, which was an innovation in organic chemistry. He, too, advanced the dye industry in Germany by dint of his aniline investigations.

The recent development of colloid chemistry, which is a phase of organic chemistry, is due, in a large measure to Jews like Jacques Loeb, who later, as we shall see in another section, became a towering physiologist, and Herbert Freundlich, who, partly Jewish, was compelled to leave the German laboratory for an English one.

Perhaps even more than in mathematics and physics, chemistry has been lagging behind in France; so that the French Jews, too, favored the humanistic and the social sciences, and yet the half-Jew, Henri Moissan (1852-1907) who was awarded the Nobel Prize, in 1906, for his great contributions to mineral chemistry was one of the leading figures at the Sorbonne. His artificial reproduction of diamonds and other minerals caused a sensation. He also devised processes which made the manufacture of acetylene simple and thus inexpensive.

England, while not equal to Germany in the sciences, could at least offer some competition in industrial chemistry; and again the Jews have come forward to strengthen, nay to build up, this branch.

One of the most esteemed chemists of his time, in England, was the cultured Raphael Meldola (1840-1915) scion of a distinguished Portuguese Jewish family, who was President of the British Chemical Society, a naturalist too, and on intimate terms with Charles Darwin. Meldola's sphere of activity was chiefly photochemistry and the dye industry, and coal-tar; and here he has a number of valuable compounds to his credit.

There were, of course, a few organic and physiological chemists, like Philip Hartog, I. M. Heilbron, who taught organic chemistry at the University of Liverpool, J. B. Cohen (1859-1935) Professor of organic chemistry at the University of Leeds and several others; but it was Ludwig Mond who founded the greatest chemical plant England had known. Discoverer of the Mond gas and nickel carbonyl, he was able, together with his son, Alfred, the later Lord Melchett, to set England on a high industrial footing. The reclamation of sulphur from alkalies (waste) is his achievement. Herbert Levinstein did something similar on a smaller scale for the dye industry in England, while Julius Lewkowitsch was the leading stereochemist in England, and director of the London Research Institute, in which capacity he was the most sought authority on oils and fats; but we cannot afford to overlook the indebtedness of England to Chaim Weizmann, who, prior to his election as President of the new State of Israel, was regarded as one of the most eminent chemists in the British Empire, and one of great service to the army and navy in both of the World Wars.

His discovery of various derivatives, his research on fluorescence, on the glycerides of amino-acids, his work on butylalcohol, which was put to use in the preparation of synthetic rubber, his more recent work on plastics, are all evidence of his highly ingenious brain; and when we take into consideration the fact that unlike most academic men, his mind was weighed down with the knotty problems of Zionism, that he was a statesman during all the years that these researches were carried on, that his continual travels on behalf of the cause had not only consumed much of his time but naturally must have interfered with his concentration and lastly that his eyesight was seriously impaired for years, we can only give him all the more credit for his achievements.

As to Russia, even during the Czarist rule, a few Jews succeeded, after conversion, in obtaining university posts in chemistry, but their number now both in educational institutions and government service is tenfold, although there are now fewer Jews in that country. It is difficult, as is well-known, to obtain statistical information of such a character, especially as many Jewish scientists bear Slavic names, and to all intents and purposes are Russian, change of faith being unnecessary. Among the leading chemists known to be Jews are Michael Altshul and Michael Goldstein of the past generation while Aron Frumkin belongs to our own time. In Warsaw, under Russian domination Jakob Natanson held the post of professor at the local university.

Among the noted Italian chemists are I. Giulio Ascoli at the Milan Technical Institute, G. Errera of Messina and Padua Universities, B. N. Pincherle of the Polytechnic Institute at Milan, and F. Jarach, who was President of the Italian Metallurgical Association.

We finally come to the United States which now harbors the greatest contingent of Jewish chemists. Many of them, of course, are research workers or teachers who have thus far not made a dent in the world, but of the score or more who have made international reputations, the following may be

singled out—C. L. Alsberg, a biochemist, for many years
Dean of the Graduate School at Leland Stanford University,
E. J. Cohn, one of the most distinguished biochemists in the
country, chairman of the Division of the Medical Sciences at
Harvard Medical School, Moses Gomberg, a former President of the American Chemical Society, Michael Heidelberger
of Columbia University, J. S. Jaffe, an expert on soils and
agricultural chemistry, M. E. Jaffa, an authority on the chemistry of foods, W. A. Jacobs of the Rockefeller Institute, a
top-ranking chemotherapist, David Klein formerly a professor
at Johns Hopkins, P. A. T. Levene, of the Rockefeller Institute, a biochemist of a high order, Lafayette B. Mendel, one
of the leading professors at Yale, and recognized throughout
the world for his work in nutrition; G. W. Raiziss, Professor
of chemotherapy at the Graduate School of Medicine, University of Pennsylvania, M. A. Rosanoff and A. Silverman, both
of the University of Pittsburgh; J. O. Stieglitz, late head of
the Chemistry Department at the University of Chicago (whose
brother, Alfred Stieglitz was probably the foremost authority
on photography in America) and L. E. Wise, one of the few
specialists in forest chemistry. Nor is it generally known that
Gerty Cori, who shared the Nobel Prize in medicine, with
her distinguished husband, is herself Jewish (Radnitz was her
maiden name). Their researches in carbohydrate metabolism
and enzymes of animal tissue signallized a great advance in
biochemistry. Both husband and wife are professors of pharmacology and biochemistry at Washington University in St.
Louis.

One of the most important biochemists in recent years,
Leonor Michaelis (1875-1949), after apprenticeship under
the great Paul Ehrlich became first professor of medicine,
then professor of physical chemistry at the University of Berlin. In 1922, probably anticipating the Hitler Walpurgis night
in Germany, he left for Japan and in 1926, he received a call
to Johns Hopkins. Later, he became head of the physico-

chemical department at the Rockefeller Institute for Medical Research in New York.

His best known book is called *The Dynamics of Surfaces*, but he has a standard textbook on mathematics for biologists and chemists; he has written on ion concentration, and on colloids, and was instrumental in developing research methods and techniques in physical chemistry which yielded a scientific harvest. This was referred to by one of his students who, in 1950, received a special award (gold medal) for discoveries which, he maintained, had been initiated by his teacher, Michaelis.

The above select list could easily be extended without including mediocrities. It may be added that because of the Nazi *"Gleichschaltung"*, many Jewish chemists are now serving the United States, either as research workers or university teachers; and the Cohens and Cohns in *American Men of Science* seem to have a special predilection for chemistry.

The Nobel Prize laureate, Otto Heinrich Warburg, who is dealt with under the Natural sciences may surely come under the present rubric, for primarily he is a biochemist.

Thus we see that although comparatively little space has been devoted to the Jews in chemistry, it is not because they have not "patronized" the science, but on the contrary, there are so many of them engaged in it that the chapter would be just crowded with names, if one were to make an attempt to be comprehensive.

In PETROGRAPHY and MINERALOGY, we shall find among the foremost the names of Henri Moissan (referred to under chemistry) and Auguste Michel-Lévy who revolutionized the methods in studying the minerals microscopically and gave us a standard classification for all igneous rocks, emphasizing the importance of mineralizing agents in processes of differentiation. Another Lévy (Armand) was a professor of mineralogy in France more than a century ago.

In Germany one of the most outstanding mineralogists of the past century was undoubtedly Emil Wilhelm Cohen (1842-1905) who taught at Greifswald, Germany, and wrote several extensive reports of his expeditions. Perhaps of a greater calibre was Victor M. Goldschmidt (1888-1947) who was professor at Heidelberg up to 1935, when he was forced out by the Nazis, settling in Oslo, Norway, and afterwards escaping to England where he was of service to the British war effort. His greatest work was the three-volume atlas of crystal formations in minerals.

In the United States, the death of Harold Berman at the age of 42 in an airplane crash during his stay in England, on a war mission, removed one of the most promising men in the field; for at the time of the tragedy, he held the office of assistant curator of Harvard's Natural History Museum and was in line for promotion to the curatorship.

HISTORY OF SCIENCE

Even in this relatively new department, one can point to Jewish scholars as well as promoters who have added a new story to the great structure.

Charles Singer and E. J. Cohn have extended our knowledge of the medical sciences. The philosopher, Emile Meyerson, was one of the recognized authorities on the history of science in general. As anyone who only thumbs through his last work *Du Cheminement de la Pensée* (3 vols.) will observe, the man was conversant with a dozen different disciplines, in addition to chemistry.

Federigo Enriques was the co-founder and editor of *Scientia,* the international periodical which is still looked up to by scientists, while, in our own country, *The Philosophy of Science* was founded by Boris Malisoff (1895-1947) whose premature death left a gap in the promotion of the subject in this country. Another journal *The History of Ideas* was also founded and edited by Jews, but this belongs rather to the philosophical sphere.

VII

THE JEW IN THE NATURAL SCIENCES

We have seen that the contribution of the Jews to mathematics and physical science was immense, but could the same be anticipated in the field of the natural sciences? The Jews for many centuries had been deprived of a natural life, in two senses. They were driven to concentrate in cultural matters, as their ghetto became barer and bleaker and devoid of the beauties which are associated with gardens, parks, conservatories, and even meadows, for landed estates were not within their sphere of ownership, and agriculture was outside of their domain for many centuries. How then could they expect to become naturalists in any sense of the word?

And yet, the natural sciences have been substantially advanced through Jewish effort. Indeed, more than one branch owes so much to its Jewish cultivators, as we shall presently observe, that without them, it might have been impeded in its growth for lack of stimulation and ingenious grafting. Let us not look for a Jewish Darwin, Buffon, Cuvier or Lamarck. Their ancestors—if we may indulge in an Irish tale, understandable enough—were probably killed off by the Holy Inquisition, The Crusades or mobs during the Black Plague as well as by the legal murders pursuant to the blood and other libels. Aside from that, it was not until about the eighteenth century that solitary Jews were admitted to university study; and it was not until much later that even converted Jews, let alone such as practiced their faith, could utilize the facilities of research which were afforded the promising non-Jewish scientist, as a matter of course.

Through what secret channels did Jewish scientists come into their own despite the restrictions and bans will not be discussed here. Partly, of course, it was through the baptismal font, partly through sheer persistence and a singleness of purpose which stagger the imagination; but there was one trend

[281]

which had been kept alive throughout the Dark Ages, despite Christian prejudice, and thanks to this, the new vistas of natural science had opened up to the Jewish investigator who further broadened the horizon and disclosed possibilities not hitherto dreamt of. It was the long medical tradition of the Jews that wafted them into anatomy, physiology, biology, bacteriology, and even zoölogy and botany including agriculture; for the common denominator of all these is *life;* and it was the task of the physician to prolong life and save lives, hence the structure and the function of the bodily organs, as well as the study of the organisms which interfered with their well-being, were within his province, and the practical purpose of healing became the foundation of the new theoretical disciplines, which turned into experimental sciences furthering human and animal life.

What is to be encompassed in the natural sciences, and where are we to begin in our survey? A systematic account of Jewish achievement in all the fields which may be subsumed under the head of the natural sciences is out of the question. The space at our disposal already has been exceeded. Perhaps it will be necessary to confine ourselves to those sciences enumerated above. Certainly the medical sciences, although they are presumably forms of anatomy, physiology and bacteriology, will have to be eliminated in the hope that they are treated in the chapter on the Jew in medicine.

As to where to begin, it scarcely matters, since it all depends on the avenue of approach. We might begin with the soil, or the microbes, plants, or anatomy and physiology. Since it is the latter that will occupy our chief attention, we might as well start with it, especially as it is in direct line with the medical pursuit which the Jews have been associated with in every country and in every age. It will scarcely be possible, in many cases, to keep the fields apart, for not only do the sciences merge into one another, but Jewish investigators, as a rule, are versatile, and, like their race, wander from one field to another.

ANATOMY AND PHYSIOLOGY

That the great founder of modern anatomy, Andreas Vesalius (1514-1564) incorporated in his epoch-making works, *Tabulae Anatomicae Sex* (1538) and the *De Humanis Corpora Fabrica* a number of Hebrew terms will be a surprise to many readers. Vesalius himself could hardly be said to have even understood the most elementary Hebrew words, but Hebrew, in its mediaeval garb, was the vogue in medical centres then, and so Vesalius, the pioneer, was in fashion. Even Arabic terms would appear in Hebrew characters in those days. C. Rabin tells us, in his learned disquisition, that "the Jewish adviser to Vesalius did not use the printed Hebrew Avicenna but borrowed from the medical jargon of Italian Jewish doctors",[25a] so far as the *Tabulae* was concerned, but the Hebrew Avicenna version was utilized for the more important *Fabrica* (1543).

It is curious that in the *Tabulae,* one may find Hebraized forms of Latin and Italian terms, and sometimes the Latinized terms would pass through the Hebrew on their way from Arabic.

Perhaps the first of important Jewish names in the medical sciences is that of G. Jacob Henle (1809-1885) who taught in several German universities, but principally at Goettingen. He was a research man, as well as a systematizer, a rare combination in science, and his range was phenomenal. As an anatomist, he was probably without an equal toward the middle of the nineteenth century. Our knowledge about the optic nerve, the cornea, the blood vessels, the intestinal cells, and the kidneys has been advanced considerably through his investigations, and the U shaped loop in kidney (vesicular canal) is called the Henle loop. Through his *Zeitschrift für rationelle Medicin,* one of the most important medical journals in the world, he promoted the cause of anatomy, physiology, and pathology perhaps as much as his illustrious contemporaries, Wunderlich, Virchow, and his own great teacher, Johannes Müller, with whom he collaborated in the volume on plagiostomi (sharks and rays). His handbooks or atlases on pathology and anatomy were standard works for decades, and his lectures on anthropology were in reality devoted to what would now be considered the psychology of personality. In William James's psychological textbooks many a diagram bears the acknowledgment to Henle.

Benedict Stilling (1810-1879) although primarily famous for his technique in surgery, having been the first to operate on the ovary without abdominal incision, and a pioneer in urethral surgery, was an eminent authority on the nervous system, particularly the spinal cord, to the knowledge of which he has added a great deal. As an extraordinarily skillful surgeon he would be in great demand throughout Germany and even France, yet he has taken the time to turn out solid works of an experimental nature.

There are several other anatomists of renown who might be referred to such as Pio Foà in Italy (1848-1923) but they were largely pathologists, and thus should be treated under the rubric of medical sciences.

That physiology should be among the sciences to have brought out the eminence of the Jews soon after their emancipation was to have been expected; for physiology is closely related to medicine; and it is in medicine that the Jews have distinguished themselves for many centuries, even during the Dark Ages. It is in Germany that their endowments seem to have realized themselves on a systematic scale, even though their ambitions did not have the same chance in that country, unless they approached the baptismal font. Scores of them raised the prestige of German science, but often they had to go to Switzerland or other countries to earn their livelihood as university teachers.

This was the fate of Gabriel Gustav Valentin, born in Breslau in 1810, who had received the award for experimental physiology offered by the Academy of Science in Paris, as a result of his Latin essay on the history of the evolution of the muscular system. The great Alexander von Humboldt interceded so that he might receive a call in Germany, but to no avail. The 26-year-old scientist accepted a professorship at the University of Berne, in Switzerland, and it was only much later that he found his place in Bonn, where he died in 1883.

Exclusive of numerous original researches, Valentin published a number of standard textbooks on anatomy and physiology, especially the nervous system. The Purkinje flicker effect which every elementary course in psychology mentions is said to have been discovered by Valentin while working together with his teacher.

It was the nervous system, and especially the brain, which attracted most Jewish physiologists, and during the '70's and '80's of the nineteenth century, the names of Munk, Rosenthal, Heidenhain, and Schiff were persons to conjure with. Sometimes casual remarks in letters are apt to give us an insight into the merit of some of the men. Thus William James, the greatest figure in American philosophy and psychology, writing to his friend, Henry Bowditch, the Harvard physiologist, describes his studies at the University of Berlin in 1867. He speaks of the series of lectures by Du Bois-Raymond and goes on to say that "two ambitious young Jews give six more a week between them, which are almost as instructive." Who these two young Jews were he does not tell us, but from the frequent citations in his *Principles of Psychology,* I should gather that one of them was Hermann Munk, who would have been only 28 then, while the other might have been Isidor Rosenthal, born in 1836.

William James, it will be borne in mind, was not only the ranking psychologist early America has produced but ranked, toward the end of the nineteenth century, as the leading scientist in the United States, according to a vote by the members of the American Association for the Advancement of Science. In his youth he had visited Germany and came in contact, as a student and instructor, with some of the greatest scientific minds in that country. I happen to have in my library a number of the textbooks which he had marked and annotated. About a dozen or more were by Jewish physiologists who are listed in this section. He was not partial to Jews, but they happen to have been the pillars of the science in the '60's and '70's, as they were, indeed, right up to the advent of Hitler. Furthermore, they all seemed to be gravitating toward neurology; and that was the closest, in those days, to psychology, which had not yet been made an academic discipline. About a hundred years ago specialization did not preclude a knowledge of allied fields and even philosophy; and James must have been drawn to the stimulating lectures of these men who were dynamic teachers as well as ingenious experimenters, and could write in a clear and attractive style.

In his *Principles of Psychology*, and even in his *Briefer Course*, James frequently cites these physiologists, anatomists, and neurologists. In 1882, he sets down his impressions of two Jewish scientists he had met in the following words:

> Yesterday I went to the veterinary school to see H. Munk, the great brain vivisector. He was very cordial and poured out a torrent of talk for one and a-half hours, though he could show me no animals. He gave me one of his new publications and introduced me to Dr. Baginsky (Professor Samuel Porter's favorite authority on the semicircular canals, whose work I treated superciliously in my article). So we opened on the semicircular canals, and Baginsky's torrent of words was even more overwhelming than Munk's. I never felt quite so helpless and small-boyish before, and am to this hour dizzy from the onslaught.

The references here are to Hermann Munk, one of two brothers famous for their brain researches, and to Benno Baginsky, one of the foremost laryngologists and otologists of this time, a brother of Adolf Baginsky, equally renowned as a child specialist.

Hermann Munk, born in Posen, in 1839, must have ranked as one of the greatest physiologists of his generation,—a generation which, by the way, teemed with distinguished names in physiology,—to have become the head of the physiological laboratory at the Veterinary School in Berlin, where he died in 1912. Munk's experimental researches on the cerebral cortex, on nerve stimulation, etc. have been discussed to this day. Immanuel Munk, a younger brother of Hermann, was perhaps even more brilliant, but he died comparatively young at the age of 51, in 1903, but even in his forties, he had become a noted figure in his field and rose to the directorship of a department of the Physiological Institute at the University of Berlin. His textbook *Physiology of Man and Mammals* went through many editions, and his chief researches were on nutrition. He was also editor of the influential *Zentralblatt für Physiologie.*

Rudolf Peter Heinrich Heidenhain (1834-1897) who at the time of his death served as Director of the Physiological Laboratory at the University of Breslau, was an experimentalist of rare distinction. His investigations on muscular metabolism, the ductless glands, and his physiological studies in general have been rated as classical.

Although Heidenhain was a convert to Christianity and may have married a non-Jewish woman, it may be mentioned *en passant* that his son, Martin, was a noted anatomist, specializing in cellular structure. He was associated with the University of Tübingen.

Like Heidenhain, Isidor Rosenthal, born in a town in the province of Posen, in 1836, was interested largely in the physiology of nerves and muscles, but his experiments in electrotherapy were among the earliest in that field of medicine, and brought prestige to the University of Erlangen where he held the chair in physiology and hygiene.

THE HEBREW IMPACT ON WESTERN CIVILIZATION

Salomon Stricker (1834-1898), although primarily a pathologist, having founded the pathological institute of Vienna, is regarded as a pioneer in several departments of physiology. His original discoveries of the subdivided cells in living tissue, as well as of the extravasation of the blood, the transformation of substance tissue into migratory cells, and the vasomotor center of the abdominal viscera, afforded him an international reputation and brought hundreds of students to his class rooms at the University of Vienna. It was he, too, who developed the theory of motor imagery in speech which the behaviorists in psychology took to be the essence of all thought. His books stressed the psychological as well as the physiological in medicine, and he might easily rank as one of the leading neurologists of his day. Had he lived a few years longer, he doubtless would have received the Nobel Prize; for, in 1920, the Danish physiologist, A. Krogh, was awarded the Prize for virtually proving experimentally the theory of the function of the capillary vessels which Stricker formulated and elaborated almost half a century earlier.

Ludwig Edinger's (1855-1918) work in neurology and anatomy was of such a high order that many of his brilliant students are still under his spell. As a comparative anatomist he had no peer during the latter part of the nineteenth century, and his *Lectures on the Central Nervous System* enjoyed many editions in German.

A physician and pharmacologist, Rudolf Magnus (1873-1927) taught at Heidelberg in Germany and Utrecht (Holland) contributing substantially to the knowledge of the central nervous system and the reflex mechanisms of bodily posture as related to the earth's motion.

Kurt Goldstein (1878-   ) has been associated with the *Gestalt* School in psychology for over 30 years, but his field is neurology, and his work on brain lesions and the more theoretical survey of the human organism have given him a prominent position in this country, where he has been residing after leaving Frankfurt during the Nazi reign of terror.

[288]

R. W. Semon (1859-1919), a practicing physician, never-theless made his mark as the originator of a biological theory which makes memory a universal function and acquired characteristics inheritable. He was well thought of by the British Darwinists, and his book *Die Mneme*, translated into English, was well received in medical, psychological, and biological circles.

Only to deal with the most distinguished physiologists in Germany, of Jewish extraction, would require a book in itself if one were to do them justice. Almost every university in Germany, Austria, and Switzerland could boast a Jewish ornament as the head of its physiological department or "Institute" as it would be called. Among the most noted in his day was Julius Bernstein (1839-1917) son of the autodidactic popular-science writer, Aaron Bernstein, who played an important part in the Berlin Jewish Community. Julius served, in turn, as professor at Berlin, Heidelberg, and Halle, where he was Director of its Physiological Institute. His specialty was the nervous system and the sense organs, while his textbook on animal physiology was the standard work for decades.

Siegmund Exner (1846-1926), professor at the University of Vienna, will be remembered for his microscopic researches on animal tissue, his optical investigations, but particularly for his work on brain localization. His special field was neurology.

Nor can one omit such a name as Hugo Kronecker (1839-1914), brother of the mathematician who received some space in another section. Kronecker, who gave us an insight into the physiology of the heart, taught at Berne (Switzerland) and at Leipzig and Berlin. G. Embden (1874-1933), of the famous Embden family, was professor at the University of Frankfurt, and Hans Friedenthal was professor at the University of Berlin, until the Nazi regime completed its programme of *"Gleichschaltung"*. Sigmund Mayer (1842-1910) was Director of the Physiological Institute at the German University in Prague; while at Cologne, Bruno Kisch served as professor until the advent of Hitler. The localization of brain function has been established through the felicitous experimentation of Fritsch and Hitzig. At the time I absorbed this information in my elementary textbook in psychology, it hardly occurred to me that Eduard Hitzig (1838-1907), who was a professor at Halle, was descended from Frederic II's Jewish banker, Daniel Itzig.

It may well be pondered in certain quarters whether all these celebrities could be of Jewish descent, but the reader may be assured that there are not a few who have succeeded in keeping their origin a secret, and I have refrained from mentioning those whose Jewish extraction is problematic.

Among contemporary biochemists and physiologists Otto Meyerhof (1884-   ) has made a mark for himself with his researches on the chemistry of muscles, which did much to explain the cause of fatigue, and for which he, in 1922, shared the Nobel Prize in medicine, with A. B. Hill. Meyerhof seems to have lasted under the Nazi regime as late as 1938, when he was compelled to leave his post as Director of the Institute of Physiology at Heidelberg and after a year in Paris accepted a research professorship in chemistry at the University of Pennsylvania Medical School.

Another Nobel Prize man who brought fame to Germany, and is now connected with the College of Medicine of New York University, is Otto Loewi, formerly of the University of Vienna. Loewi's contribution lay in discovering the chemical nature of nerve impulses and also in his researches on the structure of the heart, as well as in his investigations on metabolism and the kidneys, but his chief work was associated with the nervous system.

Again we see how chemists and pharmacologists become pillars of physiology or, perhaps better, guideposts, which physiologists must consult in their own studies.

One of the most honored scientists of the past generation was Karl Landsteiner, and even though he was a pathologist and immunologist, his service to physiology was of incalculable value, for it was he who discovered the four blood groups, a discovery which made blood transfusion a relatively safe and simple matter, thus saving millions of lives. Not only was he the recipient of the Nobel Prize, in 1930, but medals came to him from many organizations and lands.

Through some quirk of racial inferiority, this superior mind ridiculously took legal measures to prevent a Jewish biographical reference work from listing him as a Jew, which fact he attempted to conceal even in his own home.

In Poland, the name of Marian Eiger, scion of the great talmudical Eger family, shone in the annals of physiology for several decades. It was he who discovered the electric nerve-cell in the heart, which is now called the Eiger cell, and he had also a hand in the application of insulin in diabetic cases, independently of Banting.

Another luminary in the firmament of Polish natural science—and there were few among the Poles—was Maximilian Rose, probably the foremost neurologist in Poland. One of the ironies of our age was revealed when this ornament of science, lecturing in the University of Warsaw, in the thirties, would find his daughter standing together with other Jewish students, since there was a Jim Crow rule about Jewish students not being allowed to sit, on the same benches, with Gentile students.

Enrico Sereni (1901-1931), uncle of Enzo Sereni, who gave his life as a voluntary parachutist with the Jewish brigade in the Nazi war, was director of the Physiological Institute at Naples. At the University of Rome, the chair of physiology was held by Giulio Fano (1856-1930) who was also Dean of the Faculty of the Natural Sciences, while at Palermo, Simone Fubino (1841-1898) exercised a similar function.

In Holland, we find Hartog Jacob Hamburger invested with the professorship in the department of physiology, and in Belgium, T. G. Gottlieb (1812-1898) rose to eminence not only because he was physician to the royal family in Brussels, but because of his microscopic researches which led to his appointment as professor at the University of Brussels. Even Estonia had its Jewish Director at the Physiological Institute in Dorpat—Alexander Lipschütz. Indeed there is scarcely a country in Europe which does not have a Physiological Institute graced by a Jewish Director.

Botany and Plant Pathology

In the survey of the biological sciences as affected by Jews, we might have started with vegetable life, plants, the flora, etc., since life begins here, but the physiological record is far more impressive, and occupies our attention especially as it is nearer home. Our body is always with us, and we are ever aware of its processes. It would be a mistake, however, to suppose that botany has been neglected by the descendants of the ghetto denizens, as we shall see in the following pages. Experimental botany would have been in a backward state were it not for the endeavors of Ferdinand Cohn and Julius Sachs during the latter half of the nineteenth century.

Ferdinand Julius Cohn (1828-1898) was, without doubt, one of the greatest, if not actually the greatest of nineteenth century botanists. Aside from his original contributions to the morphology of algae and fungi, it was he who might be considered the father of modern bacteriology; for in the first place he established, about the middle of the last century, the fact that bacteria were plants and secondly he gave the *congé* to the doctrine of spontaneous generation, although it was Pasteur who gave it the *coup de grâce* through his celebrated experimental thesis, which won the prize of the French Academy. Cohn, furthermore, was fortunate in his students many of whom forged ahead on their own, perhaps the most distinguished being the non-Jew, Robert Koch, the conqueror of tuberculosis. The founder and director of the Breslau Botanical Institute, Cohn enjoyed the esteem and admiration of his colleagues throughout the world and on the occasion of his seventieth birthday in 1898, 250 botanists of many lands issued an album in his honor, in which were mounted the portraits of his collaborators and students.

One of the outstanding figures in modern botany was the Breslau-born Julius Sachs (1832-1897) son of an engraver. From his humble circumstances, thanks to his stimulating teacher, Purkinje, he rose to fame as the Director of the Plant Institute which he founded at the University of Würzburg. His researches, particularly on plant physiology, and the influence of ultra-violet rays and heat on the growth of plants were both numerous and definitive. His handbook of the experimental physiology of plants and his textbook on botany, as well as his history of botany, which, incidentally, stresses the contribution of his contemporary Ferdinand Julius Cohn, are still highly regarded by authorities.

Another important botanist, a contemporary of both Cohn and Sachs was Nathaniel Pringsheim, whose brother Alfred, was mentioned in the section on mathematics, and whose nephew, Ernest, was adverted to in the section on physics. It was Nathaniel Pringsheim who founded the Institute for Plant Physiology at the University of Jena. Pringsheim's many and fruitful investigations on chlorophyll and plant life led to the discovery of sexuality and the nature of cryptogamy among plants. Microscopic botany owes much to his ingenious technique.

Plant pathology had in Paul Sorauer, another Breslau-born scientist, one of its chief representatives. It must be borne in mind that a hundred years ago, the notion of diseases among plants was quite novel, and Sorauer had made the peasants beholden to him for his "preventive medicine". As founder of the first periodical devoted to plant pathology, he was instrumental in advancing this branch of botany, which was later to make such remarkable strides.

It is perhaps more than a coincidence that these four giants in botany were all born in Silesia, and three of them (Cohn, Sorauer, and Sachs) in Breslau, which is now a Polish city, so that they might have been regarded as Polish Jews. Breslau has been considered the most Jewish city in Germany, next to Frankfurt-a-M. But other towns have contributed their share.

There is, for instance, the Berlin-born Paul Ascherson (1834-1913) who accompanied Rohlf on his expedition to Libya and studied the flora of Ethiopia, Egypt, and Tripoli. Later he made a thorough survey of Central European flora. Ascherson became Professor at the University of Berlin while scarcely forty, and participated in the publication of several standard handbooks.

Plant cytology and that part of botany which deals with fertilization, and the histological phase, in general, were cultivated, on a large scale, by the Warsaw-born Eduard Strasburger, who made a career for himself as Professor of botany at the University of Bonn. The yearbooks of scientific botany which he published, as well as the cytological studies, which appeared periodically at the Bonn Botanical Institute, gave considerable prestige to the Department which he directed at Bonn.

Among the more prominent botanists of the past century were: Eugen Askenasi, born in Odessa (1845-1903), who taught at Heidelberg and published, besides many valuable papers on plant physiology, a critical examination of Darwin's theory which drew a flattering comment from the great naturalist himself; Leo Abraham Errera (1858-1905) Director of the Botanical Institute at the University of Brussels, but unlike his German synethnicists (I propose this term in place of co-religionists, since Jews and converts to Christianity can hardly be called co-religionists) he always took a keen interest in the life of his brethren; Siegfried Friedländer, Professor of agricultural technology at the University of Breslau; Paul Wilhelm Magnus, Professor at Freiburg, and many others.

In England, Dr. Redcliffe N. Salaman has been long known for his dealing with the potato virus. In Palestine, Aaron Aaronson who was the discoverer of wild wheat was a name to conjure with in the early pioneer days of the Jewish colonies. The progress of Palestine which led eventually to the emergence of Israel, was definitely associated with agriculturists and botanists of the stature of Otto Warburg (1859-1938) who, prior to his incumbency at the Hebrew University was professor of botany at the University of Berlin.

In India, we find Moses Ezekiel heading the department of botany in Wilson College, Bombay; and in New Zealand, E. B. Levy occupies a high position as a specialist on various grasses.

In the United States, Jewish investigators have reached a high level of achievement. One can point, for instance, to the work of Jacob J. Taubenhaus (1884-1937) who, although born in Safed, Palestine, into a family remarkable for the prominence of its members, received his principal training at the National Farm School and at Cornell University. Serving in the capacity of plant pathologist at Delaware College and at the Agricultural Experiment Station in Texas, where he also taught soil bacteriology and plant pathology, he was instrumental in saving the crops of this country time after time through his application of sprays, containing sulphur, and became a much sought consultant in connection with perishable foods, on the part of railroad authorities. Several of his books on diseases of vegetables, like the sweet pea, onions, sweet potatoes, etc., have attracted considerable attention in agricultural circles.

A ranking agriculturist was Jacob Goodale Lipman (1874-1939) who like his successor, Selman Waksman, brought fame to his alma mater, Rutgers University, where he founded the department of bacteriology and soil chemistry, later becoming the Dean of its Agricultural College.

On more than one occasion, Lipman represented the United States Government at the International Institute of Agriculture in Rome, which, by the way, was the brain-child of another Jew, the Polish-born David Lubin, whose centenary was recently observed with great solemnity, in Rome, on an international scale. Elected President of the First International Congress of Soil Science, in 1927, Lipman received several awards for his numerous studies on soil bacteriology and kindred subjects.

Equally recognized as a soil expert was his younger brother, C. B. Lipman (1883-1944) who like his brother had served on many committees, scientific, academic, and philanthropic and yet had the time to produce important papers on heat resistance of bacteria, the relation of plant physiology to colloidal chemistry, bacteria found alive in ancient rocks, bacteria in the sea, and the mineral metabolism of higher plants. Lipman was Professor of plant physiology at the University of California, and later became Dean of the Graduate Division there.

On a lesser scale, but certainly influential in his own sphere, was Joseph Rosen (1876-1949) whose rather eventful life took him as a young Moscow student very reluctantly to Siberia, whence he escaped to Germany. Graduated from the University of Heidelberg, he came to America in 1903. After the First World War, he returned to Russia not as a political fugitive from justice but in order to resettle 250,000 Jews on farms in the Crimea and the Ukraine. As director of the Agro-Joint, he was mainly the administrator and executive, but he was also the discoverer of a type of winter rye now grown in a large part of the United States, and highly esteemed for introducing American farming methods and American Indian maize into the frequently famine-stricken Volga region in Russia.

Zoölogy

Although the Jews are not to be credited with as much zeal and genius in zoölogy as they have shown in other branches of the biological sciences, it is curious that the man who may be said to have laid the foundations of ichthyology (the study of fishes) was Marcus Eliezer Bloch who was born in 1723 and died in 1799 at Carlsbad. Taking his degree in medicine, he abandoned the medical career in order to devote his energy toward studying the life of fish, first in the waters both of and surrounding Germany; and then elsewhere. No one before his time had such an ambitious project in zoölogy, and no one has given the world such a comprehensive and illustrated survey, together with an essay embodying a new system of classification, as did Bloch. As an ichthyologist, Bloch was without a rival for decades; and he was especially proud of a letter in praise of his work he had received from King Frederick's daughter.

But let us not suppose that Bloch was the only zoölogist of Jewish stock in Germany. There were quite a few, although not as many or as great as in other fields covered in this survey.

We can e.g. add names like Hermann Loew (1807-1879) who in his *horae anatomicae* presented a system of insect anatomy and joined the small band of entomologists who flourished at the time.

A more important naturalist was Emil Selenka (1842-1902) the author of a series of volumes on zoölogy and animal evolution, which he published while he was teaching at the University of Munich.

In Italy, the standard textbook in zoölogy was long held to have been that of Paolo Enriques (1878-1932) who occupied the chair of zoölogy and comparative anatomy at the University of Padua, and who was regarded as the dean of Italian zoölogists. If it were only for his experimental studies on protozoa and his conception of the cellular theory, he might have had an honored place in the annals of zoölogy, but the man was also an authority on genetics, as we shall see in the section on genetics.

In the United States, Libbie H. Hyman has written several excellent textbooks. Her volume on the *Invertebrates* is particularly well thought of. Ornithology is well represented by H. Friedmann, Curator of the Department of Birds in the United States National Museum of the Smithsonian Institution, who has been the head of several expeditions to distant lands. David E. Fink, who has spent many years as an entomologist with the United States Department of Agriculture, has revealed a number of interesting facts in relation to insects, particularly on the effect of certain poisons on the respiratory system of such organisms.

The British Jews, as in the other sciences, do not offer a galaxy of names in the biological sciences, but the few we encounter are significant. There is *e. g.,* Marcus Hartog (1851-1924). His work on the egg cell, on protozoa, and on rotifera has been widely discussed in the biological literature; and his *Problems of Life and Reproduction* contains a survey of his views. Born in London, he taught at Owens College, in Manchester and Queen's College, Cork, Ireland, until a few years before his death.

Salomon M. Herzenstein, who died at the age of 40, nevertheless was sufficiently recognized under the regime of Alexander II to be appointed custodian of the Zoölogical Museum of the Imperial Academy of Science in St. Petersburg. Published at the age of 30, his report on the fish and molluscs on the coast of the Murmansk Sea, brought him considerable praise from veteran scientists.

In the domain of ornithology and especially entomology, the names of Lionel Walter Rothschild (1868-1937) and his brother Nathaniel Charles Rothschild will be remembered because of their devotion to these branches of natural science. The elder of the two, Lionel, might have become the head of the great banking firm which his father built up in England, but he chose to cultivate the life of a naturalist. His collection of birds and butterflies was probably the rarest in the world, having taken 40 years to assemble and costing over a million dollars in periodic purchases. Of his million and a-half varieties of butterflies and moths, the larger part went to the British Museum.

Genetics

Genetics has attracted a fair number of Jewish investigators, both on the theoretical and the practical side. The best known is probably Jacques Loeb, who has to his credit many discoveries in chemistry, physiology, and biology, but his chief results were obtained in the genetic field where he has shown through an ingenious technique that in disparate crossings of certain organisms, the male parent contribution consists in initiating growth, but not in implanting characteristics. Let us see how Jennings, himself one of America's foremost biologists, describes Loeb's achievement.

> A method of inducing cross-fertilization between certain very diverse marine organisms was discovered by J. Loeb. By putting certain chemicals in the sea water, he found that the sperms from one type could be carried to enter the ova of very different types bringing about development. In this way he induced fertilization of the ova of the sea urchin by sperms of starfish, holothurians, and even mulluscs and annelids.
>
> It turned out that in such crosses between very diverse organisms the development of the egg produced offsprings that were not intermediate between two parental types but were like the mother only . . . showing no influence of the male parent.[26]

The explanation of this phenomenon lies in the fact that there is incompatibility between the two different organisms so the sperm merely initiates the development of the ovum but dies thereafter, and only the chromosomes of the mother play a part in further process. This laboratory technique on the part of Loeb has earned the name "artificial parthenogenesis".

Loeb, who studied in Strassburg (now part of France but at that time belonging to Germany) seemed to have been influenced by the French physiologists of the nineteenth century, breaking away from the German trend which then predominated over the scientific world. Later, his views comported with the experimental results in Russia. Both Loeb and Pavlov were intent on reducing instincts to elemental mechanisms, tropisms in the case of the former and reflexes in the case of the latter.

"Loeb," writes Emanuel Rádl, a Czech authority on the history of the natural sciences, "was the real founder of the modern school". According to Rádl, Loeb was influenced not only by his teacher, Goltz, who, as every psychology student knows, showed us that the decerebrate dog can still not only live but perform a good many functions, but by Julius Sachs's views on plant physiology.

> In his early experiments, he treated the animals purely as chemical aggregates, neglecting all the facts relating to structural differentiation or to systematic position. . . . Loeb afterwards settled in America and the result of his marvellous industry was the new science of comparative physiology. In its broad outlines, this new subject followed his teaching. No attention was paid to the facts of anatomy, but the organism was treated as a "chemical machine consisting essentially of colloidal substance".[27]

It is interesting to note that Henle and Edinger were the founders of comparative anatomy, while Loeb was the founder of a new school in comparative physiology. Loeb had given the world the doctrine of tropisms, showing that insects had no other motives in their activities than turning toward or away from light, water, earth, etc., as *e. g.,* in the case of the cockroach. It looked as if Loeb might convince a too eager scientific world that man, too, was simply a tropic animal, but Loeb's extreme materialistic system did not last. As a trained chemist, he wanted to reduce everything to chemistry or physical properties.

It may be related casually that at one time, his close friend, the Columbia psychologist, J. McKeen Cattell, proposed his election to the exclusive Century Club in New York, but Loeb was blackballed, whereupon Cattell, one of the most influential figures among men of science, resigned from the Club, attributing the rejection on the part of the majority of the members to anti-Semitism. The Club denied that this was the motive and pointed to Loeb's erratic doctrines and methods.

Few living geneticists are on a par with Hermann Joseph Muller (1890), who began his career as a zoölogist, teaching at various universities, including Columbia, and the University of Edinburgh, and now settled at the University of Indiana. Muller's chief work has been in genetics, much of which he carried on at the Institute of Genetics in Moscow, USSR. His breeding experiments on the fruit fly, drosophila, his analysis or arrangements and methods of recombining hereditary units, particularly his studies on mutation, and artificial transmutation of the gene through X-rays, changes that heralded a new era in genetics and shed a flood of light on chromosome activity earned for him the Nobel prize in medicine, in 1946. Although he has not written many books, his scientific papers, which are numerous, are marked by significant results.

RUSSIA

Our knowledge about the rôle of Jewish scientists in Russia is scant, but it must not be supposed that there were no Jewish professors of physiology in Russia during the Czarist regime. Naturally most, if not all, had to make the supreme national or religious sacrifice. Thus one may list Friedrich Arnheim (1845-1893) who taught at St. Petersburg, Natan Bernstein (1836-1891), who was a lecturer at the University of Odessa, and of course there were quite a few others, but none were of international repute, as Lina Shtern is today. Naturally since Germany or Switzerland offered a greater arena for their activities, many budding scientists in the natural sciences would leave for better opportunities. We do know that in the laboratories of Pavlov and Bekhterev, there were always a few promising Jewish assistants.

It is characteristic of the present age that perhaps the foremost physiologist in USSR at the present time is a woman of

Jewish birth, Lina Shtern (born in 1892), who is the recipient of many awards and honors both in her own country and abroad for her work on the chemistry of nerve action, endocrinology, and other related fields. A prolific and ingenious researcher, she is also an organizer of unusual ability, having been appointed by the USSR Government to take charge of research projects in several of the most important Institutes in the country. Not only has she been officially recognized as an "honored scientist" but she is the first woman to have been elected to full membership in the Academy of Science, founded by a woman (Catherine "The Great"). Her service in preparing young scientists to engage in important war activities, as well as in rehabilitation work, is outstanding; and many of her students have themselves become distinguished physiologists.

Of almost equal prominence is the Director of the Physiological Laboratories at the Institute of Experimental Medicine in Leningrad, Joseph Rozental.

As a result of the upsurge of Mitchurinism in USSR, with the stress on environmental influence in growth, we have come to learn that at least a few of those who have brought on their head the ire of Lysenko and his political biologists, or rather agriculturists, are Jews, *e.g.*, Rapoport and Shmalhausen. Whether they have lost all means of earning a livelihood because of their adherence to Western views, which means a belief in the processes of heredity as promulgated by Mendel, Weismann, and Morgan, we do not know at this writing, but it is safe to say that their scientific career is at an end, unless the party line changes in this matter; and it is very doubtful whether any other theory will suit dialectical materialists who must never compromise as to whether Marx and Darwin were infallible on the point of extra-organismic circumstances playing an overwhelming part in the shaping of an individual physically, mentally, or morally.

In genetics, Norway has scarcely a greater authority than Otto L. Mohn (1886-   ) while in Denmark, Harald Goldschmidt exercises a similar influence in the practical phase of cattle breeding.

Although genetics has not had the same following in Germany as other branches of biology, several Jews in pre-Nazi Germany have made a reputation for themselves along these lines, e. g., Richard B. Goldschmidt (1878-   ) who is at present Professor of Zoölogy at the University of California. Goldschmidt, who began with an experimental investigation of the cell, later became one of the foremost exponents of the theory of heredity. His book on the determination of sex was translated into English in 1923. Goldschmidt published the Silliman lectures, which he was asked to deliver at Yale, under the title of *The Material Basis of Evolution*. He was also the founder of the *Archiv für Zellforschung*.

Eugenio Rignano (1870-1930) who, in Italy, took over the editing of *Scientia* after the death of Enriques, was influential as a philosophical biologist, aligning himself with the school of Driesch, in Germany, and the group, in England, who believed in the transmission of acquired tendencies. He wrote on international affairs, socialism, the psychology of reasoning, biological memory; and his system or view of life may be called biological synthesis. He was strongly averse to materialistic doctrines and leaned toward vitalism. Many of his books appeared in English translation; some in French. It is scarcely surprising to find no reference to him in the *Universal Jewish Encyclopedia*, with its many omissions, but the absence of his sketch in the great *Enciclopedia Italiana* is truly puzzling.

UNITED STATES

With the decline of German science, after the Nazi purge, this country is fast becoming the world's scientific centre; and although we have had several distinguished Jewish physiologists years ago, the influx of scientists from abroad had strengthened that branch of the natural or medical sciences considerably. The name of Samuel J. Meltzer (1851-1920) who was the head of the department of physiology at the

Rockefeller Institute is one to be met with quite frequently in physiological periodicals, and Moses Kunitz, who once assisted Jacques Loeb, has now turned to biochemical problems. Selig Hecht (1892-1947) who was on the staff of Columbia University for years was regarded as one of the chief authorities in vision, and was a good physicist, too, while Harold E. Himwich, now chief of the Clinical Research Branch of the Army Chemical centre has brought out some important papers on brain and carbohydrate metabolism as well as on respiration. There is a full score, at least, of Jewish physiologists in the professoriate of leading universities, but I fear that the list would hardly be appreciated in an altogether too long section.

Although primarily a biochemist, and probably the foremost at the present time, Otto Heinrich Warburg (1883-   ) Director of the Kaiser Wilhelm Institute für Zellphysiologie (until his Semitic origin could no longer be countenanced despite his conversion) and winner of the Nobel Prize in 1931, has been regarded highly by physiologists because of his fundamental discoveries about the metabolism of tumors (which constitutes a ray of hope toward the conquest of the dreaded cancer) and the catalytic effects of living tissue.

Latterly, however, he had been directing research on vegetation, and the discovery of his group that the soil could yield a great deal more in the form of food products at a fraction of the energy which is required from the sun is on the way to revolutionize the accepted order in that regard; for it points to methods of supplying the world's needs without the recurrent fears of famine. The report read at the 1949 meeting of the American Association for the Advancement of Science was one of the most encouraging heard for a long time in these days of atom bombs.

Warburg has only returned to his old preoccupation, for as early as 1932, he had been engaged in studying the yellow enzyme and was able to separate from the crystallized protein the vitamin we now know as riboflavin. "In 1935, Warburg showed that nicotinic acid in conjunction with phosphates, certain sugars and a specific protein, was an essential catalyst in the oxidative process occurring in the living organism and indeed that a particular point in the nicotinic acid molecule was the specific locus of the oxidation reaction".[28]

Thus we see that the most recent development along nutritional lines was only the result of his earlier hypotheses and experimentation.

Of all the German scientists who were forced out of their fatherland, Otto H. Warburg is the only one who returned to rehabilitate the sadly declining sciences in that country. What is more, he is attracting some American experimentalists to his Institute.

VIII

THE JEW IN BACTERIOLOGY

At first blush, it would not be difficult to surmise Jewish interest in bacteriology, or what is now called microbiology; for that is closely associated with medicine; and since Jewish physicians have been the banner bearers of the medical sciences, such contacts might readily be anticipated.

There is, however, another angle to the story; and a story it is of rare human interest; nay, of blood and fire; and, of course, it was the Jews who were subjected to both ordeals with ne'er a chance of eluding them.

Many a reader may have never heard the phrase "desecrating the host". The present writer has known the phrase before he reached his teens, but it took another decade or more to discover what that crime really meant. I had thought till then that it was supposedly looking at the gilded cross in a Corpus Christi procession with a smile of scorn. That it had something to do with the Last Supper and the symbolic rite of Holy Communion, when the blessing pronounced over the wine and the wafer is supposed to turn the drink and food into the blood and flesh of Jesus was not even dreamed of in my student days. And yet because of the assumed desecration of this wafer which has via the blessing become the Host, hundreds of thousands of Jews were tortured, burned, hacked to death, the ghettos pillaged, and, indeed, on one occasion alone, when a German ruffian named *Rindfleisch*, in 1298, led a mob from one town to another, covering Franconia, Bavaria, and Austria no less than a hundred thousand Jews were slaughtered—possibly one third of the Jewish people—and nearly 150 communities were wiped out.

This was only the repetition, on a larger scale, of what had happened in Berlin a few decades earlier; and these brutal attacks on the strength of a "desecrated" wafer recurred almost periodically until the late Renaissance. All that some fanatical priest or bigoted demagogue had to do was to demonstrate a red-stained wafer with the splenetic outburst that the Jews had pounded the wafer into a mortar, knowing that it was the body of the Lord—and the inflamed fury of the rabble knew no bounds. Had there been a grain of reason functioning in the minds of the masses, it would have been at once perceived how monstrously absurd the charge was *prima facie*; for if the Jews had believed that the wafer could be transformed into the body of Jesus, they would have become Christians themselves. But those were not reasoning days, and centuries hence, the same will be said about our hydrogen bomb era.

What concerns us here is the connection between the particular charge and bacteria. That connection was discovered only during the last century, and appropriately enough, it was the Jewish botanist, Ferdinand Cohn, who made a thorough investigation of the phenomenon after it transpired that the polenta—a sort of maize gruel which is a favorite dish with the Italian peasant—was apparently blood-stained. The ignorant peasants naturally looked upon this as an ill omen, but the Italian scientists found that the red color was due to the multiplication of a bacillus which settled on the food in specially hot and damp weather and ingested parts of the food, so that even the bread would become moist and gummy. Now it can be understood that the wafers kept in the damp cellars of churches would precipitate a growth of these bacteria on humid days, and often overnight, the yellowish color of the wafer would turn crimson. Here was a case of a bacterium, which is no more harmful than most of the microbes we find in milk, water, or other edibles becoming the unwitting cause of a frightful extermination of a people through witless "macrobes". The particular microbe, incidentally, was named "bacillus prodigiosus" i. e. the "wonder microbe". This was no more wonderful than the moulds which have given us penicillin, streptomycin, and other antibiotics, but, I suppose the blood association made it look awesome.

This was not the only account which the Jews had to square with the microbe. While in the case of the *monas prodigiosus,* the Jews were blamed for *killing* a wafer that was supposed to be divine flesh, in another instance, where microbes were active, the Jews were charged with causing the dread scourge known as the Black Death, which took a heavy toll of both Jew and Gentile, but because of their hygienic and dietary laws, the Jews were favored by fate. Did I say favored by fate? They were favored by the germs only to be more brutally dealt with by their inhuman human neighbors.

It was reasoned that since the Jews were spared in many cases while the Gentile population was ravaged, the Jews must have had something to do with it; and since the wells were more or less accessible, it occurred to the unreasoning minds of the prejudiced that the Jews had been poisoning the water. It was in Germany that this belief was especially current, and naturally the Jews in Germany suffered the most; and those who survived the plague were slaughtered by the incited mobs. In Spain, although the Black Death carried off members of the royal family, even the king himself, there was no mass hysteria welling up against the Jews, but elsewhere they were mowed down by the frenzied hordes who were only looking for an excuse to vent their wrath and plunder their victims of their possessions.

Thus the microbes played a large part in Jewish history, and it was perhaps poetic justice that the Jews should play an equal part in the history of microbes, but curiously enough it was not from the medical side that they were first approached but from the botanical. We all know the pioneer labors of the great Pasteur, who incidentally was no medical man but a chemist, but during the same time that Pasteur was investigating these unseen devils, there was a young man in Breslau probing their life and behavior and using somewhat different methods. That scientist was Ferdinand Julius Cohn, who was the first to call that organism a *bacillus*, and to classify it under the head of vegetative life. As we have seen in an earlier section, Cohn was primarily a botanist, perhaps the greatest experimental botanist of the century, but he was also the founder of plant pathology, and thus his connection with bacteriology. One of his numerous brilliant pupils, by the way, was Robert Koch, thanks to whom tuberculosis has become a relatively infrequent cause of death.

In Pasteur's own institute, the Jewish tradition seems to have been unbroken for nearly a century; for, shortly after the famous Pasteur Institute began to function, we find Elie Metchnikoff intrenched therein as director of research; and after Pasteur's death, it was he who carried on as the chief.

Elie Metchnikoff, although his father was not Jewish, deserves an honored place in our account of Jewish endeavor because he resembled his mother, and unlike virtually all the Jewish Nobel laureates, made special mention of his Jewish mother, and probably he was named for his maternal grandfather.

Metchnikoff's colorful and hard life, in spite of his eventual triumphs was described by his devoted wife, Olga, whom he married after losing his first wife under the most trying circumstances. Born in Russia, in 1845, we find him a professor of zoölogy at the University of Odessa before he had passed the quarter-century mark. Soon he came into conflict with the authorities and left for Sicily, where he began the series of microscopic observations that were to make him famous.

We must remember that the nascent science of bacteriology was hardly in its swaddling clothes. Pasteur, its founder, was still a comparatively young man when Metchnikoff made his epoch-making discovery that there were wandering cells in the blood, the phagocytes, which wage battle on the incoming bacilli in case of disease; and thus the body is really a theatre of war, and not merely a theatrical stage.

Metchnikoff's theory was not taken kindly to in all medical circles. The Germans particularly were opposed to his conclusions. It was thought generally that the chemical action of the blood was sufficient to rise to the occasion and immunize the body, but Pasteur, genial genius that he was, recognized the man's scientific prowess and invited him to work in his Institute directing the laboratory research, which, thanks to him, yielded some of the most fruitful results in immunology. In 1908 Metchnikoff was awarded the Nobel Prize, and his co-winner was Paul Ehrlich of Salvarsan fame.

Metchnikoff's name is often popularly associated with the buttermilk fad which came into vogue as a result of the doctrine that the bacteria in this substance, a favorite food among the Bulgarians, who were particularly known for their longevity, alkalized the putrefying bacteria in the large intestine, but surely his discovery of the curative properties of calomel ointment when applied in the early stages of syphilis was of vastly greater importance.

Metchnikoff died in Paris, in 1916, a celebrated scientist, and his *Immunity in Infectious Diseases* was translated into several languages. The microbe known as *spiralis Metchnikovii,* which will be found in the dictionary, was named in his honor by an admiring disciple.

While Metchnikoff was startling the scientific world with his epoch-making theories, a young Jew from Odessa was engaged in experiments in the Pasteur Institute. That young man was destined to be regarded as a savior by millions of Asiatics. But let the Dean of medical biographers tell the story in his crisp but dramatic style.

> The Russian-Jewish physician, Waldemar Morde-cai Wolff Haffkine (1860-1930), was destined to be one of the foremost explorers of the disease-map of India. He made his mark (1891) when Pasteur, importuned by the kingdom of Siam for a remedy against cholera, placed the problem in the hands of the bacteriologist from Odessa, who discovered the method of inoculation with attenuated virus against cholera. Upon the request of the British Government that he investigate cholera in its homeland (1893), Haffkine surveyed extensive regions in India, including all of Bengal and the Punjab. Next the Indian Government (1896) asked him to study the plague in its ancient habitat, and Haffkine, in India, devised the prophylactic inoculation which robbed the Asiatic plague of its world-terrorizing power.[29]

What the article on medical explorers did not state naturally was that Haffkine, who looked, for all the world, like a high-minded French church dignitary, and was brought up without a religious training, nevertheless toward the end of his life became attached to Jewish orthodoxy and spent a large part of his time and fortune aiding its cause, not only in organization work but by writing and monetary contributions. His will left close to a quarter of a million dollars for the establishment of yeshivahs and religious schools for the Jewish youth. He was pious himself and often his prayer shawl (*talith*) or phylacteries were seen on him by visitors, who expected the world famous scientist to have shed long since the religious rites and customs of his people.

Another conquest was to be made by the Pasteur Institute and again it was a Jewish scientist who carried on the tradition. This time it was Alexander Besredka, who prepared a serum which was to kill off the dread typhus microbe.

Alexander Besredka (1870-1940) also hailed from Odessa, although he afterwards not only became a naturalized French-man but fought in the French army against the Germans. Besredka's theories on immunization represented a revolt against accepted doctrine in medical circles, and his results bore out his theory. The Besredka method in administering serums has saved thousands against the frequent accidents consequent upon anaphylactic injections. Most of his works have been translated into English and other languages.

And to complete the cycle, the Pasteur Institute has recently electrified the world by announcing the preparation of an elixir which rejuvenates the tissues. The man who was respon-sible for this elixir is the young Jewish physician, Bardach.

But let it not be supposed that all the while, the Jewish medical men in Germany were resting on their oars. Perhaps no name in modern medicine has been more signally honored than that of Paul Ehrlich, who is known to millions as the man who had given to the world an effective cure for syphilis, under the name of Salvarsan, more popularly labelled "606", because of the 605 previous attempts at such preparation which failed; but this great scientist thanks to whose efforts, the sins of the fathers are no longer visited on the innocent children and who has inspired the "Magic Bullet", a film seen by many millions, is the pioneer of a new field in medi-cine—chemotherapy, based on the theory that each bit of tissue is chemically constituted so as to react specifically to various changes. In proving this theory through ingenious dye methods, he had in Karl Weigert, an able partner.

If Ehrlich found the cure for syphilis, it was August Was-sermann (1866-1925) who discovered the blood test which is now clinical routine with everyone undergoing a thorough hospital examination. The difference between a "positive" and a "negative Wassermann" is of far-reaching significance to the examiner as well as to the patient. An equally great name in bacteriology and immunology is that of Albert Neisser, the man who discovered the microbe responsible for the development of gonorrhea.

One might be tempted to recount the exploits of the galaxy of Jews who toiled to relieve suffering or, better still, to *prevent* it—men like Joseph Goldberger, who gave us the key to the pellagra scourge, or Belá Schick, who has devised the test for diphtheria, which bears his name, and many others, but again the space restriction looms up, and it is quite likely that many of the purely medical achievements will be treated in chapters on the medical sciences. We are here confining our attention to the part Jews have played in exploring the inroads of the bacteria. When we consider that a microbe is about 1/25000 of an inch in length, in other words that it takes 25000 of them to make an inch, we can only marvel at the superhuman patience of these men who have devoted their lives in the interest of science; and let us also bear in mind that bacteria have been investigated largely by other than medical men. Those microscopic organisms are not all harmful; indeed some are very useful, and from various fields of research men converged to study them.

Even Weizmann had worked with bacteria. That was at the time of the first World War. Acetone was needed badly by the British for their shells, and Weizmann was sought out by a high officer of the navy to set his mind on the problem. First he had to find a supply of butyl alcohol. He was not interested in the ethyl alcohol which is produced through fermentation by the action of yeast bacteria. It was not long before he discovered a bacterium which gave him both butyl alcohol and acetone—and in large quantities. The manufacture of acetone became a war industry on a gigantic scale, and distilleries were set up not only in England, but in the United States and Canada as well. Just as Fritz Haber was able to produce synthetic ammonia out of the nitrogen in the air, thus making it possible for the Germans to protract the war, when they appeared to be at the end of their rope, so Weizmann solved the British problem.

It was said that when the then Premier, Lloyd George, asked Weizmann what premium he might choose for the incalculable assistance, either in the form of a royal honor or a pension, he declined to accept anything for himself but asked that his only reward be the establishment of Palestine as a homeland for the Jews, a plea which resulted in the Balfour declaration. This was particularly appropriate, since A. James Balfour was at the time First Lord of the Admiralty.

Boris Chain (originally the name was *Kheyn*, which is the Hebrew for *charm*) has written another illustrious page in the annals of science, when he, H. W. Florey and Alexander Fleming were jointly awarded the Nobel Prize.

Like Metchnikoff, Haffkine, and Besredka, Chain, too, hailed from Russia, but settled in Berlin, where he was a member at large of the Jewish bohemian colony, which had its headquarters in the Romanisches Café near the zoölogical gardens. He even belonged to the *Sholem Aleichem Club,* which would indicate that he is familiar with Yiddish. When Berlin became more of a hazard than a nuisance for Jews, he settled at Oxford, England, working in Florey's laboratory. At the time, Fleming's discovery of penicillin was known but not fully recognized even in medical circles. Florey and Chain then turned their attention to the next possibilities of penicillin, and it was through their efforts that the mould became so efficacious in therapy. Although Florey was Chain's superior, it was no doubt that the Jewish scientist had the special task of working out the specific technique of the experiments.

Chain received many honors in addition to the Nobel Prize, such as the Berzelius Medal of the Swedish Medical Society and the Pasteur Medal, and he is also a commander of the French Legion of Honor.

If this section concludes with the exploits of Selman Abraham Waksman (1888-   ) it is not because there are no other bacteriologists who deserve a place here, but because his life work represents a typical story of the Jewish immigrant boy who brought fame to his adopted country and comfort to the world's sufferers without profiting materially from his intense and arduous labors.

Like his great predecessors in the field which he has so thoroughly cultivated, he originally came from Russia, in fact close to the birthplace of Metchnikoff, Haffkine, Besredka and Chain's family, and after studying at Rutgers University, under the eminent soil chemist and bacteriologist Jacob G. Lipman, also Russian born, he took his Ph.D. at the University of California, under the latter's younger brother, and then settled down to teaching at his alma mater, where he is the most important man on the campus, for aside from the prestige which has accrued to him because of his discoveries— discoveries that should have afforded him the Nobel Prize, he may be regarded as one of the greatest benefactors to Rutgers University, in that the royalties accumulating on the drugs which Merck's has been putting on the market, are going toward the establishment of an Institute of Microbiology which promises to be the greatest in the world. But let us quote *Time*, which has had occasion to issue news stories on Waksman on more than one occasion.

> When Rutgers University needed to save some money during the war winter of 1941-42, a budget official had a bright idea: Why not fire Selman Waksman, an obscure Ukrainian-born microbiologist who was getting $4,620 a year for "playing around with microbes in the soil"? That sort of fun and games, the moneyman pointed out, had never really paid off.
>
> Fortunately for Rutgers—and for mankind—Dean William H. Martin of the College of Agriculture saved Dr. Waksman from the ax. Within two years Selman Waksman's "playing around with microbes" had paid off with one of the biggest jackpots that

has ever gushed from a scientist's laboratory. Dr. Waksman (rhymes with boxman) had become the discoverer of streptomycin, which ranks next to penicillin among the antibiotics and is the first of these "wonder drugs" to show hopeful results in the treatment of tuberculosis.

Today, the department of microbiology is the brightest spot on the Rutgers campus at New Brunswick, N. J., and its chairman, Dr. Selman Waksman, is one of the world's top microbiologists. He has won for his university not only fame but fortune. Streptomycin for a 60-day course of treatment costs $60 to $80. A dozen chemical companies are turning out the new wonder drug, and for every gram (1/28 of an ounce) sold, Rutgers gets 2¢. By last week, the university's harvest of pennies had reached more than $2,000,000.

With this money (and more still to come), Rutgers and Waksman are planning to build an Institute of Microbiology. Quiet, modest Dr. Waksman will enjoy the new equipment and the more spacious laboratories. For himself he asks little. By taking advantage of the unusually liberal Rutgers policy in such financial matters, he might have claimed all the proceeds of his discovery and become a millionaire. But he turned over his royalty rights to the Rutgers Research and Endowment Foundation with the mild observation: "Rutgers won't let me starve."[30]

And thus we see that the bacteria which have been the nemesis of the Jews because they more or less passed them by during the Black Plague became the object of intensive study on the part of their indirect victims.

There are a few other reflections which occur to one. First, the general belief in scientific circles that Jews are only good theoreticians but shy away from experimentation is not true.

[315]

THE HEBREW IMPACT ON WESTERN CIVILIZATION

In the natural sciences, particularly, the Jewish botanists and microbiologists have been second to none; and furthermore. it was the East European Jew who excelled in the fight against the microbes. Even the botanists largely came from that part of Germany which now is part of Poland; and a third reflection is that although agriculture has been thought to have been repugnant to the Jew (what had been accomplished in Palestine is sufficient disproof of the notion) the science of the soil and its products has been materially deepened thanks to Jewish efforts; and, as will be realized, the soil cannot be studied at an office desk.

Yes, the story of Jewish scientific endeavor is a long one, both instructive and revealing. Knowing the facts will go a long way toward exploding some of the myths about Jewish one-sided proclivities.

FOOTNOTES

[1] Harvey Cushing: *The Life of Sir William Osler,* vol. I, page 215.

[2] A. A. Roback: "National Traditions in Philosophy and Science." Paper read before the American Philosophical Association, 1946.

[3] Cantor's Jewish origin has been questioned by some, but A. Fraenkel, who may be regarded as a disciple of the great mathematician, tells us in his well documented monograph that Cantor's father was a Jew.

[4] G. Cantor: *Contributions to the Founding of the Theory of Transfinite Numbers* (Jourdain's translation) page 74.

[5] A. Fraenkel: *Georg Cantor*, page 61.

[5a] S. Gandz: *Isis*, Vol. 39, No. 79 (1938) p. 419.

[6] F. Cajori: *A History of Mathematics,* page 327. Cajori is, of course, not Jewish, and probably did not know that most of those mentioned in the passage were Jews.

[7] Sylvester is here referring to the Jew, Jacobi.

[8] A. Fraenkel: *Georg Cantor*, page 25.

[9] S. Brodetsky, in *The Real Jew* (edited by H. Newman) page 167.

[10] Heinrich Hertz's mother was supposed to have been a non-Jewess. Under ordinary circumstances, the son of a non-Jewish mother would, according to my own cross-inheritance theory, be regarded as a Gentile. But whether Hertz belongs to the exceptions who take after their father is something which should be examined genetically (family records). Roth makes Gustav Hertz, the Nobel Prize winner in physics, out to be a cousin of Heinrich on the father's side, but actually he was his nephew, so that Gustav Hertz was only a quarter-Jew, which

fact constitutes no good reason for the inclusion of his more famous uncle in our survey. But this omission might be considered a gap by some of the Judaeologists.

11 C. T. Chase: *The Evolution of Modern Physics,* page 142.

12 *Ibid.,* page 151.

13 E. Schuster: *The Progress of Physics, 1875-1908,* pages 110-111.

14 W. Yourgrau: *Jewish Affairs,* March 1949, page 12.

15 It is a pity that the solid essay ("Jewish Thought in the Modern World") by Leon Roth in *The Legacy of Israel* (1927), planned by the late Israel Abrahams and edited by E. R. Bevan and Charles Singer, both of whom are reputed scholars, should have been marred by such an error as thrusting upon Professor Weyl a Jewish ancestry. Once more we must realize that we cannot be too careful in investigating a man's racial origin.

16 A. Moszkowski: *Einstein The Searcher,* page 225. (English translation)

17 His investigation into the principle of gravitation has been mentioned in the chapter on Astronomy.

18 When Rutherford was asked at the time of the First World War why he did not abandon the tiny atom and turn to something more impressive, his reply was that the outcome of the work on this bagatelle would prove more important than the War itself. His prediction came true, though he did not live to see it verified.

19 Chase, C. T.: *The Evolution of Modern Physics,* page 131.

20 R. F. Yates: *Atom Smashers,* pages 153-154. (Didier)

21 H. D. Smyth: A General Account of the Development of Methods of Using Atomic Energy for Military Purposes under the Auspices of the United States Government.

22 *Ibid.,* page 17.

23 *Canadian Jews in World War II,* page 2. (Issued by Canadian Jewish Congress)

24 Another member of the Atomic Energy Commission who has resigned in February, 1950, is Rear Admiral Louis L. Strauss.

25 *The Real Jew* (edited by L. Newman) page 195.

25a C. Singer and C. Rabin: *A Prelude to Modern Science,* p. LXXVII (Oxford University Press).

26 H. S. Jennings: *Genetics,* pages 266-267.

27 E. Radl: *History of Biological Theories* (English translation) page 379.

28 E. J. Cohn: "Research in the Medical Sciences". *Amer. Scientist,* 1949, vol. 37. page 252.

29 V. Robinson: "The Physician as Explorer in Asia". *Ciba Symposia.* Nov. 1940, vol. 2, page 630.

30 *Time,* Nov. 7, 1949, vol. 54, page 70.

THE HEBREW IMPACT ON WESTERN CIVILIZATION

BIBLIOGRAPHY

BEVAN, E. R. and C. SINGER, *The Legacy of Israel*, 1927.

GERSHENFELD, L., *The Jew in Science*, 1934.

Jewish Encyclopedia (12 vols.) 1901-1906.

Jüdisches Lexikon (5 vols.) 1927-1930.

NEWMAN, CH. (Ed.) *The Real Jew*, 1925.

ROBACK, A. A., *Jewish Influence in Modern Thought*, 1929.

——, *Our Reply to Hitler*. (A series of essays on Jewish contributions in philosophy, science, art, law, medicine and music). Special edition of *Forward*, 1933.

ROTH, C., *The Jewish Contribution to Civilization*, 1937.

Universal Jewish Encyclopedia (10 vols.) 1939-1943.

WININGER, S., *Grosse Jüdische National-Biographie* (7 vols.) 1926-1932.

The Influence of the Jew on Modern Medicine

By Solomon R. Kagan, M. D.

MODERN medicine begins with the 19th century, and is characterized mainly by the introduction of systematic methods and facilities for scientific research in medicine. The new teaching of medicine as a science, experimental research in adequate laboratories, and organized studies of preventive medicine are the development of the 19th and 20th centuries. Among the factors that revolutionized modern medicine was the effect of the emancipation of Jews early in the 19th century. The admission of Jews to universities, to teaching positions, and to institutions for scientific research brought forth a great number of brilliant Jewish collaborators who have contributed substantially to the advancement of their traditional field of medicine in all its branches. The Jews have participated in the gigantic work of building a new medicine as clinicians, teachers, investigators, authors, translators, editors, organizers, educators, pioneers and leaders in the profession. They took an ever-increasing part in the progress of medicine over the world, but particularly it was marked in the German-speaking region which became in modern times for a century the center of Jewish intellectual life. In pre-Nazi Germany Jews were the best scientific exponents and creators of new ideas in medicine. They provided distinguished mathematicians, physicists and physicians in about thirty times their due proportion. Of the outstanding German mathematicians and medical researchers about twenty-five per cent were Jews. In Italy, Jewish intellectual supremacy was even higher in certain departments of science. Since 1908 eleven Jewish doctors were awarded the Nobel Prize for medicine in recognition of their outstanding contribution to medical science, which constitutes about twenty-five per cent of all Nobel Prize winners in medicine.

The Jewish doctors have contributed important work to all branches of medical science and its allied subjects, and their research work was mostly centered on the study of the minute structures and composition of normal and diseased tissues of the body and their correlation with function; on prophylactic measures against infectious diseases; on otology, ophthalmology, neurology and psychiatry. By means of their epoch-making discoveries in medicine, the German Jewish doctors were the main factor in making German medicine the most authoritative during the second half of the 19th and first quarter of the 20th centuries.

Sir William Osler, one of the greatest physicians of his time, wrote in 1884: "Should another Moses arise and preach a Semitic exodus from Germany, and should he prevail, they would leave the land impoverished far more than was ancient Egypt by the loss of the 'Jewels of gold and jewels of silver', of which the people were 'spoiled'. To say nothing of the material wealth, enough to buy Palestine over and over again, there is not a profession which would not suffer the serious loss of many of its most brilliant ornaments, and in none more so than our own." Osler's prophecy was realized. Since 1933 the German people have lost their main source of intellectual and creative work; they have lost their former claim to respect from the world of intellect. So far as the products of the intellect and science are concerned, German occupies a second place; henceforth German will be a language of secondary importance in the field of learning.

From the beginning of the 20th century American medicine started to grow rapidly. In 1930 Professor William H. Welch declared: "America has taken a position of leadership in the application of the new knowledge to the prevention of disease and to personal and public hygiene." The high development of American medicine was due partly to the genius of the American people and partly to private benefaction in the

United States of America which enabled the organization of research facilities on a large scale. The American Jewish physicians also collaborated in this great work to their full share, and directly and indirectly helped the progress of American medicine.

Among the many Jewish educators who helped the raising of the standard of medical education in the United States, the following deserve particular mention. Isaac Hays (1796-1879) of Philadelphia was the first to present a resolution at the New York Medical Convention in 1846 proposing a National Medical Association for the better management of standards of ethics and education. He was a founder of the American Medical Association in 1847, for which he composed a code of medical ethics. His code was approved, and is still accepted by every state and county medical society in the Union. By these medical ethics Hays placed our medical profession on the highest plane. He was among the earliest practitioners in this country to make eye diseases a specialty. He edited the *American Journal of the Medical Science*, called "Hays' Journal," which influenced medical thought in this country for more than a half century. He paved the way for American medical journalism, attracted the best medical writers to his journal, and inspired young gifted men to medico-literary work. He introduced some important ophthalmic instruments and wrote many scientific books on medicine. Another outstanding Jewish physician, Jacob M. DaCosta (1833-1900), also of Philadelphia, was professor of medicine at Jefferson Medical College, did pioneer work in cardiology, described a syndrome of irritable heart in soldiers. He was the ablest teacher of his time in the country, and wrote the best treatise on medical diagnosis (1859). His ideas on respiratory percussion were accepted in Europe by Friedrich. He and Dr. S. D. Gross founded the Philadelphia Pathological Society in 1857. Significant was also the accomplishments of Dr. Aaron Friedenwald (1836-1902) who was professor of eye disease at the College of Physicians and Surgeons in Baltimore. He helped to organize the Maryland Ophthalmological Society in 1898, and was elected its first president. Friedenwald's greatest service to the American medical profession was his activities with the formation of the Association of American Medical Colleges. In 1890 there was called a meeting of representatives of the Baltimore Medical Faculty to discuss the possibility of introducing a reform in medical education in Baltimore. Friedenwald, who was the president of the Faculty, suggested calling a national conference for the consideration of reforms throughout the country, and his view prevailed. As a result of his convictions, circulars signed by Friedenwald as chairman and Cordell as secretary were sent out by the Baltimore Medical Schools. The meeting for the organization was held at Nashville in 1890, and Friedenwald presided at the opening. At this meeting a permanent organization was established, of which N. S. Davis was president and A. Friedenwald the first vice-president. The newly organized Association of American Medical Colleges resulted in higher standards of instruction in medical schools throughout the United States. A great influence on American medical education was later exerted by Abraham Flexner (1866-   ) of Louisville, Ky., who, at the instance of the Carnegie Foundation for the Advancement of Teaching, made comprehensive studies of the status of medical education at home and abroad. His book, *Medical Education in the United States and Canada* (1910) served as an impetus to raise medical education in all medical colleges and hospitals throughout the country. Morris Fishbein (1889-   ), of St. Louis, was editor of the *Journal of the American Medical Association* from 1924 to 1949, and author (with G. H. Simmons) of *The Art and Practice of Medical Writing* (1925), and editor of many medical books dealing with various medical problems. As editor and author Fishbein made substantial contributions to the uniformity and advancement of scientific medical literature.

THE INFLUENCE OF THE JEW ON MODERN MEDICINE

It is not the object of the author to list in this monograph the names of all great Jewish physicians who left a landmark in modern medicine. The following will present a limited number of names of outstanding Jewish physicians who exerted a decisive influence upon modern medicine. One of medical fields in which the Jewish doctors were particularly noteworthy was internal medicine. They discovered new diseases and elucidated their nature, outlook and treatment; they described new signs, syndromes and tests for the diagnosis of many diseases; they also introduced new concepts, principles and theories relating to certain diseases. The earliest Jewish clinician of modern times was Ludwig Traube (1818-1876) of Silesia, who was one of the first Jewish doctors to become a professor at the University of Berlin in 1857. He made his mark in medicine as a founder of experimental pathology and of scientific researches of the action of drugs. He was one of the greatest teachers and clinicians of his time. Many structures of the human body are identified with his name such as Traube's space, Traube's curves, Traube's corpuscles, Traube's membrane, Traube's murmur, and Traube-Hering's waves. He was the first to introduce the thermometer in his clinic. Garrison tells that his clinics in Berlin became very popular on account of his brilliant methods of teaching and his sincere attitude toward the patient. Another outstanding German Jewish physician was Ottomar Rosenbach (1851-1907), also of Silesia, who distinguished himself by introducing revolutionary concepts in medicine. A great deal of his original ideas are accepted universally, such as his statements on functional diseases, the power of suggestion, the value of psycho-therapy, his theories on energetics in biophysics and biochemistry. His name is associated with the so-called Rosenbach bile test, Rosenbach's digestive reflex, Rosenbach's law, Rosenbach's disease and Rosenbach's sign for hemoplegia. Outstanding, too, was William Ebstein (1836-1912) of Goettingen who introduced tactile percussion for physical diagnosis and who advocated treatment of obesity by a diet from which all carbohydrates are excluded. Prominent was a French Jewish physician, George Hayem (1841-1933) of Paris who contributed fundamental work to medicine. He is most memorable for his discovery of the blood platelets. He invented the so-called Hayem's solution for preserving the red blood corpuscles in microscopical examination of the blood. He described Hayem's ventricle, Hayem's disease, Hayem-Widal disease, and a new type of acute nonsuppurative inflammation of the brain. He discovered a serum for injection in cases of infectious diseases. Simon Baruch (1840-1921) of New York described a sign for typhus fever, a sign for perforated appendicitis, was the first in the country to operate upon a patient with appendicitis successfully, established free bath houses in Chicago and New York, and was a pioneer of hydrotherapy in the country. Solomon Solis-Cohen (1857-1948) of Philadelphia was a pioneer in the field of organotherapy. He was among the first to advocate gland treatment, introduced the use of adrenal and pituitary products in hay fever, asthma and hives. Ismar Boas (1855-1938), a native of Posen, established gastro-enterology as a specialty. He founded the first polyclinic for gastro-intestinal diseases in Berlin. He is best known for the Boas-Eswald breakfast test and the Boas-Oppler bacillus. Max Einhorn (1862-   ) of New York has been the leader in the field of gastro-intestinal diseases. He invented gastrodiaphany which is the best means for mapping out the stomach, as he succeeded in introducing an electrical light into the stomach, so that it became transparent through the anterior abdominal wall. He made possible the duodenal intubation, which affords the possibility of obtaining specimens of bile and pancreatic juice for examination. He is the inventor of many important instruments and apparatus in relation to stomach and intestinal maladies, some of which were accepted throughout the medical world. Among his .inventions are the fermentation saccharometer (1887), the stomach bucket and gastrograph (1890), the stomach spray (1892), the stomach powder blower (1899), a new esophagoscope (1901), the duodenal bucket (1908) and an intestinal tube (1919). David Riesman (1867-1940) was professor of clinical medicine at the University of Pennsylvania. He made many valuable contributions to internal medicine, pathology and medical history. He described a sign of diabetic coma and a sign of ophthalmic goiter. Emanuel Libman (1872-1946) was a professor of clinical medicine at Columbia University. He did pioneer work in cardiology and bacteriology and made many contributions to internal medicine. He and B. Sacks described a new disease—a form of valvular and mural endocarditis—known as Libman-Sacks disease (1924). He was the first to describe subacute bacterial endocarditis (1906). The dean of American medicine W. H. Welch pointed out the significance of Libman's conclusions relating to the conditions favoring or opposing the entrance of bacteria into the blood stream, the possibilities of bacterial multiplication in the circulating blood, bacterial emboli, and the clinical and pathological significance of blood cultures.

Of particular importance are the achievements of Jews in the field of metabolism. Gustav Valentin (1810-1883), professor of physiology at Berne, Switzerland, was a pioneer in histology and experimental physiology. He discovered the diastatic role of the pancreating juice in the digestion of carbohydrates (1844). He also discovered the so-called Valentin's corpuscles and Valentin's ganglion. He introduced polarized light in microscopy. Oscar Minkowski (1858-1931), professor of medicine at Breslau, proved that the removal of the pancreas in a dog causes diabetes; thus he discovered the relation between the pancreas gland and diabetes. This discovery makes him one of the originators of modern treatment of diabetes with insulin. He was the first to describe hemolytic jaundice, suggested a new method of palpation of the kidney, first described the relation between dextrose and nitrogen in the urine, and discovered the etiology of acromegaly. Hermann S. Senator

[325]

(1834-1911) of Gnesen investigated the treatment of diabetes (1879). Moritz Schiff (1823-1896) succeeded in 1856 in producing artificial diabetes by his experiments on the nervous system. S. J. Plaschkes (1886-   ) of Tel Aviv, Israel, was the first to advocate the use of bean bread for diabetic patients (1932). Max Kahn (1887-1928) of New York introduced intarvin for the treatment of diabetes. Hermann Strauss of Berlin studied diabetes, and was one of the first physicians who administered insulin to diabetics in Germany. Moses Barron (1893-   ), professor of medicine at Minnesota Medical School, published a paper in 1920 in which he emphasized the role of the islands of Langerhans of the pancreas in the control of carbohydrate metabolism and thus of diabetes mellitus. This important article served as a basis of Banting's revolutionary discovery of insulin. Banting gave due credit to Dr. Barron, stating that the latter's article stimulated him to start laboratory research for securing pancreatic degeneration, and this work resulted in the discovery of insulin in 1921.

Of importance are also the accomplishments of Jews in the field of nutrition and vitaminology. Casimir Funk was born in Poland in 1884, received his degree of Ph.D. from Berne in 1904, made scientific studies in Pasteur Institute (1904-1906) and Lister Institute (1911-1913). In 1915 he emigrated to New York City, where he was connected with Cornell Medical College and Columbia University. He has done pioneer work in the field of vitamins, and has contributed original work to synthetic organic chemistry, nutrition and internal secretion. He was the first to discover certain substances of unknown composition which exist in minute quantity in natural foods and are necessary to normal nutrition, and he coined the term "vitamin" in 1912. In 1913 he advocated the application of his discovery of vitamins to practical dietetics and to certain medical problems. In 1914 he emphasized the necessity of the antineuritic vitamin for utilization of carbohydrates, and he was the first to describe some anatomic changes in polyneuritic pigeons as typical of the result of vitamin B deficiency. Lafayette B. Mendel (1872-1935) was Sterling professor of physiological chemistry at Yale University and was a recognized leader in the field of nutrition. He and T. B. Osborne were the first to describe eye changes as a sign of a deficiency of vitamins in the diet. They discovered calculi and calcarous deposits in the kidney passages in rats long deprived of vitamin A. They also found that vitamin B protects against polyneuritis. In 1918 Mendel and B. Cohen produced experimental scurvy in a guinea pig by means of certain diets. They demonstrated the existence of the antiscorbutic vitamin C and made studies of its properties. Professor Mendel exerted an influence on medicine by training his pupils and co-workers in medical research, and a number of his pupils became outstanding teachers and leaders in medical research in the country. Joseph Goldberger (1874-1929), of Washington, D. C., accomplished much in the field of public health. He is most memorable for his pioneer work in his discovery of the cause of pellagra in 1913. This is a fatal skin and spinal disease of Southern Europe, and also in the southern and central parts of the United States. Goldberger proved that the disease is caused by a deficiency of certain substances (Vitamin B^2 or G) which are contained in lean meat, milk and yeast. He demonstrated that it is not caused by infection, and he first placed it in the same group of diseases with scurvy and beriberi. With this discovery he became a benefactor of mankind. Alfred H. Hess (1875-1933) was professor of children's diseases at the University and Bellevue Hospital Medical College in New York. He was among the first to report the curative properties of vitamin D in rickets. In 1919 he and L. Unger discovered vitamin C. Hess (with Weinstock) discovered a method of radiation of food for producing a vitamin factor in it. In 1927 Hess received the John Scott Medal awarded by the Franklin Society for his discovery of a method of producing a vitamin factor in food by the influence of ultraviolet rays. Prof. Ludwig F. Meyer of Tel Aviv, Israel, found vitamin C in

milk and fresh vegetables. Barnett Sure (1891-   ), professor of agricultural chemistry at Arkansas, discovered vitamin
E. He is the author of *Vitamins in Health and Disease* (1933),
investigated the value of vitamin E in reproduction and lacta-
tion, vitamin B requirements of nursing the young, and changes
in the minute structures of the body due to a deficiency of
vitamins in the diet. He received a grant of the Committee on
Scientific Research of the American Medical Association in
1938. Simon B. Wolbach (1880-1945) of Boston (with P. R.
Howe) made studies concerning the pathologic changes in
cases of vitamin A deficiency. Israel S. Wechsler (1884-   ),
professor of neurology at Columbia, advocated the treatment
of amyotrophic lateral sclerosis with vitamin E (1940). Alfred
T. Shol (1889-   ) made scientific contributions to diseases
of children and chemical hygiene. He investigated the physiology of vitamin D (1938). He and Barnett Sure discovered
that under the influence of vitamin D a readjustment of the
calcium-phosphorus ratio is produced which requires a new
supply of these ingredients.

Among the outstanding Jewish medical teachers was Hermann Strauss (1868-1944) of Berlin, who for forty-two years
was teaching and lecturing not only in Berlin University, but
also in many countries, including the United States and Palestine, everywhere stimulating medical research work. He developed original technical methods for clinical studies, constructed new medical devices, such as the Strauss' chloridom-
eter, the Strauss' canula and an apparatus for procto-sygmos-
copy. He devised a lactic acid test and introduced a levulose
tolerance test for liver function. He was the first to describe
proctostasis, investigated the metabolic role in diabetes, and
described a salt-free diet for the treatment of kidney disorders.
He trained many German students for scientific research work,
and attracted pupils from everywhere to Berlin. But the German people mistreated their great teacher and educator Professor Strauss. They humiliated and tortured him in a concentra-

tion camp in Theresienstadt. When he learned that it was ordered to take him to the gas chambers of Oswiecim, he committed suicide in October 1944. We do not know the day of his tragic end and the place of his grave. Among the eminent Jewish hematologists is William Dameshek (1900-   ), professor of clinical medicine at Tufts College, Boston. He has made many important contributions to the study of blood, particularly in the study of the bone-marrow, chronic iron deficiency, hemolytic anemia, disorders of the spleen and the chemotherapy of leukemia and agranulocytosis. He discovered the abnormal hemolytic antibody in acquired hemolytic anemia. He trained many young men in the study of blood who later became hematologists throughout the world.

In the field of children diseases the Jews were pre-eminent not only by their scientific achievements but also by their organizational activities. Edward H. Henoch (1820-1910), professor of pediatrics in Berlin, was the first to establish a clinic for children's diseases in Berlin. He discovered the so-called Henoch's purpura. Max Kassowitz (1842-1913) of Vienna introduced the phosphorus cod liver oil in the treatment of rickets. Heinrich Finkelstein (1865-1942) of Berlin described many pediatric symptoms-complexes, and introduced a new concept in the alimentary disorders of infancy. Finkelstein's "albumin milk" was a great advance in the treatment of severe diarrhea in children. Abraham Jacobi (1830-1919) was professor of diseases of children at Columbia and is known as "the father of pediatrics in America". He was the first to establish a clinic for children diseases in New York City. Henry Koplik (1858-1927) of New York was the first to establish milk stations in the United States. He discovered the diagnostic spots of measles, known as Koplik's sign. Isaac A. Abt (1867-   ), professor emeritus in pediatrics of Northwestern University Medical School, Chicago, made valuable contributions to pediatrics. As clinician, teacher, writer and editor he was a leader of pediatrics for more than a half century. He was one of the foremost exponents of modern pediatrics, was the first to introduce in this country the Czerny-Finkelstein philosophy of nutritional disorders, and was also the first American pediatrician to use protein milk in the treatment of diarrhea in infants. Bela Schick (1877-   ) of Columbia University originated the so-called Schick test for determining susceptibility of a person to diphtheria (1913). Abraham Levinson of Chicago made original studies in spinal fluid.

Karl A. Meninger stated that although the fact is well known that Jewish physicians are distinguished for their scientific accomplishments in all fields of medicine, however, they have demonstrated a special gift for psychiatry. Records show that the Jews not only discovered new diseases and methods of treatment in neuro-psychiatry and discovered various anatomic parts of the nervous system, but also have changed the current medical thought, practice and education. They have changed the outlook of modern psychiatry and psychology in its medical application. The following may serve as an illustration. Moritz Heinrich Romberg (1795-1873) of Meningen became professor in Berlin in 1838. He was the author of a classical book on nervous diseases, which was the first formal text on the subject, and it made an epoch by its careful collation of hitherto scattered data, its clear, precise clinical picture and its attempt to systematize treatment (Garrison). He described a sign for locomotor ataxia (Romberg's sign), discovered a disease of facial hemiatrophy, known as Romberg's disease. After him is also named Romberg-Paessler syndrome and Romberg-Howship sign. He is considered the founder of modern neuropathology. Robert Remak (1815-1865) of Posen became professor at Berlin in 1859, and made outstanding contributions to medicine. He discovered the non-medullated fibers (fibers of Remak) and the ganglionic cells in the sinus venosus of the frog's heart (Remak's ganglion). He was among the first to state that the proliferation of cells to build tissue is accomplished by cell division (1852). In 1842, long before Pasteur and Koch, he separated the fungus from the genus Oidium, and using himself as a guinea pig, he produced the skin disease favus on himself experimentally, proving that this disease is caused by a specific microscopic organism. He simplified von Baer's classification of the germ-layers (1851), and was the first to describe ascending neuritis (1861). He was the founder of microscopic anatomy of the nerves, a pioneer in electrotherapy, and substituted the galvanic for the induced current (1856). Ludwig Lichtheim (1845-1928) of Breslau published original work on tumors of the brain and spinal cord, paralysis of eye muscles, progressive muscular atrophy, and meningitis. He described a disease and a syndrome, both named after him. He was among the first to perform a puncture in the brain for diagnostic purpose. Ludwig M. Hirschfeld (1816-1876) published a classical textbook on neurology, and discovered the so-called Hirschfeld's nerve. Hermann Oppenheim (1852-1919) described congenital myatonia (Oppenheim's disease), Oppenheim's cerebral infantile paralysis, Oppenheim's mouth reflex, Oppenheim's sign in spastic conditions of the lower extremities, and Oppenheim's course of multiple sclerosis. He did pioneer work in the study of traumatic neuroses. Nathan Weiss (1851-1883) of Vienna was the first to investigate the spinal cord, medulla and basal ganglia in tetany (Weiss sign for tetany). Ludwig Edinger (1855-1918), professor of neurology at Frankfurt a. M., made substantial contributions to brain anatomy. After him is called Edinger's nucleus, Edinger's fibers and Edinger's law. Joseph A. Hirschl (1885-1914) of Vienna made the discovery that syphilis is the cause of general paralysis (1896). After him it is called Hirschl's phenomenon. Emanuel Mendel (1839-1907) of Germany was the most popular psychiatrist of his time. He described the clinical picture of paranoia, epilepsy and mania, and advanced the method of treatment of mental and nervous diseases. In 1868 he founded a hospital for mental patients in Pankow, near Berlin, which won world recognition. Joseph Breuer (1842-1925) of Vienna originated the theory of equilibrium, and it has been universally accepted. He contributed much through his scientific investigations of the relation of the vagus to breathing and through his studies of the function of the semicircular. He originated the method of catharsis in the treatment of psycho-neuroses, and Freud gave him due credit for this discovery. Sigmund Freud (1856-1939) of Vienna made fundamental contributions to the study of neuro-psychiatry. In 1884 Dr. Joseph Breuer related to Freud that he was able to penetrate deeply into the causation and significance of hysterical symptoms, and that he cured them by getting the patient to recollect in a state of hypnosis the circumstances of their origin, and spoke of this method as catharsis. Freud concluded that there can be mental processes which remain hidden from the consciousness of man. On the basis of his observations, he stated that many mental processes never attain consciousness and can be exposed only through psychoanalysis. He discovered a method of free association and was able by assurances and encouragements to force the forgotten things and connections into the consciousness of his neurotic patient. He replaced the treatment of hypnosis by free association and coined the term "psychoanalysis" as a therapeutic method. Freud was a great teacher of human nature. He was a genius, a man of originality, depth of thought and vision, and influenced greatly the human conception of his time. He revolutionized psychiatry and altered the content and direction of human thought. His teachings closed a chain in the philosophy concerning the meaning of man. Alfred Adler of Vienna founded the school of individual psychology. Otto Marburg (1874-1948) first showed the association of trophic skin changes with lesions in the spinal ganglions. He and Frankl Hochward introduced neuro-surgery in Vienna.

Jewish doctors left a mark in dermatology. Moritz Kaposi (1837-1902) of Hungary described pigmented sarcoma of the skin, diabetic dermatitis, and various forms of lichen ruber. Oskar Lassar (1849-1907), of Hamburg, was the first to transmit syphilis to anthropoid apes, introduced electro-physical treatment in skin diseases, and described the so-called Lassar's paste which is still used in the practice of dermatology. He established disinfectant stations and public baths in Berlin. Paul G. Unna (1850-1929), of Hamburg, described seborrheic eczema (Unna's disease), discovered a paste for eczematous patches (Unna's paste), introduced ichthyol and resorcinol, and various staining methods in dermatology. He also described the pathology of leprosy, the plasma cells, the different foci of favus, and the so-called bacillus Unna-Ducray. Jay F. Schamberg (1870-1934) of Philadelphia was the first to describe the progressive pigmentary skin eruption (Schamberg's disease). He and Joseph Goldberger described the straw itch. He founded the Research Institute of Cutaneous Medicine in Philadelphia. A. Dostrovsky, of the Hebrew University in Jerusalem, first described the nature of endemica urticaria (1925). He and F. Sagher discovered the treatment of oriental sore of the skin by Grenz-rays (1940).

In surgery, gynecology and urology Jews also accomplished much. Samuel Kristeller (1820-1900) of Berlin introduced a method of grafting mucous membrane and described a method of manipulation in obstetrics. James Israel (1848-1926) of Berlin was a pioneer in the field of surgery and urology. Anton Woelfler (1850-1917) of Berlin contributed to surgery of the tongue, kidney, thyroid gland and gastrointestinal tract. He performed the first operation of gastro-enterostomy. Max Saenger (1853-1903) of Prague devised sutures for closure of the uterine wound in cesarean section, and modified the technic of this operation. Howard Lilienthal (1861-1946) of New York made fundamental contributions to abdominal, genito-urinary and thoracic surgery. He was the first to resect the thoracic esophagus for carcinoma without gastrostomy, and was the first in America to apply the diagnostic aid of X-ray in diseases of the jaws and teeth. He was the inventor of the two-stage operation of the prostate. He advocated a new and simple method of intestinal resection, and invented a number of surgical instruments and appliances. He invented a new portable operating table which is especially useful in operations upon the kidney and gall-bladder. This was accepted and slightly changed by the United States Army, and was employed as the regular field operating table during World War I. Dr. Lilienthal's name, however, was omitted. Dr. Lilienthal contributed to the high standard of the surgical department of the Mount Sinai Hospital. His many faceted contributions place him among the American leaders of surgery. Leopold Freund (1868-   ), professor of radiology at Vienna, advanced the knowledge of Roentgen-rays. Among other important things, he was the first to introduce X-ray treatment in certain diseases, such as skin diseases, bone tuberculosis, ischias, and in some surgical cases. He discovered the cumulative effect of the X-rays, found the effect of ultraviolet rays and the absorptive ability through the skin. Robert Lenk (1885-   ), of Tel Aviv, Israel, was the first to apply bronchoscopy for the diagnosis of tumors in the bronchi. Ernst Wertheim (1864-1920) of Vienna introduced the so-called Wertheim's operation for cancer of the uterus, modified Watkins' operation for uterine prolapse, and improved the technic in other vaginal surgical operations. Joseph B. De Lee (1869-1942), professor of obstetrics and gynecology at the University of Chicago, was the author of three standard textbooks: *Notes on Obstetrics*; *Obstetrics for Nurses* (11 editions) and *Principles and Practice of Obstetrics* (9 editions). He was the inventor of twenty-two obstetric instruments, and a pioneer in the production of educational motion pictures in obstetrics and gynecology. He raised the standard of obstetric teaching and practice, and increased the dignity of obstetric art in the United States by his contacts, lectures, writings, and visual education. Bernhard Zondek (1891-   ), professor of gynecology at the Hebrew University in Israel, is the leader of modern endocrinology. He and Selmar Aschheim originated the so-called Aschheim-Zondek test for pregnancy (1927).

Zondek described methods of preparation of the estrogenic and the gonadotropic hormones. Felix Mandl of Jerusalem, Israel, suggested a radical method of sacral operation for carcinoma of the uterus (1941). Ludwig Halberstaedter (1870-1949), professor of radiology at the Hebrew University in Jerusalem, made many contributions to the study of roentgenology. He demonstrated the destruction of ovaries in a dog under the effect of Roentgen rays (1905). In 1941 he recommended the use of artificial menopause in the treatment of cancer of the breast. Max Cutler (1899-   ) of Chicago first described transillumination as a diagnostic aid for tumors of the breast. He developed a new method of X-ray and radium treatment for cancer of the mouth and larynx. Max Thorek (1880-   ) of Chicago made fundamental contributions to the science and technic of surgery. He distinguished himself as surgeon, teacher, author and editor.

The founder of modern scientific otology was Adam Politzer (1835-1920) of Vienna who was the leading otologist of his time. He originated a method of opening up the blocked Eustachian tube and a method of illuminating the ear drum. He introduced the so-called Politzer's cone, a bag for inflating the middle ear, an ear speculum and a test for deafness of one ear. He was the founder of *Archives of Otology*, a clinic for ear diseases at the University of Vienna, and the Austrian Otological Society. Marcus Hajeck (1861-1941) of Vienna was a leader in laryngology. He improved the treatment of empyema of the sinuses, invented many practical nasal instruments and several devices for the resection of the septum. His approach to the treatment of diseases of the nose and sinuses was based on anatomical and pathological studies. Sidney Yankauer (1872-1922) of New York originated many surgical instruments, now in common use in the practice of laryngology. Robert Barany (1876-1936) of Upsala invented a caloric test for the labyrinth, Barany's pointing test of the cerebellum, and Barany's symptom-complex. In 1914 he was awarded the

Nobel prize for his work on the vestibular apparatus. Jacob Solis-Cohen (1838-1927) of Philadelphia performed the first successful operation of opening up the larynx to remove a cancer (1867). He was among the first to make otolaryngology a specialty in the United States. Gustav Alexander (1873-1932) of Vienna introduced an operation for thrombosis of the lateral sinus. He was a pioneer in organizing kindergarten classes for the early training of deaf-born children. He was tragically killed in Vienna by a syphilitic insane patient in 1932.

Among the great Jewish leaders in eye diseases was Louis Emile Javal (1839-1907) of Paris. He made many important contributions to ophthalmology. He introduced a method for the diagnosis of astigmatism, invented an ophthalmometer, and originated eye exercises in the treatment of strabismus. Louis Hirschberg (1843-1925) of Berlin introduced the electromagnet for removing particles of iron from the eye, discovered deep blood vessels in keratosis, described a method of measurement of the deviation of a strabismic eye, and demonstrated the changes in the eyes due to syphilis. He wrote the best history of eye disease. Carl Koller (1857-1944) of New York introduced cocaine as an anesthetic in eye surgery, which inaugurated a new era of local anesthesia in various branches of medicine and surgery. Stephan Bernheimer (1861-1918), professor of ophthalmology at Innsbruck, discovered the partial crossing of the fibers of the optic nerve in the chiasma (Bernheimer's fibers). Jonas S. Friedenwald of Johns Hopkins University made substantial contributions to the field of eye pathology. He suggested a new astigmatic chart and a new ophthalmoscope.

The most important achievement in modern medicine is the understanding of the complexity of the functions and the cells of the body and to learn their relations to the microorganisms that produce disease. After extensive researches the scientists discovered means of producing immunity against a number of infectious diseases and saved many millions from death. They succeeded in increasing the power of a living organism to resist and overcome infection by using certain serums for producing passive immunization and vaccines for producing active immunization. In this field Jewish discoveries are overwhelming. Waldemar Haffkine (1860-1930), a native of Russia, discovered a prophylactic vaccine against Asiatic cholera (1893) and an antiplague vaccine (1896). He became a benefactor of mankind, and in recognition of his effective work many honors came to him, including the naming of the Haffkine Institute in Bombay after him. Fernand Widal (1862-1929) of Paris discovered bacterial agglutination (1895) and its application in the diagnosis of typhoid fever (Widal test). His polyvaccine against typhoid was introduced in all armies during World War I. He introduced clinical sero-diagnosis and cytodiagnosis, and described anaphylactic hemoclastic crisis. Simon Flexner (1863-1946) of New York discovered the dysentery bacillus (Flexner's bacillus). In 1908 he originated an antimeningococcus serum used in the treatment of cerebral meningitis (Flexner's serum). Alexander Marmorek (1865-1923) of Paris discovered a serum antitoxic to streptococcus pyogenes (1896) and a serum antitoxic to the tubercle bacillus (1903). Max Neisser (1869-   ) studied immunity against staphylococci, diphtheria, typhus fever, and Friedlander's group of bacteria. His name is identified with Neisser-Wechsberg phenomenon, Neisser-Sachs complement fixation reaction for albumins, and Neisser's stain for the polar nuclei of diphtheria bacillus. Hans Aronson (1865-1919) of Koenigsberg prepared diphtheria antitoxin according to his own method. He discovered an antistreptococcus serum (Aronson's serum). Alexander Besredka (1870-1940), professor at the Pasteur Institute in Paris, discovered a method of producing local immunity, and introduced a method of anaphylactic desensitization. He originated the method of anaphylactic vaccination with small doses. This discovery is of great importance, as it prevents anaphylactic shock. After him is named the so-called Besredka's reaction and Besredka's vaccine. Israel J. Kligler (1889-1944), professor of bacteriology and hygiene at the Hebrew University, Jerusalem, developed scientific methods for combating malaria. He made extensive researches on the production of vaccines for prophylactic purposes against certain infectious diseases. Selman A. Waksman (1888-   ) of New Brunswick, N. J., discovered a new antibiotic agent called streptomycin, which proved to be a great boon in the treatment of heretofore incurable bacterial diseases such as tuberculosis, dysentery, influenza, meningitis and whooping cough. In 1948 he discovered neomycin which is of benefit in cases where streptomycin and other therapeutic agents are helpless. His purpose was to originate an antibiotic factor capable of inhibiting or destroying certain bacteria and yet non-toxic in its effect, and after isolating more than 10,000 cultures of actimycetes, he succeeded in isolating the streptomycin-producing organism which is a potent agent for destroying certain bacteria.

The following Jewish doctors are among the greatest pathologists and bacteriologists. Julius Cohnheim (1839-1884), professor of pathology at Breslau, was a pioneer in pathology. He revealed the nature of inflammation and suppuration by proving that the white corpuscles of the blood form the pus. His name is identified with Cohnheim's fields, Cohnheim's areas and Cohnheim's frog. Carl Weigert (1845-1904), of Silesia, was one of the greatest microscopic anatomists of the 19th century. He was the first to stain bacteria (1875). He introduced various methods of staining tissues for microscopic examination. By his improved technic for staining bacteria and tissues he rendered great service to modern scientific medicine. He advanced the knowledge of the structure and function of the nervous system. His name is associated with the so-called Weigert's mixture, Weigert's myelin sheath, Weigert's picrocarmine, and Weigert's stain for fibrin. Ludwig Briger (1849-1919) of Berlin described a test for strychnin, coined the term of "toxins", described bacillus cavicidus (Briger's bacillus), and discovered cachexia reaction in malignant disease (Briger's reaction). He also did pioneer work in hydrotherapy. Paul Ehrlich (1854-1915) of Silesia opened a new domain in experimental pharmacology and therapeutics, and is considered the founder of chemotherapy. He also did pioneer work in the morphology of the blood, in tissue staining, and immunology. He is most known for his discovery of Salvarsan. In 1908 he with Elie Metchnikoff (half Jew) shared the Nobel prize for his work on immunity. August Wassermann (1866-1925) of Berlin discovered the sero-diagnostic test for syphilis (1906). Karl Sternberg (1872-   ) of Vienna discovered the so-called Sternberg disease, Sternberg's giant cell, and Sternberg leukosarcomatosis. Karl Landsteiner (1868-1948) of Rockefeller Institute in New York discovered the four blood type differentiating characteristics and designated them as A, B, AB, and O. The discovery made blood transfusion a safe procedure, and saved thousands of lives. In 1930 he was awarded the Nobel prize for this discovery. Alexander S. Wiener (1907-   ) of Brooklyn, N. Y., with K. Landsteiner discovered the Rh factor. He discovered new methods of grouping dried stains of blood and secretions. Philip Levine (1900-   ), a native of Russia, with K. Landsteiner discovered the blood factors M, N, and P. In 1941 he discovered the cause of erythroblastosis fatalis, a disease of the newborn. Reuben L. Kahn (1887-   ) of Ann Arbor, Mich., originated the Kahn test for syphilis (1921). The League of Nations Health Commission recognized the significance of the Kahn test and helped to popularize it among the nations. Kahn introduced a new concept of immunity. In 1933 he received the award of the American Association for the Advancement of Science for his work on immunity.

Of great importance was the work of Jews in the field of hygiene and preventive medicine. A distinguished leader of Jewish hygienists was Milton J. Rosenau (1869-1948) who was a prime mover in the field of public health and sanitation. His textbook, *Preventive Medicine and Hygiene*, was called the bible of preventive medicine and passed six editions. Prof. W. G. Similie stated that Rosenau's book on preventive medicine has had more influence upon the advancement of public health throughout the world than any other single factor. The book was translated in many languages, including Chinese. Among his achievements was his method of standardizing diphtheria antitoxin and tetanus antitoxin. He and his co-workers confirmed and amplified the epoch making discoveries of the U. S. Army medical officers on the prevention and control of yellow fever. He popularized Schick's test, thereby saving many lives. Rosenau's organizing ability was manifested by his work at the U. S. Public Health Service in Washington, D. C., and in Boston, where he was professor of hygiene and preventive medicine at Harvard. He devised the unit for diphtheria, fought for protection of the community against smallpox by vaccination, led a battle for the pasteurization of milk, and succeeded through his effective work in lowering the death rate of infants and children. In the words of Eliot Joslin: "Rosenau has saved his native land from epidemics of cholera, the plague, and has fought smallpox, and freed Washington from typhoid."

At one time Palestine was great with scientific knowledge but had fallen into decay during four centuries of neglect under Turkish rule. During the past quarter of a century, Jewish scientists of the Hebrew University and the Jewish medical leaders have inaugurated a national public health program where none had been before. Prof. S. Ralph Harlow of Smith College has said of the country: "In 1914 when I first visited Palestine, it had been a dreaded waste of malaria-infested swamps, rocky barren hillsides, and sandy acres of unfertile soil. My second visit, in 1929, revealed a transformation that was hardly believable. Since the Balfour Declaration, the Jewish colonists had introduced modern agricultural methods, extensive sanitation projects, hydro-electric power, bringing light where all had been darkness. Most impressive of all was their courageous and constant battle with disease and the fastest lowering of the infant-mortality rate throughout the Near East." The following will serve as an illustration of the achievements of the Jews at Palestine in the field of hygiene and public health. Saul Adler (1895-   ), professor of parasitology at the Hebrew University in Jerusalem, is a world-famous authority on tropical medicine. He made comprehensive studies on the transmission of leishmaniasis which has relation to the control of kalaazar and oriental sore. This oriental sore has a marked virulence in the Far East, and the officials of the United Nations suggested to Prof. Adler to go to China to study on the spot an outbreak of oriental sore which is threatening the lives of millions of people. Prof. Ludwig Halberstaedter of Jerusalem, Israel, accomplished much in the treatment of cancer. Prof. Israel J. Kligler made fundamental contributions to the study of immunology and bacteriology. The fact that Palestine is the only country in the Middle East whose malaria is now of minor importance is due mainly to his practical methods of combating malaria. Dr. Kligler's pioneer work has been continued by Prof. Gideon Mer. During World War II, Prof. Mer was placed in charge of a malarial control unit which served in highly malarial areas in Iraq, Persia and Burma. For his meritorious contribution to the war effort, he was decorated by the British Empire.

Jews have been productive in biology and organic chemistry. Ferdinand Cohn (1828-1898), professor of botany at Breslau, was the author of the first monograph on bacteria, and is considered the father of bacteriology. At that time bacteriology was a department of botany. Cohn stated that organisms which were morphologically similar could be physiologically different. He made extensive studies in the minute fungi, and established the identity of bacteria with plants. He rendered to science a great service by his aid to a young and unknown district physician, Robert Koch. At that time many doctors entered Cohn's institute with claims of important discoveries in bacteriology, but Cohn proved that their theories were wrong. When Koch applied to him for a demonstration of his discovery that anthrax is caused by a specific bacteria, Cohn encouraged him, and he first publicized Koch's discovery in 1876. Julius Sachs (1832-1897), professor of botany at Würzburg, did pioneer work in the study of chlorophyl, and showed that sunlight plays a decisive role in determining their action in reference to the absorption. Jacques Loeb (1859-1925), head of the department of experimental biology at the Rockefeller Institute in New York, investigated the effect of electrolytic, thermal, and radiant energy upon living matter. In 1899 he demonstrated that the unfertilized eggs of the sea-urchin can develop into the swimming larvae by treating them with hypertonic sea water. Richard Willstaetter (1872-1942), professor of organic chemistry at Berlin, discovered several forms of chlorophyl in plants. He demonstrated relationship between this green coloring matter and the red coloring matter in the blood of animals. He also produced the anesthetic avertin. In 1915 the Nobel prize was awarded to him for his researches in the chemistry of chlorophyl. Otto Meyerhof (1884-   ), formerly professor of physiological chemistry at Cologne, investigated the mechanism of oxidation of the cells and the respiration of the muscles, enzyme chemistry, and fermentation. In 1922 he shared with A. V. Hill the Nobel prize for his scientific work on the physiology of the cell. Otto H. Warburg (1883-   ), professor of biology in Berlin, contributed to the chemistry of the cell. He demonstrated the peculiar fermentative type of metabolism of cancer cells. In 1931 he received the Nobel prize for his work on respiratory ferments and their mode of action. Otto Loewi (1873-   ), professor of pharmacology at Graz, Austria, made studies of metabolism, the vegetative nervous system, kidney function, digitalis, diabetes, and described a test for pancreatic insufficiency. In 1936 he received the Nobel prize in medicine and physiology for his fundamental discovery of the chemical transmission of nerve-impulses. Joseph Erlanger (1873-   ), professor of physiology at Washington University, made studies on metabolism in dogs, traumatic shock and other important problems in physiology. In 1944 he shared with H. Spencer the Nobel prize for their studies on the function of individual nerves and influence of pulse pressure on kidney secretion. Dr. Ernst B. Chain (1906-   ), a native of Russia, Professor at Oxford, England, shared with Sir Howard W. Florey and Sir Alexander Fleming the Nobel prize award for their discovery of the wonder drug penicillin. H. J. Muller, Professor at Indiana University, Bloomington, Indiana, was awarded the Nobel prize for his work in genetics. Moritz Schiff (1823-1896), professor of physiology at Geneva, was a man of great originality, displaying an almost prophetic insight into many medical problems. He anticipated Claude Bernard in pointing out the existence of the vasodilator nerves. He also anticipated Pavlov's pupils in the conception of conditioned reflex. He was the first to notice the effect of excitation of the cerebral cortex upon the circulation. He was a pioneer in the field of brain physiology. His classical experiments on excision of the thyroid made him a pioneer of the doctrine of internal secretion and thyroid treatment. He described the biliary cycle, which is named after him. Hugo Kronecker (1839-1914), formerly professor of physiology at Berne, made contributions on his specialty of a permanent nature. He investigated the problem of fatigue and recovery of muscle. He demonstrated that the heart's activity is "all or none", that means that it will either contract to its fullest extent or not at all. He invented the phrenograph, the frog-heart manometer, the perfusion canula, and the graduated induction coil. Samuel J. Meltzer (1851-1924), head of the department of physiology and pharmacology at the Rockefeller Institute in New York, was a leader in the profession. He is known as the discoverer of the so-called Kronecker-Meltzer's theory of the mechanism of deglution, Meltzer's method of anesthesia, Meltzer's treatment of tetanus, Meltzer-Lyon test for biliary disease, and Meltzer's law of contrary innervation.

W. H. Welch wrote of Meltzer as follows: "He had remarkable influence in furthering scientific research in both theoretical and practical medicine, especially upon young men." Bruno Z. Kisch (1890-   ), formerly professor of experimental medicine, physiology and biochemistry at Cologne, made important contributions to his specialty. He discovered a reflex closure of the eye, the law of irradiation of autonomic reflexes, and introduced a new test for toxic goiter. Alfred Fröhlich (1871-   ), formerly professor of pharmacology at Vienna, has done pioneer work in pharmacology and physiology. He flourished for half a century as an experimenter, teacher and author in his chosen field, and some of his discoveries have been accepted throughout the world. He describes the so-called Fröhlich syndrome in 1901. In 1910 he and Otto Loewi discovered that adrenalin following the administration of cocaine produces more intense effect. As a result of this discovery, the common use of adrenalin in combination with cocaine has been established in medical practice. In the same year Fröhlich and Hochward found that injection of hypoglysin produces powerful contractions of the non-pregnant uterus, and they recommended obstetricians to use hypoglysin during delivery, and it has been accepted in obstetric practice. He was the first to describe the stimulant effect of radium-emanation on the heart, and its protective action against anoxia in certain aquatic animals. David I. Macht (1882-   ) of Baltimore made fundamental contributions to pharmacology. Among other things he discovered a test and treatment for pemphigus.

One of the greatest anatomists of all time was Jacob Henle (1809-1885), a rabbi's grandson, who was professor of anatomy in Zurich (1840-1844), Heidelberg (1844-1852) and Göttingen (1852-1885). His contributions to medical science are of an epoch-advance in medicine. He was the founder of modern knowledge of the epithelial tissues of the human body. His name is associated with many structures of the body, such as Henle's loop in the kidneys, Henle's membrane, Henle's warts, Henle's layer, Henle's spine, Henle's fissures, Henle's cell, Henle's fibrin, Henle's sphincter, and the canal of Henle. In his *Handbook of Rational Pathology* (1846-1853) he overthrew antiquated systems and expounded new ideas. In 1840 he wrote a classical essay "Miasms and Contagia" in which he stated that infectious diseases are due to specific microorganisms. He searched for the pathogenic microbes with genius, but without technic but he did not discover them. He maintained that the germs are invisible because they differ so little from the tissues in which they are imbedded that they remain unrecognizable, and he stated that "before microscopic forms can be regarded as the cause of contagion in man they must be found constantly in the contagious material, they must be isolated from it and their strength tested." It was his pupil Robert Koch who thirty-two years later, confirmed Henle's theory by introducing his method of fixing and staining material films to discover the tubercle bacillus. Dr. Pagel stated that Koch was influenced in his epoch making discoveries by Henle. Victor Robinson pointed out that Henle laid the foundation of the germ-theory of disease. Dr. Rosen wrote that Henle gave a hint of the Virchow's cellular pathology and that Koch in later life admitted how deeply he was grateful to his great teacher Henle. Benedict Stilling (1810-1879) of Copenhagen introduced a new technic for the microscopic examination of the nervous system. His name is associated with the so-called Stilling canal, Stilling nucleus, and Stilling raphe. He also made valuable contributions to the physiology of the nervous system. Emil Zuckerkandl (1849-1910), professor of anatomy in Vienna, made significant contributions to anatomy. He described the aquaeductus vestibule, discovered a gland near suprahyoid and the so-called Zuckerkandl bodies.

Jews distinguished themselves also in the field of medical history. Max Neuburger (1861-   ), formerly professor of medical history in Vienna, enriched the literature of medical history. He is the author of a classical book *History of Medicine* (2 volumes, 1906-1910) which is the most authoritative on the subject. He founded the Institute for the History of Medicine in Vienna. He is considered the dean of medical historians. Charles Singer (1876-   ), professor emeritus of history of medicine in London, is the author of a great deal of studies on the history of medicine in antiquity and the Middle Ages, and has been the leader of the modern medico-historical school.

Jews have demonstrated their capacity as medical organizers in all its phases. As directors the Jews introduced high standards in medical institutions. Some of the greatest medical centers in the world were developed under the direction of Jewish doctors. Thus, the Frankfurt Institute reached its culmination under Prof. Paul Ehrlich's directorship; the Institute of Experimental Therapeutics in Dahlem, and the Experimental Laboratory of the Kaiser Wilhelm Institute in Berlin were ably directed by Prof. August Wassermann and other Jewish celebrities; the Pasteur Institute of Paris flourished under the directorship of Prof. Elie Metchnikoff and the collaboration of Prof. Alexander Besredka; and the Rockefeller Institute for Medical Research in New York developed under the skill and guidance of its director, Prof. Simon Flexner. Sigismund S. Goldwater (1873-1942) was a recognized authority on administrative medicine and public health, and rendered great service to the United States and many European countries in the field of hospital construction. From 1914 to 1917 he served as commissioner of health for New York City. He was the first to suggest dividing the city into health districts. He also established the first bureau of public health education in many health departments in the country, issuing newspaper releases and bulletins. From 1917 to 1929 he was director of the Mount Sinai Hospital in New York. An organized unit was formed at this hospital that served as a section of the medical department of the U. S. Army during World War I, which afterwards became known as Base Hospital Unit No. 3. Goldwater became chairman of the hospital division of the Council of

National Defense, and greatly influenced the methods of organizing army camp hospitals. Prof. W. H. Welch wrote as follows: "Mount Sinai Hospital has become an important world centre for the advancement and diffusion of medical knowledge." Jews distinguished themselves as co-founders of international institutions that serve humanity. Thus, Adolphus S. Solomons (1826-1910) of Washington, D. C., was co-founder of the American Red Cross in 1881. He is listed as a charter member of the American Red Cross, served as its vice-president, and was a delegate to the International Red Cross Conference in Geneva. He also was a founder of the Mount Sinai Hospital and Montefiore Hospital in New York, the Columbia Hospital in Washington, D. C., and the first training school for nurses.

The foregoing record shows that the medical work done by Jews since the 19th century was most efficacious in these countries, where the admission of Jews to universities and teaching positions was more freely practiced. It also demonstrates that the Jews acted as creators, pathfinders, discoverers, systematizers, teachers and leaders in modern medicine. The Jewish physicians advanced all phases of medical science and art, and their medical accomplishments are of significance and of a permanent nature.

THE HEBREW IMPACT ON WESTERN CIVILIZATION

BIBLIOGRAPHY

CUSHING, HARVEY, *Life of Sir William Osler*, Vol. 2, pp. 403-405, 1926.

GARRISON, FIELDING H., *History of Medicine*, p. 129. Philadelphia: 1922.

GOLDMAN, E., *Palestine Medical Research Aid in Rebirth of Country*, Jewish Advocate, p. 6. Boston: September 25, 1947.

KAGAN, SOLOMON R., *Jews as Nobel prize winners in Medicine*, The Hebrew Medical Journal, Vol. 2, p. 95. New York: 1944.
——, *Jewish Contributions to Medicine in America*, Second Edition. Boston: 1939.
——, *The Modern Medical World*, p. 31. Boston: 1945.

MAJOR, RALPH H., *Classic Descriptions of Diseases*, pp. 203-208. Charles C. Thomas, 1932.

NEUBERGER, MAX, *Jewish Physicians in the History of Medicine*, Medical Leaves, Vol. 5, pp. 64-66, Chicago: 1943 (translated by S. R. Kagan and F. K. Neuburger).

ROBINSON, VICTOR, *The Life of Jacob Henle*, pp. 106-107. New York: 1921.

ROSEN, GEORGE, *Jacob Henle*, Bulletin of the History of Medicine, Vol. 5, pp. 528-529. Baltimore: 1937. *Ibid.*, Vol. 6, p. 909, 1938.

SINGER, CHARLES, *The Jews, their History, Culture, and Religion*, Science and Judaism, Vol. 3, pp. 1076-1077. Philadelphia: Jewish Publication Society of America, 1949.
——, *The Jews, their History, Culture, and Religion*, Vol. 3, p. 1089, 1949.

Jewish Cultural Influence in the Middle Ages

By Cecil Roth

THE essential contribution of the Jews, as Jews, to the cultural life of the medieval world, and of medieval Europe in particular depended basically upon two factors. They were literate: and they were international. By 'literate' I do not mean that they could sign their names, and spell out a document (the acme of normal achievement among the upper classes of the Christian world at the time) but that they habitually read books, and in a large number of cases habitually wrote—or even wrote books—as well. And by 'international' I do not mean merely that they had cognisance of, and were to be found in, many countries. This was true of them also in the happier world before 1933, when the role of the Jews as cultural, economic and even political intermediaries between the various parts of Europe was so important—a factor in western civilisation to which far too little attention has hitherto been paid. A not dissimilar function was discharged during the Middle Ages by the Church, which likewise constituted a highly cultured international organisation with a footing in all countries, closely interconnected yet at the same time integrated in national life. The Jews of the Middle Ages, alert and widely-scattered though they were, could not then perform these functions, if only because they were not normally permitted to enter fully in the life of the environment. On the other hand, their circumstances and their distribution (more evenly balanced then, as between East and West, than in any subsequent age) permitted them to work on a grander scale: for by virtue of it they became the solder, not like the Church between different countries in the same orbit (that is, as one might put it, between different forms of the

[349]

same civilisation) but between warring continents, civilisations, outlooks, and cultural traditions.

There is no need to recapitulate here the details of a story that has been told so often. But it is impossible to understand the Middle Ages without a realisation of, first, the almost impenetrable veil which divided the Christian from the Moslem world, and second, the immeasurable cultural and scientific supremacy of the latter over the former. We must reverse the picture that the nineteenth century left as its heritage, of a world in which the European or Christian world was utterly supreme in every art of peace and war, and when a journey from Paris or London to Cairo or Fez was to experience a miserable decline in the standards of comfort, civilisation and knowledge. In the Middle Ages (or at least, in the early Middle Ages) the reverse was true. It was the Moslem world which enjoyed that unquestioned cultural supremacy; and to go from Paris to Cairo was to go up, not down, in the scale of civilisation, and in a not dissimilar degree.

But, while in the nineteenth century the spread of an international cultural veneer, the emergence or recognition of certain languages such as French as the medium of international relations, and the development of a superficial tolerance or apathy in matters of religion made possible a fairly easy intercourse between these two contrasting (no longer warring) worlds, there were in the Middle Ages no such amenities. Latin would carry a man through from one end of European Christendom to the other: but, if he attempted to cross the borderline into the Moslem orbit, he was at the end of his faculties. There was no common tongue, no common faith, no common outlook. He was utterly lost—in the same manner as say a Moroccan peasant would have been lost if in the middle of the last century, he had suddenly found himself, without help or guide, in the middle of London or New York. And the same was true, of course, in the reverse direction as well, with however the fundamental difference that the cultured Spanish or Egyptian Moslem who crossed the boundary line would have found in the barbarian lands to the north nothing that he on his side would have desired to emulate or to study. There was an all but impassable barrier dividing the culture, the luxury, the brilliance of the Arab world from the primitive strivings of Christian Europe.

There was, however, one element which was acclimatised or partially acclimatised on both sides of the line of demarcation: the Jews. To say that they were completely at home is of course excessive. In the Moslem world this was perhaps true sporadically, with certain qualifications; for here and there— in the courts of Spain, in Cairo, in Bagdad—we find Jewish poets, physicians and philosophers who were accepted into cultured society without reservation, though from time to time there might be and generally was an illogical, and even sanguinary, reaction. In the Christian world, on the other hand, the Jew was in the general view essentially an alien, notwithstanding the length of his establishment: though here again there are reservations, and this was perhaps less true in the Dark Ages than four or five centuries later, in the heyday of the Renaissance. But however that may be, Jews were to be found, widely scattered, on both sides of this earlier version of the Iron Curtain; and in both camps, however much despised as infidels, they were looked upon nevertheless with a certain degree of deference, as a cultured element—in the Moslem world, perhaps, as an element which shared in the culture of the environment, in the Christian rather as the votaries of a strange but (it was generally conceded) a superior civilisation: superior at least in all but the religious sense.

To the European Christian or to the Arab Moslem, therefore, the Jew whom he found on the other side of the boundary line was a little less alien than the general population of those strange lands: by this very fact, as it were, mitigating for the traveller the unfamiliarity of the background. The Jew moreover tended, by virtue of his historical experience, to be at the worst somewhat less isolated than those among whom he dwelt. He had, by virtue of his historical experience, an idea of lands other than that in which he lived, of cultures other than that which predominated in his own environment: it might even be said that his proud, exclusive sense of the mission of Judaism and the consequent superiority of the Jew helped to equalise all peoples in his eyes and thus preserve a sense of the essential unity of mankind. This may perhaps be considered sophistical. But, on the severely practical side, the Jew tended not only to preserve a sense of the unity of mankind, but also to constitute in himself a demonstration of and an instrument towards the slow realisation of that unity. Not only did he know, theoretically, of other lands, but in fact he so often had travelled thither or knew persons who had done so. Not only did he put all men on a similar ethical footing, but he so often possessed in addition the smattering of a foreign tongue (a Romance tongue in the Moslem world, an Arabic dialect in the Christian world) which enabled him to speak to other men from remote parts. The very fact that he was not completely accepted in any country implied that he could move about from country to country the more easily, finding himself only a degree less acclimatised in a new environment than he was in the land of his birth. Everywhere moreover, even though he did not know the language, he found coreligionists with whom he was able to communicate through the medium of the Hebrew of which he had at the least a rudimentary knowledge, not purely academic. (That remarkable collection of godly anecdotes, the *Sepher Hassidim* or Book of the Pious, so important for social as well as religious history, makes it clear that the Hebrew served on the Rhineland in the thirteenth century as a medium of communication with Jews from other lands.) The Jews thus provided much the same international link, between the Christian and the Moslem worlds, that the priesthood and the Church did between the various lands of Christian Europe. The specific services of certain individuals as cultural intermediaries were of outstanding importance, as will be seen. But obviously the greatest service of the Jews to European culture in the Middle Ages was the mere fact of their existence.

In the Moslem world, of course, they had the advantage of a basically similar background and linguistic affinity. (It must be remembered that the medieval Arabic civilisation stemmed from Mesopotamia and Syria, where the Jews had been from time immemorial an integral element in the population.) Moreover, although theoretically there was little to choose between Islamic and Christian intolerance, in practice the former generally though not (as is so widely believed, with complete disregard of historical fact) invariably tended to be far less stringent in application. Hence, almost from the beginning, and universally (not only in Moslem Spain, as is so widely thought) outstanding Jews took an intimate and integral part in secular cultural life, while the Jewish communities as a whole were imbued by it to an extent never equalled afterwards until the Age of Emancipation in Europe.

This cultural life, apart from its purely literary aspects (in which too the Jewish participation was marked), was based, as is well known, on the scientific and philosophical achievements of ancient Greece, which, forgotten or almost forgotten in Europe, had been discovered by the Arabs in the first flush of their expansion, translated into their own tongue, and in that medium studied, expounded, and commented with tremendous enthusiasm in the schools of Damascus, Cairo, Kairouan and Cordova.

It was their possession of this great store of knowledge and theory, basically European in origin but long since lost to Europe (or at least to Western Europe—the Byzantine Empire pursued its own curiously isolated path), which constituted the foundation of the Arab intellectual supremacy in the early Middle Ages; and the history of European civilisation in the Middle Ages is to a great extent the history of the recovery of these treasures by that curiously devious path. The translations were made sometimes direct from Arabic into Latin;

sometimes, the Hebrew translations which the Jews had made for their own use served as the intermediary.[1] Later on, systematic work was organised, largely under the auspices of the courts of Castile, Naples, and Provence, to make the Arabic corpus of knowledge available to Christendom, and in this activity Jews and ex-Jews (some of whom were actually taught Latin, at royal expense!) were widely, actively employed. Much has been written on this subject, and the precise degree of Jewish participation (universally admitted to be extremely significant) has been much discussed.[2] But perhaps the Jewish share was of greatest real importance when it was anonymous. More momentous than the work of an Avendaut or an Ibn Tibbon or an Isaac ben Sid or a Faraj of Girgenti or a Kalonymus ben Kalonymus, whose names occur so impressively in the basic monographs, was probably the unrecorded Jewish scholar in Toledo or Narbonne to whom the hungry Christian student had recourse to know what Aristotle had said on this or that matter, and who stammered out to him from the Arabic codex in his library an extemporised translation (yet a third person perhaps acting as intermediary, between the Hebrew and the vernacular), the enquirer perhaps jotting down his notes in a barbarous Latin. It was these informal and in some way almost grotesque encounters which reintroduced the lore of ancient Greece with its later Arabic developments to the consciousness of medieval Christendom, and thus prepared the ground for the systematic, but less significant, translations made at a later stage. And in such encounters, in almost every land, the role played by the Jewish intermediaries must have been of overwhelming importance.

At one vital point in the history of civilisation, in particular, this work of collaboration proved to be of peculiarly great significance. The most refulgent period of Arabic culture in Europe was not probably during the heyday of the Caliphate of Cordova, but in the so-called *taifa* kingdoms which rose on its ruins and filled southern Spain in the eleventh and twelfth centuries with a mosaic of rival and frequently warring states, both kingdoms and aristocratic republics, whose rivalry extended from the arts of war to those of peace and who developed accordingly a culture as brilliant and as widespread as that of Italy, in not dissimilar circumstances, in the age of the Renaissance. In this febrile activity, Jews played a distinguished part. But more important was the fact that when the taifa states decayed and their civilisation with them, it was the Jews who, it may be said, took the torch of learning from their hand and with magnificent success passed it on in due course to the European world, athirst for knowledge.[3] Some of the great names and achievements of this period are familiar enough to students. But it is hardly to be doubted that even in these cases what was most important was that part of their activity which could not be recorded. We are amply informed for example of the work of the Spanish convert Pedro Alfonso (Petrus Alfonsi), whose work as translator was so important and whose collection of Oriental stories under the title *Disciplina Clericalis* left an abiding trace on European literature, and ultimately influenced Shakespeare. But his personal contacts in northern Europe, as physician to Henry I of England or a visitor at Malvern Abbey, could not fail to be equally profound. The encyclopaedic activity of Abraham ibn Ezra, as philosopher, exegete, scientist, and grammarian, has always proved of special fascination to scholars, who however tend to regard his febrile travels throughout and beyond Europe—to England, France, Italy, Africa, perhaps Egypt and Greece—as no more than a picturesque element in his life; yet wherever he came he brought with him without a doubt the personal aroma of the Arab renaissance in Spain—and it would be an insult to the intellectual alertness of Christian scholars, as well as to the range of his own interest, to imagine that he was in touch only with his own coreligionists. We are specifically informed how Abraham bar Hayya of Barcelona, one of the outstanding medieval Jewish mathematicians and astronomers, collaborated in the middle of the twelfth century with the Italian Plato of Tivoli in the translation of various Moslem treatises on mathematics, as well as (in all probability) some of his own writings. It may be taken for granted however that their conversations were not restricted always to the work in hand. The same is necessarily true in a score of other instances.

Their work as intermediaries between the two mutually-exclusive cultural worlds was without any doubt the characteristic Jewish function in the Middle Ages: it was a function which they performed by virtue of their specific position and circumstances as Jews. That did not however preclude them from making memorable contributions to European civilisation as individuals.

That this was the case preeminently in the fields of medicine, science and philosophy must not be allowed to convey the impression that their interests were one-sided: for wherein else, other than in theology (in which the Jews did not of course fail to develop their own literature) did medieval culture reside before the age of Dante? The names of Maimonides and Isaac Israeli (to mention only two) were among the greatest in medieval medicine, their writings being studied sedulously down to the Renaissance period, and even later. Abraham bar Hayya's writings were fundamental for the introduction of the new mathematical studies (in particular geometry) to the European world. The astronomical writings of Abraham ibn Ezra in the twelfth century, of Abraham Zacuto in the fifteenth (once again, one forebears to multiply names, as one could do so easily) were not only widely studied, but exerted a vast influence: the latter, for example, being among the indispensable handbooks of the explorers and travellers of the Age of Columbus, who went equipped too with maps based on the work of the famous school of Jewish cartographers of Majorca and with nautical instruments drawn up to the specification of, or even manufactured by, the Jewish scientists of Provence and the Iberian Peninsula. In fact, even in the field of theology itself a considerable

Jewish influence was discernible; for, even though Maimonides wrote his *Guide for the Perplexed* from a fundamentally Jewish standpoint, his method of approach, made known to Christian scholars in an early Latin translation, profoundly affected even St. Thomas Aquinas; while the French Biblical commentator Rashi intimately influenced subsequent Christian exegesis through his Franciscan imitator, Nicholas de Lyra. The fact that Dante's *Divina Commedia*, the greatest literary production of the Middle Ages, largely depended for its cosmogony on the Almanac of Jacob ben Makhir (Profeit ibn Tibbon) of Montpellier is not merely an interesting detail; it is a symbol of the integral although concealed part of Jewish scholars and Jewish scholarship in the medieval Christian background.

It is generally assumed that immediate Jewish literary influences in the Middle Ages, at least on vernacular literature, were trivial. Slowly however material is accumulating which makes it clear that this too is an aspect that must be taken into account. The Jews were at pains to preserve only that which was written in Hebrew, but there seems to have been a far from negligible literature also in the vernacular. Recently for example there have come to light fragments of translations of the Jewish liturgy into Old French (written of course in Hebrew characters), the poetical portions being rendered into verse with the same metrical and rhyming scheme as the original—anticipating in fact the fashion which established itself again in the nineteenth century. There can be little doubt that at one time this rendering extended to the entire liturgy, being perhaps intended for recital in the women's synagogues; however, on the expulsion of the Jews from France such compositions lost their interest, so that the specimens now extant were only preserved by chance. The Old French elegy on the Martyrs of Troyes in 1288, an ancient Italian narrative-hymn of about the same date for recital on the fast-day of the Ninth of Ab, Apulian verses (said to be the oldest literary specimens of that dialect extant) preserved by the Jews of Corfu, and certain Spanish and Catalan writings of much the same type, clearly demonstrate that original composition in the vernacular was not only possible, but in fact common.

What has been enumerated was literature produced for a Jewish public, and indeed cut off from the general public because of the mere fact that it was written (like Rashi's famous glosses to Bible and Talmud, now so patiently studied by Romance philologists) in Hebrew characters. Yet there is evidence that Jews played a certain role too in ordinary literary life. A few instances must be assembled to demonstrate this unfamiliar fact. Among the medieval scientific translations there is one set which stands almost in a category by itself —that of the astrological works of Abraham ibn Ezra, which were rendered into French by the Jew Hagin f. Deulecresse, at Malines in the Low Countries, in 1273, and were thence translated into Latin. The series of vernacular translations of scientific and especially astronomical works made by 'Rabi Zag' and his colleagues at the court of Alfonso the Wise of Castile is of some importance in the evolution of Spanish prose. There are extant a few Italian sonnets and other poems by Immanuel of Rome, otherwise famous as a Hebrew poet and exegete, who in his Hebrew compositions composed a parody (rather an imitation) of Dante's *Divina Commedia.*

The writings of the German minnesinger Süsskind von Trimberg[4] in Germany, of Mathieu 'le Juif' in France (the latter indeed no great literary paladin), show that this phenomenon was not isolated. Very recent discoveries seem to suggest that these instances, some of them not unfamiliar to students, were only a few representatives of a wide-spread tendency. There have now emerged in the course of literary investigation the names of quite a number of other Jewish singers of the time: Salamone Ebreo of Ferrara, whose love-poems were highly thought of in Italy, the Provençal troubadours Bonfils de Narbonne who is attacked by Giraut Ricquier, and Charlot 'le Juif' who figures in a satirical song of Ruteboeuf, as well as the minstrels Folquet de Marseilles and Peire Cardenel mentioned in contemporary Hebrew sources; and a number of Jews even in England who were designated as 'le Romanzeur' or 'le Chanteur'. From these data, one obtains a different picture of the Jewish position *vis-à-vis* his neighbours in Europe in the Middle Ages. One sees now Jews not only conning the Talmud in the houses of study but also among the crowds surrounding itinerant minstrels in the market places and imitating what they heard—not merely in Jewish semi-liturgical ballads which they composed for their coreligionists, but in secular compositions in the tradition of the country, and taking their part in the great anonymous literary movement on which medieval European literature was based. And, when one reads of Jewish musicians in medieval Spain, or of Jewish courtiers and patrons such as Don Joseph de Ecija (who was once applied to by Alfonso IV of Aragon to send him some Castilian musicians to while away his convalescence), or of Jewish teachers of dancing and singing in Italy, we have to think of it in the proper setting, as illustrations of the integration of the Jews—or rather, of some element among the Jews—in the cultural life of the environment. And the important participation of the Marranos in the literary productivity of fifteenth century Spain (as exemplified in Fernando de Rojas, who produced in his famous *Celestina* the most important achievement of Spanish letters before Don Quixote) or the timid beginnings of Jewish contributions to general literature at the time of the Renaissance (as in the work of Salomon Usque, who translated Petrarch into exquisite Spanish verse, or in the famous 'Dialogues of Love' of Leone Abrabanel) are seen to fit into a pattern which perhaps goes back beyond the Middle Ages.

Yet all that has been said hitherto is perhaps secondary as compared with one other fundamental point. The mere fact of the presence of the Jew in medieval Christendom, and in medieval Islam, cannot fail to have had its importance. Here in the middle of a harshly uniform world there was scattered a sprinkling of persons, obviously and notoriously not less intelligent than other men, yet refusing to believe as other men believed. This mere fact—quite apart from the possibilities of personal intercourse and conscious influences—must necessarily have had a profound importance; for it made thinking men (and perhaps not thinking men only) realise the possibilities of an outlook on the verities of life which was not that of the Church or of the Mosque. The importance of this purely psychological factor, in stimulating independent thought and preventing a stranglehold of utter uniformity, cannot be overestimated. The Jew, as I have expressed it elsewhere, has played throughout history the role of 'The Eternal Protestant', and by this mere fact has tremendously influenced the world. He was the leaven of disbelief which caused the intellectual ferment out of which the modern world was born. For, in the Middle Ages as in all times, the essential service of the Jew to humanity was to be a Jew.

FOOTNOTES

[1] It is to be remembered, however, that many of the translations into Hebrew (as into Arabic) were terminal and did not come to the cognizance of the Christian world.

[2] The basic work is Steinschneider's *Hebraïsche Uebersetzungen des Mittelalters* (Berlin, 1893), a stupendous monument of erudition. From this derive a number of more popular accounts, e.g., Joseph Jacob's *Jewish Contributions to Civilisation* (Philadelphia, 1919), the chapters by C. and D. Singer in *The Legacy of Israel* (Oxford, 1927), and my own *The Jewish Contribution to Civilisation* (New York, 1940) and the relative section in my *History of the Jews in Italy* (Philadelphia, 1946).

[3] See for this now the memorable work of J. M. Millás Vallicrosa, *Estudios sobre historia de la ciencia española*, Barcelona, 1949.

[4] That Süsskind von Trimberg was a Jew has recently been questioned, but on what appears to me extremely slender grounds. 'A litigant's admission is as important as a hundred independent witnesses', in the Talmudic phrase; a principle which over-subtle literary critics of today might do well to bear in mind.

BIBLIOGRAPHY

ABRAHAMS, I. *Permanent Values in Judaism.* Oxford, 1924.

BEDARIDA, G. *Ebrei d'Italia.* Livorno, 1950.

BEVAN, E. R. and SINGER, C., editors. *The Legacy of Israel.* (Planned by I. Abrahams). Oxford, 1927.

BLONDHEIM, D. S. *Les Parlers Judéo-Romains et la Vetus Latina.* Paris, 1925.

CASSUTO, U. *Gli Ebrei a Firenze nell'Età del Rinascimento.* Florence, 1918.

FINBERT, F. J., editor. *Aspects du Génie d'Israel.* Paris, 1950.

FRISCH, E. *An Historical Survey of Jewish Philanthropy.* New York, 1924.

JACOBS, JOSEPH. *Jewish Contributions to Civilisation.* Philadelphia, 1919.

MILLAS VALLICROSA, J. M. *Estudios sobre Historia de la Ciencia Española.* Barcelona, 1949.

MYERSON, A. and GOLDBERG, I. *The German Jew: His Share in Modern Culture.* London, 1933.

NEWMAN, L. I. *Jewish Influence on Christian Reform Movements.* New York, 1925.

ROTH, C. *The Intellectual Activities of Medieval English Jewry.* London, British Academy, 1949.

———. *The Jewish Contribution to Civilisation.* Cincinnati, 1940.

STEINSCHNEIDER, M. *Hebraische Uebersetzungen des Mittelalters.* Berlin, 1893.

VERA, F. *Los Judios Españoles y su Contribución a las Ciencias Exactas.* Buenos Aires, 1948.

Judaism and Music

By Paul Nettl

THE subject "Judaism and Music" has provoked considerable discussion which, since Wagner wrote his infamous pamphlet, has become increasingly frequent. And recently Wagner's thinking was extended to its maximum limits by German-Nazism. Another non-Jew, Heinrich Berl, treated the subject in a more far-reaching and positive manner in his book which he entitled, after Wagner, *Das Judentum in der Musik*. It is his conclusion that the Jews are confronted with the solution of a very definite problem in the development of music in the Galud. Emphasizing the racial principle Berl claims that distinct and fundamental Jewish traits are distinguishable in the music of Jewish musicians irrespective of the school with which they are associated, whether it be German, French or Italian. Jewish music, according to Berl, is non-Western, but reveals a connection with the Orient that is intimate. Like the music of the Greeks, Jewish music is monophonically conceived, establishing a musical type which emphasizes melodic line to the neglect of harmony. Chordal harmony and polyphony, according to Berl, as evoked by Western culture are alien to Jewish thought.

Berl undertakes to assign Judaism a certain task in contemporary musical culture. According to him the music of the Jews belongs psychologically to the Orient and morphologically to the Occident. The expanding influence of Jews in modern music is thought to be causally connected with certain movements discernible in the history of nineteenth century music, particularly the increasing favor for linearism. It was the linear power of Schönberg's twelve-tone system that effected the destruction of romantic harmony.

And composers like Mendelssohn, Meyerbeer, Offenbach and others of Jewish extraction are characterized by an exaggerated use of the melodic line.

In an earlier publication,[1] I supported the idea that the quintessence of Jewish music in the Diaspora is found in the capacity of Jewish musicians for the development and extension of existing types through a certain exaggeration and radicalism. This notion refers to the Jewish principle of assimilation which is a basic aspect of the dualism in Jewish philosophy. It has been frequently observed that the Jewish soul is two-sided; the one is genuinely rooted in its tradition, in the faith of forefathers and its oriental home; the second, more extrovert in character, is an outcome of environment and the Jewish ability for assimilation within it. Doubtless we find here an explanation of the tremendous contrast perceptible in Jewish thought and feeling, and penetration for our insight into the musical expression of this intellectual dualism in the original and primitive neginoth and those songs of Mendelssohn like *"Wer hat dich du schöner Wald"* which became a symbol of German romanticism. Centuries of close affiliation with the Galud equips the Jew for assimilative acceptance of spiritual values and explains the ease and completeness with which he absorbs foreign thought and devotions, making them his own with new potential expressions. And it is this capacity of the Jew that enabled musicians like Offenbach, a German cantor's son of Cologne, to write music more typically "French" than Frenchmen themselves produced, notwithstanding his frequent use of synagogue melodies. It has often been observed that no music better mirrors the spirit of the French Second Empire than the operettas of Offenbach. To further illustrate the point we may mention the Jewish song writers, Pick and Krakauer who established the Viennese song-type, which tremendously influenced the course of Viennese popular music.

Before tracing the influence of Jewish activity on Western music it will assist our purpose to present a short outline of those facts respecting Hebrew music which are known. A. Z. Idelsohn in his book *Jewish Music in Its Historical Development* listed the frequent references to music which occur in the Bible. The music of the Temple in Jerusalem was in the hands of professional musicians, the Levites. It appears that instruments such as the *chatzotzra,* a silver trumpet were used in numbers up to one hundred and twenty in Solomon's time. The *magrepha,* a pipe organ of very powerful sound; the *tziltzal,* (cymbals) and others, chiefly served to announce the entry of the priests and to signal the congregation to prostrate themselves. Some instruments mentioned in the Scriptures are of Egyptian origin, as for example, the *nevel,* a fingerplayed, large harp; the *kinnor,* a lyre, plectrumplayed, similar to the Greek kithara; and the *halil,* probably used for exciting, virtuoso music. The only instrument which has survived to the present day is the *shofar,* (the ram's horn) which likewise belongs to the group of instruments used for signalling.

After the destruction of the Temple (A. D. 70) the music of the Hebrews fell into oblivion. Chanting, however, was preserved in the synagogue of both the Orient and Occident but more faithfully in the former where the art of ruling neighbors was less alien in its influence than that of Western countries. Idelsohn investigated the musical tradition of Jewish tribes in Yemen (South Arabia), Babylonia, Persia, Syria, Spain and central and eastern Europe. His studies revealed that although some of these tribes lived in strict isolation without contact with one another, many of their melodies were remarkably similar which gives irresistible evidence that they had a common origin, namely, the Hebrew Temple Song.

Dr. Eric Werner in his essay "The Music of Post-Biblical Judaism"[2] points out that two important facts must be considered respecting early Hebrew poetry. First, "the parallelism of Scriptural poetry, sometimes called dichotomical structure, which divides almost every poetical sentence into two parts, similar or antithetic in thought; second, strophic structure, especially in certain prophetic 'songs'... The principle of parallelism has to be considered the origin of all dichotomic systems of performance, such as the *responsorium*, the strict *antiphona* and the responsorial psalmody."[3] With this view we realize that one of the most fundamental principles of Western music resides in the structure of Hebrew poetry and consequently music, namely, the antiphonal principle exploited by early Christian song (Ambrosian and Gregorian song) and later in the bi-choral style of the 16th century Venetian School. And it was the Venetian School which gave impetus to the principle of concertizing, one of the most important characteristics of the Baroque which in its turn influenced the development of the modern orchestra. It is not my purpose to state dogmatically that dichotomical structure is the single source from which Western music springs. But there is slight doubt that it must be admitted that the principle of antiphony (i.e., alternation) with its extraordinary emotional and expressive power is deeply connected with the profound religious feeling of the ancient Christian and consequently the Hebrew, whose ritual is founded on the principle of question and answer.

Another basic concept of Western music is that of modality; consequently the principle of modern tonality is, according to the opinions of scholars like Idelsohn, Sachs, Hornbostel and others, rooted in the tetrachordal system of the Hebrew synagogue song. Many of the melodies of Gregorian chant which influenced the entire course of music history are based on ancient Jewish melodies. Egon Wellesz found that a Christmas mystery play (appearing for the first time in a manuscript of St. Martial de Limoges) stemmed from the same root as twelve Christmas hymns of the Jerusalem Patriarch Sophronius. In addition we find many melodies appearing in Ambrosian and Roman praxis of which the common well of all is the Church of Jerusalem and finally even beyond to the Synagogue of Jerusalem.

Medieval sources inform us of a definite animosity of the church toward the use of instruments and instrumental players. Whether the Minstrels (Spielleute) were bearers of ancient pagan or heretical ideas, or why these outlaws did not enjoy equal rights with the burghers should not be discussed here. But certainly the hostility of the church toward instrumental performance is intimately connected with the strict prohibition of any instrumental music in the synagogue, a tradition which is frequently considered an expression of mourning over the loss of the Temple and land of Judea. But as Dr. Werner observes a certain ill will against all instrumental music existed well before the fall of the Temple. Werner continues by saying "that this enmity against instrumental music was an act of defense against the musical orgiastic mystery cults in which Syrian and Mesopotamian Jews not infrequently participated."[4] It is certain that primitive Christian communities regarded instrumental music with the same belligerence, which held that it was improper for religious service.

The dualistic organization of the Christian chant, in which we distinguish two types, the syllabic (accentus) and melodic (concentus) songs, too, was influenced by the syllabic cantillation of the Scriptures in the synagogue and the melodic singing of the post biblical prayers. Also in the early church the cantillation of the Scriptures was psalmodized; whereas the prayers and hymns belong to the melismatic type.

But who was it who interpreted the early religious song? "Neither the Synagogue nor the Early Church knew of professional choirs. In the first three centuries the *sheliach tsibbur* (messenger of the congregation), an honorary precentor, performed all parts of the liturgy, supported by the worshippers' responses. The early Church used the terms 'psalmista', 'lector', 'anagnostes', or 'cantor' for the very same office. Only when monasticism attained its influence in the Church did trained monastic choruses become the rule in larger Christian communities."[5] From this time professional monastic choruses became more and more important. We see that in this respect Hebrew influence was decisive in determining the development of musical liturgy in the Christian world.

Christian liturgical music is founded upon the church modes which formed the tonal basis of Gregorian chant and early music up to the 17th century. When searching for the origins of modality we discover in ancient Syrian and Byzantine chant a system of tonal classification corresponding to the church modes of the Roman chant. These oktoechos or simply called echos are doubtless of Oriental origin. "Why eight modes seem to have constituted the generally accepted number is not quite clear... The earliest accessible sources demonstrate that the concept of eight modes was of calendaric origin."[6] Dr. Werner reminds us that "the Syro-Byzantine Oktoechos was originally a group of hymns to be sung on the eight Sundays following Pentecost", which according to Werner "reminds one strongly of the ancient Pentacontade-Calendar of the Near East in which eight holidays were inserted into a period of fifty days (seven weeks plus one day). We learn that Psalm "6 bears the inscription 'al ha-sheminit' ". Respecting this inscription the Jewish philosopher of the 9th and 10th centuries, Saadia Gaon, gives the following interpretation:

"This is a hymn ... in which the regular singers of the temple were ordered to praise God in the eight *lahan* (Arabic for "mode" or melodic pattern). The expression *"al ha-sheminit"* demonstrates that the Levites used eight modes, so that each time one of their regular groups executed one mode."[7]

We may assume that the eight modes of the Middle Ages go back by various linkages to old Hebrew ideas which, of course, may possibly have been influenced in turn by Babylonian and Egyptian usage. In as much as medieval modes which rested on Hebraic concepts are the precursors of the modern dualistic major and minor tonal system, we may go so far as to say that the entire proud construction of modern tonality has emerged from these earlier theories. In the case of the alleluia we see a direct contribution of the synagogue to the early church song, verified by Isidore of Sevilla in the phrase *"Laudes hoc Aileluja canere canticum est Hebraeorum"*. Even the word *neume,* the name for those extended melismatic passages of plain song, according to the opinion of musicologists like Riemann, dates back to the Hebraic word *Naima* or *Nagma* (sweetness).[8]

The culture of Babylonia, Palestine and Spain was affected considerably by the impact of the Arabian conquest in 711. As a result a Jewish civilization flourished on the Iberian peninsula between the years 800-1450. Among the numerous Spanish-Jews active in literary and intellectual circles, a number of writers writing in Arabic stressed the value of musical theory. One of them, Leo Hebraeus, wrote a tractate in 1343 on music "on demand of the outstanding teacher of musical science Philippe de Vitry". He even dedicated his work to that famous theoretician who was responsible for the establishment of the term Ars Nova.[9]

The most interesting document of Spanish-Jewish music is a three part motet of the second half of the 15th century discovered by Dr. Eric Werner. Written before the expulsion of the Spanish-Jews in 1492, "its text, a hodge-podge of Hebrew, Arabic and Spanish, is a Cabbalistic poem on the text of the Thrice-Holy. The music contains ancient Hebrew motifs as well as the *incipit* of a Gregorian Hymn 'Alma Redemptoris Mater' (in the contratenor)".[10] But this motet is not the oldest preserved manuscript of Jewish music. About two centuries earlier is a hymn written in four-lined Lombardic neumes.

Among the many fields of endeavor in which the Arab Jews excelled dancing figures prominently. It is truly remarkable that upon looking through the list of the unknown dancing masters of the Middle Ages and the early Renaissance, we find a number of Jews. The first dancing master of medieval time of whom there is record is the Jewish Rabbi, Hacen ben Salomo. He was commissioned in 1313 to teach a dance to be performed around the altar to the Christian parishioners of the Church of St. Bartholomeo, at Tauste in the Spanish province of Saragossa. At the court of Urbino in Italy there were two Jews from Pesaro, Guglielmo Ebreo and Ambrosio. Guglielmo, living in the 15th century, wrote a treatise about dancing. He is treated in detail in a study "A Jewish dancing master of the Renaissance", written by Kinkeldey, to be found in the memorial volume for A. S. Freidus, the New York librarian. Another Jewish dancing master was Giuseppe, a pupil of Guglielmo. Somewhat later we hear of two Jews from Ancona, Grescion Azziz and Emanuel de Rabbi Jalomacis, who were accorded the privilege of teaching dancing and singing by papal decree in 1575.

And as late as the 17th century there were Jewish musicians at the Court of Mantua—the harpist Abrahamo dell' Arpa Ebreo, and his nephew, Abramino dell' Arpa, an actor and musician. Joacchino Massarano, living in Mantua and later in Ferrara, was both lutenist and master of the ballet; and to complete the roster, we have the Jew, Simone Basilea, stage manager at the court.

After the expulsion of the Jews from Spain, the Italian Jews became important in the field of poetry and music. We must regard the series of Jewish musicians working during the Italian Renaissance as a truly remarkable phenomenon if we consider that with the single exception of Spain, neither in Italy nor any other European country either before or after the Renaissance until the Jewish emancipation of the 19th century did the Jews exert a really conspicuous influence upon the evolution of music.

In our effort to explain this short period of intense Jewish musical activity, we may suppose that the Italian Renaissance contained some peculiar conditions of fertility for Jewish development. It should be emphasized that Italy at this time was comparatively innocent of discriminatory practices. Even what anti-semitic feeling did exist in Italy never assumed such acrimonious forms as were common in Germany, a judgment which can be verified by a comparison of the German and Italian musical satires of the time.

In the literature of Italian vocal music—in the polyphonic madrigal, the "villotta", and particularly in the "mascherata", the Jew is often made the object of more or less harmless burlesque. In the famous madrigal comedy, *Amfiparnasso,* by Orazio Vecchi (c. 1551-1605), the Jewish ritual song is ridiculed; likewise other madrigals among the "villotte" by Azzaijuolo (publ. 1569) are, significantly enough, placed alongside a "Tedesca" and a "Bergamasca"; for the Germans and Bergamasques were, as we know, frequently travestied. In Adriano Banchieri's "Barca di Venetia" (1605), two comical "entrelocutori di barca", the clowns of this time, Bethel and Samuel Hebrei were introduced; in the three-part canzonette of the same composer we find a "mascherata di Hebrei"; and Banchieri, too, who seems to have a partiality for the Jewish implications, published in his *Pazzia senile* (1598), the satirical song "Sinagoga di Hebrei, Tic tac tic", which is meant to caricature the Jewish ritual song, similar to the gibberish in *Amfiparnasso.*

Such musical parodies of Hebraism are numerous in the vocal literature of the Renaissance; but they are always restrained within bounds, usually comical in purpose but never so brutal as the equivalent German satires. One of these, the contemptuous German musical caricature, "Judenleich" from the *Augsburger Tafelkonfekt* (1733) ridiculed a Jewish funeral and pokes fun at the Jewish ritual song. To these burlesques also belong numerous "Judenballette" which are found inserted between the acts of Italian operas in Vienna as in the Hamburg Opera of about 1700 and finally in the South German opera.

It would appear more important, however, to direct attention to the fact that the Jews themselves took an active part in the musical life of the period. But this is a question which has not yet been sufficiently investigated; it is more probable that Jewish historical research workers will succeed in illuminating its obscurity.

From among some of these Jewish musicians only the names are today extant. Such were Jacopo Sansecondo and Giovanni Maria, both of whom were employed at the court of Pope Leo X. (The former is said to have been the model for Raffael's *Apollo of Parnassus,* while the latter was the original for Sebastiano del Piombo's *Violinplayer.*) Others left not only their names but music as well, although these compositions have not yet received the attention deserving of their merit. Allegro Porta in 1625 dedicated two volumes of *Madrigali à Cinque* to Emperor Ferdinand II and another collection of madrigals called *Nuove Musiche* to Conte Alfonso da Porzia, chamberlain to the Elector of Bavaria.

While it appears that Jewish musicians were scattered throughout Italy, they were enlisted in quantity to the court of the Gonzagas in Mantua, in the latters' avaricious preference for Jewish artists. Among their number was Abrahamo dell' Arpa Ebreo; his nephew Abramino dell' Arpa, an actor and musician; Joacchino Massarano, a lutenist, sopranist and ballet-master, who arranged the court festivals at Mantua and Ferrara; and the Jewish musician Davidde da Civita.

The most significant of all the Mantuan musicians, however, was Salomone Rossi (d. 1628-?) who resided at the court of the Gonzagas from 1587-1628. His sister, Madame Europa, was a celebrated singer who appeared in the cast at the first performance of Monteverdi's famous opera *Arianna.* The son of Madame Europa, Anselmo Rossi, was likewise a musician, and is represented by a motet in a collection of motets (published in Mantua in 1618).

Distinguished from other Jewish musicians, Salomone Rossi clung tenaciously to his religious faith, writing a series of compositions for the synagogue which were collected and published in 1622. With this collection the foundation was laid for the vocal ritual of the synagogue throughout Italy. This first authoritative volume of Jewish Temple Songs, printed by

Bragadini in Venice, now extremely rare, has been published
in a new edition by the Parisian chief cantor, Naumbourg, in
co-operation with Vincent d'Indy. The work has an introduction by the celebrated Jewish scholar and poet, Jehuda da
Modena, whose son (so the preface states), a youth of twenty-
one and gifted with an unusual musical talent, was murdered
by his own co-religionists.

Rossi's compositions for the synagogue, written in Palestri-
na style, are peculiarly euphonious, just as are his numerous
madrigals on Italian texts. In contrast to the highly baroque
and ardent madrigals by Monteverdi, they are written in a
more conservative or popular style. Rossi was considered, like
Sulzer, Lewandowski and others, to belong to the group of
musicians who endeavored, in an artificial way, to accommodate contemporary music to the Jewish ritual. His work bears
the stamp of genius, and his larger compositions are assured
abiding fame. In any event, it is remarkable that Rossi, unlike
later Jewish composers, was not a musical innovator nor did
he participate in the revolutionary activities of the Florentines,
Peri and Caccini, although he worked side by side with the
giant Monteverdi at the Mantuan court. Only in instrumental
music was he in the vanguard of his period, being among the
first to transfer the new monodic style to instrumental works.
It is no easy task, therefore, to designate, exactly, what it is
that is Jewish in his music. Perhaps it may be said that he employed extensively Italian folklore in his sonatas and canzoni,
as was later done by Gustav Mahler and other Jewish composers. For dramatic music Rossi apparently had no great taste,
and participated only in the compositions of a religious drama
Maddalena which, according to the title, was set to music by
the most excellent musicians of that day, among them Monteverdi. Whether influenced by religious motives or by a distaste for dramatic style with the consequence that he gave his
aid reluctantly, Rossi's sole contribution was a short number,
a three-part balletto for voices and three violins, an almost
primitive piece in mascherata-style.[11]

Returning to Rossi's synagogal music, we encounter one of the most colorful personalities of Jewish history, whose protégé Salomone Rossi was. Working at the end of the 16th century toward elevating synagogal music to the high standard of contemporary art music, was the previously mentioned Rabbi Leon (Jehuda) da Modena. "Brilliant and profound scholar, anonymous pamphleteer against himself, composer and conductor, prolific writer, gambler, alchemist; in short, a jack of twenty-six trades (which he carefully enumerated), he founded a musical society in the Ghetto of Venice. One of his (converted) disciples, Giulio Morosini, gave us a good description of Modena's *Academia Musicale*. The practice of double-choirs, then the great Venetian fashion, was introduced to the Ghetto by Rabbi da Modena. He, himself, composed a series of such choral pieces in the style and technique of the Gabrielis. His chief merit rests with the fact that he induced Salomone de Rossi to compose a book of Synagogal music"[12] which was called *The Songs of Solomon* (published by Bragadin in Venice, 1622). The preface to this work by both Leon and Rossi is a most illuminating document. In the preface of Leon we learn that already in Rossi's time there existed two factions between the Jews who fought each other over liturgical questions. The fact that he directs the preface "to all those who know how to understand the truth" indicates that the work is intended not for the orthodox Jew but to those favoring liturgical reform and leaves no doubt respecting his leadership of a reform party. The preface of Rossi tells us that his music is genuinely original composition and is not based on traditional Hebraic songs.

It is strange that it is not a Jewish but a Gentile musician who must merit the distinction of having preserved parts of the old Jewish music, chiefly of the 17th century. Benedetto Marcello (1686-1739), who is otherwise best known for his operatic satire *Il Teatro alla Moda,* collected twelve traditional chants of the Venetian Jews and used them as the canti firmi for his famous collection *Estro Poetico-Armonico* (published in 1724) which paraphrases the first twenty-five psalms composed of original chants of the Spanish Jews (Sephardim) going back, as proved by Idelsohn, to the Spain of the 12th-14th centuries. To some of these psalm compositions he adds the motto *"Intonazione degli Ebrei Spagnuoli sopra il salmo"*. There is no doubt that Marcello was deeply moved by the ancient performance of the Spanish Jews in the Venetian Synagogue.

* * *

As we move from Italy to Germany we find reference to Jewish music and poetry in connection with German art in the celebrated German-Jewish Minnesinger Süsskind von Trimberg. In the famous Heidelberg Manuscript he is portrayed as a Jew richly dressed, wearing on his head a long peaked hat; standing beside him is a Bishop with a miter and staff. This portrait, perhaps, describes an attempt, evidently wasted, to convert the Jewish minnesinger born about 1220 in the village of Trimberg near Würzburg. Much has been written about Süsskind, whose songs are not typical of the German Minnesingers but are characterized by their defence of the indigent and oppressed, an attitude closely allied to Jewish thought; however, occasionally a pessimistic philosophy can be recognized in his work. He had little kinship to the Roman-Christian Minnedienst. His idea of *minne* was associated with the domestic bourgeoisie, and his songs were influenced considerably by Solomon's poetry and the Hebrew poets of the 11th and 12th centuries. But he wandered from castle to castle as any other Minnesinger, and in some of his songs we see documents of an early Jewish nationalism when he, for example, asserts that he will return to the ancient Jewish life and discontinue singing courtly songs. In Süsskind there is a certain kinship to the traditional Jewish Lezim, the jesters and clowns who under the mask of foolishness told the grandees of the world the biting truth. Unfortunately the only poems of Süsskind which have been preserved (Codex Manesse in Heidelberg) are without melodies.

[375]

But Süsskind was not the only Jew to contribute significantly to the older German poetry. There were two poets of the 14th century working in Strassburg, Clauss Wisse and Philipp Colin whose purpose it was to continue Wolfram von Eschenbach's *Parsifal* after the French poem of Manessier. As they did not understand French they used the assistance of Samson Pine, and in their acknowledgments at the conclusion, they praised the Jew for his help.

For the early German music history the Jews were not without significance. One of the most important German song books of the polyphonic period is the famous Lochamer Song Book written about 1450. The scribe of this book is, (as proved by Arnold[13]), Woelflin von Locham who dedicated, in Hebrew, the first thirty-six songs of his collection to his wife, Barbara. So we see that at that time when notation in Germany was almost a secret art, it was a Jew who collected polyphonic songs and preserved them for posterity, a historical fact which resisted the attempts of German nationalistic and Nazi musicologists to obscure it.

But in general, in contrast to Italy and Spain, the Jews in Germany did not have any influence on the general musical life of Germany. As the Jews were restricted to the ghetto, seldom did they find themselves outside their place of imprisonment. There is, however, the exception of the Jewish music bands which were common in the life of the time. Particularly in Frankfurt and Prague we hear about Jewish musical ensembles of the 16th century which played for weddings, baptisms and other occasions; and in the 17th century these grew to achieve a certain fame.

These poor minstrels who went from village to village, playing for only a few groschen for the entertainment of the people, had a very old tradition. As early as the 13th century we heard of the Jewish minnesinger, Süsskind von Trimberg, a symbol of ancient Jesters. Since his time thousands of Jewish minstrels, jesters and *marschaliks* (clowns), as they were called in Bohemia and Poland or *klezorim* which was their title in Yiddish—have brought enjoyment to Jews and Christians alike. The Jewish minstrel has even found his poetic transfiguration in a famous novelette by Perez.

In his book *Jewish Music in its Historical Development* Idelsohn has written much about this matter. As I pointed out in my book *Alte juedische Spielleute und Musiker,* the Jews, especially in Prague and Bohemia, had a musical brotherhood of their own which was greatly competitive with the Christian musicians. All the source material relating to that Prague guild of the 17th century has come into my hands so that we are informed even in regard to details about the Bohemian minstrels of the time of the Thirty Years War.

We know that after the destruction of the second temple in Jerusalem, playing on instruments was only permitted at weddings. Otherwise instrumental music could only be performed at the consecration of a synagogue or of a scroll. Meanwhile the natural musical gift of the Jews had soon become so developed that in almost all the cities in which Jews were allowed to live, *klezorim* played professionally at all the dances, both Christian and Jewish. In the 15th century Jewish musicians worked together in groups forming instrumental bands consisting of both men and women who wandered throughout the land. These Jewish musicians were everywhere hostilely received by their Christian colleagues for their greater popularity as performers. This opposition grew so intense that finally Jews were forbidden to play even at their own weddings. If we inquire into the reason for the rigid restriction by the authorities of Jewish musical performance we must ascribe it to its extraordinary popularity. As early as 1580 the Czech nobleman Peter Wok von Rosenberg reported that at his wedding a Jewish band was engaged "which played very beautifully for dancing". There are numerous such witnesses.

Prague, however, was in the 17th century a musical center for the Jews. In many records we hear about Jewish musicians in Prague who played in resorts and on different festive occasions. The recently discovered Prague sources direct a revealing light on social conditions in the ghetto. One derisive passage reads: "We would, nevertheless, be glad to see the fame of the Jews; under whom and on what basic principles they have learned their music; whether they, with their grand art, could pass a test in the fundamentals of music, in playing on the organ, other instruments, and the violin according to tablature, thorough-bass, and in all keys, in time and without error". The Jews were thus reproached for having no teachers and no knowledge of basic musical principles, but in the same breath their "grand art" is mentioned. We discover by these records that, although obscured, a flourishing Jewish musical life existed. It was doubtless this difference of Jewish melodic and harmonic treatment which led Christian musicians to complain of the inability of the Jews to keep time and tempo. It should be kept in mind that their synagogue music was of ancient Oriental origin of which modes and free rhythm were a familiar part. It appears that the Jewish instrumental bands were the counterpart of the modern gypsy band and that the rubati, portamenti, sad songs and exotic dances of the former were a particular attraction.

It appears that many Jewish musicians from Bohemia migrated to all parts of Germany. There is, for example, a record that the teacher of Isac Juda Eberst, the Cantor of Cologne and father of Jacques Offenbach, was the violin player Moses Formstecher, who was a son of the Jewish musician Abraham Wiener from Prague. He is responsible for the Jewish music tradition in the Offenbach family. We know that Offenbach's music, particularly that of the earlier period, borrows heavily from synagogue music. I also believe that his music has, in general, traces of the old Jewish "Lezim" (minstrel) tradition. Typical rhythms and melodic phrases originate there. Unfortunately that old "Lezim" music is forgotten, with few exceptions only; but this discussion could not be terminated without it being pointed out that according to the testimony of one of the most important Czech musicians of the 18th century, the Jewish minstrels exercised a great influence on their development. Franz Benda, the famous Czech composer and violinist, tells in his autobiography[14] about the company of minstrels in his native village, Staré Benatky, which was under the leadership of the old and blind Jew, Loebel. In the *Lebenslauf des H. Franz Benda*[15] it is said that he was indebted mainly to this blind man for the good tone he developed on the violin. According to his own avowal Benda also owed his unfailing accuracy of rhythm to the youthful impressions and to the performance of dance music in the Jewish band of "blind Loebel".

In the 17th and 18th centuries Jewish musicians living in obscurity participated only slightly with significance in the general musical life, although the names of a number of Jews who exerted a certain influence on European music persist. The name of Samuel Creton, evidently an Italian Jew, appears in the records of the Vienna Imperial Chapel in about 1660. The Italian *maestro di capella* Bertali warmly supports a petition of this apparently able Jewish musician who after his baptism had been forsaken by his Jewish relatives.

England of this time supported several Italo-Jewish 'cello players and composers who were active in her musical life. Among these was Giacomo Bassevi (1682-1783), a famous 'cellist and composer whose pseudonym was Cervetto (little stag), which indicates the German-Jewish name Hirshel. Dr. Burney, the celebrated English music historian, tells us that it was Cervetto in 1737 after he travelled from Italy to London who gave popularity to the 'cello in England. For many years Cervetto was solo 'cellist at the Drury Lane theater where he later succeeded Garrick as its manager. Burney goes on to say that Cervetto, whose ancestors were evidently the famous Bassevi family which spread over Europe, was of an amiable disposition but of odd appearance and manners. His large proboscis which was conspicuous inspired members of the audience to shout from the gallery with "play up nosey". He wrote a number of trio sonatas for 'cello the influence of which upon 'cello music was considerable. His son, James Bassevi the younger, (1747-1837) surpassed his father as 'cellist.

Another Jewish 'cellist living in London was Emanuele Siprutini who had been acquainted with the Mozart family during their visit to London in 1764. Evidently father Mozart had the highest esteem for his art otherwise it would be difficult to explain Leopold's diligent effort to convert the Jew to Catholicism. "I shall attack once again," Leopold writes to Salzburg, "patience I am going to become a missionary in London."

Because of the pervasive influence of the Catholic Church, Jews in Italy were not able freely to develop a high musical standard of more than local importance; and in Germany the Jews were completely relegated to obscurity, but as soon as the gates of the ghetto were unlocked a powerful stream of Jewish talent began to exert itself. The Jewish emancipation in Germany and Austria released great numbers of composers and virtuosos for active participation in international musical life. The majority figuring among the revitalized Jewish musicians of the 19th century were of Bohemian and Moravian extraction, an occurrence which is better understood if we consider the influence of the traditional Czech-Jewish minstrels of the 16th and 17th centuries some of the blood of which flows in all these Bohemian artists.

I want to mention first, by way of example, the pianist Ignace Moscheles (1794-1870) of Prague one of the most eminent pianists, pedagogues and composers of his time. His father was a Jewish merchant who entrusted him in 1804 to the tutelage of Dionys Weber, the director of the Prague Conservatory. At the early age of fourteen he performed publicly a piano concerto of his own composition demonstrating a talent which soon won for him success including the friendship of Beethoven, who permitted him in 1814 to write the piano score of *Fidelio*. Not always, however, was his musical ability equally esteemed. Between the two Jews, Moscheles and

Meyerbeer, who at that time resided in Vienna, existed a severe artistic competition which happily did not injure their personal relations. After several successful concert tours Moscheles settled in London following 1822 where he shortly became a piano teacher of great reputation. When, however, Mendelssohn founded the conservatory in Leipzig in 1843 he asked Moscheles to become a staff member; three years later in 1846 Moscheles accepted the appointment and moved to Leipzig. In his new capacity he contributed tremendously to the reputation of the already famous institution. As a matter of fact the three "M's" of music had an instrumental influence on European music in the first half of the 19th century, a phenomenon which can not be overemphasized when we remember that it was only as late as 1800 that Jews had been admitted without restriction into Western musical activity.

The compositions of Moscheles are of considerable importance. Among his seven piano concerti the third in G minor and the seventh (concerto pathétique) are today still frequently performed. Among his many chamber works a piano sextette and his piano sonatas, in particular the 'Sonata mélancolique', remain popular; but more important are his Studies, op. 70 and the 'Characteristische Studien', op. 95 which occupy such a permanent place in the literature that it is unlikely that subsequent studies will soon displace them. Outside of composition it was he who translated Schindler's biography of Beethoven into a large, edited, English version.

His life has been written according to letters and diaries by his own wife, and he has left in English the fragments of an autobiography. Moscheles's true significance resides in the fact that he for the first time gave authoritative readings of the Beethoven piano sonatas, along with his championing of the works of the other classical masters. His own works are characterized by pathos and grandeur which is an expression of his character. Although he was an exponent of romanticism, his personality may only be fully understood if we consider him as a reproductive rather than a creative artist.

The career of Moscheles opened the way to a great series of Jewish performing artists of the 19th century, which was truly remarkable in extent and ability. To mention a few the great violinist, Heinrich Wilhelm Ernst (1814-1865); the pianist, Alfred Gruenfeld (1852-1924); Mischa Hauser (1822-1887), violinist; Joseph Joachim, the friend of the Schumanns' and Brahms, who had the great merit of cultivating classical and romantic music in the 19th century; Ferdinand Laub (1832-1875); Siegmund Lebert (1822-1884); David Popper (1843-1913), 'cellist; Julius Schulhoff (1825-1898), pianist; Moritz Strakosch (1825-1887), pianist; Ignac Amedeus Tedesco (1817-1882), pianist. This group of instrumentalists listed above were all born in Bohemia or Moravia, no doubt descending in this or that obscure way from the old Jewish minstrels.

The Jewish musician has a remarkable gift for performance. In our effort to explain his unusual capacity we must remember that the Oriental musician is both creative and reproductive and that creation and reproduction are inescapably connected. The Hindu or Arabian musician has a number of musical patterns, e. g., maquams, ragas, etc., to which he is bound in composition not permitting freedom of creation in the Western sense. It is not unthinkable that in a musical culture in which creation and reproduction are equated that reproduction conceptually and practically will exist at a higher artistic level than in Western culture. The Oriental musician characteristically is more intense in his expression than the Western performer, a necessary upshot of the repetition of the maquam or raga. Likewise the art of improvisation is Oriental and southern in origin. In Italy improvisers were famous until the 18th century, and improvisation was common in ancient Greece, as we find it today among the Orientals. Following this argument we see that it is not accidental that the majority of virtuosos and other performers do not come from Germany but from Italy, Spain, the Slavic countries; and to the same category belongs the Jew who appears understandably with high frequency as conductor, pianist, violinist, singer, etc. Whereas in the 19th century the most important Jewish reproductive artists came from Germany and Bohemia, a tremendous stream of talent poured into the West during the early half of the present century from eastern countries such as Poland, Russia, Hungary and Rumania, to which I will add Austria and Czechoslovakia as they properly are ethnologically associated with the former. Among the Jewish interpreters proceeding from the above countries I want to mention a few examples in support of my argument.

Among the pianists are Anton Rubinstein; Nicholas Rubinstein; Alfred Gruenfeld, interpreter of Schubert and Viennese music; Moriz Rosenthal; Leopold Godowsky; Ignaz Friedman; Artur Schnabel, one of the classical interpreters of Beethoven, Schubert and Mozart; Wanda Landowska, who introduced the harpsichord into the modern musical world and grew to the foremost stature among interpreters of baroque music (musical performance is indebted to her for the rediscovery of the true sound of baroque keyboard music); Edward Steuermann, who became one of the most important interpreters of modern music; Franz Osborn; Rudolf Serkin; and Vladimir Horowitz to mention only a few. Among American Jewish pianists Clarence Adler and George Antheil should be mentioned. Others are Artur Rubinstein, Bruno Eisner, Dame Myra Hess, Leo Kestenberg.

As we have already seen the Jewish violinist had a venerable and old tradition. Following Joseph Joachim, I must again mention Wilhelm Ernst, the only rival of Paganini; Ferdinand David, a pupil of Spohr; C. Flesch, who as a teacher of violin ranks with Leopold Auer; Bronislaw Huberman; the excellent woman violinist Erica Morini; Efrem Zimbalist; Mischa Elman; Jascha Heifetz; Heinrich Bandler; Arnold Rosè; Nathan Milstein; Isaac Stern; Yehudi Menhuin, only to name a few.

Among the 'cellists are Heinrich Friedrick Dotzauer; David Popper; Maurice Frank; and Emanuel Feuermann.

In the end of the 18th century we find the Jewish operatic singer Hartung, who in Prague sang the part of Sarastro in Mozart's *Magic Flute* giving a performance which was mentioned by the "Prager Neue-Zeitung" of November 11, 1795 as being miraculous. Since that time a great tradition of Jewish singing and vocal pedagogy has continued to flourish influential for both opera and the concert hall. But more important has been the role played by the Jewish conductor.

For centuries, of course, the conductor had been identical with the composer, a combination which was equally true of the early 19th century when Felix Mendelssohn was at once one of the greatest composers, pianists and conductors of his time. And here in Mendelssohn is an example conspicuous of the degree to which Jews were instrumental in the promotion of world music, including even Wagner's who by no means held the Jew in high esteem. Carl Tausig (born in Warsaw, 1841; died in Leipzig, 1871) was not only one of the greatest virtuosos, called by Liszt the infallible with fingers of steel, and after Liszt the most remarkable pianist of his time but was one of the great promoters of the new German School and particularly the art of Wagner and Liszt. Besides Tausig, Heinrich Porges (born 1837 in Prague and died in Munich in 1900) founded the Porges Choral Organization in 1886 in which he propagated extensively the music of Wagner, Berlioz, Liszt and Cornelius. Another of the great choral conductors was Siegfried Ochs (1858-1929) who as director of the Philharmonic Chorus in Berlin had a tremendous influence upon the development of choral music in Germany during the second half of the 19th century. In this connection we should not forget the activities in America of Kurt Schindler (1882-1935) who founded the New York Schola Cantorum, now one of the most significant of American choral organizations.

Viewing the significant conductors of the 19th and 20th centuries we find a great number of whom should be mentioned Oskar Fried, Leo Blech, Bruno Walter, Alfred Hertz,

Joseph Stransky, Gustav Brecher, Otto Klemperer, Fritz Reiner, Egon Pollak, Joseph Rosenstock, Wilhelm Steinberg, George Szell, Artur Bodanzky, only to mention a few. And the young American, Leonard Bernstein, in recent times has achieved great success as a conductor. One of the greatest conductors of Jewish extraction, Gustav Mahler, must be considered. He was one of the first to demand accuracy and rhythmical precision of execution with a devotion to the art work itself to be explained by the intensity of his artistic personality. The merits of Mahler's conducting were preserved in a school of conductors of his own creation including such musicians as Oskar Fried, Bruno Walter, Alexander Zemlinsky, again to include a few. The intensive application of the artist to the art work is certainly characteristic of the Jewish temperament and tradition. Other Jewish conductors are Edwin Franko Goldman, Fritz Stiedry, Max Helfman, Aladar Szendrei.

Among those conductors who had the greatest influence on American musical life Leopold Damrosch and his sons Frank and Walter must be mentioned with particular praise. Leopold Damrosch, born 1832 in Posen and died 1885 in New York, belonged to the circle of Liszt and Wagner, both of whom had the greatest admiration for his talent. For ten years conductor of the Breslau Philharmonic Society he later toured with von Bülow and Tausig, conducting and performing as solo violinist. In 1871 he was called to New York to conduct the Männergesangverein Arion. His capacity for organization which had aroused active opposition in Breslau found in America free scope. In 1873 he founded the Oratorio Society followed by the Symphony Society in 1878. He conducted, in 1881, the first great music festival in New York, and it was he who was instrumental in the establishment of German opera in the metropolis. Recalling the brilliant season of opera are the words of a newspaper review of the time, "And together with Anton Seidl he conducted a season of German opera at the Metropolitan Opera House which will ever remain memorable in the musical annals in America. He was also the first to conduct Brahms in the United States." Indeed Damrosch was one of the greatest promoters of music in the United States, a distinction which he shares with his sons Walter and Frank.

What the Jews have established in the field of composition is even more remarkable and, if possible, it excells their attainments as reproductive artists. Felix Mendelssohn-Bartholdy (1809-1847), grandson of the famous Jewish philosopher, Moses Mendelssohn, received his general education in the old Berlin tradition of the early 1800's. One of the greatest geniuses of melodic invention, he continued the tenets of classicism irrespective of the fact that typologically and philosophically he belonged to the romantic era. In some areas of his creative activity he remains unsurpassed. His violin concerto in its exploitation of the violin techniques, in its melodic flow is the climax of that concerto medium. His *Midsummer Night's Dream* Music is one of the most remarkable documents of German romanticism notwithstanding the efforts of the Nazis to replace this music at productions of Shakespeare's drama. Even in the time of the Nazis it was frequently performed while mention of the composer's name was omitted. (In this respect we are reminded of the Nazi treatment of Heine's poems.) It has been observed that the sentimentality of Mendelssohn's tonal language and the intensity of his melodic power is to be explained through the monophonic tradition of Jewish music. But at once his tonal language seems to surpass in sentimentality the finest utterances of German romanticism; and some of his choruses as *Wer hat dich, du schöner Wald, Es ist bestimmt in Gottes Rat, Leise zieht durch mein Gemüt* and other compositions have come to be considered characteristic of the expression of the German spirit. The same may be said with equal truth of his *Lieder ohne Worte* and his two oratorios *St. Paul* and *Elijah*.

Apart from his creative effort Mendelssohn will long be remembered with gratitude for his rediscovery of Bach particularly through his performance of the *St. Matthew Passion.*

Even the Nazi musicologist Hans J. Moser in his *Musik Lexikon* (1935) was forced to admit that "Mendelssohn was one of the strong powers of the German musical romanticism for which all peoples must envy the Germans." No one admired Mendelssohn more than his great contemporaries Schumann and Brahms.

Wagner in his pamphlet *Judaism in Music* attacked Mendelssohn for his crystal clear forms, the perfection of his conducting and the harmony of his personality all of which must have irked the chaotic musician who felt in himself traces of Jewish blood. The question of Wagner's possible Jewish descent is still unsettled, despite the Protestant faith of his alleged father, the actor Ludwig Geyer. Certainly his psychological attitude toward Jewish musicians would be considerably more intelligible if we knew with certainty that Wagner was partly of Jewish extraction.

Among the objects of Wagner's caustic attack besides Mendelssohn was Giacomo Meyerbeer, properly Jakob Liebmann Beer, (1791-1864) who became one of the greatest and most successful operatic composers of the first half of the 19th century. A wealthy relative designated Jakob Beer his heir on the condition he would make a patronymic of his name by the prefix Meyer.

In his youth Meyerbeer met Beethoven who in spite of some animosity recognized the talent of the young pianist who played with distinction in Vienna. It was also Meyerbeer who beat the drum for the famous and sensational performance in 1813 of Beethoven's Battle symphony. As a student he worked with Hummel in piano and in composition with Karl Maria von Weber, Abbé Vogler and to some extent with Salieri.

In 1826 Meyerbeer moved to Paris where in 1831 he revealed himself with unparalleled success in the operatic world with his *Robert le Diable* with which he inaugurated his "grand opera" a descendant of the old French Tragedie Lyrique which returns together with the revolution opera and Cherubini to the old French baroque opera of Lully. With

Meyerbeer's operas *Le Prophète, Les Huguenots, Dinorah* and *L'Africaine*, the final climax of that opera type which combined theatrical effects of high dramatic force with considerable musical invention and mastery of musical forms was reached. There is no doubt that despite the hostility of Wagner the latter is highly indebted to Meyerbeer to which the operas *Rienzi* and *The Flying Dutchman* readily testify. That he influenced Verdi is to be expected.

Today, due to the disparagement to which Wagner and his partisans exposed Meyerbeer, a certain underestimation of his worth is still to be observed, as, for example, in the most recent publication on opera by the otherwise excellent Donald J. Grout.

Almost contemporary with Meyerbeer was Jacques Fromental Halévy (1799-1862), a pupil and friend of Cherubini and one of the most talented composers in the field of opera both grand and comic. His opera *La Juive* still holds the stage and is performed with invariable success. Although less successful than Meyerbeer, Halévy was an independent artistic personality of great dramatic power and excellent melodic invention. No doubt it was the unusual Jewish ability of sensing the needs and wishes of the public which assisted both Halévy and Meyerbeer in becoming the most successful operatic composers of their time. Respecting the capacity for knowing what it is that the public most wants, I should like to compare these two Jewish composers with the great film producers of our own day.

Mention has previously been made of Jacques Offenbach (1819-1880) who may be named as the third in the triad of great Jewish stage composers in 19th century France. The son of a Jewish cantor, Isaac Eberst, who in his youth was one of the wandering Lezim, Offenbach was grounded in the old Hebraic traditions. His first violin teacher, Moses Formstecher, who was received in the Offenbach Jewish community in 1792, was the son of the Czech Abraham Wiener; and so we have a continuous and unbroken linkage between Offenbach and the Prague Lezim which we mentioned in the beginning of the essay. Small wonder that the composer of the *Tales of Hoffman* often recalled the tunes which he had heard in his father's house and employed them in some of his operettas.

It should not be overlooked that Offenbach like Siprutini and Cervetto was originally a 'cellist before he turned to his brilliant career as a composer of light opera. And like Halévy and Meyerbeer he knew how to ensnare the favor of the European audiences; but unlike them he believed not in the grandeur of opera but in its possibilities for satire and parody for which the French people had considerable capacity, particularly during the second Empire. As in the *Beggar's Opera,* Gay and Pepusch at once ridiculed the great opera of Händel and the Italians and struck at the corruptions of society, so Offenbach satirized not only grand opera but social institutions as well, with wit unexampled in the history of music. Reflecting the decadence of the second Empire, he electrified Europe and America with the political implications of his operettas which were the product of his tremendous rhythmical power, sparkling melody and orchestration and an almost incredible stage consciousness. The development of opera in Vienna under Johann Strauss was strongly influenced by Offenbach's work. His opera *Tales of Hoffman* and operettas *La Belle Hélène, Barbe-bleue, La Vie parisienne, La Grande duchesse de Gérolstein,* and *Madame Favart* belong to the repertoire on the Continent, particularly in France.

The end of the nineteenth century saw the rising of such composers of Jewish descent as Paul Dukas, Charles Camille Saint-Saëns and Maurice Ravel.

Turning to Germany we find a number of Jewish composers in the romantic era who achieved some importance. Ferdinand von Hiller (1811-1885), apart from his composition, was a reputed pianist, particularly as a Beethoven interpreter. The oratorio *Die Zerstörung Jerusalems* and his operas *Traum in der Christnacht* and *Conradin* were permitted a remarkable success, but he was an Epigonus of Schumann and Mendelssohn whose strength resided in the smaller forms. Hiller's place in the history of romanticism is one deserving of honor.

In more recent times Carl Goldmark (born in Hungary, 1830 and died in Vienna, 1915) was one of the most successful operatic and instrumental composers of the late romantic period. He began his work in instrumental composition with the *Sakuntala Overture* followed by two symphonies, and various programatic overtures and chamber music in the style of the new German school. Among his operas *Die Königin von Saba* had considerable success; influenced by Wagner he showed a remarkable sense for theatrical effects combined with an extraordinary feeling for tone-color. Scarcely an opera has been written in which the biblical atmosphere is more convincingly conceived than this opera which I believe to be largely explained through his Jewish extraction. In many of his compositions as, for example, the symphony *Die ländliche Hochzeit*, op. 26; the overture, *Penthesilea*; the opera, *Das Heimchen am Herd*; and particularly in his violin concertos, many influences of his Eastern heritage can be recognized in his melodic patterns.

In the same connection Ignaz Brüll (born in Prossnitz, Moravia, 1846 and died Vienna, 1907) should be mentioned. Among his numerous operas *Das goldene Kreuz* attained success winning him the friendship and high esteem of men like Brahms, Eduard Hanslick and the great surgeon Theodore Billroth, one of the closest friends of Brahms.

If we now turn to one of the greatest composers of modern times, to Gustav Mahler, we should not forget that he was claimed as a native son by all three, the Czechs, Germans and Jews. Born 1860 in Bohemia, he died in 1911 in Vienna after a short illness contracted while conducting in the United States. We have already mentioned Mahler as one of the most important conductors of recent decades. The opera in Prague, Hamburg and particularly the State Opera in Vienna enjoyed a tremendous stimulus from his presence and work there. The Vienna Opera became the most significant opera house in the world under his baton; his Mozart performances were unexcelled. His saying was that any musician who did not give two hundred per cent of his energies to the pursuit of his art was to be despised.

But even more important than his conducting in the reckoning of music history was his composition, the center of which was his nine symphonies. Among these the second, third and fourth had choral sections as last movements and the eighth symphony, the *Symphony of the Thousands,* may be considered a choral work throughout. Formally they belong to the romantic period sharing characteristics in common with the symphonies of Schubert and Bruckner. I believe that the Jewish influences in his work are traceable to his ecstatic personality which reminds one of the Prophets and the Chassidic mysticism. He seems to be conscious in his works of the incompatibility of his existence at once as a Jew and European. It is as though he foresaw in many of his symphonic movements the catastrophe of Western civilization. Often his music suggests the prophecies of Jeremiah as an apocalypse of the Western Jewish world. By exaggeration of romantic expression and destruction of musical form he combatted traditional Western world.

Much of Mahler's thematic material, which has frequently been accused of triviality, is traceable to the tenacity of youthful impressions. Many of the folk songs, ländlers, and waltz rhythms which serve so admirably as the structure of his symphonic architecture came directly from the dreams of his youth, the penetrating understanding of which would require psychoanalytic techniques. Without doubt the folk song exerted a tremendous influence on his life. Examination of the *Knaben Wunderhorn Lieder, Kindertotenlieder,* the *Lieder eines fahrenden Gesellen* and many of the movements of the first, second and third symphonies demonstrates Mahler's ecstatic love for the folksong. (In this respect we are reminded of another Jewish composer, Salomone Rossi, who, working in the Renaissance, had a particular liking for the variation of folk melodies.)

In some of his symphonies, especially *Das Lied von der Erde,* Mahler became a pioneer of modern music through his destruction of romantic harmony. The importance of melody in Mahler's works, which are nourished by the lied, again exhibits the Eastern principle of melodic primacy. Vertical harmony, the prided prerogative of 19th century Western music, more and more lost its authority in Mahler's works; and it is from this heresy against tradition that Schönberg took his point of departure.

Arnold Schönberg, the foremost exponent of ultra-modern music in our time and one of the most incisive innovators in the field of music history, should also be understood as a composer who, in the pursuit of his art, took into account his Jewish heritage. Some believe that it is a native Jewish tendency toward revolution and radicalism which caused Schönberg to follow his chosen way with inflexible determination and unwavering purpose. Indeed, if we consider the fate of the Jewish people whose fidelity to monotheism has been unchanging, notwithstanding numerous temptations and persuasions for the abandonment of their religion, we can imagine without difficulty that the ecstatic belief of the personality in a theory once chosen is characteristic of the Jewish mentality.

In choice of principles of musical construction Schönberg stands diametrically opposed to Mendelssohn's position in music history. The latter was a champion of German romanticism in the frame of classical models, and yet Mendelssohn's inclination for melody is paradoxically akin to the music of Schönberg who is conspicuous for his denial of romantic harmony (which reached its ultimate climax in Wagner's *Tristan and Isolde*) and his emphasis of the melodic line. At first, Schönberg based his harmonic theory on the interval of the fourth which replaced that of the third; only later did he arrive at the method of the twelve tone technique. The novel achievements of Schönberg's system had already been fore-shadowed in Debussy's impressionistic devices of parallel chords, the whole-tone scale, chords not fitting in any traditional harmonic scheme; the mystic chords of Scriabin; and finally in the ingenious method of Joseph Hauer who independently devised a twelve tone system employing his tonal technique in short impressionistic compositions.

Neither melodically nor chordally did Schönberg's new music bear resemblance to the traditional tonal principles of 19th century romanticism. The most impressive examples of this style are his three piano compositions, op. 11, of 1908 and six small piano compositions, op. 19, of 1911 in which there is concentration of expression, a distillation of musical ideas unknown in earlier conventional and formal melodics and harmony. This music leaps directly from the creative motor of the composer to the understanding listener; any unnecessary phrase fragment is omitted.

Gradually Schönberg's method of composition matured to a new style (dodekaphony) which first found clear expression in his Serenade, op. 24 and the Piano Suite, op. 25. The chief principles of the style are that "every composition is based upon an arbitrary arrangement of the twelve chromatic tones, called *tone-row* or *series*. . . .The chosen succession of tones remains unchanged throughout the composition [with some exceptions]. . . . The octave position of any tone of the series can be changed at will. In addition to its original form the series is available also in its inversion, in its retrograde form, and in its retrograde inversion. [These] . . . four forms of the series can be used in transposition to any steps of the chromatic scale. . . . From this basic material melodic progressions and chordal combinations can be formed, the main principles being that the tones, whether arranged horizontally or vertically, must always occur in the arrangement of the series, and that its twelve tones must be presented in full, before the series can be used again."[16]

So Schönberg arrived at a purely constructive system which bears a certain resemblance to medieval and oriental concepts. The pure musical emotion is replaced by the intellectual and a craftsmanship deeply rooted in an extraordinary musical mind. It is a constructivism expressive of the reaction of modern man to the exaggerated personal psychology which prevailed in the 19th century romantic feeling of Schumann, Brahms and Wagner.

Schönberg's twelve tone system was adopted by his students Alban Berg, Anton von Webern, partly by Ernst Krenek and many others. Most composers, however, were not willing or able to follow his radical practice; among them Stravinsky, Bartok, Hindemith, Egon Wellesz, Honegger, Milhaud and Artur Schnabel. Whether the influence of Schönberg's constructivism will continue and increase or whether it will prove a dead end from which no development is possible is difficult to predict; but that Schönberg's music, resting on a Jewish background, has had a tremendous effect on the course of Western music is beyond dispute.

In more recent music parody has received more and more frequent use. Among the composers who have emphasized parody are Kurt Weill, Erwin Schulhoff (died in a Nazi horror camp), Milhaud, George Antheil, Louis Gruenberg, whose *Daniel Jazz, Vagabondia, Jazz Suite* and other compositions were sensational both in Europe and America. Of the Jewish expressions of modern opposition toward German romanticism in musical parody, Kurt Weill's *Drei Groschen Oper* is the most remarkable. Grounded in the ideas of the old ballad opera (*Drei Groschen Oper* in the *Beggar's Opera*) his music denies pathos, approaching the simple man. Kurt Weill, in his Broadway shows and particularly in his folk opera *Down in the Valley,* which is based on four folk tunes, demonstrates the tendency of American opera to discard subjects popular to the aristocratic and bourgeois 19th century. His operas were intended chiefly for performance by students of

colleges and universities, semi-professional and amateur organizations.

Whereas Jewish musicians responding to the situation in
European music travelled a road which led to constructivism
and esotericism, composers in America were equally able to
adjust themselves to the somewhat different musical climate
of their adopted country. One of the most distinguished
American composers, although born in Geneva, Switzerland
in 1880, is Ernest Bloch who settled in New York in 1907.
He was one of the first great musicians to become fully conscious of his ancestral tradition and to express this stern Hebraic belief in many of his compositions. It is not entirely co-
incidental that it has been in the United States that he has
expressed in music his religious feelings, in evidence of which
I quote his own words from the *Book of Modern Composers*.[17] "My faith is in justice—even delayed—on earth, in the
right of each man to live his life decently and usefully and
giving to the community what he can give, according to his
gifts, his forces. This is the great idea of our great prophets. . . ." In the paraphrase of Ewen: "Like the ancient Hebraic prophet, he has always been sublimely sure of himself,
always intoxicated with the self-assurance that the truth rested
with him, fully convinced of the significance of his artistic
mission. To Bloch, as to the Biblical prophet, love for and
faith in humanity were essential parts of his *Weltanschauung*."

Bloch was one of the first musicians to acknowledge his Jewish faith and associate it with his creative activity. In his view
racial consciousness is absolutely essential to music, although
nationalism is not. "I am a Jew. I aspire to write Jewish music not for the sake of self-advertisement, but because it is the
only way in which I can produce music of vitality. . . ."[18] Despite the fact that he pointed out that it was not his purpose
or desire to attempt a reconstruction of Jewish music or to
base his work on melodies more or less authentic, many of
his works, particularly *Shelomo* (1916) and the *Israel Sym-*

phony (1916) are, as Ewen suggests, "the proud and exultant affirmation of his race." This music which makes no claim of describing Hebrew folklore appeals in the manner of a short circuit directly to the souls of all who have read the Bible and penetrated its atmosphere.

However, Bloch by no means confined himself to the creation of "Jewish music", but extended his work to international music as well, as, for example, to America and Switzerland to which he pays respect. But even in these compositions traces of Jewish feeling are distinguishable; and one critic has rightly pointed out that the Indians in his *American Symphony* dance on Chassidic feet. Likewise, Dvořák's *New World Symphony* is more descriptive of his native Bohemia in its American atmosphere than of the Appalachians.

Carl Goldmark's nephew, Rubin, (1872 - 1936) adapted himself very swiftly to the environment of his new country. His compositions *Hiawatha*, the *Negro Rhapsody* and above all his *Gettysburg Requiem* are documents of genuine American feeling. Even more important was his capacity as teacher of George Gershwin (1898-1936) born in Brooklyn, although his ancestors came from Russia.

To be sure, American folk music was recognized as an aesthetic value by composers of the 19th century; and Dvořák in his *New World Symphony* demonstrated for future composers the function folklore could have in American art music. Since that time many composers have turned to Negro spirituals, folksong and to Indian tribal melodies for material, but it was George Gershwin who first caused the Broadway popular song to be regarded as folk music. Certainly he was not the first to use jazz in art music; Stravinsky, Milhaud, Schulhoff and many others had done so before him. But, nonetheless, February 12, 1924 was a turning point in the history of American music when Paul Whiteman gave the first performance of the *Rhapsody in Blue*. As John Tasker Howard puts it, "it was truly a shot that was heard around the world!" The importance of the *Rhapsody* is its introduction into the concert hall of jazz for its own sake (previously composers had used jazz fragments for occasional special effects), and its descriptive power so expressive of characteristic American life, in which ability Gershwin remains unsurpassed. Schönberg has designated Gershwin a real innovator. "What he has done with rhythm, harmony and melody is not merely style. His melodies are not just products of a mechanical combination, but they are units not to be taken apart. Melody, harmony and rhythm are not welded together but cast. These works have the native tang of American life."

There is no doubt that Gershwin had a powerful influence on American musical life. He is one of the most popular of American composers and in Europe is still regarded as the outstanding exponent of American music. One remembers well when he first heard the *Rhapsody in Blue* during the late twenties in Europe. People were first bewildered, astounded and finally enthusiastic, for it had in Europe, too, the same directness of appeal with which it held America spellbound.

Among the more recent American composers Aaron Copland should be mentioned. His works, which include all forms, seem to be a synthesis of French, German and American characteristics melted and forged by a great musical personality.

Of the many Jewish composers, partly native Americans and partly naturalized, I will mention only a very few. Among them Frederick Jacobi whose fine and delicate compositions frequently reveal his interest in Hebrew ritual and folklore; Leonard Bernstein, who both as a composer and conductor has impressed not only America but Europe and the Near East as well; Samuel Barber and David Diamond, whose works are included in the repertoire of the leading symphonic orchestras and are heard very frequently in concert halls and over the radio; and a group of composers who have attempted to construct a genuine Jewish national music nourished by Hebraic folklore and traditional synagogue music, including Jacob Weinberg, Lazare Saminsky, Isadore Freed, and A. W. Binder.

Austrian musicians include Eric Wolfgang Korngold, Paul Amadaeus Pisk, Karl Weigl and Hanns Eisler; and in Italy it was Mario Castelnuovo-Tedesco (now living in U. S.), a composer whose cosmopolitan attitude is happily combined with a racial consciousness as, for example, in the *King David Dances* and the *Three Chorales on Hebrew Melodies* and *The Prophets*, and the extremely gifted Lucas Foss.

Many Jewish composers imprisoned during the recent war in the horror camps of Hitler were able to escape alive, but many others, who certainly would have realized great reputation, perished in the concentration camps and gas chambers. Among those who were killed, to mention only a few, are the German-Bohemian composers Victor Ullmann, Hans Krasa, Erwin Schulhoff and Gideon Klein. Other composers who should be mentioned here are: Ermanno Wolf-Ferrari, the famous Italian, one of the most successful and genuine of composers, who became a modern exponent of the opera buffa; Sal. Jadassohn, who had equal reputation as a composer, (Epigonus of Mendelssohn), and theoretician; Ricardo Pick-Mangiagalli, of Czech-Italian parentage, shows in his composition real cosmopolitan spirit. We also should mention the "Polish" composers, Alexander Tansman, Gregor Fitelberg, (equally outstanding as a conductor), and Karol Rathaus; among the "Hungarians", Leos Weiner and Alexander Jemmitz; among the "Austrians", Hans Gal, (equally important as a musicologist), and Walter Kaufmann, now conductor of the Winnipeg Symphony. Among Americans, Mark Brunswick must not be forgotten.

One of the most significant Czech composers of Jewish extraction is Jaromir Weinberger whose folk opera *Svanda Dudàk* (The Bagpiper), Prague, 1927, enjoyed a tremendous success throughout Europe and later in America when it was given at the Metropolitan in 1931. In this opera, from which the "Polka and Fugue" has become standard in the orchestral repertoire, he uses Czech folklore in a way more genuine than is characteristic of other Czech composers. Just as the Jewish composer Pick, with the "Fiaker Lied" inaugurated the actual Viennese sentimental song which made its appeal to the entire world, and as Edmond Eysler achieved great success with his *Bruder Straubinger*, or Oscar Straus with his *Die Musik kommt, Walzertraum* and many other operettas, so Weinberger brought Czech melodies and rhythms to the world in a style more naive and popular than his great predecessors Smetana and Dvořák. Later in life he abandoned Czech folklore and replaced it with a more cosmopolitan language. It is even more remarkable for the scope of his activities that he composed a song cycle of Jewish melodies. Here in the United States where he is now residing, he has composed a *Lincoln Symphony*. It is amazing how many composers in the lighter vein are of Jewish extraction. According to a recent theory, it is worthwhile to point out that even Johann Strauss is said to have been of Jewish descendants. The father of Johann Strauss, the elder, was a Jewish innkeeper according to witnesses who knew the conditions in the family of the "waltz king". Both father and son Johann Strauss belonged typically to the Mediterranean race, and it is said that the Strauss family had Spanish blood in their veins. This riddle is solved when we authoritatively know that the family was really Jewish. As operetta and comedy composers, also Leo Ascher, Victor Hollaender, and, here in America particularly, Jerome Kern are the most important figures.

The last development in Jewish history, the political and cultural success of Israel, will without doubt have a decisive influence on the future course of Jewish music. A great many men of real talent are developing a native Palestine (Israel) music. Among them are M. Gnessin, M. Milner, S. Kisselgof, P. Lwow, I. Achron, M. Schalit, A. Schitomirsky, L. Zeitlin, S. Gurowitsch, I. Schulman, E. Sklar, I. Kaplan, H. Kopit, J. Stutschewsky and many others. The task of these composers will be to develop a Jewish national consciousness in music. Whether the result will be a Jewish national music which figures equally in the history of music in the sense of the national schools of the 19th century is difficult to predict.

In conclusion a few words should be added in respect to the contribution of Jewish writers to music and musicology. Among those who created German musicology Guido Adler deserves a position of first distinction. It was he along with P. Spitta and F. Chrysander who established musicology as a discipline ranking equally with the other studies of the liberal arts curriculum; and it was also he who founded the world distinguished collection *Denkmäler der Tonkunst in Oesterreich* which gave impetus not only to German historical editions but similar undertakings the world over.

Born in Moravia, 1885, Adler died in 1941 under the physical and psychological pressure of Nazism. One of the greatest teachers of musicology his Jewish students include such names as Egon Wellesz, Ernst Kurth, Karl Geiringer, Paul Pisk, Karl August Rosenthal. One of his pupils, Heinrich Rietsch (Loewy) became Professor of Musicology at the German University of Prague where he was prominent in the field of the German Lied. It is worthwhile to mention that the Jewish musicologists Max Friedländer and Moritz Bauer are recognized as the foremost authorities of the German Lied.

Outstanding among the figures of musicology is Curt Sachs, whose investigation of the history of musical instruments, the dance and the music of antiquity remains unexcelled. As one of the greatest Mozart scholars and an outstanding expert of Italian secular music in the 16th and 17th centuries Dr. Alfred Einstein must be mentioned with indebtedness. It was he who for years edited the famous *Zeitschrift für Musikwissenschaft* and re-edited the Köchel Mozart Verzeichnis.

Other Jewish musicologists of international importance are: Edward Lovinsky, Manfred Bukofzer, Otto Gombosi, Eric Werner, Hans Theo. David, Willi Apel, J. M. Coppersmith, Hans Rosenwald, Peter Gradenwitz, Georg Kinsky, Hugo

Leichtentritt, Erich Hertzmann, Werner Wolffheim, Wilhelm Fischer, Fernando Liuzzi, H. F. Redlich, Kathi Mayer, Lazar Saminsky, Joseph Yasser, Heinrich Schenker, and Joseph Schillinger.

In the field of comparative musicology Jewish scholars have likewise been prominent. One of the foremost men in the field of primitive music was Otto von Horbostel whose work is being continued in America by George Herzog; whereas Robert Lachmann, who formerly resided in Berlin and died in Palestine, became outstanding in the study of Oriental music. In general we can estimate that about fifty per cent of the men distinguished in musicology are of Jewish extraction.

To musical journalism Jewish writers have again contributed significantly, particularly in the large metropolitan centers of musical culture. In central Europe the key positions of musical criticism have been held by Jewish writers. In Berlin, Adolph Weissmann and Alfred Einstein; Adolph Aber in Leipzig; in Vienna, Julius Korngold, Max Graf, Paul Stefan and David Bach; Paul Bekker and Arthur Holde, in Frankfurt and later in U. S., only to mention a few. It should be emphasized that modern music has found its most zealous champions among the music criticism of writers of Jewish extraction. Without their efforts it is doubtful that contemporary music could have developed at the rapid tempo with which we are familiar. I couldn't possibly end my enumeration without mentioning one of the most important men in the history of the opera, Lorenzo Da Ponte, who occupied the key position in the field of the libretto around 1800. Born in Ceneda, near Venice, as the son of Geremia Corduangerber, he died in New York in 1838. It was he who gave the world the librettos of the greatest operas by Mozart: *Figaro*, *Don Giovanni*, and *Così fan Tutte*; and he who gave impetus to the introduction of the opera in the United States.

In summary we have seen from the evidence that Hebrew and Jewish influence on the course taken by Western music can not possibly be overstated. It is significant that the Hebraic influence became distinguishable in the early Middle Ages at the same time that Western civilization began to take shape as an individual entity. Furthermore, it appeared with greatest vigor following the Jewish emancipation during the romantic era, and in more recent times, when new and revolutionary movements have received momentum.

In conclusion it must be emphasized that the Hebraic influence on the development of Western music is only one aspect of the comprehensive cultural influence of the Hebrews on all Western civilization. Likewise we see that Christianity which permanently affected the course of Western music was germinated in the soil of Judaism. Not only the monophonic period but all the ensuing musical epochs must be considered as consequences of Hebraic religion. The whole of the Christian liturgy, the mass (cf. sanctus from Kodosh and the Psalms) and many other liturgical forms can be traced to Jewish origin.

The position occupied by the Bible in the development of Western music is unique. The Psalms and Lamentations have been the most frequently composed songs for the church. Many of the old Latin hymns and antiphons were based on the Psalms as were Luther's German chorales. Luther's battle song, "Ein Feste Burg" is a paraphrase of the 46th psalm, and the "Sanctus" of his *German Mass* is grounded in the Book of Isaiah; the Huguenot Psalter, written by the poet Clement Marot and set by Claude Goudimel, has exerted a considerable influence on following composition. The great stories of the Old Testament, too, frequently found musical setting; there are only a few of these stories which have not been composed many times. Foremost among the literature of such music are the oratorios of Händel in whom we discover the example of a great composer who, in accordance with contemporary notions, paralleled the political situation of the British with the Jewish people.

JUDAISM AND MUSIC

In Händel's oratorios the Hebrews are identified with the British who are represented as the chosen people of God in demonstration to the world of his omnipotence and omniscience. Many scenes of his oratorios (e.g. Judas Maccabaeus, Israel in Egypt and Esther) musically contrast the Jew and the pagan.

Biblical subjects have found musical setting times beyond enumeration; from Kuhnau's *Biblical Sonatas* to Bernard Roger's *Dance of Salome;* from Philipp Emanuel Bach's *Israelites in the Wilderness* to Honegger's *Judith* and *King David*; from Porsile's *Il trionfo di Giuditta* to Richard Strauss' *Salomé.*

In general it is safe to say that the entire development of Western music in countless of its characteristics and details find their origin in Hebrew sources. In every tone and every sound of modern Western music there remains a hidden fragment of times-long-ago-past-by, linking the spirit of recent music with the spirit of the holy books.

FOOTNOTES

[1] *Alte Juedische Spielleute und Musiker.* Prague, 1923.
[2] The manuscript of this essay generously provided by Dr. Werner.
[3] Werner, *op. cit.,* page 4.
[4] Werner, *op. cit.*
[5] Werner, *op. cit.,* page 12.
[6] Werner, *ibid.,* page 2f.
[7] Werner, *ibid.,* page 14.
[8] *Cf.* Neginoth in Riemann, *Heb. d. Mg.,* I, 2, p. 82.
[9] Coussemaker, *Scriptores,* III. X.
[10] Werner, *op. cit.*
[11] Nettl, *Alte Juedische Spielleute und Musiker.*
[12] Werner, *op. cit.,* page 20.
[13] Jahrbücher für Musikische Wissenschaft. II. Leipzig, 1867.
[14] Neue Berliner Musikzeitung, Jg. 10, page 32.
[15] Woechentliche Nachrichten, 1766, page 175.
[16] *Harvard Dictionary of Music.*
[17] Ewen, David, ed., Knopf, New York, 1942.
[18] Ewen, *op. cit*

BIBLIOGRAPHY

BERL, HEINRICH. *Das Judentum in der Musik.* Deutsche Verlags-Anstalt Stuttgart Berlin und Leipzig, 1926.

GRADENWITZ, PETER. *The Music of Israel.* New York: Norton, 1949.

IDELSOHN, A. Z. *Jewish Music in Its Historical Development.* New York: Henry Holt, 1929.

NETTL, PAUL. *Alte juedische Spielleute und Musiker.* Prague: Dr. Josef Flesch, 1923.

SABANEV, L. "The Jewish National School in Music". *Musical Quarterly,* XV.

WERNER, ERIC. *The Conflict Between Hellenism and Judaism in the Music of the Early Christian Church.* Cincinnati: Hebrew Union College, 1947.

——. *Preliminary Notes for a Comparative Study of Catholic and Jewish Musical Punctuation.* Cincinnati: Hebrew Union College, 1940.

——. *The Oldest Sources of Synagogal Chant.* New York: Reprinted from the Proceedings of the American Academy for Jewish Research, 1947.

The Hebrew Impact on Western Art

By Karl Schwarz

ACCORDING to Duenaburg, the historiographer, a nation's right to exist is based on two conditions: the *stability* and the *vitality* of its historical evolution. Now that Israel has entered a new phase of her history with the renaissance of her own government, it is particularly interesting to examine the factors that preserved the creative power of this very ancient nation to such an extent that, after a dispersal of 2000 years' duration, and despite the most awful collapse of an epoch that appeared to have begun with so much promise, like the one just ended, she still has the courage and the desire for a new national life.

In order to understand this phenomenon, which is unique in the history of nations, one has to go back to the archaic days and follow the development from there to this day step by step. This will enable us to recognize what the qualities of this nation consist of, what accomplishments it can show, and what relation these accomplishments had, and still have, to those of other peoples.

A short glance at the most recent past, to which we ourselves were witnesses, will show more clearly the connection between former times and now. Starting from a general survey, it will lead us to the answer of the questions that occupy us here, namely: *what part* did the Jewish people play in the fine arts, to what extent was it *self-creative, thereby furthering the arts,* and, finally, *will the future have anything further to expect from the Jewish nation in that field?*

The emancipation of the Jews, which set in with the French Revolution, initiated a completely new phase of their long history insofar as it resulted in a twofold reaction within

Judaism; a reaction that released two conflicting trends entirely unknown to Jewry before that time. The attempt at adapting oneself to a heretofore restricted environment, by assimilation to the nationality that was one's host, revolutionized traditional ghetto life; for, although it infiltrated new forces into it, at the same time it weakened its self-subsistence inasmuch as the growing urge for assimilation led to a simultaneous renunciation of many a condition that had remained intact until that time.

As man among men, the personal accomplishment of the individual improved, to be sure, showing his abilities to be quite equal to those of his fellow-men and enabling their acceptance in the general machinery of mankind; but, at the same time, assimilation estranged the Jew increasingly from his own community.

This centrifugal force was opposed by a constantly growing self-awareness which realized that preserving the essentiality of Judaism was the sole chance for its existence. For the creative element, which alone guarantees a continued development, must evolve from the *heritage* of a people so that, as axiom of a real and permanent emancipation as we understand it today—having made our experiences and gathered historical data in the interim—it is not man among men, but the nation among nations that must prevail.

And the Jewish people did preserve a healthy heritage in spite of, and all through, the tempests of the times. It was a heritage which, because of its long imprisonment, could not develop certain qualities, among them the artistic-creative qualities. However, as soon as the outward chains were removed, these qualities came to the fore. That they existed is indicated by the fact that they appeared here and there, and in all eras, but due to prevailing circumstances they could not gain universal acceptance and were, therefore, limited to individual occurrences.

In its earliest period Judaism had already developed its most important assets in the powerful spiritual-ethical structure of its Scriptures, with which it made an immortal contribution to the civilization of mankind.

When, in the first half of the last millennium B. C., the Israelitic tribes which until that time had been nomadic, began to settle down and form a national union in the land of Canaan, they first had to come to terms with already existing civilizations there, in the process of which the latter's modes of living were not without influence upon them. But what distinguished them a priori from the nations of the ancient world and, in the end, made them the givers, was the religious-ethical foundation established by Moses to which they were able to give sublime and ultimate form in their Scriptures.

The philosophies previously developed by the Egyptians, Mesopotamians, Arameans and Phoenicians were first supplied with life-giving breath by these tribes; just as they were the ones to make the human conscience aware of law and order; to clearly formulate its sense of responsibility to itself and to mankind, thus establishing the mightiest educational system of all times.

At the same time, however, they found the form in which to express emotions, in a heretofore unknown gamut ranging from the simplest word of quiet and introspect meditation to the wild eruption of extreme ecstasy; emotions in which their poets and bards, prophets and seers created pictures of immortal impressiveness. The books of the Bible echo with lyrical tenderness, epic profundity, nostalgic longing and dramatic agitation. They illustrate love and loyalty, joy as well as sorrow and, "like the eagle that soars freely above the lands," they rise from the plainest platform of the commonplace to the most translucent heights of philosophical perception.

Aside from the idealistic might of the Jewish state, their material power was the weakest, and its sovereign independence the most short-lived among the ancient nations; the others perished as soon as their external power was broken, and even the once-blooming Athens and all-powerful Rome succumbed to this iron rule. The Greeks had woven a myth around their world which Jakob Burckhardt terms "the serenity of genuine Greekdom" in his 'Weltgeschichtlichen Betracht-ungen'. It is the proper term for the carefree optimism which culminated in their artistic culture; and yet they were forced to cede to the might of the Roman Empire and dissolve in it. The Roman Empire, in turn, having forcibly subjugated the largest portion of the then civilized world, had to perish be-cause it was a structure whose intellectual culture was domi-nated by political aims which in themselves were time re-stricted.

* * *

The Jewish People, though, succeeded in preserving its cul-ture even beyond the period of its political state, and to main-tain its substance of life to the present day.

Through the centuries Jewish culture had an immediate in-fluence all over the world by means of its literature. It is not our task here to pursue the far-reaching channels in its course, via which it infiltrated into Christianity and Islamism, from the Orient to the Occident, from religious philosophies to the general scientific trends of the world. The question is rather, whether the Jewish ideology, out of the abundance of its visions and the fantasy of its narratives, inspired the fine arts; and if so, to what extent did it indirectly contribute to artistic fertility?

The works of art left by other nations did, to be sure, in-fluence and advance further art development by determining the form; archaeological explorations have again brought to light many mute witnesses of a once existing ingenuity which we may well say has to this day not been duplicated. But these very same witnesses testify to the fact that those rich civiliz-ations have vanished forever, while that which is preserved of Jewish memorials is small in number and artistically in no way comparable.

But just as the Jewish nation, although never a people of the sword, had its national heroes, who at all times were ready to give their lives for the honor and existence of Judaism, so, too, did it possess in the field of fine arts certain creative talents which, while not very important, were not altogether insignificant. The power of its words, on the other hand, was so strong that they echoed the whole world over; thus many things that the Jewish people were not to mold as a visual experience nevertheless found vivid expression in the imagery of all nations and all times.

In the second century B.C., the Bible was translated from Hebrew into Greek in Alexandria, at that time the metropolis of Jewish-Hellenistic culture. This translation acquainted the nations of the Occident with the Jewish philosophy and ideology, and subsequently was the driving force behind the early Christian art endeavors. The history of the Old Testament was repeatedly depicted in Oriental art all over; we come across it in the oldest manuscript illustrations, in the Byzantine mosaics, Roman sculptures, Gothic glass-paintings and ecclesiastical picture cycles.

The Islamic religion was to a great degree based upon the Jewish religion, tracing its origin to Abraham and his exiled son, Ismael; and it strictly forbade any sculptural portrayal except for purely ornamental forms. Yet from the 10th century on, Christian art brought to the countries of the Mohammedan world conquered by Islamism the animation for pictorial creations, which was developed further through the centuries particularly in Persian illustrative art, as set forth by Sir Thomas Arnold in his Schweich Lectures of 1928.

The Christian faith stimulated the imagination of the artists to new portrayals, by means of which they gave symbolic expression to the divine miracles associated with dogma. Art became an important medium to the Church in making comprehensible to the broad masses of the people the doctrine of Salvation, and also in leading to worship the usually illiterate layman by means of the picture. Thus were created the many biblical illustrations and other illustrated manuscripts, most of them originating in monasteries. Following the invention of typography, there was an endless deluge of books decorated with graphic pictures.

An even stronger effect was achieved by the pictorial decoration of the churches, where the glittering of the mosaics, the brilliant sunlight streaming through the stained-glass windows, the huge altar paintings and the color glory of the walls adorned with gigantic paintings captured the senses of the worshipping people. Thus innumerable artists, serving the Church, used the ideas established by Judaism and set forth in its Scriptures—ideas which today govern the entire modern world—to symbolize monotheism; many of them, spurred on by their own religious inclination, made the Bible the substance of their creations. Only Michelangelo and Rembrandt shall be named here as the greatest masters of their art to date.

In the ceiling paintings of the Sistine Chapel, Michelangelo created the mightiest imagery of the Creation and the figures of the Prophets, and in his Moses statue he typified the herald of the Divine Law. In gigantic proportions which exceed all prior conceptions of human strength, he formed these figures with brush and chisel as symbols of supreme and ultimate revelation, thereby pointing out to man his smallness and insignificance, and instilling in him fear of the power of heaven through these heroic and titanic figures.

In the works of Rembrandt, however, the greatest soul painter of all times, the biblical word became the reflection of human emotions. For this reason his art always has a conciliatory and stirring effect. It is neither heroic nor visionary like Michelangelo's, but describes everyday scenes and events, and simple, unassuming people. It does not ascend to heavenly heights, but moves upon the plane of the earth that is familiar to us. Rembrandt lived among Jews, and knew their customs, and he saw in them, in the old men and beggars on the streets, in the worshippers in the synagogues, and in the rabbis and scholars with whom he associated the living witnesses of the ancient people of the Bible, and therefore he made them the carriers of his portrayals.

The Bible accompanied Rembrandt through all the vicissitudes of his life, and was the interpreter of his own fate as well as of the universal human destiny. And so he formed into pictures the knowledge which he gleaned from the Bible in quiet hours of solitude, making quick sketches, as though he were a new prophet, and imparting immortal value to them.

*　　*　　*

Art is the heritage of all mankind, for it is an impetus innate in every man. It rises originally for purely practical purposes in the formation of tools and other objects, and also in the desire for mutual communication.

Likewise, the pleasure derived from colorful, glittering and sparkling things creates the desire to ornament oneself, while, by the same token, fear of the unknown generates the wish to make oneself unrecognizable. As a defense against evil and menaces, man makes himself amulets. And the amulet becomes an object of adoration and, finally, a deity. Among all the nations of the ancient world it is chiefly idolatry that stimulates the artistic fantasy, that directs the formative faculties towards special trends and enables them to find expression in all kinds of art forms.

When the Israelitic tribes entered history, large and mighty empires had already been in existence for a long time in which the arts flourished, chiefly in the form of temples dedicated to their gods. The Israelites also had their idols. But out of the desert they brought the mission of a new faith; faith in a spiritual God who could not be portrayed. And it was possible for them to establish their own culture only by banning from their midst everything that was connected with the physical imagery of gods. Thus was born the taboo on pictorial portrayals. The absence of pictures was supposed to educate man to concentrate his faculties on the purely spiritual, and to recognize Divine Omnipotence by meditation alone.

Since it had no chance to be active, the artistic sense within the Israelitic nation was necessarily stunted. However, there is no force that can completely kill the creative instinct inherent in everybody; at most it can suppress it temporarily. Accordingly, one can not a priori gainsay the Jew every artistic ability simply because, at a time when the art of other nations around him was flourishing, he has no achievements to equal theirs. For, even though at first the law deprived him of his desire for it, he did reveal a real talent for art that should not be underestimated. He proved it by his ability to absorb elements of foreign culture which, however, he did not merely adopt but which he always elaborated upon in his own way; and he further proved it by an urge for independent production that erupted at every opportunity given to him.

A united Israelitic state existed only under three kings. After barely ninety years, the state separated into two parts, the northern part coming under Assyrian rule after little more than 200 years, while the southern part became subject of Babylonian sovereignty after 350 years. In the south part was the capital, Jerusalem, where Salomon had built the temple. We have a fairly accurate report about its structure and interior, from which it appears that it was the work of foreign artists, as was the luxurious royal palace of Samaria, which was in the northern part. As yet there were no suitable Israelitic talents.

Following the Babylonian exile, Judea first became a Persian province for a period of 200 years. Thereafter it came under Hellenistic rule and ended up leading a sort of pseudo existence as part of the Roman Empire until, finally, its remnants dispersed over the entire globe.

After the destruction of the first temple and the temporary exile, the Jewish people underwent a spiritual change that influenced its further cultural development most decisively. Worship to an invisible God, which until that time had been conducted only by the priests as a sacrificial act in a central sanctuary, the Temple of Jerusalem, assumed new forms in that congregational prayer took its place. This led to the establishment of synagogues which could be erected at any spot simply as places for communal worship and learning, in contrast to the temples of other nations in which the deity itself was enthroned, ergo, present at its adoration.

We are in the dark about early foundations, inasmuch as synagogue buildings are known to us only from excavations dating to the Roman era. However, as far as form and decoration are concerned, they are the most important documents attesting to a specific artistic sense based on Jewish nature. This artistic sense also reveals itself in other expressions of independent forming.

There are, first, the coins. Some of them were stamped by the Maccabees, most of them, though, during the first and second rebellion against the Romans, and they were embellished with Jewish symbols. Additional testimony to the artistic talent of the Jew is given by the catacombs which the Israelites laid out in early times, as well as by the Hebrew script which they cultivated with particular care and which they developed into a special epigraphy.

Of great significance are the coin symbols which, for the first time, give expression to a definite *inclination* to art not in content alone, but in their specifically characteristic combination of *meaning and form*. From a sensual contemplation born of the ancient Jewish ideology, they created an asset of essential character which, together with other attempts that at first were only primitive, carries the germs for later achievements that were quite notable and that were to influence the general art development of the late antique period.

The ornament tradition, an important and frequently reappearing part of Jewish art production, is also initiated by the coins. The seven-branched menorah, for instance, designed after the temple candelabra which the Romans carried off to Rome, from then on appears as the symbol of Jewry, and has now become the escutcheon of the State of Israel. And the Tree of Life, which in the story of Creation symbolizes immortality, was adopted into Christian art.

Even in Abraham's days the Israelites buried their dead in caves or grotto-like pits. Later on they built subterranean chambers with benches and side niches upon which they placed the body. They collected the bones in square limestone boxes, the so-called ossuaries, which were usually decorated with simple ornaments. Such arrangements were also customary among the Jewish communities in Babylon, Egypt, Greece and other parts. They assumed gigantic dimensions particularly in the Jewish catacombs that were being built in Rome ever since the first century of the Christian Era. These catacombs are valuable both architecturally and because of their additional artistic embellishment.

In the catacomb of the Villa Torlonia, the typical symbols are portrayed upon numerous fresco paintings, and we also come across some occasional ones in sculptural form on sarcophaguses. The catacomb in the Via Appia, on the other hand, contains many inscriptions with picture decorations.

Most interesting, however, are the gold glasses with symbolic portrayals which were found in various places. These symbols, engraved in thin leaf gold and fused between two round glasses, decorated the base of small vessels. They point to Alexandria as the place of origin, whence the Jews brought to Europe the glass industry in which the Egyptians and the Phoenicians were engaged. As we shall see later on, in a different connection, the Jews practiced this industry in various places. They also manufactured glass vessels with imprinted ornaments, frequently using the seven-branched candelabrum for that purpose.

Early Christianity followed the Jewish example in its sepulchral art at first, as indicated by the Roman catacombs of Priscilla and Domitilla, dating to the second century. These catacombs also render the oldest picture types of Old Testament events in their frescoes and, according to Professor O. Wulff, who is an authority on ancient Christian art, "it can be assumed that these pictures were already given their form in Jewish custom."

The profound Jewish influence upon Christian art production lasted until the fifth century, and is apparent in the use of Palestinian ornamentation, plant and animal decoration and in symbolism. Gold glasses of the third and fourth centuries in Roman and Albanian graves bear the picture of the fish which, to the Jews, was the symbol of fertility. However, according to the Greek word it was re-interpreted to represent Christ inasmuch as the letters of the word Ιχθυς in acrostic form read: Ιησους Χρωτος θεου

After that the fish also played an important part in portrayals of the Jesus story ("The wonderful fish procession," see Raphael's tapestries), and was also to be found as an emblem on amulets and signet rings. As a matter of fact a great number of symbols used in the Old Testament frequently show up later in miniature art in the Christian interpretation.

Due to the confluence of Hellenistic and Jewish culture, and because of the reciprocal intellectual influence of the antique and Jewish concepts, a versatile art activity gets under way on Palestinian soil, beginning with the Herodian era, in which an intrinsic inclination for art can be seen that expresses itself in increasing strength.

In the outlying districts of Jerusalem, late-pagan forms with pronounced Jewish style elements were used in sepulchral structures, such as the so-called Absalom, Zacharia, Jacobus and Josaphat graves in the Kidron Valley, as well as the so-called Royal Graves which are decorated with elaborate façade ornamentation.

In Sheikh Abreiq, which as Beth-Shearim was the famous Galilean center of the Sanhedrin during the Mishnah period, excavations during the past years have brought to light the largest Palestinian-Jewish catacombs discovered so far. One of them has 16 central halls that are furnished with colored mosaic floors and decorated with many drawings of the menorah and other ritual implements and,—something that is particularly surprising—with lions, human heads, a man with a menorah, a horseman and a sailboat with two oarsmen;

also with the earliest pictorial rendition of biblical themes. A synagogue, apparently dating to the beginning of the third century, embellished with artistically designed marble ornaments is one of the discoveries which are still going on.

Israel's earth still conceals more unfound treasures especially in the regions which we know from the Bible and from history to have belonged to the Jewish commonwealth. Excavations continue to reveal secrets that throw new light upon the multifarious accomplishments of the antique era. Recently, for instance, at the banks of the Yarkon, near Tel-Aviv, in a section which it was assumed had never been inhabited by Jews, a Jewish city foundation was discovered from the period of the first Temple. As far as can be judged from the excavations, which have only begun, this city existed as late as the Roman era. And historical sites are known to exist in other parts of the country that so far have never been probed. Our knowledge, therefore, is still incomplete, which probably accounts for the fact that many associations of cultural exchange are unknown to us.

About the synagogues of the first century, for example, we know only that they existed both within Palestine and outside its borders. Our knowledge begins with the fundaments from the second to the sixth centuries which have been uncovered so far. They represent the most important links between the antique and the modern ideology, and are the most tangible proof for the historical continuity of Judaism which we mentioned in the introduction.

Abolition of the sacrificial cult assured the continuance of the monotheistic law and created new forms which the Christian and the Mohammedan religions adopted.

Arrangements at religious services such as the institution of a layman as supervisor and reader in place of the former priests, who represented a special caste; the reading of the Torah, which led to discourses and the sermon, and the resulting transformation of a temple dedicated to God into a place of meeting and worship available to everybody—all this led to re-formations that were given specific expression in synagogue structures.

The Palestinian synagogues are incontrovertible evidence of the Jews' creative talent. Here, as well as in many other feats, it demonstrates their ability to unite function and form in harmony, thereby creating artistic values of Jewish essentialness.

The synagogue structures which were handed down to us are by no means an architectonically original form system, for the Romans had introduced the basilican style of architecture for the foundation of public buildings, such as the emporiums and the exchanges.

The artistic achievement of the Jews is to be found in their ability to change the pagan style of profane architecture for religious purposes in such a manner that meaning and form became a new unity. Its eminent significance is the sacral architecture thus devised, which was continued and developed further in early Christian churches and in the mosques.

The Hebrew word for synagogue is "bet haknesset"—community house—and it already explains its purpose. For it was a combination of prayer, school, meeting and court house and, in addition, it usually contained lodgings for strangers. The main hall was used for worship and discourses, and differed from the lesser rooms in size and architectural furnishing. This main hall was reached through a pillared vestibule which occasionally served for meetings. Three portals led to the interior which was divided by columns into a wide middle nave and two narrower side aisles. Above the oblong side aisles and a rear passage ran galleries for the women.

In the center of the hall, upon a raised platform stood the reader's desk (bema). Originally the Torah scrolls reposed in a portable chest that was wheeled in for services. Later they were kept in a shrine standing in a built-in niche. A special chair was provided for the head of the congregation and placed next to this niche. The only stone bemas found were those in the synagogue of Bet-Alpha and in the sixth century synagogue in Aleppo (Syria) which was remodeled into what is today the mosque al-Hayat, and a basalt chair was discovered in Chorazin. Generally the bemas were made of wood, a fact that was confirmed by the findings in the great synagogue of Alexandria, and for this reason none of them were preserved.

On the whole the rooms appear to have been very luxurious, and furnished with mosaic floors and wall decorations.

The synagogue in Capernaum, which dates to the first century, and which was excavated in 1926, was a particularly magnificent structure of white sandstone standing upon a hill that was visible from the distance. Its ornamentation consisted of elaborately sculptured animal and plant motifs of which, however, only fragments have remained intact. Nearby is the basalt synagogue of Chorazin, but artistically it does not rank with the Capernaum building.

The mosaics frequently portray ritual implements, as well as constellations associated with the number twelve relating to the tribes of Israel, including animal and human figures. The first mosaic floor was discovered in Ain Duk, near Jericho; it portrays a Torah shrine flanked by two large seven-branched candelabra, an ornamental frame of birds and plants, and the Zodiac. The latter, however, is badly damaged. Like the mosaic floor in Gerasa, now known as Jerash, in Transjordan, it appears to belong to the early fifth century. In a frieze-like arrangement that is quite well executed, the Jerash mosaic pictures the animals leaving Noah's ark.

By far the most interesting, albeit decidedly more primitive, is the synagogue in Bet-Alpha. Not only does it have a stone bema and a built-in niche, but a mosaic floor that covers the entire interior surface, with an inscription indicating the period of origin to be between 517-528. Here we again find the Torah shrine with the two seven-armed candelabra; then, as the centerpiece, the chariot of the sun god Helios, portrayed in the Greek manner, drawn by four horses. It is circled by the Zodiac, and beneath it is a rather naive and primitive portrayal of Isaac's sacrifice. On the whole the execution is absolutely mechanical.

In comparison, the mosaic of the synagogue in Hammam-Lif, in the vicinity of what was once Carthage, is of high artistic caliber and extraordinary in its themes. A number of paradisiac motifs, distributed in several panels, are grouped together. Underneath is the spring of life in the shape of a fountain, two peacocks as symbols of immortality, and two trees: the tree of life and the tree of knowledge. In the upper section is the leviathan, the legendary fish; a wheel, probably representing the sun and, in the two lateral fields, as an ornamental border, various symbolic animals known from the Bible.

A Christian mosaic of the sixth century, likewise originating in Carthage, offers an interesting parallel.

The synagogue mosaics are unquestionably Jewish work, some of them so proven by inscriptions. However, the names appearing there indicate that the artisans involved came from Greek territories.

Of the synagogues exposed so far, the one in Dura Europos, halfway down the Euphrates, which was excavated 1932-1935, is the most memorable discovery. It represents a very specific type, thereby creating altogether new problems for archaeological research that have not as yet been solved.

The synagogue is fronted by a peristylar court, and entrance can be gained through two portals. It is a brick structure, consisting of a rectangular, non-basilican room with rounded arch. It is covered with paintings from wall to wall, and has a shell-like recess for the Torah shrine. The picture compositions contain a wealth of figures. Partly they depict Biblical stories found here for the first time, partly they show Hellenistic scenes. However, for the time being they cannot be explained unequivocally since some connecting links of the chain of development to which they belong are still missing. Also, the question as to whether they were created by Jewish or non-Jewish painters is debatable, the only definite fact being the date of origin, 245 A.D., as attested to by an inscription.

As far as the origin of the artists is concerned, we have information from two passages in the Jerusalem Talmud, from which it becomes apparent that painting was permissible at that time. One passage reads: "In the days of Rabbi Johanan, they began to paint pictures on the walls, and he did not forbid it." Rabbi Johanan died in the year 279, viz. not long after completion of the synagogue in Dura Europos. Therefore it can be assumed that paintings were done by Jews in other places, too, and that the artists of Dura Europos were Jews. A certain clumsiness in the realistic manner of portrayal would seem to affirm that fact, for it points to a lack of thorough training which the Greek artists of that period did possess.

The dearth of knowledge about similar synagogue types surely results from the fact that in times of continually re-current reaction, much art production that was a violation of the strict law against imagery was not tolerated and was destroyed by the Jews themselves, such as the relievos and mosaics in Ain Duk and Capernaum; it is also due to the fact that subsequently, synagogues were transformed into churches and mosques, or completely destroyed by Christian terrorists. Around 450, for instance, the Syrian monk Bar-sauma ravaged whole districts, thereby possibly causing the loss of just those documents that could have thrown some light on the origin of Dura Europos.

And while Judaism had to suffer under the most horrible persecutions, especially after Constantine I had given the Church political recognition, and since the first council of Nicea, held in 325, had declared that "Christianity had nothing in common any more with the murderers of the Lord"—and from the early moyen age until this day Jewish history shows an uninterrupted chain of such hardships—still, it was just this very despised synagogue which brought forth the old-Christian basilica and which played a leading part in its development.

In the synagogues is to be found the origin of the galleries, and the origin of the apse, formed after the Torah recess; the altar structure, raised in the manner of the bema, and the bishop's throne, adopted from the chair of the congregational head. Also, the perpetual light of the Catholic church is derived from the "ner tamid"—the Eternal Lamp that burns in the synagogues and that is already mentioned in connection with the Tabernacle.

Islamism, too, adopted various Jewish religious institutions which became important architectural adjuncts of the mosques. The "almimbar" is the Jewish bema, which was called "alme-mor" by the Jews ever since the 12th century, when they were living in close contact with the Mohammedans. And from the Torah niche the Islamites formed what in Arabic is called "mihrab".

The extraordinary significance of the pictures found in Dura Europos—for the time being the only ones of their type within the Jewish-Antique art sphere—lies in the echo which they evoked, chiefly in miniature painting, during the subsequent centuries.

Although the beginnings of Jewish miniature art are, for the present, still veiled in mysterious darkness, since concrete evidence is not available; and although various reports permit merely of vague suppositions, it is not improbable that biblical picture manuscripts were created by Alexandrian Jews in imitation of the Egyptian death registers and papyrus paintings and of Hellenistic parchment scrolls. (This would be a plausible explanation for the origin of the wall paintings in Dura Europos.)

The Jews had always written their Torah scrolls on parchment. Exact calligraphic rules had to be followed which, among other things, forbade the use of gilt letters. Calligraphy had been highly developed at an early stage, and even in the days of the Second Temple there had been, in addition to the plain scribes, a special class of calligraphers about whose talents, however, we know nothing.

The reports of Aristeas, Philo and Flavius Josephus to the effect that King Ptolemaeus was presented with a Torah scroll written in glorious gilt lettering by an Alexandrian Jew apparently are only a legend.

At any rate there is a wide gap of several hundred years' duration between these reports and the first appearance of illustrated manuscripts, caused, principally, by the disappearance of most documents. And if we overstep the limits of this chapter devoted to the antique era by inserting a short survey on the art of illumination, which belongs to the moyen age, we are justified in so doing because of the direct link and the significance of the Dura Europos paintings.

The earliest document is a Bible fragment in Leningrad, dated 930, which portrays among other things the temple implements but which, otherwise, shows a purely Islamic ornamentation. Other Oriental manuscripts of early origin demonstrate the same pictorial character. In the West, Jewish book illustration does not commence until after the 13th century. Its style is strongly influenced in part by the Christian monastery miniature art which was in full bloom at that time, but partly it can be traced to the pictorial art of Dura Europos.

One of the earliest manuscripts shows the handwriting of two artists. One of them follows the contemporary North-French style, while the pictures of the second are reminiscent of early window paintings in churches. Margoliouth therefore surmised that the latter must have been a Christian artist.

Several illustrated Passover Haggadas, created at about the same time, show the origin to be Dura Europos quite distinctly. In the Haggada of Serajavo, which is the work of a 14th century Spanish-Jewish illustrator, there are traces of styles belonging to the most varying periods. The ornamental scroll work is Gothic, some of the utensils are Mohammedan; the landscape elements have a certain affinity to the Psalter of Holy Louis, and the grouping of the figures resembles the

Italian trecento painting without, however, approaching the latter's elegance. Still, the severe and realistic narrative reflects absolutely the Jewish world of thought and feeling, and the compositional scheme reveals the direct descent from Dura Europos.

However, that the entire Jewish miniature art was nevertheless for the greater part dependent upon Christian art is demonstrated by a Haggada (Brit. Mus. 27210) in which the picture "Moses and his family leaving Midian" presents the Christian "Flight into Egypt".

The 46 medallions on the title page of a manuscript in the Schocken collection in Jerusalem are executed in French-German style; two others, described by Zofja Ameisenowa, belong to the North German art circle, as do the two familiar Nuernberg Haggadas and the magnificent Darmstadt Haggada. In all of them, direct copies of Christian designs occur frequently.

Since it is impossible to enumerate here all the reciprocal examples, however interesting, which Leveen discussed extensively in his Schweich Lectures, let us just say, in recapitulation, that the ancient Jewish culture has constantly remained alive, even in recent centuries, while Christianity, which had early recognized the value of art "ad majorem dei gloriam", exploited it in large measure.

That this is so becomes apparent from the earliest documents known so far. The oldest fragments, apparently from the fourth century, are the still rather primitive miniatures of the Itala manuscript, discovered in Quedlinburg in 1865, and the parchment scroll of the Vaticana. The latter depicts the conquest of Canaan by Joshua in the manner of antique-Greek murals, and is approximated by the "Cotton" Bible, badly damaged by fire in 1731, the style of which points to the Byzantine mosaics of S. Marco.

Two manuscripts of the 7th century prove the direct connection with Dura Europos. One is the Peschita Bible, now in the National Library of Paris, which originated in Syria. Its portrayal of individual figures in juxtaposition corresponds almost precisely to the four figures on the west wall of the synagogue, both as to posture and costume. The second one is the Parisian Asburnham Pentateuch, the title page of which J. C. Sloane recognized several years ago as being a combination of the portrayal of the Torah shrine in Dura Europos and the mosaic in Bet-Alpha.

* * *

The history of mankind from its inception to this day is an interplay of nations which take turns: one power displaces the other just as soon as it succeeds in developing its strength to such a degree that, it being the stronger, it is able to destroy the weaker opponent. The larger a nation becomes, the more difficult does its entire administrative machine become, and the more complicated its inner organization, for with every new expansion it must absorb the most diversified cultural elements and blend them into one unit.

Toward the second century the Roman Empire had become the ruler of almost all civilized countries of the world then existing. Spain, Gaul, Britain and all the states of the Orient were its subjects, and wealthy Egypt was more or less the emperor's private property. The empire's huge army was composed of soldiers from all nations, and its well-to-do citizens all converged upon Rome in order to share in the riches accumulated there; riches that came from a commerce encompassing lands of all the world and reaching from the Nile to the Rhine and the Danube, from Africa and Asia to the coasts of the Atlantic Ocean and the North Sea.

At first the Jews, who had settled in all parts of the empire after either having fled or been exiled from their homeland, enjoyed civil rights and religious tolerance, as did the sects of Neo-Christians that sprang up among them; but their cultural difference already carried the seed of disintegration. The growing wealth and luxury of the Roman-pagan aristocracy, and the coincident increase in the impoverishment and enslavement of the masses led the latter in growing numbers to Christendom, which enticed them with the promise of a better life in the Hereafter. Although Christianity had been suppressed and persecuted since the reign of Diocletian, it was constantly growing stronger and finally succeeded in splitting the powerful block into an eastern and a western empire.

The partition changed the entire structure of the country. The wealth once gained from world commerce was declining due to the shrinking of this world trade. Because of this the rich, who were recklessly squandering their wealth, started to extort the country with increasing harshness, with the result that the people were pauperized.

The order that had once prevailed in the state and the army disappeared, the treasury was emptied, morale sank, and the inner decline progressed rapidly. In 410 Alaric, king of the Goths, entered Rome, plundered the city and stole the treasures of the Jerusalem Temple that were kept there. In 452 the Huns pillaged Northern Italy, and three years later the country was overrun by the Vandals, and with that the fate of the Roman Empire was sealed once and for all.

The large Jewish communities in Italy and the colonies likewise lost their mutual support in the general chaos of migration and sank further and further to the point of insignificance.

The fall of Rome signified the end of the antique era, for the conquest by the barbarians threw the western countries into a state of non-culture. Only Byzantium and the Mediterranean countries were temporarily spared from ruin. Christianity, which had been given new nourishment by the influx of Judaic-Hellenistic doctrines, chiefly from Alexandria, had become dominant in those regions and was spreading with the help of fire and sword. This enabled the East Roman empire to continue its existence; but it lost its territories in the Orient, thereby causing its Jewish communities to suffer the same fate as those in Europe. The nations destroyed one another, thus undermining their own culture, and the final result was the general material and spiritual poverty of the Middle Ages.

Because of its physical weakness the Jewish people never played as deciding a political role as the other big powers. It was able to survive the collapse of the old world, in which the others disappeared completely, solely because it had developed its cultural assets in the course of preceding centuries to such a degree that its realized political strength did not assure the permanency of a nation. Thus it was psychically prepared to meet all vicissitudes of an uncertain existence. True, it had long been homeless, for it had become a people without a country; but within the Roman Empire, where most of the Jews lived, they still had enjoyed civil rights, which afforded them a certain external protection. Now, however, they were without shelter, damned to be the "eternally wandering Jew" and a powerless plaything in the hands of the world.

"The incomparable tenacious feeling of national solidarity that resulted from the peculiar position of the Jews", Theodore Mommsen writes in his Roman History—"maintained itself despite dispersion and dissolution". It preserved its vitality by preserving its heritage and fostering its cultural assets. The fragments of the Jewish nation, when given a chance, attempted to give utterance to their culture, thereby enabling them to preserve their tradition to this very day. Included among them were the artistic talents, of which early achievements give testimony. Pictorial arts of the antique era give the answer.

Only once again in subsequent years did Jewish culture experience a prime in which its talents could develop freely, under conditions similar to those in the antique period. This was in the Arabian empire, especially during the Mohammedan rule in Spain in the 10th and 11th centuries, when a strong reciprocal spiritual fertilization of the two related races took place. Philosophy, astronomy, chemistry, medicine, philology and poetry attained a high peak, and the Jews were able to demonstrate their abilities in formative art as well.

In strict observance of the Jewish taboo against imagery, Islam had developed a purely ornamental art which, however, reached the zenith of perfection as a decorative element in architecture, industrial art and book ornamentation. The extraordinary gift of the Arabian nations for the decorative expressed itself in the wealth of ornaments, in the technical and compositional use thereof and in its versatile exploitation.

There are two special reasons why, in Islamic art, the sense of rhythm stands out most purely: in the first place, the expression typical of this art was utterly preserved, and secondly, the ornamental talent which was applied to the most varied fields of art was elevated to new form values in architecture as well.

Mohammed had died in 632, and a mere 25 years later Egypt, Syria, Mesopotamia, Persia and Rhodes, followed soon after by all of North Africa, were under Arabian rule. In 750 Abd er-Rahman founded the caliphate of Cordova. And Islamic art, too, spread with the rapidity of a conflagration.

Under the caliphate of Abd el-Malik (685-705) the Dome of the Rock (often erroneously called the Omar Mosque) was erected in Jerusalem. It already demonstrates many characteristics of Mohammedan architecture: the magnificent cupola which, of course, was rebuilt after its collapse in 1016; the outside, light-blue coating of glazed plates, which was also repaired in 1561, and, in the interior, the semi-circular frieze of mosaic with gold lettering on blue ground.

The Dome of the Rock became the model for many mosques and burial vaults in Egypt, Persia, Turkestan and India. Another type, patterned after the synagogues of the Hellenistic period—the so-called temple mosques—and improved upon in the large mosque at Damascus, led to the European basilican styles which, in turn, formed the basis for some of the most beautiful synagogues of the Galuth. In Damascus we find for the first time the horseshoe-shaped arch—a combination of the Persian surmounted semicircle and the Sassanide pointed arch, and also the minaret, symbol of Mohammedan religious structures, which was adopted by the European tower architecture of all countries.

The Italian Campanile, the tower of the townhall in Verona, built in 1178, the tower of the Palazzo Vecchio in Florence, erected in 1298, as well as the tower of St. Mary-le-Bow in London, constructed between 1671-1683, are all descendants of the minaret. The minaret—a word derived from the Hebrew "menorah" (candlestick)—is the tower from which the "muezzin" proclaims the time for prayer.

Both the outside and the inside plan of the mosques testify to the great architectural ability of the Islamic world which invented new form ideas and one of the most luxurious art styles from a mixture of various elements.

In 786 Abd er-Rahman I started the construction of the great mosque in Cordova, the first of its kind on European soil. It has 19 aisles set off by 35 columns each, which are joined by horseshoe arches, and is the most magnificent of sacral structures. The Alhambra, built near Granada in the 13th century, represents the most perfect stone ornamentation in Arabian-Mooresque style.

Jewish culture in Spain blossomed forth in the lustre of this rich environment. However, it was not dazzled by this brilliance to such an extent that it could not give definite expression to its essential character. A certain congenial talent for the decorative and the rhythmic shows itself in the shape, and this constitutes one of the most important characteristics of Oriental style sense.

Toledo, where many Jewish scholars were active and which is the birthplace of Jehuda Halevi and Ibn Ezra, to this day presents the two most important synagogue buildings, even though today they are no longer regarded as such, while six others were totally destroyed.

At the start of the 13th century the five-nave synagogue was built which, in 1409, was converted into the church of

Santa Maria la Blanca. Its columns, connected by horseshoe arches, followed the brilliant style of Islamic art. The smaller, one-nave synagogue of Samuel Abulafia, now the church of El Transito, which was not completed until 1366, has a flat ceiling executed in larchwood. Its walls are richly adorned with surface ornamentation consisting of delicate stucco decorations that look like Venetian lace designs. Two friezes of Hebrew script, and the border decoration, which is reminiscent of ancient Jewish goldsmith work, are joined by naturalistic festoons of grapevines which differ essentially from the purely abstract Moorish style. A new attribute in this art sphere are the Gothic-French forms, which appear here for the first time.

The remnants of the synagogues in Cordova and Seville which, although they are now churches can still be recognized as synagogues, and the ruin in Segovia intimate a once extensive Jewish architectural art which, like miniature painting and literature, was the product of two noble cultures.

The Galuth problem of the Jewish communities, which were dependent upon their respective host nations, is brought to light most distinctly by their vicissitudinous experiences in the various countries. While Spanish Judaism was in its prime, the storms of the Crusades were already sweeping across Germany and the Jews were the unprotected prey of their persecutions. And when the auto-da-fés were flaring in Spain and, according to Jizchak Abravanel, one of the exiles in 1492, "everywhere so many terrible things were happening to Israel that had never happened to it or to any other people before", the spiritual and economic life of the Italian Jews began to flourish. And it was Holland that had opened her hospitable gates to the refugees from Spain.

Then, fifty years later, when the Italian ghettos were created—the light-less and air-less prisons that served as an example in all the countries as late as the beginning of the 19th century—Polish Jewry, consisting largely of German refugees, enjoyed a development of 100 years' duration under the liberal regime of the last Jagiello kings. Then came the Cossacks of Chmielnicki and razed the most important communities. Those who survived the terrible massacre fled back to Germany. Several years later England, which had exiled all Jews in 1290, permitted them to return.

In the same years during which Jehuda Halevi and Ibn Ezra were singing their songs, there arose in Germany the laments of dismal martyrologies. But even there, defamed as ritualistic murderers, reduced to the lowliest branches of business, and subjected to household slavery, the Jews preserved their spiritual potencies despite all physical frailties, and attempted to give them visible expression in one way or another. Neither did the arts stagnate, although, unfree as the people themselves, and dependent upon the outside world, they were able to express themselves in utilitarian handicraft rather than in great achievements.

The most important German synagogue building is the one in Worms, erected between 1175 and 1213, viz., at about the same time as the Toledo synagogue. The Worms structure demonstrates the entire contrast between the two cultural spheres: in Toledo the liberality of lavish creation, in Worms the modest retreat from the domineering ecclesiastical architecture. The Romanic dome serves as model, but neither in size nor in pomp; on the contrary, the synagogue follows the simple forms of the refectories and chapels of mendicant friars.

An arched chamber supported by two pillars—the two-nave hall is maintained until the 16th century, in contrast to the three-nave church structure—is to be found again in the synagogue of Regensburg, which is known to us only from the two etchings of Albrecht Altdorfer of 1519, the year of its destruction. The inside hall is reminiscent of the St. Ulrich Church in Regensburg, but it did not originate until the early 13th century; of still later date is the vestibule with Gothic pointed arches.

The Altneuschul in Prague, begun after 1300 and held in pure Gothic style, also has two naves. Everywhere is the same narrowness and bleakness, and a somewhat sombre appearance. The windows are small, the building does not project much from its environment, and it is always set in a narrow street. For the object is not to be conspicuous, and no special artistic demands are made.

It can no longer be determined how these synagogues were furnished inside inasmuch as almost all of them were destroyed; many of them, damaged by fire or attack, were later renovated or repaired and assumed a totally different appearance. In Prague, for instance, eleven synagogues were victims of the fire in 1684, and no part of them remained intact. And in the Cossack uprisings of 1648 over 1,800 wooden synagogues (which we shall discuss further on) were purported to have been put in ruins. On the whole neither the German nor the Bohemian synagogue architecture shows anything of special interest, since Jewish art production was limited to skill in handicraft.

As far as the 18th century there were no great changes in that respect. The oldest synagogue in Poland, the "Alt-Schul" in Cracow, which originated in the second half of the 14th century, was a two-nave Romanesque building which was rebuilt in Gothic style after the big fire of the Jewish section in 1494 had destroyed it. Then in 1640 the well-known Eisik Synagogue was built by an Italian architect in pure ecclesiastical Renaissance construction, and the first Lemberg synagogue too was the work of Paolo Romano.

In the second half of the 18th century the monastic vault type was imitated in a South-German Baroque in a number of smaller towns in Northwestern Bohemia. The most interesting example of this type is the synagogue in Kuttenplan, built in 1759.

To what extent dependence in Jewish religious institutions went is indicated by the use of the carved Jesuit altars, which were popular at that time, as Arks of the Law. Since the Jew could not and dared not be self-creative, he limited himself to imitation and handicraftmanship. That this was not due to

[431]

lack of ability, but simply because of prevailing conditions is proven by a glance at art achievements in Italy.

Due to the confluence of the most diversified interests in that country, the entire mode of living had undergone fundamental changes. Antique literature was revived, Latin documents were studied, and Hebrew likewise exercised its influence upon the learned world. Jews translated Arabian and Hebrew literature into Latin and Italian. Elias Delmedigo became the teacher of the humanist Pico de Mirandola, who studied the Talmud and the Cabbala, and lectured on Arabian and Jewish literature at the University of Padua. A Jewish physician taught Johann Reuchlin Hebrew, and Elias Levita gave Cardinal Egidio di Viterbo Hebrew lessons. The printing of Hebrew books shortly after the invention of the printing press disseminated knowledge of that language, and a chair for Hebrew was established in Bologna and Rome. Mercantile houses of globe-encompassing importance were founded; papacy, houses of nobility and city republics promoted art and science.

The Jews shared in the glory of the Renaissance, but with the result that their essentiality faded completely because of it. It seems that the prosperous congregations commissioned foreign experts to build their synagogues, including the furnishings such as the wood-carved Torah shrines. They ordered their lamps and rugs from the Orient, with which they maintained trade relations. The famous Islamic animal rug of the Berlin Museum, for example, is a relic from the synagogue in Padua.

The synagogues of Padua and Venice are pure Renaissance construction. The over-all effect is pompous and festive. The Scuola Tedesca in Venice was reportedly built by the architect Scomozzi.

However, the dream of liberty was only short-lived. The cruel Pope Paul IV initiated incarceration in the Roman ghetto, and persecutions in the Spanish vein set in so that, from then on, the life of the Italian Jews passed beyond view of the world at large.

*   *   *

Despite all diversity of circumstances, and regardless of where they lived, the Jews adhered to the laws of the Bible and the Talmud to respect every kind of manual labor, and even the most dignified and learned men plied a trade for their livelihood in which they tried to perfect themselves. Thus in the early antique era there already were efficient artisans. The Biblical books mention, among others, stone-cutters, goldsmiths and silver smiths, seal engravers as well as wood and ivory carvers. Subsequent writers have lauded their skill and emphasized the influence which they exercised upon Christian art.

In several fields of art we have to depend almost entirely upon written sources, since most of their exponents were destroyed. As we have already pointed out, archaeological research is still in the infant stage. The later history of the Jews in the Diaspora is one of constant persecutions, expulsions and, sometimes, total extirpation. The Jew never had much time for real consolidation, and with peregrinations from one country to another, the material assets were almost always lost. One has only to remember the work of destruction accomplished by the Nazis in the last decade, and of the 10th of November 1938 when most of Germany's synagogues went up in flames.

But even the confirmation of material still existing is often very doubtful since most of the products do not show any names; in other words, by far the largest part of their creators is anonymous. Also, many for whom the antagonism of their community and the oppression of the special laws made a more liberal working impossible, either were baptised or changed their names through baptism. Because of that the list of known Jewish apostates is quite long; but the number of artists and artisans about whom we do not know anything

[433]

any more must have been much greater still. So, as late as the beginning of modern times we stand before many problems that are still unsolved, and only once in a while do we see a name emerge.

In connection with ancient coin minting, catacombs and synagogues, gold glasses and mosaics, the association of meaning and form was pointed out as a characteristic. A specific gift for the decorative and the ornamental can be discerned everywhere, and the delight in colors which is peculiar to all Oriental peoples is also native in the Jew. One might also speak of a special rhythm in form and motion which appears rather geometric-formal in Arabian work, while the Jews express it naturalistically freer. And although in the course of centuries the Jew became acclimated to foreign environments under the influence of the host nations among whom he lived and due to changes in living conditions, still he never lost those characteristics.

The Italians and Greeks of today no longer have anything in common with the past history of their respective countries; they, like all nations of the antique era, were lost among subsequent conquerors. Only the Jews maintained themselves, albeit in the role of powerless minorities, and preserved their spiritual vitality. Many invisible threads still link the Jew of today with his past. Despite the fact that he has become a man of the present, in character and nature he has remained a Jew; to this day he is still a son of the ancient people.

The Jew possesses certain general qualifications for practicing professions in which, despite the most diverse influences of milieu, he was able to maintain his qualitative peculiarities. His achievements in the field of artisanry during exile prove that fact. They should not be overestimated, and in general one should not endow them with exaggerated high values. Nevertheless they are certainly not inconsiderable, especially if one takes into consideration the external conditions in which they were created. On the one hand they are an indication of the intellectual capacity to absorb foreign civilizations, and on the other hand they prove the Jew's ability to elaborate on these cultural assets independently, thereby imparting to them a new power of expression and effect.

The following review makes no claim to historical completeness, since that would exceed by far the limits set here. We suggest, instead, the wealth of material in Franz Landsberger's "History of Jewish Art". Our aim here is merely to discuss art craft, which presupposes a specific talent combined with special technical skill.

Artistic tapestries and embroideries must have been manufactured in Israel as early as the 9th century B. C. In the first books of the Bible, which were written at that time, the description of the rugs and the curtain in the Tabernacle, "of white and yellow silk with purple, crimson and gold cherubim, such as the artistic embroiderer makes them" (Exodus 26) proves the existence of this craft. In subsequent centuries the Jews had schools for weaving silks, purple cloth and rugs in Alexandria and Hierapolis. Specialists were trained there whose works the Roman author Claudius Claudianus, writing in the fourth century, praised highly.

These specialists were also highly esteemed in Greece; many of them came to Palermo in the 12th century as prisoners of war and monopolized the silk weaving industry in all Sicily. Under the Caliph Hishâm they wove costly silk flags in Cordova, and in Barcelona and Toledo they created the finest of laces up to the 15th century.

It is not known since when Torah curtains and mantles were made. In early synagogues the Torah scrolls were kept in a portable chest covered with a cloth, which was brought into the prayer hall only for services. However, in the apse of Bet-Alpha Professor Sukenik found two lateral holes for hanging up a curtain in front of the Ark, and in Dura Europos, too, a curtain was attached in front of the niche. Some gilt glasses and book illustrations show Arks with curtains. The enveloping of the scrolls with "beautiful silk bands" was a

Talmudic rule. But the first known religious textiles go back only as far as the late 15th century. The earliest is an ornamented woolen curtain in the synagogue of Padua; the next one, from the year 1630, is of brocade material embroidered in silk and was found in Ancona. But apparently it was not until the 18th century that the embroidery prowess of the Jews in various countries reached such a degree of mastery that they were given many orders by Christians.

Around 1700 Salomon Isaac was embroiderer for the court of Prussia, and in Schudt's "Jewish Curiosities" of 1718 mention is made of a Bohemian Jew who worked the gold-embroidered chasubles for the Bishop of Fulda.

At the same time Johann Sebastian Stein was active as court embroiderer in Mainz, and in 1720 Moses Samuel established East Prussia's first silk industry in Koenigsberg. Particularly noteworthy is the information that in 1738 the Jew Gerson Mayer was commissioned to embroider a precious cover with the emblems of Emperor Heinrich and Empress Kunigunde for the sepulchre built in the Bamberg Cathedral by Tilman Riemenschneider, "because no better artist could be found".

Before the Nazis destroyed almost the entire cultural assets of the Jews in Germany and in the countries which they conquered, the Jewish art collections in Berlin, Frankfort, Breslau, Munich, Mainz, Prague, Vienna and Budapest, and many synagogues had on display a great wealth of the most luxurious gold and silver embroideries. Among the artists, who usually remained anonymous, two names are prominent: Elkone Naumburg, who in 1714 had wrought two Torah curtains for Hildesheim, and two more for Augsburg and Kriegshaber some ten years later and who probably also was the creator of the curtain in the Hambro synagogue in London which has been missing since 1887. The other name is that of Jakob Koppel Gans, probably the greatest expert in this field, who designed the glorious pieces for Krumbach and Ichenhausen. He also created a masterpiece, dated 1772, which is now in the Jewish Museum in New York and which is the only one to be preserved. It represents at once the culmination and the end of Jewish embroidery art, for in the 19th century synagogical art lost all its specific significance and is only now beginning to revive.

In one branch of art which was especially cultivated by their neighbouring tribes, the old Israelites displayed decided disinterest: that was the art of ceramics, used in the Orient for the manufacture of many implements of daily life since very early times. When the Israelitic tribes came to Palestine they already found a highly developed pottery art there. They soon appropriated the technique for making plates, pots, vases, lamps, bowls and small images of idols and animals. By the stratification of the excavations the sequence of imports from Egypt, Phoenicia, Cyprus and Crete can be determined with fair accuracy. This import was so heavy that the production in the country could not keep pace with it. The ceramic art of the Israelites is rather undeveloped in comparison with the foreign vessels, which were pleasing in form and decoration. However, one of the chief causes for the above seems to have been the inferior material, which was difficult to work, for the land did not have good clay.

In the Roman-Byzantine period many clay lamps with the familiar Jewish symbols were made, to be sure, but otherwise they do not differ from the foreign form types.

Only once, in the 16th and 17th centuries, did Jewish pottery artists gain prominence in Italy. The Azulai and Fano families, who appear to have emigrated from Spain, at that time produced seder platters of fayence in Pesaro, Padua, Faenza and Urbino. These platters, elaborately decorated, represent a special type and to this day are valued highly for their characteristics.

We have already mentioned the ancient industry of glass manufacture in which the Jews had perfected themselves to such an extent that the fine glasses which they produced in the Greek colonies found wide-spread popularity and were introduced by them in France in 687. Especially fine glass types were called "glass in the Jewish manner" by the French.

Heraklius, a Roman monk living in the 10th century, mentions one glass type as "vitrum plumbeum Judaeorum scilicet", and in his travelog of the 12th century Benjamin de Tudela speaks of the Jews in Tyrus who "manufacture fine glass wares there that are famous in all countries". But after that time no special mention is made of Jewish glass workers anywhere.

All types of metal work, on the other hand, such as the art of bronze, iron, silver and gold smithery, the art of engraving and enchasing, and the production of coins and medals are among those accomplishments that form a chain connecting the ancient era to modern times.

Strabo, Pliny and Flavius Josephus already mention a masterpiece of goldsmith work that was supposedly presented to Emperor Pompeius, and a Christian writer by the name of Cosmas Indicoplaustus reports from Alexandria in the 6th century that most of the gold and silver smiths in that city were Jews.

We have so many reports from all countries, all the way up to the modern age, that, by way of extraction, we shall mention only that King John of England had Jewish goldsmiths working at his court in the 12th century, the King of Naples employed Jewish goldsmiths in 1484, and that in 1396 Jews introduced in Lyon the production and workmanship of gold and silver wire, in which they held a special monopoly up until the 19th century.

In the 16th century they had the exclusive right to manufacture wedding rings in Venice. In Aleppo they were the best gold workers, and in the 18th century they were well represented in North America, too. In 1776, as a matter of fact, Meyer Myers became president of the New York silver guild. From the 11th century to the modern age the Jews in Constantinople and Kurdistan, in all Arabia, Bagdad and Persia are the leading, if not exclusive, masters in this branch of art.

According to tradition, which, of course, is interwoven with legends, many families who worked as goldsmiths in Jerusalem are said to have migrated to Yemen during the reign of King Jojakhim and are purported to have been the exclusive artists in the enchasing of armour, filigree work and gold and silver embroidery even in pre-Islamic times. They have preserved their tradition to this day.

They furnished the Mohammedans, who were forbidden to make weapons, with the well-known Arabian enchased swords and knives; they made the richly embroidered Arabian clothes, and in the last few decades they brought back to Palestine their folk art, known everywhere as "Yemenite work". Bearing a special character of style developed in century-long seclusion, this art is now being further developed in Israel in a modern version.

One of the greatest armour enchasers of the Italian Renaissance, according to Benvenuto Cellini, was the master Ercole de' Fedeli (1465-1518), whose name before baptism was Salomo da Sessa. He furnished the courts of Mantua and Ferrara with the most excellent works of art, many of which are kept in the museums of London, Paris and Berlin. There must have been many Jewish goldsmiths at that time, a great number of them working for the Church, for in a bull of 1415 Pope Benedict XIII expressly prohibited the production of chalices and crucifixes by Jews, and even Sigismund I, the king of Poland, received a letter of complaint some time later regarding the prevalence of Jewish goldsmiths.

That many Jewish objects of worship were the work of Jews is apparent from the imitation of foreign models, which was occasionally misunderstood, and from the blending of the most diversified styles. But most of the pieces, and certainly all those that were distinguished by a mark, seem to come from Christian hands; for only guild members were permitted to sign their works, and the Jews were excluded from the guilds. However, the Jews did produce fine silver filigreed and punched book binding, as well as leather bindings, and they had always been so expert in the engraving and etching of metal and stone that they earned high honors as the engravers of arms, seals, medals and coins of many monarchs.

We should not, however, consider the Hebrew letters and words that appear on the coins of the Merovingians in the 6th century, on English coins in the 12th century, upon the Hungarian oboli of King Belas IV and the bracteates of the Polish King Mieczyslav III, to be the signatures of Jewish coin engravers. They are, in fact, nothing more than the marks of so-called "coin Jews" to whom the respective sovereigns leased the issue of those usually inferior values as compensation for delivery of the required metal. Such coin lessees, who were in reality nothing more than financiers, attained a good deal of wealth, to be sure, but they also acquired a rather bad reputation. Such was the case with Hertz Gumpert and Daniel Itzig in Berlin, and the sadly notorious Wuerttemberg court Jew, Suess Oppenheimer.

The first coin engraver in Sweden, and at the same time the founder of the Jewish community there, was Aaron Isaak, born in 1730 in Treuenbritzen, who left an interesting autobiography and who was granted special privileges by Gustav III.

Samuel Joudin, who engraved the silver rubles of Peter III, was born the same year, in St. Petersburg. The stone carver Philipp Hirsch of Stralsund became engraver to the court of Wuerttemberg after his conversion in 1813. Benjamin Goetz, the engraver, came from the same region. He anglicized his name to Yates after settling in Liverpool in 1762, but he did not change his faith, and as a matter of fact was one of the founders of the Jewish congregation in Liverpool. His son, Samuel Yates, was a noted engraver of escutcheons and heraldic bearings and exlibris, and owned a jewelry business in Liverpool.

Despite the risk of enumerating too many names, there are five Belgian masters who, because of their universal significance, should not be left unmentioned. They are Mayer Simon

(1746-1821) and his brother Jean Henry Simon (1752-1834) who was such an expert gem cutter that many of his works were thought to be genuine antiques and were acquired as such by the Emperor of Russia. Then there were the three Wiener brothers: Jacques, originator of the first Belgian postage stamps, and the engravers of the royal mint, Leopold and Charles. Jacob Abraham, royal Prussian medallist and creator of the Taler of Frederick the Great, was the father of one of the most honored portrait medallists of his time, Abraham Abramson (1754-1811) who likewise was royal Prussian coin engraver and director of the Berlin mint. He was the first Jew to become a member of the Prussian Academy of Arts and honorary member of the academies in Venice, Florence and Copenhagen. Of the huge number of portrait medals created by him we may just mention those of Wieland, Lessing, Kant and Moses Mendelssohn.

In Czarist Russia numerous Jewish medallists occupied high government posts, as for instance the chief medallist of the imperial mint in St. Petersburg, Abraham Griliches, whose father created the state seal of the last Romanoffs.

At the end of this long list are the names of Arthur Loewenthal of Vienna, one of the most eminent gem cutters of world fame (all trace of him was lost during the second global war) and Victor David Brenner who came to America from Latvia in 1890. He portrayed Theodore Roosevelt for the Panama medal, and was commissioned by the president to engrave the Lincoln portrait for the one-penny coin. Brenner wrote a book on the art of medals, and died in New York in 1924.

Whether the stone cutters mentioned in ancient literature were more than mere handicraftsmen is unknown, but we can assume that they were stone masons who prepared blocks from the quarries for building houses. The lovely Corinthian capitals and elaborately decorated friezes of the synagogue at Capernaum, as well as the sculptural work in the other synagogues are the best in artisanry.

Not until many centuries later did Jewish stone masons specialize in the production of tombstones. But even then, and up to the 17th century, the work was mostly only skilled handcraft. For the noteworthy and typically Jewish characteristic are the stones' forms, the inscriptions and the symbolic portrayals.

The Palestinian graves consisted solely of simple stones, stone flags and walled, sarcophagus-like superstructures. To make them better recognizable they were painted with a coat of white lime which had to be renewed after the winter rains. The old cemeteries in Jerusalem, Hebron, Tiberias and Safed are effective because of the rhythmic harmony of constantly recurring groups, from which no individual tombstone protrudes. Not until the moyen age in Europe did an individual tombstone art develop.

Single early mediaeval stones have been found in the Crimea, in Spain (Tortosa, 6th century), France (Narbonne, the first known date being 688) and in South Germany (Mainz, Worms, Speyer, Cologne). Most of the cemeteries are in ruins, and the stones were used for other purposes, such as the construction of houses and fortresses. Plundering and stealing had become so universal that in the 12th century various popes issued protective bulls for Jewish cemeteries, and King Rudolph of Hapsburg threatened the death penalty for cemetery vandalism. Also, the cemeteries were victims of the constant destruction of Jewish cities. Only fragments remained, and of those still in existence only a few are more than 300 years old.

Despite all similarity, the form of the tombstones was not monotonous, for they varied as to height, width and material. On the whole, they are upright, rectangular stones. At first the top was smooth, later it was surmounted with semi-circular or pointed arch and, depending on the style of the period it had a Renaissance or Baroque finish.

The sarcophagus form is to be found since the 17th century, and the most beautiful exponents are the tombstone of Chief Rabbi Loeb (1609) and that of Hendel of Treuenberg (1628) in the Prague cemetery. In East Europe mausoleum-like structures of simple masonry were erected over the graves of famous rabbis, similar to those in Palestine —like the so-called grave of the prophet Hosea in Safed and graves in Meron and Tiberias.

Among Sephardic Jews horizontal plates were the general custom, thus imparting a very special character to the cemeteries. The cemetery in Tetuan (Morocco), for instance, gives the effect of a snow field with its snow-white marble stones, and the one in Tunis, in which the stone plates do not rise above the ground, resembles a huge plastered surface.

The Sephardic cemeteries in Altona, (which were begun in 1583), Ouderkerk near Amsterdam (established in 1614) and London (planned shortly after 1655) are distinguished by elaborate and artistic sculptural ornamentation of the stones which, however, were not executed by Jews.

And finally, mention should be made of the cemetery at the slope of Mt. Zion near Jerusalem. Its innumerable graves consist of a box-like superstructure with a straight top stone plate standing upon several level steps, a form that can be found among the Arabs too. Looking like a petrified world, the cemetery makes an overwhelming impression.

A second characteristic is the writing. Up to the 16th century it consisted of sunken square types which, after that time, were worked out in relief. At first the writing was set in simple rows, then it was distributed in panels. As time went on it grew more elaborate and alternated and was also used as an element of decoration, as border strips surrounded by ornamental scrollwork. By varying the size of the letters, and occasionally filling them in with color, all kinds of variations were achieved.

Most peculiar, though, is the development of the pictorial portrayals which increase constantly as time goes on and which are so diversified that we can only mention a few of special characteristics. While the ancient portrayals consisted merely of general symbols, entirely new motifs were added since the 17th century that have direct reference to the person of the deceased. A basin and a can, or a hand pouring water from a pitcher signifies the grave of a member of the priest or Levi family. One crown, or three, a book, a Torah scroll or blessing hands indicate the tomb of a scholar. A lyre or violin decorates the resting place of a musician or cantor; frequently a broken tree or flower symbolizes a life that has ended prematurely. A small bird with a blossom in its beak indicates the passing of a child's soul. A zedaka box is used to point out the charity exercised by the deceased. Heraldic symbols refer to family names and lineage, for which animal pictures also were used—Hirsch (stag), Wolf, Loewe (lion). The fish represented Fichel, carp stood for Karpeles, etc.

This kind of tomb symbolism can be found in endless variations all the way up to the modern era, chiefly in East Europe. The rendition is often very primitive and naive, resembling a peasant or folk art. This also applies to the material used. Old millstones or erratic blocks were employed, with no further elaboration on the original form, and in some places even wood. In the western countries, on the other hand, increasing enlightenment, growing prosperity and deliberate assimilation to the forms of the respective host nation brought to a cessation a tombstone art that bore any kind of Jewish character.

The stones in the 19th century graveyards were usually ordered from stone-mason firms and were produced on a factory scale. They, together with expensive, extravagant monuments and mausoleum-like structures of costly material give the cemeteries an effect that leaves them void of the simplicity and uniformity which was once so affecting and which had lent special expression and tenor to the Jewish burial grounds.

Eastern Jewry clung to tradition much longer. The people were poor and modest. In spite of the hard work they had to engage in to eke out a bare living, they never neglected the study of the Torah. The Law was the substance of their life; all their thoughts revolved around it, and it gave them the faith and the strength to accept an inexplicable fate and to win the battle in the hope for a redemption to come. They felt safe in their small, narrow "school" and prayer houses; here was their true home, here they were amongst themselves, and here was their real life.

Without having once been in such a little "staedtl"—one of those small, dismally sad places in which the Jews constituted the preponderant part of the population—it is impossible to conceive the peculiar atmosphere of this secluded Jewish world. But, having seen such a place it is easy to understand how, toward the middle of the 17th century, at which time Jewish living assumed this specific form, a synagogue art could originate which, although constrained by its environment, was essentially derived from a combination of national feeling, religious ritual and Law, and, particularly, the Talmud. This art is the most typical utterance of Galuth Jewry insofar as in it are reflected most clearly the inherited potentialities of the Jew, re-formed by the hard school of life.

It is a folk art in which, on the one hand, the Jew's destiny of bondage expresses itself in stylistic dependency, while on the other hand his faculty for shaping his own world of thoughts and sentiments is demonstrated. The achievements in this field are the most interesting of Jewish artcraft; however, one cannot refer to them as special architecture, but as a special manner of building. By the same token it would be exaggerating to pretend to see more than a highly developed handicraft in the interior decoration. What makes it unique is the honesty and naturalness with which these people take pains. It is not their intention to create great works of art so they can be admired; the sole idea guiding them is the desire to decorate their house of worship with as much dignity as possible.

In the wooded regions of Poland, Galicia and the northern part of Russia there existed a popular profane and sacred

[445]

wood architecture which, in the 16th century, had developed a style directly resulting from the material. There are simple peasant houses, and the chapels and churches bring Indian pagodas to mind. While the wooden synagogues that were built since the 17th century display many analogies with these customary structures, especially in the roof formation and the technical performance of the wood construction, they differ otherwise in their entire planning.

The synagogues have either a simple, or a two or three-storied steep conical roof; one type, developed somewhat further, has wings annexed for the women's side, covered with plain span or lean-to roofs, while the center part is made to stand out by a steep double roof. And, in their richest form, they have small corner pavilions with closed or open galleries.

It is not known to us when the earliest wooden synagogues were created, nor how many there were. It is said that during the Cossack uprisings of 1648 some 1,800 synagogues were destroyed. Although this figure appears to be exaggerated, the greatest number of synagogues existing at the time must have been ruined. Our information is limited to a bare 100 and does not set in until 1640.

One of the most beautiful and most luxurious of these synagogues is from the year 1643. Therefore, since a very large number are certain to have been destroyed during the Cossack revolt, and since the architectural style had already reached its peak at that time, it can be assumed that quite a long period of evolution must have preceded that structure and that the first wooden synagogues were constructed no later than the last quarter of the 16th century.

However, there was also a very special kind of stone structure, but those were not built until much later, and then mainly because of the loss of so many places of worship. These were very massive one-storied brick buildings, with embrasures and ramparts framing the flat roof as a defense against attacks. One of these so-called fortress synagogues was built in 1687 in Zolkiew in place of the wooden synagogue.

Far more interesting than the exterior, though, was the interior furnishing of the synagogues, for it is absolutely original and independent Jewish folk art. Here is manifested a wealth of ideas and formation that is purest expression of the Jewish soul. The walls and ceilings are frequently covered with paintings from top to bottom which, however, with few exceptions, are executed by unskilled hands. Technically, too, they are primitive; they are painted with chalk on the white-washed boarded partitions, and the contours are then traced with black lines. Scrollwork and sayings in Hebrew characters, in the manner of Moorish painting, are interspersed with animal and human figures, occasionally even landscape pictures, and fill the entire surface in Oriental colorfulness.

Animal symbolism, whose meaning is explained in scrolls, reaches its peak here. One comes across the same motifs found in tombstone sculpture, and there exists a certain affinity between the two as far as conception and portrayal form are concerned.

In returning to the West from Poland in the 18th century, a painter from Brody by the name of Elieser Sussmann came to South Germany. Between 1732 and 1740 he decorated the wooden synagogues in Bechhofen, Horb, Kirchheim and Falkenstein in the same manner as described above.

In addition to the paintings, the forming of the bema, the Aron Hakodesch, the candelabra and other religious objects played an important part and gave wood carvers, stone masons, copper and iron smiths the opportunity to demonstrate the full scope of their skill.

The Almemor always stands upon an octangular, raised platform. First it is enclosed by a simple railing, then by a more elaborate, carved banister, or else it is surmounted by a richly decorated baldachin supported by four wooden columns.

In decorating the Aron Hakodesch, Jewish woodcarving achieves astounding results. There are simple shrines, embellished with scrollwork, that rest upon consoles. There are also some arrangements with one or two stories, and, finally, there are real works of art with shafts that are either turned or encircled by flower garlands, with filigreed foliage and scroll work, running stags and birds in flight. The over-all effect is that of a filigree design. In addition to all this, the Aron Hakodesch in Selva has a carved portal in front of the steps that lead to it. The Ark in Zabludow is executed in Italian Renaissance; and is 9½ meters high. The Ark in Wolpa is 10 meters high, and its magnificent sculptural work, carved in oak, extends to a width of 4½ meters.

Characteristic of the attitude of the artists who accomplished such masterpieces is the inscription on the Aron in Gwozdziecz, which reads: "The labor of my hand in glorification of God—the worker at the sacred work 1731." But he does not give his name!

The art of the so-called "Schnitzler"—a designation just as typical as that of the tombstone masons, who simply called themselves "mazeze makers"—was not confined to the wood synagogues of the East. We come across them again in the 18th and 19th centuries in Bohemia and West Prussia.

Samuel Goldbaum became generally known as the "carver from Kempen" for his Ark which he created in 1830 for the Kempen synagogue and which he decorated with musical instruments. His art was carried down to his son, who executed the Ark in Allenstein in 1877. And until the second global war broke out, there lived in Janowo the artist who was acknowledged to be the unsurpassed master in all Lithuania, Jizchak Dembo.

In Israel, too, beautifully carved Arks are to be found which, judging by the style and technique were made by experts who had immigrated from Poland. The Aron of the Beth Jacob synagogue, generally called "Churwah", which was only built in 1864 and which was destroyed during the recent siege on Jerusalem, carried a superstructure of two stories that was 18½ meters high, with smooth columns and expertly carved scroll work. The Ashkenasian Ari Synagogue in Safed likewise has a two-storied Ark, but the work on it is somewhat rougher.

Of the artistically wrought, large menorahs which stood on a special pedestal beside the Aron Hakodesch and which were the main ornaments of the synagogue interior, we shall mention only the two elaborately decorated brass candlesticks in Pohrebyzcze, the menorah in Brody and those in Zamosc and Grojec.

The ironsmith art also seems to have originated in the East, as indicated by the Almemor rail in Zolkiew, which has scroll ornamentation in Renaissance style and displays workmanship of highest quality. It served as model for the rococo rail of the former Gypsy synagogue in Prague. In northern Bohemia subsequent development of Almemor rails took a course similar to that discovered in the use of Jesuit altars. And, taking after the example set by the Church, the Almemor railing finally becomes an altar guard. Its characteristic vanishes, and with it the independent activity of Jewish smith experts.

A survey of the synagogue art in Eastern Europe during its 200 years prime, and the achievements produced in various fields which bear the Jewish imprint, leads to the question as to who were the creators of these works. Since for the most part they were "laborers at the holy work" who were not interested in perpetuating their name, we know only a few of them.

Simcha Weiss, from Luck, was probably one of the most efficient architects in the latter half of the 17th century. It was he who constructed the beautiful synagogue in Nasielsk. Perhaps the synagogue situated very close by, the largest and most elaborate in Wolpa, can be attributed to him also. As far as the style is concerned, this 30 meter high structure, enlarged by two corner pavilions, bears a great deal of resemblance to the one in Nasielsk, which was built only a few decades later. It is a great temptation to attribute to the same master yet a third synagogue, likewise nearby, namely that in Zabludow, of which an inscription tells us that it was restored for the first time in 1712. The date of restoration makes it quite conceivable to set the date of origin between that of the other two. Nasielsk and Wolpa have the same fundament, while Wolpa and Zabludow are built of cedar and larch respectively, i.e., of much more precious woods than the many others. Nasielsk was demolished in 1880 because of its dilapidated condition, and its material can no longer be ascertained.

According to what was just stated, it is quite possible that Simcha Weiss, who was already famous during his lifetime, was the creator of the three most beautiful structures. Not until 100 years later does a name again make an appearance: Hillel Benjamin, from Lasko, built the synagogues of Kurnik and Lutomiersk between 1765 and 1772, but he was far less important than his predecessor from Luck.

As far as paintings are concerned, those in Chodorow (1654) and Gwodziecz (1658) are artistically the best because of their elaborate and original animal symbolism, and they are the works of two masters who are known by name. There follows another gap, until we come to the versatile David Friedlaender who came to Poland from Germany at the close of the 18th century, and who was architect, painter and carver all in one. The synagogue of Wyszogrod was constructed by him, and in the interior of the Aron Hakodesch erected there he carved a Moses statue. In Piotrokow and Grojec he executed the carving as well as the painting.

With the inception of the 19th century, Jewish culture in East Europe died out. It was the final link of a closed chain and it tore when the centripetal force which had held Judaism together until then began to wane.

In certain circles of Jewish communities in Western Europe, increasing awareness of the contrast between national seclusion and a more liberal intellectual culture had awakened a desire for stronger participation in the surrounding world,

Since various business circles had come in contact with gentile circles, in consequence of increasing prosperity, they were more and more conscious of the bonds imposed on them by their confined existence. Jewish culture, until that time uniform and expression of the identical ideology and mode of living, gradually began to loosen, and both external and spiritual changes took place that led to conflicting trends within Judaism.

On the one hand they wanted to assimilate ancient traditions to those of their host nations, and set about adopting the latter's customs of daily life in habitation and clothing, social attitude and institutions of worship. Above all, the Jews acquired the language of their neighbors and with wild enthusiasm fell upon the new publications of the poets and philosophers. Social circles began to form, particularly in the salons of intellectual Hebrews.

On the other hand, the bulk of Jews living under the pressure of material poverty in the eastern countries sought refuge behind the protecting walls of an all-the-more severe conservatism which was supervised by a zealous rabbinism. This part of Jewry immersed itself more and more deeply into the mystic ideas, stemming from the old Cabbala, of a chassidism that rejected asceticism and which, instead, stressed a joyousness in God. Yiddish became the idiom and developed a wide-spread popular literature. Certain circles which, while stimulated by the enlightenment coming from the west, were not intrinsically affected by it, but which were more progressive than the broad masses, made an attempt to sever the spiritual bondage with the help of the so-called Haskala movement.

The basic difference between the two trends is this: enlightenment sought to cultivate a new culture that would liberate Judaism at the expense of Jewish-national existence, while the Haskala was trying to establish enlightenment on a national basis. Both movements had resulted from the identical conclusion, namely, that Jewish spiritual culture was in danger of becoming stagnant and, thus, that its continued existence was in jeopardy. Accordingly, means and ways had to be devised for its salvation.

* * *

The whole world stood before a spiritual and social reorientation. A new era announced its arrival with cries of Liberty, Equality and Fraternity, and for the Jews, too, liberation from the state of only-being-tolerated, and the chance of becoming citizens with equal rights seemed to loom. The emancipation that was gradually taking place in a number of countries also expedited the assimilation of the Jew. This in turn, on the one hand caused a weakening of his Jewish self-awareness and, consequently, a relaxing of his Jewish cultural affiliation; on the other hand it released forces within him in which he could prove his creative potentialities by conveying to others the new inspirations which he received.

Assimilation was (and still is, in the countries of the diaspora) the acid test for the intellectual and cultural talents of the Jewish individual who is able to point to it as the personal legitimation for an existence with equal rights among people.

For the time being it means an immense weakening of the cultural homogeneity of the Jewish heritage; for now, having survived the fire test of assimilation, this heritage first stands at the really crucial turning point at which its own cultural power makes ready to produce achievements of art, science and technology. And these achievements are the quintessence of the spiritual properties which proves the Jewish people of today, as it did during the time of its unified national existence, to be a vital element among nations.

* * *

It is one of the most curious phenomena in the history of mankind that at the very moment in which a people's continued existence—safeguarded by adhering steadfastly to its traditional foundations—threatens to break, forces awaken which prove that they had been extant in this people as they were in other peoples, and that they had merely been in concealment due to the pressure of circumstances. Talents make their appearance which very quickly bring to light an astonishing measure of ability. And it becomes apparent that the Jew, in addition to many other faculties, also has the gift for all branches of fine arts. He simply has to orient himself in his new life before he can develop this talent fully. First he gropes around, since he is not sure of himself, and copies models that come to his attention. However, he soon attains independent judgment and work, and in many instances succeeds to such an extent that he himself turns model and teacher.

It is sometimes maintained that the Jew has a special gift for adapting and adjusting himself which enables him to fit into any situation, but that he lacks the ability to immerge deeply and take root in it. History has disproved this contention a thousandfold.

The instability of a migratory life demanded a constant readjustment to new conditions; for regardless of where the Jew was, he had to adapt himself to his environment in order to even exist. Accordingly, his instinct for self-preservation sharpened his senses, especially with respect to people. He learned to observe them and to read their physiognomies, and he grew analyzingly critical.

The rest of the world did not greatly interest him, for he rarely had contact with it since it moved outside of his sphere and without his assistance. His world consisted of his narrow community within a narrow space which was barely touched by the sun and the beauties of nature. The land was strange to him, for it was not his country; the sun warmed, but it did not brighten, and the merrily chirping birds avoided the barren, noisy places where men were. Thus his appreciation of nature was stunted just as, of necessity, he was bound to become indifferent and insensible to all that was beautiful, big and free. He labored among small and petty things and lost his sense of reality.

As far as the other side of the statement is concerned: the necessity of adapting himself often resulted in a copying and imitating with which, however, a certain indifference was sometimes connected, inasmuch as it hardly seemed worth the trouble of penetrating more deeply into matters. The Jew had to guide himself in everything according to the purpose; his actions were determined by the question "what for", and not by the "why" of things, for that was in a completely different territory for him.

Art had never existed as a problem for him that he would try to solve in the pure harmony of absolute colors and forms. As this exposition has endeavored to explain about all his artistic activities, the Jew was a person whose senses, nurtured via his soul, expressed themselves figuratively in a combination of substance and form. This means that he was able to create artistic values when he could release freely the experiences of his soul. In the short periods of his freedom we at least find some beginnings, such as the coins, sepulchres and synagogue structures in the ancient era, in the Islam-Spanish period and during the relatively autonomous community living in Poland. Otherwise it is mostly a skillful handicraftsmanship which, although guided by individual talent, was still more or less environment-bound.

Now, however, with all these limitations and oppressions eliminated, his emotionalism expands. And there is yet a new impetus which thus far had been missing: active participation in the world and the incentive to prove his worth in it. The eye, which until then had been adjusted only to definite phenomena, suddenly sees much which it had disregarded. The abundance of all that now pervades his soul also at first fills the Jew with astonishment and hesitation. But then it grips him all the more firmly, and he is seized with impatience to make up for lost time. All of a sudden the repressed forces erupt and, disregarding all difficulties and many a stumble, hurl themselves at art.

The limited space of this treatise prevents us from presenting the full extent of the Jewish participation in the fine arts which now sets in. In a book issued recently by the same publisher, the author has sketched the path of the Jewish artist in the course of the last 150 years by describing a number of prominent types. Since only a short excerpt can be given here, the reader is referred to the aforesaid work (*Jewish Artists of the 19th and 20th Centuries*).

Germany had become the starting point of assimilation even before political emancipation, mainly due to the fearless stand of poets such as Lessing and Herder. In 1749 Lessing had already ridiculed gentile arrogance toward the Jews in his comedy "Die Juden", and had extolled the ethics of Judaism with his "Nathan the Wise".

In his work "Vom Geiste der hebraeischen Poesie" Herder had called attention to Jewish literature, and Schleiermacher and Schlegel were on friendly terms with the "Berlin salons", previously mentioned, to which the converted poets Boerne and Heine also had access.

This atmosphere, already estranged from Jewish spirit, was the soil upon which the first artist generation was nourished. Among the Jewish artists were the *Veit* brothers, grandsons of Moses Mendelssohn, who joined the Nazarenes in 1815 and led a canting monastery life so that they might be inspired in their art by the spirit of the Catholic Church.

Another artist was *Eduard Bendemann*, who later became director of the Duesseldorf academy. He was especially noted for his painting "The Grieving Jews".

Others were the Berlin portraitists *Eduard Magnus* and *Julius Jacob*, and *Julius Muhr*, a pupil of Cornelius and coworker of W. v. Kaulbach. All of them were excellent portrait painters whose works show absolutely individualistic-Jewish features.

For the portrait was the domain in which the Jew best knew

his way in the beginning. That this was so had been proven earlier by the medallists, whom we discussed previously, and by a number of Jewish miniature painters and portrait engravers of the preceding generation.

As far as the art of copper engraving is concerned, we know some names from the 17th century, but only the masters who appear at the turn of the 18th century are of interest artistically.

Salomon Bennett, originally named Jomtov Baneth, and a native of Poland, was active in England around 1800. Prior to that he had been made a member of the Berlin Academy for his excellent portrait engravings of Frederick the Great and Queen Louise. Likewise working in England was *Ezekiel Abraham Ezekiel,* who was born in Exeter. He was noted for his engravings after Opie and Reynolds, and for his miniature paintings.

Samuel Jesi, an Italian, made engravings after Raphael and Fra Bartolomeo (characteristically enough, his best work is the Raphael portrait of Leo X) and became a member of the academies of Florence, Paris and St. Petersburg.

Joel Ballin was founder of the Copenhagen academy for copper engraving, and *Benedict Heinrich Bendix,* an uncle of Bendemann, was an excellent portrait engraver who worked in Berlin.

The miniature painters form an even longer list, headed by one of the most talented artist families, of which five members acquired fame and honors. *Joel Nathan,* the first of the line, assumed the name *Joseph Marquand Treu* in later years. He was a miniature painter at the Electoral Court in Bamberg, and was succeeded in that position by his second son, Joseph Christian. A daughter, Katharina, was a noted cabinet painter in Mannheim; the elder son, Johann Nicolaus, painter at the court of Würzburg, became known for his altar paintings and a portrait of Pope Pius VI, created in Rome, and was the most prominent of the family. Another daughter, Rosalie, was also noted as a painter.

In the *Pinhas* family, too, the talent was inherited through four generations. Juda Pinhas was the son of the Torah scribe Samuel, from Lehrberg, and started to learn the same profession. He wrote and embellished a Megilla and a Haggadah so artistically that the Markgraf of Ansbach provided him with further training and made him his court painter. Later Pinhas also painted the King of Prussia and the latter's family. His son Salomon became painter of the Hessian court, and his grandson, Hermann Hirsch, in turn was a copper engraver in Kassel.

Born in Kassel, in 1796, was one of the most brilliant miniature painters of the 19th century, *Jeremias David Alexander Fiorino,* recipient of many prizes. His magnificent portraits are kept in Dresden, Kassel, Frankfurt, Vienna and London.

Lippmann Fraenckel, from Parchim in Mecklenburg (1772-1857) was an eminent miniature painter at the court of Denmark, and the well-known Koenigsberg copper engraver and miniature and pastel painter *Johann Michael Siegfried* (actually Moses Samuel) *Loewe* or Lowe portrayed, among others, Empress Catherine II of Russia.

Miniature painting, which was wide-spread in the 18th and early 19th centuries, and which was also very popular in the more prosperous Jewish circles, began to lose ground with the rising popularity of photography, and the engraved portrait likewise was eliminated by it.

A distinguishing feature of Jewish portrait miniatures is their characteristic traits, which are executed with calligraphic exactness. It is quite apparent that the physiognomical expression interested the artists more than the impressionistic overall effect. The finely pointed brush or the graver were the appropriate tools for these portraits, the effect of which was graphic rather than pictorial.

Of special interest as far as the hereditary talent of the Jews is concerned are the four generations of the Pinhas family, for in this particular branch of art it becomes apparent whence the gift came. Old Pinhas was a Torah scribe; in other words, a calligrapher. And calligraphy, as we have already seen, was a favorite profession of the Jews even in ancient times. The men who compiled the Holy Scriptures were not just scribes, but artists of penmanship, and their talent was passed on by generation after generation in their families.

In the Middle Ages there were calligraphers living on the island of Mallorca who claimed a lineage that went far, far back; they became famous for cartography, which was their specialty. Evidence of this particular skill is the so-called Mappa Mundi in the Bibliothèque Nationale in Paris. It was created by Abraham Cresques in 1375 by order of the King of Aragonia, who sent the map to Charles VI of France as a particularly valuable present.

From calligraphy and cartography it was only one step to graphic art. Copper engraving required the same accuracy and devoted immersion in the work, and was usually performed after a carefully executed drawing. And this at-the-table-sitting was entirely suited to the Jewish mind, which was accustomed to "study", and for the same reason it was especially well adapted to the small format and illustrative art.

The son of the Torah scribe Samuel illustrated Hebrew documents, and the decorative trend led him to miniature painting. Accordingly, there is a straight line from the original artcraft to the portrait.

Consequently, the portrait art long practiced by the Jews was the spring board for those who were the first to venture into "big art". They were fairly sure of themselves in that field and soon achieved success.

Thus it was that the portraits of Boerne, Heine and the beautiful Adele Oppenheim, wife of the artist *Moritz Oppenheim,* were the works of this first pronouncedly Jewish artist that contributed to his fame, while his picture series "From Jewish Family Life", highly praised at the time of their origin, are genre portrayals of rather stereotype art. This applies also to the painters who came from Eastern Europe somewhat later. All of them cultivated a theatrically posed sentimental painting style and a simulated ghetto poetry which, although popular because it pictured the Jewish milieu, in reality did not go beyond an academically studied skill.

All of these artists were gifted and well trained. Some of them became quite well known, particularly in Austria and Germany; among them were *Leopold Horovitz*; *Isidor Kaufmann*, a master of miniature painting; *Samuel Hirszenberg*, who had tried his hand at a monumental painting, "The Wandering Jews"; *Leopold Pilichowsky*, who created a panorama painting, composed of many miniature portraits depicting the celebration of the founding of the Hebrew University on Mt. Scopus; the painter *Jehuda Epstein*, who spent the last years of his life in Johannesburg and, finally, the unfortunate deaf-mute, *Mauricy Minkowsky*, who described the misery caused by the pogroms.

The untimely departed *Mauricy Gottlieb* (1856-1879) displayed a more outspoken artistry in some of his last designs. His monumental painting "The Praying Jews", which is considered a documentation of Jewish art, and which the artist completed at the age of 22, shortly before he died is, in reality, nothing more than a collection of magnificently conceived miniature portraits transposed to life-size, as it were. The work is overburdened with incidental accessories which, however, are well perceived graphically.

In the second half of the century the stage of adjusting and learning has been overcome by the Jewish artist who, for the most part, has come from Western countries. He has become acclimated to the world; he looks at it through his own eyes and develops into a matured master who is equal, and sometimes even superior, to the others.

Chronologically, *Jozef Israels* is at the head of the list. He was born in Groningen in 1824. As son of orthodox parents he first attended the Talmud-Torah school, and then devoted himself to art. Both in Amsterdam and in Paris, where he remained until the revolution of 1848, he learned only an antiquated academic trend of art. Not until he came for a stay in a wretched Dutch fishing village did he find his way. There he discovered the poetry of poverty and the grandeur of nature, and became its painter and the painter of Holland whose greatest master, Rembrandt, served as his model.

His paintings at first were mawkish; only much later did they reach artistic heights, yet they soon brought him fame. They won many prizes and were acquired by the state, and his fame spread quickly. And when he exhibited his painting "A Son of the Ancient People" in Paris—the picture that portrays a young Jew sitting in front of his old-clothes stall in Amsterdam's Jewish quarter—he was hailed as Holland's greatest virtuoso and as the reviver of a glorious tradition that had been doomed to oblivion.

The picture demonstrates the greatness as well as the limitations of his art; and this art rises to the top in the harmony of experiences and emotions. It is, according to Liebermann, "a simple folk song", but is frequently too pathetic. Israels is most vigorous in several Jewish themes, such as the "Jewish Wedding" which exists in a number of variations, and in his "David and Saul". Here, too, the difference in artistic values becomes apparent between the artists whom we discussed first and the matured artist.

His countrymen recognized that fact, too, and showed their appreciation by showering him with honors such as hardly any other artist had known. When he died at the ripe old age of 87, they buried him with ceremonies befitting a prince.

Israels' son, *Isaac,* likewise was a painter of note who, at 22, had already exhibited with success in Paris. He was a well-liked impressionist portrayer of metropolitan society life.

Among the impressionists of France, however, *Camille Pissarro* stands out as the co-founder and most consequential champion of this supreme and ultimate naturalistic painting trend of the 19th century.

Pissarro was born to Jewish parents in 1830 in St. Thomas, on the Antilles, and had been living in France since 1855.

He was a master in the true sense of the word, a great personality, simple, modest, serene and wise. He was a friend of Manet and Monet, was associated for years with Cézanne and was a fatherly adviser and patron of Gauguin and van Gogh.

Pissarro's production prior to the war of 1870 has disappeared. After 1874 he took part in all exhibitions of the impressionists, sharing their wants and their ridicule, as well as their subsequent glory. To really appreciate his greatness, one should read his letters to his son Lucien. They are one of the most brilliant and artistic confessions and, together with his masterpieces, which today are worth their weight in gold, they represent a permanent monument to this great man.

His was a hard life that abounded with privations, but it did not affect the cheerfulness of his art which remained throughout, and he had to wait until he was an old man before receiving full recognition. His five sons followed in his footsteps in the artistic field, but none of them achieved his greatness. Only *Lucien Pissarro,* the eldest, who lived in England since the time he was 20, was acknowledged as a book illustrator, and his daughter, in turn, using the pseudonym of *Orovida,* became a well known graphic artist.

Just as Pissarro came from a completely assimilated circle, so, too, did *Max Liebermann* descend from a rather liberal Berlin family. But no other artist's life and work reveals so clearly the problems involved in the cultural existence of a Jewish artist in 19th century Europe as that of Liebermann's personality, which for many years guided the direction of German art. Intelligence, skill, energy and ability determined his path and he had recognized that path at an early date.

He started in the barren provincialism of Berlin, studied in Paris and Holland, mainly close to his friend Israels, and was an accomplished master by the time he returned to Berlin, where he grasped the reins of art with a firm hand. He was a prosaic, keenly deliberative, incessantly active and always independent artist, equally great as painter and as graphic expert, as landscapist, delineator of daily life and portrayer of men. He was a man of great accomplishment and tremendous ability who climbed to the top rung of recognition and who became professor and director of the academy, honorary doctor of philosophy, and honorary citizen of his native Berlin.

Liebermann was the founder of the "Berlin Secession" and thus the leader of a whole generation of artists, but in his declining years he was destined to see the collapse of his beloved Germany and of the art embodied in it. He died at the age of 88, embittered, alone and forgotten by his compatriots who had once proudly called him their own.

For decades he had a tremendous following, including a large number of Jewish artists who, together with him, had made Berlin a flourishing art center comparable only to Paris.

Ernst Oppler, Rudolf Levy, Jacob Nussbaum, Eugen Spiro, Ernst Pickardt, Joseph Oppenheimer, Julius Schuelein are but a few names among the many, to which can be added, as being indirectly influenced by Berlin, the Moscovite, Professor *Leonid Pasternak,* noted for his Tolstoi portraits; the two Hungarian landscape artists *Magyar Gustav Mannheimer* and *Adolf Fényes,* and, in England *Mark Gertler* as well as the academy professors *Sir William Rothenstein* and *Salomon Joseph Solomon,* the inventor of the scientific camouflage system.

Right after Liebermann we have to mention his most important rival, *Lesser Ury,* fourteen years his junior, who never attained any notable influence. Ury was an unhappy recluse, at war with himself and the world, but he was a genius and a color expert of special character. Coming from poor environments, he had starved all through his youth and at 21 had already created works that were among the best achievements of impressionistic painting in Germany. Still he received little attention, and as long as he lived he suffered from his envy of his colleagues. He was a landscape painter almost exclusively, achieving top results in the portrayal of lonely forest and water scenes and of life in the metropolis, particularly in magically illuminated night scenes. In pastel painting, too, he is adjudged one of the best next to the French artists.

Isaac Lewithan, Ury's contemporary, and likewise raised under the poorest of circumstances, was born in a desolate Lithuanian village. He was Russia's greatest landscapist, a fact which even the anti-Semitic "Novoya Vremya" admitted in the obituary devoted to the artist who died when he was only 40, and which they couched in these words: "This full blooded Jew knew better than anybody else how to teach us to understand and love our soil and our country".

It is a peculiarity of the East European Jew that all through his life he feels an indestructible love for the soil on which he was born, even though it may awaken in him the saddest recollections. He shares this sentimentality with the Russian. When he was only 19 one of his melancholy pictures, the portrayal of a dismal autumn day, won Lewithan a scholarship to Paris. However, he soon returned from there and from then on kept painting a large number of calm landscape pictures that portray those never-ending expanses of the Russian steppes and forests which no living creature ever disturbs in their mysterious solitude. That, however, is the real Russia to which her people are attached with all their soul and which they tenderly call their "little Mother Russia" in their melancholy folk songs. In his modest little pictures a Jew transformed these melodies into colors!

In *Ernst Josefson,* Sweden, too, celebrated one of her greatest painters who contributed new values to the narrative painting trend that had been customary until that time. He spent many years in France, but his principal inspirations came to him in Spain, from the life of the people and the works of Velasquez. It was there that he painted his famous picture "Dancing Cigarette Girls" in which the fiery rhythm of the full-blooded Spaniards echoes. This work served as preparation for his masterpiece, a creation unsurpassed in depth of color and brightness of light. Josefson worked on it like a man possessed, exerting every ounce of his strength. He destroyed it, started over again and finally, after two further years, he completed it.

This symbolic painting, adapted from Nordic mythology, presents the river god Neck, aroused by wild passion, whose eerie lament echoes among the rocks and cliffs. However, in creating this picture the artist exhausted his strength. He became hopelessly insane and was unable to comprehend the enthusiastic acclaim given him by his country.

Just as Josefson's art came to an untimely end so, too, was Sweden's most prominent expressionist painter, *Isaac Gruenewald,* torn from a life of multifarious activity. Together with his wife, who was known as a painter of children, he was the victim of an airplane accident in 1946.

He had been a pupil of Henri Matisse and brought the new French style of art back to Sweden, where he taught it in his capacity as professor at the Stockholm academy. He played a leading part as portraitist, landscape, theatrical and monumental painter, and as book illustrator.

With the name of Gruenewald we have already reached the new era which, at the start of the 20th century, began to revolutionize all art life. Due to the rulers' increasing lust for power, backed by industrial magnates, and due, also, to a complacent bourgeoisie and an enslaved working class, political and economic conditions were driving relentlessly toward a world catastrophe, the travails of which were apparent in the entire mental attitude of the European nations. Under the constantly growing social pressure, people began to realize the untenability of the traditional social order, and to search for new forms of living. As a result, they were first seized by an inner restlessness which affected literature, theatre, music and the fine arts and—like life itself—was given obscure and turbulent expression in those media.

The times of a stable art development were over; the most diverse trends began to oppose one another. Yesterday's art was rejected on the grounds that it was antiquated, and one searched for an art of the future without really knowing how to go about it. There arose a jumble of the most heterogeneous opinions, one view opposed the other, one theory battled the second. Heads grew heated, whereby there was no lack of ingenious attempts by overstimulated intellect. But the main battlefield of this interesting conflict was Paris, the focal point of modern art which attracted all young talents and then sent them back into the world.

The revolutionary attitude started in 1912 with the anti-naturalist movement of "The Blue Rider" in Munich, headed by *Franz Marc* who, as noted by Professor Landsberger, originated from a Jewish family bearing the name of Markus. At the same time the Berlin secession was split by the Roumanian born revolutionary painter *Arthur Segall* (1873-1944), and *Ludwig Meidner* and *Jakob Steinhardt* belonged to a group of young artists "the Pathetiker".

It was Paris, also, that became the magnet for the young Jewish artists who were coming there in ever increasing number to study. They were beset by the same questions about the meaning of an existence in which the endowments were distributed so unevenly; and it was just these intellectually aroused Jews who saw almost no fulfillment of the promises of liberty, equality and fraternity made a century before.

This younger artist generation, born approximately around 1890, came from Poland and Russia almost without exception and had grown up among the horrors of czarist pogroms that had indelibly etched memories in their souls. They had developed into a different type of men than those who, it is true, had also sought liberty and art but who, for the most part, thought they had found both in Vienna, Munich or Berlin. For the new artists there was no more "ghetto poetry"; only a Jewish need and a Jewish lot, and that idea became the fundamental chord of their art, be it consciously or unconsciously, intentionally or otherwise.

In Paris, thirsty for knowledge as they were, they plunged headlong into the maelstrom of an alien world and of the true art which thus far had been unfamiliar to them. They saw and learned and experienced new things, but they never forgot their earlier experiences.

True, they gained new experiences in their studies, for Paris offered the best soil for artistic talents to grow in; but these artists preserved their individuality in so high a measure that the result differed from that of the others. Thus there came to be within this large international art community a special group of Jewish artists who became universally known as "The School of Paris". Masters emerged who spoke, not jargon, but a language of their own, trained by French culture, with which they enriched the artistic world.

There were a lot of them who gathered in Paris. A large number got no further than the average standard. Some got lost in the shuffle, others were merely imitators, for there were varying degrees of talent and temperament among them. Still, it was enough that some few developed into leaders of a new generation.

"The School of Paris" is not a one-sided trend, nor is it any special art method, for it employs all the expressive means of modern art. Neither does it in any way accentuate the Jewish theme, but it *is* based on the Jewish psyche. And in that respect, too, the Paris School derives from sundry sources, thereby revealing for the first time the full width and depth of the mighty torrent released by the Jewish soul; a torrent which prior to this period had never reached full artistic maturity.

Soul is not sentimentality; these two conceptions are often confused when applied to the Jew. For the soul, like the mind, is an essential part of the spirit, while sentimentality is expression of feeling. Under soul we are to understand here the spiritual potency peculiar to a nation. The short definition of the Jewish soul which follows is, therefore, not an appraisal but simply an interpretation of its particular nature.

Since a more accurate analysis does not belong here, may just a few instances and examples be sufficient, some of which have already been mentioned in other parts of this exposition.

Today's Jew, like every human being, is the product of an infinitely long chain, the links of which are forged by heritage and destiny. This chain traces its origin to distant times and lands. Every one of its links—and we have come across many of them in the course of this treatise—contributed to its formation.

All kinds of melodies resound in the soul of the Jew: the noble songs of the prophets, and the hymns of Divine Omnipotence; the laments of grief over lost freedom, the shrieks of misery from the throats of the enslaved and the cries for help from the depths of destitution and abandonment. Then again there are the solemn strains of the Jewish festivals which may grow to exuberant gaiety and proud confidence in victory, and at that point the Jew forgets all worldly cares. He has the faculty for transmuting in his fantasy the lowliest hut into a palace. "How beautiful your tents, Jacob, your dwellings, Israel!"

He can enthuse about the most minute and insignificant things by detaching himself from reality and rising from the enveloping darkness to bright heights, where his soul breaks out into a jubilant Hallelujah.

Take all these accords, interwoven with as much variegation as the colors of the rainbow, and you will understand the various visions that can issue forth from the true artist in accordance with whatever inspiration is affecting him.

Chagall and Soutine, the two greatest Jewish masters, are opposite poles of one and the same power center. The art of both originates in the primordial sources of their Jewish soul and is given its specific utterance through their geniality.

The works of Soutine heave color outbursts from the deepest crater of human destitution with such elemental force that they violate every formal order. His tortured fantasy relieves itself in uncanny seething and convulsive quivers. His entire production seems to be under a restraint, and disaster appears to be driving him so that his hand, trembling with agitation, agglomerates the forms and jolts them around pell-mell. His

[467]

palette works with the most daring contrasts, it dips into impenetrable darkness and blazes up like the flame of a rocket. The red color, above all, represents blood that flows as in a hemorrhage from his own veins until, finally, his physical strength is exhausted.

The work of *Chaim Soutine* is the most terrible indictment; a "j'accuse", in which the artist tears open with brutal candor the wounds that fate dealt him and his people. To do this he employs a language all his own, never heard anywhere else; but he speaks it with such forcefulness that the whole world hears it with horror and—understands it!

But, there is still a different-sounding Jewish language that is no less genuine, for it, too, is not studied but is the mother tongue that was sung to the child in its cradle. It forms the child's vocabulary which, in turn, guides the man's thoughts that accompany him all through life. And the more closely a man is attached to the parental home and his native soil, the more alive will the familiar melodies remain when he is away from home.

Soutine was burdened with a tragic heritage from which he could never free himself. *Marc Chagall* is the herald of a Jewish world which, instead of suffering under the incubus of terrorizing visions, lifts itself up to serenity. The tones of God-happiness inherent in him, and the echo of the chassidic songs and dances among which he grew up endowed him with the gift to see life as a vision appearing in the bright lustre of a beatifying unreality. Heaven and earth are the playground of his visions, and there seem to be no limits set for his inexhaustible imagination. In the form and in the color, in the rhythm as well as in the composition he always discovers new, unthought of, unsuspected or unseen sensations which exercise an indefinable suggestive charm.

And yet, despite all their frequently inexplicable peculiarity, these works are comprehensible to everyone because of their wonderful harmony of substance and form. They are the happy and beatifying expression of a genius whose power of formation grows out of the primordial depths of a true and genuine soul.

Soutine and Chagall are the exponents and leading masters of "The School of Paris", and the others are more or less closely associated with them. The life thread of *Issachar Ryback* tore prematurely, so that the budding flower of one of the most talented artists could not reach fulfillment. He was about to reach the vigour of manhood, after a difficult and suffering youth, and to rise toward a happier stage of life and work in the brightness of a better future, when the brush was torn from his hand.

On the other hand, it was *Amedeo Modigliani's* weak character that caused him to waste his unique artistic ability in wild orgies. His was a talent which, with more discipline, would have made him a master too, just as *Jules Pascin*, one of the greatest drawing geniuses, lost himself in sensual orgies until disgust drove him to end his life.

Among those who were accomplished artists at an early age we should mention the quiet, exceedingly tasteful, but too delicate *Eugen Zack*; the very capable *Mintchine*, who succumbed to a long illness, and the refined *Leopold Gottlieb*, a brother of Mauricy Gottlieb who was born four years after the latter's untimely death. *Louis Marcoussis* and *Jean Metzinger* became well known participants of the Cubism movement.

World War II, which put an end to European Jewry, also broke up the Paris circle. Many of its members emigrated to other countries, chiefly America and Israel, and only a few recently came back to Paris. The great epoch of the Paris School is over, to be sure, but the impulse which Jewish art received from it continues to be effective all over.

However, since for the sake of continuity we have only pursued Jewish achievements in the painting field up to this point, we shall now have to go back to that period in the 19th century when free Jewish artistry began to arise in order to recognize its accomplishments in other spheres. Then we will be able to turn to the art of our days.

In mentioning the Jewish miniature painters at the close of the 18th century, we already pointed out the graphic aptitude of the Jew. Therefore it is not surprising that he could most easily get a foothold and make progress in graphic arts. Of the great masters in painting, almost all were also active in graphic art and played a not unimportant part therein. As a matter of fact Israels, Pissarro and Liebermann, through their work, were responsible for a vigorous revival of graphic arts generally.

Jozef Israels, for instance, was the first Dutch painter of the modern era to take up etching. He made 37 prints which acted as an incentive for his painting colleagues. *Camille Pissarro* was the only one among the French impressionists to employ etching as well as lithography with the purpose of a systematic penetration and easier explanation of his working methods. Of the 104 prints that he made, the series of Rouen in particular are of high artistic caliber. His son Lucien became a book engraver of note, mainly due to his inspiration and under his constant supervision. Lucien's "Eragny Press" was held in great esteem in England.

But it was *Max Liebermann* who, on the strength of his voluminous graphic work, consisting of landscapes and portraits as well as many book illustrations, became the leader of the black and white art in Germany.

Ernst Oppler, whose expertly executed representations of the Russian Ballet are universally popular, has to be considered one of the finest and most elegant etchers. *Eugen Spiro*, who is now living in New York, has portrayed almost the whole music world of Europe in many lithographs that give the effect of hastily drawn pencil sketches. *Lesser Ury* created a number of fine landscape prints. *Hermann Struck* made a name for himself as an expert in graphic arts. Aside from his prints of Jewish content and the portraits of prominent personalities (among them his widely known Herzl portrait), he became a guide to artist and collector alike through his book "The Art of Etching". His school, in turn, turned out a number of younger graphic artists of renown, of whom we shall only name two here since they occupied a special place in Jewish art.

Joseph Budko became the reviver of the Hebrew book illustration and the Jewish ex libris, and created many characteristic etchings and woodcuts that were important both technically and for their substance. His extraordinary pedagogic skill made him the tutor of the young artist generation in Israel, where he lived during his last years until his premature death in 1940. *Jacob Steinhardt* is a master of the modern woodcut, and knows how to augment the contrast of black and white to the point of plastic effect.

Until 1933 *Gustav Wolf* was professor of graphic and book art at the State Academy in Karlsruhe. Since coming to New York his book illustrations have made him known in the United States as well, where he died at the age of 60 in 1947.

But of even greater influence upon modern book illustration was *Hugo Steiner-Prag,* both through his production and his teaching activity. For 30 years he held a professorship at the Leipzig Academy for Industrial Art. In 1933 he fled from the Nazis, going first to Prague, thence to Sweden and settling, finally, in New York. From there he directed the book illustration of the University Press in Lincoln, Nebraska, until his death in 1945. He, himself, created more than 70 illustrated works.

Emil Orlik, for many years a professor at the Berlin Academy of Art, and the most eminent drawing pedagogue of our time, died just before the political upheaval in Germany. Since the time he was 21 he had specialized in graphic art, and in untiring work; since his pencil never rested no matter where he was, he accumulated an opus of prints in all techniques such as no other artist had accomplished. In 1900 he went to Japan to study, the first European artist to do so. There he learned the technique of the colored cut and colored etching, and some exceedingly fine and delicate prints demonstrate his mastery in that field.

In Japan Orlik had also appropriated the practically secret routine of the pen and crayon stroke in which nobody was as perfect as the experts in the Far East, and with the etching needle he created an entire gallery of portraits which have no equal as far as characteristic exactness is concerned. Orlik, who was a native of Prague, without question belongs in the foremost ranks of modern graphic artists.

During the 19th century the caricature and the poster developed into special fields that played an important part in public life at large, and which to this day are of increasing significance. One has only to remember the political influence exercised by France's greatest lithographic genius, Honorée Daumier, under whose sarcastic blasts a royal throne collapsed; or to recall the ridiculer of social arrogance, Gavarni, and the scoffer in animal form, Grandville.

Frederick Burr Opper, for instance, long the chief illustrator of "Puck" and "The New York Journal", was an artist whose witty drawings had decisive influence on the presidential election of 1900 in America, and *Henry Meyer* (Hy), who went to Mexico from Germany in 1885, and later came to Chicago, exercised a tremendous moral effect with his caricatures relating to the Dreyfus trial.

Max Beerbohm, a half-brother of Beerbohm Tree, was a feared and influential theatre critic in England because of his satiric novels, his acrid reviews and caricatures of actors.

Henry Ospovat and *Edmond Kapp* play a not unimportant role on account of the portrait caricatures with which they pilloried all personalities of public life. *Walter Trier,* who was already popular in Germany for his witty children's books, now is numbered among the much-named masters of caricature in England in his capacity as editor of the well-known London Liliput books.

And last, but not least, we must mention here the greatest political caricaturist in Germany, *Th. Th. Heine,* who gained world acclaim for his drawings in the "Simplizissimus", and who died in January 1948 in Stockholm where he had found refuge from the Nazis.

Edmund Edel was a noted German illustrator of comic journals, but it was mainly through his humorous posters that he stimulated the rest of Germany's placard art. He had been correct in recognizing the fact that a funny picture which hits the nail on the head in as unequivocal a form as possible is much more effective than a lot of words. Good picture advertisements must attract the eye from afar, must be immediately comprehensible and, by their originality, must entrench themselves in a person's memory.

Words are forgotten, pictures retained. The Jew is especially well fitted for this type of intelligent aperçu, and it is therefore not surprising that a number of Jewish names are to be found among the poster artists who adhered to this method and were successful in further improving it. They are names that are inextricably linked with the conception of modern placard art. *Lucien Bernard, Julius Klinger, R. Leonard, Lindenstaedt, Louis Oppenheim, Joe Loe* (Joel Loewenstein) are but a few of those who cultivated an original combination of poster and caricature. In recent years *Abram Games* who in 1940, at the age of 26, was appointed official poster designer of the British War Office and who designed the 3d. Olympic postage stamp, became one of the most successful commercial artists in Britain.

* * *

In sculpture as well as in architecture, the Jew was confronted by far more difficult problems than in any other branch of art inasmuch as until fairly recently those two types were almost entirely beyond his scope. He did not possess the sense of the cubic and tectonic, nor a purely sensual-rhythmic feeling. The form in its purely corporeal aspect did not exist for him, he knew it only in association with a functional content.

He never had a chance to do free sculptural work since his religion prohibited the palpable reproduction of the human image. This, of course, eliminated the most essential element of sculptural production, and he was restricted to a relief-like portrayal. For a long time, therefore, the Jewish artist had to be satisfied with the purely ornamental, such as we had discovered in tombstone decoration in fanciful embellishments, and he did not attain really artistic results until he applied himself to the medal portrait at the turn of the century.

However, the surface likeness does not render the figure as such, concentrating solely upon physiognomic characteristics, while the problem of freestanding sculpture consists in the structure of symmetrically arranged forms that harmonize in the interplay of proportions. Accordingly, sculpture requires a fundamentally different attitude that results from purely intuitive physical experience.

It is quite characteristic that the first artist to venture into freestanding sculpture came from the field of industrial art, and that in so doing he stumbled. As a matter of fact, in spite of extraordinary talent and tenacious efforts, he just had to stumble since he was incapable of undertaking as radical a spiritual permutation as an art alien to his nature demanded of him.

Mark Antokolsky is apprenticed to an engraver, and in his spare time he busies himself with woodcarving, an occupation undertaken by many Jews in his native Vilna. A wealthy woman sponsors him and sends him to St. Petersburg for additional study. He learns the art of wood relief at the academy there, and earns a living by working as a turner.

A small wood relief wins him an annual prize, whereupon he executes a relief in ivory for which he receives a scholarship abroad. In Berlin he tries his hand at free sculpture for the first time, and upon returning home he immediately sets to work on a marble figure of large format. It turns out to be "Ivan the Terrible" and is acquired by the Czar. Antokolsky is made a member of the academy.

In subsequent years he creates numerous large sculptures in Rome which are celebrated by the world press in Paris as the works of one of the greatest living masters, and which win for him medals and other honors. However, his colossal statue of Peter the Great is condemned in Russia in the most contumelious manner as being the work of a Jew, inasmuch as it was claimed a foreigner had no right to portray the national hero of Russia. The incongruity, it was further claimed, was apparent in the lack of all majestic dignity and grandeur, for which a Jew could have neither the feeling nor the understanding.

As a result, Antokolsky retires from public life, works quietly in Paris for the next 20 years and dies at the age of 60 in clear consciousness of the artistic limits existing for him as a Jew.

The brief life sketch of this ambitious artist demonstrates the lot, at once triumphant and tragic, of a Jew who is not yet equal to sculptural legalities. For Antokolsky is still too deeply entrenched in the constraint placed upon his talent. True, he makes every effort to overcome his artisan traits, but the world rejects him. His big sculptures still lack the liberal touch, they lose themselves too much in analytical incidentals, which affects their compactness and they narrate instead of being effective by their appearance alone.

Antokolsky's production is a courageous attempt, and therefore a feat; it is a beginning which not he, however, but a later generation was destined to develop further.

But, before we come to those who are to be evaluated as Jewish masters of a special character among modern sculptors we must enumerate, as we did in the painting field, a group of artists who won far-reaching acclaim by virtue of works which were technically skillful rather than artistically valuable.

Almost all of them likewise came from the East and got their start under similar circumstances. *Elias Guensbourg,* a direct pupil of Antokolsky, enjoyed great popularity in Russian circles for his pleasing children's busts. *Leopold Bernstamm,* who had been living in Paris since he was 26, created many busts of prominent men there, among them Dostojewski, Rubinstein, Flaubert and Zola. The only colleague of his to equal him in elegance and technical brilliance was his compatriot, *Naum Aronson* who created, among other things, the familiar Beethoven bust in the Beethoven House at Bonn.

Henryk Glicenstein lived in Rome from 1897 till 1928, at which time he entered the United States. He spent the last 14 years of his life in America. His father had been a humble "mazeze maker" in Turek, and the son also started out as an artisan until his talent was discovered; a talent that enabled him to become the portraitist of crowned heads.

Also living in Rome, and one of the most demanded artists of his time, was the American sculptor, *Moses Ezekiel,* who had established one of the most remarkable studies in the Thermae Diocletian. *Samuel Friedrich Beer,* who spent many years in Florence, enjoyed a great deal of success with his delicate statuettes and busts of women and children.

In Hungary, two Jewish sculptors were given official recognition: *Joseph Engel,* who had started out as a carver of pipe bowls, is the creator of the Szèehenyi Monument, and *Joseph Róna,* whose memoirs, published in 1929, give an interesting picture of artistic conditions in the 19th century, created several monuments, one of which is the equestrian statue of Prince Eugene in front of the palace in Budapest.

And as Antokolsky was the first, so was his pupil and assistant, *Boris Schatz* the last representative of this artist group which has already become history. Schatz had envisioned a reorganization of Jewish art, and he had devoted himself to this idea with enthusiasm. However, he was still so unfree in his entire artistic attitude that his aspirations and his creative work dissolved like a delusive dream.

All these artists still lack the necessary discipline to be satisfied with the means at their disposal; they develop a brilliant technique and endeavor to lend particularly loud expression to it. Their manual skill is astonishing at times, and the external effects achieved therewith contribute to their transient successes.

Only a shaping born from material and form is real plastic art, and only that artist is fitted for it whose creative work masters these two fundamental elements. The greatest obstructions prevented the Jew from doing justice to this basic requirement, and there is no greater testimony to his ability in art than the fact that he succeeded in surmounting these obstacles too. The modern Jewish sculptor proves that he is able to discard traditional prejudices and to absorb new energies.

Suddenly, at the start of the 20th century, a whole new art generation of marked individualities makes its appearance, and each of them contributes to the further development of modern sculpture.

Two of these belong at the head of the list, for they are among the revivers of the medal as a personal work of art in that they replaced the coined medal—which, in the course of time had become a technical routine in which numerous Jewish artists were well versed—with the cast medal.

Following the example of the Italian Renaissance masters who, meanwhile, had been almost doomed to oblivion, and in accordance with the procedure which France had again adopted not long before, *Benno Elkan* and *Arnold Zadikow* were the artists who contributed most toward the further development of the cast medal.

Elkan moulded his likeness directly in wax, and his portraits excelled in the keen characteristics of the personality. Zadikow, on the other hand, with extraordinary sureness cut his rhythmically fine compositions as negatives direct into the slates.

Elkan's art is not confined to the medal. It also asserts itself in vivid portrait busts as well as in numerous tombstone monuments. In the latter he occasionally undertakes an interesting combination of architectonic construction and sculptural adornment. This form was originated by Elkan's teacher, Bartholomé in the famous "Monuments aux Morts" in the Père Lachaise in Paris, and Elkan's continuance of it spread its popularity.

Among Elkan's big sculptures, the monument in Frankfurt dedicated to "The Victims" of the First World War ranks first because of the impressive effect achieved by its harmonious compactness and dignified calm. In recent years he has been particularly successful with his large bronze candelabra which are elaborately embellished in the manner of the Old-German Peter Vischer. Two of these candelabra can be seen in Westminster Abbey.

The life production of Arnold Zadikow, however, had it not been for the most part destroyed by the Nazis, would have to be considered the work of a master whose genius was expressed in the most versatile forms of plastic shaping. His first efforts were small sculptures in the form of graceful dancing figurines which right off were excellent technically. However, he lost no time in progressing to increasingly larger and freer compositions and portrait busts. His cut medals were made at the same time, and later he created many glass and crystal engravings that were unsurpassable in their graceful rhythm. A number of tombstones are among the best in modern Jewish monumental art, chiefly because of the artistically decorative exploitation of the Hebrew script. And, finally, there are a number of monumental sculptures which may be considered among his greatest achievements, but only a few originals of smaller size are left.

Their creator, too, came to his end in a concentration camp, amid the horrors of the past culture-killing war, another victim of which was a second master of modern sculpture, *Moyse Kogan.*

Kogan was a quiet man who liked to give himself to intimate meditation and work. He was the creator of a timelessly serene art that contented itself with the small format. His fantasy indulged itself in musically swaying rhythms which he knew how to express in an endless variation of fine terracotta figurines and delicate women heads and reliefs cut in stone, marble and wood. The absolutely personal character of his art had aroused the admiration of the best artists of his era, among them Rodin and Maillol.

Jacques Loutchansky, who went his own way, developed his art in no less clear a manner and devoted it exclusively to the human portrayal. To this day, after almost fifty years, he still lives in Paris, a quiet master who keeps himself aloof from the general beehive of activity in art.

Chana Orlow, the first Jewish woman artist to gain universal recognition, likewise had to be counted among those whose artistic talent is expressed in a self-assured form that has remained steady from the start. From a well-marked sense for material, she develops the formal-rhythmic construction of her works, of which her portraits take on a special note by virtue of a slight intimation of irony.

The most renowned, but at the same time the most bitterly criticized and assailed artist of our age is *Jacob Epstein,* who is 70 now. Although born in America, he lives in London. One has to read his controversial autobiography "Let There Be Sculpture" in order to get an idea of the inflexible will of this independent master, who ignores all obstacles, rejections and contumely, and who just radiates strength and intelligence. It is necessary to read the story about the origin, and the explanation of his ideas, given by himself, which led him to create his frequently bizarre and extravagant, but always ingenious works, and then we can first do him justice, both as artist and as man.

Epstein's art embraces all possibilities of plastic expression, it acknowledges no rules and no limits. To him, everything seems to be presentable, and every form permissible, and he often tries to advance into regions which, for the time being, are passable only for him and which in many respects still escape our comprehension.

In no branch of art was the levelling influence of assimilation as noticeable as in architecture. That is not surprising insofar as the Jew had absolutely no experiences of his own. For never before (with the possible sole exception of the era of ancient synagogue structures) did he have the opportunity to occupy himself with the basic questions of architecture. In his mind building was solely a purpose, never a free shaping that could stimulate his imagination. The two fundamental conceptions of proportionality and sense of space had remained alien to him, since he had no use for them. What we said about sculpture applies to proportionality as well: The conception of space as inside and outside volume had no meaning whatsoever for him because of the limitations imposed upon him for centuries. The artistic lawfulness of a structure in its exterior results from the surrounding landscape, while the interior must turn the sense of volume into an event of space.

The Jew had to be content that he was permitted to build at all, and he was usually forced to take every possible advantage of the narrow space allotted to him. What good did a beautiful outside architecture that grew out of harmony with nature do him? And how was he to create large, ample rooms saturated with air and light? So accustomed had he become to narrowness and twistedness that even the smallest rooms were sufficient, so long as he could worship in them in some security.

Having grown up under such dire circumstances, the result was that the Jew lacked every conception of, and interest in architecture. This statement is borne out by the fact that of those artists who applied themselves to this branch, most of them came from a more assimilated region. The ambition of such circles was mainly to adjust their living habits to those of other people, thereby stressing their full equality. They started to build large temples and, since there was no existing form of style for synagogue structures, they borrowed from everywhere, with the result that their construction lacked all individuality.

There is nothing more disconsolate in the entire history of Jewish art than the synagogue structure of the 19th century. The general hodgepodge of style indicates absolute lack of understanding and taste; one might even say a lack of dignity. Everywhere the congregations that had grown prosperous were building luxuriously splendid structures. From the outside they were barely recognizable as Jewish houses of worship, and inside, by eliminating the central bema, erecting a preacher's pulpit, installing an organ and changing the Aron Hakodesch to resemble the form of Protestant altars, they avoided everything that might have distinguished them from churches. Germany, the pace-maker in matters of assimilation, was also trail-blazer in that respect.

As early as 1798 a synagogue with Egyptian pylons had been erected in Karlsruhe, and in 1827 a temple was built in Budapest that sported a six-column portico.

Albert Rosengarten (1809-1893), the foremost Jewish synagogue constructor, introduced the Moorish style in his Kassel synagogue. This style was subsequently widely accepted, and we find it in all sorts of combinations of cupolaed buildings with minaret-like towers in various German cities, such as Stuttgart, Nuremberg, and Ulm, which were built by *Albert Wolff*; in the Lyons synagogue, created by *Abraham Hirsch*; in the pompous synagogue of Florence, built by *Marc Treves*, which resembles a mosque in its interior, too, and, in America, in the structure of the former Temple Emanu-El, a work of *Leopold Eidlitz,* and the Central Synagogue in New York, designed by Henry Fernbach.

Edwin Oppler, father of the painter and etcher Ernst Oppler, was one of the busiest German synagogue architects who, with his buildings in Hanover, Breslau and Munich created a special adulterated Roman style. *Karl Koenig,* professor and rector of the Technical University in Vienna, built the synagogue in that city's Taborstrasse in a Renaissance style, and

Temple Knesseth-Israel in Philadelphia was a two-storied Renaissance structure topped by a cupola reminiscent of the Florentine dome, with two free-standing campanile towers as additional embellishment.

In Budweis the Viennese architect *Max Fleischer* went so far as to construct a Gothic synagogue which, with its raised, elongated center nave and the two high towers flanking it looks exactly like a church.

The cemetery parks too, especially those in America, are the worst outgrowths of architectural and taste aberration. The cemeteries of Temple Emanu-El, and Washington Cemetery in Brooklyn, for example, with their expensive mausoleums copied from Greek temples have none of the dignified aspect that distinguished the old Jewish burial grounds. The lack of every specifically characteristic achievement in sacral construction proves the failing of the Jewish architects who would have had ample opportunity to prove their merits in this particular field.

The entire construction field in the first half of the 19th century was at a low standard, for it existed only on traditional styles in accordance with an academic regime, and the few Jewish architects worth mentioning followed in the same footsteps, and not in sacral architecture alone.

George Heinrich Hitzig, whose grandfather had been the founder of the Jewish free school in Berlin which was particularly active in pursuing enlightenment, was a pupil of Friedrich Schinkel and was eminently successful with his private villas in classic style and with the construction of the Stock Exchange and Reichsbank buildings in Berlin.

In England, the well-known *George Basevi* (1794-1845) was the architect of various churches in Mooresque style, as well as of the Gothic Fitz William Museum in Cambridge.

In France we find *Alfred Philibert Aldrophe* (1834-1895), who was a noted architect of exhibits. *Henry Fernbach,* who came to New York in 1855, and *Dankmar Adler,* both originally from Germany, in partnership with Louis Sullivan constructed many public buildings in Chicago after 1879. Adler, who is considered an authority in the field of acoustics, created a number of large hotels, synagogues, theatres and concert halls and was especially noted for the "Auditorium" in Chicago, a mighty combination of hotel, opera and business house.

The social change wrought by technical and industrial progress in the course of decades entailed a break with antiquated customs, and a radical conversion in architectural tendency. The use of new building materials such as iron, cement and concrete, together with the constructive experiences resulting therefrom, led to a new economy in building. Appreciation of functional design and spaciousness gave modern architecture a completely new direction. As a result, structures sprang up that no longer hid behind false façades, preferring, instead, to announce their purpose in unequivocal language.

Modern architecture no longer would have any part of academic constructive styles; it wanted to be the expressive medium of its era and, as such, serve life and be no more than an art born from life. And this call to reality was heeded also by the Jewish artists who, in the interim, had matured to the point of independence. And just as they made a niche for themselves in sculpture, so, too, did they exercise a constantly increasing influence upon modern architecture.

The first to impart a new note to business structures by using iron construction was *Alfred Messel* (1853-1909). He designed the Berlin department store, Wertheim, which was the first large structure of this modern business-house type on the European continent.

In this building, the vertical columns between huge windows that break up the façade indicate an interior construction that consists of a huge hall with balconies all around. The total effect is still too solemn and monumental, although in a very new sense.

Erich Mendelsohn goes a step further in exploiting static possibilities with the inclusion of glass. He emphasizes the storey-construction with wall and window strips that encircle the structure like a horizontal band. This mass rhythm is demonstrated in the big factories, stores and office buildings that he erected in Germany, and during a stay of several years in Israel, and which he is now undertaking in America. With his creation he is opening new paths to industrial construction.

The rapidly mounting demands of modern living toward the close of the century placed before architecture increasingly difficult tasks. Just think of the many meeting halls, administration and railroad buildings, and the music halls, theatres and motion picture houses, all of them giant structures that have to admit thousands of people. Architecture turned into a science that combined art and technique, knowledge of material and social science.

The architects, who were busy everywhere, were joined by several prominent Jewish talents. *Julien Flegenheimer* (1880-1938), born in Geneva, became known for his construction of the Cornavin station and for his design for the palace of the League of Nations, which was awarded a prize. The Viennese *Oskar Strnad* (1879-1935), professor at the Vienna Academy of Industrial Art, was one of the most eminent pedagogues. Together with *Oskar Kaufmann,* the great theatrical constructor of our era, he became the reformer of modern theatre and stage architecture. We have to thank Strnad, among other things, for the world-famous Salzburg Festspiele, with which he introduced an entirely new form of open-air stage. His co-worker of many years' standing, *Oskar Wlach*, who has been living in New York since 1938, is the builder of numerous official structures, such as the governor's palace in Trieste.

The art of the theatre attracted many Jewish artists, not only as architects but also as stage painters. *Leon Bakst* (1868-1924), for instance, created the fabulous sceneries and costumes for the Russian ballet, and *Nahum Altman*, one of the most versatile sculptors, fellow laborer of the communist Futurists, and with *Jankel Adler* (1895-1949) who became like Chagall an outstanding master of a pronounced chassidic art, founder of the new Jewish cultural movement in Russia, won his fame through his revolutionary stage designs. *Ernst Stern* has to be mentioned as artistic adviser of Reinhardt in Berlin. Chagall designed in 1919 the stage sets and costumes for the Jewish State theatre in Moscow and in 1942 in Mexico his scenery for the ballet "Aleko" and three years later in New York for the ballet "Firebird".

A pioneer of ultra-modern architecture based on cubic forms was Bèla Lajta from Budapest (1875-1920). The great effect of the buildings he created is achieved by a severe construction that eliminates all ornamentation, emphasizing the material all the more, instead. Today many of the most recent architects follow his example.

The greatest genius of architectural dynamism that characterizes the world of today was Albert Kahn (1869-1943) who came from a modest rabbinical home in Westphalia. He had come to America at the age of 12, and had managed to eke out a living with door-to-door canvassing. At 26 he established himself as an independent architect and became so successful that he was called "The World's No. 1 Industrial Designer". In 1929 he was called to Stalingrad to design that city's huge factory plants. He sketched the first five-year construction plan of the Soviet government, and created the gigantic Ford and Chrysler aircraft plants, the mightiest achievement in exploitation of material statics the world has ever seen.

In the meantime, though, residential architecture had also undergone a radical change. The crowding of city inhabitants in unsanitary housing barracks without air and light, and a growing social sense of responsibility for national health in general sought solutions for overcoming this increasing evil. That could be made possible only by a complete remodelling of housing. And just as reasons of practicability had led to a concentration of factories, industrial and commercial houses in special districts, one now set in to create special residential sections, with the result that special housing zones sprang up around the heart of the city.

This, in turn, required systematic city planning on a new basis in order to organically separate the constantly expanding bulks of the town and then to connect them via traffic channels. In this respect the big American cities have accomplished miracles in the last few decades. And in this connection, let us not forget the New York architect and designer of a great number of monumental structures, *Arnold William Brunner* (1857-1925) who was a pathfinder in city planning. He was called in by many cities to re-organize their plans in the capacity of supervisory expert.

A further step was taken by erecting working men's settlements, consisting of rows of small, one-family houses of the villa type, which enabled the working population to dwell in sanitary conditions. This idea had been realized chiefly by *Michel de Klerk* (1884-1923) in a model plan in Amsterdam-Oost, and many city designers and architects in most of the civilized countries have since followed suit.

A pupil of de Klerk's, *Richard Kaufmann,* brought the settlement method to Israel, adjusting it to fit the special conditions imposed by that country. With it he became the founder of the huge construction task in Israel during the past 30 years.

The altered appearance of profane and functional architecture also had its effect on the forming of the sacral structure. In certain circles people began to realize the contradiction in imitating ancient architectural styles, and, above all, they recognized the lack of taste displayed in the "Protestant" synagogue structures which were quasi devoid of style, and they began to recall the tradition that had been expression of a simple and genuine conviction. "Simplicity" had become the watchword for all building, to be sure; but it had become apparent that being simple did not necessarily mean being prosaic.

The Munich architect *Fritz Landauer* risked reviving the ancient idea of combining community house and synagogue, and created a modern example in the synagogue of Plauen (1929). In a structure with a very plain exterior, community rooms for all purposes are included with the prayer hall. As in the former times, the walls are decorated with paintings consisting, for the most part, of Jewish symbols and Hebrew characters.

A second modern structure is the new temple in Hamburg, designed by the architects *Felix Ascher* and *Robert Friedmann.* It is a severely compact cubical wall, fronted at a right angle by side-aisles that form a porch through which one reaches the main building. The complex encompasses the large synagogue and a smaller chapel, a separate community hall and school rooms.

Harry Elte was one of the most deserving Dutch architects of settlements next to de Klerk. The solution which he tried in the synagogue of Amsterdam-Oost resulted in a solemnly simple prayer hall, to be sure; but as far as the outside architecture is concerned, it can be considered as having defeated its purpose; it is reminiscent of Dutch church forms. The structure is situated on a corner, and a square, chimney-like tower is set in the angle created by the main building and the wing.

Quite simple, yet grandiose is the effect given by Temple Beth Israel, built in 1936 in Hartford, Conn. by the Boston architect *Charles R. Greco,* for the very simple interior is arched by a huge cupola. Here we have the first attack against the display of luxury prevalent in American synagogue construction.

The cemeteries of the 19th century displayed the same lack of style as the synagogues. Not until the First World War caused a demand for dignified military cemeteries and honor monuments did an essential change take place. A new idea was the creation of affecting woodland cemeteries. With horticulturists, architects, sculptors and art scholars cooperating, the intersectarian "Reichsausschuss fuer Friedhof und Denkmal" in Germany accomplished something that was of great importance and could serve as a universal example.

The best solution with respect to both artistry and Jewishness is the new cemetery in Frankfurt planned in 1929 by *Fritz Nathan*. Plain buildings formed of dark red brick walls enclose an honor court, from which a three-part portal leads to the burial grounds. The same tranquillity and dignity is achieved here by severely executed tectonics. The area is divided into individual sections, each of which is identical in form, material and size of stone as well as in horticultural design. Simplicity and solemnity grew into one in this place, and thus became a model for future plans.

Modern architecture is not the secluded field of art it used to be, for in order to fulfill its destination it has to embrace everything that makes it a life-serving organism. Early style conceptions are no longer valid, for today we recognize different standards of beauty. A building is perfect in our eyes only when it is true expression of purpose in all its parts, i.e. when it does not try to deceive with a false façade, and when its interior corresponds to the function for which it is designed. Accordingly, the architect must be both exterior and interior decorator who helps decide upon the furnishing and the capacity of the rooms. It makes no difference whether the structure in question is designed as a factory, an office or residential building, a theatre or a church. The architect must possess the necessary knowledge pertaining to material and technique and, of decisive importance in connection with the building of settlements—he must know the social, economic and hygienic conditions prevailing.

Today's architect must, therefore, master many fields; above all he must be an industrial artist, as Oskar Strnad and Fritz Landauer were in exemplary fashion. And with that we touch upon the far-reaching branches of interior architecture and industrial art in which many artists specialized. Their number,

THE HEBREW IMPACT ON WESTERN ART

among the Jews, too, is so large that a mere mention of the most prominent names is impossible.

* * *

Art can prosper only in an atmosphere that is beneficial to it, for it cannot develop its creative forces by itself. These forces must be fed by various sources. Art requires inspiration, but it also needs resonance. In Italy the arts flourished under the sun of the popes and the princes, French art developed in the sheen of the Roi Soleil. In the 19th century the monarchs were replaced by a bourgeois society grown prosperous, and by the sciences.

Up to the start of the 19th century the Jew had no part in all these activities, and for this reason his artistic creations were limited to his own narrow confines. However, we have testified here as to what he was capable of accomplishing once these barriers had fallen. But he has also become a furtherer of, and contributor to the art within the scope of bourgeois society and in the sciences.

The historical and systematic exploration of art is one of the youngest sciences; it has essentially broadened our knowledge of former civilizations, and has created new aesthetic conceptions through which modern art, in turn, has received important and directive inspirations. Archaeological explorations and excavations of the last 50 years have brought to light the world that lay buried under the rubble of millennia, a world which today can be studied in museums and research institutes. Art historians are disseminating the knowledge and understanding of the fine arts, thereby animating prosperous circles to collect old and modern art and to become Maecenases of many artists and public institutions. Some big art dealers may likewise be numbered among the discoverers and promoters of the arts. And Jews, too, participated prominently in all these fields.

Jules Oppert (1825-1905), the German-born Assyriologist, and *Salomon Reinach* (1858-1932) who for 30 years was inspector general of the French museums and, prior to that time had done excavating in Greece, both became known for their numerous archaeological writings which were published in France. In Greece, too, the Koenigsberg professor of archaeology, *Gustav Hirschfeld* (1847-1895) supervised the excavations in Olympia at the request of the German government. *Emmanuel Loewy* (1857-1938) lectured in Rome as professor of Greek sculpture, as well as in his native Vienna, where his contemporary, *Emil Szanto* was professor of classical archaeology. *Leo Bloch* (1864-1918) lectured on Greek and Roman archaeology in Zurich and *Behrendt Pick* (1861-1940), the numismatist, one of the best coin connoisseurs and later director of the coin collections in Gotha, also taught in Zurich.

The Egyptologist *Wilhelm Spiegelberg* (1870-1930) was professor in Heidelberg and Munich, and *Ludwig Borchardt* (1863-1938) was director of the German Institute for Egyptian Archaeology in Cairo from 1906 to 1936. *Charles Waldstein* (Walston) who was born in New York in 1856 and died in London in 1927, was a professor at King's College and Slade professor in Cambridge, and was one of the best known archaeologists in England. He was knighted in 1912.

Mark Aurel Stein, a native of Hungary, was also knighted for his research in India, Persia, and China.

Eleasar L. Sukenik, who was born in Bialystok in 1889 and who has been a professor at the University of Jerusalem since 1926, deserves special credit for his epochal excavations in Israel and for his writings relating thereto. His son, who became a noted leader in the Israeli army under the name of Colonel Yigael Yadin, is also a renowned archaeologist.

Professor *Nelson Glueck,* who is director of the American School of Research both in Jerusalem and in Bagdad, was acclaimed for his explorations in Transjordan, and Professor *B. Maisler* gained fame for his excavations of the necropolis of Beth Shearim and for his newest discoveries near Tel-Aviv.

The list of well-known archaeologists could be lengthened essentially; yet their number is exceeded by far by the roster of prominent art historians. And in that field we must differentiate between serious scientific research, which alone is our concern here, and the popular and feuilletonistic type of art literature which has grown beyond all limits. Today, art has become a matter of fashion; it belongs to the "bonton", so to speak. Wherever one turns, there are public high schools, lectures on art and illustrated art magazines. Every newspaper publishes art reports and every layman writes or talks about art.

All along the line a dilettantism has come into existence that has turned art into a kind of conversation topic. Among the newspaper art writers, who are actually journalists and essayists, we find many Jews who distinguish themselves by the brilliance of their pen. However, our interest here is limited to their scientific participation in the promotion and advancement of culture within the general framework of nations.

Of those who, in their capacity as university professors, belong among the acknowledged great in art history, we would like to mention: *Marc Rosenberg* (1852-1930), in Karlsruhe, the best silver connoisseur and author of the history of goldsmith art and of the four-volume standard work "The Stamp of the Goldsmiths"; *Carl Neumann* (1860-1934) in Heidelberg, universally known as "Rembrandt-Neumann" for his famous Rembrandt book; *Adolf Goldschmidt* (1863-1943) in Berlin, the most prominent expert on mediaeval ivory sculpture; *Aby Warburg* (1866-1929) in Hamburg, founder of the Warburg Institute which consists of over 60,000 volumes and more than 20,000 photographs. Warburg used his own means to develop this Institute into a scientifically important research establishment with its own technical publication, and it has now been made a part of the British Museum. (The director of the Institute was Professor *Fritz Saxl* (1890-1948) who was a professor at the University of Hamburg at the same time).

Other great names in the field of art history are: *George Swarzenski* in Frankfurt, who has been working at the Boston museum since 1936; *Max Dessoir* (Dessauer), professor of aesthetics and art history in Berlin; *Max Eisler* (1881-1937) and *Heinrich Glueck* (1888-1930), who specialized in Islamic art, were active in Vienna; *Hans Tietze,* likewise formerly from Vienna, and now librarian of the Metropolitan Museum of Art in New York; *Edwin Panofsky* in Hamburg, active at Princeton University since 1935, and *Franz Landsberger* in Breslau, director of the Jewish Museum in Berlin from 1933-1938, and now a professor at Hebrew Union College in Cincinnati, where he was recently the first to be honored with the title of a Professor for Jewish Art for his research efforts in that field.

Among those who distinguished themselves as museum directors are the following: the head of the numismatic department of the Berlin Museum, *Julius Friedlaender* (1813-1884); the tapestry expert, and director of the Berlin Museum of Industrial Art, *Julius Lessing* (1843-1908); *Gustav Glueck,* director of the Vienna Picture Gallery and editor of "Graphic Arts" in Vienna, well-known for his many writings on Rubens and the Rubens era; *August L. Mayer* (1885-1941?) formerly of the Alte Pinakothek in Munich and author of many works about Spanish painting, on which he is considered to be the top expert; *John Rothenstein,* director of the Tate Gallery in London, son of the painter Sir William Rothenstein; the Bénédite brothers in Paris: *George Aaron Bénédite* (1857-1926) was chief of the division for Egyptian archaeology in the Louvre, and *Leonce Bénédite* (1859-1925) was director of the Musée du Luxembourg.

One branch in which Jewish art historians were particularly active is that of the graphic arts. *Friedrich Lippmann* (1858-1908), *Max Lehrs* (1855-1939) and *Max I. Friedlaender* succeeded one another as directors of the Berlin Copperplate Print Collection; *Kurt Glaser* (1879-1939) was the head of the modern department of the same collection and wrote, among other works, the best history of graphic arts of the modern age; *Paul Kristeller* (1863-1931) contributed among many other important writings a book of lasting value with his "Copperplate Engraving and Woodcut in Four Centuries"; *Jacob Rosenberg* has been a professor at Harvard University since 1937 and is director of graphic arts at the Boston Museum. All six mentioned were active in the Berlin Copperplate Collection.

Two deans of art history, both of them vigorous octogenarians, still enjoy the respect of the whole world. One is *Bernard Berenson,* who was born in Vilna in 1865 and who, entirely without means, began his studies in Boston at the age of 18. Since 1900 he has been living in a palatial villa near Florence that is filled with the choicest works of art. He is consulted from far and wide as the undisputed authority on Italian painting.

But it is *Max I. Friedlaender* who deserves threefold praise. Since he was forced by the Nazis to retire from office, he has been living in Amsterdam. Friedlaender is the master connoisseur of graphic art and Dutch painting; he is the reformer of museum science and one of the few classic art authors. He was born in Berlin, was a director of the Kupferstich Cabinet for twenty years, and then succeeded Wilhelm Bode in the management of the Kaiser Friedrich Museum.

A new generation of museum experts were trained under Friedlaender's guidance, and today they are in action throughout the world as museum directors who follow the scientific methods which he created.

And finally, as explorer and interpreter of art Friedlaender can be counted among the greatest and most fertile masters of the written word. A listing of his works, issued on the occasion of his 60th birthday, at that time already came close to the 600 mark! And since then various other works of lasting value have been added.

It should be sufficient to mention such widely known names as Benjamin Altman, Jules Semon Bache, Michael Friedsam, Joseph Pulitzer, Julius Rodenwald and Jacob H. Schiff in America, the Rothschilds in Paris and London, Albert

Figdor and Camillo Castiglione in Vienna, Baron Marcell Nemes in Budapest and James Simon in Berlin to demonstrate the extensive importance of wealthy personages as collectors and Maecenases.

The same holds true of the big art dealers, Alfred Stieglitz in New York; Nathan and Georges Wildenstein, who were also the founders of the "Gazette des Beaux Arts"; Charles Sedelmayer, co-publisher, with Wilhelm Bode, of the large Rembrandt work, and Raoul Heilbronner, adviser to Pierpont Morgan, in Paris; Paul Cassirer, co-founder of the "Berlin Secession" in Berlin, and the two greatest experts and discoverers of mediaeval manuscripts, Leo S. Olschki in Florence and Jacques Rosenthal in Munich—all of them have contributed valuable cultural work.

* * *

And now we have reached the fateful turning point at which the spiritual-cultural existence of Judaism is shattered by the most horrible catastrophe of all times. One third of all World-Jewry is destroyed, and the largest portion of their cultural documents ruined—but, like the legendary phoenix bird, a new Jewry that looks to the future arises from the still glowing ash.

At two opposite points of the globe energies are forming from the salvaged heritage which guarantees the proven stability of that heritage for the future, too. And it would appear as though the history of Israel were repeating itself inasmuch as today a similar process is taking place as during the heyday of Rome: when that mighty nation thought it could put an end to Judaism and discovered that the germs of its continuation had already begun to sprout elsewhere.

In America a large and strong Judaism has been growing for a long time, while upon the soil of the former homeland forces had been gathering to establish a new Israel thereon. America and Israel are the future of Judaism in this hour of destiny. They are the two energy centers, and each in its way is new and yet not new. America has the advantage in number and strength; Israel, in spite of its youth, has spiritual superiority inasmuch as it realized the 2000 year old dream of the Jewish people by establishing an independent state of its own. America already has a piece of history to show; Israel is just at the beginning of her history.

Until now we have neglected America—except for several brief references—because it does not belong directly within the period of European rise and decline which has now been concluded. Rather, it developed separately under its own laws and conditions, which we shall now bring up to date in continuity.

American Jewry existed almost as long as today's other population of the country, to be sure; but until the early 19th century it was so insignificant in number as to be unable to play any part. In 1824 there were only about 3000 Jews in all North America. It was not until after the War of Independence that the number grew, and then in increasingly rapid tempo. The Jew found altogether new living conditions in America. He was not considered inferior, was not persecuted for his faith or subjected to discriminating laws; he could live according to his customs and develop in proportion to his means and energies.

Of course, the mass immigration of poor people who were accustomed to their tradition-laden atmosphere led to social restrictions and, because of increasing over-population, to the existence of special quarters within the big cities; and while these quarters were inhabited by a huge working class whose life was similar to that in the ghettos of Europe, still there was a tremendous difference. For although the first generation could not adjust so easily in habits and language, their children overcame that problem through the schools and in their professions.

Jewish youth grew up in closest association with American youth, and each Jewish child could develop his talents without his descent or faith being an obstacle. Thus existing differences were smoothed out gradually, and the Jew grew increasingly American.

In the course of years a rapidly growing reform movement began to take shape within the Jewish community. However, unlike the assimilating dissolution of Judaism in Europe, it led to a new form of a consciously pronounced Judaism. One should pay particular attention to this factor if one would understand the spiritual attitude of the American Jew toward his new fatherland, in which his ability and accomplishments are given full recognition. And when Theodore Roosevelt, in his address commemorating the 250th anniversary of the New York Jews (the first Jews had settled there in 1655) emphasized "the full share of the Jew in the material, social and moral advancement of the nation", he was giving expression to the true spirit of the American nation. For the Jew was able to contribute to the construction of the country *with* the people, not *under* it because, although he preserved his inherited qualities, he nevertheless did not remain a stranger.

The American had not forgotten that he himself had been a foreigner when he came to these shores. For this reason he had an entirely different understanding for the Jew than the nations of yore that had considered themselves masters of their land. When the first big wave of Jewish immigration set in, the country still needed fresh supplies of people, for at that time it was just beginning its rise from colonial primitivity to world power; and toward that end the Jew was permitted to contribute in all spheres in accordance with his abilities.

Up to the first quarter of the 19th century America had no art, and what was created in the country after that time was, at first, no more than a modest provincial art. In spite of some painters of rank, the land was fairly backward since little attention was paid to the art activities of the rest of the world and the country had nothing of its own. It was the amassing of large private fortunes that first led to the collecting of foreign art production and the arousing of universal interest in art.

In the meantime, though, young folks had gone to Paris to study, and through them modern art was now reaching America. Among them were a number of Jewish artists who had already spent their childhood in the United States and had been reared in the American way. The first large exhibit of modern European art in New York became known as the "Armory Show of 1913". The chief initiators of this show were several Jewish painters and the meritorious art dealer Stieglitz. The "Armory Show" gave the final impetus to a development in art that now set in with immense rapidity and assumed proportions never thought possible, and a surprisingly large number of Jewish talents participated in ever-increasing measure.

America today has grown to be the leading world power. The concentration and incessant forward push of all forces created a new standard and trend for all expressions of life, to which art likewise is subject. The general watchword is: Dynamics! Dynamics has also become the expression of new constructive ideas which place art in a different relation to life than heretofore. Such a phenomenon could evolve productively only in a land like 20th century America, whose young civilization was open to all new talents because its hospitality was without prejudice.

Young Jewish people play an integral part in this evolution. Since they are not separated from their fellow-citizens by as deep a chasm as they were in the countries of the old world, they are given the chance of mutual assimilation. Thus we find them all over today occupying leading positions as architects, sculptors, painters and etchers. At a large exhibition of modern artists from all over the country, which was held in 1930, eleven among the 33 acknowledged best were Jews: Arnold Friedman, Bernar Gussow, Samuel Halpert, Stephan Hirsch, Morris Kantor, Bernard Karfiol, Louis Lozowick, Ben Shahn, Abraham Walkowitz, Max Weber and William Zorach. The number of prominent personalities has grown quite a bit since then. Three masters have to be mentioned right off:

Max Weber, close to 70 years old, has been the pioneer of American modernism for forty years. No less art-furthering than his dynamically expressive paintings was the effect of his writings, which speak a convincing language. His ecstasy, occasionally enhanced to the point of monumentality, has only been surpassed by *William Gropper.* Gropper, born in New York's slum district, was well acquainted with the misery that was at home there, and later met the terrors of war and unleashed passions of the most brutal violence in Europe. He is rightfully considered the master of a new symbolic art born from the storm signals of our riotous world. For, in unbelievable passion, spurred on by wrath and ridicule, he has created deeply stirring paintings and caricatural drawings of permanent validity that are a horrifying reflection of a lacerated humanity.

And as a sculptor, *William Zorach,* too, has at his disposal a masterful power of expression that is capable of transforming matter into rhythm and rhythm into life.

Among the artists already mentioned, and among many who cannot be enumerated here, we find such distinctive personalities that a characterization of each individual would result in a recital of all potentialities of portrayal and expression within the sphere of fine arts.

From the lyric impressionism of Bernar Gussow, the poetic post-impressionism of the twin brothers Soyer and Bernard Karfiol; from the delineator of country life, Aaron Bohrod, and the portrayer of city life in intimate contemplation, Morris Kantor; from Louis Lozowick and Peter Blume, who give expression to a laborious life in the rhythmic measure of steaming machines; from Todros Geller's and David Fredenthal's expressionistically powerful figures and Benjamin Kopman's Jewish types which bring to mind Rouault's dismal, heavy expressionism; and from Maurice Sterne's rhythmically elegant paintings and plastic works, the path leads to the sculptors among whom the most prominent are the master of wood sculpture, Chaim Gross; the realistic portraitist Jo Davidson; Minna Harkavy, a pupil of Bourdelle; the animal sculptor Eli Nadelman, and the most forceful exponents of the abstract trend, Ossip Zadkine and Jacques Lipchitz.

All of them have one thing in common, for which reason the part they play in the large community of universal artistry is of particular interest to us: their artistic achievements are propelled by two different energies, namely their hereditary talent and a strong life impulse. And nowhere does this impulse manifest itself as free and uninhibited as in the new America that is borne by forces which point to the future.

* * *

And now, at last, the new Israel. In the land of their fathers the descendants of the old people have aroused Israel to new life, initiating a new chapter in our history.

Emancipation had rent asunder the unity of Judaism and had made available to the Jew foreign cultures which he absorbed in increasing measure. Tempted by the advantages beckoning to him, and blinded by external successes, he was not aware that he was losing himself in the world. European Jewry was destroyed by violence, but even aside from that catastrophe it would have vanished gradually, for it was dissolving within itself, thereby contributing further to its downfall.

American Jewry did not yield to its environment in this passive sense; on the contrary, it enriched itself as an equal partner on the strength of its own assets and, since the country had no self-established culture, the Jews were able to participate directly in its construction. To what extent this state of equilibrium will continue to exist in the future, and whether sooner or later the minority may not succumb after all, is a problem that should not be underestimated.

Israel, however, wants to build up her future pursuant to her own laws, not according to those dictated by others, and

[499]

wants to convert her traditional spiritual assets into creative reality. She does not want to be merely a state of free and independent citizens who again speak their own tongue, live in their own home and plow their own soil; but, as once before, she would be the spiritual home of all Judaism. For the majority of the Jews who continue to live in the outside world are newly oriented by the centre created in Israel, both in their feeling of solidarity and their attitude towards the others, and in their spiritual tendency.

As the fountain of strength for all Jewry, Israel stands before mighty tasks which, however, are saturated with new and unlimited possibilities for her own spiritual development.

Israel did not come to pass overnight. For a long time it was no more than a vague dream, until the idea took shape and finally an entire generation invested the sweat of self-denying work and the blood of heroic pioneering to make the soil arable. At the same time people had arrived who planted the seeds of a new Jewish spirituality, without which all efforts would have led only to a material success, but never to national success as well. Spiritual culture is the foundation for the effective development of a nation's physical powers, but its growth is a process that is organically conditioned.

Of the many utterances that constitute a nation's cultural life, art is one of the most sublimated. For it cannot be "intended", it originates and grows by getting its nourishment from psychical sources. It is the visible blossom of unseen energies, and it requires a soil into which it can plant its roots. All great and genuine art needs a native earth in order to flourish. The tragedy of our lot to date was our want of a homeland and the lack of space for developing our specific accomplishments which, for that reason had to remain fragmentary.

Only now can we make our own land fertile, and we have already begun to plant the first seedlings. We have imported many of them from the outside, where we have learned how to care for them. Now, fed by the new sun and new energy sources, they shall help to beautify Israel's gardens.

It is still too early to speak of our achievements in the field of art, although some notable work is being created by the artists who came here and promising talents are to be seen among our growing youth. But everything is still too new, and we lack experiences in the special conditions imposed by the country; only time can remedy that. Accordingly, all art life is in a stadium nascendi, a state of searching and experimenting, the result of which is a colorful multiformity that does not follow any directive trend and, at most, indicates tendencies that lead to it.

It is the same in art as in other activities of daily life: one still uses strange languages and therefore cannot reach a mutual agreement. One does not master Hebrew well enough to express oneself freely and easily; one still has to translate whereby, of course, many foreign words still crop up. The younger generation, though, speaks the language fluently and naturally thinks in that language too; therefore it will arrive at an art expression that has specific character. Inasmuch as there had been no art in the whole country until just a few years ago, everything has to be built up from the very foundation.

Meanwhile, beginnings were made in all fields, and one can safely say that they are indeed promising. For we have a rich fund of talents, and from them, once they are fortified by the founts and fruits of our homeland and are deeply rooted in it, will sprout a genuine and specific art.

True, we have already achieved a great deal, having successfully fought for the freedom of our resolutions; but we must not overestimate this feat, for now we have to prove ourselves! And to that end we have to consolidate all the powers which we derive from our Jewish constitution. We have to liberate these forces from the dross of antiquity and the blemishes of foreign elements so that we may recognize their true core.

We have proved to the world that our *vitality* is strong and young enough to maintain our right as a nation of the present. We ourselves, however, must be guided by the cognition of our *stability* so that we may remain true to ourselves, thereby fulfilling our destiny as augmenters and furtherers of mankind's cultural goods in the future, too.

* * *

EPILOGUE

The facts and achievements gathered here from three thousand years of history of the Jewish People in the field of fine arts, their evaluation and relation to their nations, is the response to questions, frequently posed but never satisfactorily solved, about the artistic ability of the Jews. However, this treatise is not intended to increase by one more the large number of apologetic documents, but rather to weigh and discuss the pro and the contra in as clear and unobjectionable a manner as possible with the help of the material available.

BIBLIOGRAPHY

ALBRIGHT, W. F., *From the Stone Age to Christianity.* Baltimore: 1940.
——, *The Archaeology of Palestine.* (Penguin) 1949.

ARNOLD, TH., *The Old and New Testament in Muslim Religious Art.* (Schweich Lect.) London: 1932.

BREYER, EISLER, GRUNWALD, *Holzsynagogen in Polen.*

COHN, GUSTAV, *Der juedische Friedhof.* Frankfurt: 1930.

COHN-WIENER, E., *Die juedische Kunst.* Berlin: 1929.

GLATZER, N. N., *Geschichte der talmudischen Zeit.* Berlin: 1937.

KRAUTHEIMER, R., *Mittelalterliche Synagogen.* Berlin: 1927.

LANDSBERGER, FR., *A History of Jewish Art.* Cincinnati: 1946.
——, *Hebrew Coll. Ann.* Cincinnati, Vol. XV-XXI. (pass.)
The Legacy of Israel. Oxford: 1928. *The Legacy of Islam.* Oxford: 1943. *The Legacy of Egypt.* Oxford: 1947.

LEVEEN, J., *The Hebrew Bible in Art.* London: 1944.

LOUKOMSKI, G. K., *Jewish Art in European Synagogues.* London: 1947.

PINKERFELD, J., *Synagogues in Palestine.* Jerusalem: 1946. (Hebrew).

REIFENBERG, A., *Denkmaeler der juedischen Antike.* Berlin: 1937.
——, *Ancient Jewish Coins.* Jerusalem: 1940.

ROSENOFF, P., *Jewish Symbols on Ancient Jewish Coins.* Philadelphia: 1944.

ROSENAU, H., *A Short History of Jewish Art.* London: 1948.

ROSTOVTZEFF, M., *Dura-Europos.* Oxford: 1938.

ROTH, CECIL, *The Jewish Contribution to Civilisation.* London: 1945.
——, *A Short History of the Jewish People.* London: 1948.

RUPPIN, A., *Soziologie der Juden.* Berlin: 1930.

SCHWARZ, K., *Die Juden in der Kunst.* 2nd ed. Vienna: 1936.
——, *Modern Jewish Art in Palestine.* Jerusalem: 1941. (Hebrew).
——, *Jewish Artists of the 19th and 20th Centuries.* New York: 1949.

STRYGOWSKI, J., *The Origin of Christian Art.* Oxford: 1923.

SUKENIK, E. L., *Ancient Synagogues in Palestine and Greece.* London: 1934.

——, *The Ancient Synagogue of Beth Alpha.* Jerusalem: 1932.

——, *The Synagogue of Dura-Europos.* Jerusalem: 1947. (Hebrew).

WISCHNITZER, BERNSTEIN, R., *Symbole und Gestalten der juedischen Kunst.* Berlin: 1935.

——, *The Messianic Theme in the Paintings of Dura-Europos Synagogues.* Chicago: 1948.

WULFF, O., *Altchristliche und byzantinische Kunst.* Berlin: 1914.

ZOLLSCHAN, I., *Das Rasseproblem.* Leipzig: 1912.

Israel and the Dance

By WALTER SORELL

> " . . . *a time to break down, and a time to build up; a time to weep, and a time to laugh; a time to mourn, and a time to dance. . . .*"
>
> Ecclesiastes III:4

"NOT the epic song, but the dance," Wilhelm Wundt said, "accompanied by a monotonous and often meaningless song, constitutes everywhere the most primitive, and, in spite of that primitiveness, the most highly developed art. Whether as a ritual dance, or as a pure emotional expression of the joy in rhythmic bodily movement, it rules the life of primitive men to such a degree that all other forms of art are subordinate to it."

Dance is as old as the desire of man to express himself, to set his feelings free, to communicate his joys and sorrows with the most immediate instrument at his disposal: his body. His instinctive and organic life, his mental complexities, his spiritual desires demand communication. In this need he turns to man and turns with his fellow men to God. Movement precedes speech. Rhythm is all-embracing, cosmic. And in the rhythm of his bodily movement primitive man tries to be a part of the mystery of the divine cosmic dance. Thus dance becomes the confirmation of and the rejoicing over one's ego, the celebration of nature, the worship and glorification of God.

The ancient Hebrews differed in no way from other people in their primordial expression of love, of fear, of joy, and of awe. They sought the oneness with their like, with nature and God, and they manifested their feelings through rhythmic movements of their bodies.

During the many centuries of the Diaspora the Jews were labelled with the world's misconceptions of their essential traits, and it is only now, with the regaining of their old homeland, that their national characteristics are brought into correct focus. Their ecstatic spirit, the fervid intensity of their feelings, and the burning desire to express them through gesture and movement are some of the facts of their features which have remained intact through the ages. Hardly anyone who has not seen a genuine Hasidic dance, or the fervor of the Palestinian Jew of today dancing the Hora, can visualize the Hebrews as a dancing people. But—for the ancient Jews perhaps more than for all their neighbors—dancing played an essential and even fundamental part of the communal life.

Because of the iconoclasm inherent in the second of the Mosaic Commandments:

"Thou shalt not make unto thee a graven image
or any likeness of anything that is in heaven above
or that is in the earth beneath or that is in the water
under the earth,"

we have none but literary proof of the great desire of the ancient Hebrews to express themselves in the dance, and the Old Testament furnishes eloquent and frequent proof of it.

In spite of the fact that "there is no provision for it in the Mosaic code, which scrupulously regulates all other ritual matters," as Lincoln Kirstein writes, dancing was considered an integral part of the expression of the Jewish people. The need for this instinctive expression was fully realized. No rabbinical texts determined the manner of movement which would only have crippled what was an extemporary manifestation of one's emotion, or an artistic presentation of tradition.

The dancing will of the people was so strong that it broke forth on many occasions. Either it sprang from an instinctive urge, uncontrollable, mostly from joy, since "You shall rejoice before Jahwe Your God," giving thanks to the Invisible and, in the ecstasy of movement, coming closer to the unification of the self with God; or it was the organized artistic expression in celebration of a festive event. In both cases one person—in the role of the principal dancer—usually led the dance and, particularly in processions, was imitated by those who joined him.

After the crossing of the Red Sea, "Miriam, the prophetess, the sister of Aaron, took a timbrel in her hand; and all the women went out after her with timbrels and with dances." And Judith led a great chorus of women crowned with olive wreaths. Miriam's or Judith's dances were free improvisations, dictated by the event of the hour. And the same came to pass when "David was returned from the slaughter of the Philistine, that the women came out of all cities of Israel, singing and dancing, to meet king Saul, with tabrets, with joy, and with instruments of music." It seems that in cases of public rejoicing, the females were the dancers, expressing the feelings of the multitude, and they were also the regular chorus of the temple (Psalm 149:3, 150:4).

The most outstanding example of a principal dancer being followed and probably greatly imitated by the others was King David. In such a religious procession—organized in honor of Jahwe—as the removal of the Ark, David danced in ecstasy before the Deity "who is conceived of as being present in the Ark." It probably was a rotary dance rich in gesture, accentuated by violent leaps.

"And David danced before the Lord with all his might; and David was girded with a linen ephod.

"So David and all the house of Israel brought up the Ark of the Lord with shouting and with the sound of the trumpet.

"And as the Ark of the Lord came into the city of David, Michal, Saul's daughter, looked through a window, and saw King David leaping and dancing

before the Lord; and she despised him in her heart."
(II Samuel VI:14, 15, 16)[1]
David must have danced stripped, with no other covering than a linen ephod. This, by the way, was repeated by Mohammed who had joined the pilgrims of Mecca to encompass the Kaaba, clothed with not more than the *ihram*.

To celebrate joyous family events such as births or marriages women improvised choruses and dances to the sound of the 'adufe'. Also at the annual vintage festival at Shiloh—"a feast of the Lord"—the maidens went out to the vineyards, "And see, and behold, if the daughters of Shiloh come out to dance in dances, then come ye out of the vineyards, and catch you every man his wife of the daughters of Shiloh, and go to the land of Benjamin." (Judges 21:21). And it is said in the Song of Solomon:

"Return, return O Shulammite;
Return, return, that we may look upon thee,
Why will ye look upon the Shulammite,
As upon the dance of Mahanaim?"

This paints the word picture of a wedding dance. It seems to refer to a whirling movement, at least to a dance pattern that turns in all four directions. The passage "as upon the dance of Mahanaim" is somewhat obscure; doubt may arise whether Mahanaim is the name of a place (east of the Jordan), or descriptive of a dance in which two rows of performers face each other, or whether it is an allusion to the angels.

An unmistakable mention of artistic dancing in the Bible is found in Matthew 14:6. When Herod's birthday was celebrated, Salome, the daughter of Herodias, "danced before him and his guests and pleased Herod."

The stress of all dances however seemed to have lain on the circular form, though we are told of "moving lines" too. At the dedication of the walls of Jerusalem under Ezra and Nehemiah we find references to two "moving choruses of praise", while men of unstained character danced, threw flaming torches in the air and caught them. The Talmud describes the dances of the ancient Jewish maidens which were related to the mating dances of the primitive people:

"There were no other holidays for Israel like the fifteenth of Ab and the Day of Atonement, on which the daughters of Jerusalem went out in white dresses which were borrowed, so that no one should be ashamed if she had none. And the daughters of Jerusalem went forth and danced in the vineyards. And what spake they? Youth! lift up thine eyes and behold her whom thou hast chosen!"

On the day preceding the Feast of Tabernacles everyone went to the house of the Sho'ébáh at the appointed time and carried branches with lemons attached to them for the procession around the altar. In the court were many large candelabra, each with four arms. Four priests, or youth of priestly descent, climbed ladders, filled the vessels with oil and lit the wicks. All Jerusalem was lit from the fires. The crowd joined in the laudations that followed. Men known for their piety and good works danced with lit torches in their hands and such great scholars as Hillel deemed it not beneath their dignity to dance before the admiring crowd. The Levites stood on the steps that led from the court of the men to that of the women and made music to the dance with the lyre and harp, with cymbals and trumpets.

"No people can produce a whole race of ecstatics unless they themselves possess the gift of ecstasy," Josef Kastein says. "This Jewish ecstasy does not lie in action. It is rather a capacity for enduring, for being obliged to endure. Not one among them *wished* to be a prophet. One and all had prophecy thrust upon them. 'It' spoke within them."

This ecstatic feeling of the Hebrews found its climactic immortal expression in the language of their prophets. We are particularly interested in it here, since the movement of gesture and dance plays an essential part in prophecy. Dancing lends our physical being the feeling of freedom, of freedom from heaviness, from earth-boundness, and gives us the imaginary power of wings. Our mind is carried away on these wings. It first changes our outlook on what-has-been, our thoughts are whirled in a vortex of oblivion into a state of loftiness and in this gradual metamorphosis of losing our everyday's *corporeality* we cross the threshold of ecstasy. We are no longer ourselves. We can feel the awakening of a power which is the embodiment of the spirit in us. Is this spirit superhuman or merely the shedding of our humanness which brought us closer to God? In this state, man may believe in his ability to control the forces of nature, to call unto him all friendly powers and to banish those that are hostile to him. And those men who have grown to the stature of prophecy find in this ecstatic stage the word of God.

The medicine man, the witch doctor, or the shaman dance themselves into ecstasy with wild, convulsive movements until they collapse and thus come to again. When they hop from one foot to the other and circle around an object, or turn as if in a magic circle, this dance itself is a means to an end which is to exile evil spirit, to heal the sick, or to keep misfortune away from the tribe.

"Descended from the shaman after thousands of years of development are the Jewish and early Christian prophets, who found the spirit of God in the ecstasy of the dance," says Curt Sachs. Descended from the shaman, still rooted in the same soil of mysticism, perhaps still attached to similar means, but with ends outgrown the stage of primitiveness, the Jewish prophets danced in their communion with God and they may have danced before conveying the word of the Lord to the people. The symbolism in movement reaches man quicker than words which are too factual to be equally impressive. When the Lord, for instance, convinced Jeremiah that "I ordained thee a prophet unto the nations" it is descriptive movement that follows to make Jeremiah's communication with God understandable: "Then the Lord put forth his hand, and touched my mouth. And the Lord said unto me, Behold, I have put my word into thy mouth."

The Jewish prophets strove to rouse their people to the consciousness of their existence, to meaning and significance of their being in relationship to the higher conception of a deity. And if man is to rise above himself, above the limitations of his everyday existence, above the strata of heaviness into which earthly and worldly affairs pull him down, if man is to grasp the most comprehensive ideality of God, to embrace God in his universality, man must be lifted from the ground, he must be moved, his real self must be left beneath him and he must be carried away by his other self that is closer to God. Since this movement of flight from reality to God cannot be performed in its entirety, it is symbolized and such symbolic movement ranges from the swaying of head and trunk to the movements of the ecstatic dance.

2.

Despite the many attempts of the Church Fathers to suppress dancing, the people continued to dance. On the contrary, the many dance prohibitions in the early Christian era are the best proof for the predominance of the people's desire to dance.

The unreconciled opposition between the medieval man's carnal lust and his desire for salvation, or still better: between his ungovernable passion to live to the full and his fear of death and damnation found, among others, its emotional vent in the dance. His thoughts held on to symbols and feared facts. The Christian man was obsessed by the idea of death as a frightening spectre followed by eternal tortures. This makes us understand why the dance of death, the danse macabre, played such a major role in the Middle Ages, even before 1348 when the plague swept all of Europe and brought the horror of death, in its most cruel form, close to every man.

Reports about the 11th and 12th centuries speak of ecstatic, compulsive dancing. When someone died, men and women suddenly begin to sing and dance, most often in the church-yards where, at that time, they used to gather, but they would also disturb divine service. The priests were powerless to stop them and resorted to curse them so that they had to dance without interruption until the ban was removed. The ecclesiastical exhortations were unable to halt the dance craze, the 'evil' could not be rooted out. The Great Plague of the 14th century turned this craze into an uncontrollable madness. The symbolic power of the danse macabre took on the grimace of a last hope of man to avert the plague through the dance.

The Dark Ages were a relentless martyrdom of Judaism which reached its spiritual climax in the year 1242 when the Parisian tribunal of many dignitaries of the church condemned the Talmud to be burnt at the stake. It reached its physical climax with the Inquisition. There are hardly any records of Jewish dancing in this period, but there can be no doubt that dancing was cultivated. We know that in Spain in 1480 Jews and Moors were compelled to show their "national" dances on Corpus Christi day. At about the same time a remarkable dance spectacle developed in Spain, the "Danza de la Muerta", which was said to have been composed by a Jew, the Rabbi Santob de Carrion. The dance, a dramatic creation and apparently a counterpart to the morality play Everyman in more than one respect but with talmudic implications in its text, shows several members of society, the Archbishop, the Prince, the Cardinal and Rabbi at the very moment when death approaches them and they try to escape its clutches. There is no doubt that the Jews as the children of their time—no matter how persecuted they were and how secluded they may have lived—were affected by the medieval mentality. We hear of the dance of death being performed at Jewish weddings and other festivals, sometimes even as late as in the 19th century.

German Jewish sources of the 16th and 17th centuries speak of the professional Letzim (wandering jesters and entertainers) who would perform dances and pantomimes, who could be seen in acrobatics walking on stilts. They would play at weddings mainly and were particularly known for their torch, foil and sword dances. In their restlessness, driven from country to country, it was a natural way out for many of the Jews to become wandering entertainers. This seems to be one of the main reasons why we find such a surprisingly great number of Jewish dancers and dance teachers in the 15th century which was so important for the future development of the dance; at that time, the foundation for the dance as an art was laid by the establishment of dance teaching as a profession which was the beginning of a dance theory. We must assume that the number of these Jewish dancers and dance teachers was even greater than the existing records lead us to believe, because at that time only a few of the Italian Jews, the Spanish exiles and Marranos admitted their Hebrew descent.

One of the greatest of them was a certain Guglielmo Ebreo of Pesaro who "excelled all men in the dance". A contemporary poet, the then famous Giovanni Mario Filelfo wrote a poem about Guglielmo, the "Canzon Morale di Mario Philelfo ad Honore et Laude Di Maestro Guilielmo Hebreo", in which he not only praised Ebreo's agility as a dancer but also his skill as a musician. His great artistry was probably the final result of an old tradition. We hear of Rabbi Santob de Carrion and of Rabbi Hacen ben Salomo, "who in the year 1313 in the Church of St. Bartholomew at Tauste in the Spanish province of Zaragoza had to teach the Christians to perform a choral dance around the altar."

Not only the flattering verses written in honor and praise of Ebreo's work indicate that he was well known and considered highly by his contemporaries. There is also the fact that his one work exists in a number of manuscript copies which shows that his work was used at several places at the same time.

He wrote for people of taste and culture, for the upper strata of society. The dances he composed consisted of refined steps striving toward elegant movements. There was no longer anything folkloristic in it, it was theatrical dancing created for certain stage effects, though the stage was the ballroom floor of the Tuscan and Lombard princely courts. No longer was any space left for spontaneity of expression or simplicity of movement. For the first time a clear distinction was made between folk or peasant dancing and this complicated and refined art of movement pattern. Guglielmo's work is one of the first known to approach the dance as an art, to give in detail—although his explanations remain obscure in places—a choreographic technique and thus becomes a "monument from which descends the brilliant pedagogy of contemporary ballet," as Lincoln Kirstein says.

Guglielmo Ebreo was not the only one to write about the art of dancing. Several other Italian treatises exist on it which were done in the second half of the 15th century. His contemporary, Antonio Cornazano, wrote his "Libro dell'arte del danzare". Both Guglielmo and Cornazano were pupils of a certain Domenico, or Domenichino, of Piacenza, whose teachings were summarized in a treatise at a later date. Furthermore, a fourth work exists written by a certain Giovanni Ambrosio of Pesaro. It is in title and content identical with Guglielmo's.

But Guglielmo's manuscript, "De praticha seu arte tripudii vulghare opusculum," seemed to have been the most complete work on the art of dancing. He proves himself as the first dance esthete when he writes:

> "The art of dancing is, for generous hearts that love it, and for gentle spirits that have a heaven-sent inclination for it rather than an accidental disposition, a most amiable [amicissima] matter, entirely different from and mortally inimical to the

vicious and artless common people [meccaniche plebei] who frequently, with corrupt spirits and depraved minds, turn it from a liberal art and virtuous science, into a vile adulterous affair, and who more often in their dishonest concupiscence under the guise of modesty, make the dance a procuress, through whom they are able to arrive stealthily at the satisfaction of their desires."

This is an attempt to evaluate the dance from an esthetic point of view. We still hear through his words the echo of the bitter voices of the Christian priests censuring and condemning the corrupt spirits and depraved minds of the common people who use the dance as a means of getting at the gratification of their flesh. Guglielmo tries to free the dance from its primordial, most innate impulse, from the love or sex motive, and to elevate it to an artistic display of pure beauty, grace and enchantment. Thus, at that time, the foundation was laid for our professional theatrical dancing; and it was a Jew who was one of those very few to lay the theoretical groundwork to the monumental structure of a new art.

Guglielmo Ebreo speaks of six prerequisites for the dancer:

(1) Misuro: the dancer's ability to keep time according to the musical rhythm;

(2) Memoria: the ability to recollect the steps in correct sequence of the dance;

(3) Partire del terreno: the ability to judge the physical limits of the dance floor, briefly, the ability of the right movement in space;

(4) Aiere: a somewhat obscure term which seems to denote a "certain swaying and upward movement of the body with the corresponding settling down";

(5) Maniera: descriptive of a certain movement in the style and manner of that time. "When one performs a single or a double step he should turn his body, so long as the movement lasts,

towards the same side as the foot which performs the step, and the act should be adorned
and shaded with the movement called *maniera.*"

(6) Movemento corporeo: probably meaning the
ability to move gracefully.

Guglielmo of course was unaware of outlining the basic
necessities for the artistic dancer of all times. All he intended
was to compose dances for courtly balls. Therefore, he was
very much concerned with carriage and the general deport-
ment of the dancers. Like Emily Post, he advised the young
ladies how to deport themselves:

"Her glance should not be proud nor wayward,
gazing here and there as many do. Let her, for the
most part, keep her eyes, with decency, on the
ground; not however, as some do, with her head
sunk on her bosom, but straight up, corresponding to
the body, as nature teaches almost of herself. . . .
And then at the end of the dance, when her partner
leaves her, let her, facing him squarely, with a sweet
regard, make a decent and respectful curtsy in answer to his."

3.

Due to their continuous migration from the West to the
East and their seclusion in Ghettos, very little was heard of
Jews as prominent dancers between the 16th and 18th centuries. But Sultan Ibrahim is said to have employed Jewish
fiddlers and dancers in 1648. We also hear of Jewish dancers
and minstrels performing outside of tents at a royal banquet
in Adrianople during the reign of Mahomet in 1675. Still in
the 17th and 18th centuries, the wandering Jew as entertainer was not an unusual sight. The parents of the great
French tragedienne Rachel, née Élisa Félix (1820-1858), belonged to such a group of wandering Jewish dancers and
acrobats.

Curt Sachs mentions three famous Jews who followed Guglielmo. There were the Jews from Ancona, Grescion Azziz and Emanuel de Rabbi Jalomacis, to whom the Pope granted the privilege of teaching dancing and singing in 1775, and a certain Sieur Isaac d'Orléans, who, about 1770, played a great part at the French court and of whom the English poet Jenyns wrote:

"And Isaac's Rigadoon shall live as long
As Raphael's painting, or as Virgil's song."

The Hasidic movement, so greatly connected with the dance and movement in general, had—because of its isolation from the gentile world—only little influence on the Western dance spirit. The movement pattern employed by the Hasidim is based on the spontaneity and ecstatic expression of their feelings and fanatic beliefs. Isadora Duncan is said to have studied the Hasidic dance movements and found her principles of movement related to their emotional and expressional qualities.

However, it was not before the beginning of the 19th century that the Jewish people, then freed of the fetters of their secluded life, again had the opportunity to contribute decisively to the art of the dance. Among the great names in the romantic period we find Charles Victor Arthur Michel, better known as Arthur Saint-Léon (1815-1870), dancer, choreographer, and violinist—he studied with Paganini—who later renounced his Jewish religion to marry a devout Roman Catholic, the dancer Fanny Cerrillo, with whom he was seen in many ballets. He went from Paris—where he was born as the son of a Jewish ballet-master who had worked in the Koenigliches Theater in Stuttgart—to St. Petersburg. His most famous ballet creations, still in the repertory of most ballet companies today, were Coppella and Humpbacked Horse. He is usually named together with the illustrious dance creators of his time—Petipa, Perrot, Nijinsky—and is said to have exerted great influence on Michel Fokine.

Marie Rambert, born as Miriam Rambach, a Polish Jewess, became one of the foremost pupils of Jacques Dalcroze, the founder and father of Eurythmics. When Diaghileff asked Dalcroze for an instructor for his company, Dalcroze's choice was Miriam Rambach. She accompanied the troupe to Monte Carlo to work with the Russian-trained dancers. But she encountered stiff opposition, was nicknamed Rythmitchka, and finally faced open rebellion of the members of Diaghileff's group. Only Vaslav Nijinsky, who like her came from Poland and could speak to her in his native tongue, took to Rambach. Her influence on Nijinsky, one of the flaming names in the dance world, the immortal 'Spêctre de la Rose', was decisive. Lincoln Kirstein says about it in his dance book:

"A new dancing language was needed. Directly or indirectly, Dalcroze gave Nijinsky a weapon without which he could not have achieved his masterpiece. The reasons for the deliberate omission of Rambach's historic service in the published books are hard to guess. With the commencement of the war [World War I], Miriam Rambach changed her name to Marie Rambert. Over the last fifteen years she has done fine work fostering a national English Ballet. She adopted the *danse d'école* whole-heartedly, and some of the best English dancers have been her pupils . . ."

There are three more prominent Jewish figures connected with the Russian Ballet: The great dancer Ida Rubinstein (for whom Ravel wrote his Bolero), the designer Léon Bakst (né Rosenberg) whose stage designs and costumes contributed a great deal to Diaghileff's great success, and the son of a Jewish banker, Dimitri David Gunsbourg, who made the existence of the Ballets Russes possible; he was its financial backer and bore the honorable title of 'directeur-administrateur' of Diaghileff's company.

In the course of the impressive dance renaissance during the 20th century, we find among the foremost names those of

Jewish dancers who have helped to break through the conventional concept of the classical ballet to find a new path of modern dance expression. The third and fourth generations of the modern dance, particularly in the United States, show a surprisingly great number of Jewish dancers who undoubtedly do much to propagate the dance per se. Also Biblical themes —proving the cultural heritage for which Western civilization is indebted to the ancient Hebrews—have become a familiar feature in the program of modern dance recitals. Martha Graham, for instance, did Baal Shem and Nigun (1928) as well as Lamentations; Charles Weidman his "David and Goliath". One of the most interesting Biblical themes of more recent date was Pauline Koner's "Voice in the Wilderness" in which the dance idea was built around the prophetic words of Isaiah: "Woe unto them . . ."

Genuine Jewish spirit—profundity as the result of incessant probing and defining—can be found in the writings of André Levinson (who died in 1936), or in Akim Volynsky (who died in 1937 and whose works have not yet been translated into English). Levinson was perhaps the most erudite and authoritative critic of the ballet, and in his writings lives a creative spirit able to mold and to fashion the dancers' mentality. Among his lasting writings are: "La danse au théâtre", "Maîtres de ballets", and "La danse d'aujourdhui".

It must be said that those Jews who took to professional dancing in the 19th century and achieved stature in their art had to overcome immense obstacles. In the beginning of the last century, the Jews, tolerated in the various European countries, had no access to the Imperial Academy of Dancing and Pantomime in Milan, nor to the Kaiserlich-Koenigliche Ballet Schule in Vienna, and certainly not to the Czar's Academy in St. Petersburg and his Imperial Theatres. Later, particularly at the turn of the century, when the European Jewry had somewhat settled down, when second and third generations spoke and felt like the gentile natives and when they began to climb up the social ladder and exchanged trading with intellectual professions, they were so strongly indoctrinated with the spurious ideas of the bourgeoisie that they considered dancing beneath their rank and dignity. In the process of their gradual assimilation, they tried first to give the impression of a steady and utterly settled position, and the surest way of conveying it was to be in a learned profession or craft to which the citizenry looked up with admiration. Dancing certainly did not belong with it. On the contrary, the gypsy in the artist could have easily reminded the world of the wandering Jew. Moreover, the dance had become a female profession more and more and was, in the bourgeois mentality, mainly connected with flippancy and flirtation. All the more surprising is the great number of Jewish dancers who, especially in the last few decades, gained in number, importance and influence.

Among the living writers and teachers on the dance, Curt Sachs, Anatole Chujoy, and Lincoln Kirstein are the most prominent and have given us invaluable sources of information. Kirstein's importance to the American dance has become history. As teacher and producer, he has very likely done more for the American dance than any other single person and he can rightly be called the Diaghileff of the American ballet. His small company "Ballet Caravan" was open to experiments and discovered such a great talent as Eugene Loring ("Billy the Kid"). But Kirstein's merit lies in the organization of the American Ballet, the Ballet Society, and the more recent New York City Ballet. It was master strategy when, in 1933, he brought George Balanchine to America to head the American Ballet and to be "the key figure in a long-term plan to establish the ballet as part of the artistic life of America," to use John Martin's words. It was Kirstein's deed to have planted the ballet on the soil of the new world after its century-long itinerary from Italy to France and from there to Russia. Thanks to Lincoln Kirstein, the Italo-Franco-Russian tradition has been revitalized in America.

The great ballet renaissance in America during the last two decades saw the transplantation of such great Jewish artists as

Adolph Bolm, Ruthanna Boris, and Alicia Markova, the truly classic ballerina, and the emergence of the outstanding talent of Nora Kaye and Jerome Robbins.

Among the dancers of Jewish extraction, Helen Tamiris is probably the most interesting talent. She began her studies in the classes of Irene Lewissohn (who contributed to the development of the American dance as director of the Neighborhood Playhouse). Tamiris, after having gone through many schools, finally felt that her dancing had to be different from what she had learned and seen. Her first recitals in 1927 were experimental in a great many ways. It lay in her approach to the dance themes she selected, to the choice of accompaniment, and her movement pattern which was unconventional. She has a very clear mind and knows what she wants, even if some of her experiments led her nowhere. But she has always been sincere in her approach and, as she said herself, "sincerity is based on simplicity. A sincere approach to art is always done through simple forms."

Helen Tamiris was not only adventuresome and sometimes even extravagant in her experimentations, but also an active spirit in the development of the American dance. She organized the Dance Repertory Theatre in 1930 and was a key figure in the Federal Theatre Project for which she had done such excellent group works as "How long, Brethren?" In recent years her strongly theatrical talent made her turn to the choreography of musicals in which she continued to go her own individual ways within the framework of Broadway productions. "Up in Central Park", "Annie Get Your Gun", the revival of "Show Boat", and "Inside U.S.A." were stations of her great success.

Among the experienced dancers of the third and fourth generations in America rank first Esther Junger, Anna Sokolov, and the great dramatic talent of Pauline Koner; there are Sophie Maslow (famous for her masterpiece "Folksay"), William Bales and Joe Gifford; Nina Fonaroff, Marie Marchowsky, Felicia Sorel, and Trudy Goth (whose talent lies rather in the field of organization and who deserves great merit for her idea of dance laboratories for the young choreographer within the framework of choreographic workshops). Pola Nirenska, of Polish origin, now living in America, stunned the dance world in the middle thirties when she won the first prize in an international contest. Great reputation came to Hadassah with her oriental dance themes. Shulamith and Asaf (brother and sister) have become the leading dance stars in the Bolshoi Theatre. Asaf is maître de ballet, received the Order of Lenin, and is "Honored Artist of the Republic".

Some of the younger dancers have, so to speak, specialized in the Hebrew dance: Benjamin Zemach, who was with the Habimah and then settled in California; Lillian Shapero, who has been the dance director of Maurice Schwartz's "Yiddish Theatre"; Dvora Lapson and her group, Corinne Cochem, and the dance couple Katja Delakova-Fred Berk have done very much to acquaint Western Jewry with the Hebrew dance and have thus helped to keep Jewish folklore alive in the Occident too. And, with her Dance Bookshop on Sixth Avenue, Sally Kamin has created a veritable intellectual center for the dancers and dance enthusiasts in America.

Though it may be considered an aside, I cannot help mentioning one of the most essential influences on the dance lately, on the modern dance as well as on the ballet, exerted in a very indirect manner by a Jew who had very little indeed to do with the dance, but whose ideas and doctrines have left their indelible marks on our civilization, and thus on the development of the dance.

It was psycho-analysis which reorientated our thinking about our feelings. With the growing mechanization around us, we had, of necessity, to turn to our self and rediscover it. And this is what the modern dance has done in its own realm, and for which it is indebted to Sigmund Freud and his disciples. Freud made us realize that the interrelation of body and mind does not only permit the penetration of rhythm—that comes from the outside—by way of the body into the soul, but also the emanation of our mental rhythm by way of the body, revealing our whole personality to the world.

4.

The most perfect and ideal fusion of Hebrew and Western culture is found in Gertrud Kraus. Though never denying her Jewish heritage, she was, at the time when she began to dance, the product of the typical European artist of the 1920's, with a fervid desire to experiment, with a propensity toward expressionism. At the Munich Dance Congress in the late twenties she was, together with Mary Wigman, the greatest success. Some of her unforgettable masterpieces from that period were "The Town Is Waiting" (Nanetti-Rubin) and Gorki's "Dream of a Musician". In 1931, Hubermann asked her to tour Palestine with Heifetz and Rubenstein. She then realized that this was her home, and it was to become a fertile soil for her creativeness. She decided to give up her school and activities in Vienna, to forget the success she had all over Europe, and to settle down in the land of her fathers. That was in 1935.

Since then she has contributed a great deal to the artistic development of the Palestinian dance, not only as a soloist and choreographer, but also as a teacher and silent guardian of its artistic standard. Out of her school developed a ballet group, "a synthesis of modern and classical trends," as she defines it. Working with the Palestinian orchestra, the Kraus Ballet danced to the works of such modern composers as Prokofief, de Falla and Stravinsky. The Opera in Tel Aviv secured her choreographic talent and was followed by the "Habimah", the "Ohel" and the "Theatron Iwri". Gertrud Kraus' great choreographic successes in the last few years were "Carousel", "The Golden Cage", and Gershwin's "Rhapsody in Blue", a symbolistic pantomime of our modern social problems; and of course the Palestinian ballets, Lavry's "Emek", Boskowitch's "Semitic Suite", and Mahler-Kalkstein's "Popular Symphony".

To understand Gertrud Kraus' development we must visualize the Germany of the 1920's and, in contrast to it, the Palestine of the 1940's. We must realize the dynamic process undergone by Israel, the country of youth, of a new Jewish youth, remote from the Ghetto and the dark mysticism of yore, optimistic-healthy, agile, bound with the land, soil and sun, where the constructive will of the people is seeking new forms of living conditioned by and arising from their community spirit, turning degradation of yesterday into a regenerated strong tomorrow. In such groping and seeking for new forms of living on a soil of century-old traditions, an interplay of the old and legendary with everything new and modern is inevitable. Israel, the oldest historical place, reaching from Jerusalem to Galilee, from Bethlehem to Nazareth, from Emek to the Sea of Tiberias, the land of the prophets, the once holy land, has now also become the soil for toiling hands and for the spirit of reconstruction.

The country is rich in material and sources from which emanate creative stimulation. The desert, the rough mountains, the sea, the stony paths on which still today caravans cross the country, vineyards and pardesses (orange groves), an always blue sky and often merciless sun, a miracle of colors, brown-red soil and mountains veiled in their dark violet shadows, songs of shepherds, sounds from drums and flutes; and the multicolored mosaic of the people, beside the Jews from all over the world, the Yemenites, the Sephardim, the Arabs and nomads who, in the midst of a new growing culture, hold on to their age-old customs. A dreamlike mixture of Orient and Occident, of the young and modern Tel Aviv, the patriarchal Jerusalem, and the romantic harbor of Haifa at the foot of Mt. Carmel.

The folkloristic treasures and the cultic customs of these many peoples reach back to Biblical times and can be found in the feasts and ceremonies of the Arabs, Yemenites, and Sephardim—nothing has been lost through their contact with Western culture. On the contrary, open-minded, susceptible to the depth and simplicity of this age-old folklore, the Europeans, and particularly the artists among them, have readily absorbed the Oriental impressions and influences, and today their festivals with their Biblical and folkloristic dances clearly prove the result of their gradual growth into oneness with landscape, people, and tradition.

Gertrud Kraus' metamorphosis is symbolic for what has happened in Palestine in the last few decades: the melting of Hebrew culture with Western civilization. A bridge was built from yesterday into a new tomorrow. The result on Palestinian soil: the triumph of Israel and the Hebrew renaissance.

Beside Gertrud Kraus we find, among others, the European Gert Kaufmann, the American Rachel Emanuel, the Yemenite dancer Rachel Nadav, and the Palestinian Yardena Cohen (who has done magnificent work to help shape the folkloristic style of the Palestinian dance) and Deborah Bertonoff (Habimah).

The indomitable will of this young nation to build, to form, to create is a lasting guarantee for the preservation of the Jewish spirit, of Hebrew culture.

FOOTNOTE

[1] In contrast to the many Fathers of early Christianity, to the reformers who fought against, what they termed, profane dancing and who praisingly referred time and again to the inner grace and the sublime spirit of David's dance before the Lord, the Old Testament is frank and outspoken in its criticism of David's dance. Martin Buber, speaking of the "glorification of failure" in his essay on "Biblical Leadership" and of "the great stages in the history of the people which the Bible describes, the stages in the dialogue between God and the people" remarks about David's triumph with the entry of the Ark into Jerusalem: ". . . this triumph is clearly described as a disgrace in a worldly sense; this is very unlike the language of 'world history'. What Michal, his wife, says to David of his triumph, how he ought to have felt ashamed of himself behaving as he did in front of his people—that is the language of profane history, i.e. of history par excellence. To history such a royal appearance is not permitted, and, rightly so, seeing that history is what it is."

BIBLIOGRAPHY

BIE, OSKAR, *Der Tanz*. Berlin, 1905.

BUBER, MARTIN, *Israel and the World*. Schocken Books, 1948.

ELLIS, HAVELOCK, *The Dance of Life*. The Modern Library.

KASTEIN, JOSEF, *History and Destiny of the Jews*. Garden City Publishing Co., 1936.

KINKELDEY, OTTO, *A Jewish Dancing Master of the Renaissance*: *Guglielmo Ebreo*. A. S. Friedus Memorial Volume.

KIRSTEIN, LINCOLN, *The Book of the Dance*. Garden City Publishing Co., 1942.

MARTIN, JOHN, *The Dance*. Tudor Publishing Co., 1946.

ROGERS, FREDERICK RAND, *Dance, A Basic Educational Technique*. The Macmillan Co., 1941.

SACHS, CURT, *World History of the Dance*. W. W. Norton, 1937.
—, *The Symbolism of Dancing*. A Paper.

TAYLOR, H. O., *The Medieval Mind*. The Macmillan Co.

The Bible (The Old Testament; the New Testament).

TOYNBEE, ARNOLD J., *A Study of History*. Oxford University Press, 1947.

WUNDT, WILHELM, *Voelkerpsychologie*

The Jews in Literature

By RUDOLF KAYSER

DEFINITION

WE cannot easily give a definition for what we may justly call
Jewish Literature. The prerogatives for any national literature
are a land and a language of its own. The Jewish people possessed practically neither land nor language since the destruction of their ancient state in Palestine. They spread over
almost all countries of the world and they took on the
languages of their immediate neighbors in the course of the last
few centuries. Seemingly we may talk of a specific Jewish
Literature only in as much as works written in Hebrew or
a mixture of Hebrew and another language, e.g. Yiddish, are
concerned.

In fact, many Jewish authors who have written in European
languages display strong and peculiar characteristics which
decidedly differ from those of their non-Jewish colleagues.
This is the more evident the greater the share is which the
Jewish writers have in the literatures of all nations. Since
time immemorial the Jews are considered "The People of
the Book," and they have continued to be the People of the
Book to this day. In tracing the peculiar characteristics of the
Jewish authors through the various linguistic and geographic
spheres, we will arrive at realizing the fundamental factors
which themselves are incumbent in the history of the Jews:

1) The professed adherence to Judaism. The authors proclaim by their works that they consider themselves tied to
Judaism, to the Jewish nation and to the Jewish religion. Consequently they write on Jewish characters or problems. They
aim at presenting themselves as the Jews they are to their
readers.

[527]

2) The tradition of the Jews in literature. It has its origin in the Bible. The Bible is the source of subject matter and ideas. The Jewish writers elaborated on them. This very tradition is responsible for the character of their style of writing and of their literary themes.

3) The Jewish mentality. It cannot be properly defined because of its lack of unification and its contrasting properties. The predominant motive of this Jewish mentality is its religious and ethical orientation. On the other hand there is a strong inclination towards critical analysis and enthusiastic support of progressive ideas. Most of the Jewish poets and writers of the last few centuries were city-dwellers. This is why their writing is focused on the experiences and problems of people living in the big cities. Non-Jews often regard this mentality peculiar to the Jews as something foreign. Anti-Semites distort it for their purposes.

The product of the above given factors presents what we call Jewish Literature in the European languages. It is the subject of this paper excepting theological and scholarly literature which is another matter. Of course, we can offer only a selection of characteristic authors and works.

THE BIBLE

The Bible is the greatest religious, literary, and historic document which the people of Israel have possessed. No other book has ever exercised an influence equal to the Bible on the nations of all times. During the Middle Ages the Bible stood exclusively for heavenly revelation in the eyes of Christians and Jews alike. There was for that matter no place for any different approach. The artistic and historic qualities of the Holy Script found attention only when the era of critical analysis was initiated beginning with Baruch Spinoza (1632-1677). Protestant scholars took the lead in literary investigation of the Bible since the days of the Reformation, in the first place the English theologian Robert Lowth (1710-

1787) with his book *De Poesie Sacra Hebraeorum* (1753) and the German Johann Gottlieb Herder (1744-1803). Herder aimed at commenting on the books of the Bible as works of poetry, and as psychological history of the Jewish people, in his publications, *Die älteste Urkunde des Menschengeschlechts* (1774-1776) and *Vom Geist ebräischer Poesie* (1782, 1783). Ever since the Bible has been praised and explained as poetry of the first order, chronicle and history, laws and rulings, prophetic speeches, epics, and stories, lyric and poetic wisdom are considered its outstanding literary elements. The Deborah song is regarded as its most ancient part.

The religious and literary impact of the Bible on posterity developed very early. Individual parts were translated in all languages from the early Middle Ages onwards, and so was the entire Book. Today the Bible is the most widely distributed literary work with a translation record of approximately eight hundred languages and dialects.

The Old Testament was translated from Hebrew into Aramaic and Greek in the first place. The Greek translation the so-called *Septuaginta,* was terminated in the second century B.C. All Jews who spoke Greek read it. The Septuaginta became the stepping stone for the Christian versions. The Syrian and the first Latin translations followed. The most important Latin translation, the *Vulgata,* originated in the fourth century A.D. Simultaneously the Gothic bishop Ulfila started the first translation of parts of the New Testament into a Teutonic language. Other European languages followed in the course of the Middle Ages.

We are mentioning the most important European Bible translations only. The first complete Northern French Bible, based on the Vulgata, appeared in the middle of the 13th century. The Catholic and the Protestant Bibles in literary French did not appear before the 16th century, the Protestant one partly based on the Hebrew original. French Bibles for Jewish readers were published in the 19th century only, by Samuel Cahen (1833-1846) and Zador Kahn (1899-1906).

In Italy the first complete translation of the Old Testament appeared in the 14th century. New translations followed in the 16th and 17th centuries. In Spain the so-called *Ferrara Bible* was intended for Jews and Gentiles alike. We shall turn to this important book in another context.

Russian Bible translations have existed since the 9th century. The Russian Bible Society was founded in 1813. It took care of all future editions in Russia.

Jekutiel Ben Isaac Blitz was the first to translate the Old Testament completely into Yiddish (1776-1779). Among the Polish translations the so-called *Bible of Queen Sophia* (1455) should be mentioned above all. In Slavonic the first Bible was printed in 1581.

In Germany Humanism and Reformation renewed the study of the Bible and originated new translations. Martin Luther (1483-1546) translated the New and, later on, the Old Testament from the Greek and Hebrew originals into German. This masterly translation inspired innumerable new Bible translations in all languages. Among the Jews Moses Mendelssohn was the first to translate the Bible into German (1780-1783). Other Jewish translations followed. The *Kleine Schul- und Haus-Bibel* by Jakob Auerbach (1858) attained a high degree of popularity. Martin Buber and the late Franz Rosenzweig set out to create a modern German-language translation (since 1926).

Dutch translations of Bible excerpts appeared in the 14th and 15th centuries. The so-called *Bible of Delft* appeared in 1477, containing the Old Testament without the psalms. The year 1525 saw the first Dutch translation from the Hebrew original, followed by the first Catholic Bible in Dutch in 1548. Jews translated the Bible into Dutch not before the 19th century.

In the Anglo-Saxon sphere the earliest translations of the Vulgata date back to the Anglo-Saxon and Anglo-Norman era. John Wycliff conducted the first translation into English, based on the Vulgata and completed it in 1388. William

Tyndale published a new Protestant translation (from 1530 to 1534). The 16th century presented various new editions. The English Bible, approved still today, is the so-called *Authorized Version* or *King James Version.* It had appeared for the first time in 1611. Fifty scholars had cooperated in this work. English and American scholars published the *Revised Version of the King James Bible* in 1885. It is the foundation of all American Bible editions. The Jewish Publication Society of America has published a new Jewish Bible in English in 1917.

In all languages the Bible has become the most important instrument of religious worship, simultaneously the most popular book of education, and the most popular reading-matter. This explains the immense influx of biblical subjects and biblical style into all literatures. The Bible became one of the main sources for the European drama. There are at first the mediaeval mystery plays. The greatest dramatists such as Peele, Calderon, Racine, Alfieri, Grillparzer, Ludwig, Hebbel, Andreyev, wrote biblical plays. The psalms have widely influenced the religious as well as the secular poetry of Europe and the Americas. The works of Dante, Tasso, Milton, Klopstock, Byron, Manzoni, Thoreau, and Emerson, contain biblical subjects.

HELLENISM AND THE MIDDLE AGES

The era of Hellenism had saturated Judaism with Greek philosophy. Many Jewish authors wrote in Greek at that time, Philo of Alexandria in the first place. He lived at the outset of the Christian calendar. His numerous works did not only influence Jews, but also the Christian Fathers of the Church in the course of the Middle Ages. Philo aimed at a synthesis of Platonic philosophy and Jewish religion, in dealing with biblical subjects. His writings were translated in numerous other languages.

Flavius Josephus (Joseph Ben Mattitjahu) born 37 A.D., also wrote in Greek. As a defender of Judea he participated in the war between Jews and Romans. He lived in Rome after the destruction of Jerusalem. As a source of information of that epoch the works of Flavius Josephus are highly important. He is the author of *Antiquities*, a sort of world chronicle leading from the mythical age up to the rule of the Herodians. Besides he wrote *The Jewish War*, chronicles starting with the age of the Maccabees and ending with the collapse of Judea. This work was soon translated into Latin.

The *Talmud*, i.e. The Study, the great collective work, was completed in the 6th century A.D. It emerged in Hebrew and Aramaic out of the oral tradition practiced through many preceding centuries. It is the main work of post-biblical Jewish theology, but it contains also sagas and stories of biblical character surviving in Jewish and Gentile literature to this day.

The *Cabbala* has exercised the greatest influence of all mediaeval Jewish works on the Christian world. It is a collection of mystical writings reaching back to the pre-Christian time. It has been written down in the 12th and 13th centuries. The Cabbala (it means The Tradition, or the God-given Teaching) is considered to be of divine origin. It represents a purely mystical interpretation of the Bible in contradistinction to the mediaeval Jewish religious philosophy which mostly has been under the influence of Aristotle. As in the Christian mysticism of later days the union of the soul with God (unio mystica) is the actual aim of religion in Cabbalistic writings. The Provençal Jew Izaak the Blind (12th century) is regarded as the founder of Cabbalistic literature. The post-mediaeval Cabbalism spread particularly in Palestine. Its foremost representative is Izaak Luria (1533-1572).

The effect of the Cabbala on Christian circles was such that the expression *Christian Cabbala* came into being, used for those parts of the mystical books the religious value of which has even been recognized by Christian theologians.

The first Christian theologian who pronounced the Cabbala a divine science was Raymond Lully (1235-1315). In the 15th century Paulus de Heredia tried to prove that most of the teachings of Christianity are in accord with those of the Cabbala. Similarly Pico della Mirandola (1463-1494) pointed out the intimate affinity between Judaism and Christianity as based on the cabbalistic teachings. In 1486 he published his *Septuaginta Duae Conclusiones Cabbalisticae*.

In Germany the great Humanist Johannes Reuchlin (1455-1522) dedicated himself to the study of the Cabbala and Hebrew literature in general. He published his work *De Verbo Mirifico* in 1494 and *De Arte Cabbalistica* in 1516. Baron Christian Knorr von Rosenroth (1636-1689) translated parts of the Cabbala into Latin, published in two volumes, *Cabbala Denudata* (1677-1678, 1684).

The Jews started to have their share in the literature of the various European nations after the downfall of the Roman Empire and after their own dispersion. In the first place this share is a modest one, not to be compared with the neo-Hebrew poetry in mediaeval Spain. From the 8th to the 11th centuries the Jews in Italy and in Spain started to speak and to write the local vernacular. Arabic was dominant in Sicily and Spain, Greek in Apulia, Greece, and Macedonia. Nevertheless Hebrew still remained the actual literary idiom of the Jews. They were translators by birth on account of their linguistic versatility in the Middle Ages. Particularly in Italy they performed the duties of translators.

Simultaneously the influence of the local literature on the Italian Jews increased during the second half of the Middle Ages. It started with Italian poetical forms introduced into Hebrew poetry. Immanuel Ben Salomo Romi (1265-1330) wrote Hebrew and Italian sonnets. He also is the author of an Italian elegy on the death of Dante who apparently had been his friend. In addition, Hebrew poetry lived on in Spain and in Italy. It blossomed once again in the Italian Renaissance when Judah Leon da Modena (1571-1648) wrote his poetry. Equally the Jewish authors of the late Middle Ages wrote their narrative prose mostly in Hebrew. It comprises fables, satires, and didactic stories.

The influence of the environment on the European Jews was also a linguistic one. Mixtures of languages developed and culminated in literatures of their own. In the Orient the Judeo-Persian literature came into being during the 14th century. The so-called Yiddish (Judeo-German) developed into a language in its own right spoken by the Jews in many parts of Europe. Individual Yiddish literature has lived its life to this day, particularly in Eastern Europe and also in America. Furthermore the 16th century witnessed the formation of the so-called Ladino or Judeo-Spanish, also blessed with a rich literature.

The invention of the printing press made the era of Renaissance and Humanism as important for the Jews and their literature as it did for all other peoples. Since the 15th century great Jewish printing plants were established in Spain, Italy, later in the Netherlands. The family Soncino in Italy was particularly famous. Books in Hebrew, Greek, and Italian emerged from the Soncino Press.

The Italian Renaissance also enriched the intellectual interests and the educational standards of the Jews. Later, in the 17th century, the family of the Alatinis excelled in Spoleto and Ferrara writing essays on a variety of subjects in Latin and Italian. Their Italian style won general praise. As a whole the Italian Jews began to write their philosophical and theological papers in the vernacular. In the religious field the disputation which the Jew Bonajuto Alatini had conducted with a Jesuit pater in 1617 won fame.

In Northern Spain and in the Provence, in the age of the Renaissance Hebrew continued to be the idiom of the Jewish literature proper. The Provence was the natural bridge between Spain and the North. Consequently the "Golden Age" of Hebrew literature in Spain radiated to the Provence. Poetry and theological studies flourished in the Provence and in the South of France since the Middle Ages. The legendary Rashi

(Salomo Izchaki, 1040-1105) and his school in Troyes rose to fame. Similarly the Jewish poetry of the German Jews in the Middle Ages and the Renaissance was primarily written in Hebrew. The mysterious minnesaenger by name of Suesskind von Trimberg, author of twelve poems in Middle High German of the 13th century, remained an isolated case.

This type of the mediaeval Jew was predominant in most European countries until the 18th century. He followed the tradition of a secluded national minority which had no contact with its environments but individually. Only the era of the French Revolution and the subsequent Emancipation of the Jews provided the decisive turn. A new West European-Jewish type made his public appearance.

SPAIN AND PORTUGAL

In spite of the fact that the early beginnings of the Jewish literature in the European vernaculars date back to the Middle Ages, a clearly defined literature written by Jews in a European language came into existence during the 16th century only. This language was Spanish. The mediaeval Jews in Spain had created an impressive poetry in Hebrew. They saw its rise under the rule of the Arabs. However, the Inquisition compelled them to turn to writing in Spanish. Many Jews had become mock-Christians. These "Marranos" became the standard bearers of the Spanish-Jewish literature, upon their emigration.

The earliest important document of this literature is the *Ferrara Bible* already mentioned before. Durate da Pinel, a Marrano, whose Hebrew name was Abraham Usque, was born in Lisbon. He lived in Italy and translated the Bible into Spanish. It was published in Ferrara, Italy, in 1553. This translation became famous the world over. The German poet Lessing once said, "You ought to learn Spanish if only to be able to read the Ferrara Bible." Abraham Usque had employed a great number of collaborators at his Bible translation. He also wrote a Latin grammar. In Ferrara he founded a printing press for Jewish books to be published in Hebrew, Spanish, and Portuguese.

Equally influential are the Jewish chroniclers of the 16th century, mostly Marrano refugees from Spain and Portugal. Samuel Usque, a Marrano from Portugal who had settled down in Italy, published in 1552 his *Consolation for the Sorrows of Israel* written in Portuguese. This book is a description of the sufferings of the Jews before and during the Inquisition, executed in the form of dialogues. A third writer by name of Usque, Solomon Usque, whose Spanish name was Duarte Gomez, translated the works of Petrarca from Italian into Spanish, (Venice, 1567). He also wrote Italian odes and became one of the first Jewish dramatists of the Spanish language. Together with Lazaro Graziano he wrote a play *Esther*, published in 1619. Jacob Uziel wrote a Spanish David-epic and published in 1624 his *Poema Heroica*. Marranos were also among the last Spanish troubadours.

The expulsion of the Jews from Spain in 1492 and subsequently from Portugal put an end to the Jewish literary activities on the Iberian peninsula itself. The emigrants took the Spanish language along with them and once more, this time in Amsterdam, did the Jewish-Spanish-Portuguese literature flourish. During the 17th century Amsterdam was called "The Dutch Jerusalem". There the Marranos who now had re-professed the faith of their fore-fathers created their own seats of learning in Spanish style. A great number of important poets and writers emerged out of the midst of the Marranos, partly continuing in the Spanish tradition, partly going back to the biblical one.

Mose Ninto Delgado (1530-1590) sang the glory of the biblical women, Esther and Ruth. He dedicated his poetry written in Spanish to the Cardinal Richelieu. Delgado's lyrical poems were famous because of their beauty of language. The expulsion from Spain, the Inquisition, also Catholic reminiscences have been their outstanding themes. Numerous emigrant-authors systematically turned to religious problems. Both, their Catholic past, and their Jewish present, induced them to meditate on theological questions.

Some descendants of the Marranos faced serious religious conflicts. Uriel da Costa (1590-1640) who committed suicide had written an autobiographic confession *Exemplar Humanae Vitae*, an alarming documentation of the Marrano fate. Baruch Spinoza (1632-1677) wrote most of his works in Latin. They had a decisive impact on the development of European philosophy and culture.

Rabbi Manasse Ben Israel (1604-1657) exercized his greatest influence through his book, *Esperança de Israel* which came to the attention of Oliver Cromwell and contributed to his decision to admit the Jews to England.

In addition to the philosophical and theological writers, numerous authors of poetic works lived in Amsterdam. They also wrote in Spanish and Portuguese. Among them was Jacob Israel Belmonte (1570-1629) who pictured in Spanish verses the sufferings of the Jews during the Inquisition. Other Marranos of the Netherlands translated the psalms and wrote biblical epics in Spanish.

In the dramatic field Antonio Enriquez Gomez (b. at the end of the 16th century, d. 1662) has been called the Jewish Calderon. He wrote more than twenty dramatic works. *La Prudente Abigail* deals with a biblical theme. Besides he composed an epic, *El Samson Nazareno*, and numerous lyrical poems.

A strange personality is Moses Duarte Lopez Rosa, physician and poet. In 1668 he re-embraced the Jewish faith, nevertheless he continued to be a great admirer of the Royal House of Portugal which he elevated in numerous poems.

Reuel (Rohel) Jesurun (Paul de Pina, d. 1630) wrote religious songs for the services of the Portuguese Synagogue in Amsterdam. Daniel Levi de Barrios (1625-1701) followed the biblical tradition and wrote a *Harmonia del Mundo* based on the Five Books of Moses.

THE HEBREW IMPACT ON WESTERN CIVILIZATION

Josef Penzo de la Vega (b. 1650 in Spain, d. 1692 in Amsterdam) is considered one of the last outstanding Spanish-Jewish poets. At the age of eighteen he wrote his first Hebrew drama. Afterwards he composed Spanish poems on the Divine Law, also an epic on the City of Amsterdam. Antonio Jose da Silva (1705-1739) wrote in Portuguese. He was primarily a playwright. When he left his Dutch refuge once more for the country of his birth, he was captured and died on the pyre.

The Spanish language lived on with the Marranos in Holland through three centuries. A highly varied literature developed. Marranos gave to Amsterdam world famous printing plants producing in various languages. The books delivered by those presses were distributed all over Europe. Mose Ben Jacob Belmonte (1619-1647) founded an academy at Amsterdam in 1639. He wrote a poem against the Christian mysteries. Even as late as the 18th century, a Jewish poetess, Bienvenida Cohen Belmonte, living in London, wrote in Spanish. Her verses glorified the translation of the psalms by Daniel Israel Lopez, also done in Spanish.

The institutions of the Marrano immigrants in Amsterdam still exist in our time though many of them fell victim to the Nazi invasion of Holland.

The transition of the Jewish literature in the Netherlands from Spanish and Portuguese to Dutch was a slow process, influenced partly by the philosophy of Enlightenment of the 18th century.

THE NETHERLANDS

At the time Isaac de Pinto (1715-1780), a Marrano descendant, was among the first to take a particularly active part in the fights of the era of Enlightenment. He attacked Voltaire because of his anti-Semitism. He also wrote on the American revolutionary war, and on social questions. Most of his writings are French, e.g., his *Apologie pour la Nation Juive*, (1762). He also fought for the equality of the Jews in various papers written in Dutch.

[538]

The Jews immigrating into Holland from Germany and the East at first did not have equal intellectual standing with the so-called Portuguese Jews. (It had become generally accepted to call the descendants of immigrants from Spain Portuguese, too). The language of those Jews from Germany was mostly Yiddish, interspersed with Dutch elements. Their literature during the period preceding the emancipation had a predominantly theological character. Hartog Ullman (Naphtali Hirz Ben Juda Loeb) was a follower of the philosophy of Enlightenment, author of philosophical books in Dutch and Hebrew.

Only during the 19th century did the Jews begin to contribute considerably to the Dutch literature including journalism. Isaac da Costa (1789-1860) in spite of having embraced Christian faith continued to display a strong adherence to the Jewish people. He was a lyrical poet in the first place. A biblical poem, *Hagar*, is one of his main works. During his lifetime H. J. Koenen published the first presentation of the History of Dutch Jewry, *Geschiedenis der Joden in Nederland* (History of the Jews in the Netherlands, 1843).

Herman Heijermans (1864-1924) was the foremost representative of Dutch literature in the second half of the 19th century. He was the greatest modern Dutch dramatist alive. His works conquered the European stage, particularly the drama, *Op Hoop Van Zegen*, (The Good Hope). He dealt with Jewish subjects in some of his other plays, *Ahasverus*, *Ghetto*, and in his story, *Sabbath*.

Israel Querido (1872-1932) belonged to the leading novelists of modern Holland. His stories take place in his home town, Amsterdam, as well as in the Orient. *De Jordaan* and *Het Volk Gods* (The People of God) are among his best novels. Besides he wrote a biblical drama, *Saul en David*.

The life and work of Jacob Israël de Haan (1881-1924) reflect the spiritual unrest prevailing among modern West European Jews. He came from a rabbinical family, turned socialist, and finally Zionist. No other poet in the Netherlands raised his voice louder for the Jewish people than he did. His lyrical works manifest the way to Judaism he took. His poems were published under the title, *Het Jodsche Lied* (The Jewish Song). This work of poetry was published in two volumes. Other works of Jewish character are *Jeruzalem* and *Palestina*.

His sister, Carry van Bruggen (Carry Pit de Haan) (1881-1932) pictured in her stories Jewish life in an impressively valuable manner. They are partly of an autobiographical nature. Annie Salomons (1885-   ) took an important part in the Dutch feminist movement and fought for it in the stories she wrote.

Siegfried Emanuel van Praag (1899-   ) turns to Jewish questions in his essays and novels. Noteworthy is his book *De West Joden en Hun Letterkunde sinds 1860* (The Western Jews and Their Literature since 1860).

Maurits Dekker (1896-   ) belongs to the outstanding authors of the younger Dutch generation on account of his social-critical novels. His most successful one is entitled *Amsterdam.* He also wrote a novel on the persecution of the Jews by the Nazis, *Mordje de Jood* (Mordje, the Jew, 1940).

Het Achterhuis (The House in the Rear) by Anne Frank, born in Frankfurt, O. M. in 1929, brought up as a refugee child in Amsterdam, is another deeply moving document on the years of anguish under the Nazi rule in Holland. Anne Frank died in a concentration camp at the age of fifteen. Her diary, recovered after the war, eventually became a best-seller in the Netherlands.

Altogether the Dutch Jewish authors of the last few decades dedicated themselves more profoundly to Judaism than before, e.g., Victor Emanuel van Vriesland (1892-   ). He belongs to the great modern poets in Holland. He wrote verse, prose, and drama. In 1915 he published a valuable book on the cultural standing of the Jewish people.

ENGLAND

Jews were not admitted to England from 1290 through the end of the 17th century. Still, during the very same period two Jewish characters achieved fame on the English stage, *The Rich Jew of Malta* by Christopher Marlowe, and Shakespeare's *Shylock*, the central figure of the *Merchant of Venice*. The situation for the Jews changed only when the book, *Esperança de Israel*, by the Amsterdam Rabbi Manasse Ben Israel appeared. A Latin edition found its way into the English Parliament in 1650 and soon was translated into English. It released a general debate on the question whether or not the Jews should be admitted into England. However it took more than fifty years until they were actually allowed to land in greater number.

Those Jews who first settled down in England were of Marrano descent. They wrote in Spanish, Portuguese, or Hebrew. A Jewish literature in English developed in the 18th century.

David Levi (1742-1801) fought for his coreligionists and against anti-Semitic attacks. He translated Hebrew prayers into English. An important work in the defense of Judaism is his *Letters to Thomas Paine*. Isaac Disraeli (1766-1848) was the first English Jew of importance in the field of literature proper. He wrote lyrical poems, literary essays, oriental romances, and several novels. He was an able historian, too. The five volumes of his *Commentary on the Life and Reign of Charles I* appeared in the years 1828 through 1830. His book, *Genius of Judaism*, (1833) is an enthusiastic presentation of the Jewish history. Isaac Disraeli was the first Englishman who acquainted his countrymen with Moses Mendelssohn. He himself favored the Jewish reform movement.

His son was Benjamin Disraeli, Earl of Beaconsfield (1804-1881), one of England's greatest statesmen. Benjamin Disraeli felt himself close to Judaism in spite of his conversion. He expressed his views on the Jewish religion in several of his novels. In *Tancred* (1847) he held that Christianity was nothing else but Judaism in a more developed state. His hero of another novel, *The Wondrous Tale of Alroy* (1883), is a mediaeval Jew, David Alroy. A special chapter of his novel, *Life of George Bentinck* (1852), is devoted to Judaism.

The first English-Jewish authoress is Grace Aguilar (1816-1847) of Portuguese-Marrano extraction. She wrote stories and religious papers on Jewish subjects. Among her stories are many which deal with the history of the Marranos, e.g., her work, *The Vale of Cedars*, or *The Martyr*, (1850) which was translated into numerous languages. A religious paper, *The Spirit of Judaism*, appeared first in Philadelphia in 1842. *A History of the Jews in England* was her last work.

Lady Katie Magnus (1844-1924), too, devoted herself to the history of the Jews. In addition to *Outlines of Jewish History* (1886) she wrote *Jewish Portraits* (1901), essays on Judah Halevi, Moses Mendelssohn, Heinrich Heine, etc. She also wrote short stories.

The family Farjeon played an important role in the Jewish-English literature of the 19th century. Benjamin L. Farjeon (1838-1903) went to Australia as a young man, but a letter from Charles Dickens made him return to England. In London he published Christmas stories and some social novels. Some of them picture Jewish life.

His children continued to have an important share in the literary life of England. Harry Farjeon (1878-   ) became known as the author of a Musical Encyclopedia. Eleanor Farjeon (1881-   ) wrote poetry and stories, furthermore a history of her family, *A Nursery in the Ninetieth* (London, 1935, American edition entitled *Portrait of a Family*, 1936). Joseph Ph. Jefferson Farjeon (1883-   ) specialized successfully in adventure stories.

Gilbert Canaan (1884-   ) is as a dramatist and novelist a fighter for the freedom of the individual. His books show a critical approach to social conditions and family life. In 1916 he published the novel *Mendel*.

G. B. Stern (Mrs. Geoffrey Lisle Holdsworth) (1890-   ) wrote the Jewish novels *Grand Chain* and *Children of No Man's Land*.

In the field of the English drama of the 19th century Sir Arthur Wing Pinero (1885-1934), of Marrano extraction, became one of the leading figures. His plays belong, besides those of Shaw and Wilde, to the best works of English realism. In several of Pinero's early dramas Jewish characters are pictured. The playwright Alfred Sutro (1863-1933) became famous mostly through his Jewish drama *The Walls of Jericho*.

Harold Frederick Rubinstein (1891-   ) is the author of many tragedies and comedies dealing with Jewish and British historic subjects. He also is one of the most outstanding authors in the field of dramaturgy. He wrote a history of the English drama and edited *Great English Plays* (1928). In 1936 he published five one act plays, *Israel Set Free*, presenting episodes of the Jewish history.

Israel Zangwill (1864-1926) is the most important author who, writing in English, has devoted his entire life and work to Judaism. His first stories display no Jewish characteristics. In 1893 his sketches of the life of the poor Jews, particularly London East End Jews, appeared under the title, *Children of the Ghetto*. This book opened the door to a world thus far unknown to literature. Several similar volumes followed. His novel, *The King of Schnorrers* (1894) is laid in the 18th century. Some other works of Zangwill have no Jewish characteristics.

In 1896 Zangwill met Theodor Herzl and became an ardent follower of Zionism. In 1920 he published an essay, *The Voice of Jerusalem*, expressing the hope that a Jewish Palestine would help prevent all future nationalist wars. He set forth his particular ideas on religion in his book, *My Religion* (1925).

London Jews and Russian Jews are the central figures of the novels by Samuel Gordon (1871-1927). The socio-critical approach of the novels by Louis Golding (1895-   ) impressed the public deeply. The author made good use of his reminiscences of Manchester, England, the city of his birth. Golding also wrote poetry, travel books, e.g. *In the Steps of Moses the Lawgiver* (1937) on Palestine. He published *A Letter to Adolf Hitler* in 1933. His novel *Mr. Emmanuel*, (1939) had a strong echo in many countries. It is the story of an English Jew who falls victim to the Gestapo. Louis Golding also wrote various fundamental books on the Jewish question, *The Jewish Problem* (1938), *Hitlers Through the Ages* (1940), and an autobiography, *The World I Know* (1940).

The novels of Siegfried Sassoon (1886-   ) have a considerably autobiographical character; however they do not deal with immediate Jewish questions, or subjects. Philip Guedalla (1889-   ) became known as the author of numerous books on history. He also wrote essays on historic personalities of England and America. Guedalla was president of the *Jewish Historical Society of England* where he once delivered a much disputed lecture on *Napoleon and Palestine*.

Gladys Bertha Stern (1890-   ) is an outstanding Jewish authoress. Her novels, short stories, plays, all present the Jew as the modern European and citizen of the world who has more or less renounced his traditions. No question, her works are a valuable contribution to the sociology and psychology of modern Judaism. *Children of No Man's Land, Tents of Israel*, (1926), and *Shining and Free* (1935) are some of her most important novels.

Lily Tobias portrays English-Jewish family life in her novels, e.g. in *My Mother's House*. She paints a picture of Palestine in *The Samaritan*, (1939). She herself traveled in Palestine. In 1921 she published the volume *The Nationalists and other Galuth Studies*. Humbert Wolfe (1885-1940) hails from an Italo-Jewish family. Jewish subjects are of no major importance in his numerous epical and lyrical works. However he translated Heinrich Heine and Edmond Fleg into English. He gives an account of his position within Judaism in his autobiographical book, *Now A Stranger*.

Isaac Rosenberg (1890-1918), still a young man, died in the First World War. He was primarily a lyrical poet, besides a painter. His poems were published after his death by Gordon Bottonley (1922). They display a powerful individuality and often outspoken Jewish characteristics.

The history of the famous English-Jewish family Gollancz has been the subject of a story, *Founder of the House*, by Naomi Jacob. Simon Blumenfeld turns to the Jewish life in the London East End of our time in his novel, *Jew Boy* (1934). Mrs. F. C. Montague brought the modern Jewish-English life on the stage in her play, *Yetta Polowski* (1921).

In Canada Abraham Moses Klein (1909-), the editor of *Canadian Jewish Chronicle*, received the literary prize of the Governor General of the year 1948 for his book of poetry *The Rocking and Other Poems*.

UNITED STATES

The properties of the Jewish-American literature are of a sociological nature in the first place. In other words, this literature is sociology lived and alive. The origins of the Jewish immigrants, the memories of their old countries, the necessity of adjustment and reorientation in the New World, contrasting generations of newcomers, all these subjects are dealt with in innumerable novels and stories. A great part of this literature has been written in Yiddish to this day. Not before the 19th century did American Jews become increasingly noticeable in the Anglo-American literature. The first Jewish periodical in English, *The Jew*, appeared in 1818.

The name of *Ghetto Literature* has been given to the one that deals with the fate of the Jewish immigrants from Europe and their step-by-step Americanization. This is a misnomer since there have never been any actual Ghettos in

America. Merely those districts primarily inhabited by Jews in New York and other American cities are idiomatically called Ghettos. During the 19th century this Ghetto literature concentrated on reminiscences of the past. The Jewish-American literature of the 20th century, however, portrays either the particular present situation of the Jews or deals with the general social and intellectual currents of our time.

The number of authors and their works among the older generation is by far too great to be mentioned completely. We list here such English-writing authors whose works are representative of the history of the Jews in America. Samuel B. H. Judah (1799-1876) was the earliest Jewish author writing in English. He composed plays and novels both widely acclaimed. The Ghetto literature began to flourish in the second half of the 19th century. A novel by Nathan Mayer entitled *Differences* (1867) deals with the share of the Jews in the Civil War. Abraham Cahan (1860-   ) initiated the socialist movement within the Jewish literature of America. He himself was active in the Labor Movement. He wrote several stories collected in the volume, *The Imported Bridegroom* (1898). His novel, *The Rise of David Levinsky*, is a particularly important one because of the history of the older generation of New York's Jewish immigrants it presents. The contrast between Eastern and Western Jewry is another important theme of this novel. Francis Joseph Grund (1803-1863), who served as an American consul in several European cities, was a versatile writer and the author of two important sociological works, *The Americans in Their Moral, Social and Political Relations* and *Aristocracy in America.*

Herman Bernstein (1876-1935) professed Judaism in his stories, poems, and plays. He translated Russian poets such as Tolstoi, Chekhov, Gorki, and Andreyew into English. Rudolph Bloch (Bruno Lessing) (1870-1914) became known for his excellent stories. Isaac Kahn Friedman (1870-1931) wrote a novel, *The Lucky Number*, (1896) which has the Jewish neighborhood of Chicago as its background. Friedman became equally known for his Far East travel books and for some novels with an outspoken social theme. Meyer Levin (1905-) wrote the novel of Chicago's young generation, *The Old Bunch* (1937). He is the author of one of the most important social novels of present-day America, *Citizens* (1940). He wrote two plays on Jewish subjects, *The Pilgrim* and *The Red Robin*. Both had their premieres in 1926.

Montague M. Glass (1877-1934), the author of *Potash and Perlmutter*, has eventually become responsible for the wide popularity of the Jewish immigrant from Eastern Europe as comic figure. Glass was a lawyer in New York. Small business men were his clientele. Out of the contact with them emerged the two characters that Glass described over and over again in short stories published in magazines since 1908. They were collected in a book, *Potash and Perlmutter*, in 1910, followed by another collection, *Abe and Mawruss*, the next year, and by additional editions. As a comedy, *Potash and Perlmutter* was very successful in many countries.

Female writers, too, pictured the life of the Jewish immigrant. Anzia Yezierska (1885-) has often been called "the queen of the Ghetto." She made her start with stories of the Lower East Side of New York. Magazines printed these stories, and they finally appeared in a book, *Hungry Hearts* (1920). The New York East Side and the fate of its immigrants are also the subjects of her novels, e.g. *Salome of the Tenements* (1922) and *Children of Loneliness* (1923). Another authoress is Mary Antin (1881-) born in Russia. Her first book became the report of her travel to America, *From Plotzk to Boston* (1898). Her autobiography, *The Promised Land*, (1912) is highly informative and decidedly valuable as a piece of literature.

Edna Ferber (1887-) and Fanny Hurst (1889-) selected Jewish characters only occasionally. Edna Ferber portrays the life of a Jewish girl in her novel, *Fanny Herself* (1917). Her novel, *The Girls*, is the story of three generations in a Chicago family. In other stories she discusses the life and social conditions which face the Jews in America. Her auto-biography, *A Peculiar Treasure* (1939) is equally important. Fanny Hurst is an outstanding narrator. Her short-stories and novels are distinguished by their deep understanding of the common people. Dorothy Rothschild Parker (1893-   ) criticized modern society in verse and prose.

Ezra Selig Brudno (1878-   ) marks the turn from the realistic description of Jewish life to the psychological approach. The mentality of the Jewish artist and intellectual has been of particular interest to him. His novel, *Little Conscript* (1905), presents the sufferings of a Jewish soldier in the Russian army. A study on the Russo-Jewish intellectual in America is the novel, *Worshippers* (1906) by Henry Berman. Arthur Bullard (1879-1929) in his novel, *Comrade Yetta*, describes the rise of a Jewess within the trade union movement. George Sidney Hellman (1878-   ) is a versatile writer in the fields of fine arts, poetry, drama, and historical fiction.

The increasing influence of social thinking characterizes the way the Jewish-American literature developed in the twentieth century. In the first place the highly realistic approach prevailed, followed later by social analysis and criticism, partly even by a political radicalism.

James Oppenheim (1882-1932) published a collection of his short stories under the title, *Dr. Rast.* It was one of the first books with an outspoken socio-ethical approach. Oppenheim also wrote various novels, but particularly in his poems he became the mouthpiece of the new machine age. Again it is an outspoken social feeling that rings through his verses.

Many novels of Jewish-American authors stand for the new age. Often Jews are portrayed as the pioneers of the future. Elias Tobenkin (1882-   ) in his first novel, *Witte Arrives*, depicts the step-by-step Americanization of a Jewish family in the Middle West. Other novels he wrote deal with the problem of intermarriage. Sidney Lauer Nyburg (1880-   ) wrote the novel of a social utopist entitled *The Chosen People*

(1917). Gilbert Wolf Gabriel (1890-   ) is the author of the novel *The Seven-branched Candle Stick* which introduces the modern Jewish youth of America. Maurice Samuel (1895-   ) analyzes the position of the Jew in our modern world. *The Outsider* (1921), *You Gentiles* (1924), and *I, the Jew* (1926) are some of his books. Samuel also translated from Hebrew, Yiddish, and German into English.

A strong social approval and a sharpeyed realism characterize the prose works of Albert Halper (1904-   ), especially his novels *Union Square* (1933) and *The Sons of the Fathers* (1941). Michael Gold (1896-   ) is a socialistic publicist. He is a co-founder of the socialist magazine, *New Masses*. His most important novel deals with the Jewish proletarian in America, e.g. *Jews Without Money* (1930). Lewis Browne (1897-1949) wrote several books dealing with Jewish religion and history and personalities such as Spinoza and Heine. He became first known by his presentation of Jewish history, *Stranger than Fiction*.

Waldo Frank (1889-   ) is a particularly versatile author. Together with James Oppenheim he founded the literary periodical *The Seven Arts*. It was a short-lived one, still, his influence on American literature should not be underestimated. Waldo Frank wrote several novels. One of them, *City Block* (1922), describes life in the New York East Side. His novel, *The Bridegroom Cometh*, proclaims the era of a new social approach to religion. Frank's cultural criticism and his social conscience exercised a far-reaching influence. Nathan Asch (1902-   ), the son of the great Yiddish writer Sholem Asch, delivered a study of the white-collar worker in the novel *The Office*. He also published several short stories.

Jerome Weidman (1913-   ) dedicated some novels to the New York Jewry. His standpoint is one of strong criticism. Ben Hecht (1894-   ) is the author of novels and plays. Realism, idealism, and romanticism are strangely mixed in his most important work, *A Book of Miracles*. Jews with their particular problems walk through many of his stories and plays, e.g. *A Jew in Love* (1930) and his play, *A Flag Is Born*, glorifying the new State of Israel.

Ludwig Lewisohn (1882-   ) is a highly versatile man of letters. He wrote numerous novels, also books in the field of history and criticism of literature and introduced many European poets to the American public. He repeatedly stressed his Jewish point of view.

Robert Nathan (1894-   ) is one of the highly individualized poets of America. His novels excel in literary style. The volumes of his poetry present him as one of the most important lyricists of our time in the U. S. His novel *Road of Ages* (1934) symbolically deals with the place of the Jew within mankind. His volume *Selected Poems* appeared in 1935.

We note a number of Jews prominent in lyrical poetry as early as the 19th century. In the order of birth we mention first Penina Moise (1797-1880). She wrote primarily religious poetry. In 1856 she published a book, *Hymns Written for the Use of Hebrew Congregations.*

Emma Lazarus (1849-1887) enjoyed great fame in her time with Jews and Gentiles alike. She was only seventeen when her first volume of poetry appeared. Great writers such as Ralph Waldo Emerson praised her talents. She wrote a tragedy in verse, *The Dance to Death*, glorifying the heroism of the German Jews of the 15th century. She published this tragedy and her poems under the common title *Songs of a Semite* (1882). She is the author of numerous essays on Jewish questions. Her memory was honored in 1903 when a plaque inscribed with her sonnet *The New Colossus* was placed on the pedestal of the Statue of Liberty in the harbor of New York. Morris U. Schappes published a selection of her prose and poetry in 1944. The centenary of her birth found worldwide attention in 1949. Like no other poetess she gave voice to the basic ideas of American democracy.

Adah Isaacs Menken (1835-1860) was another Jewish poetess of the 19th century. Her volume of poetry, *Infelicia* (1868) cries for pity with the persecuted Jews.

In the 20th century there are many Jewish-American poets who in part write light verses, in part verses saturated with social ideas. Louis Untermeyer (1885-   ) published various books of verses. He also translated Heinrich Heine and wrote an autobiography, *From Another World* (1939). He edited an excellent anthology of poems of all times and all nations, *A Treasury of the World's Great Poetry* (1942).

The Jews have a particularly great share in the development of the American drama and theatre. The first Jewish dramatist of America was Isaac Harby (1788-1822) who wrote historical plays. Mordecai Manuel Noah (1785-1851) enjoyed much popularity with his plays on American history and life. Students of Columbia University in New York staged his play, *Marion, or the Hero of Lake George*, in 1932, hundred-and-ten years after it was written.

The great majority of the American playwrights of the 19th and the first part of the 20th century put theatrical skill in the production of sound entertainment first, and literary achievement second. There are many successful Jewish playwrights, e.g. Martha Morton (1865-1925), David Belasco (1859-1932), Charles Klein (1867-1915), George S. Kaufman (1889-   ). Among them Elmer Rice (1892-   ) has the highest literary standard. His epical drama, *Street Scene* (1929) belongs to the most important plays of the contemporary American stage, and so does his play, *Counsellor-at-Law* (1931) which directs the limelight on quite a number of Jewish characters.

The revival of the American drama in recent years is for a great part owed to some Jewish playwrights. Lillian Florence Hellman's (1905-   ) works have been included in several editions of the best modern plays. *The Children's Hour* had the greatest success. Other plays of hers are, *The Little Foxes* and *Watch on the Rhine*. Her most recent plays are *The Searching Wind* and *Another Part of the Forest*. The dramas of Clifford Odets (1906-   ) demonstrate a strong social feeling and compassion with suffering or oppressed people. His play *Till the Day I Die* has an anti-Nazi tendency. Sidney

Kingsley (Kirschner) (1907-   ) received the Pulitzer prize for his play *Men in White*. He also is the author of the very successful drama *Dead End*. Irwin Shaw (1913-   ) depicted the horrors of war in his one-act play *Bury the Dead*. In 1939 he published a volume, *The Gentle People, and other Plays*. He wrote many short stories, too.

Jews were largely responsible for the public efforts to raise the artistic standards of the American theatre. They were instrumental in the founding of the Theatre Guild in New York. Many important critics, essayists, editors, and translators are Jews, too.

FRANCE

The history of French literature names three great half-Jews, Michel de Montaigne (1533-1592), Anatole France (1844-1924), and Marcel Proust (1871-1922). André Suarès (1868-   ), one of the outstanding French prosaists of our time, also is half-Jewish. With each of them it is easy to trace Jewish characteristics. We also remember the courageous attitude of Anatole France during the Dreyfus trial.

Already in the Middle Ages an important Jewish cultural center existed in the South of France. Jewish theologians and religious philosophers, also fabulists and poets wrote in Hebrew. Some of their works were translated into Latin. Bonfils de Narbonne was a Jewish troubadour. In modern times the Alsacian Jews have had a particularly great share in French cultural life. Some other Jewish groups were recruited from the German and Eastern immigrants.

Beyond anything that happened in other countries, the emancipation brought along complete equality for the French Jews and enabled them to climb the social ladder to the highest offices in government. Consequently the number of authors with outspoken Jewish characteristics is relatively small. The process of assimilation in France surpassed the stage it has ever reached in any other European country.

Alexandre Weill (1811-1898) is the first French-Jewish author after the emancipation who stresses his being a Jew in his writing. He published Ghetto stories from Alsace, numerous religious essays, and an autobiography. Eugène Manuel (1823-1901) displays almost no Jewish characteristics at all. He belonged to the early realistic period and portrayed the contemporary life in the Paris of his time. Ludovic Halévy (1834-1908) made himself a name as the librettist of Jacques Offenbach. He also wrote numerous novels, short stories, satires, and comedies. Zacharias Astruc (1835-1907) was a sculptor, painter, and writer at the same time. Edouard Manet who painted him was his friend.

There are two more Jewish authors by name of Astruc, Gabriel Astruc (1864-   ), a playwright, and his father Elie Aristide Astruc (1831-1905) who took a stand for his faith in his book *Entretiens sur le Judaisme* (Conversations on Judaism).

There is no reference to any Jewish affiliation in the works of Catulle Mendès (1841-1909). His versatile literary activities during the era of the Parnassiens present him as one of the leading figures in the French literature of the 19th century.

Georges de Porto-Riche (1849-1930) has often been called the "Jewish Racine." He is one of the most outstanding French dramatists of the 19th century. In contradistinction from naturalism, he revived the art of psychological characterization. His penetrating analysis of human passion, love in particular, has been regarded as an outspokenly Jewish one by many of his critics. His best plays are *Amoureuse* (1891), *Le Passé* (1897), and *Le Vieil Homme* (1911). Georges de Porto-Riche was elected a member of the French Academy in 1923.

Bernard Lazare (1865-1903) played an important role in the trial of Captain Alfred Dreyfus. He passionately and courageously defended the innocence of Dreyfus and attacked anti-Semitism. His contemporaries called him "le Juif de la race prophétique" (The Jew of the prophetic race). In 1894 he published a study on anti-Semitism which was subsequently translated into Russian and English. He wrote various books on the Jewish question.

Gustave Kahn (1859-1936), poet and critic, was active in the French symbolistic movement. His books, *Symbolistes et Decadents* (1902) and *Charles Baudelaire* (1925) are most valuable sources of the history of modern literature.

Tristan Bernard (1866-1948) was one of the most successful French playwrights. His irony and humor display definite Jewish traits. François de Croisset (F. Wiener), (1877-   ) wrote light Boulevard comedies, also spirited aphorisms, the latter collected in the book, *L'Esprit de François de Croisset.*

Marcel Schwob (1867-1905) was the descendant of a family of rabbis and physicians. His amazingly versatile education gave him the tools to become a scholar and a critical essayist. He also excelled as a poet and prosaist. He was one of the most notable personalities of French literature at the turn of the century. A serious illness compelled him to live a lonesome life, remote from everything, and turned him almost into a legendary figure. *La Croisade des Enfants* (1896) (English, The Children's Crusade, 1898), became his best known work.

André Spire (1868-   ) stresses his Jewishness in his entire literary work. He actively stepped into the lime-light of the Dreyfus trial. In his poems he displays social feeling and profound compassion with the Jewish fate. His deep love for the Jewish people expresses itself in his *Poèmes Juifs.* He also wrote a Jewish drama, *Samael*, and philosophical contemplations.

Like Spire, Edmond Fleg (Flegenheimer), (1874-   ) is in all his works an outspoken Jew. Most of his books have a religious ethical character. Fleg wrote poems, stories, plays and essays. He is the author of an *Anthologie Juive.* Particularly worthwhile mentioning are his lyrical works, *Le Mur des Fleurs*, *Écoute, Israel*, and his great epics on Solomon and Moses. He also wrote a work on the founder of Christianity: *Jesus, Told by the Wandering Jew* (1935).

Henri Bernstein (1876-   ) is one of the most versatile and most successful French realistic playwrights. His drama, *Israel*, deals with the conflict between Jews and French aristocrats. Beside Bernstein, numerous other Jewish playwrights have come to the fore.

Léon Blum (1872-1950) was not only one of the most important contemporary French statesmen, repeatedly named Prime Minister; as a young man he was a writer and critic, too. He was the author of various books on French literature, and of one on the feminist question, *Du Mariage*. As a Jew he took his stand for a Jewish Palestine.

Max Jacob (1876-1944) has his niche in French poetry. Jacob Cohen (b. 1877) is a religious lyrical poet in the true Jewish sense, particularly known for his *Livres des Chants*. Daniel Halévy (1882-   ) is an outstanding critic and historian. His book, *L'Apologie pour Notre Passé* is an important historical document. He was the first translator of Nietzsche into French. Jean Jacques Bernard (1888-   ), the son of Tristan Bernard, has been acclaimed as a dramatist and novelist. In 1945 he published a report on the fate of the French Jews deported to a concentration camp, *Le Camp de la Mort Lente: Compiègne* 1941-1942. Henri Franck (1887-1912) was a poet with a religious, metaphysical orientation. *La Danse devant l'Arche* is the title of his great unfinished philosophical poetic work.

André Maurois (Émile Hertzog) (1885-   ) has been internationally recognized as a biographer and a novelist. His biographies on Shelley, Disraeli, and Byron have been translated into many languages. Jewish characteristics dominate in his Disraeli biography. Also, André Maurois wrote realistic psychological novels, also essays on social and political subjects, and historical studies on England. In 1938 he was elected member of the French Academy.

Joseph Kessel (1898-   ) devotes himself passionately to the adventures of our time. As a journalist he traveled in many countries. His most important novel, *Captifs*, won the prize of the French Academy. It deals with the life of a patient suffering from tuberculosis.

We also must mention Henri Bergson (1859-1941) whenever we list the great figures in French literature. No other European philosopher has influenced the intellectual life of our time the way Bergson did. His celebrated intuitive method was a turning point in modern philosophy. His works have left profound marks all along the development of modern literature, too. They are excellent in presentation and style. Bergson was honored with the Nobel Prize for Literature in 1927.

GERMANY

The era of emancipation radically altered the course of the Jewish cultural life in Germany. Long before political equality was actually achieved, many German Jews tried to join the general cultural life as quickly as possible and eventually to abandon the Jewish tradition more and more.

There existed cultural contacts between Jews and Germans as early as the Middle Ages. The influence of German mysticism on the Jewish theology is apparent. The Yiddish literature of the 15th and 16th centuries borrowed many subjects from the German Middle Ages. Various autobiographies such as the one of Glückl von Hameln (1645-1724) are important guides to the cultural history of the German Jews in the 17th century. This tradition seemingly came to a sudden end during the era of emancipation when the Jews started to write in German only and to show contempt for Yiddish which to them was a mere "jargon."

Moses Mendelssohn (1729-1786) inaugurated the cultural emancipation of the German Jews. He adhered to the philosophy of Enlightenment and aimed at reconciling Judaism with German culture. In the religious field he was the founder of the reform movement. His books, *Jerusalem* (1783) and *Morgenstunden* (Morning Hours) (1785) exercised a tremendous influence on the German Jewry. His *Phaidon* (1767) was one of the best known popular philosophical works of his time. He became particularly influential through his translation of the Bible.

Moses Ephraim Kuh (1731-1790) was the first Jew to become known as a lyrical poet in the German language. His *Hinterlassene Gedichte* were published in 1792. Isaschar Bar Falkensohn (1746-1817) wrote *Gedichte von einem polnischen Juden*, which the young Goethe reviewed in detail.

The fate of the Jewish periodicals is characteristic of the radical change in the cultural life of that period. The *Society for the Propagation of the Hebrew Language* had to close down in 1797 since the Jews recognized German only as their mother tongue. In 1806 the educator David Frankel founded a new periodical, *Sulamith*, for the propagation of culture and humanitarianism among the Jews. The contributors of this new German-language paper came from the movements of Enlightenment and reform.

Jewish writers entered all fields of literature during that period of transition. Still, most of these early works were of little significance. However, important were the efforts Moses Mendelssohn's followers made in spreading the ideas of Enlightenment more and more among the Jews. The philosophy of Kant deeply influenced the German Jewry. Marcus Herz (1747-1803), Salomon Maimon (1754-1800), whose *Lebensgeschichte* (biography) is an outstanding document, and Lazarus Bendavid (1762-1832) were the first Jewish followers of Kant.

Many intellectual Jews of that epoch renounced the Jewish faith because they wanted to stress their adherence to the German culture. Among them were the intellectual Berlin Jewesses who had turned their houses into centers of literary life early in the 19th century. Rahel Varnhagen, née Levin (1771-1833) has been the most impressive personality. Her husband published the book, *Rahel, ein Buch des Andenkens für ihre Freunde*, after her death. Dorothea Schlegel (1763-1839) was the eldest daughter of Moses Mendelssohn. She wrote an educational novel, *Florentin*.

Hartwig Wessely (1725-1805) was the last Hebrew poet in Germany, but he, too, adhered to the movements of Enlightenment and reform. Michael Beer (1800-1833), the brother of the composer Meyerbeer, was the first Jewish dramatist to conquer the German stage for himself.

Serious attempts of continuing the old Jewish tradition were made in the field of religion only. Michael Sachs (1808-1837) translated some of the great Hebrew-Spanish poets of the Middle Ages into German and also published religious poems of his own. Leopold Zunz (1794-1886) became the founder of the science of Jewish literature.

Ludwig Börne (1786-1837) was the first German author of Jewish descent who had a great impact on the German public. He was a pioneer of political liberalism and the ideas of the French July Revolution. His publications greatly influenced the development of German journalism in the 19th century.

Heinrich Heine (1797-1856) had at no time renounced his adherence to Judaism though he had been baptized. As the author of lyrical poems and ballads he achieved a unique and lasting world-wide popularity. His *Buch der Lieder* (Book of Songs) was the most popular German lyrical work of the 19th century. His relation to Judaism manifests itself in many of his poems, his prose, and his letters. He loved and admired Judaism with a tender veneration and a sarcastic irony, too. Among his lyrical works with a Jewish theme are the *Hebräische Melodien* (Hebrew Melodies), among his prose the fragmentary story *Der Rabbi von Bacharach* (The Rabbi of Bacharach).

After the Romantic era German literature was dominated by a strong realistic tendency. The individualism of the 18th century had been replaced by the social and political poetry favoring liberalism and democracy. The German Jews had great share in this development. They regarded the progress of liberalism as the best guarantee for their cultural, social, and political equality.

Karl Beck (1817-1879) was a poet fighting against social injustice. Moritz Hartmann (1821-1872) moved afterwards from the political literature of his youth to travel and realistic stories.

On the other hand the realistic tendencies of this period induced many writers to study closely the social standing of the Jews. Aron Bernstein (1812-1884) wrote numerous novels on Jewish life. He also founded the democratic daily newspaper *Berliner Volkszeitung*, and wrote numerous popular science books. Moritz Gottlieb Saphir (1795-1858) was the author of humoristic satirical sketches and became one of the best known representatives of Jewish humor. Berthold Auerbach (1812-1882) who developed the "Dorfgeschichte" (village story) stood firmly in the camp of German literature. However, his novels on *Spinoza* and *Dichter und Kaufmann*, (Poet and Merchant), the latter with Moses Ephraim Kuh as its hero, give evidence of his strong Jewish feeling, too.

Leopold Kompert (1822-1886) devotedly pictured the Jewish life of the past, particularly in his stories *Aus dem Ghetto*. Salomon Kohn (1825-1904) wrote stories on the Ghetto in Prague. The novelist Auguste Hauschner (1852-1924) portrayed Jewish families in modern Prague, too. She and Karl Emil Franzos (1848-1904) belonged to the next generation. Franzos described particularly the life of the Eastern Jews in numerous widely read novels. He also excelled as an historian of German literature and was the first editor of the works of the great dramatist Georg Büchner.

Hieronymus Lorm (Heinrich Landesmann) (1821-1902) remained in isolation independent of the currents of his time. He was blind and deaf and expressed his sorrow with a deeply felt tenderness in his poems.

Fanny Lewald (1811-1889) entertained close contact with the political tendencies of the *Junges Deutschland* (Young Germany), at the start of her career. She occupied an important place in the history of the German feminist novel. She portrayed Rahel Varnhagen in her novel, *Prinz Louis Ferdinand*.

The specific Jewish qualities seemed to suffer from the progress of assimilation in the first half of the 19th century.

On the other hand they gained from the science of Judaism newly founded by Leopold Zunz. Abraham Geiger (1810-1874), the pioneer of the reform movement, created a renewed interest in Jewish history. Heinrich Graetz (1810-1874) wrote the *Geschichte der Juden* (History of the Jews) in eleven volumes, still today an internationally recognized standard work. Ludwig Philippson (1811-1889) founded the *Allgemeine Zeitung des Judentums* in 1837. The paper achieved a very great circulation. Moses Hess (1812-1875) gave enthusiastic support to the revolutionary ideas of the Forties and to the socialism of Marx and Engels. However, later on he turned to the study of the Jewish history and published his book *Rom und Jerusalem* in 1862 advocating the national rebirth of Judaism.

Salomon Hermann von Mosenthal (1821-1877) made a name for himself in the field of drama. He was knighted in 1871. He has written a biblical play, *Deborah*. David Kalisch (1820-1872) was the author of numerous Berlin farces and the founder of the long-lived satirical magazine *Kladderadatsch*. Adolph L'Arronge (1838-1908) was the extremely successful author of many popular plays. He founded the Deutsches Theater of Berlin in 1883. Oskar Blumenthal (1852-1919) wrote some of the most successful comedies of the German stage. He, too, founded a famous theatre, the Lessing Theater in Berlin.

At the turn of the century Judaism gained new ground among many German Jews who actually had had a purely German education. This "Jewish Renaissance" was the reaction to the increase of anti-Semitism on the one side, and Zionism on the other, accompanied by certain religious and metaphysical currents in Germany. Theodor Herzl (1860-1904), the founder of modern Zionism, himself went this way from assimilation which he had favored as a successful Viennese journalist to leadership in the advocation of the national rebirth of Jewry in Palestine. Max Nordau (1849-1923), the author of critical essays, novels, plays, joined the Zionist movement of

Herzl. Ludwig Jakobowski (1868-1900) undertook to analyze the problems which faced the modern Jew in his novel, *Werther, der Jude* (Werther the Jew). Samuel Lublinski (1860-1910) dealt with religious questions and those of culture and philosophy. Georg Hermann (born 1871) tenderly recreated the period of the Biedermeier and the life of the contemporary Berlin Jewry in his very successful novels, *Jettchen Gebert*, and *Henriette Jacoby*. Carl Rössler (1864-1948) has been the author of *Die fünf Frankfurter*, a comedy the five central figures of which are the financiers Rothschild.

Jakob Wassermann (1873-1934) has most profoundly expressed his adherence to Judaism. He was one of the greatest German novelists of the first quarter of the 20th century and belonged to the best known and most translated writers of his time. He published his first historical novel *Die Juden von Zirndorf* (The Jews of Zirndorf) in 1897. Jewish characters fill the pages of many other books he has written, too. Wassermann undertook to clarify his personal relation to Judaism and Germany in his autobiography, *Mein Weg als Deutscher und Jude* (My way as German and Jew).

Arthur Schnitzler (1862-1931), the great Viennese novelist and dramatist, took his stand as a Jew in his novel *Der Weg ins Freie* (The Road to the Open) and in his drama *Professor Bernhardi*. He was the interpreter of psychological refinements and mild passions against the background of Old Vienna.

Richard Beer-Hofmann (1886-1945) had early voiced his profound love for the Jewish people in his poem *Schlaflied für Mirjam* (Lullaby for Miriam). His dramas in verse, *Jaakobs Traum* and *Der junge David*, are poetic visions projecting the mission of Israel. Stefan Zweig (1881-1942), internationally known as an essayist and novelist, wrote the biblical drama *Jeremias*. His novels, essays, and historical portraits have been translated into some thirty languages. As a congenial interpreter of human tragedies he found recognition everywhere. Peter Altenberg (1859-1919) gave in impressionistic sketches *Extracts of Life.* He was an enthusiastic admirer of all creatures near to nature, women, children and animals.

Martin Buber (1878-   ) exercised tremendous influence on the "Jewish Renaissance", particularly on its youthful followers. He became the true leader in the field of cultural and ethical Zionism. His *Reden über das Judentum* (Speeches on Judaism), his numerous religious philosophical books, his adaptations of the Chassidic Legends, all contributed immensely to the rejuvenation of Judaism. He published the journal *Der Jude* from 1916 to 1924. Together with Franz Rosenzweig (1886-1922), author of philosophical essays and translator of Jehuda Halevi, Buber set out to prepare a new translation of the Bible.

Max Brod (b. 1844) has sided with national and religious Judaism. Jews are the heroes of most of his novels. In his two volumes *Heidentum, Christentum, Judentum* (Paganism, Christendom, Judaism), he comments on Judaism from the standpoint of philosophy. Franz Kafka (1883-1924) has been the pioneer of a new novelistic art. A symbolic faith, the experience of human loneliness, and the belief in the "indestructible" in men, who always are "guilty", reflect Kafka's metaphysical thinking. Particularly in his diaries he devoted himself to an intensive study of Judaism. Most of his novels were published only after his death by Max Brod. Their influence upon present literature in Europe and America is still increasing.

Alfred Döblin (1878-   ) is another highly important representative of a new form of novel writing. His book *Jüdische Erneuerung* deals with the life problems of modern Jewry. Various novels by Julius Levin (1862-1935) represent Jewish characters. Arnold Zweig (1887-   ) proclaims the Jewish nation in novels, plays, and essays. His war novel *Der Strelt um den Sergeanten Grischa* (The Case of Sergeant Grischa, 1927) gives an intensive picture of the horrors of war and of its social causes. Joseph Roth (1894-1939) created the epic of the modern Wandering Jew in his novel *Hiob.* Other stories he wrote center around Jews. Hermann

Broch (1886-   ) couples reflective philosophy with realistic presentation in his narrative prose.

Lion Feuchtwanger (1884-   ) became famous by his renewal of the historical novel. Many of his books deal with Jewish characters and problems, e.g. *Jud Süss* and the three novels on *Josephus Flavius*.

Alfred Mombert (1872-1942), Else Lasker-Schüler (1876-1945), and Franz Werfel (1890-1945) are the greatest names among the Jewish lyrical poets of our time. Else Lasker-Schüler passionately raised her voice in her *Hebräische Balladen*. Franz Werfel displayed an inclination towards religious and metaphysical themes of Jewish coloring in his early poems. They reflect his deep faith in humanity and divine providence. He wrote three plays the central figures of which are Jews. By his great novels *Verdi, a Novel of the Opera*; *The Forty Days of Musa Dagh*; *The Song of Bernadette*, etc., Werfel became one of the most outstanding narrators of his generation. Arno Nadel (1878-   ) was a religious lyrical poet, and also an expert in the adaptation of ancient synagogual music. Karl Wolfskehl (1869-1950), was especially in his lyrical works a passionate confessor of his Jewish faith.

Jews had a very important share in the critical and essayist literature of Germany. Otto Brahm (1856-1912), himself a critic and historian of literature, introduced the naturalistic style to the German theatre. Alfred Kerr (1867-1948) was the most outstanding critic of his time. He voiced his love of Judaism in many books of criticism and travelogues. Karl Kraus (1867-1948) was one of the most influential cultural critics Austria has ever had. He presented a poetic vision of the end of the world and the final destruction of mankind in his play, *Die letzten Tage der Menschheit* (The Last Days of Mankind). Walther Rathenau (1867-1922), as a statesman and economist vastly responsible for the reconstruction of Germany under the Weimar Republic, has been the author of numerous books analyzing the social and cultural conditions of his time. Moritz Heimann (1868-1925) often turned to Jewish problems in his essays. His drama, *Das Weib des Akiba*, presents a biblical subject. Arthur Holitscher (1869-1941) expressed his Jewish convictions in his stories and plays as well as in his book on the Jewish Palestine. Emil Ludwig (1881-1948), the most versatile and successful author of biographies in our time, displayed a Jewish point of view in some of his books. Carl Sternheim (1881-1943) originated a new and powerful satirical style for the modern comedy. Ernst Toller (1893-1939) was one of the outstanding German dramatists in the period of Expressionism.

Nazism has driven the Jewish writers from Germany, Austria, and the countries occupied. Many of these writers died by the hand of the foe, or by their own hand. Many others continued their work in a new home country, particularly in Israel and the U. S. Their books continued to be valuable contributions to modern literature.

ITALY

The Italian Renaissance was another Golden Age for the Jews. During the Middle Ages the Church had been the master over all cultural life. Consequently the Jews were prevented from displaying any general cultural activities of their own. The authority of the Church weakened in Italy as it did everywhere else during the Renaissance. Philosophy and poetry became more and more secular instead of being just religiously directed. In a decisive manner the movement of Humanism rejuvenated the interest in antiquity. The Humanists studied Greek, Latin, even Hebrew. Many of them took Jews on as their instructors. Elia Levita (1467-1549) was one of the great experts in the study of Hebrew. His grammar supplied the fundaments of all future Hebraists. Aasarja dei Rossi (1513-1578) was the first to renew the Jewish-Hellenistic literature.

During the Middle Ages, Arabs and Jews in Spain turned to the study of Greek philosophy. The effect of these studies expanded to the Jews in Italy. This is why we find many Jews as students of Greek philosophy during the Renaissance.

Leone Ebreo (Juda Ben Abravanel) (1460-1535) was one of the most important neo-Platonists of the 16th century. His *Dialoghi d'Amore* (Dialogues of Love) contributed immensely to the philosophy of the Renaissance. Besides they were greatly admired because of their artful presentation. Leone Ebreo was also the author of poems in Hebrew.

Deborah Ascarelli (about 1600) translated mediaeval Hebrew poetry into Italian. She also wrote poems of her own in Italian. Only recently a comprehensive work on her has been published establishing once again her importance in the history of Italian literature. Sara Copia Sullam (1590-1641) was her contemporary, famous as a poetess and a scholar. Well known was her exchange of letters with a monk from Genoa. The monk admired her poems, but tried to convert her. The poetess, however, stressed her adherence to Judaism in her replies. There exist only a few sonnets she wrote and a manifesto, her defense against an accusation voiced by Christians who claimed that she denied the immortality of the soul.

Leone da Modena (1571-1648) wrote in Hebrew and in Italian. He was famous as a scholar and a poet. David da Pomis (1525-1588) wrote an apology of Jewish physicians.

The Renaissance of the Hebrew language and poetry lasted until the 18th century. Famous families of scholars such as the Kalonymuses and Luzzattos kept the intellectual tradition of Judaism going from generation to generation. Kalonymus Ben Judah translated philosophical and scientific works from Hebrew into Italian during the first half of the 16th century. Mose Hayim Luzzatto (1707-1746) became the father of modern Hebrew poetry. He wrote learned papers, poems, and plays. A century later Samuel David Luzzatto (1800-1865) was one of the founders of the modern science of Judaism.

Between the end of the Renaissance and the beginnings of the era of Emancipation, the Jews were once again excluded from the intellectual life in Italy. The walls of the Ghetti closed down on them. They lived a sad and painful life, particularly in the Ghetto of the Papal Rome. The days of freedom dawned for them only when the battle for the independence and unification of Italy began. Immanuel Ben David Frances (1618-1703) fought as one of the first Jewish authors, together with his brother, against the mystical movements on the eve of the Emancipation. He wrote in Hebrew and in Italian.

Salomone Fiorentino (1743-1815) became court poet to the Grand Duc Ferdinand III of Toscana and professor of poetry at the Jewish Academy of Leghorn. He also composed Italian prayers for the Jewish service. Giuseppe Prospero Revere (1812-1889) fought for the liberation and unification of Italy. He was extremely active in the fields of poetry, drama, and essay. Giuseppe Levi (1814-1874) was primarily an educational writer. In 1853 he founded the magazine *Educatore Israelita.* He also published an autobiography. Tullio Massarani (1826-1905) was a versatile author. He translated Heinrich Heine into Italian and wrote on history, politics, literature, and art in Italian, French, and German. His works were published in twenty-two volumes after his death. Sabatino Lopez (1867-) was one of the first Italian Zionists and took active part in the Jewish life of Milan. He wrote a number of social plays on the Italian middle class.

The Jews contributed extensively to the Italian narrative prose during the past five decades. They displayed characteristically a penetrating psychology, a sort of anatomy of the human soul, partly influenced by psychoanalysis. Italo Svevo (Ettore Schmitz) (1861-1928) became the most important one among these novelists. His books were translated into most European languages. James Joyce had discovered him, the French critics were full of praise for him, and, finally, he was recognized in his fatherland. Italo Svevo wrote three novels, some stories, one play, all displaying an equal psychological penetration. His main work is the novel *The Confessions of Zeno.*

Annie Vivanti (1868-1942) was the author of poems, novels, and short stories. Her works found the attention of Italian writers like Carducci and Croce. Other critics pronounced her the most outstanding woman in modern Italian literature. *The Devourers* is considered her best novel. Angiolo Orvieto (1869-   ) demonstrates an outspoken Jewish feeling in his writings. His *Il Vento di Sion* tells of a Hebrew poet of the 16th century who has a like passion for Florence and Zion.

Alberto Moravia (1907-   ) figures prominently in the most recent Italian literature. He, too, applies a new sort of psychological realism to his novels. Already his first novel, *The Indifferent Ones*, shows him as one of the most interesting representatives of the young generation in Italian literature. Like Moravia, Guido da Verona became known after the first world war. A strange atmosphere, laden with sex, gives tension to his novels.

The alliance between Hitler and Mussolini put a temporary end to the activities of the numerous Jewish writers, critics and journalists in Italy.

EAST EUROPE

The East European literature has exercised little influence on the West. The great Russian writers are the only exception. Otherwise the East European literature is a cultural bridge between Europe and Asia.

The isolation of the Eastern Jews lasted much longer, socially and culturally, than the one of their Western coreligionists. Equality was granted very late, in Russia not before the Bolshevik Revolution. Consequently a secluded Jewish literature in Hebrew and Yiddish has lived on in Eastern Europe, particularly in Poland and Rumania, to the present time.

The Eastern Jews mostly had come from Western Europe during the Middle Ages and had brought their language along. In Bulgaria Simeon Set wrote a story in Greek during the 11th century. It was subsequently translated into Bulgarian under the title *Stephanit and Ichnilat*. During the 14th century Hungarian Jews came to the Balkans, later others from Germany, Spain, and Portugal. These Sephardic Jews took over the leadership among the Bulgarian Jews. Their language, the Ladino, a mixture of Spanish and Hebrew, has remained the vernacular of many Bulgarian Jews to this day.

Russia had the largest Jewish population, particularly after the repeated partition of Poland. But the lack of political and social equality continued to exclude the Jews from the Russian literature for quite some time.

Joseph Rabbinowitsh founded the first Russian-Jewish magazine in 1860. Semjon Juschkewitch (1868-1927) portrayed the life of the Russian Jews in his stories and plays. His greatest stage success was his comedy *Sonkin and the Lucky Hit*. David Eismann (1869-1922) was one of the most important Russian novelists in the time preceding the bolshevist revolution. Several of his novels describe the life of the Jewish intelligentsia in Russia. Andrei M. Sobel (1888-1926) was a member of the Social Revolutionary party and therefore an opponent of the Soviets. His most important work is the novel *Dust* (1915). Ossip Dymov (1878-   ) writes in Russian and Yiddish. A deep melancholy, characteristic of the East, goes through his works. His play, *Nju*, and his novel, *The Boy Wlas*, were translated into many languages. Mark A. Aldanov (1889-   ) wrote novels, sketches, and essays. He had close contact with Jewish life. He is best known for his historical novels, e.g. *The Ninth Thermidor*, *The Conspiracy*, and *Saint Helena*. He wrote a number of biographies, too.

Ilja Ehrenburg (1891-   ) is the best known writer and journalist of Soviet Russia. As an author of novels and stories he possesses a versatile ability of presentation and the sharp eyes of a keen observer. He lived in Paris for quite some time and, therefore, entertains intimate relations with European literature.

Isaak E. Babel (1894-   ) comes from an orthodox family in Odessa. He never renounced his intimate contact with the

Jewish tradition, more so he stresses it in his most important books, e.g. *Odessa Tales* and *Jewish Tales*.

Jewish poets played a great part in the history of Russian lyrical poetry, beginning with the symbolistic movement. Nikolai M. Minski (1855-1937) was a leading figure among the Russian decadents. As an adherent of Social Democracy he went in exile. Besides poetry he wrote a dramatic trilogy and a volume of criticism. He became famous as a philosopher, too. His greatest influence was in the field of philosophy of religion. His work *The Religion of the Future* (1905) established a new kind of mysticism and attracted many religious readers among Christians and Jews.

Leo Shestov (Leo Isaakowich Schwartzmann, 1868-1938) belonged to the greatest and most influential Russian philosophers of the twentieth century. He wrote books on Pascal, Tolstoy, Dostojevski, Nietzsche and Kierkegaard. Other essays deal with numerous great figures in European philosophy and literature. They often have a religious and metaphysical character.

Boris Pasternak (1889-   ), the son of the famous painter, developed a very personal style in his poems. He is known to be the outstanding futurist in Russian poetry. He also is an excellent translator of foreign literature. In 1941 he published a highly acclaimed translation of *Hamlet*.

In the rest of Eastern Europe the number of Jewish authors who wrote in the vernacular of the country of their birth is small. Julian Klaczko (1825-1908) has been well-known in Poland, in the age of Romanticism. He wrote in Polish, Hebrew, French, and German. His *Florentine Nights* were translated into many languages.

Wilhelm Feldmann (1868-1914) was the most important critic in Polish literature. He also wrote a novel, *The Jewish Boy* and plays presenting Jewish subjects. His work *The Contemporary Literature of Poland* continues to be recognized today as being of fundamental importance. Cezary Jellenta (Napoleon Hirschbrand, 1860-   ) was known as prosaist and lyrical poet. Alfred Nossig (1864-   ) displays a Jewish national point of view in his novels and plays. Joseph Wittlin (1896-   ) wrote poems and novels often expressing a pacifist tendency.

Jews lead the Hungarian drama to world-wide recognition. However, the theatrical effect of these plays is often more convincing than the profoundness of thought or art. Alexander Brody (1863-1924) is the author of the realistic rural comedy *The Lady Teacher*. Ferenc Molnar (1878-   ) is by far the most successful and talented of all Hungarian playwrights. His tragi-comedy *Liliom* bristles with social feeling. Ludwig Biro (1880-   ) wrote various plays dealing with Jewish subjects. Melchior Lengyel (1880-   ), a successful playwright, became famous especially by his play *The Typhoon*. Among the younger generation Béla Zsolt (1895-   ) and Károly Pap (1899-   ) are best known.

In Bohemia of pre-Hitler days the Jewish populace adhered predominantly to German culture. Jews contributed to Czech literature only since the establishment of the Czecho-Slovak Republic. Jaroslaw Vrchlicky (1853-1912) wrote the epic *Bar Kochba*. Ottokar Fischer (1883-1938) was a lyrical poet and translator. Frantisek Langer (1888-   ) has been acclaimed as playwright and novelist.

SCANDINAVIA

The Jewish population of the Scandinavian countries is very small. However a considerable Jewish cultural life developed in Copenhagen, Denmark, during the 19th century. A playwright and lyrical poet, Henrik Hertz (1797-1870) was the first Jew in Danish literature. Meir Aron Goldschmidt (1819-1870) wrote Jewish stories and an autobiographical novel culturally and historically important. Peter Nansen (1861-1918) was the author of impressionistic novels of great tenderness.

Georg Brandes (1842-1927) is one of the greatest writers Denmark has ever had. His books on the history of literature and his biographies made him well known the world over. He wrote on the Jews Benjamin Disraeli and Ferdinand Lassalle and composed an autobiography comprising three volumes.

Henri Nathansen (1868-1944) became Georg Brandes' own biographer. A profound Jewish feeling was the driving force in his work and life. Notable is his play, *Behind the Walls*. Nathansen committed suicide when he had fled from Nazi-occupied Denmark to Sweden. An important Swedish writer of Jewish descent was Oscar Levertin (1862-1906) who wrote novels, poetry, and essays.

Ludwig Oscar Josephson (1832-1899) was the author of many plays and as a stage director a pioneer of Ibsen and Strindberg.

CONCLUSION

The preceding survey does not claim completeness. It rather aimed at presenting the great variety of the Jewish literature in Europe and in the U. S. Therefore, the point of view was not a historical one, but rather a cultural-sociological one with the aim of analyzing the grades and varieties of Jewish thought and tradition within the boundaries of the Western nations. Literature always is the best mirror of human life and it certainly fits our purpose.

The contribution of the Jews to the intellectual life of Europe has been very great, compared with their own small number. Whether they deal with social realities or religious visions, they follow the Jewish tradition in affirming life and in looking toward eternity. Thus Jewish literature fulfills its ancient mission. Martin Buber defined this mission once as "the human answer to the divine, uniting spirit and world."

BIBLIOGRAPHY

BEVAN, EDWYN R., and SINGER, CHARLES, ed., *The Legacy of Israel.* Oxford, 1927.

GRAETZ, HENRICH, *History of the Jews.* 6 vols. Philadelphia, 1891-1897.

Jüdisches Lexikon, Berlin, 1927-1930.

KARPELES, GUSTAV, *Geschichte der jüdischen Literatur.* Third ed. Berlin, 1921.

ROTH, CECIL, *A Bird's Eye View of Jewish History.* Cincinnati, 1935.

—, *The Jewish Contribution to Civilization.* Cincinnati, 1940.

SAKHEIM, ARTUR, *Das Jüdische Element in der Weltliteratur.* Hamburg, 1914.

The Universal Jewish Encyclopedia. 10 vols. New York, 1939-1944.

WAXMAN, MEYER, *A History of Jewish Literature from the Close of the Bible to our own Days.* 4 vols. New York, 1930-1941.

The Jew in Drama, Theatre and Film

By Curtis Lubinski

THE people of the Book has eventually become the people of the drama, of the tragedy, and of the comedy. Since the word of the Old Testament is truly a living one, it has released the desire to dramatize the laws for which it stands in order to impress them the more on the masses. The playwrights of all times have looked upon Adam, Noah, Abraham, Jacob, Moses, Samson, and David in his fight against Goliath as highly dramatic figures. They are the heroes of the Bible, they took the place of the mythical ones previously elated in the legends of the Greeks and Romans. The psalms of the prophets, the Sweet Singers of Israel, and the odes of King Solomon possess the prerequisites for stage effect and drama. They are largely responsible for the literary concepts in our modern civilisation which is the synthesis of the aesthetic and philosophical fundaments developed in Greece, of the political and juridical contributions made by the Romans, and of the religious, ethical and literary principles delivered by the Jews.

The very name of Europe which stands for the cradle of our Western civilisation points at drama, at the capture of the Semitic young lady of that name by Zeus, the King of Olympus. She was the daughter of the Phoenician King of Tyre and thus of Palestinian birth.

Jewish actors were acclaimed in antiquity. Jewish poets composed plays on strictly biblical subjects in Alexandria at the time of Christ's birth. The writer Josephus mentions one Alityros as the favorite performer of the emperor Nero. The feast of Purim has been the forerunner of the European Carnival with Esther as the leading lady of a legitimate show.

These performances were famous and attracted numerous Gentiles in the period of the Italian Renaissance. We know of a document in which Marino Sanuto reports in the year 1531 "there was performed by the Jews in their Ghetto a very fine comedy, but no Christian was permitted to be present, by order of the Council."

The ghetto of Venice early had its permanent theatre. A Marrano poet of the 16th century composed a formal Purim play presented before a mixed audience. Marrano playwrights of the succeeding generations were Paulo de Pinno, Moses Zaccuto, Moses Chajim Luzzatto who took his allegorical dramas from place to place, and Josef Penso de la Vega.

The most important influence of the Jewish theatrical groups concentrated on Mantua in the 16th century. The enterprising Gonzagas were the rulers of this principality. They introduced command performances of the Jewish players at all official festivities whether a foreign Grandee came to visit or a princess was to be given away in marriage. But the obligation to perform was not all that rested upon the Jews. It was up to them to carry the burden of all the expenses involved. To perform for the prince was just an additional way they were expected to pay their taxes. Still, their religious laws were respected by their masters who permitted the shows to end before sunset on Fridays and not to take place at all on Saturdays and all feast days.

The Jews of Mantua did not only provide the actors. Leone da Sommi Portaleone lived in their midst. He was a master of the Italian prose. The plays he provided them with were pastoral ones according to the temporary fashion. Their subjects were almost completely secular. Actually, Portaleone was the first professional all-round showman of Jewish birth, playwright, producer, director. The Italian poet Manfredi turned to him to have one of his plays staged. Portaleone was also the first theatrical critic who gave to the Western world a handbook on practical and theoretical theatrical studies under the title of *Dialogues on the Dramatic Arts* written in 1556.

It was his own theories which Portaleone put to work on the stage of Mantua and which were adopted first all over Italy and subsequently all over contemporary Europe. We can regard him as the first exponent of two gifts the blend of which has made the Jews particularly apt for their contributions to the theatre of modern times, a freely flowing, idealistic productivity and a keen critical sense fit to analyse the problems of the theatre as an art and as a social institution.

Italy continued to offer a rich field to Jewish performers. There were itinerant ones who went from town to town and appeared as professional jesters at weddings and banquets wherever Jewish communities had established themselves in the Europe of the Middle Ages. Samuel Romanelli had quite a reputation as a wandering playwright. In the Rome of the 18th century Jews were allowed to present their comedies in the Ghetto, in Siena permission was granted for the performance of a *tragedia sacra* on Passover. Giuseppe Revere (b. 1812, d. 1889) wrote historical plays which were very popular all over Italy. In modern times it was Sabatino Lopez who rose to the highest rank in Italian literature. He was president of the Italian Society of Authors from 1911 to 1919. He taught Italian literature in Genoa and at the Academia di Brera of Milan. His plays which courageously tackled the problems of the Italian bourgeoisie of his days were not only performed in his home country, but also in France, Poland, Austria, and the South American countries.

The emancipation of the Jews all over Europe in the 19th century gave them the first great opportunity to prove that they have not been made to be the world's money-lenders, but that they are inspiring idealists and artists. The two actresses who became the idols of France both were of Jewish descent, Rachel and Sarah Bernhardt. Rachel (born Elisa Rachel Felix in Mumpf, Switzerland in 1820) had a uniquely brilliant career which was abruptly ended by death from tuberculosis when she was only thirty-eight years old. She rose to fame from the most humble environments. Her father was a peddler. She and her sister used to sing for tips in cafés until a famous vocalist recognized the genius in Rachel. She became the star of the Comédie Française, the declared Queen of Tragedy. All France mourned her early death.

Sarah Bernhardt, originally Rosine Bernard, lived to become seventy-nine years old, active on the stage almost to the end as the foremost actress of her time. The circumstance of her education at a convent led to her baptism at the age of twelve, but she always was a typical Jewess in that strange combination of physical fragility and dramatic personal power, a synthesis which returned to our age on a modern level in another Jewish actress, Elisabeth Bergner. Sarah Bernhardt had her debut in the Comédie Française in 1862. She often was the chief attraction of the London theatres and first toured the United States in 1882, returning often with never failing success. A Paris theatre was given the name of Théâtre de Sarah Bernhardt in 1899. Acting was so much her only purpose in life that she continued touring the world even after she had undergone the amputation of a leg. Her idealistic fire, making her "golden voice" unforgettable, never left her. She even went to the front playing for the soldiers of the Allied armies of World War One. She once more made her appearance in the United States, this time as Hamlet. The "Divine Sarah" who had carried the beauty of the French language from continent to continent was given a state funeral in Paris. She lies in the cemetery of Père-la-Chaise.

The French stage saw the rise of many other Jewish performers. The brother and the sister of the great Rachel established a reputation of their own. Georges Berr (b. Paris in 1867) became prominent as a comedy and lyrical actor who also wrote plays. He was elected a member of the Comédie Française in 1893 and served on the board of the Conservatoire where he taught the art of declamation for twenty years. But the one French actor whose performance has survived his death is Harry Bauer, an Alsatian Jew. The films in which he played have continued to be shown wherever high class cinematographic art is appreciated, *Les Misérables, The Life and Loves of Beethoven* and *Un Carnet de Bal*. Harry Bauer was an unusual character actor. The aged men he has created carry a burden of sorrow which is as much a Jewish one as is the patriarchic fatherly love radiating from them. Harry Bauer was arrested by the Nazis for forging an "Ahnenpass" in 1942 and died soon afterwards.

The unique way the French language lends itself to the expression of wit and wisdom, of delight and pain, has early fascinated the Jewish intellectuals. Out of their midst have come some of the most successful playwrights of the 19th and 20th centuries.

Adolphe Philippe d'Ennery (b. Paris 1811, d. 1899) was the model of a Jewish intellectual and gentleman during the most brilliant period of the emancipation. He is credited with over three hundred plays and novels, which he wrote independently, in part together with Alexandre Dumas and in part as dramatisations of the works of Jules Verne. Two of his plays, *Marie Jeanne,* and *Les deux Orphelines* were particular stage favorites. The use he made of the money which he had earned as a writer remains memorable. He had a bathing resort, Cabourg-Dives, reconstructed so that the poets and artists of his time could have a relaxing get-together. He was its mayor for some time. His last will left his house and an important art collection to the French government which turned it into the Musée d'Ennery.

The playwright Georges de Porto-Riche influenced French public life in a different way. As it used to happen to the progressives of his period he was once imprisoned by the government. After his play *Un Drame sous Philippe II* had been successfully produced at the Odéon in 1878, he became the outstanding representative of the French drama of his time. He was the first to picture man and wife without romanticism, but instead in the true relations which are the consequence of the egotism of love emanating from the same inevitable fate which was the driving force in the great Greek tragedies. A collection of his plays is entitled *Théâtre d'Amour*. The former inmate of a prison was elected a member of the most distinguished organisation of his country, the French Academy, in 1923.

His disciple was Henri Bernstein who has been recognized as one of France's leading dramatists and as the master of the French "esprit" all over the world. His interest in the fate of his coreligionists has never been subdued by his overwhelming success. He analysed anti-Semitism in his play named *Israel* in 1908 and in a comedy *Judith*. His influence on the cultural life of France has not been limited to his playwriting. He was a director of the Théâtre du Gymnase. He was made an officer of the Legion of Honor. The order of St. Maurice and Lazare was bestowed on him by Mussolini. He returned it to the Duce later with an open letter in protest against "persecution in the name of racism". Henri Bernstein found refuge in the United States when the Germans entered Paris in 1940. He returned to Paris after the war.

Tristan Bernard was his contemporary. All lovable dispositions of a Jew and of a Frenchman were united in his talent. He knew how to hide melancholy behind a joke, he was just as sarcastic as is agreeable to an audience in search of selected relaxation, and he always provided a superior smile in presenting the weakness of mankind in his comedies. He was unequaled as the "national humorist of France". In recognition of this achievement he was made a Commander of the Legion of Honor and a member of the Société des Lettres. He was as prodigiously productive as only a Latin playwright can be. A collection of his comedies has been translated into English. His son Jean Jacques Bernard is a dramatist in his own right.

The unique structure of Germany offered to the Jews of the 19th century an opportunity greater than anywhere else for entering the field of the dramatic arts. The many excellent theatres managed by the individual princes, the independent cities, and by private producers had a permanent demand for good performers.

Bogumil Dawison (b. Warsaw 1818, d. Dresden 1872) became the greatest actor of his time. It was on his tour through the United States that he exhausted his strength. He never recovered and died insane. When Dawison still performed at the Vienna Burgtheater, a young man from Budapest sought the privilege of meeting him. The young man's name was Adolf Sonnenthal. He made his own debut at the Burgtheater in 1856 and remained its most distinguished member to his death in 1909. The rank of a nobleman—Adolf Ritter von Sonnenthal—was conferred upon him by the Emperor Franz Joseph in 1881. Never before had any actor, Gentile or Jewish, been equally honored. (Another Jewish actor was knighted by the Bavarian Prince Regent in 1895, Ernst von Possart.) Sonnenthal presents the admirable example of a great idealistic actor who went through all stages of his own development together with one and the same theatre since he considered his art not as an object of business transactions. He had started with juvenile leads, transferred to bon vivants, finally followed by patriarchic parts, each one monumental, of biblical shape, his Faust, his King Lear, his Wallenstein, his Fuhrmann Henschel. The American public had ample opportunity to admire Sonnenthal in 1882, 1899, and again in 1902.

The development of the theatre in Vienna was eventually coordinated with the one in the Reich. Ludwig Dessoir was the first Jewish actor who established his fame in Berlin. He was praised as the greatest interpreter of Shakespeare on the German stage to his death in 1874. Ludwig Barnay, son of an official of the Jewish community in Budapest, became a disciple of Adolf von Sonnenthal. He joined the most famous theatre troupe of those days, the Meininger, and the Deutsche Theater of Berlin in 1882. He headed the Berliner Theater and the Königliche Schauspielhaus in later years. His name will live on as the founder of one of the world's earliest actors' unions, Genossenschaft Deutscher Bühnenangehöriger, organized at Weimar in 1871.

Barnay's contemporary was Maximilian Ludwig who played important classical and modern parts at the Königliche Schauspielhaus of Berlin for thirty-four years. The length of his service has been surpassed by Max Pohl who was with the State Theatre from 1894 to his death in 1935. He was a character player of distinction and served as president of the German actors' organisation for many years.

During the same time Jewish directors were responsible for a brilliant cultural climax in the German theatrical history. Otto Brahm, one of the early supporters of Henrik Ibsen and of the new style the Norwegian dramatist had initiated, the Naturalism, was the founder of Die Freie Bühne in 1892. He took Adolf l'Arronge's place as director of the Deutsche Theater and opened the Lessingtheater. Brahm's greatest deed was perhaps the discovery of a young actor who became his heir in the Deutsche Theater and eventually world-famous as a director, Max Reinhardt. (b. Baden near Vienna 1873, d. New York 1943.) Max Reinhardt's name stands for the most colorful, most inspiring and inspired period the German stage, perhaps even the international stage, has ever seen. He merged the orthodox drearily one-sided naturalism with a new sensual and ever so versatile style mustering the services of all allied arts, the dance, the pantomime, the music, the song, the painting, and the architecture. His cycle of the works of Shakespeare extending over many years is unique in the history of all theatre. The greatest actors were cast in it. The other classical dramatists and all important contemporary authors of all nations had their turn. Max Reinhardt set the example for a new type of modern playhouse with the Kammerspiele, the tiny intimate theatre fitted with club chairs only, and its counterpart, the all-dimensional theatre-circus of the masses. He invaded Berlin's Kurfürstendamm with the theatre, Die Komödie, specially built for the showing of the sophisticated English comedy to a sophisticated Berlin audience. He had a foot-hold in Vienna, the Theater in der Josephstadt, and he became definitely an international figure as the founder and theatrical director of the Salzburg Festivals. The old morality play of *Everyman* (Jedermann) rewritten by Hugo von Hofmannsthal is still performed there today as staged by Max Reinhardt. It was seen in New York in 1924 and so was Reinhardt's other great medieval show, Carl Vollmoeller's pantomime *The Miracle.* Reinhardt saw the happy days for the creative Jews in Germany and saw their end. Himself a victim of Hitler's anti-Semitic laws he emigrated to the United States. On Broadway he staged *The Eternal Road,* a saga of the wanderings of the Jews, and in Hollywood he founded a workshop for the training of the young theatrical generation. He held quite a number of honorary degrees, among them a professorship and a doctorate conferred upon him at Oxford in 1933, the year of the advent of Hitler. A Berlin street was named Max Reinhardtstrasse after Hitler's fall.

The story of this entire generation in the Berlin theatre as far as it has been a Jewish one ends as the story of the emigration and/or expulsion of the Jewish artists from German and Austrian soil. Another Jewish director who held the highest official position in the theatrical life of Germany died in America, Leopold Jessner. He became the head of the Berlin Staatstheater. His expressionistic approach to staging made history. The modern way he presented Shakespeare's *Richard III* (with Fritz Kortner) and Schiller's *Wilhelm Tell* (with Albert Bassermann) has been discussed all over the world. He was a pious Jew and became an early pet target of anti-Semitism in Germany.

Victor Barnowsky who was the director of three Berlin theatres is now a lecturer in New York City. His predecessors in the "Theater in der Königgrätzerstrasse" were Carl Meinhard and Rudolf Bernauer, once famous for their Strindberg and Wedekind productions. Dr. Georg Altmann, for many years director of Das Kleine Theater in Berlin specializing in the comedies of Carl Sternheim, went to California. Felix Holländer, a faithful follower of Max Reinhardt and the discoverer of many actors who have risen to fame died in Berlin. But his nephew, Frederic Holländer, became one of the busiest film composers in Hollywood. Eugen Robert, a Hungarian by birth who directed with gusto the comedies of his compatriot Ferenc Molnar, died in London and so did Hermann Haller who flavored the Anglo-American type of musicals for the Berliners with their own idiom. There were a great number of excellent Jewish directors in other cities of Central Europe, among them Rudolf Beer in Vienna and as the head of the municipal theatre of Chemnitz Intendant Tauber, father of Richard Tauber, the great tenor. Berthold Viertel belongs in a class of his own having been one of the finest German-language poets, an inspiring director on the stage and in the movies. He modernized the repertory of the Dresden Schauspielhaus, he opened a literary theatre in Berlin and introduced Eugene O'Neill to his audience. Viertel came to Hollywood in 1927 and directed pictures for Fox, Paramount, and Gaumont-British. His wife is the former Yiddish actress Mea Steuermann-Viertel who has become Greta Garbo's script writer and chief adviser.

A listing of the Jewish actors and actresses who emerged from the theatres in Germany and Austria in our time coincides with the tribute we pay to the generosity of the United States where many of them are featured performers today. All of them brought along almost no property, but an unrelenting idealism and a load of the best continental approach to the art of acting.

Rudolf Schildkraut who died in Hollywood in 1930 made his mind up early to come to the United States. He was unequalled in his portrayal of fathers with a Jewish heart which befits a King Lear as much as a Shylock. He appeared on the English-speaking stage in Sholem Asch's *God of Vengeance* and finally on the screen in Carl Laemmle and Cecil de Mille productions. His son, Joseph Schildkraut, is a well-known American stage and movie actor. He appeared on Broadway as the leading man in the thriller *Uncle Harry* and in Tchekow's *Cherry Garden*.

Emanuel Reicher was an immediate success when he established himself in New York back in 1915. His pathos had overwhelming emotional qualities. Another Jewish actor who like the Schildkrauts and Emanuel Reicher came from the Deutsche Theatre in Berlin to the United States early was Oscar Beregi. He committed the great mistake of returning to his home land, Hungary where he was soon banned from the stage though his non-Jewish colleagues had interfered in his behalf.

Most of the others emigrated for good in the crucial years between 1933 and 1939. Elisabeth Bergner, who has grown to stardom under the direction of Max Reinhardt and Victor Barnowsky in Berlin, first went to London. There she was seen in Sir James M. Barrie's *The Boy David*. Queen Mary kissed her on the cheek in tribute to her acting. Elisabeth Bergner was Catherine the Great in the motion picture which found world-wide acclaim in 1934. It was shown even in Germany until barred by the Nazis. During the same season she made her debut on Broadway in *Escape Me Never*. The critics unanimously selected her as the actress giving the best performance of the year. She repeated her success in *The Two Mrs. Carrolls* and returned to Broadway as the *Duchess of Malfi*. Movie goers admired her in *Escape Me Never* and *Stolen Life*.

Grete Mosheim, daughter of a physician, was the Berlin Eliza in G. B. Shaw's *Pygmalion*, Berlin's leading lady in Elmer Rice's *Street Scene*, and the Gretchen in *Faust*. Her glowing strength and sweetness of expression always carried her audience away. She appeared on Broadway twice, in *Letters to Lucerne* and in *Calico Wedding*. Lilli Palmer also is the daughter of a Berlin physician. But unlike Grete Mosheim she embarked on her acting career after her emigration, first to Paris, then to London where she quickly rose to stardom, followed by a Hollywood contract. Lilli Palmer is married to the English actor Rex Harrison. Her most recent Broadway success was Cleopatra, in Shaw's *Anthony and Cleopatra.*

Two more actresses who have escaped from Nazism have become familiar figures on the London stage as well as in the London film studios, Lucie Mannheim and Sybille Binder. The former was Puck and Juliet in Leopold Jessner's Shakespeare productions. Her impersonation of Ibsen's Nora established her in the first rank of English performers. Sybille Binder was a leading lady of Victor Barnowsky. Her tender exotic appearance and her talent of subtle characterisation were readily recognized in London.

There is one actor who must be mentioned for having become a leading man around Piccadilly, Anton Walbrook whose name on the stages of Vienna and Berlin once was Adolf Wohlbrück. He scored as the Prince Consort opposite Anna Neagle in *Queen Victoria* and in the motion picture *The Red Shoes* only recently.

Luise Rainer who was with the Dumont Theatre of Düsseldorf and with Max Reinhardt has frequently appeared on the stages of New York and London. The motion pictures *The Great Ziegfeld* and *The Good Earth* made her famous. Her extraordinary sensitive acting won her the Award of the Motion Picture Academy for 1936 and 1937.

Dolly Haas who makes her bow on Broadway once in a while is in private life Mrs. Hirschfeld, wife of the famous theatrical cartoonist of the New York Times. Else Bassermann née Schiff came to this country together with her actor-husband Albert Bassermann who though himself a Gentile insists on speaking only of "We the Jews..." His true genius as an actor is no doubt responsible for Else Bassermann's high standard. She usually appears together with Albert Bassermann who still is performing in New York, in Hollywood (*Foreign Correspondent*), in the film studios of London (*The Red Shoes*), and elsewhere in Central Europe at the age of eighty-two.

Lili Darvas, Mrs. Ferenc Molnar, who was seen as the Queen in the Maurice Evans production of Hamlet was acclaimed on Broadway when she appeared in the Kaufman-Ferber comedy of 1948 *Bravo*. She played actually the part of a refugee actress.

Fritzi Massary (b. Vienna 1882) has not performed any more after her arrival in the United States. She last played at His Majesty's Theatre in London in Noel Coward's *Operetta* in 1938. The part was meant as a tribute to her unique past. For she was the undisputed Queen of the German operetta for twenty-nine consecutive years as the star of the Berlin Metropoltheater. Its composers composed their music with her spirited art of interpretation in mind. Champagne transformed into action was her performance in Johann Strauss' *Rosalinda*.

In the latter she appeared together with her husband, Max Pallenberg who died in an airplane accident. He was an outstanding comedian endowed with a tender understanding for the actual tragedy in the life of the poor creatures he impersonated. He was unique in *Imaginary Invalid* in Molière's comedy and he remained unequalled as the Czech soldier Schweijk in Erwin Piscator's history-making production.

Fritz Kortner, the foremost character actor of Leopold Jessner in his expressionistic approach to the theatre as Richard III, Othello, and Shylock, went straight to Hollywood. His Alfred Dreyfus, Dimitri Karamasoff, and Abdul Hamid are masterpieces. Kortner wrote quite a number of screen plots and had two plays produced on Broadway, *Another Sun* in collaboration with Dorothy Thompson, and *Somewhere in France* together with Carl Zuckmayer.

Two of Hollywood's most sought after comedians fled from Nazism in Central Europe to this country, Szöke Szakall who is not expected to lose his delightful Hungarian accent, which is part of his success, and Felix Bressart who early had rejected the fabulous salary the German film industry had offered him if he would continue with his comedy impersonations of men in the army. Bressart last appeared on Broadway in the Bush Fekete-Helen Fay play *The Big Two*; he died in Hollywood in 1949.

Oscar Karlweis, son of a Viennese playwright and a favorite player of the pre-Hitler era in Vienna and Berlin, was unanimously praised when his personal charm made Franz Werfel's *Jacobowsky and the Colonel* the hit of a Broadway season.

Peter Lorre first scored in the Fritz Lang motion picture called *M*. He became world-famous when as a Hollywood actor he added a modern psycho-analytical touch to the villains he was given to play. (In the *Maltese Falcon* and many pictures before and after.)

It is impossible to include a complete listing. Among the others who injected their enthusiasm into the theatrical life of this country are: Sig Arno of *Song of Norway* fame, Herbert Berghof, Curt Bois, Ernst Deutsch, Ilka Grüning, Hans Jaray, Erwin Kalser, Kurt Katsch, Reinhold Schünzel whose degenerated characters are very much in demand in Hollywood and on Broadway, and his daughter Marianne Stewart, in private life Mrs. Louis Calhern.

Two lovable personalities died, Paul Graetz in Hollywood and Alexander Granach in New York while appearing in the Broadway cast of *A Bell for Adano*. He appeared together with Greta Garbo and Felix Bressart in *Ninotchka*. The film performance of the late Conrad Veidt as Jud Süss is an unforgettable one.

The playwrights come and go with the actors. It may work the other way around. Any way, when the Jewish performers rose to fame on the German stage, the heydays had dawned for the Jewish dramatists. Their present day generation left Germany and enriched the literature of their new chosen fatherland.

As long as they were writing in the Old World, they gave to their fellow-citizens one masterpiece after the other. Adolf l'Arronge was actually the first showman among them who knew equally well how to satisfy the average playgoer and how to call upon the intellectuals. As the founder of the Deutsches Theater in Berlin he gave to the German nation one of its most important cultural centers for the rebirth of the great classics and as the author of *Mein Leopold, Hasemanns Töchter,* and *Doktor Claus* he gave it three plays of lasting popularity, still today favorites in the repertory of the German-American amateur societies.

Ludwig Fulda as many Western Germans of Jewish or Gentile extraction alike has many characteristics in common with the neighboring French, his fondness for the flow of beautiful language, his gracile approach to the subjects he tackles in his plays. He eventually became foremost translator of the works of Molière. He was decorated with the Cross of the French Legion of Honor in 1933 at a time when Hitler's Germany ignored his work. The American theatregoer got acquainted with quite a number of his plays, *The Talisman, The Lost Paradise, Robinson's Island* among them.

Frank Wedekind who was a half-Jew combined the qualities of literature, cabaret, comedy, and tragedy in his unique sophisticated plays which were the delight of the theatregoers during the first quarter of our century. He satirized the sex problems of society.

Carl Sternheim wrote the comedy satire of the German bourgeois proper. His *Der Snob, Bürger Schippel*, and *Die Hose* were the hits of the Kleine Theater Unter den Linden. Sternheim died in Switzerland in 1939.

Emil Ludwig, the world-famous author of many biographic works, created a sensation with his play on *William II*. Emil Ludwig died in Switzerland in 1948.

Walter Hasenclever, a half-Jew, gave voice to the spirit of a new generation after the First World War in his expressionistic drama *Der Sohn.* He committed suicide in France when the Germans closed in on him.

His contemporary, Ernst Toller, committed suicide in New York. The Germans had closed in on him, too, in an allegorical sense. Toller, the author of *Masse Mensch,* was a sincere and great idealist whose pacifistic and humanitarian ideas commanded world-wide respect.

Lion Feuchtwanger, now a reputed American novelist, saw his plays such as *Vasantasena* and *Warren Hastings* first performed on all German stages, then banned from them.

Alfred Neumann, now equally at home in Hollywood and in Florence, Italy, has given modern suspense to the historical drama, in *The Patriot* in the first place.

Bruno Frank, author of delicate comedies, died in Hollywood.

Hans José Rehfisch is a lecturer on drama with the Dramatic Workshop of Erwin Piscator in New York now. He wrote such important plays as *Chauffeur Martin* in search of God and *Die Affair Dreyfus* in cooperation with Wilhelm Herzog.

Bert Brecht, the author of *Mahogany* (music by Kurt Weill), *Drums in the Night, Baal,* and numerous other plays fights the spirit of Nazism from his new American home.

Walter Mehring, once an anti-Fascist German song-writer of distinction and the author of *The Merchant of Berlin* produced by Erwin Piscator, now lives in New York City.

The names of two authors of light comedy, Oscar Blumenthal and Gustav Kadelburg, will not disappear from the repertories because they wrote one of those never failing farces *The White Horse Inn.*

Franz Arnold, now a resident of London, gave a large number of similar light comedies to the international theatre.

The greatest Jewish writers and poets were at work in Vienna during the area of emancipation which not by accident coincided with the flourishing of that city as a center of German-language culture.

THE JEW IN DRAMA, THEATRE AND FILM

Arthur Schnitzler (b. 1862, d. 1931) was the son of a highly respected citizen. His father was a professor on the medical faculty of Vienna University. Arthur Schnitzler, becoming a doctor himself, turned to neurology. He was a great thinker and a rare poet. His dramatic work will live on, *Liebelei, Der Reigen* which unleashed an early storm of anti-Semitic protests, as did *Professor Bernhardi* the drama of progress versus dogma. A conscientious Jewish doctor defends his medically and psychologically justified approach to a dying patient against the dogmatic demands of a Catholic priest. This subject brought the discussion of anti-Semitism to a forum of hundreds of thousands.

His son Henry Schnitzler emigrated to the United States in 1938 and has been active as a lecturer and dramatic instructor in California ever since.

Richard Beer-Hofman was a Viennese like Arthur Schnitzler, but unlike the latter he was more concerned with the great Jewish heritage than with contemporary social problems. Still, in an early play, *Der Graf von Charolais,* he created the figure of Red Isaac who—long before Hitler—voiced on the stages of Berlin and Vienna a protest against religious persecution. Beer-Hofman reached the poetic qualities of the biblical psalms in his drama *Jacob's Traum.* It was translated into Hebrew and performed by the Habima in New York. Beer-Hofman was a true poet exercising the greatest economy as to the quantity of his writing all his life. An exile himself, he died in the United States.

Hugo von Hofmannsthal had the lyrical quality of his writing in common with Beer-Hofman. It was not accidental. Hofmannsthal not adhering to the Jewish faith himself was the grandson of Isaak Löw Hofmann who was knighted in 1835. The entire approach of his grandson to poetry points to the Jewish heritage. The dramatic as well as the operatic stage owes much to Hofmannsthal. He wrote *Everyman,* the chief attraction of the Salzburg Festivals, and the librettos for three operas composed by Richard Strauss, *Elektra, Ariadne auf Naxos,* and as the most popular one *Der Rosenkavalier,* which reappears in the repertory of the Metropolitan Opera House in New York every season.

The name of a Viennese Jewess must be mentioned here not so much for her contributions to the lasting treasures of dramatic literature, but for her ability to provide the stage and screen with timely entertaining subjects, Vicki Baum. She became internationally famous when Max Reinhardt produced her Grand Hotel in Berlin. The Theatre Guild introduced it to the American audience in 1930 and Metro-Goldwyn-Mayer to the movie-goers in 1935. Vicki Baum herself settled down in California and continued producing works with an excitingly colorful international background.

Many of the finest Jewish writers in the German language hail from Prague, Czechoslovakia. It has been the birth-place of Franz Werfel, equally great as a lyric poet, a novelist, and a playwright. In his drama *Juarez and Maximilian* he confronted two worlds which will clash for ever, the one of the despotic ruler who is humane when he so pleases and the other one of the true representative of a nation demanding its natural freedom. Werfel's comedy *Jacobowsky and the Colonel* was a Broadway hit. The screen is indebted to him because of his famous novel *The Song of Bernadette* which has become a truly great Hollywood product.

Paul Kornfeld belonged to the same literary circle of German-language writers in Prague as Werfel. Kornfeld's dramas and comedies furthered the expressionism of the stage. Max Brod, the author of *Clarissa's Half-Heart* and *The Bunterbart Case,* now lives in Israel.

Stefan Zweig gave to the stage his *Jeremiah* and Arnold Zweig *The Mission of Semael.*

No other dramatist ever has reached the national standing of Herman Heijermans in the Netherlands. His dramas *Ghetto* and *Good Hope* strongly exposing the social shortcomings of our age were world-wide successes. The greatest contribution towards them was made by the actress Esther de Boer van Rijk. She became famous as Kniertje, the old seaman's wife in *Good Hope*. She played the part everywhere in Dutch, in German, in French, in English. She was the undisputed Queen of the Dutch stage. She helped the establishment of the Netherlands' Actors Society, she was made a Knight in the Order of Orange-Nassau and in the Crown of Belgium, a canvas painted by Eduard Frankfort showing herself as Kniertje obtained a place of honor in the Municipal Theatre of Amsterdam. At the age of seventy she won a swimming diploma, at eighty-three she performed in Palestine, and she died in the midst of the preparations of another tour to Eretz Israel in 1937.

The Netherlands would never have been as honorably mentioned as they are in the chronicles of the international theatre were it not for their Jewish performers. Louis Bouwmeester toured Europe and the United States. He played his greatest part, Shylock in Shakespeare's *Merchant of Venice*, at the age of eighty for the delegates of the Hague Conference in 1922. He was immensely popular in his home country. They just called him "Onze (our) Louis."

Denmark had her Jewish playwright in Henrik Hertz (b. Copenhagen 1798, d. 1870). He embraced Protestantism in 1832. All his rhymed lyrical plays and historical dramas were performed at the Danish National Theatre as well as all over the rest of Scandinavia.

Ludwig Oscar Josephson was a playwright and director in Sweden who firmly guided the Scandinavian theatre of the 19th century. He headed the Royal Theatre of Stockholm in 1864 and the Christiania Theatre of Oslo, then Christiania, in 1873. Due to his judgment and courage Ibsen and Strindberg found their way to the stage.

Hungary has almost become legendary as the original home of glamorously gifted playwrights. The legend owes its international recognition to Ferenc Molnar and his world-wide success. He is, no doubt, one of the most brilliant dramatists of Europe. His comedy *The Play Is The Thing* has been successfully revived during the Broadway season of 1948, preceded by *Carousel* which has been the musical version of Molnar's *Liliom* seen on Broadway before. Actually, it was a play entitled *The Devil* that first established his reputation. There is even a comprehensive English edition of *The Plays of Ferenc Molnar* covering his writing until 1937. It presents the author as what he wants to be, a witty entertainer, a psychologist who holds his office hours on the comedy stage. Molnar lives in the United States since the start of the Second World War.

His compatriot, Manyhert Lengyel, made the United States his home in 1925. As a playwright he is a satirist primarily concerned with the cracks in our social structure. Otis Skinner starred in Lengyel's *Sancho Panza*. Lengyel dedicated himself extensively to the writing of film scripts such as *Catherine the Great* for Elisabeth Bergner and *Ninotchka* for Greta Garbo.

Ossip Dymow is the only Jew from Czarist Russia who has established an international theatre reputation outside the Russian and Yiddish language domains. Three of his plays were produced on Broadway, *Nju*, *Personalities*, and *Bronx Express*. As the title of the latter indicates, the author has become quite a New Yorker since his immigration in 1913.

Jews started to contribute to the theatrical life in England as soon as they were admitted to its shores. Moses Mendes wrote plays which were produced in the Covent Garden and Drury Lane Theatres of the 18th century. A particular success must have been his play *Double Disappointment* which drew crowds to the Drury Lane in 1746.

The Portuguese Jewish families who immigrated to England brought with them a deeply rooted love for arts and letters. The original name of Sir Arthur Wing Pinero had been a Jewish-Portuguese one, Pinheiro. He was an actor until 1881. His principal, Henry Irving, encouraged his desire to become a playwright. In his early drama *The Squire* Pinero reveals himself as a brother-in-arms of Henrik Ibsen. Pinero introduced sincere discussion of the pressing problems of his time to the English stage with *The Profligate* and *The Second Mrs. Tanqueray*. He was the one who gave to the young British generation the evidence that no subject worthwhile presenting for the benefit of human society should be "taboo" on the stage. Pinero was knighted in 1909.

Alfred Sutro, too, to judge by his name was of Portuguese-Jewish descent. With the production of his play *The Walls of Jericho* he became the favorite of the Londoners in 1904. A new play by Sutro was a prerequisite of all theatrical seasons until 1929 with the exception of the first World War. Sutro became the provider of sure entertainment with *The Perfect Lover, The Fascinating Mrs. Vandervelt, The Perplexed Husband,* and as many other plays as there were happy seasons in London.

The author and actor Leonard Merrick must be mentioned here, not for any playwriting, but for his theatrical novel *The Actor-Manager* which placed him in one line with the greatest novelists of world literature.

The first Jewish performer to play on an English stage was a Mrs. Manuel in 1663. When Sheridan's *Duenna* came to the Covent Garden in 1775 it was Myer Lyon who under the name of *Mr. Leoni* played the part of Isaac. There were no performances on Friday nights on account of him. The chief attraction of the Covent Garden Theatre was at that time a Jewish actress, Hannah Norsa. She played Polly Peachum in *The Beggar's Opera.* Her niece Maria, by the way, married into the highest aristocracy. Her first husband was the Earl of Waldegrave, her second one the Duke of Gloucester.

Isaac Isaacs and his daughter Rebecca, Charles, Henry, and Edward Salomon were stars of the 19th century in London. Edward's daughter is Claire Romaine. John Braham, a celebrated tenor of the Hanoverian period, built the St. James's Theatre. Benjamin Lumley was His Majesty's Theatre's most successful manager. The Edwardian period had its great star and virtuoso in Sir Herbert Beerbohm Tree. He made Shake-speare who had almost been a forgotten man in the West End worthwhile again. Beerbohm Tree was knighted in 1909. Those who saw his performance remember his passionate and idealistic approach to acting.

Jews have played a decisive part in bringing to America the banner of supreme excellence in the field of dramatic arts. The first playwright of Jewish origin in the history of the American drama, Mordecai Manuel Noah (b. Philadelphia 1785, d. New York 1851), was a highly colorful personality, his life adaptable for dramatization for the stage. He was the perfect example of a daring American pioneer.

His father had served in Washington's army. Noah became an orphan when he was still a boy. He became a carver for his living, but by going to school in his spare time and by intensive reading he prepared himself for a career. He became a newspaperman, an editor, a columnist, and American con-sul to Tunis, North Africa, in 1813. This territory was a hot one at that time. The notorious pirates had captured American sailors. It was Noah's task to liberate them and to impress upon the nations sailing the Mediterranean the dignity of the young United States. He created a precedent of fundamental historic importance in his dealings with the British. They took objection to his activities as violating a treaty governing the relations of a Christian power to Tunisia. Noah, however, gave documentary evidence proving that the United States could not be classed as a Christian power. His diplomatic move was highly successful as to the discharge of his duties, but not as to the continuation of his consular career. His opponents back home availed themselves of this splendid opportunity to have him recalled.

But Noah continued to be prominently active in New York. His theatrical work became popular. The American scene and American history were his subjects. One of his plays, *Marion or The Hero of Lake George*, was performed at Columbia

University in 1932 in celebration of the bicentennial of George Washington's birth.

At no time did Mordecai Noah forget the strife of the Jews in their diaspora. He founded the dream city of Ararat on the Grand Island in the Niagara River as a refuge for his coreligionists from Europe. He appointed himself "by the Grace of God Governor and Judge of Israel" anticipating the name of the future Zionist state. But Ararat had not the magnetic power of Palestine. The foundation stone is now an exhibit of the Buffalo Historical Society. Mordecai Noah was basically a great showman, even at times when he did not write plays.

Isaac Harly was his contemporary, though not equally versatile. He wrote the dramas *Alexander Severus*, *The Gordian Knot*, and *Alberti*. Harly was the object of admiration of the great Americans of his days such as Thomas Jefferson and James Madison. As one of the first professional critics he exercised a far-reaching influence on intellectual life. However, he died in poverty.

No other man has meant so much to the American stage as David Belasco (b. San Francisco 1854, d. New York City 1931), the son of Sephardic parents. His father, Abraham Humphrey Belasco, had been a famous harlequin in London who with his wife, Reina Martin, hoped to strike gold in California. They did not. Young David was given in the care of a Catholic priest, but he soon escaped with a touring circus to become its *"Davido, the boy bareback-rider"*. A subsequent career as colorful as it could be only in the century that produced men like Thomas Edison, Teddy Roosevelt, and P. T. Barnum led Belasco from obscure beginnings in the mining camps of the West to the unchallenged position of pre-eminence in the international theatrical world. He was the fore-runner of the Provincetown Players and of the Theatre Guild. He made theatre a matter of importance for every American.

At the age of nineteen he was an actor and stage manager

in San Francisco and developed his own ideas of naturalistic stage lighting, setting, and acting. His New York career began with a failure. His and his companion James A. Herne's play, *Hearts of Oak,* was by far too much saccharine for the sophisticated metropolis. But when Belasco returned in 1882 he came to stay. He was the first to introduce electric lighting to the stage when he managed the Madison Square Theatre. His own play, *May Blossom,* established his name as an author-director firmly in the American theatre. Its history is identical with Belasco's biography for almost five decades. He revolutionized the appearance of the stage and the style of acting. The extravaganzas of his naturalism were named Belascoism. He was a great coach of new talent, he brought to the fore such performers as Mrs. Leslie Carter, Frances Starr, David Warfield, Leo Dietrichstein, Leonore Ulric, Blanche Bates, E. H. Sothern, Henrietta Crosman, Ina Claire, Robert Lorraine, and Judith Anderson. He discovered and trained America's sweetheart, Mary Pickford. He developed the architectural and technical blueprint for modern theatre buildings. The Belasco Theatre of New York City still carries his name. In his lifetime he produced about four hundred plays, the works of one hundred and twenty-five different authors, and one hundred and fifty plays of his own. His *Return of Peter Grimm* was an important event on Broadway in 1911. Most of his plays were written to meet the taste of his period. However his dramatization of *Madame Butterfly* and his *Girl of the Golden West* will live on together with the scores of Giacomo Puccini. Toscanini conducted the world premiere, Caruso, Amato, and Emmy Destinn were heard in the chief roles. Shakespeare's *Merchant of Venice* had in Belasco's staging the longest run ever remembered on Broadway. All his productions were superbly presented. He did not save any labor to bring a performance as close to real life as possible, idealized by all the glamour the stage can provide. This was his credo as an artist. Whatever we may think about it today, he was the first to secure for the American theatre its recognition as the temple of fine art, not as a place of business.

One of Belasco's favorite playwrights was Charles Klein (b. London 1867) who died in the sinking of the Lusitania in 1915. Klein who had come to the United States at the age of sixteen had first been an actor. He became famous with his play *The Music Master*. Belasco had given the lead to David Warfield. Klein developed a particular efficiency in plays executed without taking refuge to the customary love story. An outstanding example is his play *The Lion and the Mouse*. Here Klein unmasks the brutal money-makers who vehemently oppose any government official just because he proves himself not to be accessible to bribe.

Channing Pollock, author and co-author of numerous plays and motion picture scripts, has found the acclaim of Broadway with his dramas *The Pit, Napoleon the Great, The House Beautiful*. Public recognition had its further expression when Colgate University conferred upon him the honorary degree of Litt.D., followed by an honorary LL.D. of the Northeastern University.

Elmer Rice has become an international figure in the theatrical world. The money he made with his first play, *The Trial*, reflecting his own experiences as a lawyer, enabled him to experiment on new approaches to the stage. Consequently *The Adding Machine* represented an outstanding example of impressionism in drama, and *Street Scene* satisfied his literary ambition as to originality. It won him the Pulitzer Prize in 1929 as the first documentary play of its kind. Its success was repeated when it was made into a musical with a score by Kurt Weill.

Rice discussed legal ethics once more in *Counsellor-at-Law*, with a Jewish character the center of interest. It became the vehicle of Paul Muni and many other great actors all over the world.

Practically Elmer Rice inaugurated the modern American theatre. His plays are today as exciting to see as when they first were performed. Personally he is actively paving the way for an American theatre of high ethical standards, not subject to business considerations. He was Regional Director for New York of the Federal Theatre Project, became president of the Dramatists' Guild and a director in the Playwrights' Company.

George S. Kaufman has only recently given evidence of his ties with the plight of his co-religionists when he wrote together with Edna Ferber the comedy *Bravo* for the Broadway season of 1948/49. Nobody can say that the play is laden with wisdom, still it creates sympathy for the fate of the refugees from Nazi-Europe.

Kaufman is the greatest practitioner of the American comedy stage today. His name is linked with some forty plays. As collaborator with Marc Connelly he wrote *Beggar on Horseback*, with Moss Hart *Once in a Lifetime, I'd Rather Be Right, You Can't Take It With You*, awarded the Pulitzer Prize, and *The Man Who Came To Dinner*, another hit. All of them reveal his special gifts as a never erring technician in the developing of a good plot, with a superb sense for a wisecrack at the proper time, a sure understanding for contemporary worries which he selects as targets for his satirical attacks. Many of the plays made great motion pictures.

Moss Hart, George Kaufman's comrade in success, recently wrote single-handed, *Lady in the Dark*, psychoanalysis cleverly applied to the musical and wrapped in glamour, on the stage the vehicle for Gertrude Lawrence, on the screen for Ginger Rogers. Moss Hart's splendid contribution to the war effort was his Air Force Show, *Winged Victory*. The season 1948/49 saw his latest satire, *Light Up The Sky*.

Edna Ferber is the other author who has conquered Broadway as an ally of George S. Kaufman. They both are responsible for such hits as *The Royal Family, Dinner at Eight, Stage Door*, and as mentioned earlier, *Bravo*. It was *Show Boat*, first a novel, then one of the most successful musicals ever produced in America, and twice a motion picture, that established her name for good in the annals of the Theatre. Among the honors bestowed upon her are the membership in the National Institute of Arts and Letters and the honorary degree of Doctor of Letters of Columbia University.

Clifford Odets is the most conscientious and powerful critic among American playwrights. He reviewed the shortcomings of Hollywood in his latest play, *The Big Knife*. All those who earmarked Odets exclusively as the herald of the pre-war generation have been wrong. He continues to be the outstanding anatomist of the ailing body of our society.

He made his start in the theatre as an actor and came to join the youthful Group Theatre in 1930. His one-act play *Waiting for Lefty* inaugurated a sequence of full-length dramas dictated by Odets' distinct social conscience. The refreshing language in which his *Awake and Sing* was written, the uncompromising anti-Nazi theme of *Till The Day I Die* established him not merely on Broadway, but wherever a progressive theatre ensemble was looking for a congenial play. Clifford Odets puts his dramatic talent, his ability for dealing with hot subjects and of developing fascinating stage characters exclusively in the service of his convictions as citizen of the United States and of the world.

Lillian Florence Hellman belongs in the same category of highly serious and ethical playwrights. In the *Children's Hour* she explored an old Glasgow law case dealing with two teachers whose existence was undermined by a child's slander. In the *Little Foxes* she depicts what she knew of the troubles of families in the South where she herself was born. And in *Watch on the Rhine* she lent her voice early to the fight against the Nazi pest. This drama gained her the Award of the New York Drama Critics' Circle.

S. N. Behrman early chose the occupation with the drama as a career. At Harvard he acquired the degree of M. A., he started out as an assistant editor of the New York Times Book Review, and finally became a master of the lightly and elegantly written comedy, first with *The Second Man*, subsequently in collaboration with Ruth Gordon on *Serena Blandish*, with Alexander Woollcott on *Brief Moment*, with Ina Claire on *Biography*, and with quite a number of other celebrities on other plays. His play *Rain from Heaven* opened the eyes of the American theatregoers to the threat of Nazi tyranny early in 1934. One of his successes in later years was *No Time For Comedy*. Hollywood frequently called on him for such important scripts as *Queen Christina* and *Tale of Two Cities*. In 1938 Behrman joined forces with Robert Sherwood, Sidney Howard, Elmer Rice and Maxwell Anderson in founding the Playwrights' Company, a theatrical organisation of the highest literary standard dedicated primarily to the production of the work of its founders independent of the business men of Broadway. The late Kurt Weill was the most recently enrolled member.

As did Behrman and many other dramatists Ben Hecht started as a newspaperman. His short stories have become American classics. He wrote numerous plays and motion pictures all of them disclosing his artistic personality, in part tending towards extreme realism, in part towards high flying romanticism. He composed the stage hit *Front Page* together with Charles MacArthur. Hecht stands out among his colleagues of the Great White Way as the most ardent fighter for the independence of the State of Israel. He wrote many a pageant to arouse the general interest in the plight of Palestine and brought to Broadway as a benefit *A Flag Is Born* in which Paul Muni enthusiastically took the lead.

Sidney Kingsley wrote *Men in White* with so much skill that doctors who saw the drama did not question his being a member of the medical profession. This is significant, as the medical profession would object to the slightest deviation of a playwright from the correct presentation of their activities. The Pulitzer Prize awarded Sidney Kingsley in 1934 affirmed their judgment. His *Detective Story* was the hit of the Broadway seasons 1949 and 1950.

Bella and Samuel Spewack are a playwriting couple. Bella

was born in Hungary, Samuel in Russia. She learned the theatre technique from all angles, as an actress and as a press agent for Max Reinhardt's *Miracle*. Her husband has been an outstanding newspaper correspondent. Together they were extremely lucky in all their theatrical ventures: *The Solitaire Man, Clear All Wires,* a satirizing summary of conditions in Russia and their experience as foreign correspondents. The drama *Spring Song* had the Jewish East Side of New York as its scene. The Spewaks turned to the musical in *Leave It To Me* supported by the music of Cole Porter. It delighted its audience with a prophetic moment in 1938, the American ambassador to Russia, impersonated by the comedian Victor Moore, kicking the Nazi envoy. The behind-the-scenes-knowledge of the Spewacks exposed book publishing and ghost-writing in the light comedy *Miss Swan Expects*. They hit the jackpot of Broadway with *Kiss Me Kate*.

Irwin Shaw displayed persuasive power in the defense of pacifist ideas in his one act play, *Bury The Dead*. The Group Theatre produced *The Gentle People* with long lasting success. Shaw also wrote *Salute*, an episode of the Civil War in Spain, and *Retreat to Pleasure* in 1940. Hollywood has filmed *The Gentle People* under the title *Out of the Fog*. Irwin Shaw served in the army during the Second World War.

The English-born playwright Benn W. Levy came to Broadway with *The Devil Passes* and *Mrs. Moonlight*. The united skill of Jerome Chodorov and Joseph Fields made the grade with *My Sister Eileen* and *Junior Miss*.

Garson Kanin was hired by Samuel Goldwyn to direct pictures and was successfully set to work by RKO. By now his fine reputation as a motion picture director has been overshadowed by his work as a playwright-director for the legitimate theatre. *Born Yesterday* is one of the finest contemporary comedies.

The unfortunate fact that the basic structure of theatre life on Broadway is a business structure has done much harm to the flourishing of American dramatic literature. Arthur

Laurents is the author of one of the finest war dramas ever written, *The Home of the Brave*. Its run on Broadway was curtailed in consequence of a discord between the producer and the house owner. In this play Arthur Laurents at the age of twenty-seven presented the American spirit of true democracy in an excitingly dramatic action centering around an American Jewish army private who returns from a mission to a Japanese Island with a psycho-pathological shock. Laurents reveals in a convincing manner the fundaments of the prejudice which regards the Jews as "different". The solution of the problem he offers is equally convincing, "Everybody is different, so what?" His play has since been turned into a truly great motion picture.

Arthur Laurents is an established radio-writer. While he was in the army he composed training films for the Signal Corps. For Alfred Hitchcock he wrote the screenplay for *Rope*. He turned to Hollywood, but there is no doubt that he will find his way back to the theatre.

Arthur Miller has become the most successful and most internationally known American playwright since his *Death of a Salesman* reached Broadway. He was born on the lower East Side of New York. His success story comprises the plays *The Grass Still Grows*, *The Man who Had All the Luck*, and *All My Sons*. Three famous Jewish actors, Lee J. Cobb in New York, Paul Muni in London, and Fritz Kortner in middle Europe have played Willy Loman, the salesman.

Some other Jewish dramatists are: Hyman Adler, Marc Blitzstein, Lowell Brentano, Edward Chodorov, Lester Cohen, Nat Dorfman who also holds office as a theatrical press agent, Rose Franken who wrote *Another Language* in 1932, I. J. Golden, Samuel R. Golding, Fanny Hurst, Harry Segall, Rita Wellman who wrote *The Gentile Wife*, and Victor Wolfson. Even this listing is far from complete.

The American art of acting has been made world-famous in the 19th century by a Jewess born in Milneburg near New Orleans in 1835, Ada Isaac Menken. She was also a poetess possessed by an ardent love for the wisdom of the Bible. Her glamorous beauty, her romantic temperament, her declamatory talent eventually led her to the stage. When she played the part of *Manzeppa* in an adaptation of Byron's work she became the sensation of the American stage. Mark Twain adored her and so did Charles Dickens when she came to London in 1864. Her triumph became truly international upon her stage appearance in Paris during the great exhibition there. Poets such as Alexandre Dumas and monarchs of many nations sought her friendship. Thomas Buchanan Reed and a rabbi were comforting her when she died at the age of thirty-three. Swinburne wrote in her memory, *"Lo! This is she that was the world's delight."* Baron Lionel Nathan de Rothschild of London erected a monument on her grave in Montparnasse out of personal gratitude for the relentless public support Ada Isaac Menken had given his cause when he had fought for his rightful seat in the English Parliament in 1857.

David Warfield rose to stardom at the turn of the century. It was David Belasco who guided Warfield from the burlesque to the legitimate theatre. The Jewish characters Warfield presented on the stage were always pleading for sympathy. His fame was at its peak when Warfield appeared in *The Auctioneer, The Music Master,* and as Shylock in Belasco's production of the *Merchant of Venice.* He was honored with a gold medal for "distinguished service to the theatre" on his seventy-fifth birthday in 1941.

Louis Mann at one time performed together with Edwin Booth. He was a comedian of nation-wide reputation and a particularly engaging personality. Herbert H. Lehman, Alfred E. Smith, William Randolph Hearst were his close friends. President Woodrow Wilson paid personal tribute to his art. Mann's wife, Clara Lipmann, an actress, occasionally engaged in playwriting as did he himself.

Florence Reed gave a performance of great humane effect when she appeared in Michael Morton's play, *Yellow Ticket.* She portrayed one of those unfortunate Jewish girls who were forced by the Czarist regime to register as prostitutes if they wanted their freedom of movement.

The actor who made history on Broadway as well as in Hollywood and on the radio has been a Russian Jew, Al Jolson. He was seven years old when he arrived in this country. He rose from local minstrel shows to unique international stardom. His career has been turned into two film musicals. His appearance as the blackfaced "Gus" in many Winter Garden productions established his fame. He became the first singing star of the sound film in the *Jazz Singer* in 1927. He created a particular style of radio entertainment combining monologue and song. He last was seen on Broadway in the musical *Hold On To Your Hats*. Whoever heard him sing the Kol Nidre will never forget the touching force of his voice. The screen musicals *The Jolson Story* and *Al Jolson Sings Again* rediscovered him as the greatest box office attraction among the singers of our time. He passed away in 1950.

Eddie Cantor is the comedian who like Al Jolson has entertained New York on Broadway, all of America over the radio, and the entire world by his film musicals. Florenz Ziegfeld, one of America's great Jewish producers, made him the center of attraction of his Follies. He is responsible for Hollywood's funniest pictures such as *Strike Me Pink* and *Kid From Spain*. Personally he is the example of a good American citizen never missing an opportunity for the discharge of his responsibilities towards his country and his co-religionists in accordance with the means at his disposal. He served as president of the Screen Actors Guild of America, of the Federation of Radio Actors, of the Jewish Theatrical Guild. He simultaneously is an honorary member of the Catholic Actors' Guild and of the Episcopal Actors' Guild. A national *Eddie Cantor Week* was observed in October 1937 with personalities such as James A. Farley, Mrs. Eleanor Roosevelt, Herbert H. Hoover, and the late Cardinal Mundelein on the Committee.

An entertainer who shares with Eddie Cantor the modest beginnings between the Bowery and Coney Island is George Jessel, perhaps America's wittiest master of ceremonies.

Charles Chaplin expresses his Jewishness in all the world-famous characters he created for the screen from the little tramp who never in all his misery loses his wit nor his hope to the enterprising barber who in *The Great Dictator* takes the place of Hitler and addresses his followers in an unmistakable Yiddish. Anti-Semitic Hungarian papers attacked Chaplin when he was to visit Budapest, and so did papers of similar low type elsewhere on other occasions. Chaplin, however, stands above any such mere expressions of jealousy as an international phenomenon, the first and only actor who made six continents laugh for more than thirty years. Actually, he entered American motion pictures in 1913. First there were only one-act comedies, followed by full length features since 1921, *The Kid* together with Chaplin's discovery, the child prodigy Jackie Coogan, then *The Gold Rush, The Circus, City Lights, Modern Times*, though screened in 1935 still silent, *The Great Dictator*, semi-talking in 1940, and finally *Monsieur Verdoux* as a regular sound film.

All of them were entirely his own work, the leading part, the direction, the script, and the production. All of them reveal his sense of responsibility towards his fellow-men. He exposed the thoughtlessness of those who live in plenty, the bewilderment of mankind confronted with the terrorizing machines of our technical age, the stupidity of dictatorship, and the little man's vain hope for peace. He always has been the little man himself in each of his pictures.

Paul Muni, originally Weisenfreund born in Lemberg, Galicia, in 1895, is regarded today as the most versatile character player of America. Beyond his art of the make-up he never fails to present a true human being. Together with his parents he started out on the Yiddish stage. He had his first Broadway success as the old Morris Levine in *We Americans* in 1926. The lead in Elmer Rice's *Counsellor-at-Law* won him fame. But it was left to the motion picture to reveal the comprehensiveness of his art. *Louis Pasteur* was the part which won him the Award of the Motion Picture Academy of Arts and Sciences for 1936. He was the poor hard-toiling Chinese in *Good Earth,* he was *Emile Zola* and Mexico's heroic Indian president, *Juarez.* He equally fascinated the film audience in *We Are Not Alone* and in the anti-Nazi picture *The Commandos Strike At Dawn.* Though one of the busiest actors from coast to coast, he always takes time out to support the cause of Palestine. He visited there in 1938 and enacted a scene from the Emile Zola film. He appeared in Ben Hecht's *A Flag Is Born* on Broadway in 1948, waiving all remuneration.

John Garfield born on the lower East Side of New York City in 1913 takes a similar commendable attitude. When Clifford Odets staged his *Golden Boy,* Garfield did not hesitate to leave a three hundred dollars a week part for the forty dollars a week which the Group Theatre offered to him because this was an organisation seriously concerned with the ethical message of the theatre. When Garfield had the choice between appearing in a Broadway production guaranteeing a long-run star salary and Jan de Hartog's *A Skipper Next To God* for eighty dollars a week and an uncertain share in the profits, he decided to appear in the latter because it was the story of a man aware of his obligations towards those who are persecuted. The Experimental Theatre staged the show as a benefit for the American National Theatre and Academy. Though a top ranking film star himself, John Garfield readily appeared in the minor part of the Jewish-American officer in *Gentlemen's Agreement* in view of the fight against anti-Semitism which is its basic theme. The outcome was the unanimous praise all critics had for his treatment of the role. He was last seen on Broadway in Clifford Odets' drama *The Big Knife.*

John Garfield made his career the hardest imaginable way. His father was a presser in a factory and a cantor in his spare-time. John did not get along within the narrow boundaries of the daily bourgeois routine. After expulsion from various public schools he was given by the authorities into the care of a principal, Angelo Patri, who at his school specialized in problem children. This man immediately recognized Garfield's great talent. He permitted the "problem child" to take up boxing as an outlet of his temperament; he supported the young man with six dollars weekly to enable him to take up dramatic lessons. The outcome is generally known. No actor's name has ever appeared in bigger letters on Times Square than John Garfield's on the occasion of his picture, MGM's *Force of Evil.* His earlier pictures include *Air Force, Destination Tokyo, The Pride of the Marines,* and *Humoresque.* During the war he entertained the troops overseas in a world-wide foxhole-circuit.

Edward G. Robinson came from Rumania to the United States at the age of ten. In the period between 1915 and 1929 he became a successful Broadway actor. Hollywood, however, made him the Number One Gangster of the Screen. His two departures from this line increased his reputation as an artist tremendously. For his lead in *Dr. Ehrlich's Magic Bullet* he received the gold medal of the American Humane Association in view of his "humanitarian interest in children and animals". *The Tales of Manhattan* earned him world-wide recognition as a great character player. During the First World War Robinson served in the U. S. Navy; during the Second World War he gave $100,000 to the USO "as a small down payment for the privilege of being an American."

The following is a rather incomplete listing of other Jewish actors and actresses well known to the American public.

The Marx Brothers, Groucho, Harpo, and Chico; Alla Nazimova who successfully turned to the American stage and movie after she had come from Russia to the United States as a member of the Paul Orfenoff Company; Sylvia Sidney, Bertha Kalich; the film stars Joan Blondell, Melvyn Douglas, Paulette Goddard, Hedy Lamarr, Lauren Bacall, Dinah Shore,

Danny Kaye, Adolph Menjou, Paul Lukas, the Ritz Brothers.
Stella Adler of the famous family of Yiddish actors has been
seen on the Broadway stage. Other well-known Jewish per-
formers are Edward Arnold, Belle Baker, Phil Baker, Theda
Bara, Binnie Barnes, Edward J. Bromberg, Milton Berle of
stage and television fame, George Burns, Kitty Carlisle, Sue
Carol, Ricardo Cortez, Morris Carnovsky, Mary Ellis, Sally
Eilers, Alice Faye, Joe Fields, Sidney Fox, Bert Gordon, Phil
Harris, Louise Henry, Lou Holtz, Eugene and Willie Howard,
Sam Jaffe, Bert Lahr, Broadway's funny man; Francine Larri-
more, Lou Lehr, Sam Levene, Aline MacMahon, Helen
Menken, Jack Osterman, Jack Pearl, Martha Raye, Al Shean,
Sid Silver, George Stone, Akim Tamiroff, George Tobias,
Sophie Tucker, Lew Weber, Louis Wolheim, Ed Wynn,
Keenan Wynn, and Harry Weiss who under the name of
Houdini was the sensation of six continents.

The medium of the radio led eventually to a specialization
of a score of American performers. Most successful among
them has been Gertrude Berg who rose to nation-wide popularity over N.B.C. and the Columbia Broadcasting Systems
with *The Goldbergs,* a series which she wrote, directed, and
as to the part of Molly enacted herself. She turned the lovable
Jewish radio family into the subject of a Broadway comedy
named *Molly and Me* in 1947.

The comedian Jack Benny was voted not less than five times
the most popular radio entertainer of the country and Fanny
Brice has been the delight of listeners from coast to coast as
Baby Snooks.

Behind the actors and directors of the legitimate stage stands
the enterprise of the producers. The American theatre of the
19th century was wide open for men with keen foresight.
There were hardly enough theatre buildings in the country
nor was there enough entertainment to be had. One of the first
to recognize the big chance was Oscar Hammerstein. He was
a self-made man who rose from bricklayer and worker in a
tobacco factory to financial leadership on Broadway. On the

side he was an ingenious man who made millions of dollars with his inventions. All in all he built at least seven theatres in New York City. He opened the Victoria Theatre on Times Square in 1899 when it still was Longacre Square and considered by far too much uptown for show business. He competed with the Metropolitan Opera House in his own Manhattan Opera. He gave an opera house to Philadelphia, to London, and another one, the Lexington, to New York. He supplied David Belasco with a theatre where the playwright-director could produce unhampered by any competitive theatrical combine. In short, Hammerstein gave to Broadway the prerequisites for the reputation it has today.

The Hammersteins stayed in business, Arthur, the son, as a producer and inventor like his father; Oscar Hammerstein II, the grandson, as America's most popular librettist, in part responsible for such hits as *Rose Marie, Show Boat* and *South Pacific*, wholly responsible for many famous songs such as *The Last Time I Saw Paris*.

Another family of producers are the Frohmans. Charles Frohman got the first taste of theatre business when he sold tickets in Brooklyn as a boy. He rose to conceive the idea of a nation-wide theatrical circuit. He was the first American who sent shows step by step from New York to San Francisco the tour of which would otherwise have been entirely prohibitive because of the expenses involved. Later he formed with the firm Klaw and Erlanger the Theatrical Syndicate. He produced about four hundred plays of such authors as Oscar Wilde, G. B. Shaw, Rostand, Galsworthy, Ibsen, Schiller, and Belasco. The Barrymores, Maude Adams, Otis Skinner performed for him. The last play he put on was Justus Miles Forman's *The Hyphen*. It had a patriotic theme, the dangers of divided allegiance. Its author died together with Frohman in the sinking of the Lusitania. G. B. Shaw called Charles Frohman "the most romantic and adventurous man of my acquaintance." As a business man he was famous for never writing a contract, but always sticking to his word.

He was associated for some time with his brothers, Gustave and Daniel Frohman. The latter was largely responsible for the production of American plays at a period when it had been the customary thing to show only foreign products to the American theatregoer. In later years he turned to the movies introducing Sarah Bernhardt as *Queen Elizabeth* of the screen, Mary Pickford as *A Good Little Devil* and Lillian Gish as a child actress. He was president of the Actors' Fund of America to his death and a member of the Actors' guilds of the three denominations, the Jewish, the Catholic, and the Episcopal one.

Abraham Lincoln Erlanger made the firm Klaw and Erlanger the backer of most theatrical events from coast to coast between the years 1888 and 1919. As an associate of Charles Frohman he gave to the American theatre its modern nationwide possibilities. Florenz Ziegfeld and David Belasco also were Erlanger's partners at various times.

The Shubert Brothers came to Broadway with the next generation, Lee, Sam S., and Jacob J. Shubert. Lee turned to strict business transactions, and Jacob to the production of musicals. John Shubert, a son of Jacob J., and Milton Shubert, a nephew, are the next in succession.

Edgar B. Selwyn, first an actor, then a partner in the Goldwyn pictures enterprises, became a theatrical producer who made considerable contributions to Broadway introducing Noel Coward, Beatrice Lillie, and such hits as *Gentlemen Prefer Blondes.*

Sam H. Harris brought Mary Pickford as a child actress to Broadway in *The Fatal Wedding* and is responsible for such memorable productions as *Of Mice And Men, The Man Who Came To Dinner,* and *Lady In The Dark.* He was the partner of George M. Cohan for fifteen years.

Frank Harris must be mentioned because of the unique success he had with Thornton Wilder's *Our Town* that was awarded the Pulitzer Prize and became a part of America's dramatic treasures.

Herman E. Shumlin belongs to the most literary-minded

producers of our theatre. He has been responsible for Vicki Baum's *Grand Hotel,* for Lillian Hellman's *Little Foxes* and *Watch on the Rhine,* and for Emlyn Williams' *The Corn Is Green,* both of the latter two being named the best plays of the year by the New York Theatre Critics' Circle. He put on Lillian Hellman's *Children's Hour* in 1934. Shumlin stands for good theatre, for theatre with a mission that makes its audience think about the problems of our time.

It is hardly possible to give a complete picture of the Jewish contribution to Broadway enterprise. Theresa Helburn's and Lawrence Langner's leadership within the Theatre Guild must be mentioned and so must the name of Max Gordon who is one of the most active sponsors of talent among playwrights and actors. Gordon made a fine contribution to the American film when he produced *Abe Lincoln in Illinois.* Other Jews, each one of them leading in a specialized field of Broadway business, are the producer Morris Gest; the star among the impresarios of our time, Sam Hurok; and Billy Rose who has given the *Diamond Horseshoe* to the night life of New York, the tremendous *Carmen Jones,* modern Negro version of Bizet's immortal opera, to the theatre of our time, and the liveliest column to our newspapers.

The motion picture offered an entirely new field to the performer, the technician, and the businessman at the beginning of our century. There were no traditions, no prejudices. The Jews who entered this new field were given the unique opportunity of proving to the world their ability to develop an entire industry, an entire medium of art, and to set up the standards for new world-wide entertainment and for the morals involved. The men who made Hollywood the unique metropolis of the film provided the six continents with a scheme of how to organize their entertainment that is totally without precedent in our history. What all these men did was true American pioneering beyond our own frontiers.

Many of those who were the first to become responsible for the film as the newest important object of our international trading are dead, among them Carl Laemmle and his one time secretary, Irving Thalberg, who paved the way for the production of truly significant films.

Carl Laemmle originally intended to open a Five and Ten Cent Store. He invested instead in the Laemmle Film Service which soon supplied three hundred theatres in Chicago. He became the president of the Independent Motion Picture Company and of the Universal Film Manufacturing Company in 1912. He retired in favor of his son, Carl Laemmle Jr., in 1936. Among the innumerable pictures he produced is Erich Maria Remarque's *All's Quiet on the Western Front*, an example of Laemmle's unrelenting efforts to raise the standard of motion pictures above the level of light entertainment.

Marcus Loew rose from operator of penny arcades to top rank in the motion picture industry. He purchased the Metro Pictures in 1919 and was the first producer to spend the sum of $640,000, then considered fabulous, for one single picture which was a product of literature, *The Four Horsemen of the Apocalypse* by Blasco Ibañez. It brought a return of more than four million dollars. Loew opened theatres in all parts of Greater New York from Times Square to Brooklyn and everywhere in the States. In recognition of his contribution to the national wealth by organizing the Gaumont chain the French Government made Marcus Loew a member of the Legion of Honor.

William Fox like Marcus Loew got acquainted with the mechanical possibilities of reproducing art in his own "Automat". Phonographs and slot-machines were suddenly no longer the attraction of the arcades, but those celluloid strips displaying people moving in unnaturally abrupt motions, were. Out of similar beginnings developed the Fox organization with hundreds of theatres and with agencies all over the world. The Fox Company at one time produced one picture a week. Among them were the greatest works of literature, *A Tale of Two Cities* by Charles Dickens, and Victor Hugo's *Les Misérables*. William Fox' belief in the cultural mission of the film expresses itself in a house rule of all his enterprises—any priest or rabbi could obtain any Fox film free of charge for the showing in any church or synagogue. Fox himself gave twenty per cent of his earnings as well as of his working hours to the service of others.

Samuel Goldwyn started as a glove-maker. He joined forces with his brother-in-law, Jesse Lasky, in 1913 as they both were convinced that the film could be turned into a medium of a new dramatic art. Goldwyn's name, originally Goldfish, originates from the fusion of his firm with Edgar Selwyn. To Goldwyn's credit are many great pictures such as *Arrowsmith, Dodsworth, Wuthering Heights*. Will Rogers, Edgar Bergen, Anna Sten, and countless others were made by him.

Louis Burt Mayer came from Russia to Canada as a child and as a young man to this country. A store show, followed by a chain of New England theatres preceded the foundation of the Louis B. Mayer Pictures Corporation. It added production so successfully to the mere distribution that a merger with the Metro and the Samuel Goldwyn firm into the Metro-Goldwyn-Mayer Corporation turned out to become an event of far reaching importance to the international trade. Louis B. Mayer himself took care of the production until 1942, relentlessly pioneering, developing new technical methods, discovering new performers, Luise Rainer, Paul Muni, Robert Montgomery, Robert Taylor, Mickey Rooney, Norma Shearer. She starred in Mayer's first talking picture, *The Trial of Mary Dugan*.

He was a delegate to the Republican Convention in 1928, and a president of the Motion Pictures Producers Association. Many honors have been bestowed on him, the Legion of Honor in France, the Cross of the White Lion in Czechoslovakia, an honorary degree of LL.D. at Rutgers University. President Hoover offered him the ambassadorship to Turkey in 1929.

Jesse L. Lasky had a picturesque start as a cornet player, a gold-digger in Alaska, a manager of a magician. This way he landed in Vaudeville production and eventually as an associate of Samuel Goldwyn and Cecil B. de Mille in the Jesse L. Lasky Feature Players Company, merged with Adolf Zukor's Famous Players in 1927. He was producer for Fox, RKO, and Warner Brothers in later years. Together with Hal B. Wallis he is responsible for *Sergeant York* starring Gary Cooper.

Adolph Zukor like Loew and Fox learned his first steps at the birth place of all mechanized entertainment, the Penny Arcades. But ambitiously he was looking for a way upwards. The success he had with the presentation of Sarah Bernhardt in her motion picture *Queen Elizabeth* strengthened his faith in the eventual union between cinematographic technique and art and encouraged him to turn to production himself. He founded together with Daniel Frohman *The Famous Players Film Company,* subsequently incorporated in the Famous Players-Lasky Corporation, and the Paramount Pictures Corporation. Adolph Zukor was its president until 1935 when he became chairman of the board.

The Warner Brothers, Harry Morris, Albert, Samuel L., and Jack Leonard, have given an outstanding example of the strength that underlies a family enterprise. The first theatre they opened was a little half-broken down place in New Castle, Pa. Jack used to accompany the tremulous events on the screen with a song. The brothers were publicly recognized as pioneers after they had produced the first important propaganda picture in the history of the film, *My Four Years in Germany* after James W. Gerard's book, the bestseller of World War I. They brought to America the best director of that period, Ernst Lubitsch, they introduced to the screen audience John Barrymore in his first full-length picture, they were among the first to abandon the silent picture in favor of the sound when they produced *The Jazz Singer* with Al Jolson, they designed many new types of pictures, the gangster film in documentary fashion, the historical one in form of a screen biography, *The Story of Louis Pasteur, The Life of Emile Zola, Juarez.* They continued to pioneer in the field of patriotic pictures. *Sons of Liberty* received the award of the Motion Picture Academy of Arts and Sciences in 1939; *The Confessions of a Nazi Spy* exposed the activities of the Gestapo in the U. S. of 1941. *Yankee Doodle Dandy, Casablanca, Air Force,* and Joseph E. Davies' *Mission to Moscow,* a production of far-reaching national and international importance, followed closely upon each other.

Albert Warner was a major in the R.O.T.C. during the First World War, Jack L. Warner a Lieutenant Colonel in the U. S. Air Corps during World War II.

Max Fleischer is credited with the first practical device for the production of those animated cartoons which have become the delight of the movie-goers. The Fleischer Studios which originally was founded with a capital of $600, the smallest amount in the history of all Hollywood enterprise, rose to do an annual business of several million dollars. The Fleischer characters became popular all over the world, *Popeye*, the Sailor, and *Betty Boop*. *Gulliver's Travels* was one of the first full-length cartoon features. Fleischer made numerous inventions supplying the production of animated cartoons with indispensable tools.

Max Fleischer served under General Pershing in 1917. His film designed to speed up the training of troops proved to be useful still in 1941. Fleischer applied his animated cartoons to educational films in many other fields. In cooperation with Garrett P. Serviss he produced a seven-reel feature popularizing Albert Einstein's theory of relativity and a similar one on Darwinism when a nation-wide debate of evolution emerged from the Scopes Trial in 1925.

David Oliver Selznik, the president of the production company named after him, is actually the second in succession of a family in the motion pictures. His father, Lewis J. Selznik, was among the early pioneers of the industry, fabulously successful at first, out of luck later on. His son David inherited from him the broad outlook on things, combining artistic sensibility with courageous enterprise. He spent $4,250,000, production costs never heard of before, to screen *Gone With The Wind* in 1939. The gross returns were $32,000,000. He has been regarded ever since as the outstanding box office attraction among the producers.

Joseph Leo Mankiewicz is the son of a professor of education and the brother of Herman Jacob Mankiewicz, writer and stage producer. He collaborated as a script-writer in the filming of numerous pictures and finally turned producer himself with such films as *Fanny, Strange Cargo,* and *The Philadelphia Story* to his credit.

Dore Schary is generally praised as the most powerful personality among a new generation of Hollywood producers. He turned out *Crossfire*, a film from the book by Richard Brooks exposing the destructive influence of discrimination and anti-Semitism. The picture produced at negligible cost was not only an extraordinary propaganda weapon for our American democracy, it became a box office success at the same time. Earlier Schary was awarded the Academy Award for his script for the picture *Boys Town*. Schary himself said in an interview, "Sincere character is the only sure guide to successful film production. I am convinced that any audience prefers to spend money for valuable pictures."

Darryl F. Zanuck is responsible for at least two of such valuable pictures, the film biography of *Woodrow Wilson* and the screen version of Laura Z. Hobson's *Gentlemen's Agreement*.

Felix Jackson, originally Joachimsohn, has become the producer of Deanna Durbin's best pictures. He had his first public success as a playwright in Berlin when Leopold Jessner presented his comedy *Fünf von der Jazzband* at the State Theatre. The film producer Joe Pasternak helped Joachimsohn out of Nazi Germany and made him the script writer of his entire output of pictures. Pasternak took him along to Hollywood where he became Felix Jackson, the author of such films as *Back Street* for Margaret Sullavan and Charles Boyer, *Destry Rides Again* for Marlene Dietrich and Jimmy Stewart, and subsequently producer of the Deanna Durbin pictures for Universal. He wrote for her *Bachelor Mother*. Felix Jackson married Deanna Durbin.

One of the producers who has been most instrumental in establishing early relations between the German pre-Hitler film industry and the American film is Erich Pommer. He emigrated to the United States and went back to Germany to reorganize the German film as an envoy of Washington. One of his best known early productions was *The Congress Dances*.

The names of other German-Jewish film producers and directors are Friedrich Zelnik, Richard Oswald, Richard Eichberg, Fellner and Semmle, Julius Haymann, E. A. Dupont, Joe May, and Seymour Nebenzahl, the latter highly active in Hollywood today.

Ernst Lubitsch was one of the most disarming directors who gave to his pictures what Max Reinhardt gave to his stage productions, glamour combined with realism, wit combined with powerful characterization, continental flavor seasoned with international sophistication. He actually started as an actor at Max Reinhardt's theatre in Berlin. Hollywood immediately fell for Lubitsch. He was with Warner Brothers, MGM, the Famous Players-Lasky Company, and was appointed managing director for Paramount in 1935. Some of his pictures which will return to the screen for many years to come are *Lady Windermere's Fan*, *The Shop Around the Corner*, and *Ninotchka* with Greta Garbo, supported by Felix Bressart and Alexander Granach. Lubitsch was made a Chevalier of the French Legion of Honor.

It will again be quite impossible to present a complete listing. Paul Ludwig Stein who like Ernst Lubitsch received his early training with Max Reinhardt first went to Hollywood and is now directing pictures of the light musical comedy type in the London studios.

William Wyler proved to be an inspiring director, with *Dodsworth*, *Wuthering Heights*, *The Little Foxes*, and *Mrs.*

Miniver. He was a major in the Army Air Force during the war.

The world wide reputation of being dramatic prodigies which Ferenc Molnar established for his compatriots has been confirmed by many a career in the motion picture industry. Sir Alexander Korda has been a film pioneer of genial qualities. His great achievement is the new life he has given to the ailing British film. The pictures he produced were not only great hits within the British empire, each of them figured as number one in the English export revenues. Most famous among his productions are *The Private Life of Henry VIII, The Scarlet Pimpernel,* and *The Four Feathers.* Knighthood has been bestowed on him. When he was still with the film studios of Budapest, Vienna, and Berlin, he was married to the one time film star Maria Korda. His second wife was Merle Oberon.

Another Hungarian, Mike Curtiz, formerly Michael Kertesz, was one of the first to win a scholarship for the study of cinematography back in 1912. He directed films in Budapest, Berlin, Vienna, Copenhagen, and in Stockholm when Greta Garbo was a rising star there. Warner Brothers brought him to Hollywood to replace Ernst Lubitsch in 1927. He has firmly consolidated his reputation as one of the most competent technicians and as a great master of suspense.

Lajos Biro who as a writer excels in stories on Jewish subjects is one of Alexander Korda's favorite script writers. In his domain he is responsible for *The Last Command, The Private Life of Henry VIII, Catherine the Great,* and many other pictures of earlier date.

Ludwig Wechsler has become to the Swiss Film industry what Alexander Korda has been to the British one. Wechsler is the head of the Praesens-Film Gesellschaft in Zürich, a man who injects his humanitarian credo into all the pictures he makes. They have become internationally famous because of their touching sincere humane qualities as much as because of their artistic merits, *The Last Chance, Marie Louise,* and *The Search.*

A few more names of men who served the British film should be mentioned. Isidore Ostrer was the president of Gaumont-British until 1941. Oscar Deutsch organized the Odeon Theatres Ltd. Michael Balcon is responsible for the production of many fine British films, some of them produced by the Ministry of War. Arnold Pressburger who came to England from the studios of Central Europe is the co-producer of the international hit, *Stairway to Heaven.* He made history by producing the first full-length sound film of British make in 1930, *The City of Songs* starring Jan Kiepura.

Jean Benoit-Lévy is the French international authority on motion picture art. Hundreds of educational and professional feature pictures are his work. Being a Jew he was early discriminated against in Germany. The firm who had acquired his famous *La Maternelle* requested his permission to drop the "Lévy" from the announcements of his name. He, however, insisted on complete billing. After all, his family had lived for two hundred years under its full name in France. During the war Benoit-Lévy came to the United States and was a much sought after instructor in his field. He holds the Certificate of Honor of the International Photography and Cinematography Exposition, became a Chevalier of the Legion of Honor, of the Order of Leopold of Belgium, and of the Santé Publique. He was elected president of the French Organization des Artisans d'Art du Cinéma.

There is one Russian film artist of Jewish descent who has widely influenced the art and the technique of the motion pictures, Sergei Michailovitch Eisenstein. Originally a civil engineer, then a theatrical director, he turned to the film attracted by its wider possibilities which he set out to determine in his greatest pictures, *Potemkin, Ten Days That Shook The World,* and *Alexander Nevsky.* He introduced a new powerful star to the screen: the people, the masses.

Eisenstein went to Hollywood in 1931, but nothing came

out of this visit. He made a picture in Mexico released under the title *Thunder Over Mexico*. His American expedition remained a failure. The Soviet Government made him a professor at the State Institute of Cinematography.

Many scenic artists of international reputation are Jews. Leon Bakst (b. Grodno, Russia in 1868, d. Paris in 1924) won the Nobel Prize for his presentation of *Scheherazade*. His designs meant a new approach to theatrical production. They gave beauty to many renowned Paris opera productions.

Lee Simonson, one of the founders of the Theatre Guild, has been leading in the field of stage setting in the United States. He was a director of the International Exhibition of Theatre Art in the Museum of Modern Art in 1934, a director of the National Theatre and Academy, his private collection of costumes is now with the Museum of Costume Art which he founded in New York City. He was the adviser of college theatres at the universities of Wisconsin, Indiana, and at Hunter College. He wrote books and articles, all of them in propagation of the artistic stage setting as an essential part of valuable theatre.

Mordecai Gorelik came to this country from Russia at the age of six. His modern approach to stage designing made him a frequent contributor to the productions of the Theatre Guild and the Group Theatre. He was an instructor in stage craft at the School of the Theatre, scenic director of the American Academy of Dramatic Arts, and was twice awarded a fellowship of the John Simon Guggenheim Foundation. His settings do not merely decorate the stage, they are conceived to express the mood of the dramatis personae and the basic idea of the author.

Jo Mielziner is one of the most successful stage designers of our theatre. His settings to Tennessee Williams' *Glass Menagerie* and Elmer Rice's *Dream Girl* are only two of his Broadway achievements. Two periodicals of the theatrical profession, *Variety* and *Billboard*, voted him the best scenic designer of the season 1945/46. During the war he put his art at the disposal of the U. S. Air Force as a camouflage officer. He has lectured for the theatre seminary of Fordham University.

Ernest Stern's name as a designer will be mentioned whenever theatre enthusiasts pay homage to the scenic beauty of Max Reinhardt's productions.

The guardians of all theatrical standards are the critics. There have been outstanding critics of Jewish faith in every country. Gustave Cohen of Paris was an early authority of the medieval stage, Alessandro d'Ancona wrote the criticism of the Italian theatre.

In our time all Jewish critics saw their mission clearly in the defense of great works of art against stupidity and prejudice.

Georg Brandes (originally Morris Cohen, born Copenhagen in 1842, d. in 1927) was the unique intellectual liaison officer between the Scandinavian countries and the rest of the world. He made Henrik Ibsen and Björnstjerne Björnson the international figures they have become.

In this country Alfred J. Cohen (pseudonym Alan Dale) first established the aesthetic and literary standards in the evaluation of American theatrical events. George Jean Nathan wrote many volumes on the American theatre and was a president of the New York Drama Critics' Circle 1937-1939.

The German theatre of the pre-Hitler era was reviewed by many outstanding Jewish theatre critics. They were Otto Brahm who later became famous as the director of the Deutsche Theater, Arthur Eloesser who was the biographer of Elisabeth Bergner, Monty Jacobs and Alfred Kerr who both died in their London exile. Manfred George, one time Berlin critic, is now reviewing Broadway, and so is Julius Bab. Kurt Pinthus has become lecturer on drama at Columbia University.

Joseph Pulitzer, the great journalist, publisher, and philanthropist who was born in Budapest in 1847 and died in Charleston Harbor, S. C. in 1911 has been beyond his death as instrumental as the critics to the development of the American theatre and to its ever rising standards. The Pulitzer Prize of his foundation is equal to a national honor awarded any worthy playwright.

BIBLIOGRAPHY

Current Biography. New York: H. W. Wilson Company.

EMDEN, PAUL H., *Jews of Britain.* London: Sampson Low, Marston & Co. Ltd.

JACOBS, JOSEPH, *Jewish Contributions to Civilization.* Philadelphia: The Conat Press, 1919.

MERSAND, JOSEPH, *Traditions in American Literature.* New York: The Modern Chapbooks, 1939.

MYERSON, ABRAHAM and GOLDBERG, ISAAC, *The German Jew, His Share in Modern Civilization.* New York: Alfred A. Knopf, 1933.

OSBORNE, SIDNEY, *Germany and the Jews.* London: The Soncino Press, 1939.

Philo-Lexikon, Handbuch des Jüdischen Wissens. Berlin-Amsterdam: Philo Verlag, 1937.

ROTH, CECIL, *The Jewish Contribution to Civilization.* Cincinnati: The Union of American Hebrew Congregations, 1940.

——, *Short History of the Jewish People.* London: East and West Library, 1936.

——, *The Jew as a European.* Presidential Address delivered before the English Jewish Historical Society.

——, *The History of the Jews in Italy.* Philadelphia: The Jewish Publication Society of America, 1946.

——, *A History of the Jews in England.* Oxford: Clarendon Press, 1941.

STERLING, ADA, *The Jew and Civilization.* New York: Aetco Publishing Co., 1924.

The Universal Jewish Encyclopedia, Inc., New York.

ZWEIG, ARNOLD, *Insulted and Exiled.* London: John Miles.

The Jewish Influence on Journalism

By RICHARD VAN DYCK

Is THERE a Jewish influence on journalism? We say decidedly: yes. But before we endeavor to prove our point, we had better agree upon the starting point of our detailed examination and its scope.

Journalism, as we know it today, is a child of the 19th century. To be sure, there were journals and gazettes even before that revolutionary Napoleonic era, which widely opened the gates to all forces and currents that have molded our modern world and influenced its final pattern. However, when we speak of newspapers in the true modern sense of the term, we can only refer to the beginning of the 19th century as the approximate birthdate of modern journalism. In other words, any Jewish influence upon this relatively young brain-child of the human mind—a child which we call the free press—must necessarily be confined to the last hundred years.

So much for the starting point. As for the scope of our investigation, its limits are self-evident. If there is such a thing as Jewish influence on modern journalism, then all we have to do is to ask whether this impact has been a creative and constructive one; of what kind and variety it has been; whether it has put a lasting mark upon the various types of newspaper writing and reporting and, finally, whether Jewish journalists, by their writings, have influenced or helped to shape certain developments and movements in modern history. Therefore, what we have in mind is to show that Jewish newspapermen gave new impulses to the modern press, developed new forms of news communication and even made history in quite a few cases.

We have said before that the press as we know it today came out only after the fall of French emperor Napoleon I. The rise of dailies on the European continent and elsewhere is a natural and logical consequence of the travails of an epoch that strove to initiate an entirely new conception of the relationship between the state and its citizens.

The French revolution and the American revolution had proclaimed the inalienable human rights, among them the freedom to think, speak and write. But under the consulship of Napoleon Bonaparte already and even more so under his imperial regime, the idea of a truly free press had completely vanished. Like any dictator of modern times, the Corsican hated the idea of his subjects having access to a free flow of information and of an unhampered interchange of ideas. By a series of draconic measures the emperor fettered the press of France, shackling at the same time the newspapers of subjugated European countries by a severe censorship.

Typical and most significant of Bonaparte's mental attitude towards the press and its members are certain statements he made in 1809 during a session of the State Council: "A printing plant is an arsenal, which should not be accessible to everyone. Only people who enjoy the confidence of the government should be entitled to publish something." And one year later, the emperor addressed his docile State Council with these unmistakable sentences: "Within the framework of the English constitution, the government must be influenced by public opinion. Thus, you cannot prevent the press from denouncing the Ministers, from blaming and censuring their acts. The disastrous effects of principle are counterbalanced by certain institutions and characteristics of the English people ... In France, where the nation has been gifted with quick understanding, vivid imagination and impressibility, unrestricted freedom of the press would have the most sinister results."

No wonder that in 1810 this man established the most far-reaching censorship one can imagine. Inasmuch as Napoleon's ideal was a one hundred percent controlled press, directed from above, he suppressed or eliminated all but four of the so called "independent" newspapers. These, then, were given instructions to reprint the political editorials of the official "Moniteur". It is true, however, that later on the emperor changed his mind as far as freedom of the press and censorship were concerned. During the ill-fated "100 days", there was no censorship at all, France enjoying full freedom of her press. And the Exile of St. Helena once said: "There are certain institutions—freedom of the press is among them—where the problem is not whether they are good or bad, but whether or not one can resist the current of public opinion. To rob a people of this freedom under a constitutional government, would be an insulting anachronism, an absolute folly!"

The "Decline and Fall of the French Empire" had a wholesome effect upon the upbuilding and organization of the modern press as we understand it. Politically and economically, the new life sought and found its best expression in the newspapers. Dailies and periodicals began to reflect the general political trends of the nations, their main cultural currents and outlooks. England was the first European country to enjoy the privilege of a press free from any kind of censorship. But even this model country of liberty attained the enviable goal not before the last quarter of the 18th century. In any event, the London "Times", founded in 1785, soon became a model for the entire political press of Europe and North America. In France and in the United States, the press developed very much along the same lines. Only Germany lagged far behind. The land of Goethe and Heine had to wait till after the year 1830 until a network of political newspapers, comparable to the press of more progressive and liberal countries, had been built up.

As a result of the ideas of philosophers and writers of the Enlightenment era and the French revolution, the obedient subject of the Ancien régime became a free, full-fledged citizen of the new state. This fact completely changed the noble task of the press. A bourgeoisie had come into existence which now entered the full life of the modern state. Hence, the political education of the nations falling predominantly to the newspaper, became its foremost duty. A modern state, complete with constitution and parliament, with government and political parties and, mainly, with a preconceived notion of all of its citizens participating in its political life cannot function without newspapers. Undeniably, the press of the 19th century has materially contributed to fostering this political development in the days of our grandfathers.

The citizen, however, was not merely a "zoon politicon", but a man who could not escape the necessities of a more and more powerful economic life. In the wake of the industrialization of Europe and the growth of international commerce, nobody could afford not to read and study reports about the economic situation at home and abroad, about the rise and fall of stock exchange quotations, etc. Advertising developed into an indispensable medium for sales and purchases; no merchant, who took his business seriously, could omit studying the advertisements.

Last but not least, the newspaper fulfilled a highly cultural and educational mission. The more the sciences and arts gained momentum in the national life of a people, the more the press served to interpret and popularize them, to disseminate religion and education. This function of teaching the nation, of becoming a permanent source of knowledge and information, could not and did not always measure up to the highest intellectual standards. Under the compelling pressure of writing daily for the day, a certain superficiality was often inevitable. To satisfy the curiosity of the reading masses, it seemed more important at times to hunt for sensations than to build up a solid core of well-checked political, social, cultural and economic facts.

On the whole, however, it must be said that the development of the modern press during the last hundred years was a remarkably sane one. The modern newspapers can be credited with many achievements which do honor to their professional ethics, honesty and efficiency. Jewish journalists in all countries have done their best to help build the tremendous structure of the modern press in all its fascinating grandeur and awe-inspiring world-wide ramifications. That the modern newspapers today are what they are, seems to us, to a not inconsiderable part, due to the toil of many a Jewish newspaper publisher, writer, columnist and reporter. Quod erit demonstrandum.

* * *

I

Looking into the special conditions, which paved the way for a first appearance of Jewish newspaper men in the general press, it takes no great pains to discover the decisive factor, which was responsible for the rather amazing Jewish "invasion" of the newspaper world in the first decades of the 19th century. It was the emancipation of the Jews in most civilized countries.

If it had not been for the generous act of Abbé Grégoire, member of the French convention, who introduced in that revolutionary assembly his famous motion to bestow upon the Jews of France the same political rights and liberties enjoyed by their Gentile fellow-citizens, it is very doubtful whether the world would have seen the significant phenomenon of Jewish journalists at so early a stage. The emancipation which broke down the walls of the ghettos not only physically but spiritually, most timely coincided with the opening of the newspaper profession to Jewish writers; this is clearly confirmed by the testimony of an authority in the field of contemporary Jewish history.

Cecil Roth, Anglo-Jewish historian of great distinction, states in his book "The Jewish Contribution to Civilization": "In the first impetus of their emancipation the Jews flocked to journalism and played a considerable part in that profession. But there was never any distinctively Jewish quality in their contribution; and the new conceptions and ideas which they introduced became common property before long. The rapidity with which the Jews grasped the potentialities of the new instrument is attested by the fact that in the 17th century two Jewish newspapers were established in Amsterdam, one in Spanish and one in Yiddish".

The author, blending these observations with some picturesque and nearly unknown details from the early history of British journalism, informs us further: "Yet for Jews to engage in general journalism was as yet impossible. It is true that Oliver Goldsmith writes of a Jewish journalist in 1771, in his "Haunch of Venison". But this instance, if not jocular, was isolated, and from certain points of view the earliest English journalist in the modern sense was Lewis Goldsmith, a violent pamphleteer of the Napoleonic era".

Here Cecil Roth, like the prompter on the stage of a theatre, gives us the cue. Speaking of "their contribution", the question arises at once what was the specific kind of contribution Jewish journalists made to the modern press. This contribution has many aspects and angles; it cannot be described by a one-or-two-word definition.

What Jewish newspapermen in the course of the 19th century did, is this: they gave the French-born "feuilleton" the final polish of perfection lifting this particular kind of newspaper writing to heights unknown before; they created new forms of political reporting and commenting; they established ingenious new systems of telecommunications and organized large official and private news agencies; they developed new types of daily newspapers with an appeal to millions of readers. Their critical mind was particularly well suited for the introduction of new methods of political analysis and dissection; their articles and editorials influenced the course of history in many ways; it may safely be said that without them the world of today would have a different face.

THE JEWISH INFLUENCE ON JOURNALISM

This seems to us, by no means, an overestimate on Jewish merits; they belie most convincingly the often repeated assertions of foes of the Jewish people that the activities of Jewish newspaper men are not constructive, but destructive, not positive, but negative. Such attacks are just as false and misleading as another old-timer from the arsenal of anti-semitic calumny and vituperation: the fairy-tale of a Jewish controlled press. We shall have ample occasion in the course of our investigation to refute this anti-Jewish legend that, because of human gullibility, apparently never will die out.

The first countries in Europe where Jewish influence on journalism produced remarkable and tangible results were Germany and Austria. This is probably not a mere coincidence. It is a fact that talented Jewish writers in these two countries chose journalism as the best means to express themselves, preferring it on a large scale to the writing of poetry and fiction —even tried to be both, journalists and poets; after their liberation from the darkness and narrowness of the ghetto, it may be explained by the eruptive force of the emancipation which hurled the best Jewish minds into the whirlpool of a political life entirely new to them. We must not forget that this was the first era of political liberalism when Jews had their first real social contacts with their Christian surroundings, when in Berlin, for instance highly refined and educated Jewesses like Henriette Herz and Rahel Varnhagen von Ense (née Levin) received in their Berlin "salons" the flower of Christian society and intelligentsia.

Germany—and to a lesser degree Austria—was then a hot-house of progressive ideas, of new philosophies such as the systems of Fichte, Schelling and Hegel, of new literary movements such as Romanticism. In these stirring years of the early 19th century, when the German press was about to grow into a press of opinion, Jewish talents cheerfully plunged into this new world of newspapers.

Their restless spirit was not satisfied with merely following the established rut of newspaper writing-technique. They longed for something new and they found it. As we have pointed out before, it was Jewish journalists who brought to perfection a type of newspaper article "sui generis": the "feuilleton", that first came to life in France.

How are we to describe this strange thing, the feuilleton, a species utterly unknown to the Anglo-Saxon press and its readers? First and foremost, the feuilleton is a work of art, belonging as such essentially to literature. When we say that it is a piece of art of the literary type, we mean that it is of a more lasting nature than the common fugitive newspaper articles. Feuilletons written by great Jewish masters of this special art, by Heine and Boerne, by Herzl and Nordau, by Daniel Spitzer and Moritz Saphir, by Ferdinand Kuernberger and Alfred Polgar, to name only a few highlights of German and Austrian feuilleton writing—have, up to this day, not lost anything of their special flavor and charm, of the melody and cadences of their sentences. This is the acid test of any feuilleton written in the past: that we are not bored by it today.

The specialty of the feuilleton is its outspoken subjective character. More than any other writer, the "feuilletonist" tries to show the world exactly as he sees it with his own, individual, eyes. He is not like the scientist, who prefers to disappear behind his work. On the contrary, the "feuilletonist" insists on bringing his individuality into focus, whenever and whatever he may write. Newspaper articles of this special kind cannot be created without a penetrating and understanding mind and without a highly developed sense of form.

Reviewing the beginnings of modern political and literary journalism in the period just described, we see two towering figures dominating the scene in Germany. They are two men of genius who belong to literature no less than journalism: Heinrich Heine and Ludwig Boerne. One is a poet of world fame, the other not so much a "darling of the muses" than a "sweetheart of liberty"; both widely differing in character and style, but resembling each other as citizens of the world and yet fervent German patriots.

If there were any doubts about whether or not the writings of outstanding journalists are to be considered as pieces of literature, Heine and Boerne must do away with them. Today even the most stubborn historian of literature will no longer deny that Heine's and Boerne's purely journalistic work is definitely not to be classified as minor writing. There is today a general consent to the contrary. From a retrospective point of view, the political and cultural opinions and outlooks expounded by these two Jewish writers of genius in their newspaper reporting, seem just as valid today as they were when put to paper. More than that, they sometimes reveal a prophetic vision, a sharpness of analytic power, an awareness of things to come which are really admirable. Thumb whatever page you may in Heine's "Reisebilder", "Franzoesische Zustaende", "Lutetia", or in Boerne's "Pariser Briefe", you will immediately feel: this is journalism at its best.

And they are certainly among the highlights of European "Feuilletonism". In a sense, we may even safely say that Heinrich Heine and Ludwig Boerne are, so to speak, fathers of the German "feuilleton". Banned from their fatherland and forced to live in exile abroad, both made their home in Paris, which, then, was the spiritual capital of the world. Here in the "city of lights", Heine the poet and Boerne the political moralist, discovered the fragrant flower called "feuilleton" in the garden of French journalism. They took the seeds, watered them and cultivated them until a plant of their own breeding grew out of the foreign soil. Then they set out to transplant the product of their gardening to Germany.

However, the results were not identical in Heine's and Boerne's journalistic writings. They could not be identical. For the psychological ground in both writers was fertilized by very different chemicals. We shall have to make this clear. Heinrich Heine was not made to become a political martyr.

Nor could he ever be integrated into the rank and file of any political movement. He constantly vacillated between extreme poles and, worse than that, he lacked in faith; faith in a religious or political dogma, faith in mankind and in his own self.

Therefore, Heine was never so strongly possessed by political ideas as Boerne was, taking, however, a deep interest in social problems. This easily explains why he became so enthusiastic about the doctrines of the Count Saint-Simon, French philosopher, who was a forerunner of modern Socialism. How great the impact of Saint-Simonism on Heine was, is proven by many a passage in the political "feuilletons" published later on under the collective title of "Lutetia". They are still the best mirror of that epoch—and the most stirring reflection of French history a hundred years ago.

It is futile to describe the power and brilliance of Heine's prose, the lucidity and elegance of his style: let him speak for himself. The following is a short excerpt of one of Heine's articles from "Franzoesische Zustaende" (French conditions). Commenting on Prussia's perfidy against the Polish insurgents of 1830, Heine says:

"... I watched with anxiety this Prussian eagle, and while others boasted that he looked so boldly at the sun, I was all the more observant of his claws. I did not trust this Prussian, this tall and stilted, white-gaitered hero with a big belly, a broad mouth, and a corporal's cane, which he dipped in holy water before he laid it on. I disliked this philosophic Christian military despotism, this conglomerate of white-beer, lies and sand. Repulsive, deeply repulsive to me was this Prussia, this stiff, hypocritical Prussia, the Tartuffe among states... Oh this Prussia! how well it understands how to make the utmost of its people—even its revolutionists! For its political comedies it employs assistants of every color. It even puts to use zebras with tri-colored stripes. So it has of late years set on its most fiery demagogues to preaching everywhere that all Germany must become Prussian. Hegel must justify the permanence of servitude as reasonable, and Schleiermacher is compelled to protest against freedom, and advocate Christian submission to the will of superior authority. And it is irritating and infamous, this turning philosophers and theologians to profit, in order to influence the people. They are thus compelled, by treason to God and common sense and reason, to dishonor themselves publicly. How many a noble soul, how much admirable talent has been thereby degraded for worthless aims!..."

This could have been written in our days. Was there ever more intuition, a clearer vision of things to come? In these bitter words of sarcasm Heine anticipated the infamous mental attitude shown by German writers and scholars during the first world war, and he reminds us of the notorious manifest of the 93 German intellectuals who did exactly what Hegel and Schleiermacher had done.

But there is an even more convincing piece of Heine's amazing foresight. Who has ever depicted Hitler's totalitarian Germany in all her ugliness with such cruel sharpness:

"... Should that subduing talisman, the Cross, break, then will come crashing and roaring forth the wild madness of the old champion, the insane berserker rage, of which Northern say and sing. That talisman is brittle, and the day will come when it will pitifully break. The old stone gods will rise from long forgotten ruin, and rub the dust of a thousand years from their eyes, and Thor, leaping to life with his giant hammer, will crush the Gothic cathedrals!...

German thunder is indeed German, and not in a hurry, and it comes rolling slowly onward; but come it will, and when ye hear it crash as naught ever crashed before in the whole history of the world, then know that "der deutsche Donner", our German thunder, has at last hit the mark. At the sound the eagles will fall dead from on high, the lions in remotest deserts in Africa will draw in their tails and creep into their royal caves. There will be played in Germany a drama compared to which the French Revolution will be only an innocent idyl..."

And Heine to warn the world:

"...Let happen in Germany what may...keep your armor on, remain quietly at your posts, weapons in hand...Among the naked gods and goddesses who there (on Olympus) make merry over nectar and ambrosia, you may see one goddess, who, though surrounded by much festivity and gaiety, ever wears a coat of mail and bears helmet on head and spear in hand.

It is the Goddess of Wisdom."

At this point, I would like to take issue with the aforementioned remark of Cecil Roth to the effect that there was "never any distinctively Jewish quality" in the contribution of Jewish journalists of the post-emancipation period. The political writings of Heinrich Heine and Ludwig Boerne clearly testify against Mr. Roth. There are very distinctive Jewish traits in the articles and "feuilletons" of both. Although Heine and Boerne adopted the Christian faith, they never could get rid of their Jewishness, and they confirmed this many times and on many occasions.

Heine's wit, his self-irony, his inclination to rebel against established authorities and dogmatism, his dialectic gifts, his literary egotism—all these are essentially Jewish. They shaped and determined his unique style to a considerable degree. Boerne, too, was deeply imbued with predominantly Jewish qualities, which, consciously or not, penetrated beneath his skin and tinted all his thinking and writing. All his life, he carried with him the memory of the Frankfurt "Judengasse" (Jewish lane), hating it and caressing it at the same time.

While in Heine the poet normally was stronger than the journalist, Ludwig Boerne lived, felt, thought and fought a journalist exclusively. Accordingly, the ways and means of both writers differed in every respect. Heine used to battle for his ideas with the skill of a fencer, handling most elegantly the rapier of his Aristophanic wit. Boerne's was a sacred wrath in the grand style of the biblical prophets, whenever he fought for religion or liberty. And this trait in him was Jewish too. Boerne had the "furor judaicus", although he would never admit it.

Heine and Boerne, these two incomparable leaders of what is called in German literary history "Das junge Deutschland" (Young Germany), were antipodes in almost all issues and problems they were confronted with. Bitterly feuding against each other, their life-long and only intermittently interrupted controversy ended with Heine's most questionable book "Ludwig Boerne", which was a kind of literary execution of the unfortunate victim. However, when you strip this book of its polemical contents, you will find it a fascinating settling of accounts with Heine's enemies in the fields of politics and art and, in this sense, a confession and a credo.

As stated above, Heine practiced journalism only occasionally and mainly to make a living, as the revenues of a poet in exile were rather lean. Boerne, on the other hand, was driven by an inner vocation to embrace journalism. Georg Brandes, Danish literary critic of international reputation—himself a Jew—makes the following statement in his classic standard work "The Main Currents of 19th Century Literature": "He (Boerne) never was able to create a political, poetic, critical or historical work of any sizable scope; he could not write books, only single pages. He was essentially journalistically-minded. The specific kind of Boerne's humour is just based on that".

Brandes is right. While Heine, so he explains in analysing the poet's personality, was "probably the wittiest man who has ever lived, at least the wittiest of modern times", he calls

Boerne "the first journalist in the grand manner appearing in German literature and the one who made the periodical press in Germany a power". In another passage of his work, Brandes, very correctly, characterizes Boerne as an "agitator of the moralist type in the political field". Thus he puts the yardsticks to the demarcation-line between Heine and Boerne: the one a writer and poet of genius in addition to being a newspaper man, the other a great journalist, but nothing else.

Compared with Heine's "Reisebilder", "Franzoesische Zustaende" or "Lutetia", Boerne's "Pariser Briefe" (Letters from Paris) have not stood so well the trial of the years. This, in my opinion, is due to several causes. First to the style; Boerne's is less enduring than Heine's.

The poet-journalist was the true heir of Voltaire, Swift and Sterne, who helped shape his magnificent prose, climaxed in the "Reisebilder" with that "wonderful mixture of French esprit, British spleen, German irony and Jewish wit" (Karpeles). The glory of Boerne's prose faded faster, because the themes discussed in the "Pariser Briefe" are mostly obsolete. Furthermore, we should always bear in mind that Boerne's "Letters from Paris" were not "feuilletons", not newspaper articles in the strict sense of the term, but actual letters written to his friend and confidante, Mrs. Jeanette Wohl-Straus. He wrote them without any thought of having them published and only later, upon the request of Madame Wohl, gave his consent to their publication.

Boerne's style was influenced by Jean Paul (Jean Paul Richter), a German writer, who is today almost forgotten. Like Johann Gottfried von Herder, he preached fraternal love among all mankind. His was a long-winded, tortuous style, rich in flowery language and abounding in imagery and parables. Boerne's predilection for word images evidently stems from Jean Paul, all changes and adaptations notwithstanding.

A second reason for the dwindling of Boerne's impact is his often baffling "naiveté". It speaks for his spiritual honesty that he allowed his letters to be published exactly as he had written them, without any editing or corrections. This did much harm to his fame, for there were numerous passages categorically refuted by later events. Thus, the trust in Boerne's political prophesies and judgment was thoroughly shaken. Sometimes the contrast between what he had predicted and what actually happened was so abysmal, that the effect was almost comical.

Yet, as a whole, the "Letters from Paris" still are one of the masterpieces of political journalism; they reveal a man with sharp eyes, with unusual sarcastic wit and humor and, at times, with an astounding gift for seeing future developments. In short, while their author was a political idealist and a faithful follower of liberty, he lacked in statesmanship and political insight. Whatever we may think of Ludwig Boerne today, one thing is certain: his satire and humor appealed tremendously to the German readers of his time and his brilliant criticisms had a deep influence on European thinking.

* * *

II

Once Heine and Boerne had set the pattern for the art of the "feuilletonist", this new category of newspaper writing found numerous followers all over Europe, particularly in Austria. In Vienna, there arose a whole school of feuilleton-writing, which culminated in a galaxy of real masters of the art.

In this long line we find the names of men who not only knew how to write a perfect feuilleton in the Heine vein, but also wrote their names into the annals of history—such as Theodor Herzl and Max Nordau. Most representative of the Viennese species of feuilleton seem to us writers like Daniel Spitzer, Moritz G. Saphir, Theodor Herzl, Max Nordau, Alfred Polgar. Many other names (Felix Salten, Raoul Auernheimer, etc.) could be added. Each writer on this list may be looked at as a prototype of the highly specialized Vienna school of feuilletonism.

[637]

Take for instance Daniel Spitzer whose collected articles constitute a classic of 19th Century journalism. His famous "Wiener Spaziergaenge" (Viennese Promenades) are documents of an epoch. They portray the Vienna of young Emperor Francis Joseph I far better than any lengthy description of a historian could. Spitzer was a master of what is classified as "Genre-Malerei" in German painting. Painters of this kind choose their subjects from every-day life: a drinking bout; a street vendor peddling his merchandise; a barefooted urchin begging at the door of a farmer's house; a village parson walking in his blossoming orchard; lovers sitting on a bench in a park—these are favorites of a "genre-maler". And this is exactly what Daniel Spitzer has done with words. With words he painted the everyday-life of the Viennese. He told, in charming pictures, how the citizen of the Austrian capital felt, what he thought, how he lived. The joys and sorrows of the Viennese of that era are rendered with the precision of a camera. And no one has ever sketched the famous high-spots of the Viennese landscape, the Prater, the Kahlenberg, the Semmering, more glowingly than Daniel Spitzer. This Jewish feuilletonist has truly been one of the most faithful and most loving chroniclers the metropolis on the banks of the "Blue Danube" has ever had. Spitzer's "Wiener Spaziergaenge" up to this day still outrank scores of later books about Vienna. Literary connoisseurs know that his journalistic craftsmanship has preserved the very essence of life in Vienna during the 19th Century, its perfume, its atmosphere, its color, to the delight even of the most exacting reader.

Hungarian-born Moritz Gottlieb Saphir might not have Spitzer's talent for realistic observation, but he had something else instead: a satirical and humorous vein that made him a kind of Austrian Mark Twain. However, a comparison between the laughing American sage and the Austrian-Jewish jester is not possible, if only for the very decisive reason that Mark Twain's humour has all the qualities of immortality, whereas Saphir's satire was of a more transitory type. Moritz

Saphir, who founded newspapers in Vienna, Berlin and Munich, attained literary fame and material success from 1837 on. In that year, he published "Der Humorist" (the humourist), a satirical paper, in Vienna. Within a few years, this publication became to Central Europe what, let us say, "Punch" was to Great Britain. In Germany, Austria, Switzerland, Bohemia, Luxembourg, Alsace, in the entire orbit of German-speaking peoples, each issue of Saphir's paper was impatiently waited for and read with chuckles. Saphir was a man of stunning productivity. His complete works were published in 26 volumes in 1886. As a whole, this bulky "oeuvre" has greatly lost its spell upon posterity. What remains, what still may amuse are Saphir's extremely witty puns, his "bon mots" which became popular everywhere, while his sharp polemics made him far less popular. It might be worthwhile to select from Saphir's innumerable feuilletons and articles those, which show his journalistic penmanship "sub specie aeternitatis". For quite a few of them bear that distinctive mark, adding Saphir's name to the honor roll of European journalism.

We have mentioned before that men like Theodor Herzl and Max Nordau—the former to become the father of political Zionism, the latter his first lieutenant—started their journalistic careers as typical feuilletonists. And we may add that they rose to stardom in Austrian journalism, not only as recognized masters of this art, but also as political reporters.

It is significant that an outstanding Swiss scholar and literary historian, Dr. Jonas Fraenkel, professor of the University of Bern, devoted a detailed essay to Herzl's "Art of Feuilleton-Writing", which appeared in the "Theodor Herzl Jahrbuch" (Vienna 1937). From this, we quote:

"The feuilleton accompanied the life of this man. Although he devoted his life to a high and sacred purpose that led him far beyond the needs of the day, he did not discard feuilleton writing like a cumbersome past. He stuck to it, like a poet who pours his feelings into delicate poems and who always returns to making verse, even after having mastered more comprehensive forms of literary art..."

This remark of the Swiss scholar is very true. The lyrical trend in Herzl's feuilletons can never be overlooked. They are, as Dr. Fraenkel puts it, pure creations of a poet who knows how to express the quiet voices of the soul. Strangely enough, this man, who later on stirred the Jewish masses with the passion and pathos of a visionary and a prophet, lacked pathos and passion in his feuilletons; they always sprang from a poetic mood, never from rational inspiration. In these articles —which were later collected in several volumes—Herzl unfolds his best qualities, the wisdom of a sage who knows about Good and Evil, an undertone of philosophical seriousness even in themes of lighter weight, a grace of expression, which might have been French, and the tender love of a poet for the beauties of nature and human life.

Herzl's intimate friend Max Nordau—both writers came from Budapest but used the German language as their medium of expression—undeniably was one of the greatest journalists of all times. Nordau (his real name was Suedfeld) reached journalism via the medical profession which he never ceased to practice. Herzl was a political thinker, Nordau a philosophical thinker—that makes the radical difference between the two friends, explaining at the same time why Nordau's stature as a journalist frequently overshadowed Herzl's. Nordau's provocative and militant books ("Conventional Lies of Our Civilization", "Paradoxes", "Degeneration")—best-sellers in the eighties and nineties—were heatedly discussed all over the globe. Max Nordau's pen became an international force. The leading newspapers in Europe as well as in North and South America vied in obtaining his collaboration.

THE JEWISH INFLUENCE ON JOURNALISM

In the loving biography his wife and his daughter, Anna and Maxa Nordau, published in 1943, we read this striking passage:

"... In 1916, Nordau wrote a series of articles for the 'New York American' of which several were reprinted in many countries. He foresaw an enormous exodus of Europeans to America from the ever heavier burdens of taxes and the ever more menacing impingements on the most elementary rights. He predicted the stranglehold of American gold on all markets of Europe:

"The disaster of Europe will make the fortune of the United States. Providence seems to have created the New World as a remedy for the crimes and follies of the Old.

"After every historic collapse, tortured creatures turn their eyes toward America, and every European revolution has witnessed an exodus to the new continent ... America is destined to enjoy an era of magnificent prosperity after the war. Those elements which are most energetic and most deeply imbued with the ideal of liberty will preponderate not only in number but in quality."

Even more than this passage, another one illuminates his powerful gift of prophetic insight. On January 1, 1914, in his annual news summary for the "Neue Freie Presse" of Vienna, Max Nordau uttered this anguished and amazing cry:

"Europe offers a hallucinatory spectacle. The very earth is hidden by barracks and parade grounds, millions of men are under arms, on foot, on horse, on bicycle, on motor cars, in aircraft. The sea is crowded with dreadnoughts, submarines, hydroplanes. Everywhere the demands of the state swell like a torrent thundering beyond its bed. Everywhere taxes grow fantastically like the poodle in Faust behind the stove which grew big and fat and sud-

[641]

denly arose like a hippopotamus. Everywhere debts for armaments devour the people's savings and the insane rise in prices causes the life of the common people to be more and more difficult and poverty-pinched. In all countries tumultuous minorities, whom the majorities are too timid to curb, raise sinister cries in favor of cannibalistic ideas of preponderance of power, of conquest, or dividing up the earth, above all, of war...

"Morality has never played much part in international relations. Now reason is banished too. The individual who has kept his simple common sense looks with terror upon this mass delirium. He is tempted to close his eyes to this spectacle of all civilized humanity rushing toward a precipice of ruin, while there is no warning voice to recall it to reason."

This is an excellent sample of the fiery, passionate prose which made Max Nordau a journalist whose voice was heard in every corner of the globe. Whether he wrote on politics, art, literature, science, philosophy, his word had decisive weight and very often practical consequences. When Nordau defended causes which were dear to his heart "because he thought truth was on their side" (Anna and Maxa Nordau) he battled fearlessly, even ruthlessly against institutions, opinions, social phenomena, individuals. Fearlessness is the salient trait of this splendid journalist and thinker whose philosophical work—unjustly forgotten in our time—should be revived. For Max Nordau, even if he may have erred now and then, has much to say to anyone who needs an intrepid guide through the maze of the conventional lies and perverted phenomena of our social body.

In his famous book "Degeneration", he was one of the first to combat the idols of his generation, Tolstoi, Nietzsche and Wagner. Nordau, who wrote for the international press reports datelined Berlin, St. Petersburg, Copenhagen, Stockholm, Paris, London, Rome, Madrid and Iceland, was the first to realize the immense danger that lurked behind Nietzsche's ideal of a "herd of blond beasts of prey, a race of conquerors and masters, with a military organization" (Genealogie der Moral). Adolf Hitler's ghastly Third Reich has confirmed and justified every word Nordau has written. His refutations of Nietzsche's theories from the anthropological, historical, philological and biological points of view have not lost anything of their validity, up to this day.

A great part of "Degeneration" was devoted to the rise of antisemitism. Nordau thought and wrote as a German. Even at a time when he mastered half a dozen other languages, he wrote "We Germans". It was, to quote his biographers, "a cataract on his far-sighted eyes". And they continue:

"The growth of antisemitism proved to be the painful operation which removed that cataract forever. Nordau came to the conclusion that antisemitism had originated in Germany and was a result of the special German nature and conditions... The fierce assault he launched against Richard Wagner was to a great extent the result of the latter's antisemitic inclinations and theories."

It certainly is deeply to be regretted that Max Nordau did not live to see the rise and fall of National Socialism in our days. In him Dr. Joseph Goebbels would have found his master. For Nordau was not only a great writer and journalist, but a great orator as well. Herzl said of him: "Every time I hear our great friend speak, his personality impresses me anew. This extraordinary man masters all forms of linguistic expression, no less amazingly than he commands all the treasures of human knowledge..."

We shall meet Herzl and Nordau again, when taking a look at Jewish journalists who have made history. For the time being, we now bid farewell to Viennese "feuilletonism", introducing its greatest living exponent: Alfred Polgar. His is a prose as beautiful and clear cut as a precious gem. Polgar writes with the same loving care a diamond cutter applies to the facets of the stone he works on.

Alfred Polgar, too, is a philosopher, but not in the sense of the thinkers who built up a "Weltanschauung" of their own. This lovable Viennese writer, whom the Nazis sent into exile and who has made his home in New York, knows the secret of music in words. It was a French statesman, Gambetta, who once coined the phrase: "Les mots sont là pour cacher les pensées" (We have words to hide our thoughts). Alfred Polgar could and would never have said that. He has words to express his innermost thoughts. And he plays the instrument of language so masterfully that he enchants by the magic of his style.

The Polgar style is just as inimitable (and just as untranslatable) as, for instance the style of the Frenchman Chamfort, whom he resembles in more than one respect. Like Chamfort, Polgar possesses the grace and elegance to say even the most daring things, to scoff at human frailties and stupidities in a delightful way. Anyone who reads one of Polgar's short essays, which sparkle of an almost Voltairian irony and contain a great deal of laughing wisdom in the marvelous filigree of their sentences, will immediately feel how much they are tinged by a "latin esprit". If this heir of Austria's finest cultural traditions were not so truly Austrian in every line he writes, one might be tempted to say that only by an "accident of birth" Alfred Polgar did not come into this world on the soil of France.

* * *

III

Of course, these "Big Five" of Viennese journalism do not give the whole picture. They are but a small group among a host of other newspaper writers in Germany and Austria, many of whom had brilliant minds. Let us go back once more to the period of Jewish emancipation in the first half of the 19th century. What do we see? There were many Jewish talents who set out as journalists, only to become powerful politicians. Such a man, for instance, was Gabriel Riesser.

Gabriel Riesser may truly be called the champion of Jewish emancipation (1806-1863). Born in Hamburg, where he also died, he founded, in 1832, his famous review "The Jew", "a periodical for the freedom of religion and conscience". In the stormy year of 1848, the year of revolution all over Europe, he was elected a member of the National Assembly; the deputies of the revolutionary German parliament then in session in St. Paul's at Frankfurt, held their Jewish colleague in such high esteem that they made Riesser twice vice president of the assembly. He also belonged to the historic delegation which offered King Frederick William IV of Prussia the crown of the German emperors. Among the many distinguished orators of the Assembly, Riesser was one of the most illustrious.

Riesser knew how to combine journalism with politics. More than anyone else, he was aware of how much his pen could contribute to building up a political career. Therefore, one year after having started his magazine "The Jew", he joined in 1833 the editorial staff of the "Hamburgische Abendzeitung". As a political newspaper man with a fighting spirit, Riesser always wanted to broaden his political horizon, to deepen his knowledge of foreign affairs and foreign nations. This was the main reason that, in 1856, prompted him to make a trip to North America. Here, in our country, Gabriel Riesser learned what democracy really meant; in speeches and letters, he has stressed many times how deeply his visit to the United States influenced his entire political outlook as a German democrat. In 1860, Riesser was appointed a member of the Hamburg High Court, the first Jew to become a judge in Germany.

The eminent Jewish historian Ismar Elbogen characterizes Gabriel Riesser's historic position in his book "A Century of Jewish Life" as follows:

"Like his contemporary, T. B. Macaulay, he emphasized that whether a man worshipped in a church

[645]

or a synagogue may be decisive for his election as
bishop or rabbi, but not for his value as citizen.
Riesser warned them (the Jews) not to sacrifice
their religious freedom to concessions of a political
nature, because there was no freedom, where freedom of conscience was denied. He admonished his
fellow-Jews to organize themselves and to fight for
their right, to fight under the name of 'Jew', which
he gave to the monthly dedicated to their cause.
Riesser was fascinating in his pathos and brilliant in
his polemic. With irresistible logic he analyzed the
absurdity of the arguments against the emancipation
of the Jews proferred in parliamentary debates, governmental decrees, or political essays of the period."

In Riesser's very comprehensive correspondence with the
leading liberals of his time, we often come across the name
of Johann Jacoby. Like his friend Riesser, he occupies an
outstanding place in the phalanx of German-Jewish publicists who fought in the forefront of liberation.

Johann Jacoby was active as a physician in his native town
of Koenigsberg in East Prussia, where he was born in 1805
and died in 1877. A fellow-citizen of the immortal Immanuel
Kant, he gained his political reputation by a pamphlet published in 1841; it was entitled "Four Questions Answered By
An East Prussian" and called for a constitution.

Over night, it made Jacoby famous all over Germany. It
earned him arrest and imprisonment. When freed he called
again and even stronger for a constitutional monarchy.

Of course, a man made of this stuff was a natural leader
of the revolution of 1848. In the course of this most stirring
event in Germany's history of the 19th century, Johann Jacoby
showed remarkable civic courage. A member of the deputation
which, calling on King Frederick William IV, that romantic
reactionary on Prussia's throne, to ask for the dismissal of
his conservative ministry, Jacoby countered the king's ada-

mant stand with the famous words: "It is the misfortune of kings that they do not want to hear the truth!"

In later years Jacoby, the parliamentarian, fought Prussian Junkers and Prussian militarism with speeches and articles; he did not even spare Bismarck when opposing the annexation of Alsace-Lorraine by the "Iron Chancellor" in 1870. Again they put him in jail. Toward the end of his political activity, Johann Jacoby joined the Social-Democrats and allied himself with the rising labor movement.

In the same category of German-Jewish journalists, who made politics their career, we must not omit two men who played a very influential role in the Bismarckian Reich. They are Eduard Lasker and Ludwig Bamberger.

Lasker, the son of a Jewish merchant, was born in 1829 in Jarotschin in the Prussian province of Posen; he studied law and then lived for some years in England where he became an enthusiastic admirer of British liberalism. On his return to his native Prussia, he embarked on a journalistic career by contributing numerous articles to the influential political review "Deutsche Jahrbuecher" during the years 1861-1864. They won him a wide recognition and assured his election to the Prussian parliament in 1865. One year later, Lasker was one of the co-founders of the national-liberal party. When elected to the Reichstag, he campaigned against the country's speculation rage and bitterly attacked the German railway magnate Strousberg and his aristocratic associates. The collapse of Strousberg's empire was largely due to Lasker's intervention in the Reichstag which aroused greatest admiration on the part of the German people.

The fame of Eduard Lasker did not stop at Germany's boundaries. In 1883, he visited the United States and travelled extensively all over the country. He died unexpectedly in New York on January 5, 1884. On January 9, 1884 the House of Representatives passed a resolution honoring the memory of Eduard Lasker and sent it to the German Chancellor with the request to convey it to the Reichstag. But Bismarck flatly refused. The House resented this as an offense to the American people. According to Ismar Elbogen, Bismarck had a hard time placating the irate congressmen; he attempted to settle the incident under a rather flimsy pretext that he considered the wording of the resolution a condemnation of his own political course. "The repeated discussions in the House gave occasion to eulogize Lasker's high idealism and great statesmanship". (Elbogen, loc. cit.)

Mentioning Eduard Lasker is tantamount to linking his name with that of another famous German member of parliament, Ludwig Bamberger. Anybody familiar with the history of the Hohenzollern Reich knows that these two Jewish politicians belong together like Castor and Pollux in Greek mythology. Both were standard bearers of a liberalism which, more often than not, had an anti-Bismarckian touch. Both were not only very clever party-leaders but also brilliant orators, whose speeches sometimes echoed far beyond the frontiers of the empire.

Ludwig Bamberger who, in 1848, fought in the ranks of the German revolutionaries for freedom and unity, had to go into exile when the uprising pitifully failed. The years he spent in the Netherlands, in England and France were fruitful because they taught him an invaluable lesson in economics; later on, as a deputy in the Reichstag, he could exploit to the fullest his experience in these countries as a banker. In Paris, he became one of the managers of the Banque des Pays-Bas, and it was this practical activity which made him, later on, the German parliament's foremost expert of all monetary and currency problems. The creation of a unitary German currency and the structural framework of the Reichsbank as a highly centralized financial body was to a large extent based on the ideas of Ludwig Bamberger.

It goes without saying that Bamberger, as did Lasker, looked to journalism as the best medium to publicize his political and economic opinions and thoughts. When the amnesty granted in 1866 allowed him to return to Germany, Bamberger immediately plunged into politics, first as a member of the national-liberal party, then, after the secession in 1884 of the more progressive elements, in the ranks of the liberal party. In his articles and writings, Bamberger developed with stupendous mastery the pros and cons of his primary theme: *Free Trade*. As long as Bismarck did not deviate too much from his own politico-economic conception, Bamberger staunchly supported the "Iron Chancellor". But when Bismarck turned to tariff protectionism and social insurance, it was too much for Bamberger. The "classical representative of orthodox liberalism and consistent opponent of both Marxism and State Socialism" (Sidney Osborne, Germany and Her Jews, London 1939) simply could not stomach that and the alienation between the two men grew consistently.

Only a few patient research workers or diligent students of Central European journalism in the 19th century, have come across the name of one Joseph Lehmann, who died in 1873 in Berlin. Lehmann was a friend of Heinrich Heine and a business man with international connections. Partner of the highly respected merchant, David Veit of Berlin, he mastered almost all languages of Europe. This linguistic talent brought Lehmann into journalism.

For when the Prussian government set up an official newspaper, the "Preussische Staatszeitung", Lehmann exchanged his desk in the house of David Veit for an oak-paneled office in the presidency of the Prussian cabinet. He directed and edited this official Prussian gazette so skillfully and successfully that grateful King Frederick William IV presented him with the "Magazin fuer die Literatur des Auslandes" (Magazine for foreign literature), a supplement that Lehmann edited for 42 years. The journalistic spokesman for the Prussian government, he was, at the same time, one of the co-founders of the famous "Hochschule fuer die Wissenschaft des Judentums" (Academy for the Science of Judaism).

If Austria had Moritz Gottlieb Saphir, Prussia had David Kalisch. They have an adage in Berlin which says: "A genuine

Berliner is born in Breslau". This is true for David Kalisch,
too. This man, whom all of Germany considered the most
typical representative of Berlin popular wit and humor, was
a Silesian from Breslau and definitely not a native of "Athens-
on-Spree", as the Berliners liked to designate their city. David
Kalisch from Breslau became so much of a Berliner, not only
in the flesh, but in the spirit, that even now he is considered
the father of that biting political satire and mockery every
Berliner has in his blood. This lust for jeering and sneering,
this dry sarcasm and matter-of-fact sense that permeates the
thinking and speech of the Berliners, has made all of Germany fear their quick tongue. The vernacular of the population
of the German capital, incidentally, lends itself marvelously
to aiming hard-hitting blows at a political opponent.

No one can deny that David Kalisch mastered the special
brand of Berlin wit and sarcasm to perfection. So much so,
that he became the incarnation of the authentic spirit of his
adopted city. About the year 1846, he started his journalistic
career in Leipzig. Two years later, he moved to Berlin, where
he founded the satirical weekly "Kladderadatsch", which made
him famous all over Europe. Immediately, this weekly became immensely popular. In a relatively short time Kalisch's
"Kladderadatsch" was the most efficient weapon the democratic elements in Prussia had at their disposal, and even the
victims of his often deadly satire enjoyed it.

Kalisch's humor was, as one of his biographers justly remarks, "artistic enough to captivate his victims. The King of
Prussia impatiently waited for each new issue of the magazine, and the Czar of Russia was said to have learned
Kalisch's political poems by heart". These crowned admirers
of his did of course nothing to save the satirist from going
to jail. Prussian police always had a sharp eye on Kalisch's
alleged offenses against his sovereign and other princes. But
he was not a man to be easily intimidated. Even the great Bismarck was not safe from frequent attacks by "Kladde-

radatsch". Bismarck's answer was prosecution, though he, himself, thought highly of Kalisch as a writer and journalist.

There is still another aspect of David Kalisch's creative faculties. He gave to the German stage a new dramatic form —the popular farce, Berlin style. These plays, rich in buffoonery and brilliant political couplets, have never been surpassed; they are the direct Berlin counterpart to Vienna's Johann Nestroy and his plays. Until the Nazis came to power, Kalisch's farces never disappeared from the stages of the German capital.

The reader who has followed us to this point, might have gained a misleading impression, which we hasten to correct. After what we have said so far, it might look as if Austria's Jewish contribution to 19th Century journalism has been feuilletonistic exclusively, whilst Jewish journalists in Germany were more or less of the political kind. This, however, is not the case. Austria, too, had her ample share of outstanding Jewish publishers and editors of a pronounced political attitude. Such a man, almost forgotten in our days but in his time one of the most influential Austrian journalists, was, for instance, August Ludwig Frankl. (Ritter von Hochwart).

In literary and historical textbooks, he is mostly remembered by his famous poem "Die Universitaet" (The University), which he composed one night while standing watch as a citizen-guard in the stormy year 1848. His verses became the "Marseillaise" of the Viennese; more than a quarter of a million copies were circulated, and his poem has been set to music 27 times. From poetry, Frankl turned to journalism.

Under his inspiring leadership his papers, the "Oesterreichisches Morgenblatt" and later on the "Sonntagsblaetter", which he founded himself, became a first rate political and literary forum. Frankl himself contributed many outstanding literary articles and essays about his friends Grillparzer, Lenau, Hebbel and Raimund, all of them eminent writers. We even venture to say that Frankl's penetrating articles and essays are still readable and a valuable chronicle of German-Austrian history of literature. August Ludwig Frankl's role as a writer is probably almost forgotten today—not forgotten, however, is his record as a Jew and philanthropist.

The Jews of Vienna will always remember him as one of their great leaders. From 1866 to 1882, he was President of the Jewish Community of Vienna, building it up to a widely respected center of European Jewry. His devotion to works of charity determined Emperor Francis Joseph to knight Frankl and to confer upon him the title of Ritter von Hochwart. Yet, Frankl had still another love: Palestine. Safed and Tiberias gave him the freedom of their cities; Jerusalem presented him with the title of "Nasi (prince) of the Holy Land". Just as he took many themes of his poetry from the Bible and the Haggada, he was under the spell of Oriental Palestine which he magnificently described.

There were others like him, Adolf Fischhof, Ignaz Kuranda, Leopold Kompert, Karl Emil Franzos. The two last mentioned are of interest here as gifted writers and journalists, whose entire work was steeped in genuine Jewish feeling and thinking. Leopold Kompert gained reputation by his famous Ghetto stories, the first of which, entitled: "Der Schnorrer", appeared in Frankl's "Sonntagsblaetter" and made the author known all over Germany and Austria. It remains his lasting merit to have introduced Jewish ghetto life into European literature. Karl Emil Franzos was an extremely talented representative of Galician regionalism. He introduced, so to speak, the then Austrian province of Galicia with its colorful and strange Jewish population to the European reader. Through him, Central and Western Europe learned for the first time about the culture and social problems of Eastern Europe's Jewry. Franzos started his journalistic career as an editor for the "Neue Wiener Illustrierte Zeitung". In 1886, he moved to Berlin and made the German capital his permanent domicile up to his death in 1904. In Berlin, he edited the excellent literary journal "Deutsche Dichtung".

THE JEWISH INFLUENCE ON JOURNALISM

Though, among the Jewish writers and journalists of Eastern Europe, Karl Emil Franzos was the only one who identified himself one hundred percent with the German nation, it is a fact that none did more to familiarize Western readers, Jews and non-Jews alike, with life in Jewish Galicia. In addition to many newspaper articles on the subject, he wrote a series of fine novels: "Die Juden von Barnow" (The Jews of Barnow); "Judith Trachtenberg"; "Moschko von Parma"; "Der Pojaz", the latter undoubtedly being his best work. The fame of Franzos rose to international heights, inasmuch as his Jewish novels were translated in more than 15 languages.

All these writers gave new weight to the Jewish impact on journalism in German-speaking countries. Today, they have faded into a past that has not much in common with our exciting present. To most of us they are names without a distinct meaning. However, we have to mention three more journalists, one Austrian, one Bohemian and one German, all born in the last quarter of the 19th century, who are still very much alive, although they have been dead for quite some time; they are: Karl Kraus, Egon Erwin Kisch and Kurt Tucholsky.

Karl Kraus holds a particular position among the Jewish writers of Austria. His beginnings were purely reactionary. In his famous review "Die Fackel" (The Torch), Kraus campaigned bitterly against socialism, liberalism, democracy. He opened the columns of his periodical to an outspoken reactionary, such as Houston Stewart Chamberlain. Widening the front of his attacks, Karl Kraus finally rejected the whole civilization of his time. But he did this with such independence of judgment and criticism and in such a brilliant style of his own, that even the generation of young Viennese Jews was truly captivated by the Pied Piper of modern satire who was Karl Kraus.

It is not easy to convey the extremely personal style of Karl Kraus to any one who does not command German. Cleverly he blended local and personal allusions with brilliant critical remarks and delighted his readers—who belonged to the most discriminating kind of intellectuals—with a combination of pun and pathos. In the eyes of many, Kraus is considered the Jonathan Swift of our times. This, above all, because as a radical in social morals and an inexorable fighter against any kind of injustice, he used the weapon of corrosive satire. With the outbreak of World War I, Karl Kraus changed in many respects. Not only did he abandon his violent anti-liberalism, but he became one of the foremost pacifists. He poured his hatred of war, of Pan-Germanism and militarism into his dramatic pamphlet "Die letzten Tage der Menschheit" (The last days of humanity), realistic portrait of the first World War, in dialogue, which has hardly a parallel in modern writing.

Prague-born Egon Erwin Kisch, like Karl Kraus, is a man of the outgoing 19th century; yet, his writings bear the marks of our own age. As a journalist, he is a man of the 20th century which imbued him with the nervousness, the quick pace, the sensitivity and restlessness so typical of the days we live in. He called himself the "Rushing Reporter", and we know of no better label to describe his characteristic style of writing and reporting.

Indeed, Kisch has created a new type of modern newspaper reporting; it may be added that quite a few writers have tried to imitate him, yet none has equalled him. He was unique in blending amazing personal experiences into a masterly woven story which mostly centered around the oddities of life, or a reportorial scoop. Egon Erwin Kisch, leftist in his political opinions, had an extraordinary gift for running into thrilling adventures or tracking down scurrile types. When he was after a sensational story—such as that of the notorious Austro-Hungarian master-spy, Colonel Redl—he became so involved that he identified himself one hundred percent with the object of his reportorial search, dissecting the latter's innermost feelings like a surgeon the organs of a patient on the operating table.

THE JEWISH INFLUENCE ON JOURNALISM

There is something unusual and new in the approach of Kisch to the manifold subjects which incessantly offered themselves to his eagle-eyed reportorial genius. Whatever material he touched was magically transformed and became glitteringly fascinating. Later on, Kisch collected his newspaper stories and published them in books, which show this master reporter at his best. He lacks nothing: there is shrewd insight, a striking angle, color and brilliance of style (a very personal style), wit and irony and, above all, a warm heart aroused by social or political injustice. Even today, more than twenty years after these stories first appeared, "Der Rasende Reporter" (1924), "Hetzjagd durch die Zeit" (1925), "Zaren, Popen, Bolschewisten" (1927), "Paradies Amerika" (1930), etc., are more thrilling than any fiction could be.

This great Jewish reporter became a victim of Hitler and Nazism. He had to go into exile, first to his native Czechoslovakia, then to Australia. In Perth he was jailed for six months on the charge of having disseminated communist propaganda. In 1939, he came to the United States and finally moved to Mexico City. He died in 1948, a few months after having returned to his native Prague. Mention must also be made that Egon Erwin Kisch edited an anthology entitled: "Klassischer Journalismus" (Classic Journalism), a standard reference book for all students of the art of newspaper writing.

Another victim of Hitler is Kurt Tucholsky, who committed suicide in 1935, in the Swedish town of Goeteborg. When he died by his own hand, Tucholsky had only reached the age of 45 years. He was born in Berlin. That is to say that he inherited the typical Berlin spirit—the "Mutterwitz", the dry sarcasm, the juicy vernacular, the lust for mockery. In this respect, we may call Kurt Tucholsky the only true heir of David Kalisch.

All through his life Tucholsky, who loved to disguise himself under the pseudonyms of Theobald Tiger, Peter Panther, Ignaz Wrobel or Kaspar Hauser—by-lines which have become famous—was a radical pacifist. Siegfried Jacobsohn, founder and chief editor of the "Weltbuehne", (one of Berlin's most progressive and courageous weeklies covering politics, art and theater), invited Tucholsky to contribute to his review. Tucholsky accepted and, throughout Germany, the response to his innumerable articles carried by the "Weltbuehne" was extraordinary. Soon Kurt Tucholsky was one of the most hated and most beloved German journalists. His enemies howled when hit by his well-aimed blows, which were the delight of all the progressive elements in Germany. Tucholsky was about to become Germany's leading political satirist, when Hitler came to power, cutting off a most promising journalistic career. Tucholsky's name was one of the first on Hitler's proscription list; he fled at once, going into exile in Sweden. Evidently, he had not the stamina to face the stark and brutal reality of a Hitlerized Europe; in utter despair, he killed himself—like other Jewish writers, such as Stefan Zweig, Ernst Toller, Walter Hasenclever.

Tucholsky's voluntary death brings into focus the fact that this militant political satirist had much more lyrical sentiment and sensitivity than he ever would have admitted. In the deepest recesses of his soul, Tucholsky concealed the tender feelings of a lover, who idolizes nature, life and life's crowning glory: woman. In the tradition of Heinrich Heine, he wrote two delightful love stories, "Rheinsberg" and "Schloss Gripsholm", which will outlive many of his other writings. However, the journalist in him was stronger than the poet, a fact which was borne out by his travelogues. His "Pyrenaeenbuch" (Book of the Pyrenees), written in 1927, has been unrivalled as a portrait of the French-Spanish border region and its Basque population. Nobody, not even a Frenchman, has ever painted the Catholic pilgrimage to Lourdes and the miracle of Bernadette's grotto in such glowing colors and gripping words as Tucholsky, the Jew.

We now stand at the threshold of the 20th century. Men like Kraus, Kisch and Tucholsky belong to the transition period of Central European journalism. They paved the way to new heights of modern Jewish journalism when eminent Jewish publishers with great initiative—such as Rudolf Mosse, Leopold Ullstein and Leopold Sonnemann—built up their imposing press empires and publishing houses in Germany. They established nationally and internationally reputed dailies, such as the "Frankfurter Zeitung", "Berliner Tageblatt", "Vossische Zeitung", which represented German public opinion at its height and grew into political and cultural media of international radius and reputation. Before and after World War I, outstanding Jewish journalists, such as Theodor Wolff and Georg Bernhard, were, for many years, the most respected spokesmen of a democratic minority in Germany which, although comparatively small, was listened to by the entire nation whenever they raised their voices in matters of foreign politics.

We shall hardly find two men of more different temperament and character than Theodor Wolff and Georg Bernhard. Though antipodes, they were united in their common faith in democracy. Theodor Wolff, editor in chief of the "Berliner Tageblatt" until 1933, was definitely not the militant type of newspaper man. His famous editorials were written with painstaking care and always based on detailed research. His lengthy articles, which enjoyed great popularity and were widely quoted by the domestic and international press, captivated the reader with elegance of style, logic, validity of argument and clear insight into future developments. Still, many readers of Theodor Wolff's editorials considered them somewhat stuffy and pompous pronunciamentos.

The crucial test for Theodor Wolff came when Hitler crushed the Weimar republic and built his Third Reich on its ruins. However, the man, whom most Germans considered *the* spokesman of German Democracy, became silent. Theodor Wolff, to whom thousands and thousands had looked for political guidance throughout decades, never raised his voice against the brutal tyrant. An exile on the French Riviera, he apparently had not the moral strength to stand up and fight for his coreligionists. He, who could and should have been the conscience of tortured humanity, stood aside in European Jewry's direst hour.

This, of course, is a bitter indictment of one of the most highly regarded journalists, but it must be said in all frankness that, at the end of his glorious career, Theodor Wolff failed,—failed as a man and as a journalist. Here was his great chance to take the lead in a crusade against the greatest criminal of all times. He preferred to live in secluded retirement, to remain a mute spectator of the political holocaust developing around him. However, his aloofness did not pay. The ruthless persecutors finally caught up with him. Theodor Wolff was arrested by the Germans when they took over the whole of France. They dragged him through 13 prisons and eventually brought him to Berlin in 1942, where he was allowed to die in a hospital bed instead of under the hands of the executioner.

Unlike him, his colleague Georg Bernhard, once editor-in-chief of Ullstein's "Vossische Zeitung", never hesitated a minute to battle the Nazis as fiercely as he could. Bernhard, like Theodor Wolff, one of the strongest pillars of the short-lived German Republic, had perhaps not the same brilliance of style, but he was a courageous and aggressive fighter, who had no fear of the Nazis. He, too, sought refuge in France; the first thing Bernhard did in Paris was to found a political daily. His "Pariser Tageblatt" (later "Pariser Tageszeitung") was the first anti-Nazi newspaper in the German language which appeared outside the boundaries of the Third Reich. In his Paris Emigré-paper, Georg Bernhard almost single-handedly waged a furious battle against the brown tyranny, warning the French and other democratic governments of forthcoming perils. Too late, and to their great detriment, these governments recognized how right Georg Bernhard had been in his political predictions.

[658]

THE JEWISH INFLUENCE ON JOURNALISM

No wonder that Dr. Joseph Goebbels hated the "Pariser Tageblatt" in general and Georg Bernhard in particular more than anything else and did whatever he could, though unsuccessfully, to snatch it from under his feet. At one time, there were conducted secret negotiations between the Russian-born financial backer of the paper and the German embassy in Paris to rob Bernhard of his dreaded anti-Nazi weapon. Fortunately, the coup failed at the last minute by the vigilant staff of the paper.

It is true that Bernhard did not always write with the scrupulous care and the profound historical knowledge of Theodor Wolff, and it is equally true that he sometimes erred in his political judgment. On the other hand, he had one gift that his rival Wolff lacked: Bernhard was a financial and economic expert of the first order. His once famous financial review "Plutus" was, for a long time, the leading organ of its kind in Germany, enjoying the same authority as the "Economist" in Great Britain. And many times it was suggested that he be appointed Minister of Finance in one of the Weimar coalition cabinets.

These two great Jewish journalists differed fundamentally in still another important point: Theodor Wolff was a typical German-Jewish assimilationist, whereas Georg Bernhard was very Jew-conscious. He worked in Paris for the World Jewish Congress as its economic and political adviser. He never was silent when Jewish rights and interests were at stake. Thus Georg Bernhard through his entire life in exile, was an unflinching and valiant champion of the suffering Jews, a noble defender of Judaism at the peak of Jewry's most tragic disaster.

We cannot leave the Central European scene without mentioning briefly one of the special fields of journalistic activities which have always appealed so strongly to Jewish newspaper writers. We mean art criticism in its broadest sense, embracing music, drama and painting. The last fifty years of

German and Austrian journalism saw the blossoming of creative criticism that fostered arts and artists in an unprecedented manner. Jewish art critics were leading in giving new directions, explaining new trends, promoting new talents.

Music critics like Paul Bekker, Adolf Weismann, Oskar Bie in Germany, Paul Stefan, Ernst Descey, Richard Specht, Julius Korngold in Austria, were heralds of contemporary music. Max Osborn, Fritz Stahl, Adolph Donath, Julius Meier-Graefe, Max Deri and many others initiated the art-loving public into the rather esoteric ways of modern painting and sculpture: into cubism, surrealism, abstractivism. But the richest harvest came from the ceaseless efforts of Jewish drama critics. Men like Alfred Kerr, Siegfried Jacobsohn, Felix Hollaender, Manfred George, Kurt Pinthus, Monty Jacobs, Arthur Eloesser, Julius Bab, immensely helped the German stage build up entirely new techniques of acting, directing, stage setting, and to inspire new authors to search for new dramatic means of expression.

There was a time when the word of Alfred Kerr was almost law in Central and Western Europe as far as the theatrical world was concerned. This extraordinary Jewish drama critic of the "Berliner Tageblatt" not only beautifully and wittily handled the German language, enriching it with many self-coined words and slogans, but he undoubtedly did most, singlehandedly, to bring into international focus the new giants of modern drama. Henrik Ibsen, Bjoernsterne Bjoernson, Gerhard Hauptmann, Arthur Schnitzler, Maxim Gorki, Oscar Wilde, Eugene O'Neill—to name only a few—owe a great deal of their world-wide fame to Alfred Kerr, who spread the gospel of the "new drama" all over Central and Western Europe. Modern drama and modern stage as well as modern acting could hardly have grown up to its present grandeur without the writings of Alfred Kerr, great popularizer of the works of these creators of contemporary drama.

IV

So far, our theme has mostly been Jewish journalism in Central Europe, i.e. in Germany and Austria. The reason which compelled us to devote so much space to Jewish newspapermen writing in German, is the undeniable fact that 19th Century Jewish journalism on a large scale developed first and almost exclusively in Germany and Austria. We have seen that eminent Jewish newspapermen fertilized in many ways the domain of the press. They found new forms of newspaper writing; they perfected feuilletonism to hitherto unknown heights; they developed new techniques of newspaper reporting. But all this, of course, does not mean that such uplifting of Jewish journalism was to be observed in the German speaking countries only.

The following condensed survey will show that most European countries shared more or less in giving newspapermen of Jewish descent a chance to display their special talents and gifts. In England, in France, in Italy, in Russia, even in small countries like Denmark or Sweden, Jewish publishers, writers, editors and reporters proved to their countrymen and to the world at large how much could be expected of their own, particular brand of penmanship.

The Jewish contribution to British journalism seems comparatively greater in the field of publishing newspapers or building up news agencies than actual newspaper writing. Whereas Germany had her Ullsteins, Mosses and Sonnemanns, Great Britain produced even bigger press lords. Men like Ralph D. Blumenfeld, Joseph M. Levy, Paul J. Reuter, Sidney Low and Laurie Magnus were co-builders of a British press empire which became indispensable to the greatness of the British empire as a whole. The career of Ralph David Blumenfeld illustrates best what Jewish initiative and talent did to provide British imperialism with one of its most powerful tools.

Blumenfeld was not a native Briton. An American Jew, he was born in 1864 in Watertown, Wis. He started his journalistic career that was to lead him to the peaks of continental journalism and to make him one of the politically most influential men of his time, at the age of 20. At that time, he was a beginner on the staff of the Chicago Herald.

In 1887, he was assigned to cover Queen Victoria's Golden Jubilee in London. He filled this assignment so well that it established him as a first class reporter. But Blumenfeld's ambitions were not satisfied. He felt his chances in the printing business were even better; so he entered the type-setting business and made a considerable fortune. However, Blumenfeld could not escape the truth of the saying "Once a journalist, always a journalist". When he came back to visit London again, he re-entered journalism as an editor for the "Daily Mail".

In 1904, at the age of forty, Blumenfeld shifted to the editorship of the "Daily Express". Together with the Canadian millionaire Max Aitken, who later bought the "Express", he built up this newspaper's circulation to 2 million. From then on, Ralph D. Blumenfeld was a power in the politics of the British empire. The great of his time, monarchs and statesmen, sought his advice and friendship: Queen Victoria, Bismarck, King Edward VII and many others.

Blumenfeld steadfastly declined to have himself knighted. He preferred to be elected a member of the exclusive Carleton Club to which he was the first Jew to be admitted. In 1932, Blumenfeld visited Palestine. He returned to England as a convert to Zionism. The man who had made the "Daily Express" England's most popular newspaper and a medium of mass appeal never equalled in Europe, lived long enough to see the rise of Hitler. Ralph D. Blumenfeld did not waver; he became one of the most active opponents of antisemitism in the British Isles.

Joseph M. Levy is another British-Jewish publisher of eminence. To him, the "Daily Telegraph" owes its political influence and significance. It is to the merit of this far-sighted Jewish publisher that the "Telegraph" held its own beside the London "Times", and became a highly regarded voice of moderate British toryism all over the British Commonwealth.

Sidney Low and Laurie Magnus, publishers of the "St. James Gazette" and the "Morning Post" respectively, close the circle of prominent Jewish publishers, who helped to make the British press a national institution which is admired and envied all over the world.

Most representative of Anglo-Jewish newspaper writing are Lucien Wolf, Israel Zangwill, Adolphe Oppert-Blowitz, Harold J. Laski. They give a good cross-section of what Anglo-Jewish journalism has achieved in all branches of press activities.

Lucien Wolf, editor of the "Daily Graphic", has a special place in the early history of political Zionism. He will be mostly remembered as the influential spokesman of Anglo-Jewish assimilation who, most vehemently, opposed Theodor Herzl. Even though this negative attitude towards the great mass movement of Jewish redemption, whose significance he did not realize, somewhat obscures Lucien Wolf's record as a writer, he was considered one of the finest and ablest journalists of his time the British press could boast of.

Lucien Wolf's name is almost forgotten today, known mostly to students of Zionist history. But Israel Zangwill's writings are still very much alive. Zangwill, too, played an important role in Herzl's life. He did much to pave the way for the founder of Zionism in England; he attended the first Zionist congress in Basle, but he was not always convinced of the correctness of Herzl's ideas.

The famous author of "Children of the Ghetto" and "King of the Schnorrers" wrote a great deal for American-Jewish publications. His journalistic connection with the "American Hebrew" was a very fruitful one, and Philip Cowen, then publisher of that still existing Jewish review, devotes a whole chapter to Zangwill's work for the "American Hebrew" in his most interesting "Memories of an American Jew". Zangwill himself frequently visited the United States where he had many friends and admirers. It was the eminent American jurist Mayer Sulzberger in Philadelphia, who suggested that Zangwill write "The Children of the Ghetto". Zangwill, son of Lithuanian immigrants to Great Britain, won the English speaking public by his heartwarming tales and stories about a world that was entirely unknown to it. Thus he did what Leopold Kompert and Karl Emil Franzos had done for the German speaking world. But in one respect, at least, he was far superior to these two: in the quality of his typically Jewish humor. Israel Zangwill's humor, though Anglo-Saxon, is very much colored by ancestral hues and tints from Eastern Europe. I might even say that it goes back to those famous Yiddish humorists who, like Mendele Mocher Sforim and Sholom Aleichem, gave birth to the folklore and anecdotes so typical of the mentality of Eastern Jewry in pre-Hitler times. Instead of labeling Zangwill a Jewish Mark Twain, we better call him a kind of English Sholom Aleichem. With his master, he shares many traits: a kind soul, a "naiveté" of the heart, a gift to see men and things through rosy spectacles.

The most outstanding Jewish journalist in Great Britain, in my opinion, was the late Harold J. Laski. The world knows his threefold achievements as one of the leaders of the British Labour Party and its supreme authority in all matters of theory, as a scholar in the field of economics, and as an eminent political writer. Prof. Laski, who lectured quite often at American universities, has won international reputation by his many books and newspaper articles; the latter did a remarkable job in helping the peoples of Britain and the United States to better understand each other.

Laski's writings on British socialism and American democracy show him a clear-sighted political thinker who combines a master intellect with profound analytical ability and a highly refined style. Indeed, Harold Laski presented the cases of evolutionary British Labour socialism and of American democracy so well that, in the eyes of most Europeans and even of many Americans, he was considered one of the classic exponents of both government systems. We may not always agree with Laski's opinions, we may even strongly disagree with him, but we cannot escape the charming and unusual way in which he exposes his often daring theories, and the crystal clear logic of his arguments. As a political journalist, I think, Harold Laski had few rivals.

The name of Mr. Adolphe Oppert-Blowitz does not mean anything to this generation. Not so to our grandfathers, however. They knew this queer and somewhat mysterious member of British journalism to be the most famous of all foreign correspondents. As a matter of fact, Oppert-Blowitz was the first journalist of the type the French call a "correspondent diplomatique". In the days of the memorable Berlin congress of 1878 with Bismarck, Disraeli and Gortshakov as the central figures, Oppert-Blowitz, then correspondent of the London "Times", was on an almost equal footing with all the illustrious European statesmen that had gathered in Berlin to settle the Russo-Turkish peace treaty.

Among those who knew Mr. Oppert-Blowitz, who represented the "Times" in Paris, was Prince Bernhard von Buelow, later Chancellor of the German Kaiser. In the fourth volume of his most entertaining memoirs, Buelow says that he considered Oppert-Blowitz one of the greatest and most versatile journalists he ever met. His real name, we learn from Buelow, was Oppert; to make it sound better, he added the name of his native town in Bohemia. As a young man, Oppert-Blowitz went to France and became tutor in the family of a French merchant in Marseille. Rumor has it, continues Buelow, that the wife of his employer fell in love with the handsome tutor. During an outing in a rowboat in the harbor of Marseille, Blowitz and his lady allegedly threw the sleeping husband overboard and let him drown quietly.

Be that as it may, it is fact that, while in Paris, Mr.

Oppert-Blowitz became acquainted with Prime Minister Thiers. This connection with France's chief of government and other leading French politicians was extremely valuable for, after having been naturalized in France, Oppert-Blowitz became permanent French representative of England's most powerful political daily. Buelow thinks that Thiers himself was responsible for the appointment of Oppert-Blowitz as Paris correspondent of the "Times". The French Premier provided him with most valuable information, in order to influence British public opinion. At the time of the Berlin congress, Oppert-Blowitz enjoyed an internationally recognized position as the dean of European political reporters. Many of his disclosures in his letters to the "Times" such as the text of the Treaty of Berlin, which he forwarded to his paper before it had been signed, created much excitement throughout Europe. To give an idea of how this famous diplomatic correspondent treated the statesmen as his peers, let me quote this significant story Prince Bernhard von Buelow tells in his memoirs:

"Mr. Walter, owner of the 'Times', once came to Paris to check certain denunciations of Oppert-Blowitz which had been planted by Herr von Holstein, notorious 'Gray Eminence' of the Berlin Foreign Office. Mr. Walter decided to investigate on the spot and appeared unexpectedly in Blowitz' Paris home. Without losing countenance, the journalist asked his boss for dinner the following day. When Mr. Walter entered the drawing-room in the swanky apartment of his Paris representative, he found a gathering of all ambassadors accredited with the French government, headed by the papal nuncio. Casually Mr. Oppert-Blowitz asked the nuncio: 'Dear friend, would you graciously act as the host and take the seat opposite of me?' Then the guests sat down for dinner. Mr. Walter found himself between the ambassadors of Great Britain and Germany, Lord Lyons and Prince Chlodwig von

Hohenlohe. Before Mr. Walter left, he asked Oppert-Blowitz to allow him to considerably raise his salary. A man of such social position, so he said, deserves a 'golden setting.' "

An even more striking personality in the British press domain was another Jew, who may rightly claim to be the founder of the largest and most influential telegraph agency in the world. He is Baron Paul Julius von Reuter, originally a commoner whose real name was Israel Josephstal. Baron Reuter, founder of the world-famous Reuter News Agency, was born in Cassel, Germany, in 1821. In Berlin he started the publishing house of Stargard & Reuter. When his business affairs led him to Paris, he came in contact with the newly established Bureau Havas, a French telegraphic agency. Reuter was immediately attracted by this kind of work and became active in the Havas agency. Having learned all the tricks of the trade, he thought it wise to set up an enterprise of his own. In 1849, he founded in Paris a news agency which maintained the fastest pigeon-post service with Brussels and Aix-la-Chapelle.

His further plans, however, were thwarted by the French government. So, upon the advice of German industrialist Werner von Siemens, he went to London in 1851, where he established the Reuter Telegraph Agency. He laid his own cable between England and Cuxhaven in Germany, and in association with the Anglo-American Telegraph Company, laid the cable between America and France in 1865. This pioneer of modern news communication was raised to the baronage by the duke of Saxe-Coburg-Gotha in 1871. Under his direction, the Reuter Agency developed into a globe-circling news service whose dispatches were famous for their reliability and speedy transmission. Baron von Reuter died in 1899 in Nice, France.

Another German Jew, incidentally, became Reuter's most dangerous competitor in the field of international news communication. With the help of private backers, Bernhard Wolff, originally owner and publisher of the "Berliner Bank-Boersen-und-Handelszeitung" and of the "Nationalzeitung", founded the German counterpart of Reuter's: the "Wolff'sches Telegraphen-Bureau". For a time the Wolff Bureau acted as the German branch of Reuter's. But after the Franco-Prussian war of 1870-1871 "W.T.B." became a joint stock company; Bernhard Wolff remaining its director until 1875. It was largely used by the German government and later had official standing.

* * *

Curiously enough, France, homeland of so many great poets, novelists, playwrights, thinkers, scientists, painters, sculptors and musicians, since medieval times cultural and spiritual center of Europe, had not produced a long or impressive line of Jewish journalists. This makes us wonder why, for the French press, though not always comparable to the high moral standards of the press in other countries, at least saw to it that all available talent in the country used the newspapers—more than any other medium—as a forum and an arena for their first public jousts. Looking for eminent Jewish newspaper men in France, we find only one or two dozen who really excelled in the art of newspaper writing.

In France there is general consent that one of the best French journalists of our times was the late Léon Blum. As a leader of masses, as a politician and statesman, we shall meet him later among the Jews, who have made history. At this point of our survey, however, we are only interested in Blum, the writer and journalist.

Léon Blum, born in 1872 in the Saint Denis quarter of Paris, came from Jewish-Alsatian stock. His father, Auguste Blum, was a wealthy wholesaler in the ribbon trade. The house Blum Frères, an extremely prosperous enterprise, exists to this day. Nothing in his surroundings or his social position predestined this young man from a typically Jewish bourgeoisie family to become a future leader of proletarian masses. But the fact that Blum grew up in a purely Jewish atmosphere has left an enduring mark on his soul. One of his biographers made a very true remark to this effect: "His Jewish training has given him some of those gifts which have always been the mark of the Jew. It has acted upon his imagination as a fertilizer, it has sharpened his sympathy with the oppressed, it has quickened his sense of justice—or perhaps it would be more accurate to say: of the injustice of our social world".

Already in High School, young Léon took to writing. Together with his schoolmates André Gide, Pierre Louys, Paul Valéry and others, he edited a review that, today, is a collector's item. Another friend, Philippe Berthelot, later on right-hand man to Aristide Briand, introduced him to Parisian society and into horse-racing. Believe it or not, Léon Blum, one of the most serious-minded and lofty idealists of modern French statesmen, wrote a column on horse-races in the famous "Revue Blanche", for many years, while his friend Tristan Bernard did the other sports notes.

Blum's first contact with the ideas of modern Socialism came through a fellow student of his, Louis Revelin. But after his admission to the "Ecole Normale", France's foremost institution for the training of brilliant minds in the service of the state, Blum became acquainted with Lucien Herr, librarian and teacher at this extraordinary school, under whose influence he began to study seriously the philosophy of Karl Marx. It may well be said that it was Lucien Herr, who made Léon Blum a socialist.

At this time of his student years, Léon Blum literally "crashed the gates" of the editorial sanctum of the "Revue Blanche". This was a monthly review directed by Thadée Natanson; it played a very important, almost revolutionary part in the intellectual life of France at the close of the 19th century. Though not socialistic, it was a vanguard publication. Among its regular contributors were such men as André Gide, Pierre Louys, Marcel Proust, Maurice Barrès, Anatole France, Tristan Bernard, etc.

Blum's first article in the "Revue Blanche" appeared in 1892. It was to be the first of numerous pieces, the most important of which were critical essays on eminent writers like Anatole France, Rudyard Kipling, Paul Bourget, etc. For years, until the disappearance of the "Revue Blanche" in 1903, Blum wrote regular book reviews that made him a kind of literary arbiter in France. Even Anatole France praised the "maturity of his judgment". Léon Blum also contributed other pieces to the "Revue Blanche", sketches, short stories, a sports column, reviews of plays. His fame rose even more when he published his "New Conversations of Goethe with Eckermann". This splendid book, which first appeared in the "Revue Blanche" between 1892 and 1896, is by far the best of all the works of Léon Blum. To grasp fully the boldness and originality of the underlying idea, it suffices to say that Blum projected Goethe into the present and, a century after his death, made him speak of men and events as if he knew them and had been in daily intimate contact with them.

I think the reader will better understand the character of this unique book, if we quote a significant passage:

"I said to Hegel: I will take up the defense of tradition against you. But let us be clear about it. I will not give that word the same meaning as do Barrès, Maurras, Bourget. . . . For me, tradition does not imply standing still; it expresses the continuity of nature and history. Natura non facit saltus, such is the correct formula of tradition. There is, in my view, in the present state of things nothing sacrosanct or eternal. . . . Every institution, every nation, past or present, that impedes the progress of civilization, of justice, must disappear; I admit that readily. But I hold this process is regular, is bound by stable laws. To determine future state of mankind, the philosopher or the politician may legitimately call as well upon the experience of history as upon the pure yield of reason." — "Must one conclude from this reply to Prof. Hegel that you blame revolutions?" — "How should I blame them?" said Goethe. "They are a natural phenomenon. After a certain time the dead oak tree falls to the ground and that, too, is a natural phenomenon."

A second work of Blum's which contains as much food for thought as the "New Conversations of Goethe with Eckermann", is his volume "Du Mariage" (On Marriage). In it Blum strongly revolts against the unequal standing of the sexes and their unequal treatment. The book aroused storms of indignation after its publication, but today it is generally recognized as a defense of women's rights: it is felt that the author's purpose in writing it was not to weaken marriage as an institution but, on the contrary, to strengthen it. A third work of Léon Blum's became of highest importance for French literary history: "Stendhal et le Beylisme" (Stendhal and the Beylism) is no doubt the best and most exhaustive critical study of Stendhal written in our time. No other book has done more to reveal the personality of the great French writer in an entirely new light. Our real knowledge of Henri Beyle (Stendhal) dates from this work of Léon Blum's.

Other works belong more in the purely political domain. But of all of Blum's writings his political editorials in the socialist newspaper "L'Humanité" (today in the hands of the French Communist party) and later in "Le Populaire" did most to bring him close to the working masses of the French people and everywhere else. These articles, little gems of political prose, were widely admired for their clarity, lucidity and brilliant style. One may say that, as a journalist, Léon Blum was the only true heir of his master Jean Jaurès, who taught him not only the art of parliamentarian eloquence but also the style of one who speaks for the people. Léon Blum despised nothing so much than the tricks of cheap demagoguery; the convincing force of his newspaper articles lay in the deep faith of their author, in his belief in mankind, his fiery and yet luminous presentation of ideas and opinions.

In the heydays of France's Third Republic, another Jewish publicist gained general esteem and political influence. Joseph Reinach was an intimate friend and collaborator of Léon Gambetta. The Reinachs were a Jewish family which gave three famous brothers to France: Salomon, Théodore and Joseph. Salomon became a world-famous archaeologist and philologist, Théodore an eminent Jewish historian, while Joseph made politics and journalism his career. Joseph Reinach, brother-in-law of unfortunate Captain Alfred Dreyfus, stood in the forefront of the "Dreyfusards" and largely contributed to proving the innocence of the Jewish officer. During the First World War Joseph Reinach wrote newspaper articles—military and political chronicles—which did much to sustain the morale of the French people in the most critical hours of the French nation. How highly Joseph Reinach was esteemed may be seen from the fact that the republican parties wanted him to run for President of the Republic. But indirectly and without his fault being involved in the Panama Canal scandal, he withdrew his candidature although the voters kept their confidence in him.

The third of the great French-Jewish journalists of the 19th century was Bernard Lazare. His close friend, Poet Charles Péguy, likened Lazare to the Jewish prophets, and really Bernard Lazare had the fire and the vision of the prophets of old. The son of an assimilated Sephardic family all of a sudden awoke to Jewish consciousness, when he came from his native town of Nîmes in Southern France, to Paris. He not only wrote a brilliant two-volume history of antisemitism, analyzing its causes, but also fought most vehemently for the cause of Dreyfus. His pamphlet "Une erreur judiciaire—la vérité sur l'affaire Dreyfus" (An error of justice—the truth about the Dreyfus affair), published in 1896, had almost the same bombshell effect as Émile Zola's open letter "J'Accuse". Clemenceau, Jaurès, Zola himself became more than ever convinced of Dreyfus' innocence, after reading Bernard Lazare's splendid apology.

However, the real importance of Bernard Lazare lies somewhere else. Chronologically almost coinciding with the publication of the writings of Moses Hess and Theodor Herzl, who first revived the idea of Jewish nationhood in our times, Bernard Lazare proclaimed the doctrine of Jewish nationalism. He joined the young Zionist movement as an ardent follower, but as he was a natural "dissenter", he broke away from the movement after some time, just as he did with Socialism. A man like Bernard Lazare could not be regimented into the rank and file of a mass organization. And because Bernard Lazare carried in his soul the burning fire of prophetical vision, he could say to his people: "I shall have the courage to point out the ulcers of my people and to cure them. I have overcome the pride of being a Jew, I know why I am one, and that binds me to the past of my own people, links me to their present, obliges me to serve them, allows me to cry out for all their rights as men." ("Job's Dungheap", Schocken Library, p. 44/45).

These are the "Big Three" of Jewish journalism in France. Of course, there are others, but compared to them, they are minor figures. Still, some well-known French journalists of Jewish faith have made good, their names being familiar to the international reading community: Tristan Bernard, one of the great humorists of our time, creator of jokes and "bon-mots" which have spread around the world; Arthur Meyer, a man of great talent but of no character, a renegade Jew who, as editor of "Le Gaulois", took the side of clericals, antisemites and reactionaries in the thick of the Dreyfus battle; Marcel Hutin, Pierre Lazareff, Géo London, Jacques Kayser— all of them excellent reporters of international standing; Louise Weiss, woman journalist of manifold talents, André Spire, grand old man of Jewish poetry in France and a qualified newspaper man too, André Maurois, world-famous biographer of Disraeli, Shelley, Chateaubriand, and writer of numerous enlightening literary articles; Edmond Fleg, journalist and fiery poet of Hebrew revivalism; the late Aimé Pallière, gentle Catholic priest converted to Judaism and thereafter the flaming defender of the Jewish faith in many books and articles; Bernard Lecache, editor of "Le Droit de Vivre" and valiant champion in the battle against racism.

* * *

Turning to Italy, the output seems even more meager. But if we consider that Italian Jewry amounted only to 50,000 in a total population of 45 million, the Jewish contribution to the Italian press gains more weight and momentum. Perhaps Samuel David Luzzato cannot be called a journalist in the strict meaning of the word. However, this fascinating figure of Italian-Jewish belles-lettres—at the same time an eminent scholar and Hebrew poet—contributed to all leading periodicals of his time in Hebrew, Italian, French or German. Therefore, we may list him as one of the earliest Jewish journalists in Italy.

In Daniele Manin, founder and chief of the short-lived Venetian Republic of 1848, we meet an Italian half-Jew, who played a memorable role as a statesman and journalist in Italian history. Manin, in many respects a forerunner of Garibaldi, and a liberal of the noblest idealism, went into exile to France, after the Austrians crushed his Venetian republic. In Paris, he made a living as a journalist. His articles in the French press did much to arouse vivid sympathies for the Italian cause.

The famous epoch of the "risorgimento" saw the rise of many other talented Jewish-Italian journalists. Cesare Rovighi, later a colonel and aide-de-camp of the king, published and edited the first Jewish review "La Rivista Israelitica". Giuseppe Revere became the successful editor of Mazzini's "Italia del Popolo" and signed, with him, the famous appeal to the French republic. Angiolo Orvieto, together with his brother Adolfo, founded the important Florentine weekly "Il Marzocco". Right hand man of Camillo Cavour, Italy's great unifier and liberator, was Isaac Artom, who widely influenced the movement of the "Risorgimento" by his newspaper "Opinione", directed by Giacomo Dina, who also was Jewish. Artom was one of the first Italian Jews to be appointed a senator of the Italian kingdom and Undersecretary of State for Foreign Affairs.

Greatest of them all is Luigi Luzzatti. This economist of international reputation is generally recognized one of the best ministers of Finance Italy ever had. Luzzatti devoted considerable part of his writings to newspaper articles, which always tended to improve the economic status of the people. It was Luigi Luzzatti, who first and foremost taught the Italian people by articles to understand the advantage of a sound cooperative movement.

What about Jewish-Italian journalists in Mussolini's fascist state? It is a credit to Italian-Jewish journalists that only very, very few of them succumbed to the temptations of Fascism. As a matter of fact, we know only two: Carlo Foa, prominent physiologist, who edited the Fascist review "Gerarchia". This publication became familiar to many newspaper readers inside and outside of Italy because it largely helped to shape the Fascist party's opinions and policies in the earlier period of Italian totalitarianism. The other was a Jewish woman journalist who made headlines all over the world press: Margherita Sarfatti who, for quite some time, was the Egeria of "Il Duce". This very talented journalist belonged to Mussolini's inner circle and was one of his favorites. Signora Sarfatti collaborated with the Duce in his journalistic work and later became his biographer. Margherita Sarfatti's book about the life of Benito Mussolini makes highly entertaining reading. But as a historical source it should be studied with due reservations.

* * *

It may be of surprise that even Czarist Russia, which oppressed the Jews heavily in the days before World War I, produced at least one Jewish journalist of more than local importance.

This man, Ossip Aaronovich Rabinovich, who died in 1869 in Meran, is almost unknown even to well informed students of European journalism. Nevertheless, Rabinovich was a creative power in imperial Russia and as such of much concern to the Czar's authorities. He was responsible for the foundation of the first Jewish journal on Russia's soil. This newspaper, "Razsvyet", in the Russian language, did not exist very long. In the long run, the resistance and the malevolence of the imperial authorities proved unsurmountable obstacles for the survival of "Raszvyet". Nevertheless, Rabinovich's short-lived paper exerted an immense influence upon the Jews of Russia. Not only did Rabinovich and his editorial staff introduce the basic problems of Russian national culture to the masses of Russian Jews, but, beyond that, they inspired the younger generation of Russia's Jews to strive for higher education and seek contact with the culture of Western Europe. This is the great and lasting merit of Rabinovich, which alone should secure him an honorable place in the ranks of Jewish journalism. But he will also be remembered as an excellent story-teller. In the times of the czars, Ossip Aaronovich did more than any other writer to awake sympathies for the Jewish situation in the hearts of Russian Gentiles; his stories about Jewish life in Russia were widely read and admired by both Gentiles and Jews.

One of Poland's most esteemed Jewish journalists is Ignacy Schwarzbart who for years directed the most important newspaper of Lemberg (Lwow). Schwarzbart, during the war years in exile in Great Britain, was a member of the Polish National Council and a close adviser to General Sikorski, chief of the Polish government in exile. Today he lives in the United States and devotes all his activities to Jewish affairs as a member of the Zionist Executive and head of the organizational department of the World Jewish Congress.

Jewish contribution to Soviet Russia's journalism is considerably more important, but it belongs to the chapter of Jewish writers who have made history. That is the proper place to speak of men like Vladimir Jabotinsky, Leon Trotsky, Ilya Ehrenburg, etc.

In the meantime, let us switch from gigantic Russia to tiny Denmark, only to point out that the smallness of a country does not necessarily entail a small-sized intellectual output. Little Denmark offers conclusive proof to the contrary. The country, which produced geniuses like Ludwig Holberg, Adam Oehlenschlaeger, Hans Christian Andersen, Soeren Kierkegaard and Jens Peter Jacobsen gave to the world also a journalist genius: Georg Brandes.

As a literary critic this Dane of Jewish descent has justly won world-wide fame, comparable only to that of his erudite French colleague Charles-Augustin Sainte-Beuve. But Sainte-Beuve, author of the immortal "Causeries du Lundi" (Monday Talks) and of the "Portraits Littéraires" (Literary Portraits), had not the stupendous knowledge typical of Georg Brandes; whereas the latter was at home in all cultures, all literatures, the Frenchman only mastered his own national literature. As historian of modern world literature, the Dane has no rival. Therefore, I think, we should look to Georg Brandes as one of the few high peaks in contemporary Jewish writing.

Reviewing the bulk of Georg Brandes' work, including his numerous newspaper articles, one is truly amazed to see its enormous scope. Brandes indeed is the most universal, the most cosmopolitan, the most progressive mind the 19th century has produced in the special field of literary history and criticism. The realm of Georg Brandes was the world at large. An intellect like his could never be confined within the narrow boundaries of a single country, say his native Denmark.

This universalism of Brandes embraced all kinds of cultural themes. He described the intellectual position of Europe as he saw it, i. e. broken away from the orthodoxy and romanticism of the beginning of the 19th century. Thus, in the years 1872-75, he built the powerful and perennial monument of the "Main Currents of 19th Century Literature"—a work that will outlive all other literary histories on account of its beauty of language and style, the wealth of original ideas, the penetrating analysis of the creative European mind. Here at least, in fascinating sentences, an unusually able writer has committed to paper a diary of a modern intellect.

Beyond that, Georg Brandes was attracted by spiritual grandeur wherever he met it. He gave us literary portraits of Shakespeare, Goethe, Voltaire, Disraeli and Lassalle, which compare favorably with the best of Sainte-Beuve's vignettes. But they surpass them by far in the boldness of their conception, the vivacity of their colors, the artful composition of a great man's life-drama. Stefan Zweig, André Maurois, Emil Ludwig—three Jewish masters of what the French call "biographie romancée" could never have done what they did without the pioneering of Georg Brandes, who laid the groundwork for this new kind of biography-writing. No worthier man, no greater journalist could close our general survey of Jewish journalism in Europe than this genius from Copenhagen, who greatly influenced the shaping of the modern European mind.

We have shown what impulses the European press as a whole was given by many journalists of Jewish descent in the course of the last century; we have demonstrated how the Jewish impact on newspaper publishing and writing was a very constructive one; we have explored the diverse new forms they introduced into the modern press, and the technical improvements they brought to news gathering and news transmitting. All we need to round off our picture, is a short summary of Jewish newspapermen who have made history, and of the Jewish contribution to the press of the United States.

* * *

V

Think of what our modern world would be today if there had never been a Karl Marx—and you have the most conspicuous example of a Jewish journalist who made history! Both socialism and communism consider him the patron saint of organized labor. Indeed, Karl Marx, son of a Jewish lawyer in Trier, Germany, editor of the "Rheinische Zeitung", has been one of the most powerful revolutionaries of all times. Says Sidney Osborne in his book "Germany and her Jews":

"When one considers the many stupendous changes in the political, social and economic worlds of all countries, which were set in motion by the spoken and written thought of this one man, there can be no doubt that his place in history is with other revolutionaries, the greatest the world has known—namely, Moses, Isaiah, Jesus, St. Paul, Maimonides, Spinoza, Albert Einstein—all of them Jews, as it happens."

This is, by no means, an exaggerated evaluation of Marx's historical position. The ideological force of Marxism as represented by the political and economic philosophy of the modern communist state has been demonstrated to the western world in a way we all know too well. Leninism-Stalinism, the revised modern bolshevist version of Marxian theory, seems an intellectual dynamite that is about to split our world in two halves.

We need not retrace here the details of the life and literary works of Karl Marx. They are too well known; suffice it to say that the author of "Das Kapital" reveals himself in his famous newspaper articles which appeared in the "Rheinische Zeitung" and later the "Neue Rheinische Zeitung" as an editorialist, who has the journalist's flair right in his fingertips. His journalistic work cannot be detached and isolated from the political and social effects of his revolutionary activities. Both belong together as history has proven. Socialism, labour parties, trade-unionism, Soviet Russia—they all owe their existence to Karl Marx. Whether or not we like it—the thoughts of this Jewish writer and journalist, who discovered and scientifically described the laws of class struggle, are a domineering power in many parts of the world.

Frequently the name of Ferdinand Lassalle has been linked with that of Karl Marx. This other Jewish star of rising German socialism was a political pamphleteer, an orator of genius, but no journalist. Lassalle hated the press and despised journalists. Therefore, this unusual spokesman of the people, who aroused the masses of German workers and tragically died in a duel over a beautiful woman, never really tried his hand at journalism. As far as I could find out, the entire literature about Ferdinand Lassalle mentions only one single newspaper article he ever wrote. This article, Georg Brandes tells us in his Lassalle biography, appeared on July 19, 1864, in the Berlin "Kreuzzeitung" and asked for compulsory education of the working classes on the largest scale possible. There are still other radical differences between Karl Marx, the journalist, and Ferdinand Lassalle, the agitator and leader of masses. Georg Brandes puts it this way: "Marx always has the whole world before his eyes, Lassalle only Germany or, to be more accurate, Prussia. Marx was an internationalist, Lassalle a nationalist and an open admirer of Bismarck whom he expected to accomplish sweeping social reforms in favor of the working class.

In our days, we saw the miracle of the birth of a Jewish state called Israel. The man who dreamed and planted this miracle fifty years ago, was Theodor Herzl. We have already given him due credit for his achievements in the fields of feuilletonism and newspaper reporting. Here is the place to pay tribute to the great statesman.

On February 14, 1869, a little book entitled "Der Judenstaat—Versuch einer modernen Loesung der Judenfrage" (The Jewish State—Essay on a modern solution of the Jewish question) appeared in Vienna. The first edition of this history-making little book which was published by M. Breitenstein, was limited to 3000 copies. Theodor Herzl knew very well, what he did, when he wrote his immortal message to the Jewish people. For in 1895 he began to write a diary "The Jewish Cause". This unusual work, unique confession of a political visionary, begins with the following sentence: "For a certain time, I have been working on a book of infinite scope. I do not yet know if I shall be able to carry it out. It looks like a powerful dream".

Theodor Herzl, endowed with the infallible instinct of a political genius, saw very clearly the way he had to go in order to reach his goal. At the first Zionist World Congress in Basle he spoke these memorable words: "We want to lay the cornerstone for the house that one day will accommodate the Jewish Nation!" His was an unshakable belief in the feasibility of his plan as expressed in the famous phrases: "If you will it (the Jewish State), it is no myth" and: "The Jews, who want it, will have their state. At long last we shall live as free men on our own soil and die in our own homeland."

We acknowledge to the fullest degree the greatness of Herzl's conception; still, it is a fact that the Viennese journalist built his scheme of a Jewish state along the lines of thinking of an earlier Jewish journalist. It certainly is no minimizing of Herzl's importance to point out that the first Zionist concept of Palestine as the future home of the Jewish people was advocated as early as 1862 by the German-Jewish journalist Moses Hess (1812-1875). Hess was not only one of the co-founders of modern socialism and as such associated with Karl Marx and Friedrich Engels, Lassalle and Bakunin, in his capacity as editor of the "Neue Rheinische Zeitung", but he was just as well the first Zionist theoretician. In his outstanding work "Rome and Jerusalem" he presented the first complete philosophy of Jewish nationalism. And, what is more, unlike Herzl, who at first did not always think of Palestine as the central point for rebuilding Zion, Moses Hess, from the very beginning, fought for the Holy Land as the core of Jewish nationalism.

If in the history of political Zionism Theodor Herzl justly holds first place, second place should go to Max Nordau, Herzl's lieutenant. In November 1895 Herzl came to see Nordau, and read his book "The Jewish State" to him. His first

[681]

words were: "My friend Schiff says that I am crazy!" Nordau listened for days, then at last he rose, and embracing his trembling friend, he said: "If you are crazy, let's be crazy together! You may count on me!" It might well be said that in this very minute the Jewish state was born.

Nordau's intimate friendship with Herzl bore most rewarding fruit as far as the young Zionist movement was concerned. Nordau willingly recognized Herzl's leadership, he was fully satisfied with the role of Herzl's political guide and mentor. As such he rendered historical services to the movement. For Herzl had neither Nordau's practical experience in politics, nor his skill in dealing with people. It was Nordau, who created the term "Jewish National Home", later officially incorporated into the Balfour Declaration. At Herzl's special behest he added the words "legally guaranteed". The term "Zionism", however, had not been coined by Nordau. The real author of this word which today has become part and parcel of the modern political vocabulary, was Nathan Birnbaum, member of the Jewish sport organization "Kadimah" and one of Herzl's first followers.

Max Nordau only once presided at a Zionist World Congress—the seventh, which was held in 1905. It was then—one year after Herzl's premature death—that he eulogized his friend in a commemorative speech which shows how much he subordinated himself to Herzl's genius: "Our people had a Herzl, but Herzl never had a people. That does not depreciate him, but it casts a slur upon us. . . . He straightened the back of a broken people. He gave them hope, he showed them new ways and means. The seed will sprout, and his people will garner the harvest."

We cannot leave the fathers of political Zionism without having mentioned the name of a third eminent journalist, who added to the Zionist movement an activist touch that has culminated, in recent days, in the actions of "Irgun Zvai Leumi". The brilliant Russian-Jewish journalist Vladimir Jabotinsky has his place in Zionist history as the founder of

"Revisionist Zionism". Together with his friend Joseph Trumpeldor, leader of the Russian socialist Zionists, Jabotinsky organized the famous battalions of the Jewish Legion, which, in 1917, fought under the command of British General Allenby and helped him conquer Palestine. After World War I, Jabotinsky found the official leadership of Zionism far too lenient in their reaction to the efforts of the British government to minimize the implications of the Balfour Declaration. Therefore, at a conference in Paris, in 1925, "Revisionism" was born. Jabotinsky became the leader of this militant wing of Zionism. The Revisionists left the original Zionist Organization in 1935 and established in the same year in Vienna their own "New Zionist Organization". After Jabotinsky's death in 1940, Revisionism began to disintegrate. In 1946 the Revisionists returned officially into the fold of the mother organization.

We have already met Léon Blum, the writer and journalist. But Léon Blum, the politician and statesman, is even more striking. As a leader of France's Socialist Party, Blum was not only responsible for drafting the party platform but he also saved the party from certain political decline. By his decisive intervention at the dramatic party convention in Tours (1920), Blum influenced a minority to secede from the old party and build up a newer and stronger one.

One of Léon Blum's biographers has compared him to Franklin D. Roosevelt. The experiments of both men, so he states, are "essentially social attempts to solve without violence vital problems that have arisen out of the decaying system of private capitalism . . . and both are attempted within the framework of free democracy". I think this remark hits the spot. Indeed, the New Deal of Franklin D. Roosevelt may very well be likened to Léon Blum's Popular Front. Both political programs have been attempted "to bring order out of chaos, prosperity out of ruin, content out of deep-seated revolt".

THE HEBREW IMPACT ON WESTERN CIVILIZATION

Although in 1936, when Léon Blum became Prime Minister of France and set up his much-hated and much abused "Front Populaire", the social reforms introduced by his administration had been long overdue, the masses of the French people felt they were at long last on the way to social progress. Vacations with pay, the forty-hour week, collective bargaining, were innovations which seemed almost revolutionary in that citadel of conservative capitalism called France. The great experiment of the Popular Front certainly had many weaknesses but, as a whole, it lifted the standard of living of the French worker just as much as Roosevelt's New Deal did in his country.

Léon Blum's foreign policy was much less praiseworthy than his domestic program. He committed the unpardonable blunder of underestimating Hitler's aggressive plans against France. But when the Nazi invasion engulfed his country and the Third Republic meekly yielded to Marshal Pétain's totalitarianism, Blum's moral strength and true greatness became evident to all, to the French nation as well as to the world. Neither imprisonment in Pétain's jails nor internment in Hitler's infamous concentration camps could break the strong soul of a Léon Blum. His own splendid defense before the court of Riom will be remembered a long time after those, who were his jailers and judges, will have gone to dust and oblivion. Even today, under the Fourth Republic, Léon Blum has been one of the most respected elder statesmen of France, who always had the ear of the nation.

"Here I was in New York City, city of prose and fantasy, of capitalist automatism, its streets a triumph of cubism, its moral philosophy that of the dollar. New York impressed me tremendously because, more than any other city in the world, it is the fullest expression of our modern age. . . ."

This is a quote from the autobiography of a man, who in life and death transcended all normality, who was a unique amalgam of action and abstract intellectualism: Leon Trotsky.

Official historiographers of Soviet Russia have done all they could to make people forget that once the name of Leon Trotsky was second only to that of Lenin, being cited all over the world almost with awe as the synonym of revolutionary heroism. Today, the falsifiers of Russia's great revolution may have succeeded in obliterating Trotsky's part in the historical days that changed the world—but before the incorruptible tribunal of history his achievements are recorded once and for all as deeds of a political and military genius.

No one knew this better than the man, who hated Trotsky most and "liquidated" him by murder. Stalin himself once paid glowing tribute to Trotsky's leadership in the October Revolution of 1917. Believe it or not, the great Stalin, in Nr. 241 of "Pravda", confirmed the official account of Trotsky's role in the following words: "All the work of practical organization of the insurrection was conducted under the immediate leadership of the President of the Petersburg Soviet, Comrade Trotsky. It is possible to declare with certainty that the swift passing of the garrison to the side of the Soviet, and the bold execution of the work of the Military Revolutionary Committee the party owes principally and first of all to Comrade Trotsky."

And did not Vladimir Ilyitch Lenin emphasize many times how much the Russian revolution owed to "Lev Davidovich"? We have a striking testimony in a conversation between Lenin and the writer Maxim Gorki. At that time, rumors of some discord between Lenin and Trotsky came up. Lenin declared to Gorki: "They lie a lot it seems, an awful lot about me and Trotsky!" And then, striking his fist on the table, he exclaimed: "Show me a man, who could organize almost a model army in a single year!"

As builder of the Red Army and as creator of the theory of "Permanent Revolution", Lev Davidovich Trotsky—his real name was Bronstein—had an impact on European destiny comparable only to that of Karl Marx. Undoubtedly, Leon Trotsky was one of the greatest journalists and propagandists of all times. The American writer, Max Eastman, who knew Trotsky intimately, says in his book "Heroes I Have Known":

"There is no doubt of his great place in history. His name will live, with that of Spartacus and the Gracchi, Robespierre and Marat, as a supreme revolutionist, an audacious captain of the masses in revolt. . . . He played, next to Lenin, the major role in founding the Soviet state. And when it was done, he wrote a three-volume history of these events that holds a permanent place in the world's literature."

Another American, Edmund Wilson, states in his book "To the Finland Station. A study in the Writing and Acting of History":

"One finds in his (Trotsky's) writings not only the Marxist analysis of mass behavior but a realistic observation in the tradition of the great writers; and not only a sense of development and form which give dignity to the least of his articles but also a vein of apt imagery, which lends beauty to even his polemics and makes some passages in his books unforgettable."

All in all, we must agree with Max Eastman that Trotsky was one of the few men, who ever wrote history as brilliantly as he made it, but that he finally lost power because he could not wield it. "He could not handle men. He did not live among men. He lived among ideas."

In the Stalinist regime, other Jewish journalists like Ilya Ehrenburg and David Zaslavsky occupy honorable places in the Soviet press. But they have neither the all-persuasive force of Trotsky's writings nor his giant stature as a political leader of the masses.

Maximilian Harden and Walter Rathenau are the two Jews, who in contemporary Germany rose to the pinnacle of political influence and had their part in making German history. Maximilian Harden (Felix Witkowski) became a great power in German politics by the trenchant articles which appeared in his famous periodical "Die Zukunft" (The Future). The older generation of European readers remembers him as a fearless critic of the absolutist government of William II.

When the Kaiser dismissed Bismarck, Maximilian Harden defended the Grand Old Man of Friedrichsruh with a civic courage unheard of in imperial Germany. Harden's fierce attacks on corruption in public life and on infamous conditions at the imperial court, resounded throughout Europe. It was he who exposed the machinations and the disastrous influences of a camarilla of courtiers led by Prince Philip Eulenburg. Harden's sensational revelations about the abnormal disposition of this favorite of the Kaiser led to the downfall of Prince Eulenburg and his elimination from the Berlin court. After World War I, Maximilian Harden was a staunch supporter of the Weimar republic although denouncing many of its weaknesses. Wounds from an attempt to assassinate him compelled Harden to retire from public life. He died in 1927.

It was Harden, too, who introduced in his "Zukunft" a writer, who later became Minister of Foreign Affairs of the German Republic: Walter Rathenau, outstanding economist and industrialist, who published his first essay in 1897 in Harden's review. He was more of a philosopher and an aesthete than a statesman. But when he was called to organize Germany's war economy during the First World War and, later, to direct the foreign affairs of the Weimar Republic, he showed real statesmanship. The treaty of Rapallo, the first to link the Soviet Union to Western Europe, was his work.

Walter Rathenau, we might say, was the archetype of the perfect Jewish assimilationist in Germany, and this is the pivotal point in his life. The inner tragedy of this writer and statesman was his inferiority complex of being a Jew. He strove with all his heart and soul to prove to himself and to others that he was a German and nothing but a German: "I have, and I know of no other blood than German blood, no other stem, no other people. Even if I am driven from my

German soil, I shall remain a German and nothing will be different. . . ." These lines he wrote in his first article "Hear, O Israel!", which Maximilian Harden published in the "Zukunft", in the same year in which Theodor Herzl issued his call for the first Zionist Congress. The charges that this article—an appeal to the German Jews to discard all ethnic characteristics—might foster antisemitism was indirectly confirmed by Rathenau himself. He later withdrew that piece from a collection of his writings; furthermore the Nazis widely used it for propaganda purposes.

Yes, Walter Rathenau all his life suffered from being a Jew, and it made his suffering even more painful that the Germans did not respond to his love calls. On the contrary, to most Germans Rathenau became a symbol of Jewish influence in German politics and industry. The antisemitic propaganda of the Nazis went still further and openly accused him of being the leader of the so called "Elders of Zion", of having worked for the defeat of Germany throughout the war years.

No wonder, therefore, that finally the fierce and venomous attacks against Walter Rathenau were climaxed by murder. Two young nationalist gun-men killed the German Foreign Minister by well-aimed bullets, while he drove in his car through the streets of Berlin's fashionable Grunewald suburb. The shots, which killed Walter Rathenau, also killed the German Republic. Dr. Joseph Goebbels banned and burned Rathenau's books. But more than ever they have preserved their vitality. For their author, though somewhat aloof and esoteric in his approach to the external world, wrote the finest political prose in modern Germany and his writings stood for the best traditions of a noble humanism and universalism. Rathenau, the political thinker, will have to be rediscovered in our days because he may serve as a useful beacon in the bewildering entanglements of our political and social worlds.

VI

So far we have unfolded the panorama of Jewish journalism in Europe. Our remaining task is a presentation of the Jewish contribution to the press of the United States.

Here, at the very beginning, a clear-cut distinction must be made, a dividing line drawn. In the United States we have the phenomenon of a specific Jewish press which consists of its own group of Jewish, or to be more precise, Yiddish journalists; in Europe, on the other hand, all Jewish writers and journalists worked for the general press and wrote in the language of their country. Consequently, we must now survey a two-sided journalism: newspaper people who work for the English written press and those who write for the Yiddish press.

As far as the general American press is concerned, it may positively and definitely be stated that Jewish influence on the newspaper world of the U.S.A. is virtually negligible. Specifically, what I mean is this:

To be sure, there are among the many thousands of America's dailies and periodicals a handful of Jewish-owned publications, some even of great importance such as the "New York Times". Also, we find quite a few American newspapermen and columnists of Jewish faith, who won a nation-wide or even international recognition. However, on the whole, the European record of Jewish journalists cannot be matched in this country. Whatever creative impulse may be discernible in them, they are mostly to be found in the specific field of Yiddish journalism. The Jewish writers of the general press, however excellent and outstanding they may be, have, as a rule, not created new forms, new techniques of newspaper writing. There were no radical innovators among them, no makers of history. They were satisfied with following routine. Therefore, a Jewish journalist working on the staff of a U. S. newspaper is in no way different from his Gentile colleague. In terms of newspaper business, he is "assimilated", although he may be a strictly orthodox Jew.

Such is not the case with the Yiddish journalists in the United States. They have contributed to the American scene something of their own. Their newspapers have a physiognomy that clearly differentiates them from the rest of the U.S. press. They have transplanted something of European journalism and its methods to this country, whereas the Jewish journalists on the staffs of the general nation-wide press have been entirely integrated into the American routine of newspaper-making.

Naturally, this does, by no means, imply that there are no great American-Jewish journalists. As a matter of fact, there are a great many and we shall present their most remarkable types. The first Jewish journalist of significance whom we meet in the United States is also the most colorful of them all: Mordecai Manuel Noah.

This strangely fascinating personality was "a journalist and a diplomat, a judge and a visionary, a lawyer and a prophet. He was a Zionist before the word Zionism was coined" (Paul Masserman and Max Baker, "The Jews Come to America", N.Y. 1932). Born in 1785 in Philadelphia, Mordecai Manuel Noah started his career as a newspaperman in the Pennsylvania Legislature in Harrisburg. Reporting parliamentary sessions was his first experience. Five years later, he studied law in Charleston and edited the "Charleston City Gazette". The good citizens of that South Carolina town were not always pleased with the behavior of this 26 year old firebrand, who "was eager for war with the British, fought duels, killed his opponent in one of them, and enjoyed himself hugely". But they could not deny that this man Noah had not only a lively prose, but utter common sense which made him popular all over the state.

His patriotic speeches and newspaper articles soon attracted wider attention. His ambition to get into active political life was sharpened. One day President Madison offered to

Noah a diplomatic post. He was appointed U.S. Consul to the "Barbary States" of the beys of Algiers and Tunis, with the special assignment to free American prisoners held as slaves by the corsair rulers of the Mediterranean. Noah was successful in this specific task, but meanwhile his enemies undermined the chief executive's confidence in him. Secretary of State James Monroe abruptly dismissed him, saying: "At the time of your appointment as Consul to Tunis it was not known that the religion which you profess would form any obstacle to the exercise of your consular functions". Noah did not take it lying down: he found it incredible that America should betray her high ideals by discriminating against her Jewish citizens. He answered: "I thought as a citizen of the United States I was protected in my religion as well as in my civil rights. My religion was known to the government at the time of my appointment."

Once back in the United States, Mordecai Manuel Noah quickly established a true picture of what he had achieved in Algiers and Tunis. His enemies were silenced and his great services to his country officially recognized. Nevertheless, bitterly disillusioned, he decided to resign from the diplomatic service and to return to journalism.

In 1816 he settled in New York, where he remained for the rest of his life. From then on, Mordecai Noah led a life of hectic activities. The list of his editorships in this busiest period of his journalistic career is just as long as it is impressive. He successively edited the "National Advocate", "New York Enquirer", "Evening Star", "Commercial Advertiser", "Union", "New York Sun", and "Times and Messenger".

Mordecai Noah, journalist and diplomat, was a man of practical thinking, of worldly experience. But there is another Mordecai Noah, who seems even more attractive. This is Noah, the Jewish dreamer and visionary. His is a case of what the modern psychiatrists would call a "split personality". The same man who devoted the best of his abilities to the service of his country and to American public life, kept in the innermost recesses of his soul as his dearest dream Israel's rebirth as a nation and a Jewish state. Thus Noah was the first American Zionist "avant la lettre". If posterity remembers him, it is for this most spectacular aspect of his life.

"We will return to Zion", said Noah as early as 1824, three quarters of a century before the first Zionist Congress in Basle proclaimed the same goal. And immediately he put his dream to action. "He busied himself writing letters to leading rabbis and Jewish leaders all over the world. Some Gentile ministers in the U.S. favored the project. Finally Noah obtained a tract of land on Grand Island near Niagara. Thus 15th of September, 1825, was proclaimed as the great day when the foundation for the new home for the Jews would be laid. There were speeches and music and the boom of cannon. All was in readiness to welcome the thousands who would flock to the settlement. But, alas, no one came. The project had failed. Noah was ridiculed for his Messianic dreams." (Oscar Leonard, "Americans All", N.Y. 1944).

The dream of the Jewish city of Ararat on Grand Island in the Niagara river did not come true, but the Jewish state did, more than one hundred and twenty years later. And one of the first, who had this vision long before Theodor Herzl, was Mordecai Manuel Noah, the Jewish boy from Philadelphia. This makes him unforgettable.

In Emma Lazarus we greet not only America's greatest Jewish poetess but also an extremely gifted newspaper woman. The fact that the author of the immortal stanzas on the pedestal of the Statue of Liberty once contributed to newspapers and periodicals will be news to many, who see in her only the tender lyrical poetess.

Deeply shocked by the Russian pogroms in 1881, Emma Lazarus, who up to then had not shown much enthusiasm for Judaism and the Hebrew language, all of a sudden awoke to pronounced Jewish consciousness. Henceforth, she was no longer content to write beautiful verses and translate Goethe and Heine into masterful English; she took to the pen to defend her persecuted coreligionists. This she did first in the Jewish periodical "The American Hebrew".

Philip Cowen, founder and editor of this still existing review, tells in his most entertaining and instructive "Memories of an American Jew" that in her first article for the "American Hebrew", Emma Lazarus showed her Jewish spirit in her criticism of Longfellow's famous poem: "In the Jewish Cemetery at Newport". The poet says: "And the dead nations never rise again". Emma's answer to this is unmistakable:

"The rapidly increasing influence of the Jews in Europe, the present universal agitation of the Jewish Question hotly discussed in almost every pamphlet, periodical and newspaper of the day, the frightful wave of persecution against the race, sweeping over the whole civilized world, and reaching its height in Russia; the furious zeal with which they are defended and attacked, the suffering, privation and martyrdom in the name of Judaism, prove them to be very warmly and thoroughly alive, and not at all in need of miraculous resuscitation to establish their nationality".

But her journalistic master-piece is the series "An Epistle to the Hebrews". In this sequence of sixteen articles, which Cowen considers "her most fruitful work", Emma Lazarus frankly expresses her views on all the Jewish topics of the day. Herzl's "Judenstaat" had just appeared. The book was thoroughly discussed by her in the "Epistle to the Hebrews". Many years later the series was reprinted by the Zionist Organization for propaganda purposes.

On the other side of the press fence, I mean on the publisher's side, there is a Jewish giant, who built up the most famous and most influential newspaper in the United States. How Adolph S. Ochs, born in 1858, in Chattanooga, came to New York, bought the declining and almost financially bankrupt "New York Times" and, in the short space of 25 years, converted this newspaper into one of the most respected and prosperous papers of the world, belongs to the history of the American press. Details of his amazing career in the newspaper publishing business cannot be told here. But a single figure may illustrate what the genius of Adolph Ochs achieved: when he bought the "Times", the paper had a circulation of only 9000 and a daily deficit of 1000 dollars. Today the "New York Times" can boast of a circulation of 500,000 and of business worth many millions.

Another eminent American newspaper publisher of Jewish descent was Joseph Pulitzer. Editor and publisher of the New York "World", Pulitzer was a born crusader. Whenever this Hungarian immigrant fought for a cause close to his heart he was victorious. A significant example: without Joseph Pulitzer, New York Harbor would never have seen Bartholdi's Statue of Liberty on the pedestal which now carries the goddess with the torch on Bedloe's Island. When Pulitzer's "World" came out with a front page story "The Unfinished Pedestal", money contributions were sent from all parts of the United States in a steady flow. 120,000 Americans contributed 100,000 dollars for the pedestal through Pulitzer's "World". In commemoration of this campaign the United States Postmaster General has honored the Jewish newspaper publisher —a rare distinction—with a special stamp in 1947. The stamp shows the Statue of Liberty together with a characteristic phrase of Pulitzer's: "Our Republic and its press will rise or fall together!" The annual distribution of the Pulitzer Prizes keeps alive the memory of this magnificent newspaper man who bought from Jay Gould a rather dull newspaper and made it the most interesting of all New York papers in his era.

Moses Koenigsberg, another "tycoon" of the American press, was 16 years old when he bought and published the "San Antonio Evening Star". This boy from New Orleans worked his way up through reporting and editing until he entered the field of systematic news gathering. In 1913 he organized the "News Feature Service" and became its general manager. Koenigsberg did so well that he was able to build up a worldwide news service. As general manager and president of "King Features Syndicate" and of "International News Service" he gave the American press one of its finest instruments to provide its readers with reliable and speedily transmitted news from all corners of the globe. In 1927 Moses Koenigsberg was one of the five American delegates to the first international conference of press experts summoned by the League of Nations to Geneva. In 1940 he published his autobiography "King News", a work abundant in details, important for any student of the modern American press and its development.

Mordecai Noah, Emma Lazarus, Adolph Ochs, Joseph Pulitzer—all these are names of a glorious past in American newspaper history. But the present can compare quite well with the past. It is equally plentiful of Jewish personalities who enrich American journalism. We may even claim that never before in the history of the U.S. press were there so many Jewish newspaper men of professional distinction as today. Numerically, they are only a relatively small group, perhaps no more than two or three dozen of them. The position they gained is not due to quantity but to quality. If today Jewish journalists have a say in domestic and foreign policies, in all fields of cultural and social activities, if they have made the nation receptive to their opinions, this can be attributed not so much to their number but far more to the fact that most of them are "syndicated" writers—writers whose articles are simultaneously published in hundreds of newspapers all over the U.S.A.

This holds particularly true in the case of "columnists". The columnist of the type we know here is an American specialty. It is a fact that this kind of journalism had magnetic effects on gifted Jewish newspaper men. Among America's famous columnists of today, there are at least two Jews with a world-wide reputation: Walter Lippmann and Walter

Winchell. Both are very different in their approach, but both are extremely influential in their own way.

Walter Lippmann is a sort of high priest of U.S. Foreign policy. His opinions on external affairs, of what the United States Government should do or not do in its relations to foreign nations weighs often heavily in the deliberations of politicians and government officials. This is so, because Lippmann is an utterly conscientious writer who explores the problems with honesty and detachment. His famous column "Today and Tomorrow" in the "New York Herald Tribune" is syndicated and brings his message to millions of readers who seek and find enlightenment there, a direction based on sound principles, and the product of a first-class mind. It is true that Walter Lippmann's articles are sometimes written in a style resembling that of the scholar than of the journalist. He, therefore, is often jestingly called a "pundit". But the fact remains that, in all matters of foreign politics, Walter Lippmann is generally recognized as America's Delphian oracle. The unique position of this columnist is best indicated by the many honors which were bestowed upon him. The French made him an officer of the Légion d'honneur; he became a member of the National Institute of Arts and Letters and of the American Academy of Arts and Letters. Numerous universities and colleges—to mention only Columbia, Amherst, Dartmouth, etc.—awarded him honorary degrees.

Walter Winchell seems like the antipode of a Walter Lippmann. It was the late Damon Runyon, one of America's most beloved writers and journalists, who gives this flattering evaluation of Broadway's No. 1 columnist: "The importance of Winchell has been underestimated for years by persons who persisted in thinking of him only as a Broadway "gossip columnist" even when he had reached the stature of a fighting journalist addressing a great audience by radio and newspapers. Certainly, his was a powerful voice for his own people and for the democratic way of life. It seems strange that anyone could fail to recognize the true measure of Winchell, yet no man has had more detractors through his fabulous career, which began as a vaudeville performer and subsequently made him one of the highest salaried men in the history of the newspaper business".

The secret of Walter Winchell's tremendous influence on the readers of his column or the listeners of his broadcasts is his absolute fearlessness. He attacks injustices and crimes against humanity wherever he meets them. He was, as Damon Runyon put it, a great "editorial force for the right". Furthermore, what makes his column so attractive to millions, is that queer mixture of journalese and slang, giving his style a very personal touch. In our opinion, there can be no higher recognition than the fact that a Damon Runyon calls Walter Winchell a "great newspaperman and a great American", who has "the courage to shout his convictions from the house tops".

Beside these stars of ink and newsprint, there were or are many others of hardly lesser talent. There was the late Charles Michelson, an old hand in American domestic politics and a power as the unofficial "ghost" of the Democratic Party. It was said of him that he was the author of more important public statements than any other man of his time. Charles Michelson, for years publicity director for the Democratic National Committee, became Franklin D. Roosevelt's press agent in 1932. There was scarcely an important speech delivered in F. D. R.'s various campaigns that Michelson was not supposed to have written. In his amusing book "The Ghost Talks", Michelson ("Old Poison Pen") revealed much of his thrilling political adventures all centering around the White House.

There is David Lawrence, the editor of the outstanding political magazine "United States News and World Report" and one of President Woodrow Wilson's righthand men. At Princeton, for the first time, David Lawrence came in contact with the spiritual father of the defunct League of Nations. He remained with Wilson after the latter went to Washington to assume the presidency. Since 1933 David Lawrence heads the staff of the brilliant "U.S. News"—the magazine which many think the best-informed in this country. Samuel Grafton and Max Lerner won distinction as sharp-minded columnists. The late Simeon Strunsky, who wrote the delightful "Topics of the Times", was the American columnist who came nearest to the European concept of "feuilleton". Arthur Krock of "New York Times" fame is the experienced specialist of the Washington scene.

Ludwig Lewisohn deserves a special place of honor among the leading American writers and journalists of Jewish faith. He excels in each and every domain of literature. Not only is he one of the most scholarly historians of American literature, but a high-ranking novelist too. As a fiction writer he stands out among American authors. As a connoisseur of world literature he has few rivals in this country. Just recently Ludwig Lewisohn enriched our knowledge of Goethe with a highly original portrait of this greatest of all Germans based exclusively on documents, memoirs, letters of the poet and his contemporaries. As a journalist who devotes much of his time to the topics of Jewish cultural life and to the burning questions of the day, he is held in wide esteem by Gentiles and Jews alike.

Adding to these names those of Herbert Bayard Swope, Lester Markel, I. W. Stone, Albert Deutsch, Ben Hecht, Ira Wolfert, Meyer Levin, Benjamin de Casseres, Cyrus L. Sulzberger, Curt L. Heymann, as celebrated members of the working press and mentioning among Jewish publishers of today Arthur Hays Sulzberger (New York Times), Eugene Meyer (Washington Post), Dorothy Schiff (New York Post), we have a pretty good cross-section of Jewish achievements in the general American press.

But when it comes to final conclusions resulting from what we have said so far, we can only state: In this country, Jewish publishers and journalists have helped, to a certain extent, in molding American public opinion. That much is true. But the antisemitic charges that the Jews control the

American press are simply preposterous, in view of the fact that they are only a handful in the vast realm of American newspaper business.

We now turn to the other side of the story of Jewish journalism in the United States. Yiddish journalism in America goes back to the 80's and 90's of the last century. Then the Russian pogroms brought tens of thousands of Jews to America, among them a good deal of talented writers. Immediately a definite need for a Yiddish press arose. "They were homesick, these immigrants; they did not know English; everything was new and fearful to them; they clung to each other; they wanted some explanation of the American scene around them; they wanted to know what was going on in their old homes; they wanted to know how other Jews were getting on; they wanted information on a thousand different topics, and the Yiddish press was started to give them this information." (Masserman and Baker "The Jews Come to America", Chapter XXI, p. 410).

Today the Yiddish press in America is losing ground. Quite a few of the Yiddish newspapers and periodicals have died. The reasons are obvious. The Americanization of the younger Jewish generations has largely reduced the "raison d'être" of a Yiddish press, let alone the other influential factor that the Hebrew language made astonishing progress among Zionists and Zionist youth. Only four Yiddish dailies remain in New York City: "Forward", "Morgen Journal", "Der Tog" (The Day) and "Freiheit" (Liberty). The "Vorwaerts" (Forward) is by far the largest of them all. Once the spokesman of Jewish labor, it is now only mildly socialistic. The "Morgen Journal" has a distinct orthodox and Zionist tint; in American politics it used to lean toward Republican opinions. "Der Tog" is liberal, Zionist and non-partisan in politics. The "Freiheit" is the organ of Jewish communists and strongly anti-Zionist.

Undoubtedly the greatest figure in American Yiddish journalism is Abraham Cahan. Eighty-nine years old, he is the Nestor of the American press at large. A young immigrant from

Lithuania, he became one of the great leaders in American Jewry in the course of half a century. When Cahan took over the "Vorwaerts", things looked pretty gloomy for the paper. Its circulation was barely 6000, its columns were filled with boring abstract economic controversy in a highbrow language. Cahan changed all this. He threw out all the long essays and substituted instead interesting little stories from Lower East Side life as it was. Not only did he modify from scratch the contents of the paper, but also the entire appearance of the "Vorwaerts". He introduced headlines, he employed the make-up of a really American newspaper, in short, he Americanized the Yiddish press. This was the secret of his great success.

Other pioneers of the Yiddish press in America were Jacob Saphirstein, founder of the "Morning Journal", and Herman Bernstein, founder of "Der Tog". Both were remarkable news-paper men who realized that the Jewish masses of the Lower East Side were longing for knowledge and information.

Yiddish journalism has also some curious sidelights. Who knows, for instance, that the man who wrote Israel's national anthem, the "Hatikvah", led the life of a Bohemian in New York? From Haifa, where he had lived with the family of the Anglo-Palestinian romantic, Sir Laurence Oliphant, Naphtali Herz Imber came to the shores of the Hudson. Philip Cowen tells us the amusing detail that Imber left a calling card on his office desk bearing the imprint: "N. H. Imber, the National Hebrew Poet". In the description of Cowen, the poet of the "Hatikvah" had, as journalist, the genius of a vagabond, whom it was difficult "to separate from his bottle". And now we quote Cowen: "I shall never forget a Zionist meeting at Cooper Institute where Imber was thrown out because he was in his cups and had become obstreperous. I had come late to the meeting and he button-holed me outside. As the meeting was about to close and they sang "Hatikvah", he opened the door and leered through the crack and said to those about him: "They may kick me out, but they must sing my song!"

Another amazing character in Yiddish journalism is Abraham Goldfaden. Most people know him only as the father of the Yiddish theatre and the composer of so-called Jewish operettas. However, only few know that Goldfaden worked as a journalist for years. He first published a humorous magazine, later in Czernowitz, in Rumanian Bukowina, the "Bukowiner Israelitisches Volksblatt". Who, of all those who hum in the Yiddish theatres in New York City's Second Avenue the charming tunes of "Bar Kochba" or "Shulamith"— Goldfaden's most popular musicals—would guess that their favorite composer also made good as a very witty Yiddish journalist?

At the end of our Yiddish cavalcade, we place the great Morris Rosenfeld, the genius of Yiddish poetry. Born in Russia, he had been a diamond cutter in Amsterdam and a tailor in the sweatshops of New York. Morris Rosenfeld was the poet of the toiling masses and of the poor. His poetry is a flaming protest against the social conditions of his time. Many of his poems were translated into English by Prof. Leo Wiener of Harvard. But Rosenfeld was also an outstanding journalist. For long years a permanent contributor to the "Forward" with striking stories and "features", Rosenfeld made journalism the basis of his livelihood. In later years he lived in his home in Yonkers, a sick man without means. The "American Hebrew" brought the poet's plight to the attention of the public and his lot was eased.

* * *

We are at the end of a long winding road. We believe we have amply demonstrated the value of the Jewish contribution to journalism, its wide scope, its constructive character. Wherever the glorious annals of journalism are written, Jewish newspapermen will be prominent and thus help refute effectively the age-old lie that Jewish journalism necessarily is subversive.

BIBLIOGRAPHY

BEIN, ALEXANDER, *Theodor Herzl*. Vienna: Fiba-Verlag, 1934.

BRANDES, GEORG, *Main Currents in Nineteenth Century Literature.* New York: Boni & Liveright, 1923.

COWEN, PHILIP, *Memories of an American Jew*. New York, 1932.

DUBNOW, SIMON, *Weltgeschichte des juedischen Volkes*. Vol. 9.

EASTMAN, MAX, *Heroes I Have Known*. New York: Simon & Schuster, 1942.

ELBOGEN, ISMAR, *A Century of Jewish Life*. Philadelphia, 1944.

GOLDBERG, ABRAHAM, *Pioneers and Builders, Biographical Studies and Essays*. New York, 1943.

HERZL, THEODOR, *Jahrbuch*. Vienna, 1937.

LAZARE, BERNARD, *Job's Dungheap*. New York: Schocken Library, 1948.

LEVINGER, LEE J., *A History of the Jews in the United States*. Cincinnati, 1930.

LIPTZIN, SOLOMON, *Germany's Stepchildren*. Philadelphia, 1944.

MARCUS, JACOB R., *The Rise and Destiny of the German Jew*. Cincinnati, 1934.

MASSERMAN, PAUL and BAKER, MAX, *The Jews Come to America*. New York, 1932.

NORDAU, ANNA and MAXA, *Max Nordau, A Biography*. New York, 1943.

OSBORN, SIDNEY, *Germany and Her Jews*. London, 1939.

ROBACK, A. A., *The Story of Yiddish Literature*. New York, 1940.

ROTH, CECIL, *The Jewish Contribution to Civilization. History of the Jews in Italy*. Philadelphia, 1946.

RUPPIN, ARTHUR, *The Jews in the Modern World*. London: Macmillan, 1934.

TROTSKY, LEON, *My Life*. New York: Charles Scribner's Sons, 1930.

Universal Jewish Encyclopedia. Works of Heinrich Heine and Ludwig Boerne.

VON BUELOW, FUERST BERNHARD, *Denkwuerdigkeiten*. Berlin: Verlag Ullstein, 1930.

WILSON, EDMUND, *To the Finland Station*. New York: Harcourt, Brace & Co., 1940.

The Jewish Contribution to the Exploration of the Globe

By HUGO BIEBER

FROM antiquity up to the present times, Jews have taken an active, often a leading part in exploring the world.

As early as in the sixth century B.C.E., Jews, living in dispersion, undertook long and dangerous travels to Jerusalem, the center of worship and the destination of numberless individual pilgrims and of missions sent by remote Jewish communities which wanted to maintain spiritual connection or advice in matters of religious rites and doctrines. These travels through countries inhabited by hostile peoples and often through unknown areas, induced the Jews to collect information about the safest ways and the opportunities to buy provisions or to repair their carriages, in order to facilitate pilgrimage. Very soon commercial interests joined the spiritual purposes. When Xerxes was king of Persia, a steady traffic between that country and Jerusalem was established. The more the Roman empire extended its domination, the more frequently the leaders of Jewish communities had to go to Rome for political reasons, whether to obtain privileges or to prevent anti-Jewish measures. Akiba Ben Joseph, the founder of rabbinical Judaism, who lived from about 40 to about 135 C.E., visited all places of Palestine, and wandered to Arabia, Cappadocia and Media to support his coreligionists morally and materially. He went to Rome to defend successfully the cause of the Jews before emperor Nerva, and to Parthia to perform religious ceremonies. Until Christianity became the official religion of the Roman empire, Jewish missionaries visited all of its provinces to win adherents to their religion. According to a statement in the New Testament (Matt. 23:15), the Pharisees compassed land and sea to make one proselyte. All these traveling activities involved investigations of the local, economic and social conditions of the visited places.

In the Middle Ages, Jewish merchants were the first to dare travels to the wilderness of Northern Europe and Central Asia for the exchange of goods, for tracing new avenues of trade and commerce, and often for diplomatic purposes in the service of non-Jewish rulers. In Asia and Africa they met with Jews who lived in places unknown to Europeans, understood Hebrew, supported their itinerant coreligionists and provided them with goods and information. In this way, the Jewish travelers often combined their commercial interest with more or less scientific aims while collecting economic and geographical lore, acquiring books or oral intelligence, above all learning from foreign mathematicians and astronomers. In the times of Charlemagne who sent the Jew Isaac as ambassador to Bagdad, the Radanites, Jewish merchants, organized commercial expeditions which went to China in regular intervals. A Jewish adventurer, Eldad Hadani who lived from 880 to 940, wandered through East Africa and struck the imagination of his audiences and readers with reports claiming to have discovered the descendants of the Ten Lost Tribes. While large parts of his story, translated into several languages, met with skepticism, some of his reports on Ethiopia proved to be reliable. Abraham ibn Ezra, a versatile poet and scholar, born in Toledo, Spain, in 1092, died probably in Rome in 1167, wandered in France, England, Italy, Palestine, Egypt, and eastward to India, studying peoples, their languages, their way of living, the state of learning, mathematics and astronomy in Islamic countries. The most famous Jewish explorer of that epoch was Benjamin of Tudela, Spain, who started his journey in 1160 in Saragossa, Spain, to return only thirteen years thereafter. From Spain he went to Provence, Italy, Greece, Asia Minor, Palestine, Mesopotamia, Persia, India, to the frontiers of Tibet and China, and, on his way back, to Yemen. His vivid descriptions of about three hundred towns are of unique documentary value. The knowledge of several peoples that disappeared completely because they were destroyed by the Tatars, is based upon Benjamin's reports only. A Bohemian Jew, named Pethahiah, born in Prague but commonly called Pethahiah of Regensburg or Ratisbon, began his journey in that city about 1195. He traveled in Poland, Russia, Crimea, Armenia, Babylonia, Persia and India, and returned to his Bohemian homeland by way of Syria, Palestine and Greece. Estori Ben Moses Farhi who was born in Provence about 1282 and died in Palestine about 1357, became the first to investigate scientifically the topography, archaeology and folklore of the Holy Land, dealing with its history, geography, architecture, numismatics, weights and measures, and the way his Jewish, Christian and Moslem fellow inhabitants of Palestine used to live.

In 1375, Abraham Cresques, a Jew from the Mediterranean island of Majorca, accomplished his "Catalan Atlas", which is considered "one of the most prized maps in the history of geography". Mapmaking had been for a long period in the hands of Majorcan Jews, almost exclusively. Cresques utilized for his map the reports of Benjamin of Tudela and of numerous of the latter's Jewish disciples who had penetrated into Africa, opened unknown areas to European trade and crossed the Sahara from Algiers and Morocco to Timbuctu. Abraham's son Jehuda Cresques who, in 1391, during a pogrom, was forcibly baptized and assumed the name Jaime Ribes, was also a great scholar and an authority on geography. He founded the famous "School of Sagres", a center of studies that became of primary importance to explorers and navigators. Prince Henry the Navigator of Portugal was the protector of the school whose teachers, most of whom were Jews or crypto-Jews, gave the prince highly valuable advice for the preparation of his expeditions. Jehuda Cresques was also a famous maker of nautical instruments. Mecia de Villadestes, another crypto-Jew from Majorca, and a disciple of Cresques, was an expert of inner Africa. In our days, tanks and autocars use the road across the Sahara which was at first traced by Mecia de Villadestes. Among the Jews of Majorca were also Gabriel de Vallsecha whose map was used by Amerigo Vespucci, and Abraham Farrisol who explored Africa on camel-back, climbed high mountains and brought immense treasures to Europe in exchange for salt.

Jehuda Cresques was not the only Jew who excelled in making nautical instruments. Nautical science was in medieval Europe principally a Jewish domain. Already in the eleventh century, Jewish astronomers introduced the use of the astrolabe. Jacob Ben Mahir Ibn Tibbon, a Jewish professor at the university of Montpellier, France, who lived from 1230 till 1312, invented the quadrant. His astronomic tables were used by sailors until the middle of the eighteenth century. Of greatest importance and influence was Abraham Zacuto, professor at the universities of Salamanca and Saragossa until the expulsion of the Jews from Spain, then court astronomer of king John II of Portugal, finally a refugee in Tunisia. Zacuto was consulted before Vasco da Gama could start his expedition which succeeded in discovering the maritime route to India, and improved de Gama's astrolabe and tables. When Vasco da Gama landed at the Indian coast he was greatly surprised to be greeted by a Jew who had come to the same spot overland from his native town of Posen. This Jew later assumed the name of Gaspard da Gama and became famous because of his valor while participating in Cabral's expeditions to South America.

There are continued debates about the presumably Jewish descent of Columbus. But without any doubt, the men who prepared his first travel to America scientifically and financially, and a large number of his crew were Jews. Columbus was taught by Abraham Zacuto and carried the latter's works on his voyages. Crypto-Jews, of whom Santangel and Sanchez were outstanding, defended his cause before Ferdinand and

Isabella of Spain and provided the money for the purchase and equipment of his ships. Santangel and Sanchez were the first to receive the announcement of his success by Columbus. Luis de Torres, a Jew baptized shortly before the expedition started served Columbus as interpreter. He was the first European to set foot on an American island. Bernal, the ship's doctor had narrowly escaped death because the Inquisition had sentenced him for adhering to Judaism. Alonzo della Calle, Rodrigo Sanchez and Marco, the cook, were also Jews participating in Columbus's first expedition while the Jewish origin of other members of the crew is less certain.

A great Jewish contemporary of Columbus, Joseph Vecinho, was also a disciple of Abraham Zacuto. He is blamed by Columbus because he did not favor support of Columbus's project by the king of Portugal. But Vecinho aided him with scientific information. Previously Vecinho had been sent by king John of Portugal to Guinea to determine the altitude of the sun throughout that area, and was highly respected because of the accuracy of his measurements.

About 1586, the Marrano Pedro Teixeira began his long travels which were of major importance to the development of reliable geographical knowledge. Teixeira explored the Amazon River and other parts of America, furthermore China, the Philippines, India, Persia and the Middle East. His reports, written with literary skill and scientific solidity, were highly appreciated for centuries after his death. Tobias Cohen, one of the greatest physicians of his time and a precursor of modern medical science, who was born in Metz, France, in 1652 and died in Jerusalem in 1729, made use of his journeys in the Near and Middle East for careful and exact studies of diseases, plagues and hygienic conditions. As the representative of the Jewish communities of Palestine, Haym Joseph Azulai traveled, from 1753 to 1758 and from 1772 to 1778, in Turkey, Egypt, Italy, Germany, France, Holland and England, Tunisia and Algiers. His diary is full of highly interesting notes about the economic and cultural life of the Jews of his time in Europe and Africa, interviews with rabbis and scholars, and descriptions of libraries and manuscripts. At the end of the eighteenth century, Samuel Aaron Romanelli explored North Africa, and acquired especially intimate knowledge of Morocco. His book on that country, published in Hebrew in 1792, was translated into English as late as 1887, and attracted even then general attention.

Search of the Lost Ten Tribes induced Jews continually to explore remote countries. In the seventeenth century, the Marrano Antonio de Montezinos penetrated into Ecuador for that purpose. From 1831 to 1834, Baruch Ben Samuel of Safed, Palestine, went to Yemen to trace there the Tribes until he was killed by the Imam. For the same purpose, the Roumanian Israel Joseph Benjamin who called himself, in memory of Benjamin of Tudela, Benjamin the Second, traveled from 1845 to 1853, in Syria, Kurdistan, India, Afghanistan and Algeria. His reports aroused the interest of the great explorer Alexander von Humboldt and numerous geographers.

Frequently it was longing for adventures that dominated itinerant Jews. Thus Simon van Geldern, a grand-uncle of the poet Heinrich Heine, and originally an excellent scholar, wandered, in the second half of the eighteenth century, from town to town, from country to country, visiting all capitals of Europe, delivering lectures and becoming implicated in various plots and affairs. In his diary he proved to be a keen observer. He died on the road. Jacob Philadelphia, a physicist and mathematician, born in Philadelphia, Pa., probably in 1720, enchanted many European princes as well as his learned audiences in the most important cities of Europe. He tried to promote trade between Prussia and the United States, and, in 1784, king Frederick II of Prussia adopted Philadelphia's ideas in his commercial treaty with this country. Philadelphia's successes, however, stirred up jealousy and caused him adversity on the part of many enemies. The last years of his life are veiled by legends. Perhaps the most fortunate Jewish adventurer was Alexander Salmon. He was the son of a banker in London but refused to enter his father's business. He became a sailor, and for many years he was on board a whaler. Then he came to the island of Tahiti, married the female ruler of that paradisic island, and was the principal adviser of the ruler. His daughter became a queen. His son was the intimate friend of Robert Louis Stevenson who made Tahiti famous in world literature. Salmon wrote important books on the social and economic conditions of Tahiti.

The eras of enlightenment, liberalism and democracy, removing many disabilities and discriminations, facilitated also the activities of Jewish explorers in many regards. The heroic age of the itinerant Jew, traveling alone and being exposed to greater dangers than his non-Jewish colleagues, came to an end. Instead Jewish explorers began to cooperate with scientific institutions, academies, learned societies, governmental enterprises, and their exchange of knowledge with non-Jewish scientists as well as their contributions to learned reviews became more frequent. While the exploring activities of the Jews became more and more integrated into the general progress of science, their individual initiative and adventurous spirit remained existent and effective.

The first Jew to participate in a modern scientific expedition which was undertaken by non-Jews was Israel Lyons, noted mathematician, astronomer and botanist. In 1774, he accompanied Captain Phipps who later became Lord Mulgrave, on his expedition to the North Pole, serving as chief astronomer. In the nineteenth century, five arctic expeditions were accompanied or led by American Jews. Isaac Israel Hayes was surgeon in the second Grinnell Arctic Expedition, commanded by Captain Kane, which, during the years 1853 to 1855, made investigations in Smith's Sound. In 1860, Hayes himself led a Polar expedition to Foulke Fjord, and proceeded from there to regions never before reached by a white man. In 1869, he directed an expedition to Greenland. Emil Bessels who previously had participated in a German voyage to the Arctic Ocean, was, in 1871, appointed surgeon on the *Polaris*, commanded by Captain Charles Francis Hall whose attempt to reach the North Pole ended tragically. It was Bessels who proved, on the ground of tidal studies, that Greenland was an island. After being associated with the Smithsonian Institution in Washington, D.C., Bessels participated in the voyage of the United States steamship *Saranac,* bound to make ethnological studies on the northwest coast of America, but wrecked in Seymour Narrows, British Columbia. Edward Israel, astronomer of the Lady Franklin Bay Expedition under the command of General A. W. Greely, became a victim of his daring spirit before the expedition went home. Angelo Heilprin, after exploring the geological structure of Florida, Mexico and the Bermudas, became world-widely famous in 1892 when he led the Peary Relief Expedition to Greenland. Later he explored the island of Martinique after the eruption of Mt. Pelee, North Africa and Alaska. Another famous relief-expedition was led by the Russian Jew Rudolph L. Samoilovich which, in 1928 rescued Umberto Nobile and the crew of his dirigible in the Polar region. Previously Samoilovich had explored Spitzbergen, and subsequently he directed an expedition to Franz Josef Land, each time making important discoveries.

Jews also contributed to the exploration of the Americas in modern times. Arthur Poznansky discovered antiquities in remote and almost inaccessible areas of Peru and Bolivia. Eight important expeditions were conducted by Charles Leopold Bernheimer who began as an office boy in New York City, and then became of national renown as an arbitration authority. Bernheimer explored the "bad lands" of Northern Arizona and Southern Utah, and excavated prehistoric settlements in New Mexico. He extended his investigation to southern Mexico, Yucatan and Guatemala. Leo Joachim Frachtenberg, from Atlanta, Georgia, studied the life, customs and history of North American Indians. Morton C. Kahn and Melville J. Herskovits did the same in Surinam and the Caribbean islands. Kahn also studied tropical diseases in Costa Rica and British Guinea, and became an authority on the life and history of the Bush Negroes. Herskovits was respected as an expert on Haiti and American Negroes. Julius Popper, born in Roumania, made a trip around the world, and finally concentrated his studies upon the island of Tierra del Fuego on the southern tip of South America, previously unexplored. He took possession of the island, ruled it as a sovereign, exploited it commercially and described it with scientific exactness from the geographic and geological point of view. Paul Radin excelled in geological and anthropological research. He discovered important traces of American aborigines and threw new light upon the psychology and the social life of American Indians. Franz Boas, the greatest anthropologist of his time, had previously become renowned because of his meteorological expedition to Baffin Land in 1882. Then his interest turned to the culture of the Eskimos, and subsequently the American Indians. In 1886, Boas began to study the life of the northwestern tribes of Canada. From 1900 to 1905, he was the leading spirit of the Jesup North Pacific Expedition whose principal scientific result was the proof of the cultural relationship between the Siberians, Eskimos and American Indians. This and several other expeditions conducted by Boas to Mexico and Porto Rico gave him the broad fundaments for the development of his anthropological and sociological theories.

In the Far East, Heinrich Agathon Bernstein explored the Moluccan islands and New Guinea for the Dutch government, and died on one of the islands in 1865. Samuel Fenichel, noted ornithologist and entomologist, observed the fauna of New Guinea, discovered numerous birds and butterflies unknown until then, and made valuable contributions to the knowledge of the native population. New Guinea was also the object of Lamberto Loria's investigations. Loria, descending from an old Italian Jewish family, also traveled through the Australian continent. The results of his studies were deposited in the Ethnographical Museum of Florence, Italy, which was founded by Loria. Charles Gabriel Seligman, British physician, ethnologist and anthropologist, was a member of the Cambridge Anthropological Expedition to Torres Straits and Borneo, and turned his special attention to native medicine and surgery, and gave interesting information about popular rites and customs. Married to Brenda Z. Salaman, noted zoologist, who assisted him in his anthropological research work, Seligman directed expeditions to New Guinea, Ceylon and the Sudan. His books on *The Veddas* and *The Races of Africa* which became standard works show the steady enlargement of his point of view. Seligman embraced physical anthropology, archaeology, comparative religion and sociology. Elio Modigliani, member of a well-known Italian Jewish family, explored the island of Sumatra and the neighboring regions, penetrating into areas on which no European had set foot, and describing both the peoples and the fauna with artistic skill and scientific accuracy.

The exploration of Northern Asia is of special interest because the Russian Jews who contributed to it began their scientific careers as political convicts, exiled to Siberia. A rare exception was Georg Huth, born in Krotoshin, Poland, who was invited by the Russian Academy of Science to make an expedition, intended to investigate the language, history and ethnography of the Tunguses in the Yenisei region. Thereupon Huth participated in an expedition to Eastern Turkestan. Vladimir Jochelson, sentenced to three years' imprisonment and ten years of exile to Siberia because of his revolutionary activities, studied there the language and folkways of the Yokashirs, and published the results of his research work after he had served his time. Subsequently, Jochelson took part in expeditions to Kamchatka, the Aleutian islands, Alaska and Eastern Asia. His wife, Dina Jochelson-Brodsky, assisted him in his research work. Leo Sternberg, a member of the Russian socialist party, was sentenced to ten years of exile on the island of Sakhalin in 1910. There he studied the language of the Gilyak, Orok and Ainu tribes. He made expeditions to the Amur region which yielded valuable results. Sakhalin and the Amur region were also explored by Berthold Laufer, curator of anthropology at the Field Museum in Chicago. Laufer collaborated with Boas as a member of the Jacob Schiff Expedition to China, the Blackstone Expedition to Tibet, and the Field Expedition to China.

A daring explorer of Central Asia was Ney Elias. In his early years he traveled without any companion or escort from Pekin to St. Petersburg, crossing the desert of Gobi by a route hitherto completely unknown. Thereupon, Elias was sent by the British government to Yunan, to Ladakh, India, and to Chinese Turkestan. In 1885, he undertook a long and dangerous journey, along the Pamir mountains, through Badakishan and Afghan Turkestan to Afghanistan. In 1889 he was entrusted with demarcating the frontier between Siam and the Burman Shan States, and accomplished this highly difficult task with bravery, energy and fairness. The inquiries of Sir Marc Aurel Stein made epoch not only in the history of scientific exploration of Central Asia but also in the general history of archaeology and art. Stein had been appointed principal of the Oriental College in Lahore, India, in 1888, and registrar of Punjab University. After making antiquarian investigations in various parts of India, Stein began, in 1900 his great expeditions to Central Asia which completely changed the aspects of the historical studies of art. Traveling from the Near East to China, Stein discovered the ancient frontier wall of China; in the "Cave of the Thousand Buddhas" he picked up very old paintings and manuscripts. He traced the campaigns of Alexander the Great on his way to the conquest of India, penetrated into unknown territories, rediscovered forgotten periods of art and civilization, and saved an immense number of works of arts from oblivion or destruction. Sven Hedin, another explorer of Central Asia who became popular because of his vivid narrative of his adventures, was of Jewish descent.

In the Near East, Joseph Judah Czorny was one of the earliest explorers of the Caucasus which he investigated for ten years, from 1864 on. He also made journeys to Daghestan, Persia and Afghanistan. Eduard Glaser contributed to the topography of Southern Arabia by conducting four expeditions to that country, where David Heinrich Mueller discovered important inscriptions and literary documents. Joseph Halévy, born as a Turkish subject, later a naturalized French citizen, made a dangerous journey to Yemen to study the Sabean inscriptions, of which he brought about 700 to Paris. He also explored Ethiopia and inquired into Babylonian and Assyrian antiquities on the spot. In the disguise of a dervish, Arminius Vambery traveled in Persia, Turkey and Armenia. Gottfried Merzbacher, an international banker and trained Alpinist, did much to explore the Northern Caucasus. He also climbed mountains in Africa and America, and became famous because of his ascents in Central Asia. A chain of the Tian Shan Mountains was called, in his honor, the Merzbacher Range.

In the nineteenth century, Africa, called the "dark continent", attracted the explorers particularly, first because its map showed many and large white spots, and above all because political aims were combined with scientific interests. African soil was considered as unclaimed property to be annexed by those who were the first to set foot on it. In this way, the explorer was bound to become a conqueror in the name of his nation. He had to meet with armed resistance on the part of the native population, and was exposed to intrigues on the part of competing colonial powers. Emin Pasha whose original name was Isaac Eduard Schnitzer, penetrated into inner Africa beyond the Sudan, after reaching the sources of the White Nile. At first he served the Khedive of Egypt, then he went over to Germany, and planned to conquer a great African empire for emperor William II. He was, however, assassinated before he could realize this idea. By far more successful was Louis Gustave Binger in his efforts to enlarge the colonial possessions of France. Binger was one of the greatest explorers of his time. He was an eminent geographer and philologist, an outstanding expert of African languages and dialects, a far-

sighted organizer, tactful and energetic administrator, a painstaking scholar and a steadfast and intrepid man. He was devoted to both science and conquest, to the enlargement of
human knowledge and to the great aims of French colonial
policy. For many years, the French government had deliber-
ated upon the plan to consolidate its African possessions by
linking the Sudan and Senegal with the Guinea Coast. Binger
was the man to accomplish this task. In 1887, he proceeded
from Senegambia to regions until then unknown, concluded
treaties with the native chieftains, and, after two years
of extremely dangerous and adventurous marching through
the wilderness, reached a French outpost on the Ivory Coast
which, due to Binger, was completely annexed by France in
1891. In the latter year, Binger began to explore the territories
along the Niger river and thereupon, by a travel of more than
twelve hundred miles, he took a decisive part in determining
the frontier between the French Ivory Coast and the British
Gold Coast. Binger's books on Africa, the history of geography
and the explorer's calling are considered classical, and his
maps of unsurpassed value.

Another French explorer, Edouard Foa, descending from a
distinguished Italian Jewish family, traveled through Morocco, Central and Southern Africa. He made highly valuable
contributions to the study of the Congo river and the territories of Dahomey and neighboring areas. His great performance was the careful investigation along the Zambesi river.
The expeditions undertaken by Nahum Slouschz, a native of
Odessa, Russia, who became a French citizen and lecturer at
the Sorbonne, Paris, were mainly devoted to researches on
the history and antiquity of the Jews in North Africa and the
vestiges of Phoenician civilization. Slouschz became intimately
acquainted with the population of Tripoli, Algeria, Tunisia
and Morocco, and discovered many inscriptions, manuscripts
and documents of forgotten civilizations. Later on, he directed
excavations in Palestine. After daring adventures in Indo-
China and Malaysia, Raimondo Franchetti, a member of a

widely ramified Jewish family, concentrated his exploring activities upon East Africa. The accounts of his perilous journeys in Ethiopia and Kenya made him famous as "the Italian Lawrence". Franchetti, born in Venice, was killed in an airplane accident in 1934, while on a mission for the Italian government. Valuable contributions to the knowledge of the Islamic populations and the Jews in North-Eastern Africa and the Middle East were made by Hermann Burchardt who was murdered in Southern Arabia in 1900.

The exploration of South Africa was initiated by Nathanael Isaacs, a native of Canterbury, England, who was a pioneer settler in Natal. He was called by the Zulus "Tamboosa", the valiant warrior, and was wounded on the battlefield more than once. Besides penetrating into unknown territories, Isaacs took an important part in the foundation of the city of Durham, South Africa.

A daring American Jewess, Sarah Lavenburg Straus, the widow of Oscar S. Straus, American ambassador to Turkey and cabinet member, financed and accompanied, in 1929, an expedition of scientists to explore the African fauna for the American Museum of Natural History. She traveled more than 15,000 miles and collected thousands of specimens many of which were of greatest zoological importance.

The development of the modern sciences, especially astronomy and meteorology, requires that the scholar sometimes has to leave his study or observatory to confirm statements or theories on remote places. Thus the theory of Einstein was confirmed by expeditions to exotic countries. A pioneer in this field was Sir Arthur Schuster, who, in 1875, was chief of the "Eclipse Expeditions" to Siam, and, in 1878, 1882 and 1886, directed, or participated in, the Solar Expeditions to Colorado, Egypt and the West Indies. Maurice Loewy, director of the Paris Observatory, had to undertake long travels to determine the longitude of many important cities more precisely.

Modern journalism called forth a new type of investigating traveler, the reporter and foreign correspondent whose profession often involves adventure, hardship and risk of life. The first modern journalist who succeeded in being present wherever something of political importance happened, was Henri Oppert de Blowitz, for many years foreign correspondent of the London Times. He was an eyewitness of revolutions and wars, an eavesdropper at international conferences of leading statesmen and secret plots, and seemed to be ubiquitous. He had many successors who combined rapidity of reporting with solid knowledge of the history of the countries on which they had to write and who showed sound judgment on the political, economic and cultural situation, and described their experiences with artistic skill. In the French language Joseph Kessel became noted because of his faculty in narrating both his adventures and contemporary events in a cultivated form. Arthur Koestler impressed even more readers by his experience, views, ideas and sentiments. In America, Hermann Bernstein, Isaac Don Levine, Elias Tobenkin, Isaac Marcosson became renowned as war correspondents and subsequently reporters on foreign affairs. They were followed by Louis Fischer, Eugene Lyons, Waldo Frank, I. F. Stone and many others who made American readers acquainted with the situation in various countries. The youngest roving writer who feels the pulse of the peoples of Europe, while traveling from country to country, is Cyrus L. Sulzberger.

BIBLIOGRAPHY

ADLER, ELKAN N. *Jewish Travelers*. London: 1930.

——, Introduction to *The Itinerary of Benjamin of Tudela*. Oxford: 1907.

BAKER, J. N. L. *A History of Geographical Discovery and Exploration*. Boston: 1931.

DE MADARIAGA, SALVADOR. *Christopher Columbus*. New York: 1940.

EDMUNDSON, L., "The Voyages of Pedro Teixeira", *Transactions of the Royal Historical Society*. Vol. 3. London, 1920.

GERSHENFELD, LOUIS. *The Jew in Science*. Philadelphia: 1934.

GILLESPIE, J. E. *History of Geographical Discovery*. New York: 1933.

GRAETZ, H., *History of the Jews*. Philadelphia, 1927.

GRAYZEL, SOLOMON, *A History of the Jews*. Philadelphia, 1947.

JACOBS, JOSEPH. *The Story of Geographical Discoveries*. London: 1899.

JOHNSTON, HARRY H. *A History of the Colonization of Africa*. London: 1913.

KAYSERLING, M., *Christopher Columbus and the Participation of the Jews in the Spanish and Portuguese Discoveries*. New York, 1894.

KEY, CHARLES EDWARD. *The Story of Twentieth Century Exploration*. New York: 1937.

KIMBLE, GEORGE. *Geography in the Middle Ages*. London: 1937.

KOMROFF, MANUEL, *Contemporaries of Marco Polo*. New York, 1931.

LEBESON, ANITA LIBMAN, "Jewish Cartographers", *Historia Judaica*. Vol. 10, No. 2, October 1948.

ROTH, CECIL, *A Short History of the Jewish People*. London, 1948.

——, *The History of the Marranos*. London, 1932.

The Jew as Soldier, Strategist and Military Adviser

By WILLIAM B. ZIFF

DURING the recent campaigns in Palestine, there were few of the experts who were not startled by the military prowess demonstrated by the Jews in their successful defense of the new State of Israel against the invading armies of six neighboring Arab nations.

It had been commonly held that the Jews would be pushed into the sea in a swift and easy campaign, with the converging Arab armies making juncture before the indefensible Jewish city of Tel Aviv, and dictating the peace there with bombs and artillery. Not only were numbers, strategic situation and weight of arms overwhelmingly on the side of the invaders, but the Jews appeared to have neither weapons nor organized forces, and indeed, no organized government. From the conventional military view, they were neither an army nor a state, but a disordered rabble composed of tradesmen, farmers, and shattered refugees who had fled Europe in panic. Even more important, an almost universal bias ascribed to them qualities of meanness, servility and cowardice which would make any calculated defense virtually impossible.

When by unaided raw courage and brilliant tactical capacity, the Jews demonstrated an ability first to hold their ground, and then to rout their opponents completely in a series of successive engagements, the gentlemen in the chancelleries and the top military echelons still could not conceive the situation. With an almost superstitious reverence for the traditional misinformation in which their opinions had been anchored, they were at the beginning disposed to credit the wildest of rumors to explain the miracle—Russian generals; Russian heavy tanks, munitions and airplanes; overwhelming superiority in fighting planes and pilots somehow smuggled out of the American and British air forces.

Yet any competent survey of the history of the Jews would indicate that as a fighting people they have not been excelled anywhere.

It is true that as the traditional People of the Book, and as a race which has been scattered, ghettoized, and imprisoned everywhere in the iron chains of prejudice, they did not give the appearance of a military people. They seemed to lack much which is deemed essential to the warlike spirit. Their generally mild demeanor and high disproportion of intellectuals and tradesmen, for whom the military mind has had an habitual contempt, easily fitted into the legend of Jewish weakness and slavish self-seeking. In Palestine itself, the British commander, Sir Evelyn Barker, angered by the guerrilla exploits of the Jewish underground, epitomized this belief in the remark that he would force the Jews to their knees by a boycott of Jewish tradesmen, thus "hitting the race where it would hurt them the most—in their pocketbook."

What must be recognized is that in organized warfare, battles are not necessarily won by individual truculence and ferocity alone. As far as the human factor is concerned, the preponderant weight of arms is determined rather by organizability, skill, fortitude, determination, know-how and the capacity for strategy and maneuver. Here devotion, high intelligence, and the will to endure, give the martial spirit its real meaning. The superior capacity of a gifted and endowed people thus is as much reflected in the art of war as in any other type of human activity, and rests on exactly the same elements of character which allow for success in other competitive human endeavors. The whole history of the Jew, his intellectual resource, his tenacity, his quiet determination in the face of adversity, and his willingness to sacrifice well-being and life itself to his spiritual beliefs, all bear witness to this fact.

THE JEW AS SOLDIER, STRATEGIST, MILITARY ADVISER

In the perspective of human affairs, it is perfectly clear that the Jews have always been a great military people, and given opportunity, excel both as soldiers and military organizers.

The Hebrew people were originally a colonizing offshoot of one of the great fighting peoples of antiquity, the Chaldeans.[1] The neighboring Phoenicians and their descendants of Carthage, were of identical stock, speaking a like language, possessing and displaying the same traits and the same adventurous fighting spirit.[2] The Old Testament *Apocrypha* declares the kinship of the Jews with still another great military people, the Spartans. In a letter to the High Priest Onias, Arius, King of the Spartans remarks "concerning the Spartans and Jews, that they are kinsmen and that they are descended from Abraham." The High Priest Jason, forced to flee for his life, is described as "crossing the sea to the Lacedaemonians, hoping to find protection there because of his relationship to them."[3]

However one may accept the accuracy of these accounts, it is certain that the Jews were among the ablest soldiers of ancient times. Inhabiting a little state caught in the pathway of many huge military juggernauts, their record is a saga of human endurance, of military ingenuity and boundless personal courage. Throughout their history they had to fight powerful and aggressive nations, far better equipped, situated and numerous than they, including the successive lords of the earth, the Egyptians, Hittites, Babylonians, Assyrians, Greeks and Romans. Access to metal for armor and weapons was poor. An even greater weakness from the aggressive viewpoint of the ancients, was the Jewish preoccupation with moral problems under a philosophy of living dominated by what the baffled Romans described as "the superstition of an invisible god". As a people the Jews were thus diverted from the prime business of enslavement and conquest which galvanized the purposes of ancient society.

Whether in their own land of Israel or in their collective history later as "dwellers among strangers", their dependence in military contest had to be on a superiority of tactics, mobility, courage and discipline.[4] In ancient Palestine, as later in the Twentieth Century, when Jews again fought as organized bodies under their own banners, their arsenals had largely to be built by seizing them from the enemy.

Ancient Hebrew military prowess must be considered of far greater importance than as a mere unique incident for historical reference. Its impact on Western civilization had decisive effects; for had the Jews succumbed to the massive forces around them as did the Hittite Empire, Moab, Edom and Philistia, Hebrew thought would have perished from the memory of men; Christianity and Moslemism would never have been born, and the course of Western history would have been unrecognizably different. The resistance of the Maccabees alone to the victorious march of Hellenism in the ancient world, possessed a determining influence on the final course of world events.[5]

Recent archaeological findings, plus the internal evidence of the Bible stories, indicate that the Commanders of ancient Israel anticipated by long centuries the military planning which distinguished Greece and Rome. Fleischer in his *From Dan to Megiddo* insists that the tactical formation of Jewish armies during the Exodus was later copied by the Romans. The British major, Vivian Gilbert, declares that during the Allenby campaign in Palestine, he and his commanding officer "were inspired by the Biblical account of the strategy used in the Battle of Micmash, and reproduced it exactly, and with the same excellent results."[6]

It was the Hebrew King, Uzziah, who first invented engines of war, some 500 years before the advent of Philip of Macedon. Similarly, Uzziah was the author of the general staff, and planned campaign, as well as the use of uniform military equipment for his entire host. Even Philip's use of the first standing army not composed of mercenaries, seems to have been long anticipated by David. The attack principle used by Titus against Jerusalem, that of a mound built in a moat, had been used by Joab as early as the Eleventh Century B. C. in his successful investiture of the fortified city of Abel.[7]

As early as Joshua, we find a very real mastery of the importance of thorough intelligence work preparatory to a campaign, and his understanding of espionage and reconnaissance were unique for his time. The training and organization of his men has been described as "a model of military art." The crossing of the Jordan into a bitterly hostile country, "points to a carefully planned, completely successful exploit such as had never been seen. An entire nation passed over a major topographical obstacle, without loss or confusion, and under perfect discipline."[8] The fall of the Walls of Jericho was a minor masterpiece of military operation, starting with the intelligence obtained from the spies who visited the local harlot, Rahab, and ending with a perfectly contained sapping operation. Joshua's capture of the fortified city of Ai showed the same understanding of the value of early and thorough reconnoitering, and of the type of strategic deception used so ably later by Alexander at Tyre and Hannibal at Cannae.[9]

Almost the entire principle of modern guerrilla warfare was anticipated in the ancient wars of the Jews. We shall see that this is particularly true in the desperate struggles against the Romans, but it was already the case in the feats of the Maccabees against the Greco-Syrian conquerors. After the crushing defeat of Judas Maccabaeus at the Battle of Elasa, the Greco-Syrian victor, General Bacchides, nevertheless found himself exposed to an endless succession of small raids, surprise attacks, ambuscades, and planned disruption of his communications, until "he was worn out and his army almost completely destroyed."[10]

II

Throughout the long course of their existence as a nation, the Jews enjoyed the reputation of being the finest fighting men in the ancient world. Overwhelmed time and again by the enormous forces of great world empires, they never yielded, and fought on to the last. Almost alone among the peoples of the earth they were not cowed by the power of Imperial Rome. The Jewish wars against Rome were epic in their proportions. Time after time, this small nation, pitting itself against the mightiest empire of the world, broke out in bloody armed rebellion.[11]

In the earliest of these, led by Judah the Galilean, the rebel watchword, never to be abandoned, was: "We have no master but God." Resistance to Roman rule culminated in a violent upheaval under the reign of the Emperor Nero. The Roman general Cestius Gallus who invaded from Syria, was thrown back with immense slaughter, the worst disaster to Roman arms to occur since the defeat at Varus. Nero promptly appointed the celebrated general, Vespasian, to prosecute the war. The rebels were led by a simple Galilean farmer called John of Gischala, and another independent force by an intellectual named Simon Bar Giora.[11a]

After six terrible years of struggle in which quarter was neither given nor asked, the Jews finally retreated to their capital, Jerusalem. The attack was now in the hands of Titus, famous son of Vespasian, who had under his command five Roman legions, together with 340 catapults. Titus in a series of magnanimous gestures, offered to parley with the insurgents. The Jewish answer was always the same—a contemptuous refusal of any terms save unconditional freedom and the total withdrawal of Roman troops from their country.

The Jewish troops conducted their campaign with such determination and ability, that twice Titus came within a hair's breadth of disaster, and once was himself almost taken. "So unconquerable was the ferocity of the Jewish soldiery," comments Dr. Adams, "that it may be doubted whether even the stern discipline, the high military spirit, and the overwhelming numbers of the Romans would not have been compelled ultimately to give way before them," had Rome not acquired two new and invincible allies—famine and dissension among the ranks of the defenders themselves.[12]

The Roman side of the war was conducted by an apostate Jew, Tiberius Julius Alexander, General of the Army and Chief of Staff, considered one of the outstanding military geniuses of his time. It was he who conceived the device of heaping up a mound against the fortifications so as to enable the Romans to bring their engines of war to bear, perhaps based on his memory of the traditional Jewish account of Joab's maneuver at Abel. Even here the defenders gave a terrifying account of themselves.[13] Dion states that the "Jews made night and day sallies as often as the occasion offered, set fire to the engines, slew numerous combatants. . . . As for the rams, they lassoed some of them and broke the ends off, others they seized and pulled up with hooks . . ."

When after six months of siege the city finally fell, the Jews still refused to capitulate. As they were later to do in the Battle of the Warsaw Ghetto, they fought for every house. The last resistance took place on the hill on which the Temple stood. Again, says Dion Cassius, "Titus made a new proclamation offering them immunity. They, however, even under these circumstances held out." The Roman writer relates almost in awe that "Though they were but a handful fighting against a far superior force, they were not subdued" until the Temple itself was on fire. "Then they went to meet death willingly, some letting themselves be pierced by the swords of the Romans, some slaughtering one another, others committing suicide, and others leaping into the flames. It looked to everybody, and most of all to them, apparently that so far from being ruin, it was victory and salvation and happiness to perish along with the Temple." Thus, this sober, pedestrian Greco-Roman got an inkling of something strange in the ancient world—of a great moral victory in the face of physical defeat.[14]

The reduction of Jerusalem was perhaps the most difficult undertaking in Roman military annals. Returning to Rome after seven years of grueling and costly warfare, the weary conqueror was honored by the erection of an arch to mark his achievement, a recognition only given to commemorate a victory over the most formidable of enemies.[15]

As a result of this deadly struggle, Judea was reduced to ashes. Yet a scarce forty-five years later, during the reign of Trajan, the Jews again found the strength to revolt. In Cyrene, Egypt and Cyprus, as well as in Judea, the rebellion blazed in uncontrollable fury, throwing the entire Empire into an uproar. Two hundred and forty thousand Greeks were alleged by Dion Cassius to have been slain in Cyprus alone. Before the rebels were shattered in Cyrene, the country was turned into a desert.[16] In Egypt, the Jews after driving their opponents to take refuge in Alexandria, were finally crushed by the Roman prefect, Q. Marcius Turbo. Meanwhile in Judea itself, under the generalship of a remarkable leader named Bar Kochba, the Romans were beaten everywhere. In one year, the Jews had reconquered fifty fortified strongholds and 985 towns and villages, and had even succeeded in reoccupying the ruins of Jerusalem.

Again the Romans did not take this contest lightly. Hadrian put the war in the hands of his greatest general, Julius Severus, who was recalled from Britain with his legions for the purpose.

When the resistance of this small land ceased after four years of unrelenting struggle, Judea had become a wilderness, almost without people. Says Dion Cassius . . . "fifty-eight myriads of men were slaughtered."

Even these disasters did not quell the fighting spirit of the Jews. Under the reign of the Emperor Constantine in the Fourth Century A.D., there was another of the usual desperate rebellions, which was put down by a powerful Roman army with indiscriminate slaughter. Still later when King Chosroes made war against Byzantium, the Jew, Benjamin of Egypt, created a Hebrew army of 30,000 men, which managed to reconquer Palestine and to hold it under Jewish rule for fourteen years. After the conclusion of a treaty of amity with Emperor Heraclius of Byzantium, that ruler, on the urgings of the Church, ambushed the Jewish troops without warning and succeeded in destroying them.

III

The hatred of the Church for the scattered remnants of the Jewish nation was without let. Throughout the civilized world, Jews found themselves scarcely in possession of the most elementary human rights, reduced to sunless ghettos, and treated with all the indignity of a pariah people.

It will be observed that the ancient legend concerning the Jews indicts them as an incorrigibly quarrelsome race, given to reckless violence and only happy in armed contention. Dion Cassius accuses them of every manner of atrocity against the Romans. Tacitus, too, refers dourly to the fighting qualities of this most irreconcilable of Roman foes, crediting them with almost superhuman truculence, obstinacy, and reckless desperation. Their indifference to death and ferocity in battle were a byword in the Roman world. Jewish captives were the favored gladiators in the arena, and Jewish mercenaries were highly regarded as professional soldiers until the end of the Fourth Century. They were numerous in all of the Roman wars. The Roman writer, Macrobius, declares that a large contingent of Jewish fighting men served in Caesar's legions. Both the Persians and Egyptians utilized Jewish mercenaries in considerable numbers. The Ptolemys relied heavily on Jewish fighting men. The founder of the dynasty, Ptolemy Soter, entrusted all of the major fortresses of Egypt to Jewish hands, settling Jewish military colonies in conquered areas he was anxious to hold. This was a system followed in turn by Ptolemy Philadelpus and his successors. Josephus tells us that Ptolemy II, called Philometer, and his wife, Cleopatra, "committed his whole kingdom to the care of Jewish troops" commanded by the Hebrew generals, Onias and Dositheus.[17]

The contrary legend that the Jews were a mild and non-military people, or actually a cowardly and servile race, was fostered during the long dark period when the power of the medieval church consigned the race to the dark confines of the ghetto, and forbade them to take any active part in the life of the countries in whose midst they lived. Just as Jews might not own or cultivate land, or participate in the normal life around them, generally speaking they also were barred from the military profession everywhere.

Even under these withering conditions, however, there were indications that the Jewish fighting spirit was far from dead, and that the character of the race had by no means changed.

When Italy was invaded by Theodoric, King of the Ostrogoths, the suppressed Jews flocked to his banner. When his successor, Theodohat, was attacked by Emperor Justinian, whole units of the defending armies were formed of Roman Jews, who gave a magnificent account of themselves. When Justinian's troops landed on the toe of the Italian peninsula, the people of Naples, dejected and frightened, sought to surrender unconditionally. The Jews of Naples, however, refused to allow the city to submit. Led by Isaac Mender and Saar ben Gutta, they vigorously repelled the assault. When Justinian's great fleet attempted to occupy the port, every Jew up to the age of 70 served, holding positions along the entire coastline, and forcing the fleet to retire. Justinian's historian, Procopius, concedes that it was the stubborn Jewish resistance which gained badly needed time for Theodohat and thus postponed Justinian's conquest of Italy for another 20 years.

The conquest of Mauretania (Morocco) by the vandal king, Genserich, was largely due to the presence in his ranks of a strong body of Jewish troops. Shortly after, these *Bahuzim,* or Berber Jewish warriors, succeeded in consolidating the mountainous zone, or Jebel area of North Africa, into a strong confederacy. Under a noted fighting queen known as the Damia al Cahina,[18] they even succeeded in beating back the first waves of the great Arab invasion. The Cahina was subsequently defeated in pitched battle and slain. Many of the Jewish tribes were then converted to the creed of Islam, and participated in the later Moslem conquests. The Cahina's two sons are reputed to have been among the Moslem commanders during the military reduction of Spain.

Many Jews served in the Arab armies during the period marking Arab capture of both North Africa and Iberia. According to Arab writers of the time, conquered Spanish cities were often as not left in charge of Jewish garrisons. The Moorish invader, Tariq Ibn Zeiad, from whom Gibraltar takes its name,[19] was himself described as a Jewish Berber and former officer of the Cahina, and his Moslem army as a Jewish Berber force, augmented by a few Arabs.[20] In the Eleventh Century, the noted Samuel Hanagid was State Minister in charge of military affairs for the Moorish kingdom of Granada and Malaga.

In Christian Spain, where for a period the Jews were a reasonably free people, they participated actively in the military life of the nation. In Tulaitula in 838, they rose in revolt together with the Arabicised Christians against the tyranny of Moslem rule.[21] At the Battle of Zallâka in 1086, King Alfonso VI of Castile is reported to have had 40,000 Jews in his armies, an extremely large force for those times. The opposing armies of Moslem Seville also contained so many Jews that among other considerations the day of the battle was mutually arranged so as not to fall on the day of the Jewish Sabbath. Jews fought fiercely for Pedro I, a king who had always treated them well. They made up a large proportion of Pedro's armies "and great numbers fell fighting in defense of their king and country."[22] Pedro's chancellor and major strategist was the Jew, Don Samuel Ben Meir Allavi. The city of Toledo in a historic siege, is described as having been defended by Jewish troops fighting on the side of Pedro. Under Alfonso VII of Castile, Judah ibn Ezra was raised to the position of commander of the important frontier fortress of Calatrava and later became Court Chamberlain. Alfonso VIII, who also treated the Jews well, was repaid amply by them in loyalty and service given in his wars against the Moors.

During the earlier Medieval period there were many exceptions to the general rule which sought to forbid Jewish military service, and many instances of outstanding Jewish heroism and quality on the battlefield. It was only in later Medieval times, when the strictures of church and state against them became so rigorous that Jews no longer were allowed to bear arms for any cause, that history presents us with a blank page as far as Hebrew military genius is concerned. Even here, however, we occasionally find the names of converted Jews in high military position.

Jews were considered to be especially proficient as crossbowmen, and in some countries were admitted in considerable numbers to the noncommissioned ranks. Abramo Colorni was famous as an innovator in military defense works. We read that Hanuchim, a French Jew, was given special license to live in England because he had fought so gallantly in Normandy under King John. King Philip is reported to have had 30,000 Jews in his army in the war against Count Guy of Flanders. The Bohemian chronicler, Hajek, reports that in 995 A.D., it was armed Jews who decided the great victory of the Bohemians over the pagans. Even during the mass pogroms conducted by the armies of the Crusaders on their way to the Holy Land, the attacked Jews, though overwhelmingly outnumbered and largely without arms, defended themselves well. At Halle in Germany, in the year 1096, they succeeded in defeating the Crusading armies and in a pitched battle with the Crusaders at Carenton, France, forced the attacking knights to withdraw. In other cities where they were assailed by these wandering armies, they sold their lives dearly.

There were many Marranos (secret Jews) who figured prominently in the ranks of the *conquistadores* in the conquest of the New World. Among these was Luis de Torres, who sailed on all four trips with Columbus and was killed in a battle with the Indians in Haiti. Nunas Cabeza de Vaca, who adventured from the Texas coast southward, was the conqueror of Peru. Luis de Carojal y de la Cueva fought in Mexico, and was famous for his feat in capturing Hawkins' buccaneers. Gil Gonzales, a sanguinary ruffian of the stripe of Cortez, discovered Nicaragua in 1519, and at the head of a small body of infantry and horse, wiped out a considerable share of the Indian population of Central America. Alonzo Hernando fought for five years at the side of Cortez. Also well-known in the conquest and sack of Mexico was Alfonso de Avila, cousin of Gonzales, who was killed in a battle with the Indians in 1537. In the following generation, another Gil Gonzales and Alfonso de Avila, of the same family, were executed as rebels in the early abortive attempts to secure the freedom of Mexico.

Among the long list of adventurers of the period was Simon Fernando[23] who sailed the seas with Sir Francis Drake, and was captain of the Admiral's ship, and who before this was reputed to have been a pirate. Many Marranos also participated in the Portuguese expeditions to India and the Far East as well as to the New World, and their names are still perpetuated among many distinguished military families in Latin America.[24] Antonio Vaaz Henriquez prepared and led the Dutch expedition which captured Pernambuco in 1630. Another Jew, David Peixotto, was in command of the eighteen vessels sent for the relief of that city. Francisco de Silva, a Marrano fighting in the Spanish service, was instrumental in defeating the French at the siege of Treves in 1673. Simon de Caceres was military adviser to Cromwell, and the Portuguese emigre, Edward Brandon, was a Yorkist hero during the Wars of the Roses.

In far away Surinam, Jewish settlers, rejoicing in their new-found freedom, became famous for their military prowess. Under Samuel Nassy, they fought brilliantly against the French assault in 1688-9, and again in 1712, under the noted Captain Isaac Pinto.

IV

The Napoleonic conquests, which smashed with cyclonic force against the stockades of feudal Europe, brought into these twilight areas the bright light of French equalitarianism. Once more Jews were allowed to bear arms and to take part in the general military life. Learned debates now took place throughout the continent as to whether this queer race of Jews who had just been released from the crushing enervation of the ghetto, were physically or morally capable of fulfilling the role of citizenship, and particularly that of military service. It was certainly true that the stamina and physical strength for which the Jew once had been famous, had deteriorated under the blight of the ghetto. Abject poverty, enforced degradation, and the type of occupation to which the race had been relegated, had left their cruel marks on the Jewish personality; but these effects vanished with miraculous rapidity under the warm sun of freedom.

Jews were first admitted to the Prussian army in 1813. The historian Buchholz remarks upon the outstanding quality of Jewish valor in the wars with Napoleon. The much decorated Prussian war heroine, Esther Manuel, fought against the French Emperor disguised as a man, in a regiment of lancers. How well Jewish soldiers acquitted themselves may be judged from the fact that the Chancellor, Prince Hardenberg, found himself writing much to his surprise (January 4, 1815), that "young men of Hebrew faith prove to be excellent fighting comrades of the Christian soldiers, and we have seen in their midst examples of true heroism and of most praiseworthy disdain of the dangers of war."

In the Franco-Prussian war of 1870, more than 100 Jews were commissioned officers, and 373 decorated for valor. Though they constituted a fraction of less than 1% of the total population, 5,000 Jews fought on the Prussian side, 10% of whom were killed or wounded.

In the War of 1866 the Jewish general, Von Henikstein, was chief of the Austrian General Staff. The situation in Austro-Hungary was such as to cause the Emperor Franz-Josef to write to his minister, Dunayevsky, that to him the anti-Semitic movement in Austria was actually painful when he considered the heroic service rendered to the throne by Jewish soldiers in the wars of 1878 and 1882. "Even now", he exclaims, "in my desk are piled up numerous orders rewarding Jewish soldiers for their distinguished deeds." It is interesting to note that by 1893, though Jews composed some 3.9% of the Emperor's army, roughly corresponding to their percentage in the general population, those in the officers corps constituted 8%, including the celebrated naval engineer, Rear Admiral Siegfried Popper, and the Austrian Naval Chief, Rear Admiral Ludwig Tobias Freiherr von Oesterreicher. By 1909 there were on active duty in the Austrian army one Jewish lieutenant general, three major generals and a large number of lesser officers. Among the Jewish officers of the period was Lieutenant Field Marshal Joseph Singer, who was responsible for the complete reorganization of the Austrian officers corps.

In Italy, Jews enjoyed complete equality since 1848. Until the time of Mussolini's conversion to Hitlerism, the familiar type of social anti-Semitism could scarcely have been said to have existed. From Jewish ranks was drawn the distinguished General Giuseppe Ottolenghi, known as "the father of the Italian army," who, after a brilliant military career which included a professorship of military history and tactics in the Royal Military School at Modena, became Minister of War in 1902-03. In 1911, there were some 500 Jewish officers in the Italian army, an almost fantastic ratio when one considers the minuscule Jewish population of that country.

In all of the states but Imperial Russia, the story was much the same during this period. Jews played a role in all wars and in all revolutionary movements. They fought behind the barricades with Kosciusko. A Jewish enlisted man named Wolff died in the Alamo. Captain Ullman of the 5th Cavalry fell with Custer in the Indian massacre of Little Big Horn. Jews stood with Houston in all the battles for Texas' independence and earned immortal glory at San Jacinto, Goliad and Neches. Among these was the noted Captain Levi Charles

Harby, who later commanded the Neptune during the Civil War; David Kauffman, who had a Texas county named after him; and Moses Albert Levy, who was Surgeon General for Houston's army throughout the Texas-Mexican War. A Jewish regiment served under Kossuth in the Hungarian Revolt of 1848, and two Jews, Michael Heilprin and Fishel Friend, were among the Hungarian leaders' principal lieutenants. In the Greco-Turkish War, 1,500 Jewish soldiers served in the Greek ranks and carved out an undying name for themselves in the Battle of Previsa. Among other Jewish soldiers, General Jacob Baiz fought in the Central American battles for freedom, and Captain Luis H. Brie in South America. The records of all the Spanish-American wars for independence are heavily sprinkled with the names of fighters descended from old Marrano families, though these were no longer identified as Jews.

Ernesto Nathan, later to become Mayor of Rome and to enlist for active service in World War I at the age of 70, was an associate of Mazzini. The Italian revolt against Austria of 1848-9, centering in Venice, was led by the converted Jew, Daniel Manin. In his service were many Jewish enlisted men and a dozen Jewish officers. High in the upper echelons of Garibaldi's command were Giuseppe Ottolenghi, Giuseppe Finzi, Enrico Guastalla and a number of lesser officers. Jewish military adventurers include the unique Elias Pasha (Elias Cohen) who was at one and the same time general in the Turkish army and vice admiral in the Turkish navy; General Mazar Pasha (Stephen Lakeman) who fought professionally in the Turkish army and also served in South Africa, India and Britain; and Simon Bolivar's fighting comrade, General Isidore Borovsky, later to fall in battle while soldiering for the Persians.

In Bulgaria, saturated with virulent anti-Semitism, Prince Alexander Battenberg found it necessary to address his Jewish soldiers after the victory at Pirota as follows: "Valiant

Jews, your heroic conduct today proved that you are direct descendents of the Maccabees."

Russia of the Czars remained untouched by the great broom of the French Reformation. Its Jewish population continued to be herded into the restricted area known as the Pale, and made the subject of repressive laws up to the time that Kerensky took power. Jews, who had reason to detest the monarchy, nevertheless fought ably in its behalf wherever they were called upon.

Advancement in the army, or recognition even of outstanding valor, were impossible to Jewish soldiers.

Jews in military service were subject to the harshest restrictions. They could not serve in fortresses, artillery, navy, border patrols or local reserves. They were not allowed to take examination for officer's rank, and though not specifically forbidden by law, in practice were denied the possibility of becoming non-commissioned officers. The usual encouragement given to soldiers, such as medals and promotions, were not allowed to them except for rare exceptions. Nevertheless, there were many instances of individual Jews surmounting these discouraging barriers, such as Chaim Zaitchikoff, who showed such lionlike courage at the defense of Sevastopol that the Supreme Commander singled him out for a ceremonial shaking of hands after the battle.[25] The famous partisan leader, D. V. Davydov, in his *A Diary of the Partisan Wars of 1812*, remarks on the brilliant exploits of a certain Uhlan, adding: "It is very strange that this Uhlan, having received the Cross of St. George for his heroism, could not wear it. He was a Jew from Berdichev." During the Russo-Turkish war, General Kuropatkin wrote that "the Jews showed that they knew . . . how to fight and die as heroically as the rest of the Russian soldiers."

The heroism of Joseph Trumpeldor became a byword in the Russo-Japanese War. Though Trumpeldor had lost an arm during the siege of Port Arthur, he wrote to his commanding officer, "I have but one arm left; but this one arm is my right arm. And, therefore, desiring to share as before the fighting life of my comrades, I beg Your Honor to petition for an issuance to me of a sabre and a revolver." Despite the fact that he was a Jew, Trumpeldor was promoted to junior non-commissioned officer's rank, decorated with all four classes of the Russian Military Order of St. George, and finally given command of a company which distinguished itself in the defense at Port Arthur—the first Jew ever to receive a commission from the Czar.

The Russians had some picture of the fighting quality of Jews when engaged in a cause in which they believed, during the Russo-Polish War of 1794, where many Jewish young men flocked to the banners of Kosciusko. The Austrian official, Anton Baum, reported to the Minister of War that these pale and narrow-chested denizens of the ghetto had nevertheless formed a corps of border patrols, incongruously dressed in the ghetto garb of the time, yet carrying sabres and pistols, and declared himself amazed at their heroism. In his book, *Berek Joselowicz,* the Polish author, Ernest Luninsky, recounts that during the siege of Warsaw, Jews showed miraculous courage in the face of the heaviest losses under fire. He comments of Berek Joselowicz's all-Jewish regiment of light cavalry, that though its members were pale, poorly-nourished men who still wore the caftans and somber raiment of the ghetto, the regiment "was impressive in its austere firmness and discipline." Almost the entire regiment perished in a single day during the terrible assault on Warsaw of November 4, 1794.[26]

For Holland, Belgium, and Britain, Jews served at all fronts. In the latter country, Sir Jacob Adolphus, after being baptized became a major general in 1770. In the early Nineteenth Century, both Sir George Aguilar and Sir David Ximinez reached the rank of lieutenant general. Jewish sailors fought under Nelson; and Wellington specifically cites for commendable performance, fifteen Jewish officers who served under his command at Waterloo. Major General Albert Goldsmid fought in all the British wars of the period, including those against

Napoleon.[27] In far-away India, where only a few thousand native Jews, known as Bene Israel, exist, "Bene Israel soldiers . . . constituted almost half of the number of native officers of each Regiment of the Bombay Presidency for nearly a century and a half of British rule".[28] During the Napoleonic wars, Vice Admiral Alexander Wilmot Schomberg[29] was considered one of Britain's ablest commanders. Colonel Sir David Harris took part in many colonial wars. Hugh Culling Eardley Childers was Secretary of War under Gladstone, and Ralph Bernal Osborne was Secretary of the Admiralty during the Crimean War.

A strong contingent of Jews served in the British army during the Boer war, including Colonel Albert Edward Goldsmid, Chief of Staff with the 6th Division. Colonel Sir David Harris commanded the Kimberly Guard. Major W. D. Karri-Davis was the first to enter Johannesburg and Mafeking. There was a whole Jewish regiment known as the Pietersburg Light Horse. Many Jews also served on the Boer side. Among these were the two French engineers, Léon Gruenberg and Samuel Léon, in charge of artillery and sappers, whose exploits became legendary in Afrikaans' patriotic tradition.[30]

It is one of the ironies of history that just as it was the Jew, Tiberius Julius Alexander, who was instrumental in bringing the Roman siege of Jerusalem to a victorious conclusion, it was the Jewish Minister of State, Farchi, who was the presiding genius at the defense of Acre, whose successful resistance frustrated Napoleon's plan to march east to India.[31]

In the ranks of Napoleon's armies were many Jewish fighting men, as well as a sprinkling of officers. Most famous of these was Andrea Menasse, whose name was later changed to Massena. He became Napoleon's most important marshal, and was referred to by the French conqueror as *"L'enfant chéri de la victoire."* Like almost all the Jews of his time, Massena came into prominence the hard way, with very little conventional military instruction. He had volunteered to the Italian army and later to the French army. His military career was one long succession of personal triumphs, including the conquest of the Maritime Alps in 1794, and the decisive victory over the Austrians and Sardinians at Loano. It was Massena who was credited with saving the day at Lodi, and with the victories at Castiglioni, Rivoli, Mantua, Friedland and Wagram. In his memoirs, Napoleon lauded him as "one of the greatest men of his age."

After the fall of Napoleon, a bitter reaction set in, swallowing up many of the Emperor's reforms. The European attitude toward the Jew once more hardened. France was no exception to the disease of anti-Semitism which once again swept over Europe to capture the souls of men, as was soon seen in the notorious Dreyfus affair.

At that time there were serving in the French army some 337 Jewish officers. L'affaire Dreyfus is too well known to be recounted here, but this conspiracy against a distinguished comrade by the ruling officer caste of France, offers the clearest evidence of the difficulties both Jewish soldiers and officers were under in attempting to requite their duty as citizens in the lands of their birth.

V

Even in America, deepseated social prejudice actuated against the Jewish population. The Governor of New Amsterdam, Peter Stuyvesant, refused arbitrarily to allow Jews to serve in the military guard duty of the colony, imposing instead a discriminatory tax. The Jewish population though minor, spiritedly resisted this affront. In 1655, Asser Levy demanded that Jews be allowed to stand guard. When Stuyvesant remained adamant, Levy bought uniforms for himself and other Jews, and proceeded to stand guard just the same.

From the scattering pre-Revolutionary records we learn that Captain Isaac Isaacs served with the first expedition against the French stronghold of Crown Point; Aaron Hart was on the staff of General Amherst at the capitulation of Montreal; and

Captain Isaac Myers and two Jewish enlisted men marched with Washington in the Indian expedition across the Alleghenies.

In 1776, there were less than 2,500 Jews in the Thirteen Colonies, including women and children. By ordinary standards, this meant perhaps 800 men capable of bearing arms. At least 600 of these fought through the entire War of Independence, serving on all fields from Valley Forge to Yorktown. Among a distinguished group of officers was the able Colonel David Salisbury Franks, who was later to fall in a fight against the Indians; Benjamin Sheftall of Georgia, whom the British referred to by official proclamation as "a very great rebel"; Francis Salvador of South Carolina, who became known as "the southern Paul Revere" and was later killed in battle; David Emanuel of Georgia, later to become Governor of the State; and young Isaac Franks, who enlisted at the age of 17 and later became a lieutenant colonel in the Pennsylvania militia. Isaac Nunez Cardozo, great grandfather of the late Supreme Court Justice Cardozo, was a member of a company of fighting men said to be almost entirely Jewish. Lieutenant Colonel Solomon Bush, Major George Bush and Major Lewis Bush fought with distinction; Captain Jacob Cohen of Virginia commanded a cavalry company. Isaac Myers of New York organized a company of men, of which he was chosen Captain. In South Carolina, there was a "Jews' Company" commanded by Captain Richard Lushington, the majority of whose members were Jews. Major Benjamin Nones volunteered from his native Bordeaux, France, and became aide-de-camp to Washington. Nones' Legion of 400 men attached to Baron de Kalb's command, was composed largely of Jews. When de Kalb fell mortally wounded at the Battle of Camden, he was carried off the field by three Jewish officers, Major Nones, Captain Jacob de la Motta, and Captain Jacob de Leon.

Among other figures was Mordecai Sheftall, Commissary General of the troops of Georgia, and the immortal Haym

Saloman, who is best known for having been instrumental in financing the Revolution and in its economic organization. What is less known is that he "displayed great personal courage also in carrying on daring enterprises to destroy the fleet and storehouses of the enemy,"[32] and that he once was tortured and condemned to be hanged for his Revolutionary activities, but managed to escape to Philadelphia.

During the War of 1812, it is probable that the number of Jews in the United States was around 3,000. In this war, too, they served with distinction.

One of the great fighting men of United States naval tradition was Commodore John Ordroneaux, who in one sea battle defeated and sank five British frigates. The British referred to him as "the terror of the seas". He is reported once to have halted a retreat on the part of his men in the face of a British boarding party, by lighting a match near the powder magazine and threatening "to blow the ship to hell" if his men retreated further. Another brave naval officer was Commodore Uriah P. Levy, who is also said to have been responsible for the abolition of corporal punishment in the Navy. Among Jewish officers in this war were Brigadier General Joseph Bloomfield, Major Abraham A. Massias, who was instrumental in the defense of Charleston, Colonel Nathan Myers, and a considerable group of lesser rank. Captain Mordecai Myers distinguished himself in many engagements, and wrote the stirring words: "Sum must spill there blud and others there ink. I expect to be amongst the former. . . ." Among the enlisted men was the grandfather of the author, Bret Harte; and Levi Myers Harby, who volunteered as a boy of 14 and later was to distinguish himself for heroism in the Mexican War. At the defense of Fort McHenry, whose triumphant resistance to heavy British battering inspired Francis Scott Key's *The Star Spangled Banner,* the records show a considerable proportion of Jewish names.

In the war with Mexico, General David de Leon who became known as "the fighting doctor", led cavalry charges as well as attended to the medical needs of the army. His gallantry in action caused him twice to receive the thanks of the United States Congress. There was the usual complement of lesser officers and enlisted men. One company composed almost entirely of Jewish immigrants from Germany was organized in Baltimore.

At the time of the Civil War, Jews constituted less than one-half of 1% of the 31,000,000 people then living in the United States. Their number in both armies was disproportionately large. John Seddon, Confederate Secretary of War at the time, is reported to have refused a request for High Holy Day furloughs for Jewish soldiers, on the ground that there were 10,000 to 12,000 Jews in the Confederate army and that "it would disintegrate certain commands if the request were granted." Observers at the time placed the number of Jews in the Union armies at fifteen to twenty thousand.[33] These figures include whole families of brothers, fathers and sons, as for example, the five Moses brothers of South Carolina, the five Wenk brothers of New York, and the Jonas family, which sent four brothers to the Confederate army, with the father and one brother enlisting on the Union side.

Among the Jewish soldiers serving in Blue and Gray uniforms were nine generals, twenty-one colonels, and 647 officers of lesser rank. The most prominent of these, perhaps, on the Union side, was General Frederick Knefler, a brilliant tactician who served on Sherman's staff in the famous March to the Sea in 1864.

The Union general, Oliver O. Howard wrote of the German officers and men under his command, that "so many were of Jewish lineage that I am unable to designate them. I had a Jewish aide-de-camp, one of the bravest and best, in the first battle of Bull Run . . . I had another aide who was killed at the Battle of Chancellorsville, a true and brave officer. Two of my brigade commanders answered to the above description." During the first two days of the Battle of Gettysburg, the brunt of the Southern attack was borne by the regiment under the command of Colonel Edward S. Solomon, which repeatedly repulsed the desperate charges of the Confederate cavalry leader, Pickett. The 27th Pennsylvania Infantry, which covered the retreat of the Union army in the first battle of Bull Run, was commanded by Brigadier General Max Einstein of Philadelphia, and included 30 Jewish officers and a considerable number of Jewish enlisted men. William Durst, a sailor on the Monitor, so conducted himself in the historic battle with the Merrimac,[34] that the ship's commander, John Lorimer Worden, on receiving the thanks of the Congress for his valiant action, observed that Durst, too, was "eminently worthy to be recognized by some action on the part of Congress." Among others who served with distinction was General Leopold Blumenberg, who commanded the 5th Maryland Regiment and who left one of his legs on the field at Antietam, and the legendary captain, J. B. Greenhut, of the famous 82nd Illinois. Among other citations and awards for heroism, seven Jewish soldiers won the coveted Congressional Medal of Honor, the highest award for bravery. Leopold C. Newman was promoted from colonel to brigadier general during a personal visit by Lincoln, as the former lay mortally wounded in a military hospital.

On the Confederate side, Jews served with equal gallantry, and considering their small numbers, left a most remarkable record. There were at least twenty-three Jewish staff officers in the Confederate forces. Judah P. Benjamin of Louisiana, became Secretary of War and later Secretary of State for the Confederacy. There were two assistant adjutant generals, J. Randolph Mordecai and Lionel Levy. The Surgeon General of the Confederate armies was David Camden de Leon of South Carolina, the gallant officer who had so distinguished himself under fire at the Battle of Chapultepec in the Mexican War. Captain L. G. Harby, also a veteran of the Mexican War, became a commodore in the Confederate fleet and commanded the defense of Galveston.

The great Confederate military hero of his time was the Jewish soldier, Max Fronthall. His name became a synonym for heroic conduct under fire, so that any man cited for conspicuous bravery was described as "a regular Fronthall". During an account of the Spottsylvania Courthouse battle in which Fronthall took a conspicuous part, the writer, A. T. Watts, exclaimed: "I now understand how it was that a handful of Jews could drive before them the hundred kings; they were all Fronthalls".

In the Spanish-American war, Jewish fighters again were conspicuous, bearing their full share of the national burden. Five thousand[35] Jews saw service in this struggle, a ratio 20% higher than that applying to the American population as a whole.

Fifteen Jews went down with the crew of the battleship Maine. The executive officer of the Maine, and later vice admiral of the U. S. Navy, was Adolph Marix. The first to fall in the Battle of Manila was a Jewish sergeant, Maurice Juster of California; the first to capture an enemy flag was Sergeant Morris J. Cohen of the 20th Kansas Volunteers, later killed in action; the first American sailor killed in an engagement with the Spaniards was the Jewish seaman, Ernest Suntznich, during the bombardment of Cienfuegos; and the first to reach the top of San Juan Hill in the famous charge of Colonel Roosevelt's Rough Riders was Irving Peixotto of the 6th U. S. Infantry.

VI

In view of the brutal anti-Semitism which was to engulf them immediately after World War I was concluded, the heroism of the Jews in this terrible struggle, and their passionate faith in its purposes, comprise one of the bitterest gibes the Fates have ever written into mortal history.

The estimated total of men under arms on both sides was 65,000,000. The number of Jews engaged was about 1,506,000 or 2.3% of the total under arms. The proportion of Jews to the total population of the countries concerned, approximated 1%. The Jewish dead totaled 171,375 or slightly over 2.6%. Over 100,000 were decorated for valor.

Even in Germany, where pre-Nazi anti-Semitism was already real and crushing, the ratio of Jews in the armed services was more than 12% greater than the ratio of Jews to the total population.[36] Of the 100,000 Jews in the German army, at least 78% served at the front, and some 35,000 were decorated, including 900 who received the Iron Cross, 1st Class, and four who were awarded the rarely bestowed Prussian Gold Medal for exceptional heroism under fire. About 23,000 were promoted to non-commissioned ranks, and over 2,000, not including the Medical Corps, were commissioned, a remarkable record since previously no Jew could be commissioned in the Reichswehr.[36a]

Of the handful of German fliers, 200 were Jews. Among these were the celebrated ace, Lieutenant Frankel, who was killed in action, and the gallant Lieutenant Weill, also killed in action. The oldest German flier was 48-year-old Jakob Wolf. The leading instructor in the German naval air service was Ellis Dunitz. The famous Baron Manfred von Richthofen and his brother, Lothar, would have been liquidated by Hitler as non-Aryans. So would General von Mossler, commander of Wilhelm's Hussar Guards; General Max Hoffman, who played a leading part at the great German victory at Tannenberg; and General Otto Liman von Sanders, who won the title of "Lion of Gallipoli" for his successful defense of that strategic spot, and who later was defeated by Allenby in 1918 while commanding the Turkish army in Palestine.

The first member of the Reichstag to fall in battle was the Jewish Social-Democrat, Ludwig Frank. The youngest German volunteers were all Jewish lads, Joseph Steinhardt, 15, Richard Bing, 14, and Joseph Zippes, 13, the latter losing both legs on the field.

Outside of the armed services, the German Jews gave themselves fully to the war effort. The work of Walter Rathenau in mobilizing the Germany economy for war was instrumental in keeping German resistance alive for so long. So was that of Fritz Haber, Director of the Kaiser-Wilhelm Institute for Physics and Chemistry, and in charge of German Chemical Warfare. His discovery of the means for extracting nitrogen from the air kept Germany from military collapse long before her final defeat at the hands of the Allies. Karl Arnstein was chief builder and designer for the Zeppelin works, and the principle of the rigid airship itself was discovered by David Schwartz, a Hungarian Jew, whose widow subsequently sold his plans to Count Zeppelin who named the ship after himself.

In Austria-Hungary there were 320,000 Jews in the armed forces, or more than 14% of the entire Jewish population. More than 12% of the Jewish servicemen died under fire. In the Austrian divisions alone, 6,000 were decorated for conspicuous heroism. Although anti-Semitism was ineradicable in the Dual Monarchy, the policy of Emperor Franz-Josef was completely opposed to discrimination. In his service were two Jewish field marshals, six generals and 691 other officers. These included Lieutenant General Felix Schreiber, who led the Emperor's armies in the advance on Serbia, Colonel Joseph Knerber, the first Austrian officer to be killed at the front, and the noted General Emil von Sommer, who later had his medals torn from his uniform by Hitler's minions because he was a Jew.

In almost all of the countries engaged in the war, including Greece, Rumania, Serbia and Turkey, "the Jews furnished a greater proportion of fighters and a greater proportion of dead and wounded."[37] In Belgium, 6% of the Jewish population served as against 3.6% of non-Jews. Twelve percent of the Jewish soldiers were killed in battle as compared with 5% of the non-Jews. More than 25% of the Belgian Jewish soldiers received one or more decorations. Among the Jewish officers in the Belgian army were General Louis Bernheim,[38] valiant defender of Antwerp, and Leopold Wiener who entered the war a major, and came out a general, with eight decorations for bravery.

In the British Empire 2.3% of the total population was mobilized. Among the Jews of the Empire, 12% served in the armed forces. Twenty per cent of the Jews in the armed forces were volunteers. Of the non-Jewish subjects of the King, only 2.3% volunteered. Before conscription came into effect, a total of some 10,000 Jews were in the British Army, of whom 1,130 were officers.[39]

Ten per cent of the fighting British Jews fell.[40] The figure for non-Jews was 4.8%. Of the comparatively few Englishmen who received the Victoria Cross, five were Jews. All told, Jewish fighters received 1,596 awards and citations. Many gained distinction as aviators.

Voluntary enlistments in the Dominions were high. Canada, with 80,000 Jews sent 6,000 overseas. In Australia, out of a Jewish population of 17,000, there were 2,000 enlistments. Of these, 260 died in action. The proportion of Jewish volunteers was 11%, against 9% for the country as a whole. The commander of the Australians was the brilliant Sir John Monash, who was in charge of the great offensive which finally crushed the spirit of the German army in the summer of 1918. Next in command in the Australian forces was Major General Sir Charles Rosenthal. Another Jewish soldier, who was also to distinguish himself in the fighting in World War II, was General Bernhard Cyril Freyberg, who commanded the New Zealand troops. A tough, fighting officer, Freyberg had become a brigadier general at the age of 27, was wounded in action no less than nine times, and among other decorations, wore the Victoria Cross.

Jewish officers in the British forces included Brigadier General H. J. Seligman who commanded in the Royal Artillery from the beginning to the end of the war. Lieutenant Colonel Solomon J. Solomon was instrumental in converting the British army to the use of camouflage. Chaim Weizmann, later to become President of Israel, played a key role by finding a way to produce acetone, indispensable to the production of cordite. Lieutenant Colonel Sir Albert Stern was the first to recognize the immense potentials of tank warfare; and the engineer, Sir Alfred Yarrow, was responsible for the design and building of the high speed torpedo boats and destroyers which so greatly affected the nature of naval warfare.

Also fighting under British command in the Middle East were a number of wholly Jewish units, who marched under the blue and white banner of Israel.[41] Joseph Trumpeldor and the Zionist leader, Vladimir Jabotinsky, had offered to form a Jewish legion to fight on the Allied side against the Turks. At Cairo, the British commanding general, Maxwell, refused the offer, but suggested instead a Zion Mule Corps for service at Gallipoli. Jabotinsky was indignant but Trumpeldor philosophically decided to make the best of the situation and accept. The Mule Corps was placed under the command of the noted British soldier, Dublin-born Colonel J. H. Patterson. For the first time in modern life, 720 volunteers, though recruited for non-fighting service, marched proudly under the ancient flag of David. Shortly, the Zion Mule Corps found itself in the thick of the fighting. Trumpeldor, whose characteristic cry was "Kadimah!" (Forward!) and who was again wounded on the field, was described by Colonel Patterson in his reports as "the most courageous man and the best soldier whom I ever met."

The failure of the Gallipoli expedition resulted in the disbanding of the Mule Corps; but with the issuance of the Balfour Declaration in November 1917, Jabotinsky finally succeeded in obtaining permission for the organization of a Jewish battalion recruited for Palestinian service, the 38th Royal Fusiliers. Colonel Patterson again was placed in command. Two other units, the 39th and 40th Battalions, commanded respectively by Lieutenant Colonel Eliazer Margolin and Frederick Dudley Samuel, soon followed. It was the 38th Battalion, known as "The Judeans", which held the difficult position on the extreme right flank of the British army, at the Wadi Mellahah, and which participated together with the 39th and 40th Battalions in the final drive which resulted in Turkish collapse. It was they who pursued the Turks across Jordan, finally capturing Es Salt.

In France, over 55,000 Jews, comprising 22% of the Jewish population, fought. Seventeen percent of this number were killed. Of the non-Jewish French population, 14.9% fought, with a casualty record of 16%. Over 2,000 Jewish soldiers received war decorations. One hundred and one Jews received the Croix de Guerre; 140, the Medaille Militaire; and 311, membership in the Legion d'Honneur.

A like pattern existed for the Empire as a whole. The 11,000 Tunisian and Moroccan Jewish troops who joined the Tricolor were all volunteers. Not being French citizens, they were not subject to the draft, and not being Moslems, they could not be recruited in the native contingents. Many of the best fighters in the Algerian Zouave regiments were native Algerian Jews. The Jewish population of Algeria was about 65,000. There is no documentary evidence to establish the exact number called to the colors, but, preliminary lists showed 29 decorated with the Legion d'Honneur, 94 who received the Medaille Militaire, and about 800 citations for heroism under fire. Whole regiments of Algerian Zouaves who conducted themselves so remarkably in the war, were found under analysis to be made up one-third to one-half of Jews.

The foreign Jews residing in France in 1913 numbered 30,000, including women and children. Of this number, 12,000 volunteered for service in the French Foreign Legion. In the attack on Carency of May 9, 1915, the regiments of the Foreign Legion which bore the brunt of the fighting, consisted mainly of these Jewish soldiers, less than 20% of whom survived the battle.

At the start of World War I, there were two Jewish generals in active service. Four in the Reserve Corps resumed service. Eight other officers became generals, making fourteen in all.

General Georges Valabrégue, head of the Artillery School and the Paris Military Academy, commanded the 3rd Army Corps. General Heymann who had reached the over-age limit, had the 15th Region of Marseilles. General Lucien Lévy commanded the engineers of the 4th Army Corps, General Geismar, the artillery of the 4th Army Corps, Brigadier General Camille Lévi, a division of shock troops, Brigadier General Dennery, a territorial division of infantry, Brigadier General Grumbach, the brigade of infantry which performed so heroically at the Marne, and Brigadier General Mayer, the expeditionary forces to French West Africa. Lieutenant General Naquet-Laroque was a member of the Superior Council of Inventions at the Ministry of War. General Francfort commanded the fortress of Epinal and was killed in action. General Bloch was one of the chiefs of the garrison of Maubeuge which defended itself so well against siege. General Mordecai Valabrégue was a member of the Supreme War Council. General July Heym commanded the 15th Army Corps. The Artillery General, Paul Edouard Alexandre, is generally credited by military men as being the real hero of Verdun, not the vacillating Pétain. Any list of French military leaders of World War I must also include the superb tactician, Brigadier General Chanville Levy, and the formidable General Andre Weiller, who was wounded eight times and received six decorations. Alexandre Millerand, the great French Minister of War, also would have been liquidated under Hitler's Aryan laws.

A long list of lesser officers commanded and fought in all the combatant branches. That these were for the most part field officers rather than desk sitters, may be judged from the fact that some 250 French Jewish officers were killed, exclusive of alien Jews, Algerians, Moroccans and others who served under the Tricolor banner.

Even though Russia had been the land of pogroms and violent Jewish persecution, the Jews of that state rallied to her defense during the war. Though with rare exceptions Jews previously could not be commissioned as officers in the

Russian army, "there were several hundred Jewish officers in 1916-17, indicating that they had achieved this rank by sheer merit on the battlefield," [42] By July of 1917, 60,000 Jews in the Russian army had been decorated and 2,600 recommended for commissions. The figures necessarily must be pieced together due to the destruction of records following the Red Revolution, but the indications are that some 650,000 Jews, or 9.4% of the Jewish total in the Czar's Empire, fought in the armed forces, as compared to a general total for all Crown subjects of 7%. Jewish casualty figures "have been estimated as at least 100,000 dead, or over 15% of the Jewish enrollment."[43]

In Rumania where the Jewish population constituted 3.19% of the total population, they nevertheless made up 4.6% of the mobilized forces. The anti-Semitic bias against Jews was largely identical in Rumania with that of Russia. Nevertheless, at least 900 received war decorations and 218 became commissioned officers, achieving this rank through valor in the field.

In Italy, whose entire Jewish population was only 43,929, or slightly more than one percent of the total population, there were no less than 700 Jewish officers, including two full admirals, one rear admiral and eleven generals, two of whom, Aristide Benedetti and Allegro Pavia, were killed in action.

Jewish officers were also prominent as air fighters and submarine commanders. The Gold medal for valor, given to only 57 men, was won by four Jews. Over 500 Jewish soldiers received decorations. Baron Sydney Sonnino, Italy's wartime Foreign Minister, was killed in the Air Corps. Lieutenant Colonel Benedette di Benedetti died in action at the age of 77. Among the outstanding heroes of World War I were Admiral Umberto Pugliese, and General Achilles Levi-Biancini.

Some 250,000 Jewish soldiers served in the U. S. armed forces during World War I, constituting 5.7% of the total American mobilization. The Jewish proportion of the total American population at the time was 3.27%.[43a]

More than 20% of the Jewish contingent, as shown by the files of the American Jewish Committee, were volunteers.

In the A.E.F. the infantry, artillery, cavalry, engineers and signal-aviation branches together constituted 60% of the total personnel. The distribution of Jewish soldiers in these branches, however, was 75%. The infantry was 26.6% of the entire army but constituted 48% of all Jewish soldiers. The signal-aviation corps represented 6.5% of the U.S. army total, but 15% of the Jewish fraction. The proportion of Jews in the medical corps was 8%, as compared to the general average of 9%. In the marine corps, 3.4% proved to be Jewish.

There were nearly 10,000 Jewish commissioned officers. These included Rear Admiral Claude C. Bloch, in charge of Naval Transport, and later commander-in-chief of the U.S. Fleet, Rear Admiral Joseph Strauss, Rear Admiral Edward David Taussig, Major General Milton G. Foreman, who became the first commander of the American Legion, Brigadier General Abel Davis, and Brigadier General Charles H. Lauchheimer of the marine corps. The navy had at least 900 Jewish commissioned officers, and the marine corps another hundred.

The total of Jewish dead was more than 5.7% of the total American death roll. Of the 63 American volunteer dispatch runners who died in the performance of this exceptional duty, 37 were Jews. The youngest American in the war was thirteen-year-old Albert Cohen of Memphis, Tennessee, who fell in the Meuse-Argonne offensive. Altogether, 1,100 Jewish soldiers were cited for conspicuous valor. Of 78 Congressional Medals of Honor awarded during World War I, Jews received at least three.[44] Four received the rarely conferred French Medaille Militaire; 174, the Croix de Guerre; and 150, the Distinguished Service Cross.

The youngest American soldier to receive the Distinguished Service Cross was Louis Abend, who enlisted at fifteen and was already a corporal when he landed in France at seventeen. Another Jewish soldier, Sergeant Sam Dreben, was referred to by General Pershing as the "finest soldier and one of the bravest men I have ever known." Dreben received the Distinguished Service Cross for single-handedly rushing an enemy post and killing 23 of the 40 Germans located there. Another to receive the Distinguished Service Cross from the personal hands of Pershing was Abraham Krotoshinsky, an immigrant from Poland, cited for his spectacular heroism in the battle of the Argonne Forest.

Sergeant Sydney Gumpertz, on a mission to silence a machine gun nest, found his companions killed, but went on alone in the face of heavy fire and succeeded in capturing a crew of nine Germans at Bois de Forges. For this, he won the Congressional Medal of Honor. Sergeant Ben Kaufman, later to become a Brigadier General in the Army Reserve, advanced alone with an empty gun upon a German machine gun nest, despite a shattered right arm, took one prisoner and scattered the balance of the crew. For this his country gave him the Congressional Medal of Honor.

Numberless instances of heroic conduct on the part of Jewish fighting personnel dot the records. All told, they gave a proud account of themselves and served their country well. On another front were still other patriots, advising in the war effort and doing the thankless work of organization back home. The most illustrious of these was Bernard Mannes Baruch, Chairman of the War Industries Board and the author of the American system of wartime controls. During this period, Felix Frankfurter, later to become Associate Justice of the Supreme Court, was an Assistant Secretary of War.

VII

One of the most remarkable military thinkers of our time was the Polish Jew, Jean de Bloch. Although largely forgotten today, his exhaustive six-volume work, *The Future of War in Its Technical, Economic and Political Relations,* written in 1897, was a matter of great controversy in his time, and was translated into many languages. The well-known British military writer, Major General J. F. C. Fuller, comments on the fact that aside from Bloch, neither Von Moltke nor Foch, nor the other military geniuses of the past, had grasped the meaning and nature of modern war, especially in its relation to industrial world interdependence. Whenever Fuller mentions some radically new military development, he states that "even Bloch could not have foreseen it." He remarks that Bloch's "description of the modern battle is exact, for it is exactly as it was fought seventeen years later, and his prediction of the coming war is no less so."[45]

Bloch's estimates of the course of the Boer War were so accurate that R. E. C. Long, writing in the *Fortnightly Review*,[46] declared that Bloch "had predicted, even in number and detail, the course of events in the South African war." Bloch clearly foresaw both the tactical and strategic functions of the modern air arm. He recognized the obsolescence of cavalry and the gradual obsolescence of navies, as well as the regrouping of power potentials which has destroyed the war-making ability of minor states. Almost alone, he foresaw that the day of cold steel was over, and predicted with uncanny insight, not only the trench fighting in World War I, but the precise conditions under which the battle would seesaw back and forth, as well as the ultimate role industry, science and civilian production would play in military decision.[47]

The collapse of the Russian state and the almost complete disintegration of the Russian armies in 1917-18, brought into prominence the brilliant organizing genius and great military gifts of another amazing figure, the Communist theoretician, Leon Trotsky. Together with his chief lieutenant, Efraim Markovich Skliansky, a Jewish physician with as little practical military experience as Trotsky himself, the Communist leader was responsible for hammering the Red Army into an effective military instrument, despite the deadly chaos which gripped Revolutionary Russia.[48]

Trotsky was easily one of the pre-eminent military figures of our time, not only for his practical achievements in the organization of the Red Army, but for his deep insight into the future of military operations. In an article written several months before Munich, he estimated with amazing accuracy the course, nature and outcome of World War II.[49] He foresaw that the English theory of the small army would have to give way to conscription, despite the advent of high mechanization, and visualized in essential detail the "totalitarian character of the next war," though in this respect, he may possibly have been influenced by the writings of Bloch.

In the revolutionary and turbulent post-war period, Jews served prominently in all of the fighting movements, with the exception of that of the Nazis. Even here, there were outstanding figures such as Colonel Dusterberg, one of the co-leaders of the powerful ex-servicemen's organization, the Stahlhelm, who had to retire because of Hitler's racial laws, though his organization in the pre-election campaigns collaborated with the Nazis. There were also others who might be presumed to be at least half-Jewish by blood, as for example, Goering's Chief of Staff for the Luftwaffe, Field Marshal Eberhard Milch, who legally had himself declared a bastard in order to disacknowledge his Jewish father.[49a] Nor did Hitler neglect to utilize the work of Jewish military inventors and thinkers on behalf of his warrior state, or disdain to have the important German psychological warfare branch rest on principles evolved by such men as Hirschfeld, Stern, Lippman, Bergson, Freud, Lazarus, Steinthal and Stransky.

In the Irish Rebellion, one of De Valera's top lieutenants was Robert Briscoe of Dublin.[50] The Jewish general, Morris A. Cohen, known as General Ma, organized the first modern Chinese army, and for a period of time was virtually Minister of War for Chiang Kai-shek. Jews marched with D'Annunzio in the seizure of Fiume. In the Spanish civil war of 1936-39, among the foreign volunteers who rallied to the side of the Republicans, the Jewish percentage was high. Of the American contingent of 3,500, 630, or about 20%, were Jews. Two hundred and seventeen of these were killed and 90% of the rest wounded. Both of the leaders of the Abraham Lincoln Brigade were Jewish boys, Lieutenant Colonel John Gates, and the battalion commander, Milton Wolff.

Just as Jews were numerous in the leadership of the Red Revolution, so they were also disproportionately so in Mussolini's march on Rome. Half a dozen Jews were among the small group of leaders who founded the Fascist party. Three were among the "martyrs" who gave their lives in its early struggle for supremacy. The Duce's righthand man during the whole early period was Aldo Finzi, the airman. Another Jew, Carol Foá, as editor of the official Fascist journal, Gerarchia, was instrumental in molding the party's opinions and policy and Marghereta Sarfatti was the Duce's literary collaborator and close adviser during the whole early Fascist period.[51] Even after the Aryan laws which Mussolini had placed into existence at the insistence of Hitler, some Jews had to be called back by him for wartime service as advisers. Among these were the noted General Modena, Admiral Pontremoli, and Admiral Umberto Pugliese, considered Italy's greatest naval designer. Though Jewish participation in the armed services was thus rigorously brought close to zero, a Jew, Bruno Jesi, nevertheless managed to win the rarely bestowed Gold Medal "for outstanding valor under fire," in 1939.[52]

VIII

World War II as is well-known, proved to be the graveyard of a large section of the Jewish people. More than 6,500,000 were wiped out in the Nazi extermination camps alone. During this time, anti-Semitic calumny reached a pitch of fury hitherto known only to the darkest period of the Middle Ages. Jewish patriotism was assailed, and the quality of their soldiering made the butt of vicious jibes. Even in those parts of the world where Jews had not been deprived totally of human rights, the mass effect of carefully nurtured propaganda was to derogate them in the eyes of their neighbors as a craven people. Yet the records which exist indicate that in this war, too, Jewish soldiers bore themselves with dignity, and fought with all the fine courage and manliness which has distinguished the registers of the race over the centuries.

It is known that a total of more than 1,000,000 Jews served in the armies of the United Nations; but the collapse of the various governments in the death struggle over Europe, and the virtual disappearance of organized Jewish life on that continent, has made exact data on the fighting forces of many countries almost impossible to secure. By far the best information available on the performance of Jewish soldiers as patriots and fighting men, is from the United States, the British Empire, and the Soviet Union.

Though the Soviets showed an increasing tendency to restrict the participation of Jews in the higher circles of state leadership, they were by no means allergic to Jewish fighting intelligence and skill. Among the Soviet generals warring against Hitler, 313 were Jews. These included General Isserson, whose infantry tactics were greatly admired by German military leaders and copied by them in the initial campaigns of World War II; Lieutenant General Jacob Kreiser, master strategist of the Battle of Moscow; General Lev Dovator, victor in the crucial first Battle of Rostov; General Michael Rabinovitch, commander of the tank troops; and Marshal Jakob Smushkevich, commander of the Soviet Army Air Forces. The Jewish poet, Israel Fisanovich became the most feared of all the Russian submarine commanders. The development of guerrilla warfare, so important to the final outcome of the war, may largely be credited to heroic Jewish officers.[53]

Although the Jews were hardly 2% of the population of the Soviet Union, they took fourth place among all the national groups decorated for gallantry in battle during World

War II. Altogether, 185,000 Soviet Jewish soldiers were cited by the Soviet High Command for bravery.

In the American forces during World War II, there were 550,000 Jews in uniform, or approximately five per cent of the total under arms. The Jewish proportion of the whole American population at the time was 3.55%.[33a] Of the Jewish total, 80.59% were in the army, and 19.41% in the navy, coast guard and marine corps. In the quartermaster corps, a traditional source of anti-Semitic ridicule, despite a familiarity with this type of work which should have qualified them for a far higher proportion, the percentage of Jewish servicemen was only 3.43%, whereas 33½% of the Jewish army men were with the Army Air Forces. Jewish flyers constituted close to six per cent of all AAF flying personnel.

Jewish voluntary enlistments were extremely high. A survey of Jewish refugees made early in 1945, showed that 10% had entered the armed services. At the identical period, 8.9% of the total American population was in the service. A survey of 22 cities covering 3,050 physicians, of whom 20% were Jewish, showed that 44% of the Jewish physicians were in service against 25% of non-Jews.

The grand total of awards to American Jewish soldiers, including citations and awards by foreign governments, was 61,448.

Jewish officers were about 20% of all Jewish men in uniform. These included seven major generals, thirteen brigadier generals, one admiral and two rear admirals.

Jewish names were sprinkled throughout the news of the war, including such men as Sergeant Barney Ross, one of the heroes of Guadalcanal; Sergeant Meyer Levin, the bombardier for Captain Colin Kelly, whose plane put the Japanese battleship, Haruna, out of commission; and Major General Maurice G. Rose, commander of the famous 3rd Armored Division, the first American unit to reach German soil, and who was killed in action in western Germany. The last American word sent from Corregidor was wirelessed by a young Brooklyn soldier, Sergeant Irving Strobing. Rear Admiral Ben Moreell, later to become a four star admiral, organized and commanded the Seabees, who played so important a part in operations in the Pacific.

Among a long list of heroic officers, Lieutenant Colonel Robert S. Levine, air squadron commander, of Columbus, Ohio, received 16 decorations of valor, the Distinguished Flying Cross, Silver Star, Air Medal, and Croix de Guerre, together with eleven oak leaf clusters to the Air Medal. Lieutenant Raymond Zussman of Detroit, a tank officer who had been a street fighting instructor at Fort Knox, proceeding on foot in a hail of hot lead, when his tank bogged down in the Rhone valley drive, wiped out two snipers' nests in succession, killed 17 Nazi soldiers and captured 32, together with a quantity of antitank guns and other war materiel. For this feat, he received the Congressional Medal of Honor.

In the fields of communications, engineering and scientific discovery, so vital to modern warfare, the record is studded with Jewish names. It was Professor Raymond D. Mindlin who was the main designer of the proximity fuse. The atomic bomb itself, on which America relies so much for its security today, is largely the product of Jewish minds. It was Albert Einstein and the Russian-born economist, Alexander Sachs, who successfully urged upon President Roosevelt the practicality of the research upon which the bomb was founded. It was Einstein, together with other men and women of Jewish blood, such as the professors Isidore Rabi, Niels Bohr, Lise Meitner, O. R. Frisch, Rudolph Peierls and Franz Simon, who supplied the all-important theoretical work in nuclear physics, and another brilliant Jewish physicist, Professor J. Robert Oppenheimer, who planned, organized and directed the subsequent work which produced the bomb itself.[53b] It is worth mentioning, too, that it was Rear Admiral Joseph K. Taussig who predicted before the Senate Naval Affairs Committee in December 1940, the subsequent Japanese attack on Pearl Harbor. His warning at that time caused him to be looked on as a firebrand, and to be passed over for promotion.

In the United Kingdom, out of a Jewish population of 400,000, over 60,000 served in the British armed forces. Fourteen thousand were in the Royal Air Force, and 15,000 in the Royal Navy. These figures do not include Dominion personnel, or the 30,000 men and women who volunteered for the British forces from Palestine.

Among a prominent list of others, Leslie Hore-Belisha, Minister of War, 1937-1940, was chiefly responsible for the mechanization of the British army at the beginning of the hostilities. Sir Philip A. G. D. Sassoon, who had been Under Secretary of State for Air, is generally credited with responsibility for molding the RAF into an effective fighting arm. There were a number of generals, including Major General R. H. Lorie, Brigadier W. R. Beddington, Brigadier E. F. Benjamin, and Brigadier F. H. Kisch. Among the pilots killed in the air struggle over Britain was the son of Chaim Weizmann.

The names of Jewish fighters figured prominently in the dispatches during the early battles in France, the evacuation at Dunkirk, the air war over Britain, and in the subsequent fighting over the globe. Lieutenant A. N. Abrahams who had fought in both the Boer War and World War I, was killed in action while on patrol duty in the North Sea, though over 70. Lieutenant Colonel Claude Beddington fell at sea during the Dunkirk evacuation, at the age of 72.

In South Africa, where Jews constituted 4.7% of the population, they contributed 10% of the total enlistments. They were especially numerous in the RAF and the armored divisions. In Australia and New Zealand, out of an estimated Jewish population of 35,000, provisional figures show 3,872 in all services. In Western Australia, the single place where complete figures are available, Jewish enlistments were 14% of the total Jewish population of 2,200. In Canada, out of a

Jewish population of 176,500, there were 16,883 serving in the armed forces, 5,889 of whom were in the Royal Canadian Air Force. An additional 1,631 Canadian Jews fought under the flags of other state members of the United Nations.

The number of awards for gallantry to Jewish soldiers of both the United Kingdom and the Dominions, was substantially large.

Authoritative information on Continental Europe for World War II is scattering. Among the details which are available, we note that in Greece, 100% of the Jews eligible for military service joined the colors. There were 7,000 Jewish soldiers from the single city of Salonika, who took part in the heavy fighting on the Albanian front. Six thousand five hundred Greek Jews registered for military service with their consulate in Jerusalem alone. The first officer in the Greek army to be killed in battle was Colonel Mordecai Frizis.

Jews, strangely enough, formed an actual majority in the Czechoslovak army fighting in France. Twelve hundred of these volunteered from Palestine. Gervasi observes that "a high proportion of the Polish army's officers are Jews."[54] These included at least one high-ranking officer, General Mond. Jews are declared to have been prominent particularly in the Polish air forces.

On October 9, 1939, the Polish General Staff announced that 32,216 Jews had already fallen in defense of Poland. The Polish army organized in France was 12% Jewish. Two of its Jewish members received the Order Virtuti Militari, an award comparable to the American Congressional Medal of Honor. General Anders, head of the Polish army in Russia, declared that more than 15% of his troops were Jewish volunteers, certainly an under-estimate, since the Polish corps which marched from Russia to Iran and the Middle East, is believed to have been no less than 30% Jewish.

The French Foreign Legion again had a heavy proportion of Jewish members. In June 1940, a regiment of the Legion composed entirely of Polish Jews, showed such violent resistance to the German advance that out of 3,000 only 400 survived.

More than 80,000 Jews, of whom half were foreigners, served in the defense forces of France, a truly astounding figure. Forty thousand of these were volunteers. The French armed services included a large complement of Jewish officers, with at least eleven generals and two admirals. The names of Generals Darius Bloch and Charles Huntzinger were particularly outstanding in the pre-Vichy dispatches. The leader of the first French company to cross the frontier into German territory was the Jewish captain, Pierre May; and the last official resistance, continuing for two weeks after France signed the articles of capitulation, was that of 1,300 men led by the Jewish colonel, Schwartz, who held out on the Maginot Line until Pétain forced him to lay down his arms.

After the fall of Europe to the German Wehrmacht, Jewish soldiers were numerous among those who rallied to the support of De Gaulle in London. When the Free French began recruiting in the Middle East, "the highest response was from the French Jews."[55] There were many Jews also in the ranks of the Free Dutch. The same is true of the Belgian Army-in-Exile as is noted from the statement of Baron Silvercruys, Belgian Minister to Britain, who called attention to the fact that "many Jewish names appear in the list of Belgian martyrs," and that a great number of Belgian Jews "risking not only their own lives but those of their families, had joined the Belgian forces in Great Britain."

IX

It was the Jews principally who resisted the Nazis in occupied Europe. Even though Jews were relentlessly hunted down, and automatically herded into small concentration areas, they were an important factor in the guerrilla resistance everywhere. Their percentage in these forces throughout the Continent was phenomenal, and their courage and ingenuity outstanding. Whole Jewish guerrilla units became famous for their exploits. Their desperate courage in battle was such that the Germans were said to have feared them particularly.

Judge Leon Meis reported that at least 40% of the French Maquis were Jewish, including whole independent Jewish units.[56] The number of Jews among the Maqui fighters is indicated in the reproach made by collaborationist Radio Paris to the French Committee of Liberation in Brazzaville, for acclaiming ten saboteurs in Paris as "liberators and true Frenchmen." Expostulated Radio Paris: "Is Grieswachs, the perpetrator of two outrages, a Frenchman? No, he is a Jew, a Polish Jew. Is Elek, who was responsible for eight derailments and the deaths of dozens of people, a Frenchman? No, he is a Polish Jew. The other terrorists are also Jews: Lifshitz, Fingerweiss, Stockwerk, and Reiman."[57]

A French Jew, Roger Carcassone, became the leader of the resistance movement in French North Africa, which played a decisive part in causing Algiers to fall into American hands. José Aboulker, Pierre Smadja, and Raoul and Edgar Bensoussan, also Jews, organized the underground itself, while still another Jew, Bernard Karsenty, became the liaison officer between the underground and the Allied Military Intelligence. The record here is superb. When the appointed hour arrived, the underground methodically seized and arrested enemy officers and leaders, occupied police and staff buildings and cut telephone wires. Raphael Aboulker commandeered the main radio station and broadcast the news of General Giraud's return. José Aboulker seized the Central Police Office. Alfred Pilafort, another Jew, blockaded and held the main street; and when the regular army rose in opposition under the influence of Vichy dictates, still another Jew, Lieutenant Jean Dreyfus, led the partisans into battle to protect the work of the underground. He and his men fought successfully until dawn, when the American troops landed. In this action Dreyfus was killed.[58]

Four thousand Jews succeeded in escaping the systematic extermination in Greece and took to the hills, fighting as guerrillas.

In Yugoslavia, Jewish partisans liberated whole concentration camps. There were 68,000 Jews in Yugoslavia in World War II, of whom 6,000 fought in Tito's forces. Other thousands fought with Mikhailovich. One Jewish officer was Mikhailovich's aide-de-camp, and another directed operations of 50,000 men.[59] General Velebit, head of the Yugoslav military mission in London, said in January 1945: "The leaders of the National Liberation Army feel deep gratitude for the magnificent contribution of the Jews in their ranks." One of the leading figures of the Yugoslav resistance, and later one of the three Vice Presidents of the Provisional Government, was Moische Pijade. Another was Dr. Alkalay.

An extremely high percentage among the Czech guerrillas were Jews. A much feared, purely Jewish guerrilla group, known as the "Jewish Patriot Brigade," operated from a mountain stronghold.

Reports coming out of Hungary through underground channels at the end of November 1944, indicated that the armed resistance against the Nazi Government in Budapest was largely carried out by Jews.

In Poland, the guerrilla fighters had a high percentage of Jews who had escaped the ghetto, men who distinguished themselves by their resourcefulness and reckless courage in action. Jewish partisans out of all proportion to the existing numbers, served in every one of the raids on German outposts, estates and communications. Cases of extreme individual heroism and daring were numerous. Baruch Goldstein who brought the first flame thrower into the ghetto, was responsible for the wrecking of four German ammunition dumps. Engineer Isaac Ratner ingeniously contrived delayed-action chemical gadgets by which many German gasoline reservoirs were wrecked. A Jewish partisan group which called itself "The Avengers," became a minor scourge, wrecking trains, destroying bridges, factories and German ammunition dumps. When the Red Army began its attack on Vilna, the first to enter the city were the Jewish partisans, who engaged the barricaded Germans in a bloody encounter in which neither side expected, or received, mercy.

The savage struggle of the Warsaw Ghetto was not a battle in the ordinary sense. It was more than that—a kind of terrible epic which occurs seldom in history, a last supreme test of human dignity, courage, endurance, and moral strength. Originally the overcrowded ghetto area had held some 200,000 people. An influx from the provinces in the wake of the German army brought it to 400,000. About 50,000 died in a nightmare year of disease and deliberately induced starvation. In July 1942, mass deportations began to the Eastern extermination camps, which had been described to the deportees as mere labor camps. More than 300,000 Jews from the ghetto had thus perished before the horrible truth dawned upon those who remained.

Now within the ghetto walls were 45,000 human creatures, without human rights, sick, emaciated, ragged, inexperienced in war, and without arms. The leaders of the ghetto remnant met, and despite the disheartening conditions the determination was made to fight.

The plan of defense was astonishingly well-conceived, and in an area filled with German informers, involved a miracle of discipline and secret organization. The Polish underground, made aware of the impending struggle, refused to help, regarding the moment as inopportune. However, a secret tunnel was built from the headquarters on Muranowska Street, into the Aryan sector, through which weapons were smuggled, to be stored in underground arsenals. Jewish partisans from the forests infiltrated into the area to furnish military instruction. Weapons and bombs were manufactured right in the ghetto.

The Germans meanwhile had gotten wind of the fact that something was brewing. On April 18, 1943, the ghetto was surrounded by heavily-armed battalions of S. S. Elite guards, and regiments of their Lithuanian, Latvian and Ukrainian allies. The blue and white Jewish flag was suddenly raised and the Germans were met with machine gun fire, hand-grenades, Molotov cocktails, knives, clubs and stones. More than 250 Germans fell in this first full-scale rebellion against Nazi rule and outrage. The rest retreated in wild disorder. The next day, a special Jewish shock troop group broke through the walls of the ghetto, attacked German arsenals and factories and took possession of a considerable quantity of Nazi uniforms and war materiel, together with badly-needed food stores. The following night a body of four hundred Jewish commandos dressed in German uniforms, stole out of the ghetto through the secret tunnels, and stormed the great Pawiac prison, liberating several thousand Jews and a number of Christian Poles, who joined the fighters.

Now followed an amazing struggle which lasted for forty-two bloody days, in which an untrained rabble army, overwhelmingly outnumbered and outweighed, and more resembling emaciated scarecrows than men, held out against the most powerful and best equipped army in the world.

The tactics, discipline and organization would have done credit to any professional army, much less to the ragged tubercular ghetto men, women and children who constituted the defenders. The Jewish plan of organization utilized every street corner and every house as a point of support for a general blueprint of defense. All possible tactics were foreseen and prepared for. Barricades were improvised, a system of medical stations created for expected casualties, and even a commissary provided by which orderly resistance could be maintained. Everything that could be used in a fight, including vitriol and boiling water, was utilized against the heavily-armed enemy.

During the course of the battle, Colonel von Sanmern, commanding the S. S. troops, was removed, and Police General Stroop placed in command. He sent an ultimatum to the defenders ordering them to give up "the senseless fight" and release German prisoners, threatening otherwise to destroy the ghetto in a day. The Jews replied that they would be glad to exchange prisoners—ten Jews for one German, and refused to discuss the other points of the ultimatum.

The gates of the ghetto were mined. The Germans now came in with heavy artillery and tanks. When they crossed into the ghetto, the mined gates blew up causing dreadful havoc. The German armor was met by well-camouflaged anti-tank guns, resulting in the annihilation of the advance guard of tanks. The tanks which had been able to retreat were stopped by Jewish men in German uniforms who jumped on board, throwing hand-grenades inside, and often blowing themselves up with the enemy. Again the Germans hastily retreated with heavy casualties. That night, Jewish hand-picked troops in German uniforms attacked Gestapo guard-houses, liquidated the occupants, commandeered arms and brought them back to their own headquarters on German trucks. Now the fight went on in deadly earnest, with the Germans bringing up their heavy cannon, using flamethrowers, bombers and poison gas. Hundreds of German tanks and cannon were destroyed in a single day. Every house was fought for and had to be burned out before the defenders could be routed. Throughout the struggle, fighting within a veritable sea of roasting corpses and stinking flesh, the Jews counterattacked in orderly ranks against the guns and heavy armor with which they were met.

Ceaselessly blasting artillery and incendiary bombs, rained on the ghetto from attacking planes, finally turned the entire area into a roasting inferno of flames. A desperate last appeal to the Polish underground to join the battle was met by renewed refusal, and the Jews determined to fight it out to the bitter end alone.

By June 3 only one house was left standing amid the ashes of what had once been the great Jewish ghetto of Warsaw. With the exception of its occupants, and some 300 who had managed to escape into the forests to join the partisans, all the defenders had been killed. They had laid down their lives in a battle, not for victory, which the Jews knew was a hopeless dream, but for the honor of their name. This remaining structure was defended stoutly, floor by floor. The last survivor, a young Jewish boy of 14, was finally trapped on the roof, his ammunition gone. In a last incredible gesture of defiance, he grasped the blue and white Jewish banner which still floated from the roof, wrapped it around his body and leaped to his death in the smoldering ruins below, rather than surrender.

German losses had been heavy, both in men and material. It is said that they used more fire power in liquidating the virtually defenseless ghetto than during the entire siege of Warsaw.

Revolts followed in other cities, including Sobibor, Bendin, Minsk, Vilna, Slutsk, Rovno and Bialystok. In Bialystok alone, 40,000 Jews, men, women and children, fell after eight days of desperate fighting. The Germans learning from their costly experience in the Warsaw battle, no longer took the Jewish defense lightly. They brought up their big guns at once, coordinated with a massive weight of incendiaries dropped from the sky, systematically turning the entire ghetto into a flaming furnace. The Battle of the Ghetto of Vilna lasted for a full week, with the Germans using bombing planes and heavy artillery to break down the walls.

X

It is in Palestine, the ancient cradle of the race, that the Jews have relived the heroic days of the Maccabees, of David, Gideon, and that host of heroes who have been for the Christian world the very symbol of valor in battle. It was this vanguard of returning expatriates whom Britain's foremost military expert, Captain Liddell Hart, was finally to refer to with unstinted admiration as that "fine fighting race . . ."

During the period following the Balfour Declaration, the Jews of Palestine had learned a deep distrust and hatred for their British overlords, whom they had come to regard as tyrants and conspirators bent on destroying the fetal Jewish state before it could be born. Immediately upon the outbreak of war, however, practically every able-bodied Jewish man and woman eligible for service volunteered, and offered themselves to the British War Office as a body, to fight under the Jewish flag. Altogether, over 137,000 individuals registered for military service in September 1939.

The British, notwithstanding the peril of their own position, refused the offer. The explanation was that to accept the Jews without a compensating number of Arabs, would "disturb the delicate balance of Jewish-Arab relationship." The British attempted instead to organize a Palestine division, half Arab and half Jewish. The Arabs, however, would not enlist in substantial numbers, so the project had to be abandoned. The British thereupon decided to accept a limited number of Jews into the British armed forces themselves. Some 10,000 were promptly inducted into the RAF, including mechanics and air crew specialists. After the collapse of France, this first Palestinian pioneer unit was suddenly dispatched to that country, where it was given the ungrateful task of covering the retreat of the British expeditionary force, a job it discharged with so much daring and courage that it became known as the "Suicide Squad."

On the whole, British reluctance to accept Jewish servicemen from Palestine continued for more than a year. Only a limited number were taken, and at the beginning these generally were assigned "to shoveling dirt and truck driving, but not to combat duty."[60] Although they were forbidden to fight under their own banner, 30,000 Palestine Jews finally were permitted to join England's fighting forces.

By the Summer of 1942, the situation of the British army in Egypt had become little short of desperate. It had lost more than half its manpower and the better part of its mechanized equipment to Marshal Rommel, who confidently expected to be in Cairo in a matter of weeks.

Farouk of Egypt had refused to fire a single shot in defense of his invaded country, and was openly pro-Nazi. Iraq had revolted in favor of a Nazi alliance. The German timetable envisaged a descent through the Caucasus and thence down the ancient pathway of the Middle East, to make final juncture there with the seemingly unbeatable Japanese war machine. To the north, the Vichy regime was preparing Syria as a base for a German invasion.

In response to a request from the worried British authorities, twelve young Jews volunteered to blow up the all-important oil establishments in the Syrian port of Tripoli, well knowing that they would never return. Dashing off at night in a speed boat loaded with high explosives, they succeeded in overpowering the French guard and demolishing the refineries. All were killed.

The Jews specialized in these suicidal expeditions, where their record as fighting men is literally incomparable. Before the reconquest of Iraq, the British received information that a German crew was arriving to destroy the vital Mosul oil wells and installations. They had in jail David Raziel, leader of the Jewish underground. Raziel was released and given the assignment to protect the Mosul installations. With 24 of his picked fighters, he made his way to Bagdad in Bedouin disguise. The little band managed to locate the special crew of 150 German engineers and mechanics who had been landed by German transport plane and were waiting on the outskirts of the city to complete their job of demolition, if the British were to advance on Iraq. Raziel possessed only ten machine guns, a number of cases of hand-grenades, and one revolver for each man. Commandeering five cars, he ambushed the German crew that night, destroying almost all of them together with their trucks and equipment. Raziel was killed as were almost all of his men, but "a fantastic mission had been successfully completed—a mission upon which hinged the life and death of the British Empire."[61]

In 1941, with the Germans poised in Greece, and ready to make juncture with the Vichy French in Syria, 50 Jewish volunteers dressed in German uniform crossed the Syrian border, mingling with the collaborationist soldiers, contacting Free French forces behind the enemy lines, sabotaging valuable military equipment, and transmitting by wireless the intelligence necessary to the success of the forthcoming Syrian campaign. Not one of the 50 volunteers was ever seen again. Two days before the British invaded, another group of fifty young Jews led by Moshe Dayan, who previously had been jailed by the Mandatory Government for possessing "unauthorized arms," was sent on a mission to seize three essential bridges. Their task was to prevent the destruction of these vital arteries by the French, an action which well might have turned the invasion of the Australian spearhead into disaster. The Vichy stronghold, Fort Gouraud, which dominated the approaches to these bridges, was built on the site of an ancient crusader's castle, and manned by a garrison of 300. Dayan and his boys took the fort by a ruse, and in a fierce, uneven struggle in which the greater portion of them were killed, managed to hold until the Australians and Free French came up.

Another group of thirty-two Jews was dropped from British planes into Yugoslavia, Rumania, Slovakia and northern Italy, under instruction to organize Jewish resistance groups and train them in sabotage. Among these was the famous girl officer, Hanna Szenes, who was shot by a Nazi firing squad in Budapest in 1944.[62]

It was Jewish desert scouts, able, daring, acquainted with the type of terrain, and speaking German so that they could mingle undetected with German troops, who provided Montgomery with his military intelligence and guides. It was Jewish engineers who organized and manned the coastal defense and signal services of the entire Middle Eastern coast, and the Jewish coast guard which ran the hundreds of speed boats along the dangerous Mediterranean line.

Until Montgomery took over from Auchinleck, the British at no time had more than 45,000 men on the African front. Of these almost a full quarter were Jews. In the crucial battle of Egypt, which was won by the British 8th Army, the 30,000 Jewish volunteers from Palestine played an indispensable part. There were 2,500 Palestine Jews who served "with the Royal Air Force as bombardiers, pilots and observers. Six thousand more Jews were in the ground crews of the Egyptian airdromes."[62a] Under the direction of Brigadier General Frederick Hermann Kisch of Haifa, chief engineer of the 8th Army, Jewish engineers constructed Britain's so-called impregnable forts at El Alamein. It was Kisch and his men who organized the tremendously difficult supply line which enabled Montgomery to undertake his successful 1,300-mile trek through Libya and Cyrenaica to Tripoli. It was at the gates of Bizerte that Kisch himself was killed.

In June 1942, a company of Jewish engineers at Mechili in Libya, led by Major Felix Liebman of Tel Aviv, disrupted Rommel's inexorable advance for the first time. Laying down a mine field to prevent Rommel's forward thrust aimed at turning the flank of the 8th Army, which stood with its back to Alamein, they were spotted by German scouts. The Germans immediately attacked in strength with Stukas, heavy bombers and tanks. Liebman wirelessed the British for antiaircraft and antitank guns, reinforcements and instructions. The guns and reinforcements did not arrive, but instructions did—to finish laying their mines and hold the position at all costs.

The ill-matched contest lasted for almost a month, with the Jews tenaciously holding their ground. Surrounded on three sides by enemy armor, the engineers received a German emissary who demanded that they hoist the white flag of surrender. Liebman replied that he had no white flag, that he only had the blue and white flag of Zion, and that he was going to fly it. He did. His camp was promptly assaulted by three German columns totaling 110 tanks, together with a number of Stukas. The Jews replied with Molotov cocktails and tommy guns, conserving their ammunition by waiting for close combat before they counterattacked. One sergeant alone accounted for seven tanks. Daily the German assaults against these obstinate men continued in mounting intensity, with Liebman and his remaining men forced back into a deep central dugout, where they made their final stand in the intense desert heat. Their food was gone, and small amounts of water were dropped to them in cans by the RAF.

When they were finally rescued by a column of Free French under General Koenig, the Jews had managed to destroy a considerable portion of Rommel's armor, and had held their position. Only 42 of the 500 remained alive.[63]

It was Major Richard Perach who led the battalion which turned the flank of the Mareth line at another critical juncture in the war. It was a Jewish suicide task force of 85 men, carrying only machine guns and small arms, which at another dangerous moment in Montgomery's campaign, under instructions to create a diversion behind Rommel's lines, instead accomplished the impossible by capturing the important stronghold of Bardia intact, together with all its military booty and 9,000 enemy prisoners. Jewish suicide task forces landed in Tobruk and helped take that city as they had captured Bardia earlier.[64] The expendables used by General Sir Archibald Wavell as the spearheads for the capture of Sidi Barrani, Solum, and Fort Capuzzo, were Jews from Palestine.

There were no engagements in Africa or the Middle East in which Jewish boys did not play a prominent part. In Eritrea, it was Jews who covered the left flank of the advance to Karen, which cut off the Italians. In Ethiopia, they operated as advance suicide squad spearheads, and played a vital role in the capture of Gondar, the last Italian stronghold. Among the 10,000 British troops reported missing in Greece and Crete, 1,023 were Palestinian Jews.

At the moment when he was facing a seemingly invincible Rommel, Montgomery himself had stated privately that only a miracle could save him. "Jewish Palestine," remarks Van Paassen, "was part of that miracle."[65] In addition to the participation in the military forces, the Jews turned all of Palestine into an industrial bastion for the British armies, supplying them with the precision instruments and vital equipment of all types which are needed by modern armed forces. With typical ingenuity, the Jews created almost overnight some 432 new industries for war, furnishing as well the skilled technicians, medical, meteorological and other experts required by a modern mechanized army.

On the plea that such a course was necessary "to avoid inflaming the Arab-Jewish question," the extraordinary and significant service of Jewish Palestine was virtually ignored in the wartime acknowledgments released by British leaders and information services. Nor were Jews allowed to serve as Jewish nationals until September 1944, when intense pressure from the United States and elsewhere forced Britain to agree to the formation of a Jewish infantry brigade group under its own flag. Commanded by Brigadier E. F. Benjamin, this brigade moved into Italy in November 1944, becoming a complete combat group and winning for its personnel many citations for distinguished conduct in the field.

XI

The fighting record of the Jewish Yishub, standing on its own as the new State of Israel, in repelling the invasion of the armies of six Arab countries, trained, equipped and led by the British, is almost without parallel.

Over the years, the sharp clash which had developed between the aims of restive Jewish Palestine and those of its

British rulers, had resulted in deep tension, and a bitterness bordering on hatred. The growing Jewish underground, described to the writer by the French military as the finest guerrilla force this age has produced, had succeeded, after a series of daring operations, in destroying both the peace and security of the British stationed in the Holy Land, together with the all-important prestige of the British raj elsewhere in the Colonial areas. Forced into a dramatic action, London announced its intention of withdrawing from Palestine, leaving the Jews to contend alone with the combined armies of the suddenly bellicose Arab states. When the British finally evacuated, it was confidently expected by most military men, and certainly by those in the British Foreign Office, that there would be a quick end to Jewish pretensions.[66]

For years, the British had made possession of arms by Jews a criminal offense. Regular searching parties had raided Jewish settlements in an unending search for military contraband. At the beginning of the Israeli-Arab war, it may safely be said that there were not enough small arms and ammunition in Jewish hands to equip 2,000 men. The departing British had deliberately drained all known stocks of oil out of the country in an effort to freeze its vehicular services. Administrative services were left in chaos. There was not even a postal service; the phone service was in a hopeless jangle. No effort had been made to train and turn over to the new Jewish authority any of the departments of government. A world wide blockade had been instituted, allegedly for the purpose of localizing the conflict, but operating with massive force against the hopes of the Jews in particular. The key points in Palestine's military economy had been transferred to the Arab Legion, nominally headed by Abdullah, but up to the final moment of withdrawal, used as an integral part of the British policing operation against the Jews. Not only did the British assist the Legion in fortifying itself in the very heart of Palestine, but placed at its disposal the large amount of war material concentrated in the Transjordan British bases.

In addition to the Palestine Arabs themselves, the armies of Iraq, Transjordan, Syria, Lebanon and Egypt were poised on the borders. Saudi-Arabia was prevented from marching[66a] only by a distrust of Ibn Saud's intentions on the part of Arabs occupying intervening territory.[67] The Arab armies possessed heavy armor and squadrons of modern military aircraft. They had the expert advice of top British military personnel, and in the case of the Transjordan Arab Legion, were equipped, financed and led as a virtual arm of the British military forces themselves.

Pitted against this imposing host was a hastily organized volunteer militia, with some broken-down, antiquated aircraft,[67a] almost without a central authority, and possessing only a few makeshift, home-armored vehicles, a few home-made mortars, and a limited quantity of small arms and ammunition.[67b]

The territory the Jews occupied was not only attenuated but lay in lowland country caught within the surrounding hills; strategically it could be regarded as being in an almost impossible position.

That any people could have successfully survived this crushing set of circumstances is a phenomenon from beginning to end. The Jews were always short of arms and munitions. At the time of the first big Arab Legion assault on Jerusalem, the total Jewish arms in that city consisted of a small quantity of rifles, and three 3-inch mortars with a daily ration of 16 shells delivered to an improvised airfield by light plane. There were two Beza machine guns which arrived on May 13, but only one man in the city was found who knew how to handle them. A considerable stock of Molotov cocktails were discovered, however, providentially left behind by the departing British. Against these meager arms stood an iron wall of heavy guns, ringing the city almost completely. The attacking Arabs were estimated at two infantry brigade groups, supported by a field artillery regiment and strong armored elements, two batteries of 25-pound cannon, two batteries of 4.2-inch mortars, large units of tanks and armored cars, and various small artillery units.

For the most part, the Jewish militia was green and inexperienced. Months later, the American, James F. Metcalf, remarked that if the recruit received instruction "for twenty days between conscription and combat, he has had a lot more than the earlier trainees."[68] He described the Israeli troops as "a fighting element reduced to its barest essentials, a man and his weapon, with little in the way of artillery or other support." He observes that though "the invaders were driven from positions that appeared impregnable," there was never any parity of weapons, and that these striking victories were achieved by small detachments of determined men "relying almost entirely on surprise, dash, night attacks and a will to win."[69] The greatest weapon the Israeli soldier had was what Captain Liddell Hart described as the fact that the Arab was "more careful of his own skin than the Jew."

Desperately lacking munitions and arms, the Jews attacked at night with cold steel. The Arabs proved to have little stomach for this type of campaign. In every case of hand-to-hand fighting the Arabs gave ground, abandoning their equipment in headlong flight. The Jews also benefited by a superb and daring intelligence service which allowed them to peg the movements of their foes in many cases well in advance.

Meanwhile by a combination of circumstances, including the capture of war material from the Arabs, raids on British arms trains and depots, and the acquisition of arms purchased in many countries abroad and run in one way or another through the blockade, the quality of Jewish equipment improved enormously, though at no time did it compare with the heavy armor, artillery and planes in the hands of the invaders. Within a matter of weeks, the impossible had occurred, and the beleaguered Jews, fighting tanks with rifles, and bombers with machine guns, relying largely on their courage, initiative, endurance and resourcefulness, succeeded in passing to the offensive. Jaffa, a city of 70,000 Arabs, bulwarked by a considerable army of irregulars from Iraq and Syria, was attacked by some 400 men of the Jewish underground. As the Jews advanced in the narrow streets, British artillery began to shell their positions. Nevertheless, after heavy street fighting and a series of brilliant tactical operations, considerably aided by the panic which had overtaken the Arabs, the Jews succeeded in running up their flag over the central part of the city. The great bulk of the Arab inhabitants fled, together with the irregular units who had been the advance guard of the Arab armies.

Haifa fell in a similar lightning attack, and again the British opened up on Jewish troops with cannon and tank fire, as they evacuated. The overwhelming majority of Haifa's 66,000 Arabs bolted, both before and after the battle was joined.

At Safed were 1,200 Jewish inhabitants, in a town containing 16,000 Arabs, and completely surrounded by 40,000 Arab fellaheen and tribesmen. Confident that the Jews had no arms, the Arabs attacked in force. From hidden recesses the Jews dug up some old shotguns and rifles secreted against this very need. When the struggle was over, a small number of Jews and Arabs lay dead; the balance of the Arabs had hurriedly packed what they could and ran, leaving the entire area in the undisputed possession of the surprised Jews.

Quite different from the circumstances which clogged the roads of Europe before the German advance, and which caused the numerically preponderant Arab population of Palestine to flee almost in a body, the Jews yielded nowhere. Isolated outposts and farming communities dug themselves in and held out against whole armies.

The typical case of Negba, known as the "underground kibbutz," became an Israeli legend. The village lies in a hollow one kilometer below fortified heights which were handed over to the Egyptians and Iraqians by the British military. The whole area of the Negba settlement was hardly more than 150 acres, and its able-bodied male population not more than 90. These were equipped with 80 rifles, 35 machine guns, five two- and three-inch mortars, one short-range anti-tank gun and several hundred hand grenades. In possession of the attackers, in addition to regulation armament, were several batteries of heavy artillery, numerous Bren carriers, planes, tanks and other heavy armor. On one day alone more than 6,000 shells are reported to have fallen into the settlement. All houses were completely demolished by constant shelling. The settlers dug themselves underground, holding their fire until the enemy was within rifle distance. During the five-month siege, the settlement was swept daily by heavy artillery shells and aerial bombs. On a single day four waves of Egyptian infantry led by ten tanks, thirty-six armored cars, and supported by heavy artillery, mortars and the Egyptian air force, attacked. On June 12, 1948, the Egyptians opened an all-out assault on this obstinate settlement, strafing it from the air and advancing on it with infantry and artillery units behind a spearhead of twenty-four giant Sherman tanks. The Jews replied with machine guns and their single anti-tank gun. They concentrated with this and with Molotov cocktails, hitting seven of the armored vehicles in the first column. The Egyptians turned back.

At Ramat Naftali, Yad Mordecai, and other tiny communities, the Jews defended themselves with the same fierce determination. In this battle of armor versus human flesh, a typical report states: "One of the settlers stood at his post, absolutely exposed, working his Bren gun as though he were punching a time-clock in a factory. Another went straight up to an enemy tank in the closing phase of the battle, throwing a hand-grenade into it, and blew himself up together with the enemy."

During the shelling of Jerusalem, there were 4,300 casualties out of the city's 100,000 population. Food, fuel and water were scarce, and a large part of the city reduced to rubble. But the Jews held.

The enterprise and valor by which the Jews contrived to supply the "New City" of Jerusalem with badly needed food and arms for defense, must literally be described as Homeric in its dimensions. Jerusalem was totally cut off from the rest of the Jewish territory. The single tortuous road passed through Arab-held areas. Each time supplies were run, the road itself had to be cleared by a frontal attack. The Jewish supply trucks were compelled to run a gantlet of fire down this narrow ribbon of road whose surrounding heights were manned by Arab sharpshooters and artillery. The road was quickly littered with the blasted shells of Jewish trucks and cars. The casualties were heartbreaking, but the Jews kept coming.

Meanwhile the Arab Legion, already anchored in the old City of Jerusalem with the help of its British mentors (who had also given the Legion possession of Jerusalem's source of water supply as well as the important military positions and approaches to the city) made a supreme attempt to take the all-but-isolated New City.

In addition to confiscating Jewish weapons, disclosing Jewish positions to the enemy and blocking Jewish lines of communication, the British opened up on the Jewish defenders with their own mortars and artillery. It was British heavy guns which dislodged the Jews from the strong defensive position they held at Sheikh Jerrah.

The single strong point remaining to the Jews which would hold back the Legion long enough for the defenders to consolidate their positions in the New City, was the Kfar Etzion Bloc in the heart of the Hebron hills. The entire fighting force consisted of 100 Jewish women and 400 men. These were surrounded by a well-armed Arab population of 60,000, stiffened by the Arabs of Abdullah's Legion. The Jews possessed no antitank weapons nor heavy arms of any kind. Only one-half of the Jewish defenders could be equipped with the arms available. The function of the defenders was to engage the thousands of villagers and Legionnaires who would otherwise have converged upon the city with irresistible force.

Strong assaults by the Arab "liberation army" were beaten back with heavy losses. The Arab Legion finally began an offensive under cover of a merciless ten-hour bombardment from the surrounding ridges. The Arabs used among other vehicles heavy British Sherman tanks, numerous infantry and a large complement of guns. Wave after wave of this armored assault was repulsed. A large proportion of the defenders were killed outright or badly wounded, but the enemy nevertheless was thrown back. The Jewish tactic was always to permit tank advance until the attackers were within range of rifle fire and hand-grenades, and if possible, to turn the battle into a hand-to-hand encounter.

On the morning of May 12, after a protracted defense, the Arabs opened up an all-out attack employing two Legion battalions, thousands of villagers and 40 armored vehicles. In this fierce and bloody struggle, positions continuously changed hands. Kfar Etzion finally capitulated after the Jews had run out of ammunition completely. Only a handful of the 500 defenders survived this ordeal, but they had played their part well. They had held long enough to give Jerusalem's Jewish defenders the breathing spell they needed to dig themselves in. And meanwhile, too, the resolute Israelis had accomplished another minor miracle by cutting a new road along the southern flank of the Judean Hills which linked up Jerusalem with Tel Aviv through wholly Jewish-held territory.

In the end, each of the Arab armies was beaten in detail, beginning with the forces of the Iraqian adventurer, Fawzi Bey Kauji, who was shattered in the battles of Tirat Zvi in the Jordan Valley, and at Mishmar Haemek, scene of the Biblical Armageddon, losing most of his armor to the Jews.[70]

In the decisive Second Battle of the Negev, the Egyptian army was broken with crushing rapidity. By a lightning attack, Jewish jeep units had taken the desert center of Beersheba. In the final movement, perhaps the most daring operation of the war, swiftly moving Jewish troops swept around a wide arc over the southern desert to completely outflank the Egyptians, turning up in Egyptian territory at its rear.

The Egyptian forces lay in two arms, one based on the "impregnable" fortress of Asluj, and extending to Auja, and the other along the southern coast to Gaza. Occupying what apparently was an unbeatable strategic position, the 30,000 Egyptians had at their disposal two modern armored regiments in addition to numerous aircraft.

The Israelis secretly managed to make a circle through the desert, bypassing Asluj and exposing Auja to direct assault. Their desert scouts had found the course of an all-but-obliterated Roman road. This narrow desert track with its dangerous soft sand shoulders, was followed silently through the black night by the Israeli army train, whose travel-weary soldiers were scheduled to arrive after fifteen hours of foot-slogging, at an early morning hour on the main Auja-Rafah road.

Appearing unexpectedly like the very wrath of God, these ferocious, wraithlike warriors descended on Auja, putting the defenders to immediate rout. The road to the south of Asluj was cut at El Musharafa and the position of the supposedly impregnable fortress rendered hopeless. With one of their armored regiments trapped between Auja and Asluj, and completely annihilated, the Egyptians fled across the frontier pursued by Israeli troops, who penetrated 50 miles to the great Egyptian base of El Arish. From this base, the Israelis systematically destroyed Egyptian airfields, capturing some aircraft, and shooting down others. The greater part of the fine Egyptian air armada was smashed on the ground. Hundreds of tanks and armored vehicles were left a twisted and blackened mass of iron or abandoned, together with gasoline, ammunition, small arms and other booty to the triumphant Jews. The remaining Egyptian forces in Palestine found themselves suddenly cut off from all communications with their home bases.

This operation introduced Israeli marine commandos for the first time. In addition to developing a small war industry

THE HEBREW IMPACT ON WESTERN CIVILIZATION

of their own, the Jews had succeeded in running the blockade with enough materiel to produce a small but efficient air force, and a swiftly moving jeep unit. In an operation perfectly synchronized with the movements of the ground troops, Jewish aircraft simultaneously hit all enemy strongpoints, destroying railroads, munition dumps, troop concentrations and airfields, and took complete control of the air. At the same time, the fledgling Israeli navy took over command of the coastal waters, and in its sole naval contest sank the Egyptian flagship and pride of the Egyptian navy, the King Farouk.

The same total victory was achieved over the Lebanese army which had advanced into Palestine headed by a mechanized column. This was attacked, cutting off the Lebanese armored vehicles, and throwing the entire column back into Lebanon in precipitate retreat. Similarly, the Syrians were soundly trounced in the Jordan and Huleh valleys and forced to turn back into Syria.

The Arab Legion itself, despite the carefully nurtured British legend to the contrary, was decisively beaten in every encounter it had with Israeli troops. The Legionnaires fled in disorder from Lydda and Ramleh, which the Israeli army took in a series of sharp blows. In a few days of fighting, the Legion lost some 20% of its personnel and a whole squadron of armored vehicles. At the time of the final truce, which was insisted upon by the great nations of the world, the Legion's military position was a precarious one. During the nine days of battle between the first and second truces, the combined Arab armies lost about 22% of their total strength of approximately 56,000, together with much of their armor. It is conceded that the Armistice forced on the Jews by British pressure in the United Nations, saved the Arabs from complete annihilation. There is little question in the minds of competent military observers that had the Israeli Prime Minister, David Ben-Gurion, given the word, his forces could have marched successfully on Cairo, Amman, Beirut and Damascus at any time in the latter days of the campaign. The British, in fact, felt compelled to warn the Jews that if they crossed over into Trans-Jordan, they would be met there by the British army. This perhaps deterred the top echelon of Israeli planners. The fighting Jews, however, were not intimidated when armed British reconnaissance planes appeared over the battle area in the Negev, for they promptly shot down five of them.

XII

In a century trembling under the impact of stirring events, none has been more impressive than the succession of victories by which Palestine has disappeared forever. In its place stands Israel, inhabited once again, as if the continuity of their residence had never been broken, by a fighting people who have taken up again where their forebears in the militant days of antiquity had left off. The cost has been heavy, for there is scarcely a home in Israel which is not draped in mourning for loved ones who have fallen in the field. It is this record which speaks for itself in reply to the calumnies which have assailed the character and martial qualities of the Jewish people; for here the record is clear, and may be read without debate as to the value of comparative figures.

Elsewhere the evidence amassed over the centuries would appear to point indisputably to the conclusion that the record of the Jewish fighting man is among the best the world has produced. It is the record of a stanch and devoted people whose loyalty to all causes to which they have been pledged has been proved on all of the battlefields of Western civilization.

FOOTNOTES

[1] See Sir Leonard Woolley, *Abraham*; see also *The Apocrypha*, Book of Judith, and Josephus, *Antiquities,* Book XIII, Chapter 5. The remnants of the Chaldaic-Assyrian nation, still living in the Middle East, acknowledge this relationship to this day, and still speak Aramaic, the language of the Jews during the time of Jesus and the Apostles.

[2] Joseph J. Williams, *Hebrewisms of West Africa*, pages 188-196.

[3] Mentioned in both the First and Second Books of Maccabees.

4 It was only in the time of Solomon that a really well-equipped Jewish army existed. According to I Kings, 10:26, the great philosopher-king had 1,400 chariots and sufficient horses for 12,000 horsemen, together with a navy whose principal port was Eziongeber at the present site of Aqaba on the Red Sea.

5 The triumph of Judas Maccabaeus over Nicanor at Adasa in the Judean War of Independence "was certainly as decisive as the victory of General Gates at Saratoga over Burgoyne in the American Revolutionary struggle, over 2,000 years later. The effects of Judas' success were still influential when Mother England retired from the contest with her daughter colony across the Atlantic."—Israel Abrahams, *Campaigns in Palestine*, page 3.

6 *The Romance of the Last Crusade.*

7 " . . . and they cast up a bank against the city, and it stood in a trench; and all the people that were with Joab battered the wall, to throw it down." II Samuel, 20:15.

8 Rogers MacVeagh and Thomas B. Costain, *Joshua*, p. 91-165.

9 How well advanced the early Jews were in the military arts may be inferred from Lyn Montross' observation that "by the fifth century B. C. the Greek line of battle consisted of a hedge of spears bearing down upon the enemy . . . it was seldom that either general resorted to surprise, maneuver, flank attack or any other variation from the plain frontal assault."—*War Through the Ages*, page 9.

10 Joseph Kastein, *History and Destiny of the Jews*, page 101.

11 Describing the quality of Jewish character which led to these conflicts, Dion Cassius observed in his *Annals*: "the race is very bitter when aroused to anger . . ."

11a Bar Giora, or Bar Gurias, as his name indicates, was said to have been the son of a convert to Judaism; hence, at most, he could only have been part-Jewish. The interesting and oft-mooted question as to whether the term 'Jew' connotes a religious, racial or purely social definition, cannot be answered here. However, the question does pose certain difficulties in reference to the purposes of the present study. In the case of a famous American general killed on the battlefield, his wife is alleged to have declared that he could not be Jewish because he was a Protestant, notwithstanding the fact that he was the son of a Jewish rabbi. On the other hand, if Hitler's definition that a single Jewish grandparent was sufficient to confer Jewish identity were to apply, the list of known Jewish military figures would be enormously enlarged. It may be added, also, that absolute records often as not, were not kept at all. It is also a fact that numerous military figures have concealed their Jewish antecedents, which under circumstances of the prevailing anti-Jewish bias, were felt to be prejudicial to their careers.

12 Rev. H. C. Adams, M.A., *The History of the Jews*, page 34.

13 The military writers, Spaulding, Nickerson and Wright, remark with true insight into the stream of Jewish history: "They resisted the Romans desperately, with the intense determination familiar to modern students of Jewish character."—*Warfare: A Study of Military Methods from the Earliest Times,* page 205.

14 "So they fell," writes Tacitus, "with swords in their hands, contending for liberty, and, in the act, preserving it . . . "—*History* VII:13. After this unmitigated catastrophe to Jewish arms, the fortress of Masada, at the southwest corner of the Dead Sea, continued grimly to hold out. Dr. Adams, who regarded the rebels with as little sympathy as did his Roman sources, remarks that Masada was "garrisoned by men as fierce and resolute as the defenders of Jerusalem itself." (*The History of the Jews,* page 38). After a protracted and harrowing siege, the Romans succeeded in breaching the outer walls of the fortress and firing the inner wall. When they entered finally, a terrifying silence greeted them. The defenders, men, women and children alike, had taken their own lives during the night rather than capitulate. There had not been a single outcry to act as a sign to the Romans as to what was transpiring.

15 This arch has endured the destructive hand of time and still stands in Rome.

16 Before they were finally beaten by the Roman legions, the Jews had held the greater part of Cyrene and had even proclaimed their leader, Andreas, as king.

17 *Treatise Against Apion,* Book II, Chapter 4. See also Nathan Caro Belth, Universal Jewish Encyclopedia, Book IX, page 597.

18 She is referred to by French scholars as the African Joan of Arc.

19 *Gebel al Tariq,* or Rock of Tariq.

20 Joseph J. Williams, *Hebrewisms of West* Africa, page 210.

21 A short decade before, they had erupted against the Caliph in Andalusia in a characteristic bloody rebellion against repressive taxation, and were put down with great slaughter.

22 E. H. Lindo, *The History of the Jews of Spain and Portugal,* page 153.

23 Fernando also sailed with Sir Walter Raleigh on four voyages to America, and was the discoverer of Virgina in 1584.

24 When the Portuguese explorer Vasco da Gama arrived in India, he found there a Jew from Posen, who had made his way to India years before, and was now admiral in the fleet of the Viceroy of Goa. Cecil Roth, *The Jewish Contribution to Civilization,* page 9.

25 A special monument was erected at Sevastopol to Jewish soldiers who fell in defense of that city.

26 Joselowicz, its leader, managed to escape and later took a prominent part in the Napoleonic Wars, falling in combat finally at the battle with the Austri-

ans at Kotzk in 1809. He was known at the time as "the famous Polish colonel". In 1830, Berek's son, Joseph Berkowitz, again called his fellow Jews to revolt in the cause of Poland; and in 1860-63, Jews stood stanchly beside their Christian compatriots in the abortive revolution.

27 Goldsmid belonged to another well-known British military family. His three brothers were officers, as were his sons after him.

28 H. S. Kehimar, *The History of the Bene Israel of India,* page 218.

29 Sir Wilmot's father, Sir Alexander Schomberg, was also a noted naval officer, as was the latter's cousin, Captain Isaac Schomberg. A brother of Sir Wilmot attained the rank of rear admiral, as did two of Sir Wilmot's sons. A third son was General Sir George Schomberg.

30 Jewish captains had earlier commanded pioneer militia forces in the wars against the native tribes. Among these were Elias de Pass and Joshua Davis Norden, killed in the Kaffir wars. Nathaniel Isaacs became military leader to the great Zulu king, Chaka, and principal Chief of Natal. He was called by the Zulus "The Brave Warrior." Part of Britain's claim to Natal was based on the charter received by Isaacs from King Chaka.

31 Bonaparte had announced his sympathy for the project of a renascent Jewish state in Palestine and had called on Jews to rally to his standards.

32 Universal Jewish Encyclopedia, Vol. IX, page 622.

33 Together with the figure estimated by Mr. Seddon for the South, this would come to the high figure of sixteen to twenty-one percent of the then 155,000 Jewish population. For this reason, and since exact statistics were not kept at the time, the estimates made then have been questioned later by Jewish sources.

34 On the luckless Merrimac, too, was a Jewish officer, Lieutenant Moses.

35 This constituted five-tenths of 1% of the approximately 1,000,000 Jews in the country, as against four-tenths of 1% for the population as a whole.

36 Jews constituted 1.1% of the armed forces; their population ratio in Germany was 0.93%.

36a These Jewish officers whose commissions thus were born on the battlefield, actually constituted 2.5% of all the officers of the German army. This figure comprises only officers of the Jewish confession, and not so-called non-Aryans in the Nazi sense of the word, who were also numerous.

37 Ralph Nunberg, *The Fighting Jew,* page 172.

38 It was Bernheim who held the Germans on the Yser for fifteen days until the sagging line could be reinforced, and who commanded the Belgian North Division when it made its decisive break-through.

39 The Sassoon family contributed ten officers, of whom three won the M. C. All five sons of Mrs. Arthur Sebog-Montefiore held commissions, and one

was killed at Gallipoli. The Beddington family contributed 37 members. One, Lieutenant Colonel E. H. Beddington, was mentioned six times in the dispatches. The Spielmann family gave 41 members, of whom one was killed in France, one at Gallipoli, and 12 were wounded.

40 "It is a striking fact," remarks the *American Jewish Yearbook, 1919-20,* "that a large majority of Jews engaged in active service belonged to the fighting units of the army, such as the infantry, artillery, tanks, machine-gun units, and the special brigades of the Royal Engineers who were in charge of gas operations." In the administrative departments, there appear to have been comparatively few.

41 After the Kerensky Government came into power, Joseph Trumpeldor, hero of Port Arthur, and the engineer, Pinchus Ruthenberg, conceived the idea of recruiting an army of Jewish volunteers who would invade and liberate Palestine through the Russian Caucasus. When the Bolsheviks came into power, they immediately declared their opposition to the "imperialistic war," and outlawed Zionism by decree as a counter-revolutionary movement. Five thousand Jewish volunteers who succeeded in reaching the ports of Vladivostok and Kharbin were disbanded, and both the doughty leaders were thrown into prison.

42 Bernard Postal, *The Jews in the World War,* page 12.

43 *Ibid.*

43a J. George Fredman and Louis A. Falk, *Jews in America,* page 78.

44 The Universal Jewish Encyclopedia lists six, but other sources authenticate only three. The latter figure though probably erring on the side of conservatism, is used by the author. Much of the same difficulty in absolute authentication of names undoubtedly has served to reduce the actual Jewish figures throughout.

45 J. F. C. Fuller, *Armament and History,* page 125. This tribute is all the more marked in view of the fact that Fuller is politically a follower of Sir Oswald Mosley.

46 Issue of February 1902.

47 A convert to Calvinism, Bloch became influential at the Court of Czar Nicholas II. The Hague Peace Conference is said to have been called at his instigation.

48 D. Fedotoff White in his book, *The Growth of the Red Army,* credits Trotsky with not only molding the Red Army into a powerful fighting force, but with the tactics and strategy by which it achieved its triumph over the White Guards of Denikin, Wrangell, Kolchak and Semenoff. He refers to Trotsky as the Soviet "père de la victoire."

49 *If World War Comes Again,* The Yale Review, June 1938.

49a The dean of German military men, *Generaloberst* Alexander von Linsingen, noted for having held the Russians on the Bug, and for having led the later advance into the Ukraine, though a so-called non-Aryan, had not, as a professed Christian, considered himself Jewish. The classic story was that after the ascent of Hitler, the doughty old general made application to the Reichs Union of Jewish War Veterans, with the following words: "Since Herr Hitler has promoted me to be a Jew, I have the honor to make application for membership in your Society."

The distinguished Prussian military writer, Adolf Caspary, himself of Jewish descent, observes in a letter to the author that Hitler was forced quietly to mitigate his actions against Jews under the "Aryan paragraph", where it came down to the officers corps in the Reichswehr, so that two Christian grandparents in practice were sufficient to make a man Aryan. Otherwise, remarks Caspary, the higher echelons of the Prussian military caste would have been disastrously affected, and the German army crippled. He points out that the Prussian nobility, among whom the military career was practically hereditary, provided the great bulk of high-ranking officers for the German army, and had since the days of the elder Von Moltke, inter-married in a powerful and steady stream with wealthy or important Jewish families.

50 Out of Ireland's minuscule Jewish population a number of Irish patriots of Jewish antecedents made themselves immortal in the wars for freedom. The best known of these was Charles Stewart Parnell, whose Jewish mother referred proudly to the fact that her famous son sprang from fine fighting Jewish stock.

51 Of the fifteen jurists who drew up the Fascist Constitution, three were Jews. Cecil Roth, *The History of the Jews of Italy*, page 509.

52 Among the tragedies caused by Mussolini's racial policy was that of Colonel Ascoli, scion of the famous military Ascoli family, one of whose members, Aldo Ascoli, commanded the Italian fleet in the Aegean, and another, General Ettore Ascoli, who was director of the Central Military School in Civita Vecchia. Colonel Ascoli in the presence of his regiment, draped the regimental flag over his shoulders and shot himself, rather than resign.

53 A particularly flaming figure was a girl, Reizel Teitelbaum, who led a famous guerrilla unit, and for her extraordinary exploits became known as "The Manager of the Bryansk Forests."

53a This figure is based on the general assumption that the American Jewish population was close to 5,000,000, a calculation arising from the 1937 estimate of the Jewish Statistical Bureau, of 4,771,000. The American Jewish Year Book for 1948, after systematically compiling the figures for 1,200 communities, suggests that the earlier estimate is an exaggeration, and that the true population figure may not exceed 4,000,000.

THE JEW AS SOLDIER, STRATEGIST, MILITARY ADVISER

53b The specially selected 20th Air Force group given the duty of organizing and carrying out the historic atomic bomb missions against Japan, included a high proportion of both Jewish officers and enlisted men. Among the officers were Captain Joseph Slusky, technical inspector and flight test engineer of the Group, Major Guy Geller, squadron adjutant, First Lieutenant William Schiller, armament officer, Captain Bernard H. Budmen, ammunition and delivery officer, First Lieutenant Meyer Rothenberg, adjutant of the maintenance squadron, First Lieutenant Richard Podolsky, electrical officer, and First Lieutenant Jacob Baser, who flew on both the missions to Hiroshima and Nagasaki. Also on the Hiroshima mission was radio operator, Sergeant Abe H. Spitzer. Flying as bombardier-navigator on one of the observation escorts was Captain Charles Levy. The navigator of the photo reconnaissance plane which followed to photograph the stricken city, was First Lieutenant Frederick Charnes.

54 Frank Gervasi, *The Jew as a Soldier,* Collier's Magazine, April 22, 1944.

55 Frank Gervasi, *The Jew as a Soldier,* Collier's Magazine, April 22, 1944.

56 *Black Book—The Nazi Crime Against the Jewish People,* page 416.

57 Marie Syrkin, *Blessed Is the Match,* pages 305-6.

58 The first American troops to land in Algiers were commanded by Lieutenant Colonel A. H. Rosenberg. Corporal Bernard J. Kessel of Brooklyn manned the guns of the first U. S. tank to enter Oran. It was Squadron Leader Julius Cohen who managed to bring Duff Cooper and General Lord Gort from Britain to Rabat, Morocco, to make contact with the refugee French ministers there. The New Zealand general, Freyberg, led the Anzacs in the North African campaign. The final surrender of the Nazis in North Africa by General Fritz Krause and his staff at Bizerte, was made to another American Jewish army officer, twenty-three-year-old Lieutenant Albert Klein. It is of some interest, too, that the leader of the American expedition, General Mark Clark springs directly from an old Jewish military family on his mother's side.

59 Israel Cohen, *Jews in the War,* page 77.

60 Frank Gervasi, *To Whom Palestine,* page 92.

61 Mac David, *Jews Fight Too,* pages 103-106.

62 Though this number does not appear large, at no time did the entire British Empire have as many as 250 parachutists working behind enemy lines.

62a Pierre Van Paassen, *The Forgotten Ally,* page 225.

63 Van Paassen gives a stirring account of this incident in his *Forgotten Ally,* pages 193-96. He recounts that Major Liebman himself, wasted with hunger and seriously wounded, was embraced by General Koenig, and then immediately took down the Jewish flag. "Why?" asked Koenig, astounded. Liebman explained that flying the Jewish flag was against regulations—he had only raised it because he thought everything was lost. The indomitable Koenig replied that he did not give a damn about such regulations, and placed the Jewish flag next to the Tricolor on his own car, causing his men to pass it in salute.

64 In Tobruk, there is a street called Rehov Tel Aviv, honoring the Jews who were so essential a part of the defense of the city.

65 Pierre Van Paassen, *The Forgotten Ally,* page 232.

66 The tenor of the British view may be gained from Foreign Minister Bevin's contention to President Truman that if further Jewish immigration was permitted into Palestine, it would require a half million American troops to protect the Jews from the wrath of local Arabs.

66a A token force of Saudi Arabian troops consisting of several battalions of infantry, actually did accompany the Egyptian invasion armies, along with elements of the Defence Force of the Anglo-Egyptian Sudan.

67 There were at the time 650,000 Jews in Palestine, and about 1,100,000 Arabs. The attacking Arab states possessed a population of around 40,000,000.

67a The Jews had managed to buy 20 obsolete single-seated Auster trainers, which were in such poor condition that the British had considered them worth nothing except as scrap. By a great effort the Israelis were able to make a portion of these flyable. These rickety and almost wholly unairworthy planes constituted the nucleus of what was to become the Israeli air force. They were used for airlift of besieged settlements, and also for a type of primitive dive-bombing, and the strafing of enemy troops with Browning machine guns.

67b There were also a small number of homemade two and three-inch mortars, but these were extremely short on munitions, and their use had to be limited to the amount of captured British munitions which became available. The most important of these weapons, known affectionately as the Davidka, was a homemade Napoleon gun, which possessed no rifling and had to be muzzle-loaded. This primitive artillery piece had its principal value as a noise-maker. When the war started, the only artillery the Israelis had were two 75-millimetre guns mounted on Cromwell tanks, which the Jews had managed to get away from the evacuating British forces. The Jews possessed only a limited quantity of light weapons—rifles and homemade Sten-guns, though Jewish shops soon began turning out efficient submachine guns. Even the armed escorts on the vital supply road to Jerusalem, in the early fighting, had no rifles, and were compelled to use short-range machine guns.

68 Infantry Journal, March 1949.

69 *Ibid.*

70 Fawzi Bey with the blessing of the Arab League, had appeared in Palestine with his well-equipped "volunteers" from all of the Arab countries, with an ultimatum addressed to all Palestine Jewry: "Surrender, or we wipe you out." Fawzi Bey's army consisted of 3,000 Syrians, Iraqis and other trained volunteers, assisted by German, Yugoslav, Syrian and British officers. The Israeli forces engaged at Mishmar Haemek consisted of less than 2,000 members of the Haganah, the Israeli militia.

BIBLIOGRAPHY*

ABRAHAMS, ISRAEL, *Jewish Life in the Middle Ages*

American Jewish Historical Society, Publications Nos. 3, 26 and 33

American Jewish Yearbooks, 1919-1920, 1920-1921, 1946-1947

American Jews in World War II, (Jewish Welfare Board)

BERG, MARY, *Warsaw Ghetto*

Canadian Jews in World War II, (Canadian Jewish Congress)

CASPER, BERNARD M., *With the Jewish Brigade*

DUKER, ABRAHAM G., *Jews in World War I*

EMDEN, PAUL H., *The Jews of Britain*

FREDMAN, J. GEORGE AND FALK, LOUIS A., *Jews in American Wars*

FRIEDMAN, LEE MAX, *Jewish Pioneers and Patriots*

GRAETZ, H., *History of the Jews*

JOSEPHUS, *The Jewish War*

LEVY, HERMANN, *Soviet Jews at War*

MCCALL, SAMUEL WALTER, *Patriotism of the American Jew*

MILLER, MADELAIN AND LANE J., *Encyclopedia of Bible Life*

NATHAN, DR. MANFRED, *Jews in the Boer War*

PARKER, JAMES, *The Jew in the Medieval Community*

RADIN, MAX, *The Jews Among the Greeks and Romans*

SHILLMAN, BERNARD, *The Jews in Ireland*

South African Jewish Board of Deputies, *They Answered the Call*

USOV, M. L., *Jews in the Army*

ZIFF, WILLIAM B., *The Rape of Palestine*

* Additional bibliographical material may be found in the footnotes.

BIBLIOGRAPHY*

ABRAHAMS, ISRAEL, Jewish Life in the Middle Ages

American Jewish Historical Society Publications, Vol. ...

American Jewish Yearbook, 1919-1920 (1920), pp. ...

American Jews in World War II. (Jewish Welfare Board)

BINH, MARY, Warsaw Ghetto

Canadian Jews in World War II. (Canadian Jewish Congress)

CASPER, BERNARD M., II with the Jewish Brigade

DUKER, ABRAHAM G., Jews in World War I

EMDEN, PAUL H., The Jews of Britain

FRIEDMAN, ... GISOWER AND FALK, LOUIS A., Jews in American Wars

FRIEDMANN, LEE MAX, Jewish Pioneers and Patriots

GRAETZ, H., History of the Jews

JOSEPHUS, The Jewish War

LEVI, HERMAN, ... Jews at War

McCALL, SAMUEL WALKER, Patriotism of the American Jew

MILLER, MADELEIN AND LANE, ... Encyclopedia of Bible Life

NATHAN DE MODERNO, Jews in the Army ...

PARKER, JAMES, The Jew in the Medieval Community

RABIN, MAX, The Jews among the Greeks and Romans

SHIPMAN, BERNARD, The Jew in Poland

South African Jewish Board of Deputies, They Answered the Call

UKOV, M. J., Jews in the Army

ZEITZ, WILLIAM H., The Role of Judaism

* Additional bibliographical material may be found in the source.

The Jew and the Law

By MARTIN L. WOLF

THE fact that the Jew has been one of the greatest makers, interpreters, and enforcers of the law since time immemorial should not come as a surprise to anyone possessing even a smattering of knowledge concerning Jewish history, understanding, or culture. The impact of the Jew upon law is as strong as—if not considerably stronger than—his impact upon any other field of endeavor (and there are many) in which he has distinguished himself.

The tremendous *why* behind his consuming interest in the law through the centuries cannot be explained on the basis of any single proposition, although a considerable part of it is merely a reflection of his natural desire to create and maintain a level of civilized society at which all could exist in security and in harmony. The ages of aimless wandering, the heritage of persecution and homelessness, the filial piety and desire for community peace . . . these were some of the factors which contributed to the stirring events and achievements stemming from Hebrew expertness in the law.

No group has greater right to the title *The People of the Law*; the Old Testament is a vast storehouse of law, legal principle, and legal philosophy, much of which is incorporated —almost word for word—in the modern law of numerous jurisdictions and systems throughout the civilized world. Even more technically legal than the Old Testament is the great repository of law known as the Talmud, closely allied by scholars with the effective machinery of Roman law.

Hebrew law has been defined generally as the combined system of ritual observances and jurisprudence, believed to have been the consequence of divine revelation to Moses on

Sinai, and carried by him into the Pentateuch, the 'Five Books of Moses.' In reviewing the life and legal importance of Moses, the great British Chief Justice, Sir Edward Coke, stated that he was the first reporter of the law known to the world. Although other compilations of Hebrew law appeared on the scene from time to time, including the famous Mishnah of Rabbi Judah the Patriarch, and certain Spanish, Franco-German, Italian and Turkish treatises based on original Hebrew concepts but varying somewhat in liturgical and ritual details, the Bible and the Talmud have remained the two chief sources and authorities throughout.

* * *

One of the most distinguished leaders in the early history of law was Hillel (30 B.C.-9 A.D.), Jewish teacher of legal interpretation and philosophy who entered Palestine from Babylonia and soon became the leading authority of the period. He is acknowledged as the first teacher ever to have formed specific hermeneutic principles, devoting his life to the science of laws, their interpretation, explanation, and history.

Judah the Patriarch (135-220 A.D.), known also as *ha-Nasi* (The Prince) and *ha-Kadosh* (The Holy), was disturbed by the chaotic variances in Hebrew law and ritual, and sought to resolve all rules then existing into a system of unified observances, legal and religious. Rabbi Judah was a scholar and legal philosopher of Sepphoris, Palestine, succeeding his father Simon ben Gameliel II as Patriarch. In the compiling of the Mishnah, famous digest of laws, Judah made use of all earlier collections and codes available to him; thus, many of the elements of the Mishnah, functioning as Eastern and Western law alike, embodied precepts which preceded by far the Christian era. His masterful handling of the subject, coupled with his position of great prestige, resulted in an almost unanimous acceptance of the work over widespread regions, and brought the needed clarification of the entire system of law. Prominent among the parts of the Mishnah adopted by or rewritten for other peoples throughout the world are those on domestic relations (sec. III), and on civil and criminal law (sec. IV).

An early and important contribution to the judiciary and enforcement elements of the law was the famous Sanhedrin, supreme seat of legal judgment in the Jewish state, founded at some time in the third century B.C. (or even earlier), and existing until its destruction by the Romans in 70 A.D. While there is considerable disagreement among scholars regarding various aspects of this court, most historians are in accord on one important point: that there were *two* Sanhedrins. One group of authorities believes that there was a supreme council, the highest judicial and ecclesiastical tribunal of the ancient Jewish nation, having 71 members, and in addition, a similar Sanhedrin of subsidiary character, having 23 members. Others are of the opinion that the courts enjoyed a parity of importance and membership, one dealing with the administration of justice in political, criminal and civil matters, and presided over by the High Priest, and the other concerning itself with religious matters only. Both convened in the Temple of Jerusalem, though in different chambers.

It is to the first, or highest Sanhedrin that the Gospels refer, and in this connection it may be interesting to observe that some students of the subject are convinced that the Sanhedrin which met for the purpose of sitting in judgment of Christ was without jurisdiction for the reason that the court was called into session on a Friday evening, the Sabbath, and also (because it *was* the Sabbath), that a quorum was not present.

In any event, the rules of procedure and evidence governing the Sanhedrin(s) were of such simple, basic and efficient justice (requirements as to reliability of witnesses, presumption of innocence, written evidence as against oral, etc.) that the system was not only adopted by contemporary courts, but can be found, practically intact as to basic elements, in many of the courts of the world today.

Hillel was active in interpreting the laws and philosophies controlling the operation of the Sanhedrin, although his views were frequently in conflict with those of Shammai, eminent doctor of the Jewish law at the time of Herod the Great. Shammai's strict, severe requirements gave way to the patient, understanding methods of Hillel, who was president of the Sanhedrin; Shammai was vice-president.

The eighth century gave to the world the man who is probably the father of legal research. Achai Shabcha was the compiler and editor of an important collection of decisions on juridical questions, and he furnished authorities with a collated picture of numerous cases on a single point of law, enabling tribunals to render judgments consistent with those of other courts bound by the same laws and procedures. His work influenced Western law-making and law-enforcing bodies which executed similar compilations on other points of law. Shabcha's collection was one of the strongest factors bringing the system of legal bibliography to the fine state it enjoys today.

Eleventh century Spain was the temporarily secure home of a vast number of Jews, and prominent among them was Bahya ben Joseph, legal philosopher and judge who presided over the Rabbinical Court at Saragossa. Preceding Moses Maimonides by about one century, he wrote *Guide to the Duties of the Heart* in Arabic in 1040, and this book came to be recognized as the first systematic presentation of Hebrew ethics to the world. It exerted profound influence on the makers and interpreters of the laws of most Eastern and Western countries for hundreds of years thereafter. Chasdai Crescas (1340-1410) was likewise a Spanish Jew, and his liberal beliefs in legal philosophy appear to have been the inspiration and guide for Spinoza. Crescas' profound and deeply moving *Light of the Lord*, showing clearly the utter necessity of certain acts committed by man, had a marked effect in reducing the number and severity of punishments meted out for crimes. He is frequently referred to as the author of the oft-quoted but seldom executed maxim "True justice is tempered with mercy."

THE JEW AND THE LAW

One of the unsung heroes of Jewish law and the Jewish cause was Menassah ben Israel (1604-1657), scholar, Rabbi, and legal philosopher, who abandoned his life's work of religious pursuit in order to frame the magnificent legislation which, when presented forcefully and logically to Cromwell, bespoke its own purpose so well that it left the government with no recourse other than that of enacting it into British statute, allowing for the readmission of the Jews into England.

* * *

The philosophy of law, a never-ending labyrinth of blind alleys, hair-splitting distinctions, and exasperating minutiae when studied in relation to the conduct of man, has always posed a seducing challenge to the Jewish thinker. While legal philosophy is generally considered an element of interpretation of the law, many famous jurists (notably Brandeis and Cardozo) sought to have their philosophies actually written as practical law through their decisions; in their later years, convinced more than ever that their philosophy of changing the law with the times was the correct philosophy, the two were rewarded by concordance of the United States Supreme Court with their views.

Moses Maimonides (1135-1204), known also as The Ramban and Rabbi Moses ben Maimon, was one of the most 'practical' legal philosophers of all time, excelling also in medicine, mathematics, and theology. Born in Spain, he studied with zeal under Arabic scholars, but after the Moslem capture of Cordoba in 1148 he was obliged to escape to Cairo, where he later became the personal physician to Saladin, Sultan of Egypt, and in 1177, the Chief Rabbi of Cairo. His philosophy sought to reduce the differences between Rabbinic Judaism and Aristotelian philosophy, bringing in some elements of Arabic interpretation as the 'blender.' Basically, he believed in the complete and unfettered freedom of the individual human will, he condemned asceticism, and he urged upon all people the threefold care of body, mind, and soul. Among his outstanding works are the Hebrew *Mishnah Torah* (Second Law), the Arabic commentary on the Mishnah entitled *Siray* or *Siraj* (Illumination), the Arabic *Book of Precepts*, the Arabic *Guide of the Perplexed*, and numerous others on all of his varied branches of study. In law, his monumental *Yad Hahazakah*, commonly known as *Code of Maimonides*, compiled in the late twelfth century, remains the most comprehensive and authoritative restatement of the Jewish law since the Talmud. This enormous work covers the complete history of more than fifteen centuries of continuous legal development of the Hebrews, for whom the law was not only a practical consideration, but a mode of worship as well. This famous code is at present being prepared as a fifteen-volume project by Yale University under the Louis M. Rabinowitz Foundation.

More specifically a true legal philosopher and sociologist than Maimonides was Baruch (or Benedict) Spinoza (1632-1677), who concerned himself with the 'naturalistic philosophy of law' leading to pin-pointed individualism in the treatment of any case before the bar of justice, as first advocated by Crescas three hundred years before him. Spinoza's studies broke all of society down into its irreducible elements—the isolated individuals—disregarding completely all aspects of social reality and communal existence. However, some understanding of the individual's rights and obligations was, he stated, a promise of order and peace under public power. He persisted in his belief that the law must be sufficiently flexible to fit the needs of the person being tried under it; that law can be both methodological and personalized; that it is the purpose of law "neither to laugh nor weep, but solely to understand" when studying human conduct and its aberrations. Spinoza's own life was a difficult one. In 1656 he was excommunicated from the synagogue for his 'advanced' teachings, and while writing he supported himself by working as an optical lens grinder. Although offered a professorship at Heidelberg University, he felt that to accept it would fetter his unrestrained freedom of thought and expression, the freedoms he found through his studies of Maimonides and Crescas. Spinoza is regarded today as one of the most independent thinkers of all time, and the outstanding exponent of pantheism.

Another strong force in the philosophy of law was the Frenchman Emmanuel Levy who, with Duduit and Hauriou, founded the great principles of the sociology of law in his native country in the early twentieth century. His efforts were devoted almost exclusively to the problems of the original requirements, the creation, and the precipitating causes for the existence of laws, especially those in force at the time of his studies (late nineteenth century). His investigations centered about the recent changes in the law as provoked by variations in group activities, beliefs, and needs, evaluating the evolution of the people against evolution of the law, and affording the greater part of his research to the psychology of law and its effects upon changing trends. He brought to public attention the needless power of the spontaneous, loosely-constructed law, and suggested the practical means whereby it could be crystallized into organized law, applicable in fairness to all persons and all situations, with individual considerations nevertheless possible. Basing his concepts upon psychological factors, his principles of law consider the aspects of confidence, good faith, and 'normal expectation' in human conduct. The present French law of individual case psychology is built largely upon the foundation constructed by Levy.

The death of Morris Raphael Cohen in 1947 (born 1880) brought to a close a career in legal philosophy that can scarcely be matched in modern history. Born in Minsk and arriving in the United States at the age of twelve, his subsequent years of work, study, writing and teaching earned him the reputation of one of America's foremost thinkers, contributing vastly to the improvement of the American social order by renewing with vigor the importance of the philosophy of law in jurisprudence. He served as assistant to George Santayana, Josiah Royce and William James, and was invited with great frequency to lecture at leading colleges, universities and law schools throughout the country. Although he never sought admission to the bar, his philosophical interpretation of the law had deep effect and influence upon Holmes, Brandeis, Cardozo, Frankfurter, and other leading jurists, many of whose decisions are directly traceable to Cohen's sociological and philosophical concepts which, while differing in many respects from those of Spinoza, nevertheless found their common basis in the strength of individuality and the free and fearless exercise of individual reason.

*   *   *

There is not—nor has there been—any individual branch of the law of particular or exclusive specialization by the Jew. He has been the pioneer, developer, and practitioner in all of the wide classifications of the vast subject including, surprisingly enough, Roman law and canon law. Nor is the fact that the Jew finds the law vital to his existence (and consequently vital to his devoted attention) any factor contributing to a localization of his interest to any specific point or points in time or geography. The entire civilized world has found him (where permitted) leading or assisting in the analysis of group problems, setting up structures of law, and interpreting and enforcing the law. In the days of early Australia, for example, the name best remembered by students of historical and legal development is Chief Justice Isaacs, later to become Governor-General; prominent in preserving the legal backbone of New Zealand were the two famous Chief Justices Sir Arthur and Sir Michael Myers, who judged the cases before them with strength and vision; from the moment of California's entry into the United States in 1846 the Jew was instrumental in knitting the vast and varied threads of Mexican hatred, gold rush lawlessness, and early confusion into a strong fabric of orderly existence. Washington Bartlett, first mayor of San Francisco, was a Jew. His task was an enormous one, but he set the legal pattern upon which one of America's great cities is now founded. One of his vigilantes, Morris Schloss, brought to an end with courage and tact the difficulties experienced with the feared Mexican revolutionary and bandit Joaquin Murietta, adjusting differences and rendering Murietta one of the state's most valuable supporters and his own good friend. Louis Rose was the postmaster and city treasurer of San Diego; Emanuel Linoberg, Polish immigrant, was the town councilman of Sonora; Solomon Heydenfeldt was Chief Justice of the state Supreme Court, Abraham C. Lebatt the alderman of San Francisco, Elkan Heydenfeldt a member of the state legislature, Samuel Mark the United States appraiser of the port, Joseph Shannon the county treasurer at San Francisco, and Marcus Katz the county treasurer at San Bernardino. The efforts of all, devoted and sincere, combined to create a state of exemplary legal structure. The beginnings of other states were similarly formed by Jews of outstanding legal stature and prestige.

The American law of the sea and the naval code can be attributed to the untiring efforts of Admiral Uriah Phillips Levy (1792-1862), flag officer of the United States Navy in the Mediterranean under Lincoln. Levy was responsible for the abolition of corporal punishment in all of its many forms, and for the present equitable system of justice prevailing in naval courts.

Of the same period, although in a different part of the world, a brilliant career was taking shape . . . a career that was to have its force felt throughout many countries, throughout many years. Benjamin Disraeli (1804-1881) was the English Conservative statesman who played the leading role at the Congress of Berlin where he strove with every device at his command to obtain the enactment of laws which would furnish equality of civil rights for the Jews. His efforts were especially notable in view of the fact that he and his three younger brothers had been baptized at an early age in the Anglican Church by their father, Isaac Disraeli, English literary figure; however, there is doubt as to his own feelings in the matter, just as there is no doubt at all in the case of Felix Mendelssohn, grandson of the great Jewish philosopher Moses Mendelssohn, who affirmatively sought and received conversion at a mature age, and added the hyphenated Bartholdy to his surname. Disraeli was Prime Minister of Great Britain, the author of numerous well-received works on a variety of subjects, a Member of Parliament for the astonishing period of forty-three years, Chancellor of the Exchequer under Lord Derby, and was created Earl of Beaconsfield in 1876. His elevation to posts of such great importance—particularly in times of general suppression of Jewish endeavors in public life— served as a source of pride and inspiration to Jews throughout the world and encouraged other nations to heed the ability of their Jewish citizens and their value to government.

It was said that Disraeli's brilliant oratory and keen mental acuity, as a combination, surpassed by far that of any other man in public history . . . except one; but Disraeli probably did not mind this subordinate comparison with the most fabulous figure ever to appear on the legal scene. Lawyers the world over will never cease to exclaim, to admire, to marvel, and to dream, when the talk turns to the name of Judah P. Benjamin (1811-1884). Born on the island of St. Croix, his family moved to the southern United States where he received his early education. He was admitted to Yale University at the age of fourteen, but left three years later under mysterious circumstances and without a degree. Although the whisperers were convinced that he had been apprehended in an act of dishonesty, such rumors were inconsistent with the contents of his letter to the school's president, in which he stated that he "regretted the disrespect shown to a member of the faculty."

He studied law in New Orleans while working and tutoring, and was admitted to the bar in 1833. His marriage in the same year to a French girl of sixteen ended in failure, and she subsequently returned home to Paris with their daughter. Benjamin's success at law was immediate, and he was arguing

cases in the Louisiana Supreme Court before his third month
of practice; he wrote standard, authoritative books on law before the end of the first year. In 1842 he was elected to the
state legislature, and in 1852 to the United States Senate (he
was the second Jewish senator; the first was David Levy
Yulee of Florida). After election but before he was seated,
President Fillmore nominated him to the United States Supreme Court, the highest honor ever offered a Jew, but he
declined, preferring a more active political life. After a distinguished career in the senate, characterized by sparkling
orations, almost superhuman insight into national problems,
constant wit and cheerfulness, and chairmanship of numerous
Senate committees, he resigned after the election of Lincoln,
convinced that civil war was imminent.

His good friend Jefferson Davis appointed him Attorney-
General of the Confederacy, later Foreign Secretary, and finally Secretary of War. His escape from the country just before Lee's capitulation reads with the fascination of a juvenile
adventure story. Disguised in the dress and tongue of a Frenchman, he traversed Georgia by horse and wagon, and sought
passage to the West Indies by boat from Florida. The small
boat he succeeded in hiring was stopped by a northern warship
and searched, but his cook's disguise was effective. The
boat crashed against rocks at the Bimini Islands, but Benjamin
saved his life and procured another boat which foundered and
went down. He and three Negroes escaped in a one-oared rowboat, and were rescued by a British yacht which took them to
Nassau. He obtained passage on a ship sailing for England,
but it caught fire one day out and scarcely succeeded in making the trip back to Nassau. These incidents failed to damage
his perpetual state of hope and optimism, probably because he
knew that he would have been tried for treason if he had remained in the United States.

The next endeavor was successful, and he was barely settled
in England when the bank to which he had entrusted his

money failed and wiped him out. He started life anew at the age of fifty-four, penniless but ambitious. He supported himself by writing specialized articles for the *Daily Telegraph* until admitted to the English bar in 1866, and after a year of unsuccessful practice (blamed by many on his American mannerisms and accent) he devoted his time to the writing of his famous *Treatise on the Law of Sales*. It was the leading publication on the subject, and is considered the classic of English law today. From then on (1868) his rise was meteoric, and in 1870 he was appointed Queen's Counsel. In 1883, shortly after his retirement, bench and bar joined to sponsor a dinner in his honor, an event reported by *The Times* as "a function without parallel in the long history of the bar." In the principal speech of the evening the Lord Chancellor stated "No man within my recollection has possessed greater learning or displayed greater shrewdness or ability, or greater zeal for the interests entrusted to him. . . . His high honor is united with the greatest kindness and generosity." Attorney-General Sir Henry James added "This is the one man of whom it can be said that he held conspicuous leadership at the bar of two countries."

Upon his death in May, 1884, *The Times* said in a leading article "His life was as various as an Eastern tale, and he carved out for himself by his own unaided exertions not one, but three several histories of great and well earned distinction. Inherent in him was the elastic resistance to evil fortune which preserved his ancestors through a succession of exiles and plunderings. He possessed the refined insight of one who would fathom the subtleties of the Talmud." Such was the acclaim with which this strange career came to an end . . . a career so successful, so fantastic, and so brilliant as to render Judah P. Benjamin an almost legendary figure in the history of law.

One of Benjamin's outstanding contemporaries was Sir George Jessel (1824-1883), successful English lawyer who was elected to Parliament in 1868. However, his greatest ability was shown as a judge, in which capacity he performed the phenomenal feat of never once reserving decision, despite the fact that he presided over and rendered judgments in more than a thousand cases, some highly technical and complicated. The speed and accuracy in the workings of his mind can best be appreciated in connection with the noted *Epping Forest* case which required twenty-three full days of trial. More than a hundred witnesses testified, exhibits and documents were piled high, figures and statistics were both astronomical and conflicting, and precedents and statutes dating back to King John were cited and submitted. Nevertheless, Jessel delivered an oral decision (later reduced to sixteen printed pages) immediately upon conclusion of the arguments of counsel, displaying his power of analysis even in complicated matters, and his ability to strike swiftly and accurately at the very core of a problem. Appeals from his determinations were rare, for experience had shown English lawyers that his decisions were as unerring as they were just and spontaneous

This remarkable quality often led to criticism, for his alacrity in seizing upon the heart of a case was so great that in some instances he did not afford counsel sufficient time for the development of their arguments. Jessel was once reprimanded in open court by a lawyer for cutting him short, reminding Jessel that "while it was important that people should receive justice, it was even more important that they should be made to feel and see that they were receiving it." The lawyer, incidentally, was Farrer Herschell, a Jew by race who preserved his heritage despite the fact that his father, Haim Herschell, a Polish Jew, had changed his faith and adopted the name Ridley. Herschell was elected to Parliament in 1874 after having succeeded Judah Benjamin as Queen's Counsel, and was appointed Solicitor-General in 1880. He refused the offer of Jessel's judgeship after the latter's death, but in 1886 accepted the Lord Chancellorship. He died while on a mission to Washington in 1899. It is interesting to observe that while

Benjamin, Jessel and Herschell were contemporaries in the same vicinity, there does not appear to have been any attachment between the three, or any two of them.

Jessel was one of the first judges of the world to apply quick changes in the law to changing conditions, and he encouraged other judges to do likewise. In his abrupt but clear manner he scorned antiquity and exhibited great speed in his process of deleting dead wood from the law. A large number of his decisions commence with the words "To my mind the matter is clear" or "I have no hesitation in creating a precedent." His clarity of thought is well illustrated in all of his observations, and there is not a single vague or fuzzy sentence among them. In his own words, "I may be wrong, but I am never uncertain."

Sir George Jessel was the first Jew in British history who took a share in the executive history of the country, the first Jew sworn as a regular member of the Privy Council, and the first Jew to take a seat on the judicial bench. His bust was placed in the Royal Court of Justice as a memorial to one of England's greatest judges. The fact that he was one of England's greatest judges cannot be open to doubt; the only question is whether he was the greatest of all time.

While English law was being strengthened and dignified through the efforts of its famous Jewish barristers and judges, another Jew was working laboriously in France, endeavoring to open the doors that had been closed to the Jews in the arts and professions. He was Narcissus Leven (1833-1915), lawyer and philanthropist who founded and devoted his life and fortune to the *Alliance Israélite Universelle*, and surrounded himself with such patriots as Charles Netter, Aristide Astruc, Jules Carvallo, Isidore Cahen, and Eugène Manuel. France at the time (1860) was still characterized by prejudices against the Jews—prejudices which broke out into the open with decisive regularity—despite the fact that seventy years had passed since the Revolution which was presumed to have been based upon utter liberty and freedom of individual endeavor. The Alliance, finding its problem as much with the depressed, even disgusted Jew who was leaving France forever, as it did with the arbitrary government and its outmoded laws, did much to bring pressure upon legislators and Jews alike to give and to accept a pattern of equality and confidence in government previously lacking.

Leven's Alliance spoke hopefully of the unrealized dream of the centuries—a union of all the Jews of the world, allowable under laws promulgated by every government, not necessarily promoting, but at least not repressing such a spiritual unification. The Alliance felt that the Jews, scattered throughout all the nations, had lost contact with each other's problems and needs. What did the German Jews know about the Jews of Russia? What did the Jews of the Orient know about those of France and England? In fact, what did the Jews in one sector of any given country know about those in another, burdened as they were with their own local difficulties? When tragedy struck (as it did all too frequently), the cry was heard and help was invariably forthcoming, but it constituted little more than a brief, fleeting contact with the geographically removed brother. The emergency concluded, for better or worse (generally the latter), isolationism returned, along with the characteristic, divided weakness of the Jew. The Alliance believed that in union was salvation. In his *Cinquant Ans d'Histoire* Leven wrote "If you believe in the progress of humanity, the triumph of truth and eternal reason, then all the living forces of Judaism must be united, small in volume but mighty in love and good will." Despite criticism, Leven persisted that the unification he sought was not one of militarism, politics, or any form of physical strength, but purely of a spiritual and religious contact. Although but a dream, the thoughts and hopes of Leven provoked in many Jews and governments the feeling that there was need for international understanding of mutual problems, and in direct

[807]

consequence of the work of the Alliance, Jews in many countries were permitted to participate in alleviating the difficulties of their brethren elsewhere.

* * *

The first Jew to be elevated to the Supreme Court of the United States was Louis Dembitz Brandeis (1856-1941), Boston lawyer whose parents were Czechoslovakian immigrants. The formation of the great trusts, corporations and industrial empires in the last quarter of the nineteenth century interested Brandeis, particularly with regard to the labor problems that grew alongside. He devoted considerable of his time and effort to the furtherance of harmony in the relations of industry with labor, often embarking on a one-man crusade to correct what he believed to be a case of exploitation of labor. At the same time, he enjoyed a highly successful private practice.

In the course of his numerous fights (in and out of court) against trusts and power-lobbies, he made many enemies among the industrial tycoons, and when Wilson did not appoint him his Attorney-General in 1912 to the surprise of many observers (Wilson appointed instead James C. McReynolds, later Supreme Court Justice McReynolds), Brandeis' opponents relaxed with the thought that their foe was finally and decisively shelved from public life and government-backed power. But the shock came in January, 1916, when Wilson nominated him to the Supreme Court. The consent of the Senate was exceedingly doubtful, and it required five months to entertain the hearings at which numerous persons (among them lawyers) voluntarily appeared to give evidence against him, denouncing his qualifications for the position. With the ardent assistance of Elihu Root, his nomination was confirmed in June, 1916, by a vote of forty-seven to twenty-two, and the first great liberal era of the court was born. He joined Holmes in the latter's numerous dissents, but whereas Holmes' conflicts with the court were founded on his desire to broaden the general philosophy of the law, those of Brandeis were based on his understanding of the need for practical, down-to-earth interpretations of the individual cases heard; he stated repeatedly that his colleagues on the bench were out of date on political and economic matters; that the law was out of touch with contemporary goings-on; that there was immediate need for 'judicial surgery;' that the court was losing the respect of the people.

In most of the more than six hundred decisions he rendered during his twenty-three years on the bench he was in the minority, and his judgments were characterized throughout by the firm conviction that since commerce, politics, and general national conditions were not static, the law could not be static, but rather must flow along with the tide to meet the requirements of the ever-changing elements. The conservative majority nevertheless continued to defeat much of the liberal legislation fostered by President Franklin D. Roosevelt, but the picture slowly changed, and prior to his retirement in 1939, the aging Brandeis, now eighty-three, saw his prophecies and beliefs welded into the framework of the law. The letter of farewell from his fellow justices stated "Your long practical experience and intimate knowledge of affairs, the wide range of your researches and your grasp of the most difficult problems, together with your power of analysis and your thoroughness in exposition, have made your judicial career one of extraordinary distinction and far-reaching influence." Supplementing his legal interests, he was an ardent Zionist until his death on October 6, 1941.

The enormous contribution made by the Jew as a lawyer and lawmaker in all parts of the world is enhanced even further when it is considered that the Jew was excluded from the bar and from many universities until the mid-nineteenth century, and the force of Jewish interest in law, therefore, was held in restraint until the latter half of the century; exclusions were particularly severe at the universities of Oxford and Cambridge. An outstanding exception to the restrictions was Sir Francis Goldsmid, admitted to the British bar in 1833. However, his acceptance came about as the direct result of invitation based upon recognition of his ability, and not as a matter of right. Later, conciliatory arguments offered in support of a quota system were regarded by many as a device of anti-Semitism.

These attempts at limitation had tapered off somewhat when Rufus Daniel Isaacs (1860-1934) started the career which led him to the highest rank of nobility ever attained by a Jew in England. Shortly after his entry into the legal profession he was acknowledged as one of the outstanding practitioners in the country. He was quickly elevated to the post of King's Counsel (prosecutor) and later elected to Parliament. In 1910 he was appointed Solicitor-General, filling the position earlier occupied by Sir George Jessel, and a few months thereafter became Attorney-General, head of the English bar. After several successful visits to the United States to procure loans, he accepted the difficult and delicate post of Viceroy of India, and it was upon his return to England in 1926 that the king conferred upon him the title First Marquess of Reading. He concluded his career as British Foreign Secretary.

He was one of the few lawyers who exhibited absolutely no dramatics in the courtroom. He knew that his strength existed in patience, tactics of calm but shrewd procedure, and the almost endless collating of the facts in preparing for trial. As a judge, his explanations to juries were famed models of fairness and insight. As his country's servant, he did much to integrate the loose ends of national and international feeling, commerce, and politics into a dominion-wide structure of unity. He was an unusually handsome man, often referred to as 'The Dark Apollo', and had been an excellent athlete. His wit was strong and caustic, and his quiet but deadly attacks in the courtroom during cross-examination were classics of subtlety and tact.

Bernard Lazare (1865-1903) was more important to law and its application to tolerance than the omission of his name from most writings on the subject would appear to indicate. This French writer on legal and political matters took a leading part in the vindication of Dreyfus, and his best known work is *Anti-Semitism, its History and Causes*. He strove for the enactment of laws which would effect the accomplishment of his lifelong dream—laws granting complete freedom of profession and unquestioned equality to the Jew. He (as others before and after him) felt that the inclination of the Jew toward law was a natural one, since the restrictive political and social conditions under which he existed through the ages had established the need for law and order to fortify him in his uncertain existence and daily struggle.

Joseph F. Fishman branched away from the practical aspects of the law and looked into its effects, particularly with respect to procedures and punishments under criminal law. As the United States Inspector of Federal Prisons he wrote and labored extensively through the 1930's seeking prison reforms designed to humanize the penal system and some of its vicious consequences. Nevertheless, he drew a strong line of separation, preserving discipline with modernization, but not incorporating any pampering or coddling into the plan. He was responsible for the effecting of numerous humane changes in the prison systems of the world.

Another Jew who left the active bar for public service was David Lilienthal, until recently the key figure in atomic development. The terrifying possibilities posed by the bombing of Nagasaki and Hiroshima in the summer of 1945 precipitated the end of World War II, but also presented to all civilization the problem of controlling the destructive element of this new force and diverting it to the promotion of mankind's welfare. Laws were needed—national and international laws—to allay the fears and to put the hopes into accomplishment, and the great step in this direction was the *Lilienthal Report* of April, 1946, now considered one of the important public documents of the American government. Drafted by a committee of atomic experts headed by Lilienthal prior to his resignation, the paper set forth American willingness to disclose the secrets of atomic development to international authority and control. Before his assumption of the chairmanship of the Atomic Energy Commission, Lilienthal served as chairman of the Tennessee Valley Authority.

Perhaps the greatest student of and authority on the common law in the world's history was Benjamin Nathan Cardozo (1871-1938), the sweet, kindly man who started life in the reflected humiliation of his father's disgraceful career and completed it under a shower of world acclaim and honor so great and so sincere that scarcely another in the field of law has received, or ever may receive, its equal. Albert Cardozo, his father, was given a judgeship in 1862 by Boss Tweed, notorious leader of the corrupt Tammany political machine, and it is a matter of common knowledge that he repaid his 'benefactors' with favors from the bench. His receivership of the Erie Railroad was marked by such open and flagrant misconduct and resulting scandal that the public demanded a thorough investigation, during the early stages of which Albert Cardozo resigned from all public posts and interests.

Benjamin, born in 1870, was aware at an early age of the stigma brought to the hitherto excellent family name, and it is obvious from many facts in his personal, legal, and public history that he had resolved firmly to redeem it. It is believed by many who knew him that his shyness and reclusive life stemmed from his early desire to avoid people for fear of provoking remembrance of his father's disgrace. In his early years he was tutored by Horatio Alger, who later became famous as the author of popular boys' books invariably characterized by the poor but worthy lad who rose to success by courage and hard work, despite an unbelievable quantity of insurmountable obstacles thrown before him. Cardozo took a somewhat improved interest in life and people in consequence of Alger's closeness to him. Despite his modesty and reticence, he delivered the class oration at his graduation from Columbia University; in it he attacked the advocates of absolute communal government who urged rigid equality of wealth for all. He was, at the age of fifteen, the youngest student at the university.

After the death of his partner and brother, Albert Jr. in 1909, he distinguished himself as a 'lawyer's lawyer,' and in 1913, when a particularly strong wave of political vice was extant, a committee asked him to run for justice of the New York State Supreme Court in the Fusion Party, organized for purposes of political reform. He acquiesced reluctantly and did little campaigning, and no one was more surprised than Cardozo himself when he was elected. This outcome of the election in the face of strong power and unity in the opposition was probably the result of an accident; of the mistaken belief on the part of the extensive Italian vote in New York City that Cardozo was Italian. In any event, accident or otherwise, it was a happy occurrence, as the years bore out in ever-swelling evidence. Within one month Governor Glynn appointed him to the New York State Court of Appeals, the court acknowledged by many as the strongest and most influential in the United States on matters of common law.

Cardozo's decisions were highlighted by deep recognition of the historical development of any matter brought before the court, many of them setting forth amazingly detailed features of the growth of the object or principle in question, all leading to the important point at issue and his reasons for holding one way or the other. He insisted throughout his career that the process of law must be one of conciliation and compromise, and he, perhaps more than any other judge of that court, pulled and strained at the bonds of the law to the extent that, without committing error, he brought what he believed was (and it invariably *was*) true justice to the case before him. He was quick to realize that all too often the law was one thing, and justice another, far removed.

[813]

His famous *MacPherson* and *Haynes* cases (1916 and 1935) pointed out so sharply the inadequacy of the law of torts (negligence) that not only did New York and other states adopt his changes, but England, as well, cited them in bringing the same improvements to the British law.

When the resignation of Holmes, at ninety, created a vacancy in the United States Supreme Court, it did not appear that Cardozo would receive the nomination, for two practical reasons. First, there were already two New York judges on the bench of the high court (Hughes and Stone), and geography had ever been a motivating factor in the choice by the president, who sought to 'spread' the membership of the court across the country. Second, there was a Jew incumbent in the Supreme Court (Brandeis), and many were bitterly (though quietly) opposed to the elevation of a second Jew for the 'quota' reason that such a move would be in vast disproportion to the population percentage. Yet, there was no alternative, and despite the nation-wide screening of possible candidates, one name and one name only persisted in popping up not only as the logical choice, but also the inevitable choice. In February, 1932, President Hoover submitted the name of Cardozo to the Senate, and he was rapidly approved by unanimous vote.

His six years in the Supreme Court were sad years, sad because of the continual state of controversy prevailing among its members. He was unaccustomed to such internal discord, having come from a court possessing a high degree of unity without sacrifice of individuality of philosophy or opinion. Although his decisions on constitutional questions were clear, just, convincing, and of high legal caliber, they seemed to lack some of the spirit, depth, and magnificence of language found in his common law work; it is in the latter tradition that he will be best remembered. In the spring of 1938, tired and ailing, he was offered cloistered refuge at the home of his friend Irving Lehman, Chief Justice of the New York State Court of Appeals, and he died there on July 9th of that year.

At a memorial service in the Supreme Court, Chief Justice Hughes observed "His gentleness and self-restraint, his ineffable charm, combined with his alertness and mental strength, made him a unique personality. With us who had the privilege of daily association there will ever abide the precious memory not only of the work of a great jurist but of companionship with a beautiful spirit, an extraordinary combination of grace and power." Bench and bar were shocked at the irretrievable loss, and law school professors mourned. Their beloved Cardozo was gone, no longer to thrill them with his words, his quiet brilliance, his masterful treatment of the cases heard by him. His never-ending search for secluded retirement was finally over, after the more-than-successful mission to bring honor to the name of Cardozo once again. The sound of the name today bespeaks completion by the addition of *Benjamin* only, for his work has relegated Albert to the domain of the obscured, to the unremembered.

The number of important Jewish names in law is legion. So great, in fact, that no one book—let alone a mere section or chapter—can grant sufficient recognition to all. Many prominent Jews in the field deserve biographical notice equal to that of some recorded herein, but in view of the limitations necessarily imposed, let it be said that while their specific identification may be glossed over or omitted, their work is not forgotten, if for the only reason that it cannot be forgotten because of the harrowing odds against which their efforts commenced. The Middle Ages produced a galaxy of Jewish legal figures despite the educational and intellectual stagnation of the period, and the Jew forged a chain of continuous progress extending, stronger than ever, into the present day.

European law was enriched incalculably by such men as Hermann Kantorowicz, Otto Lenel, Heinrich Dernburg, Arthur Cohen, Friedrich Julius Stahl, Eugen Ehrlich, Georg Jellinek, Paul Laband, and a host of others; American law by Jerome N. Frank, the Lehmans, Bernard Mannes Baruch,

Felix Frankfurter, Benjamin Cohen, Anna Rosenberg, the Untermeyers, Samuel Irving Rosenman, the Steuers, etc.

Somewhat tangential to the precise field of law, but nevertheless allied with it, are the accomplishments of those Jews who reached the supreme level of statesmanship within their respective states. The sixth governor of Georgia was David Emanuel, elected in 1801. Louisiana selected Michael Hahn as its leader during the threatening days of 1864, and Moses Alexander was twice governor of Idaho, first elected in 1897. Simon Bamberger was the first non-Mormon governor of Utah, elected in 1916. The troubled economy of the 1930's brought Jews to the leadership of five states: Julius L. Meier in Oregon (elected 1931), David Sholtz in Florida (elected 1933), Henry Horner in Illinois, Arthur Seligman in New Mexico, and Herbert H. Lehman, four times the governor of New York. Lehman subsequently acceded to the public demand for his services despite his avowed intention to retire from politics, and won a seat in the United States Senate.

While the Hebrew contribution to law was hurt by its share of Abe Hummels, and of inefficient, corrupt, or unethical practitioners, bondsmen, etc., these setbacks were infinitesimal when weighed in the balance against the priceless treasure of justice founded on strong government that has been—and continues to be—the gift of the Jew to the world.

* * *

It is obvious from his past and present efforts that in the future, with wider freedom of education and profession becoming available to him, the Jew will go on to even greater accomplishments in this important and fascinating work of the world and its civilizations, furthering the strength of his country and the freedoms of its citizens, protecting its commerce, preserving internal order and harmony, and improving its position of esteem in the world family of nations.

THE JEW AND THE LAW

BIBLIOGRAPHY

ADAMS, *The Epic of America*. Little, Brown & Co., 1931.

BARBE-MARBOIS, *Our Revolutionary Forefathers*. Duffield, 1929.

BEROLZHEIMER, *The World's Legal Philosophies*, 1924.

BRIDENBAUGH, *Cities in the Wilderness*. Ronald Press, 1938.

BRIERLY, *The Law of Nations*. Oxford, 1949.

BROWN, *We Hold These Truths*. Harper & Bros., 1948.

CALISSE, *History of Italian Law*, 1928.

CARDOZO, *The Growth of the Law*, 1927.

COHEN, *History of the English Bar to 1450*, 1929.

Dictionary of American Biography. Scribner, 1936.

Dictionary of National Biography. London: Macmillan, 1885.

DORN, *Competition for Empire*. Harper & Bros., 1940.

FAULKNER, *American Political and Social History*. Appleton, 1948.

FOUILLÉ, *Modern French Legal Philosophy*, 1921.

FRIEDMAN, *Jewish Pioneers and Patriots*.

GILLIN, *Criminology and Penology*, 1927.

GOODHART, *Five Jewish Lawyers of the Common Law*. Oxford, 1949.
——, *English Contributions to the Philosophy of Law*. Oxford, 1938.

GRAY, *The Nature and Sources of the Law*. (2nd ed.) 1927.

GURVITCH, *The Sociology of Law*. Philosophical Library, 1942.

HOLDSWORTH, *History of English Law* (12 vols.), 1903-38.

HUNT, *History of England*. London: Longmans, Green, 1905.

HURST, *Growth of American Law; the Law Makers*. Little, Brown, 1950.

JENKS, *Law and Politics in the Middle Ages*, 1905.

JIRKU, *Das weltliche Recht im alten Testament*, 1927.

Journals of the Continental Congress. U. S. Gov't. Printing Office, 1910-28.

KELLY & HARBISON, *American Constitution, Origins & Development*. Norton, 1949.

KUTASH & BRANHAM, *Encyclopedia of Criminology*. Philosophical Library, 1949.

LAVISSE, *Histoire de France*. Paris, 1911.

LOTH, *Chief Justice John Marshall*. Norton & Co., 1949.

THE HEBREW IMPACT ON WESTERN CIVILIZATION

MAIMONIDES, *The Code (Mishnah Torah) of Maimonides*. Yale University, 1949.

MILLER, *The Triumph of Freedom*. Little, Brown & Co., 1948.

MORISON & COMMAGER, *Growth of the American Republic*. Oxford, 1937.

NETTELS, *Roots of American Civilization*. Crofts, 1938.

PARRINGTON, *Main Currents in American Thought*. Harcourt, Brace, 1930.

PRICE, *Observations on the American Revolution*. London, 1784.

ROUCEK, *Slavonic Encyclopedia*. Philosophical Library, 1948.

SAMUEL, *Jewish Anthology*. Behrman, 1925.

SEAGLE, *The History of Law*. Knopf, 1941.

SMITH, *Origin and History of Hebrew Law,* 1931.

STEPHEN, *History of English Criminal Law* (3 vols.), 1883.

SUMNER, *The Science of Society* (4 vols.), 1927.

WARREN, *History of the American Bar,* 1913.

WILLOUGHBY, *Principles of Judicial Administration,* 1929.

The Fountainhead of Western Religion

By Vergilius Ferm

IT IS strange when one comes to study the thought of a person or some ideological movement how much clearer it becomes when one sees and understands the sources out of which it emerges. Strange it is because one tends to think of a man's ideas or some thought current as an isolated phenomenon and then comes the almost surprising realization that these thoughts have a history which removes the illusion of utter novelty. Not do we mean to say that the genesis of an ideological current constitutes a full explanation; for, nature and growth have a way of adding novelty to history. Nevertheless, it has become a truism that no man or movement is wholly cut off from its setting.

How much, indeed, is missed in Platonism, for example, apart from an understanding of its natural setting in the Greek view of life, from the Socratic method and conclusions preceding it, from the great Pythagorean movement which taught the doctrine that forms and patterns underlie the structure of the world and give meaning to it. How little of Aristotelianism can be understood apart from the Platonism which preceded it and which undergirds the whole tenor of its approach. How much of the Old Testament literature remains obscure without a knowledge of the borrowings, the imitations and reactions which the ancient Israelites carried over from the Canaanites from the day they entered the Promised Land. How little of later Mohammedanism is understood apart from the acknowledged influences of the religions of the Jews and the Christians.

In this essay, we set our limitations to that phase of Western religious thought commonly called Christian which carried on, consciously or unconsciously, the great religious tradition of the Hebraic-Judaistic culture. It is no surprise to be reminded of how great was this influence since, for the most part, Christians have acknowledged their commitment to the ancient Jewish Scriptures; but it is surprisingly strange how much of it that came to be called Christian was, in fact, the lengthening shadows of Hebraic ideas and influences.

Strong was the consciousness of these ancient people of a destiny to which they felt called and around which so much of their lives revolved. This characteristic alone makes any people genuinely religious. For it is of the essence of the religious mind that it is aware that life has a meaning which reaches out beyond the everyday tasks of living to something big and great and momentous. Ancient Israel was not the only group in the old world that possessed this consciousness strongly. The Hindus and the Iranians had a consciousness of destiny equally strong; in fact, all ancient peoples took the hinterlands of life seriously as witness the rituals and cult-practices and the gropings for an understanding of life's meaning.

Why the Hebrews had this sense of destiny in such striking measure and why they were able to pass it on to successive generations so persuasively calls for a number of interpretations. The ancient and persistent explanation was that the God of the Universe had especially selected them to convey His message and direction to all sons of men. But an equally strong conviction was in the minds of devout Hindus who also claimed the doctrine of a universal insight to which all the peoples of the earth are called. The traditional *religious* explanation of the Jews—accepted even by Christians—is a matter that cannot be settled dispassionately since it belongs to whatever religious commitment favored by the interpreter. For a more objective interpretation one must not overlook the fact that time and circumstance and sheer quality of offerings play their rôle in the measure, the reach and the breadth of a people's influence.

THE FOUNTAINHEAD OF WESTERN RELIGION

The descendants of the ancient Israelites lived strategically; they lived at the cross-roads of the world of their day; they moved about, willingly and forcibly, among other people and were relatively free from cultural isolation; they were made stronger in their religious convictions and commitments in the measure that they were politically weakened by invading conquerors; their experiences with unwelcome strangers of the world made them strong as extroverts in carrying on their difficult rôle in economic struggles and, at the same time, prevented their religious pattern to follow (as did the isolated Eastern Hindus) the path of inward isolationism and asceticism. And when Western civilization emerges it is Western and the Jews were there on its borders and in Roman and Greek centers to make their contribution—even though by subtle infiltrations. But this is not, of course, the whole story. They had a way of looking at life which caught the imagination of many of those whose own outlook was less satisfactory. Their dramatic picture of creation was not without appeal. Their religious commitments called for a welcome response because of a certain sanity which appealed to men of vigorous nature: they did not ask for withdrawal from life but called men to rise to their full stature as moral creatures with moral responsibilities in a moral Universe. The finer sensibilities of men have a way of responding to life as a noble adventure—in spite of life's crudities and absurdities. Their utter sense of destiny—in spite of the reverses of personal and political fortunes—kept their optimism high and never failed to impress others who lacked it. They were not easily to be removed in the struggle. They may have been down; but they never did quite count themselves out. Their experiences had been rough enough to cause them to forge for themselves an outlook which could carry over the rough edges. But what is more—they had great prophets who measured values with depth of insight. And they, as a people, were the ancestors of the greatest of their prophets, Jesus of Nazareth, who captured the imagination of not only the children of their own faith but those who by birth and circumstance had been strangers to it in the early generations and in the long generations which followed.

In spite of what traditional scholars have been saying, the Jewish people were as rich in philosophy as they were in religion. What is fundamentally the difference between the two? Only one factor: a religion represents a *commitment* to a way at looking at life and destiny; a philosophy is an exposition of what life is held to be. The two are ideally one in content. And surely the Jews excelled in trying to come to an understanding of the Universe. This was to them a serious matter, so that their philosophy was not a mere theory: it constituted a commitment which then became their religion. Extroverted in terms of a vigorous moralism as was their religion, it was not, like Confucianism, at the expense of an inward conviction of deeper philosophical meaning and cosmological significance. True, they were not scientists in the earlier day, but neither were the Greeks in any modern sense of the term. It is not true, as many historians would say, that Western philosophy began with the ancient Greek culture; it is equally untrue to say, as is heard from many sources, that high ethical insights began with the Hebrew prophets. Dating beginnings is always precarious business when one sees how far back lie the sources of men's insights and the origins of ideological movements and practices.

The theory of strongly marked racial characteristics, with attending socio-psychological distinctions, in so far as these are deep in the blood of peoples, is one that is today much in question. There is evidence, of course, that certain peoples have distinguishable biological characteristics such as stature-types and pigmentation. There is, for example, evidence too from recent genetic studies that the Negro race exhibits blood phenomena such as sickle-cell-anemia which points to some affirmative conclusion of group-blood characteristics. Although this question is an open one for biological and psychological studies, sociologists realizing the complex intermixtures of peoples are on surer ground when they speak of cultural heritages which distinguish groups from others. Cultural heritages are as distinguishable in the Hebrew lineage, even as they are among the Irish, the Nordics and even among smaller social units such as American Yankees or Southern aristocrats. Great cultural changes, it is clear, are now moving at a rapid rate due to an age of increased intercommunication and intermixture which technological advances have forced upon man.

The cultural inheritance of the Jewish people like any others is to be explained by climate, source and character of food supply, proximity to the great routes of communication, topography, strategic localization, isolationism or its opposite by virtue of geographical factors, and a thousand others. The strong feeling of Jews for loyalty to their own kith and kin can surely partly be explained by the geographical location of their homeland: for centuries their backyards were the highways between north and south and they must for self-protection fortify themselves and unite to survive. That their religious philosophy should be affected by this cultural circumstance is only evident: a strong protective nationalism, a conscious struggle to preserve self-integrity, the dynamic of the idea of a peculiar destiny. Any people fated to live closely together by circumstance will inevitably develop codes of cleanliness, regulations for the details of living, moral norms and some unified philosophy. For such people to believe themselves the elect of God was not the result of some mystic contemplation (as it could have been for others) but issued in the roots of insecurity of their homeland, of themselves and their families and the need for strong ties to bind when the temptation to falter was strong—as it often became. Even an intense monotheism has a cultural rootage.

For the Jews morals and religion were one. The Lord God was the focal point of an ultimate destiny and the promise of a better and securer day. Loyalty to the will of a father-God would pay delayed dividends far surpassing the sufferings of this present world. To follow after the light of the Divine promise—vouchsafed to selected leaders—was the *summum bonum* of life. Man can not expect to strive to be less than the character of God demands; the holiness which is in God demands its reflection in man. (Lev. 19: 2) To sin against these promises and this high election of God's special revelation is no light matter; it is sheer rebellion which can only end in disaster both for the individual and the people.

Life with its concrete demands for living is a serious business before the God of the Universe. Hillel, a leader and patriarch of Palestinian Judaism of the early Christian era, taught the essence of the Judaistic faith to be: "What is hateful to thee, do not unto thy fellowmen; this is the whole Law; the rest is mere commentary." (Compare also Lev. 19: 18 which is the earlier expression of the Golden Rule.) The concrete virtues of life to which men are to dedicate themselves, according to Jewish religious thought and standards for ideal practice, were unsurpassable by any ethical standard: honesty, truthfulness, justice, mercy, purity, honor of parents, solicitude for the weak, reverence, obedience, love of fellowmen (brotherhood), kindness to animals, sexual purity and regard for family relations. All these were Jewish before they were Christian; even as (so we are coming very slowly to realize) they are a part of the bundle of teachings in other great religions of the world.

It is interesting to note how, centuries later in medieval Catholicism, the same list of the cardinal sins of men recurs as was taught in the developed Judaistic faith: the shedding of blood, sexual impurity and apostasy. A sturdy morality it was that issued from the voices of the ancient prophets of Israel and a strong respect for a sense of obligation to the moral order of the world lay at the heart of Israel's traditional teaching. It is wrong to accuse the whole of Judaistic religion of the extravagancies of the priesthood which fell victim to trivial requirements turning values upside down and preferring the lesser to the greater. This is the common fate of all priestly religions everywhere, including Christianity.

The Christian religion was born in the matrix of Judaism but it was born as a reaction not against essential Judaism but against its eccentricities. The three competing schools of Judaistic religious thought at the time of Jesus did not represent Judaism at its best any more than do the derivative cults of any great religion which shoot off into radical expressions. Pharisaism though soaked in the parent culture was not Judaism at its best, although its sincerity would match the sincerity of any religious cult. It was a priestly religion with meticulous observances made prominent, fanatical in behavior, in thought and expectation. Saducceism and Essenism, the one the religion of the privileged and charged with political intrigue to the point of advantageous assimilation, the other a semi-communistic Quaker movement strongly touched with ascetic motives, both fanatical, did not represent the best in the great tradition. Against these did the new prophet from Galilee pit his quiet strength, calling down a holy curse upon those who distorted values and calling for a return to the great prophetic religion of the fathers.

Not enough is objectively known about the beginnings of this modest religious movement to give a detailed and accurate picture. What is known can be gathered only from broad outlines and these, for the most part, by religiously committed witnesses. We do know that it was content with the anonymity of its disciples (with the exception of a few) and with no organization for its effective propagation. How far Jesus remained loyal to the religion of his fathers, in essence or in detail, and how far he launched a movement totally different from it, is a question which has been settled with prejudice on both sides. The Jews of broad appreciation would claim him as among the greatest in their prophetic lineage but would set certain limitations to what they would regard as extravagant claims of Gentile admirers. The Christians who followed soon after saw in him a person so unique that they tended to forget that whatever else he may have been, he was a Jewish prophet and belonged to the ages out of which he and his ancestors came.

A more balanced interpretation—doing no harm to the *essential* claims of either camp—would be, perhaps, to say that while he belonged—most strikingly, to be sure,—with the greatest Jewish prophets, both he and they belonged also to the prophetic world at its best; for many of the insights which they had in common concern all men of whatever the lineage and cultural background and to those prophetic voices which men may believe issue from Reality. Universality is the real *basis* of the greatest religious values. And no true judgment can be made without a sure sense of universality. One thing seems clear: He protested against the current religion of his day but, at the same time, he was as eager to recognize the truths and values of the religion of his fathers as he was quick to recognize the qualities of values from whatever sources they came—even from those who were rooted in the less promising soil of official Gentilism.

The Christian religion did not emerge from Judaism with any pretense of founding itself upon a literature apart from the accepted literature of the Jews. True, it soon began to interpret that literature after its own heart and later to work out a literature of its own. But Judaism's Old Testament remained in this primitive period the only authorized literature, quite understandable to Palestinian Jewish Christians and more or less so to those far from the traditional Jewish centers. It would only be natural to expect that Hellenistic Jewish Christians would gravitate toward an understanding of the message of their Teacher in ways more adaptable to their own peripheral environment. The Peter Christians were Jews of one type; the Pauline Christians in that larger world out-beyond the holy shrines would be something different. Paul, most naturally, saw to that. And — what is more! — Hellenistic Christians without the Jewish background would see to it that their understanding would not be ignored. Gnostic Christians, for example, saw to that.

It was Paul, the Jewish Pharisee, who swung open the gate to allow interpretations wider than the strictly Jewish homeland would permit—except perhaps the Prophet himself. His earliest outlook upon life—although we cannot be certain—was presumably that of a normal Jew living outside the homeland but in contact with the traditional culture of his family. His parents were probably orthodox; for it is clear he knew well the keeping of the minutiae of the Law. But the open air of a more cosmopolitan commercial city, Hellenistic in influence, together with the privileges of Roman citizenship must have operated, however slowly and painfully, to release him from the religious fundamentalism of his heritage. Some scholars would point out the probability of the liberalizing influence, even indirectly, upon Paul of the contemporary Jewish philosopher, Philo of Alexandria, in coming to terms with Greek thought. We do know that he had not seen the Prophet of Nazareth in the flesh; but he had felt the breath of the Teacher from the heroic witnesses already bent on proselytizing their kindred. They say it was a miraculous conversion from Judaism to Christianity that saw the birth of Pauline Christianity. Paul himself may have been convinced of some sudden Divine intrusion upon his life. Certainly one would not expect a carefully worked out auto-psycho-analysis on his part. His own religious interpretation will be affirmed or denied only in so far as one's own religious commitment persuades. One thing is clear: a man of his varied gifts, training, cosmopolitan contacts, could hardly have failed to note in his maturing years the awareness of a strong dualism between the religion of his fathers on the one hand, and the wider religion (return to essential Judaism?) of the Prophet of Nazareth, of the provincialism of many of his kinsmen as compared with the wider world of everyday experience, of the impossible exactitude of a life of conformity to a circumscribed past with the freer air of a wider culture. Pharisaism

[827]

must sooner or later come to look quite small in compariso
with that other very real world of the Gentiles, also sons o
God.

And so Paul receives his conversion (however gradual
and he begins to declare openly his convictions and to wri
letters and, unconsciously, to contribute to a new and sporad
sacred literature. A distinctive religious philosophy emerge
in which the world outside and the world within are sharpl
distinguished, a world of flesh and a world of spirit, the ol
Adam and the New Adam, the here-and-now and the grea
hereafter, the Law and the Gospel, the works of righteousnes
and the grace of faith, principalities bad and principalitie
good. The religious philosophy of the Prophet of Nazaret
was much more on the side of harmony and a world not to
foreign to its God—much more monistic, in the terminolog
of philosophy. For Paul the world became split into a violenc
of disharmony; and there was need of effecting some ultimat
harmony. Thus, the idea of salvation which implies a two
fold sphere (away from and toward) became accentuate
(typical with the Greeks) in his thought and reflects his ow
torn personality. The Greek and Oriental mystery cults of th
Roman empire furnish a dramatic fulfilment of this emphasi
upon salvation and this was something Paul understood an
certainly could incorporate into his religious experience an
interpretations.

So secure in the early Christian tradition was the acknowl
edged link with the Jewish Old Testament by the early Chris
tian church that any movement to cut the church off from
that tradition would find the going hard. The classic attempt
of course, was that of Marcionism (and, naturally, Gnosti
cism). According to the wealthy Marcion, Christianity had se
its course in the wrong direction. That course was set by it
too friendly relations with traditional Judaism, particularly i
holding on to the cosmological faith as taught in the Ol
Testament Scriptures. It was his aim to correct this error and
to launch the church on a course with a commitment to a

much simpler type of Scripture, a new canon, of which he was to be the reforming editor. The Old Testament, he said bluntly, depicts the God who is the Demiurge rather than the one true God revealed by the Christos. Moreover, the religion of the Jews, with its submission to the Law, belonged to a religion of yesterday, altogether inferior to that of the new faith in the Gospel so emphasized by Paul.

Marcionism constituted a formidable threat to sever the Christian religion from its deep roots in Judaistic thinking. From the middle of the second century until its close, while Catholicism was beginning to work out some self-conscious organization, Marcionism continued to be the church's greatest threat. Why did Marcionism fail? The answer seems evident: Marcion, though earnest and committed to high morals and a liberal, failed to take into account how deep in the consciousness of the early Christian Church was its dependence upon the religion of the Jews. The unfailing emphasis of Jewish monotheism would never permit a material world to be created by one God and a spiritual world as belonging to a greater. The Greek mold into which his mind was cast, and, for that matter, the minds also of many fellow Hellenistic Christians of that time, while calling for an interpretation in keeping with Gnostic philosophy could not, however strong, cope with the mighty stream of Judaistic tradition. The shadows of a towering, historic Judaism fell across the Greek Christians and they were unable to ignore them. Jesus did live in Nazareth; his disciples were from that far-off Judean country; the Old Testament had long been the one Bible; Paul had set forth his own message but Paul too was a Jew and belonged originally with the faith of his fathers; and, too, the so-called Gospel could hardly be meaningful without the Law which is emphasized as its contrast and which became interpreted as the stepping-stone. -

The Roman stage was set for the post-primitive chapter in the history of the Christian religion—a chapter which takes into account the gains made and the way to preserve them.

Christianity must now be fortified. The presbyter-priests now take over and unruly prophets of reform are brought into subjection.

It was Tertullian (born c. 160 A. D.) who, in general outlines, drew the map of the future for Christian belief—a map which, although filled in here and there by different colors of crayon and sharper lines due to the changing theologies of time and the provocation of heresies, was to remain normative for subsequent Roman Catholicism. The Tertullian map (anti-Marcionite) revealed in bold strokes an acknowledgment of the unbroken Jewish heritage: its monotheism, its sturdy morality, the normative character of that whole tradition and the high place of the ancient sacred literature. He, of course, did more. Jesus of Nazareth had become the promised personal Messiah and the Christos. The mysteries of worship and ritual (e. g., communion) with their more or less fantastic and elusive interpretations as practiced by the mystery-cults of the Graeco-Roman world were put to sanctified use in the gathering tradition. Nevertheless the lengthening shadows of the Jewish faith continued to fall over the established church and to prevent the recurrence of another serious anti-Jewish threat like that of Marcionism.[1] It would be centuries before any radical reformation would appear—and then the church would have established for itself a mighty tradition.

The Judaistic heritage must remain secure if for no other reason than the simple fact that one cannot deny one's parents or the land of one's birth. But that was not, of course, all of it. Who would fail to discern the voice of a moral God in the moral passion of the Hebrew prophets? Who could deny that Deity was not to be found in much of the Jewish law, e. g., in the ten commandments? How could the function of the ancient priesthood be abrogated in view of the growing powers of a new priesthood in the Christian church? How could there be a divorce from the ancient sacred literature when the new carries on references to it on every scroll? Who would dare think that Abraham and Isaac and Moses were altogether strangers to the ways of God and as not forerunners of the new faith? If there be any trouble in making them a part of the developing drama of the new faith one need only a set of principles of interpretation to understand all this and make it clear to others. Clement[2] and Origen (born late in the second century)—and Philo before them with his interpretation of the Old Testament—helped to that end with their famous method of allegorization—a principle which was destined to bind the Old and New Testaments solidly together into one whole, *only if properly understood.*

By the end of the second century, the main body of the New Testament had been canonized. The canon of Jewish scriptures was also finally settled in the second century of our era by the rabbis at Jamnia. The Jewish canon included the three-fold division: the Law, the Prophets and the Writings.

It is interesting to note that a chief principle by which selections were made for this New section of the enlarged Bible was that the writings were supposed to show the mark of reversion to origins. A writing must be apostolic and carry some apostolic name (whether the authorship permitted it or not). Thus, the Christian mind had in the day of the canonization of its literature the will to proclaim that Christianity had roots which must never be forgotten. But what is more—these roots stretched far back into the Old Testament literature and beyond to the antecedent Hebraic culture. Many of the apologists of the second century stated their conviction that the great truths of Christianity had been taught before Christ, that Christianity was not something new but a confirmation of truths already known. Moses and the Hebrew prophets, they said, were teachers of Christianity.

When it came time to draw up its first ecumenical confession, the Christian Church at Nicea in 325 did not hesitate to proclaim its allegiance to Jewish monotheism in spite of its long practiced worship of Jesus as also somehow God. Moreover, it followed the lead of bishop Irenaeus (late second century) who insisted so strongly that the Old Testament was to be honored as part and parcel of the Christian faith (as well as the Jewish moral law). Said Irenaeus of the Christian faith: It is "in one only God, the Father almighty, who created heaven, earth, sea and all they contain." Said the Nicene creed: "We believe in one God, Father almighty, Maker of all things visible and invisible."

The Christians followed the pattern of the Jews who had come to regard the canon fixed and that further revelation could be, at most, only an illumination of what had already been given. Thus ended the age of revelation. Further generations needed only to look back for their religious norms and at the same time look around suspiciously upon any who would claim some new and even reformatory apocalyptic insight.

The unity toward which the church strove and which was brought to so successful conclusion in Roman Catholicism had its historic counterpart in the fundamental unity which underlay the religion of Israel. The idea of a chosen people with a special revelation and a destiny—so highly cherished in the minds of the Hebraic-Judaistic people—now became a fundamental doctrine of the Christian church—amended, of course, with emphasis upon the person of Jesus Christ as the Incarnation of the living God. The church, like Israel of old, was to be the homeland of its people, the anchor for every storm and the sure guarantee of Divine favor and prosperity. Cyprian (died, 258) used the symbol of the Ark of Noah for the church—outside of which no one can be saved. The institution of the church, in its very beginnings, had been modeled after the Jewish synagogue—even its form of worship[3]—(attested to by the literature of the earliest days). The older men naturally took the leadership. Time and circumstance were to bring changes—such as the pre-eminence of urban centers such as Rome giving prominence to priestly leadership—but the pattern was still there. Again, the lengthening shadows of Judaistic influence reached down and touched even the area of administration in the new households of faith.

[832]

The Jewish people were exiled from their own land in the year 70 A. D. Until recently they had been a people without their own country. Throughout the long centuries, their devout hope and prayer remained for a return to their ancient home as they believed was vouchsafed them by their God. Their ritualistic prayers never forgot the land of Israel. Not even the attempted suppressions by the two great competing religions, the Mohammedan and the Christian, could blot out this religious conviction.

During the Middle Ages the Jews were regarded as a nation and each Jewish community as a fragment of that nation. From the late eighteenth century they were granted the rights of citizenship and expected to become loyal members of nationalistic groups. Thus nationalism came in as a temptation to curb the traditional hope and desire to return to their own homeland of Israel. But to traditional Jews this conferred citizenship was still a temporary experience; they were still confronted with two loyalties. In the developing modern states they were expected to discard their allegiance to both their Written and their Oral Laws in favor of the reigning civil laws—all of which was an aggravated affront to their very religion since the revealed Word of God and its accepted interpretations (e. g., the Talmud) covered the rules for all living. Moreover, emancipated as the Jews were in the days of the Enlightenment their emancipation was not complete. They still suffered humiliation socially; and the worst offenders were those from whom it should least be expected, the Christians. Christians might have accepted the Jews had they forsworn their fathers' religion in favor of the church. Likewise the Mohammedans. Their Hebrew tongue was preserved in their sacred literature and in their rituals and holy festivities in spite of the necessity to use the language of the nation into which they became adopted. Compromise languages they created which shows the strength of their own group-feeling and at the same time their loyalty to the civil authorities. They created out of German the Yiddish; and out of Spanish came the Ladino.

It was their religion, however, which bound these people together. Their Torah was their chief group-interest and their rabbis continued to be the symbol of their unity in dispersion. They idealized the future and lived in it. And it was a future which stretched out into eternity.

Claim has been made that Mohammedanism has been strongly conditioned by the Hebraic faith. Not all scholars are agreed that Islam imported its strong emphasis upon monotheism from the first and great commandment of Israel. Mohammed's own ideas may have been affected more strongly by Jewish thought than by Christian; but the record is not too clear as to the development of his religious ideas. The *Qur'an* has numerous references to Judaism and the Old Testament but this is no proof of Mohammed's own early dependence upon those ideas. It is unquestionably true that Judaism (together with Christianity) prepared the way for Mohammedanism, negatively by weakening the traditional religions of Arabia and positively in the later formulation of Islamic ideas— especially in the interchange of peoples in the day of Moslem conquest. Both Jews and Christians had to be subtle in the propagation of their own faiths to avoid the penalties imposed upon them by the great Islamic victories. For the Moslem was as certain of the truth of his faith as others were of theirs. Although theoretically tolerant of both Judaism and Christianity the Moslem victors sought converts; and Jewish and Christian pagans had to make choice between refusal with burdensome taxation or conversion with its promise of death for apostasy. Neither choice was too good. From the seventh century on Judaism and Christianity were to suffer losses to their missionary enterprises in successive waves of Arabic victories. Islam by 1500 dominated the Western religious scene —even the sacred shrines and holy places of Israel. Not only Jews but Christians became minority groups by the avalanche of a new religion which claimed to be a corrective of both.

The close of the fifteenth century brought the final elimination of Islamic political power in Spain and the tide was turned in favor of the Christian church. It must be remembered, however, that, in spite of the long and exacting period of Moslem domination, the main features of the Christian faith did not differ in the church from those of the fifth century. This meant that the Jewish heritage as transmitted through its sacred Scriptures persisted together with that which was carried over and transmuted by Paul and others in the normative New Testament. This same tradition was held in the Greek churches which had creedal differences of slight variation and which ran its course more or less separately because of political fortunes.

Thus the fate of Judaism in the ongoing centuries of Western civilization was sealed: to surrender its treasures—its main contributions—to the two big competing religions, Islam and Christianity, both of which in time absorbed much of which it had gloriously to offer; and to be content with an identity within small and almost negligible minority groups. The rôle of Judaism as a religion followed a course much like that of later Unitarianism—which by being gradually absorbed by liberal Protestants contributed its characteristic ideas quietly and anonymously, continuing its own identity as small and unobtrusive minority groups.

Measured in terms of the long centuries which preceded it, Protestantism burst upon the scene almost overnight although there were warnings of the coming rebellion. It turned out to be a reformation that proved good both for the Roman church (acknowledged by the Catholic Church since Trent as the "Catholic Reformation") and for the plurality of Protestant offspring.

Through the Augustinian monk, Martin Luther, the Jewish apostle Paul came again to his own. Those who followed the path of this leadership carried on the stream of Jewish influence by maintaining the sacredness and the fully normative character of the Jewish Scriptures and the Pauline interpretation of the great Prophet of Nazareth, now long worshipped by Christians as Lord and as an integral part of the Godhead and as the One foretold in the Old Testament through Whom comes ultimate salvation.

The other line followed a course which, in many respects, was more like a genuinely Jewish renaissance. Wherever the Protestant groups followed the leadership of Calvin and the Calvinists, an even stronger consciousness of Jewish heritage became evident. The Old Testament is dusted off and re-studied and its normative character taken seriously. Calvinism, in many respects (although, of course, Protestant), represents in Protestantism the revival of Jewish traditional faith. The Puritanism which became vocal in this sector strongly suggests its affinity with the ancient proclamations from Mt. Sinai and the tradition of the Law.

John Calvin's dream of a theocracy at Geneva (with, however, a representative government) is the new Israel dressed in Protestant garb. Calvinists like the Jews of old regarded themselves as peculiarly chosen, the true keepers of the temple of the Lord and appointed interpreters of God's will. The absolute sovereignty of God was the theme song even as it was of ancient Israel. Excommunication was a privileged prerogative of the church for those who would not fit into the chosen community, the elected of God. Even as in Israel offenders were put out of camp, so in Geneva there was to be the same expulsion from the new Israel. Children were given Jewish names: Abraham, Andrew, Daniel, Zachariah, Isaac, Ruth, Esther and Mary, replacing the names of Catholic saints. And when the heirs of those Protestant Israelites were privileged to name new settlements in America many of the towns took on names of Israel: Salem, Bethel, Mt. Carmel, Kidron, New Canaan and Zion. The Psalms remain the inspired hymns of the church. What hymn writer dare stand up to compete with David's songs? The Sabbath must be observed in truly legal fashion as a day especially hallowed of the Lord (although perchance it was now the first day of the week). The

Old Testament was to be read and the stories about Israel and its Divine commission and experience must be learned, not merely as the prophets would have it but as the scribes prescribed. Gentile theological students must continue (the medieval way) to sweat through years of study of Hebrew (as well as Greek), certainly not for cultural attainments but in order to acquaint themselves first-hand as students of God's inspired Holy Word. (This, of course, became the continued practice of other educated non-Calvinist Protestant groups.) Tithing was the Lord's expectation as it was in ancient Israel and it was sure to bring its special blessings. The doctrine of predestination, with the help of Paul, went well with the doctrine of the peculiar call of a chosen people. Calvinism was a religion of severity and solemnity rather than of spontaneity and joy; the sin of Adam continued to impose itself with a holy curse down to each and every individual including those yet unborn. A philosophy of history there was in which the outcome is already fixed from the beginning even to the number of those to be saved. God's justice and exacting character were re-emphasized. The day of inspiration was long ago closed and no new novelty of doctrine was to be permitted. An ethics in which rules and regulations for detailed living were sharply set by ministers and with this a sensitive conscience was brought to focus. A Bibliolatry much after the pattern of Pharisaism-in-the-best-sense postponed the day of objective scholarship in Biblical studies. An organized effort of the church set clear the line of demarcation between regenerate saints and unregenerate sinners, thus marking the character of missionary efforts.

It is true that the mind of John Calvin was severe and that his thinking followed legalistic lines. It is not difficult to see, accordingly, how appealing the priestly type of religion depicted in the Jewish Scriptures would be to such a mind. But this is not the only reason, nor even perhaps the chief reason for Calvin's predisposal toward this ancient Jewish emphasis. Rather, it must not be overlooked that there was in him a deep desire to make Christianity a visible thing and the pattern of ancient Israel was already there to serve. Moreover, it was a pattern set by God which current Catholic practice with its alleged abuses could not match.

Calvinism became enormously influential in Protestant Christianity down to the present era; and in the lengthening shadows of Jewish influence—on the side of its institutional, sacerdotal and puritanical expressions—stretches into our day. Lutheranism, the strongest competing Protestant influence, together with the lesser groups which stressed (theoretically) the Pauline heritage and the freedom and release of mind to more spontaneous expressions, soon came under the spreading influence of Calvinism and, in America, at least, failed to carry through the implications of its own peculiar genius.

Modern Judaism has sought consciously to set its influence upon Western civilization in sharper focus in six ways. First, late in the last century the Reform group came to life. As its name suggests it conceived of the faith as sound in essence provided ideas become modernized: revelation must be conceived to be natural as well as unique; creation can operate through evolution; the chosen people can be chosen in the sense of being foremost rather than unique; Palestinian hopes may give way to common cause with sons of men in a sense of mission wherever fate has decreed one shall live; the Torah can be followed as a spiritual and moral guide but need not bind modern man to ancient mores; ceremonies may be kept but made modern.

Second, the conservative-reform group (a minority) would reform ancient Judaism only modestly: the retention of the Hebrew ritual, the keeping of many of the laws (such as feasts and fasts, more rigorous Sabbath observance, dietary rules and ceremonies). Third, the fundamentalist group which would hold to the old orthodoxy and make clear that it is still reasonable and binding; philosophical speculation to be subject to the Scriptures and tradition; the goodness of obedience to God's declared will; Israel remains the instrument of God's high purpose to teach men the only true way to God and to life; the dispersion is the work of God and the sense of mission is seen in it.

Fourth, the conservative group which began about the middle of the last century, a group today effective in their call for a return of the sons of Israel to the faith and practices of their fathers but at the same time sympathetic toward revisions in matters regarded as less essential. Fifth, the small but liberal group of reconstructionists (of recent origin) who see the Jewish faith as a civilization worthy to be preserved and of value to the total cultural life of mankind. Sixth, Zionism which only recently has come to its magnificent fruition by the turn of political events is a religious-political movement inaugurated during the last decade of the nineteenth century seeking to re-establish Palestine as the homeland of the Jewish people. Attracted to this cause were Jews of various schools of thought, from conservative to liberal, each with its own peculiar set of hopes but all having faith that the return will revitalize the whole cause of historic Judaism.[4]

It must be remembered that, as a whole, there is no one authoritative Judaistic religion today. There are rabbis who lead their groups by virtue of no apostolic succession other than that they succeed in convincing their followers that they are worthy interpreters of the ancient faith and culture. These range from the orthodox to the liberal. One factor which has contributed to a continued self-consciousness and, more or less, to a privileged sense of destiny has been the persistent habit of restricted marriages, a habit consciously striven for and eminently successful. No religious group in Western civilization can match this success—not even the Roman Catholic nor certainly the Protestant Christians who have sought to set up corresponding restrictions within their separate households of faith.

It is no part of this essay to predict the wave of the future. But the temptation is great enough, at least, to express an opinion if not a prophecy.

One thing seems clear enough: the new age in which we are entering will call for changes in religious thought far more revolutionary than any of the preceding centuries of reform. Intimations of such a revolution are to be seen in the swift changes now in progress throughout the whole cultural life of man: in technology, in medicine, in physical and biological concepts, in sociological areas of thought, in impending political reforms. Men's philosophies and religions move with much heavier feet—but they do move!

Religions need not aspire to become one other than in the appreciation of their fundamental and universal values. Judaism has a large share to contribute toward this end—especially in the prophetic stream of its heritage. So also have Christianity and Mohammedanism—to name only the three great Western religions. But such appreciation will not come from the priests of these religions but from the new prophets which each in time will produce. Already such prophetic voices have been raised but to heed them will take time—a long time if the changes come without too much external pressure and a short time if some cataclysmic experience (such as an even more hideous war) takes place.

The orthodoxies in each faith will not be expected to surrender. Only through liberal minds within each faith, receptive to the growing revelation of events, will there come the necessary leadership in the acknowledgment of values in the several households of faith, wider appreciations and the genuine spirit of *rapprochement*. Unity in essentials must naturally be expected in a world that is growing into one world; but differences in detailed theologies and practices, properly understood, will probably continue with more good than harm. A Christian need not give up his idealization of the Jewish Prophet of Nazareth as a revealer of God, nor the best in his tradition, nor the cultus which has sprung up around that Name and conditioned Christian devotees with strong emotional feeling. Jesus may well remain for those of the Christian heritage the Son of God and the Voice and Mediator of the supreme Way of Life. On the other side, the Jew need not give up his idealization of the best in his tradition and may well welcome the supreme idealization which others have given to the Prophet of Nazareth as perhaps the greatest which his own heritage has produced without harming his own strong feeling for monotheism and the greatness of the other teachers in his tradition. Nor need he give up the rich heritage of his cult-practices, feasts and festivals, around which center he holds ties of deep feeling and affection.

By whatever term we may call the revered saints of our faith, we may be reminded of the truth that a term or name does not make them qualitatively what they were or are to us. The variant Messianic concepts about which schisms have played so strongly in the past need not divide. All truly supreme religious prophets have more than a name to keep—they had a cause, a moral cause, which far exceeds in importance the names we give them. Jesus, it seems clear, was not bent upon setting up a new religion; rather, he was bent upon fulfilling the best in a hallowed tradition and leading it from more to more. This a liberal Jew might well accept and so may the Christian with a larger vision. On other points of interpretation there is room for variant theological and soteriological theories; but on the main issues Jews and Christians belong together in a closely knitted heritage—and not only they, but those of other faiths, also, who in their own heritage must have had their share of prophetic voices consecrated from beyond the veil.

FOOTNOTES

[1] The last major threat to *primitive* Catholic Christianity was that of Montanism which the Christian priests successfully squelched.

Christian Manichaeism with its rejection of the Old Testament came later but was not a serious threat especially since the towering Augustine, after tasting of it, came to disavow it.

[2] Clement made the extravagant claim that the Greeks had borrowed their best thought from Moses and the prophets!

[3] A striking example is the continued practice in ritualistic Christian churches of reading the Epistle first and then the Gospel after the pattern of the synagogue which consisted of reading first from the Book of Moses and then the Prophets.

4 For an exposition of Reform Judaism, Conservative Judaism and Reconstructionism see articles by their respective exponents in *Religion in the Twentieth Century* edited by Vergilius Ferm (Philosophical Library, 1948). Brief accounts of Orthodox Judaism and Zionism appear in *An Encyclopedia of Religion,* same editor (same publisher, 1945).

BIBLIOGRAPHY*

CRANSTON, RUTH, *World Faith*. New York, 1949.

EISENSTEIN, I., *Creative Judaism*. New York, 1941.

ENSLIN, M. S., *The Ethics of Paul*. New York, 1930.

FRIESS, H. L. and SCHNEIDER, H. W., *Religion in Various Cultures*. New York, 1932.

KAPLAN, M. M., *Judaism As A Civilization*. New York, 1934.

——, *Judaism in Transition*. New York, 1941.

KOHLER, K., *The Origins of the Synagogue and the Church*, edited by H. G. Enelow. New York, 1929.

LATOURETTE, K. S., *The First Five Centuries*, Vol. I of *A History of the Expansion of Christianity*. New York, 1937.

——, *The Thousand Years of Uncertainty*, Vol. II of *A History of the Expansion of Christianity*. New York, 1938.

MCGIFFERT, A. C., *A History of Christian Thought*, Vol. I. New York, 1932.

* For recent bibliographies recommended by representatives of various Jewish schools of thought see the works cited in Footnote 4 (above).

Jewish Philosophers

By KURT F. LEIDECKER

HEBREW thinking has seldom run into mythology or pantheism, but it has always been fundamentally religious. Religion, however, is not to be separated from philosophy and ethics, especially not in Jewish speculations, because all these tendencies meet and revolve around the problem man. Jahveh is man writ large, even though he may be regarded as so holy that he is unapproachable. All ideals tend to become worshipped rather than practiced or communed with. God, then, is the ideal man, person, personality, I, Thou. As such he has passed into Christian thinking, with certain reservations. In Christian thinking God is no longer fully man writ large, having become divested of some of the human failings that clung to Jahveh. He is one only, not many, as Man also is one, and no picture can be made of Him just as no image can be made of a unique individual. Even in Christianity God's essential manhood is not sacrificed. Nor has man ever been consistently suppressed by either Jew or Christian in a sort of Oriental mysticism and asceticism.

To know that all of Jewish thinking has as its base man and his problems is to possess the key to Jewish philosophy in nearly all of its phases to within the recent past and measure the greatness of its impact on western civilization. Hebrew monotheism is thus nothing but a veiled moral and sociological philosophy superimposed on a custom and habit controlled society which evolved in several stages and gradually emerged on the reflective level. All ethical thinking, by necessity, must concern itself with man, and God as Man or Person, which is equivalent to the conglobation of man's ideals. What concerns man must concern Man, and a dialectic ensues between man and God which, in religion, takes the form of revelation, and in philosophy becomes insight into the true nature of man's mind and aspirations. In the Old Testament, God and man are as little distinguishable—except in the magnitude of power—as in the latter-day Society for Ethical Culture founded by Felix Adler (1851-1933),* or in the conception of God as the ethical ideal of man in Hermann (Ezekiel) Cohen (1842-1918).

It is this ethical and practical point of view which is the principal contribution of Judaism to western civilization. In fact, Samuel David Luzzatto or Shadal (1800-1865) contrasted Abrahamism, or the ethically oriented Jewish point of view, with Atticism, or the rationalistic-esthetic Gentile outlook. The forte of Jewish thinkers has never been ontology; it is ethics, and the essence of the moral life as conceived in the West from the beginning of the Christian era down to the present time are the Shall and Ought of ancient Hebrew speculation. All problems, even the most abstract, can be interpreted as sublimations of ethical thought peculiar to the Jewish people and reflecting their social and political vicissitudes. Their interest in religion, ethics, logic and symbolism, for instance, was suggested by their quest throughout the ages for the whence and whither, for justice, for structure and meaning, for universality and particularity. It was only with the emancipation beginning toward the close of the 18th century, notably since the *Toleranzedikt* of Joseph II, that Jewish thinking lost its peculiar tone with the aid of the political action of men like Gabriel Riesser (1806-1863) and Jewish philosophers everywhere entered the intellectual life vigorously in all fields and disciplines.

The basic ethical significance of the Old Testament is especially evident if we study it in the division of Torah or Law, Nebiim or Prophets, and Ketubim or Writings. The begin-

---

* The fact that an author is Jewish is either expressly stated in the following or may be inferred from an indication of his birth and/or death as given in parenthesis.

ning of wisdom is the fear of the Lord, not free philosophic enquiry, and it is this attitude· which Christianity inherited from the study of the Bible. Christians merely liberalized the habit and custom bound ethical speculations and injunctions.

The western world adopted as its ethical code the decalogue which Moses, the Hebrew (end of 14th cent. B.C.), gave his people on Mount Sinai. The socio-political problems of Samuel and Saul impressed the Christian world until the overzealous rationalizations of a James I of England spoiled our taste for the divine rights of kings. The wisdom of Solomon is proverbial throughout the world. Elija's spectacular triumph over the four hundred and fifty Baal priests on Mount Carmel meant victory for the concept Jahveh as the sum total of the ethical ideals of Israel. That victory, ephemeral though it was, miracle-working Elisha and every last Christian evangelist is trying to consolidate in helping the one, jealous, personal God to worldwide recognition.

When Jahveh speaks in the *Books of Samuel* and *Kings,* it is the social conscience becoming vocal and changing the original Shall into an Ought. The prophets, one and all, were moral philosophers who appeal to us without benefit of technical terminology or reference to basic philosophical principles. The name of philosopher is more appropriate for those among the greater prophets who were political theorists as well. This is true of the shepherd Amos (ab. 800 B.C.) and mighty Isaiah (active between 758 and 700 B.C.), the latter a poet and statesman and a master in both. Morality for them is possible only in the larger context of international relationships, a concept which was taken over by the western world and is still in the process of clarification. Hebrew ethical thinking did implicate individual acts in national and ultimately international destinies, and it is here where the roots of modern thinking lie which implements educational, social and political reforms with international events. The capstone of this development is the ethico-political philosophy of western democracy embodied in the Four Freedoms and the Atlantic

Pact. But beyond that the literary and esthetic impact likewise has caused reverberations in the sphere of individual and social ethics, as when the 102nd Psalm inspired Friedrich von Schiller's "Ode to Joy" which Beethoven set to music at the end of his Ninth Symphony.

No need to name all other moral preceptors whom every Christian knows from the study of the Old Testament, such as Hosea (died 784 B.C.), the prophet of love, Micah (ab. 700 B.C.), and Ezekiel (after 596 B.C.), or to elaborate on the ethical problems and solutions offered by the compilers of the story of the fall of man, the *Book of Job,* the psalms, *Proverbs, Ecclesiastes* and other documents. Their significance in having shaped the moral conceptions of the West individually, socially, politically and every other way, is too obvious to require comment. They have set and still set for us the problem of good and evil in all its ramifications. The western world is generally not disposed to lending an ear to any other ethical theory than that which Jewish moralists worked out long ago and presented us with, and the early Church Fathers chose to preserve for later generations in the selections they had made of Hebrew writings which were incorporated into the Bible which, in turn, has, truly, become the book of fate for many a century.

The greatest of the Hebrew moralist philosophers, however, was Jesus of Nazareth. In that he preached the doctrine of love and forgiveness he was and is, in Jewish conception, but one of the rabbinical teachers. Considered as a moralist alone, Jesus is of subordinate importance in Christian thinking to Christ, the divinity and theological figure created by another great Jewish religious thinker and philosopher, Saul of Tarsus, called Paul (born before 10 A.D., died after 63 A.D.). In so far as Jesus, the prophet, suggested by word and deed his divinity and pushed the concept of God way beyond the concept of Man, he fell outside the great Jewish tradition and retained his place in the Hebrew commonwealth of thought only in that he also claimed to be the Son of Man.

The well of ethical speculation among the Hebrews did not dry up with Paul. Nor is all Hebrew moral philosophy contained solely in the books of the Old and New Testaments which the compilers of the Bible declared inspired and hence worth including in the collection. Some books are apocryphal but on that account not less important, ethically and philosophically. Sibylline books of the Jews were adopted by Christians and edited by them. Other writings were accepted in part only or rejected entirely. For example, the *Book of Maccabees*, four in number, were rejected in their entirety by the Protestants, including the fourth book which is highly philosophical in character. The Catholics, however, declare the first two books canonical, in fact regard them as ethically very significant. Do they not recognize the Maccabees as the only Old Testament martyred saints?

The influence of ancient Hebraic ethical thinking upon the West became self-operative after the canonization of the various books of the Bible. It became greatest when Protestantism, along with the art of printing, made the Book of Books available generally. Some of the writings of the Bible, it must be remembered, however, were not pure products of Hebrew genius. The cosmopolitanism of the Jews expresses itself distinctly in many features which bear the stamp of the diaspora character of the Jewish community. Yet, Platonic and Stoic concepts, the Logos idea, mystical strains, allusions to the virtues, the Iranian conception of light, are all woven into the texture of some Old and New Testament books. Jewish thinkers in Alexandria and elsewhere who tried to assimilate Greek thinking during the Judeo-Hellenic period, did not exert a vital influence upon western thought with their ideas which were typically Hebrew. Only in so far as Philo the Jew (born about 25 B.C.), of Alexandria, worked out the Logos idea and allegorized his concepts, was he of influence in Neoplatonism and early Christian philosophy. Some early Church fathers thought that he possessed a useful solution to the problem of how to reconcile the unity of God with the divinity of the Son.

It would be impossible to trace even perfunctorily in the compass of a tome the actual influence of the Bible on western philosophy. Heinrich Heine (1799-1856) once said in his *Confessions* that it is to the Jews that the world owes its God, and Francis J. Oppenheimer (1881-   ) states in *Ezekiel to Einstein* (1940), p. 118, that Christianity is "a Jewish invention in religion". In so far as Christian theology, Catholic and Protestant, is also philosophy, it must accept from the Bible the basic ethical anthropomorphism. Any philosopher, also, let him be scholastic or modern, who does not borrow his concept of the personality of God from the Stoics or some Oriental source, must likewise acknowledge his indebtedness to Hebraic thinking. In this connection it may be mentioned that some think Zeno (336/5-270 B.C.), the founder of Stoicism which had such a tremendous influence within the Roman empire on slave and emperor alike and produced such admirable philosophers as Seneca, Epictetus and Marcus Aurelius, was of Jewish origin. The point is, however, not proven. Of schoolmen, influenced by Hebraic thinking, we should name all those who believed in the divine as well as human aspect of Christ, and among other philosophers we mention but those who, like Lotze, have been persuaded of the personality of God, idealists in the camp of Josiah Royce, and most of those who call themselves personalists. It is interesting to note that one of the greatest of Royce scholars is Professor J. Loewenberg (1882-   ) of the University of California.

The further development of Jewish thought in the Jerusalemite and Babylonian Talmuds, with their Mishnahs and Gemaras, their Halakhahs and Haggadhahs, all more or less complete at the end of the 5th century, has not had such a great influence on western philosophy because of its strictly legalistic and rabbinical tendencies. But the esoteric Cabala with its Platonically integrated mysticism originating in

Gnosticism and the apocalyptic literature of the first Christian centuries did make a thorough impression. If we consider the magical and alchemical outlook of the Middle Ages which captured the imagination of many a sober thinker, we cannot help but believe that, for instance, the *Sepher Jezirah* (Book of Creation), composed in the ninth century, and the *Sohar* (The Splendor of Light), composed in the 13th century, must have been implicated in the general conception of life all through the centuries. Despite the language barrier which Hebrew represents, the mode of literary interpretation, the number symbolism and the number mysticism which were cultivated in cabalistic circles, lent color to the thinking of many of the darker centuries of the western world. Occultism, a phase of half philosophical and prelogical thinking, has not lost its fascination even today and often derives, as in theosophy and anthroposophy, renewed vigor from Jewish symbolizing, allegorizing and cabalistic mystic literature. Among the interesting attempts to combine Cabala, Catholicism and Schelling's philosophy should be mentioned that of Meir Heinrich Landauer (1808-1841). More recently, Sigmund Isaiah Gelbhaus (died in 1928) wrote on the Cabala and Spinoza, and Joseph Leon Blau (1909-   ) just published his findings regarding the Christian interpretation of the Cabala.

Of men of note in the history of philosophy who have been influenced by Jewish mysticism we name, among others Johann Reuchlin, humanist and student of Jewish literature who wrote *De Arte Cabbalistica;* Agrippa von Nettesheim, the sceptic and physician who fought scholasticism, yet believed in the all-soul and extended his researches deep into the magical; Theophrastus Bombastus Paracelsus, the great philosopher-physician who was devoted, as one of the first, to experiment, but respected Neoplatonism in the garb of cabalistic thinking; his noted pupil, Johann Baptist van Helmont; Giordano Bruno, whose wide and deep knowledge embraced some of Jewish mysticism as well; Jacob Boehme, the great mystic who found much in the Cabala that was congenial to his own experience;

Henry More, the Cambridge Platonist who derived many a thought from the Cabala; Franz von Baader, who combined independent Catholic thinking with epistemology and a gnostic-cabalistic outlook; and Franz Josef Molitor, who thought Christianity could be enriched by the Cabala.

Mention must also be made of the prophesies of the Jewish physician and astrologer, Michel de Notre Dame, best known as Nostradamus (1503-1566), which are studied with renewed vigor in some quarters, and the influence, passing though it was, of Rabbi Isaak Bernays (1792-1849) who wrote *Der Biblische Orient* which appeared in 1820 and represents a curious mixture of symbolizing and rationalizing tendencies, allegedly following Herder's interpretation of the spirit of Hebraic literature.

All through the Middle Ages the Jews were in close touch with Islam. By virtue of their peculiar position as the Biblical people, they represented a bridge, religiously and theologically speaking, between themselves and Christianity and Islam, and between all the derivative faiths. But the diaspora fitted them especially for the task of passing on the views of the great Greek philosophers as well. For some centuries preceding the Renaissance, the Jews were in possession of more knowledge —indirect though it was over Islamic speculations—of Greek philosophy than western scholars dreamed was in existence. Together with the Arabian thinkers they knew Plato and Aristotle far better than any Christian. As chief interpreters for centuries they also were the carriers of Arabian Aristotelianism, the transformers, along with others, of Platonism, and the retellers of Oriental lore in general. In the revival of classical learning the Jews were, thus, a step ahead of western scholars. In the ninth century Jewish philosophers were beginning to make themselves independent of Islamic speculation. The Logos doctrine of Philo was not entirely lost to memory. One of the first Jewish philosophers of that age, Isaac ben Salomo Israeli (about 850-950), was a Neoplatonist whose influence, however, was felt only centuries later. Far more important than he was Saadia ben Joseph (882-942) who hailed from Fajjum in Egypt. The fact that many of his writings were polemical is proof that he was not merely writing for the benefit of Jews, but was in active exchange of opinion with Christians, Mohammedans and even followers of Zoroaster. His eudaemonism does not stray far from traditional Judaism.

The author of *Fons vitae,* a widely read book of metaphysics, was considered by many schoolmen to have been a Mohammedan or even a Christian. But it has been established by Salomon Munk (1803-1867) that he was the Jew Salomo ibn Gabirol (about 1021-1070). This amusing incident alone, involving a Latin translation of a work originally written in Arabic, shows beyond doubt that Jewish medieval philosophy had a tremendous influence on the thought of the Middle Ages, especially when it represented a recast or further development of Neoplatonism to which Jew and Gentile were both favorably disposed. More specifically, the men whom Gabirol influenced were William of Auvergne, Albertus Magnus, Thomas Aquinas and Duns Scotus.

Jehuda Halevi (1086-1142) somewhat obliterated the fundamental distinctions between Neoplatonism and Aristotelianism which only a century later appeared in greater clarity, especially when Abraham Ibn Daud (died about 1180) presented a type of Aristotelianism that seemed in perfect agreement with the philosophy of Judaism. It was not till Moses Maimonides' (1135-1204) writings that Aristotelianism and Judaism were discovered to be at variance. Maimonides was *the* Jewish philosophical genius of the Middle Ages who exerted the greatest influence upon his contemporaries as well as later generations. It was he who laid the basis for philosophy within Judaism and was studied by Alexander of Hales, William of Auvergne, Albertus Magnus, Thomas Aquinas and Nicolaus Cusanus. Meister Eckhart knew his work, and even Leibniz was impressed with him.

[851]

To be sure, none of the Jewish philosophers of the Middle Ages was so well known as Maimonides, but there were other thinkers who attained renown outside rabbinical circles, such as Levi ben Gerson (1288-1344), whose *Milchamot Adonai* was studied by Pico della Mirandola, Reuchlin, Kepler and others, Chasdai Crescas (about 1340-1410), and Isaac Abravanel (1437-1509).

The first fruit of the emancipation of Jewry in the 18th century was a regenerated consciousness of the Hebrew spirit itself and a realization of its importance in world history. In a sense, men like Isaak Bernays, the Hegelian Nachman Krochmal (1785-1840) called the "Mendelssohn of Galicia", Joseph Salvador (1769-1873), Salomo Jehuda Rappoport (1790-1866) known as Shir, Leopold Zunz (1794-1886), Samson Raphael Hirsch (1808-1888), Abraham Geiger (1810-1874), Zacharias Frankel (1801-1875), Moses Hess (1812-1875), Hirsch (Heinrich) Graetz (1817-1891), Elijah Benamozegh (1822-1900), Max Nordau, pseudonym for Simon Südfeld (1849-1923), and Simon Dubnow (died in 1943), were philosophers of history. Though they were primarily concerned with the Jewish people and its vicissitudes, they tended in Krochmal and Geiger to interpret the Hebraic spirit as the World Spirit, in analogy to Hegel. There was, of course, every reason to treat the unique Hebrew contribution from the point of view of world history, because the West had placed Christianity in its banner, and Christianity was unthinkable without its basis in Hebrew monotheism and the Hebrew interpretation of morality as a constant interplay of human and divine factors. As a militant and missionary faith, Christianity gave at the same time the stamp of universalism to the ethical and religious core of Judaism, thus fulfilling for Judaism that great and holy destiny among the nations of which the prophets of old had such a grand vision.

This sort of philosophic pattern of history was implied in the very acceptance of the Bible by the West, but it was never formulated by Christian theologians and philosophers of history with such emphasis on the Hebrew warp. In that this Jewish philosophy of history was messianic throughout and became involved in a dialectic which passed through Chassidism, Restoration and Autoemancipation to Zionism on the one hand, and the assimilation movement on the other, sponsored as early as 1770 by Moses Mendelssohn (1729-1786) to which such brilliant Jewesses as Henrietta Herz (1764-1847), Dorothea Mendelssohn (1763-1839) and Rahel Lewin (Rahel Antonie Friederike Varnhagen von Ense, 1771-1823) succumbed along with other literary minds, the Hebrew World Spirit became as it were concretized politically.

In the field of philosophy of religion, Jewish thinkers exerted an influence supplementary to the Scriptures, yet not so vital, first because they did not stress the unique importance of Christ and, secondly because they leaned too heavily on other thinkers. Thus, Salomon Ludwig Steinheim (about 1789-1866) accepted along with other philosophers in religion the view that revelation is the essence of religion and rationalism is its death. But, Samuel Hirsch (1815-1889) and Hermann Cohen were thoroughly rationalistic in their views. Salomon Formstecher (1808-1889), a Schellingian originally, held to the transcendence of God, yet interpreted the development of religious consciousness as one passing from objectivity to subjectivity, that is, from recognition of God Old-Testament-style to God as the creative power of spirit in self-realization. These thinkers reinterpreted, thus, Hebrew ethical ideals in the light of Kantean, Fichtean and Hegelian speculation. Efforts, such as David Friedlaender's (1750-1834), to find a middle ground between Judaism and Christianity, were too obviously motivated by seeking political advantages in a Jewish Christianity and diluting if not mocking the essential doctrinal content of Christianity and consequently failed to gain the support even of the well-meaning, such as Schleiermacher.

A good many Jewish authors have occupied themselves with the problem of the philosophy of religion in its comparative and cultural aspects. A long list of names and titles could be assembled, from Daniel A. Huebsch, the translator of Pfleiderer, Maurice Flügel (1832-1911) who made many significant comparative studies, and Salomon Reinach (1858-1932), the French author of *Orpheus, A History of Religion,* to James Henry Leuba (1868-1946) and his psychological approach, Claude Joseph Goldsmid Montefiore (1858-1938), Rabbi Joshua Loth Liebman (1907-1948) and his much-read *Peace of Mind,* and Sholem Asch (1880-   ) whose *Nazarene* and *The Apostle* created quite a sensation. Their appeal, and hence influence, rest upon a certain daring or unorthodoxy in the interpretation of religious experience which does not concern us here directly, since the interest often stems from fresh points of view gleaned from psychology, psychiatry, psychoanalysis, or the general hygiene of mental life.

Some believe that the concept of humanity was the creation of the Jewish people and they point to the phrase "the nations of the earth", which occurs in the Bible. Be that as it may, on the basis of the panorama of Jewish life in which *galuth,* exile (see the recent translation of the book entitled *Galut* by Yitzhak Fritz Baer, 1888-   ), and diaspora are the most persistently recurring disasters, we can well believe that such universalistic concepts as mankind or humanity could easily arise, first because of the wider acquaintance with all manner of races and nations, secondly on the strength of their own farflung communities which nevertheless preserved their spiritual bond in the Torah and rabbinical literature (the Jews were always known as *Ahl' ul kitab,* the people of the Book, among Arabs as elsewhere), and, thirdly, and antithetically, as an ideal or a hope for a world-wide humane humanity. The latter, of course, is well-known from the problem in Lessing's *Nathan the Wise,* and the biblical longing for the kingdom of God on earth, which is the essence of messianism.

Now, the philosophic position of humanism may be easily traced to this quasi-religious and economic origin. Humanism is the point of contact which philosophy maintains with the pulsating life of the age. Characteristically, humanism, in the understanding of the Jewish thinkers, is ethically oriented, a fact which Arthur Liebert (1878-1946) who belongs to the Marburg School and who, with the editorship of the *Kant-Studien* and later *Philosophia* succeeded in gathering about himself quite an international following, again and again emphasized in his various books. Humanism is too broad a classification to allow us to name all humanists among Jewish philosophers. Even such specialists as Albert Einstein (1879-   ) should be called humanists if their more popular writings are taken into account. Again, even the most critical and rationalistic among Jewish thinkers, such as Hermann Cohen who speaks of an ethics of pure will, should be counted among humanists as they have given the plight of the Jewish people through the centuries a more than passing consideration and hence have dwelt on various occasions on the problems of humanity, society, the state, nation, "one world", liberalism, humanistic studies and attitudes, a free world and similar concepts as vital to their own existence and happiness and, by extension, to everyone else. The tradition of humanism is, indeed, carried wherever Jewish thinkers have established themselves in positions of influence, as for instance, in South America where Ricardo Levene (1885-   ) was instrumental in starting a series called *Humanidades* at La Plata University. In this connection should, perhaps, be mentioned Alejandro A. Zascalevich (1894-1936) who, as philosophical and psychological essayist, was active in Buenos Aires, Argentina.

From humanism it is but a step to pragmatism. The Jewish thinkers who are also pragmatists are not too many in number although the majority of all Jewish philosophers are against all absolutism in any form. Outstanding among those who achieved a larger hearing among their contemporaries in

Europe where pragmatism has never risen to such dignity as a philosophic ism as it has in the United States, we can name but a few, such as Wilhelm Jerusalem (1854-1923) who expressed himself strongly against Neo-Kantianism as well as all systems that are interested in logic as a pure science, himself assuming the genetic and social point of view, and Theodor Lessing (1872-1933) who worships action and is fierce in his condemnation of all metaphysics.

Nothing has been said as yet about the best-known of Jewish philosophers, Benedict de Spinoza (1632-1677) who exerted a very great influence upon western philosophy. His doctrine of the intellectual love of God, his deification of nature and naturalization of God in the phrase *deus sive natura,* his contention that nothing happens purposefully but only *more geometrico* (we should say according to logical laws), seems at first sight so completely outside the pale of Hebraic tradition as to negate our original statements regarding the main burden of Jewish philosophy. Spinoza seems to land in an outright intellectualism with the spontaneity of the moral life completely sacrificed in an uncompromising determinism and egotism. And yet, often the antitheses meet. Man, we said, was the prime concern of the Hebrew philosophers, and hence they arrived at the Thou of God. But in that man is also a social being beset by a million misfortunes and, wishing to control nature for his own purposes, he casts about for a method which will assure him control, well-being and universality. The rational or logical method with its mathematical structure fulfills the requirements of universality, prediction of behavior and control,—all elements compatible with the desire of the Jewish people to overcome the bad effects upon them of the diaspora and endeavor to form a close-knit community despite language and national barriers, their messianic hope, the urge to break the ghetto walls of their existence, physically and spiritually, and the longing for equality, peace, shelter and leadership so long denied them. Here is intellectual dynamism to supplement the ethical dynamism of monotheistic thinking.

Spinoza was not the first to try the rationalistic approach. Sophistry and logistic reasoning, legalistic and formalistic thinking, have sometimes been considered synonymous with rabbinism and Talmudism. To be critical and sceptical was the natural result of the economic and social position of Jewry. Keen and cutting critique was thus the characteristic acquired by Jewish thinkers in their long struggle to survive. Already Philo spoke of a sober intoxication brought about by much thinking and reflection, and Saadia ben Joseph appointed reason as judge over Torah and Talmud. Even Jehuda Halevi, poet and Neoplatonist that he was, recognized that logic and mathematics give us certain knowledge while traditional metaphysics in its aberrations will not. Abraham ibn Daud strove for a philosophy of reason that has as uppermost aim knowledge and the love of God. Joseph ibn Zadik (died 1149) used didactic logic in his book entitled *Microcosm*. Moses Maimonides laid an even better foundation for a rationalism in his definition of logical terms. The Cabala, finally, strange though it may seem, contributed to intellectualism by suggesting the geometric method in its number symbolism.

The ground was, therefore, well prepared for Spinoza's dogmatic rationalism to which Stoicism, Giordano Bruno, Hobbes and Descartes contributed heavily, besides the Jewish philosophers Maimonides, Gerson and Crescas. He was completely persuaded of the efficacy of the logico-geometrical method in the demonstration of God as the one and only substance, the immanent cause of all things which emerge with logico-mathematical necessity from his being. God's freedom is his inner necessity. Man does not possess freedom of will; he must overcome his emotions by reason and when he has won clear and distinct knowledge of God, his relation to God is that of intellectual love which constitutes freedom, highest virtue and perfect happiness all at once.

Spinoza was excommunicated from the Jewish community because of his pantheism which, as we saw, is foreign to Hebraic thinking. But on that account he was not less a Jew; his *Tractatus Theologicopoliticus* proves this. He was in advance of his age and his confreres who were not ready for the integration of Jewish thought with the stream of European thinking. What is significant is the fact that Spinoza's influence upon other thinkers has been inordinately great, but mainly in the things that were not up to that time characteristically Hebraic. The German philosophy of identity of Fichte, Hegel and Schelling, the latter's pantheism, Schleiermacher's theological speculations, Karl Christian Friedrich Krause's Panentheism, some of the great conceptions of Herder, Goethe, Shelley, Byron, Coleridge, Flaubert, Renan and even Nietzsche, must be held indebted to Spinoza in not a few particulars. The Jewish thinkers who made a name for themselves by expounding Spinoza are numerous. We mention only Leo Baeck (1873-   ), Constantin Brunner, a pseudonym for Leo Wertheimer (1862-1937), Julius Lewkowitz (1876-   ), Fritz Mauthner (1849-1923), Max Grunwald (1871-   ), Harry Austryn Wolfson (1887-   ), René Worms (1869-1926), Jacob Freudenthal (1839-1907), David Neumark (1866-1924), Richard Wahle (1857-1935), and more recently Abraham Wolfsohn.

Once the breach was made and intellectualism joined to the geometrical method in an effort to understand the world around and in us, Jewish thinkers applied the keen edge of their reasoning to the systems that were springing up in Germany, to where the torch of philosophic enquiry had passed from France and England. We soon find them self-conscious critics of Kant. In the person of Moses Mendelssohn (1729-1786) Judaism had its first modern philosopher who was recognized by western philosophers, yet did not compromise his Hebraic heritage. Rising to prominence from the ghetto, autodidact, he became the Jewish Socrates. He achieved this place because the ideas and tendencies of his time were receptive to the religious spirit as it had traditionally manifested itself in Judaism. While breaking with medieval rationalism, Mendelssohn searched Torah and Talmud for the formula which would adapt Jewish thinking to the engulfing enlightenment without sacrificing Hebraic essentials. This "Jewish Enlightenment" which some date from Mendelssohn, really had its antecedents not only in Spinoza, but in Judah Abravanel, also called Leo Hebraeus or Leone Medigo Ebreo (about 1460 to about 1525) and Judah Aryeh Leon of Modena (1571-1648). Mendelssohn found the solution of the conflict in a religion of reason, rejecting the thesis that revelation concerns religion rather than the law. This now famous solution, foreshadowed, of course, in Spinoza, cleared the way for his being appreciated in circles which believed in a religion within the bounds of reason but, more significantly, liberated Jewish speculation and philosophy for all time from the shackles of revealed religion. The ethical heritage of Judaism was, thus, left untouched and safe.

Even though Kantian thinking held the stage and overshadowed this approach of Mendelssohn's, the door to further developments in Jewish rationalism was opened wide. At first it oriented itself on Kant. Kant, who really never had a full appreciation of the problems of Judaism and of the Bible, nevertheless engaged in a very important correspondence with Markus Herz (1747-1803), the husband of the famous Henrietta. He had a follower in Salomon Maimon (Salomon ben Joshua, 1754-1800) who achieved some note in the history of philosophy as a critic of the Kantian thing-in-itself which he regarded as an impossible concept *per se* and took it in a Leibnizian sense as a differential of consciousness. With this criticism we see in our discussion for the first time the very pronounced bent of the Jewish philosophical mind toward quanticizing and the mathematical in general. In Lazarus Bendavid (1762-1832) Kant had another devotee who lectured vigorously on his philosophy and conception of religion, but whose influence, like that of David Friedlaender's, was principally directed toward education and reform among the Jewish community.

A somewhat larger audience listened to Otto Liebmann (1840-1912), the reawakener of interest in Kant who also bears out the trend of Jewish thinking in philosophy toward intellectualism in his oft-quoted thesis that correctness of thought consists largely in the precision with which we make distinctions. But the greatest contributions to modern philosophy within the confines of modified Kantianism were made by Hermann Cohen. In him Jewish rationalism celebrated its greatest triumph, for he considered Being and Thought identical, a thing-in-itself completely inadmissible, science to be of the nature of mathematics, religion a thing of reason, and logic pure knowledge. Characteristically, however, he extended his interest to ethics in which he also sought purity for will and feeling. His thinking was vigorous enough to have led to the founding of the so-called Marburg School of Neo-Kantianism whose main protagonist arose later in Ernst Cassirer (1874-1945), the author of the widely read *Substanzbegriff und Funktionsbegriff* which established his fame.

A lesser Neo-Kantian who combines Spinozistic and Schellingian ideas with those of the Königsberger, is Léon Brunschvicg (1869-1944). Also under the ban of Schelling and influenced by Hermann Cohen was Franz Rosenzweig (1886-1929). Related to the spirit of Kant were the *Kant-Studien* known internationally in philosophic circles, whose editorship was, in part, in the hands of Arthur Liebert mentioned previously. In this connection reference might be made to Richard Hönigswald (1875-1947), a humanist in the broadest sense and a Kantian of sorts, and to various others who have furthered or popularized criticism, such as Ernst Marcus (1856-1928), Benzion Kellermann (1869-1923), Hans Israel (1881-   ) who also dealt with the theory of relativity, Julius (Judah) Guttmann (1880-   ), and many more whose contributions to western philosophy were less spectacular than those of Cohen and Cassirer. The study of Kant by Jewish thinkers was furthered also by the edition of his works in Hebrew, done by Juda Junowitsch.

Here, perhaps, is the place to name some Jewish philosophers who had a considerable influence without founding schools. Eduard Gans (1798-1839) was cofounder of the *Jahrbücher für wissenschaftliche Kritik* and, more than that, tried to apply Hegel's categories to some phases of jurisprudence. Hugo Spitzer (1854-1937) is well-known for his contributions to esthetics as well as his tenet that matter possesses some internal organization which develops into consciousness. Jonas Cohn (1869-   ) devoted himself to problems of esthetics which he defined as a critique of value; in epistemology he is regarded as a pupil of the idealist Heinrich Rickert. Emil Lask (1875-1915) has likewise developed Rickert's ideas in the important study in the logic of philosophy and the doctrine of categories, but his work was interrupted by death on the battlefield. Moreover, he is associated with the well-known philosophical journal *Logos* which Richard Kroner (1884-   ) continued later on. The latter, by the way, made significant contributions toward an alignment of scientific and moral concepts.

A number of noted Jewish philosophers have leaned toward the esthetic. To those already mentioned we add Max Dessoir (1867-1947) who had considerable influence with his *Introduction to Philosophy* but more so with his quarterly *Zeitschrift für Aesthetik und allgemeine Kunstwissenschaft*. Emil Utitz (1883-   ) likewise gained recognition for himself with his analysis of esthetic experience.

Georg Simmel (1858-1918), firmly grounded in Kant and Hegel, was an idealist and ethical formalist who believed that spirit created nature. He is better known as a sociologist of some stature. Karl Joël (1864-   ) taught in Basel and his name is associated with German Neo-idealism, and particularly with that of Rudolf Eucken. Anna Tumarkin (1875-   )

taught in Bern and established her reputation with her work on Herder, Kant and Spinoza.

If the Marburg School made a decided impression upon modern western philosophy, the phenomenological school made one perhaps even more profound. It too had a Jew as its founder, Edmund Husserl (1859-1938), of Freiburg. Phenomenology has had a history of nearly two hundred years, but in its formulation by Husserl as an eidetic, transcendental science it had its antecedents principally in Kant, Hegel, Bolzano and Franz Brentano. However, abroad, where Husserl founded the influential *Jahrbuch für Philosophie und phänomenologische Forschung,* and in the United States, where phenomenologists publish the *Journal of Philosophy and Phenomenological Research,* phenomenology has taken many different turns. Among the more prominent pupils of Husserl's are Moritz A. Geiger (1880-1937), Adolf Reinach (born 1883, killed in World War I), and Max Scheler (1874-1928). The latter became the head of the Köln School. Alfred Brunswig (1877-1927) was likewise a follower of Husserl; he endeavored to synthesize psychology and pure logic.

In following through the purely rationalistic, intellectualistic, mathematical strain of Jewish thinking we should mention those who have attained to international fame, beginning perhaps with Ferdinand Eisenstein (1823-1852) and his theory of complex numbers, and Russian-born Georg Ferdinand Ludwig Philipp Cantor (1845-1918) who taught in Halle, Germany, and laid anew the foundations of mathematical analysis and established the theory of transfinite numbers. In his mathematics of infinity he chose the Hebrew letter aleph as the symbol for a class of transfinite numbers. Cantor, along with others in the field of mathematics, opened up significant prospects for the development of logic and particularly mathematical and symbolic logic in which field much work has been accomplished by contemporary Jewish thinkers. Inasmuch as the borderline between physics and the philosophy of science is seldom sharply drawn, we should mention once again in this paragraph Albert Einstein, and besides him Hermann Minkowski (1864-1909), Max Born (1882-   ), Ludwig Silberstein (1872-1948), Tullio Levi-Civita (1873-1941), Philipp Frank (1884-   ), and Emile (Ariel) Meyerson (1859-1933) who, in his more philosophical writings, placed himself definitely into the camp of realism, a rather exceptional affiliation. The latter also is noted for his philosophical interpretation of the theory of relativity. Many a Jewish philosopher pursued some profession besides speculating, as did the lens-grinder Spinoza. Of examples of recent times we mention Israel Wolf Vladislaus Asch (died in 1928) who was chemist and philosopher, and Jacob Block (died in 1923), who was both surgeon and professor of philosophy in Kansas City, Missouri.

Before mentioning other stray philosophers who have exerted an influence in western philosophy, it is well to point out another current in Jewish thinking, antithetical to the intellectual one, which tends towards the biological and psychological. Here the name of Henri Louis Bergson (1859-1941) stands out above all others. His work *Creative Evolution* attained great popularity and laid the foundation for a spiritualism and a skepticism with regard to intelligence to comprehend life and organic forms. The soul balks at the mathematical comprehension of reality, at materialistic naturalism. His intuitionism and panvitalism, however, did not find too many defendants, and one of his most eloquent antagonists was the prolific essayist Julien Benda (1867-   ).

With Bergson we have made the transition to the psychological, coming full circle back to man who has always been the concern of Jewish thinkers. But in psychology it is no longer man writ large, but simply man. The psychologizing tendency, as a conscious or instinctive reaction against extreme intellectualism fostered by most post-Kantians as well as by the admirers of the logico-mathematical method, made itself felt in many a philosopher. We shall name only those who have not gone all out for the experimental or psychiatric.

[863]

Heymann (Khayim) Steinthal (1823-1899) and Moritz Lazarus (1824-1903) are known as the founders of psychological ethnology or *Völkerpsychologie,* a branch of psychology greatly developed later by Wilhelm Wundt, but their researches into language, myth and custom morality led them into the philosophical. Steinthal was a Herbartian, and in his ethics he maintained that "objective" feelings possess absolute value. Lazarus in his studies acknowledged that it is ideas which work in history; his philosophy of history is idealistic throughout.

Ludwig Stein (1859-1930), who wrote extensively also under the pseudonym Diplomaticus, the founder and editor of the *Archiv für systematische Philosophie* and the *Archiv für Geschichte der Philosophie* as well as the editor of the *Bibliothek für Philosophie* and the *Berner Studien zur Philosophie und ihrer Geschichte,* devoted himself to demonstrating that criticism, in Kant's sense, if it is to survive, must somehow incorporate the concepts of Darwinian evolution. The unity of the self or I must mirror the unity of the cosmos in which God is conceived in a dynamic pantheism as the energy of the universe. Man is not free as a creature of nature, but, as a being establishing a civilization, he is. Thus, in history, we perceive psychical factors at work. History exhibits tendencies, not natural laws, and sociology is essentially philosophy applying the psychogenetic and historical method. Here again, society is conceived as an ethical endeavor teleologically and voluntaristically conditioned.

Heinrich Gomperz (1873-   ) is related in his thinking to Avenarius. The name of his system, panthempirism, suggests a purely psychological introspection which reduces the concepts of substance, identity, relation and form to feelings. The *Philosophy of War in Outline,* which achieved popularity in Germany, is also a work of his. He was the son of Theodor Gomperz (1832-1912), the translator of John Stuart Mill who was, however, better known as a Greek scholar, historian of Greek philosophy and decipherer of the Herculaneum papyri.

Oskar Kraus (1874-1942) had, at first, a decided influence upon the philosophy of law and economics to which he applied the psychology of Franz Brentano whose work he edited. He became not only a champion of the cause against positivism but even more significantly developed a critical attack upon the theory of relativity. In this he was rather much alone among Jewish philosophers. Other followers of Brentano are Hugo Bergmann (1883-   ), Max Brod (1884-   ) and Felix Weltsch (1884-   ). Perhaps Christian von Ehrenfels (1859-1932) should be named among Brentano's pupils, although he may be regarded more properly a pupil of Meinong's. He is usually regarded as the father of the Gestalt school in psychology. Before he devoted himself entirely to the ethics of the sexual life, he contributed much to the theory of value and the development of an evolutionary ethics. His following was considerable.

Hugo Münsterberg (1863-1916) is a big name not only in psychology but also in philosophy in that he strove for a synthesis of Fichte's moral idealism with physiological psychology. In epistemology he could be classed with the Marburg School. The world of physics and psychology is of a derivative nature, produced by the activity of mind upon that which is given in experience. Louis William Stern (1871-1938) is perhaps better known as a psychologist and, as inventor of the I. Q., a pioneer in the testing of intelligence, but in philosophical circles he is associated with the doctrines of pantelism and critical personalism. He belongs, properly, to the idealistic school also. Another famous name is Alfred Binet (1857-1911), the professor at the Sorbonne, who was among the first to apply measurement to intelligence.

By contrast we mention Eugenio Rignano (1870-1930) whose Neo-Lamarckism combines with a psychological interpretation of reason and a biological basis of memory. As editor of *Scientia,* which serves an international audience, he attained a name far beyond the borders of Italy. In England, Samuel Alexander (1859-1938) rose to fame with his work

entitled *Space, Time and Deity* in which he represents a species of neorealistic point of view. He draws upon the findings
of physics as well as recent developments in other sciences.
Deity is an emergent, something novel which is brought into
being by a nisus tending toward new and higher levels above
mind. In both these thinkers various elements meet and the
basically ethical orientation is somewhat obscured.

If any psychological school has attained to prominence in
philosophy as well by virtue of a Jewish thinker it is the Neo-
Friesian School whose main representative was Leonard Nelson
(1882-1927). Jacob Friedrich Fries had interpreted Kant psychologically in that he considered all knowledge a psychic
function. This thesis was upheld by Nelson who denies that
knowledge carries objective validity or consists in judgments.
There is, likewise, no epistemological basis for ethics. All
our moral concepts are given. Everything is psychologically
grounded. In his philosophy of law he established a juridical
criticism. Pure psychologism is the avowed tendency of this
school which Nelson, who taught at Göttingen, brought to a
new high. Several among his followers were also Jewish,
Kurt Grelling among them.

It is not necessary to point out that the writings of a large
number of Jewish psychologists contain much matter of interest to the philosopher. To those already alluded to we add
some of the leaders in the important *Gestalt* group, Max
Wertheimer (1880-1943) and Kurt Koffka (1886-1941, Jewish on his mother's side) who, together, founded the journal
Psychologische Forschung, David Katz (1884-   ), Otto
Lipmann (1880-1933), Kurt Lewin (1890-1947), who came
forward with a criticism of Hans Driesch and coined the term
genidentity, and Alfred Adler (1870-1937) of "inferiority
complex" fame and founder of the individual psychology
school. Josef Breuer (1842-1925), who has sometimes been
credited with the discovery of the psychoanalytical method,
and Sigmund Freud (1856-1942), the master and philosopher
of the art, have influenced philosophy in many respects, also

in the theory of the levels of consciousness and symbolism. Joseph Jastrow (1863-1944), the professor of psychology at the University of Wisconsin, is well-known by his philoso-phizings in professional and other circles.

Jews, ever since the diaspora, have been physicians of note and the profession of being a minister to the bodily ailments invariably entailed also ministration as *Seelenarzt*. Hence it is not surprising that many of the Jewish philosophers who are named in this article were also practicing physicians. Being in positions of trust and respect, their influence can be fathomed to a degree.

Three names of editors, typical of the internationalism of all the movements initiated by Jewish thinkers, should not be forgotten, as the articles which they printed were frequently more philosophical than psychological in character: Charles Samuel Myers (1873-   ), editor of the *British Journal of Psychology,* Ignace Meyerson (1888-   ), editor of *Journal de Psychologie,* and Alfred Adler, already mentioned, who edited the *Zeitschrift für Individualpsychologie.*

The borderland of parapsychology, with emphasis also on the speculative and metaphysical in occultism, has been fructi-fied by many Jewish thinkers and the *Zeitschrift für kritischen Okkultismus und Grenzfragen des Seelenlebens,* established by Richard Baerwald (1867-   ), is symptomatic of the dar-ing of many of the Jewish philosophers with which they pry into the controversial. Max Dessoir likewise occupied himself with these problems. In Levi Oscar Kuhns we get a treatment of the transcendental, the infinite and the unseen in a popular form.

This leads us to the prelogical whose main expounder was Lucien Lévy-Bruhl (1857-1939) and who has made basic contributions to our understanding of primitive mentality. Through his editorship of the *Revue Philosophique* he be-came influential in the field of philosophy, while as sociolo-gist and anthropologist he is mentioned in every textbook in these sciences. As a matter of fact he continued the school founded by another Jew, David Émile Durkheim (1858-1915) whose theory of the collective mentality of groups as well as other ideas have recognized ethical significance. Only one more name shall be added here, and that is René Worms, editor of the *Revue Internationale de Sociologie,* whose definition of society as a superorganism has both scientific and philosophic implications. Ideologically, the theories of Franz Boas (1858-1942), the anthropologist, had the greatest moral significance in recent discussions of politics and racism.

At this juncture it is well to recall that the core of Jewish thinking is ethical. The list of names of Jewish thinkers in the field of ethics could be extended considerably to include not only the already mentioned Moritz Lazarus, but Emil Fuchs (1874-   ), Rudolf Goldscheid (1870-1932), Heinrich Ehrenberg, Otto Weininger (1880-1903), the somewhat psychopathic author of the much-discussed work *Geschlecht und Charakter,* Moritz Goldstein (1880-   ), Max Brahn (1873-   ), a pupil of Wundt, Bernhard Münz (1856-1919) who made pre-Socratic ethics one of his fields of research, and Gerardus Heymans (1857-1930) who endeavored to introduce an empirical, analytical method into ethics. Leon Roth (1896-   ) who made contributions to our understanding of Spinoza, Descartes and Maimonides, also wrote on morals, expressing a skepticism as to the reconciliation of science and ethics. In America especially we could mention many a textbook writer not only in ethics but in philosophy as well, Nathan Krass (1879-   ), A. S. Rappaport and Grace F. Landsberg among the earlier ones; but the influence of this type of literature is not always in the direction of new ideas in the field. An exception might, however, be made of such men as Moritz Schlick (1882-1936) of the Viennese circle who is coming into his own in America through English translations.

We must not omit reference to the editors of some well-known ethical journals and leaders of widely-known ethical and pedagogical movements. David Koigen (1879-1939) was the founder, together with F. Schneersohn, of the quarterly

Ethos, a periodical which always tended to take in the broader cultural and even political developments in addition to the strictly ethical ones. More on the philosophical side is the *Revue de Métaphysique et de Morale* which was edited by the Jew Xavier Léon (1868-1935) who also became editor of the bulletin for the French philosophical society. In the Ethical Culture Movement, whose founder was Felix Adler whom we mentioned earlier, ethics joins with religion and becomes a powerful drive toward social reform. This tendency is particularly noticeable in William Taussig, the Ethical Culture leader of St. Louis, Missouri, who died in 1913 at the age of 87. In the widely-read columnist Walter Lippmann (1889-   ) whose *Preface to Morals* is a must for intellectuals, ethics and politics come together in a vigorous synthesis. The decided tendency toward a pure ethicism freed of all religious admixtures, was considered by Ahad Haam, pseudonym for Asher Ginzberg (1856-1927), the very soul of Jewish nationalism. The Dutch philosopher Leonard Polak (1880-1942) devoted himself to promoting free thought as the natural consequence of an ethical activism.

To the reader it must become obvious that the majority of the Jewish thinkers mentioned are in the idealistic camp, that their problems are those of an ideal community in which freedom and tolerance are supreme. Ludwig Stein once pointed out that in F. A. Lange's *History of Materialism* there is not listed a single Jew of eminence and that if there is any united front among Jewish philosophers, it is that against materialism. The individual religious attitude is not so much one of dogmatism, of harping on conservative points of view, nor driving toward absolutism or overstressing faith. Already Mendelssohn maintained, as we have noted, that the Jewish religion is less revealed doctrine than it is revealed legislation. This being so, the spirit of free enquiry was never curbed while a critical attitude could develop unimpeded. Reasoning *a priori* took the place of revelation.

[869]

However, in the philosophy of Bergson we see a dynamism come to the fore in the conception of the *élan vital*, which is also apparent in Einstein's concept of relativity and in Freud's unconscious and subconscious drives. Here is to be sought the origin not only of the reaction against rationalism, but of irrationalism itself. It would, indeed, be surprising if Jewish thinking had not taken this turn in view of Jewish collective social and economic experience. The abiding never had any place in Jewish life—*omnis determinatio est negatio*. The Ahasuerus nature influenced Jewish thinking in seeking forever the answer to a perpetual whither. It is prophetic, and in the striving for the place of rest becomes revolutionary and negative. Thus, Jewish thinking became quite naturally the focus of radical and even revolutionary thinking.

It is somewhat strange that the highly abstract and idealistic philosophy of Hegel should have become the breeding ground for radicalism. It was Ferdinand Lassalle (1825-1864), the Jewish thinker who had written creditably on Heraclitus the Dark, who applied Hegelian development to the economic and social reality and discovered the moving principle of the dialectic not in the quivering, fluctuating shades of thought experienced by Hegel, but in the class struggle, and thus became the father of German socialism. Karl Marx (1818-1883) at last worked out a consistent social philosophy which, in being based on historic materialism, makes him the one great exception to the rule that Jewish speculators do not incline to materialism. He repudiated, together with Friedrich Engels (1820-1895), his collaborator and fellow anticapitalist, all philosophy as a purely intellectual pursuit. All three agreed that philosophy should change the world in a material way. Indeed, no philosophy has had such world-shaking power as that incorporated in the *Communist Manifesto* and *Das Kapital*. There were other Jewish thinkers who, like Max Adler (1873-1937) gilded Marxism with idealism, or, like Boris Stolpner (died 1937) mingled Marxism and religion, or, like Siegfried Marck (1889-   ),

Louis B. Boudin and Heinrich Levy-Suhl, made comparisons with Hegelianism or treated Marxism from yet other points of view. V. G. Simkhovitch (1874-   ) contrasted Marxism and socialism. Dov Ber Borochov (1881-1917) campaigned for Zionism on the basis of Marxism and interpreted the fate of the Jewish people in terms of class struggle and victims of the conditions of production. In this connection reference should be made to Sidney Hook (1902-   ), the Marx interpreter and professor at the College of the City of New York.

This is not the place to discuss David Ricardo (1772-1823), known in economics as the author of the law of diminishing return and the theory of free competition, or Walter Rathenau (1867-1922) with his radicalism in political economy, or the noted sociologist and political economist Franz Oppenheimer (1864-1943), author of *The State*, or Joseph Fels (1854-1914), Harold J. Laski (1893-1950), Abraham Epstein (1892-1942), the vigorous advocate of social security, Julius Goldstein (1873-1929), professor of philosophy at Darmstadt, Giorgio del Vecchio (1878-   ), Hans Kelsen (1881-   ), and other social and political thinkers of note whom Judaism has produced. Their number and influence are large, especially if we also include men of the caliber of the well-known economist and political scientist Edwin Robert Anderson Seligman (1861-1939), or the juridical philosophers, such as Benjamin Nathan Cardozo (1870-1938), Louis Dembitz Brandeis (1856-1941), and Felix Frankfurter (1882-   ) who have left their mark indelibly on the legal thinking of this and possibly later generations in America.

Just to indicate the range of Jewish philosophic thinking we shall pick at random a very few philosophers in education, such as Millicent Baum (1863-1943), the well-known Andrew Sloan Draper Junior High School principal and educational adviser to Mayor LaGuardia; Frank Mankiewicz (1872-1941), the reporter who became professor of education at the College of the City of New York; Isaac Leon Kandel (1881-   ), the editor of *School and Society* who in his various activities and writings combines the philosophic spirit with education, and Mortimer Jerome Adler (1902-   ) who preserves great breadth of vision in the field of education, politics and philosophy.

A very interesting experiment was conducted toward the end of the last century by Thomas Davidson, the Scottish philosopher, and continued by William Torrey Harris, the Breadwinners' College for poor Jews in the lower East Side of New York City. Out of this educational venture which was largely based on a thorough study of philosophy, a number of men and women have attained to prominence, one of them being the well-known philosopher and mathematical logician Morris Raphael Cohen (1880-1947).

The name of Morris Cohen calls up that of Ernest Nagel (1901-   ) whose logical studies and work in scientific method are well-known. Rudolf Carnap (1891-   ) with his logical syntax of language, and Otto Neurath (1882-1945), the sociologist and logical empiricist who acted as editor in chief of the *International Encyclopedia of Unified Science,* and Hans Reichenbach (1891-   ); also M. Milhaud who held the position of professor of the history of philosophy in its relation to science, at the University of Paris.

It would seem almost paradoxical in view of the fact that so much of Jewish thinking in philosophy followed rationalistic, intellectualistic or/and ethical channels to find some philosophers worshipping power and egotism, preparing the stage for Nietzsche. It was Paul Rée (1849-1901) who drew the moral conclusions from Darwinism and deterministic science, preaching that it is ignorance to believe in freedom of the will and that the whole of evolution points to an increase in man's antisocial tendencies. When Nietzsche, then, modeled much of his *Genealogy of Morals* on Rée, other Jews became exponents and popularizers of Nietzsche, as the panpsychist Raoul Richter (1871-1912), Paul Mongré, a pseudonym for Felix Hausdorff (1868-1932) and Georg Morris Brandes (born Cohen, 1842-1927). Still others like Max

Brahn, K. Eisner, Henri Lichtenberger (1864-), Daniel Halévy (1872-), Georg Simmel, Oskar Ludwig Levy (1867-), Julius Wilhelm Kaftan (1848-1926), Karl Joël, Leo Shestov-Schwartzmann (1866-1938) who has been called the Nietzsche of Russia, Moritz Kronenberg (1865-), the Kantian idealist and ethical thinker, Ludwig Stein and many more used Nietzsche dialectically. Henry Louis Mencken (1880-) of *American Language* fame, likewise published a *Philosophy of Friedrich Nietzsche*. As in the case of Schopenhauer who also has been popularized by many a Jewish writer, it accords well with Jewish thinking to get away from conventionality and to seek a challenge in morality and ethics.

With this we have touched upon the contributions of Jewish philosophers to historical problems. A number gathered around Wilhelm Dilthey, among them Anna Tumarkin, Georg Misch (1878-), Arthur Stein (1888-) who revived the *Archiv für Geschichte der Philosophie*, and Hugo Krakauer. Others again, like Kurt Sternberg (1885-), adhere to the Marburg School, and still others, like Alexandre Andre Koyré (1892-) belong to Husserl's circle.

Most of our knowledge about Jewish philosophy which we have in the West, particularly as developed during the Middle Ages, we owe practically exclusively to Jewish scholars and historians of philosophy. Solomon Munk, Moritz Eisler (1823-1902), Solomon Schechter (1847-1915), David Kaufmann (1852-1899), Saul Horovitz (1859-1921), Israel Pollock (about 1885-1945), David Neumark, Max Leopold Margolis (1866-1932), Cyrus Adler (1863-1940), Martin Schreiner (1863-1927), Jacob Guttmann (1845-1919), Julius Guttmann, Manuel Joël (1826-1890), Benzion Kellermann, Israel Davidson (1870-1939), Max Seligsohn (1865-), Harry Austryn Wolfsohn, Israel Isaac Efros (1891-), James Pyle Wickersham Crawford (1882-), Isaac Husik (1876-1939), Jacob Lewkowicz, Albert Lewkowitz (1883-), Julius Lewkowitz, Zevi H. Wolf Diesendruck (1890-1940),

Isaak Heinemann (1876-   ), Leo Strauss (1899-   ), Joël
Julian Obermann (1888-   ), Moses Behor Ventura (1893-
    ), Meyer Waxman (1887-   ), Abraham Heschel
(1907-   ), Salo Wittmayer Baron (1895-   )—all have
made significant contributions to the history of philosophy by
throwing light on the development of Jewish thought within
the Jewish community and in dialectics with Greek, Arabian
and Christian philosophy. Others, having published mainly or
exclusively in Hebrew, such as Simon Bernfeld (1860-1940),
Eliezer Isaac Scheinbaum (1853-1928), Nachman Krochmal,
Joseph Klausner (1874-   ), Moses Joseph Glickson (1878-
1939) who, by the way, was a pupil of Hermann Cohen,
Simon Rawidowicz (1897-   ) and Jacob Klatzkin (1882-
1948), did not, of course, exert any appreciable influence because of the language barrier. Special mention, however,
should be made of Martin Buber (1878-   ) who made
known to the West the great movements of Hasidism and
Chassidism.

In the field of Oriental philosophy other than Jewish
should be named a number of Jewish scholars of prominence.
Thus, Otto Strauss (1881-   ) who made a significant contribution to our interpretation of Indian philosophy, as did
the following who remained more strictly within the field of
philology: Isidor Scheftelowitz (1875-1934), Moriz Winter-
nitz (1863-1937), Maurice Bloomfield (1855-1928), Silvain
Lévi (1863-1935), and, more recently, the already mentioned
Heinrich Gomperz. James Darmesteter (1849-1894) was a
great Avesta scholar. Averroës (1126-1198), Gustav Weil
(1808-1889), Ignatz Goldziher (1850-1921), Edward Glaser
(1855-1908), Israel Friedländer (1876-1920), Eugen Mitt-
woch (1876-1942), and Max Joseph Heinrich Horten (1874-
) are big names in the field of Islamic or Arabian phi-
losophy. Richard James Horatio Gottheil (1862-1936), as
Head of the American School of Oriental Research in Jerusalem and particularly as editor of the *Columbia University*

Oriental Series and the *Semitic Study Series,* contributed generally to an understanding of the Oriental mind, and so did Gustav Solomon Oppert (died in 1908), Hartwig Derenbourg (died in 1908), Hugo Gressmann (1877-1927), Morris Jastrow, Jr. (1861-1921), and L. Scherman (1864-1946).

The great service to philosophy that has been rendered by philosophical dictionaries should not be overlooked, especially in view of the fact that if edited by Jewish scholars an international outlook and an appreciation of not only Jewish but generally Oriental philosophy is being helped to the fore. Of dictionaries of philosophy that have received wide popularity should be mentioned those edited by Adolphe Franck (1809-1893), Rudolf Eisler (1873-1926), Fritz Mauthner and Dagobert D. Runes.

The list of influential Jewish philosophers has by no means been exhausted. Some were only of regional importance, as Frédéric Rauh (died 1909) at the University of Paris, Rodolfo Mandolfo at the University of Bologna, or what their names and positions at various colleges and universities throughout the world might be or have been. Others, like Jean André Wahl (1888-   ) who currently interprets existentialism, are becoming gradually known internationally. We have also been sparing with names, such as Michel de Montaigne, Rudolf Stammler and Ilya Metchnikoff, for instance, who were only half Jews. Furthermore, we have avoided mentioning those whom we are not certain of as to their Jewish origin. Especially with reference to American Jewry we found ourselves in a peculiar predicament. For, unless the philosopher has no objection to his being known as a Jew or has not given up his title to be counted among the Jewish community by having accepted baptism and thus been converted to one or the other of the Christian denominations, it would not be well to print his name. Nevertheless, we shall mention at least two well-known men whose influence upon present-day thinking is not inconsiderable: Horace Mayer

Kallen (1882-   ), the editor of William James' unfinished
work and literary executor of Benjamin Paul Blood, and Irwin Edman (1896-   ) who is professor of philosophy at
Columbia University and whose recent books on philosophy
have caught the popular fancy.

BIBLIOGRAPHY

Agus, Jacob B. *Modern Philosophies of Judaism*. New York: 1941.

Baron, Salo Wittmayer. *A Social and Religious History of the
Jews*. New York: 1937. 3 vols.

Baumgardt, David. "Philosophie", in *Jüdisches Lexikon, ein zyklo-
pädisches Handbuch des jüdischen Wissens in vier Bänden*, vol.
IV. Berlin: 1930.

Eisler, R. *Die jüdischen Philosophen des Mittelalters*, 3 vols. Wien:
1878-1883.

Finkelstein, Louis, ed. *The Jews; Their History, Culture, and Religion*. Philadelphia: 5710-1949, vol. 2, chapter 14 by Alexander
Altmann, chapter 15 by Mordecai M. Kaplan.

Gartenhaus, Jacob. *The Influence of the Jews upon Civilization*.
Grand Rapids, Mich.: 1943.

Grunsky, Alfred H. *Einbruch des Judentums in die Philosophie*.
Berlin: 1937.

Guttmann, Julius. *Die Philosophie des Judentums*. München: 1933.

Husik, Isaac. *A History of Jewish Mediaeval Philosophy*. New
York: 1946.

Janowsky, Oscar Isaiah, ed. *The American Jew. A Composite Portrait*. New York: 1942.

Joel, M. "Einfluss der jüdischen Philosophie auf die christliche Scho-
lastik", in *Frankel's Monatsschrift*, IX. Jahrgang: 1860.

Landman, Isaac, ed. *The Universal Jewish Encyclopedia*. New
York: 1939-1940. 10 vols.

Lewkowitz, Albert. *Das Judentum und die geistigen Strömungen
des 19. Jahrhunderts*. Breslau: 1935.

JEWISH PHILOSOPHERS

MUNK, SALOMON. *Philosophie und philosophische Schriftsteller der Juden.* Leipzig: 1852.

NEUMARK, DAVID. *Geschichte der jüdischen Philosophie des Mittelalters.* 2 vols in 3, incomplete. Berlin: 1907-1928.

ROBACK, A. A., *Jewish Influence in Modern Thought.* Cambridge, Mass.: 1929.

ROTH, CECIL. *The Jewish Contribution to Civilization.* Cincinnati, Ohio: 1940.

SINGER, ISIDORE, ed. *The Jewish Encyclopedia.* New York and London: 1925. 12 vols.

STEIN, LUDWIG. *Die Juden in der Philosophie der Gegenwart.* Berlin: 1926.

The Jewish People, Past and Present. New York: 1946, 3 vols.

Index

Authors and Book Titles listed in the Bibliographies appending chapters are not indexed.

A

INDEX

Asser, Tobias, M.—135
assimilation—560, 687, 825, 853
Assyrian—54
Astrachan, Max—222
astrolabe—706
astronomy—230 ff
Astruc, Aristide—553, 806
Astruc, Gabriel—553
atom and energy—256 ff
Auchinleck—771
Auer, Leopold—383
Auerbach, Berthold—559
Auerbach, Jakob—430

Auernheimer, Raoul—637
August the Strong—110
Augustine—841
Aurelius, Marcus—848
Auvergne, William of—851
Avenarius—864
Avendaut—354
avertin—342
Avila, Alfonso de—731
Azkenazi, Salomon N.—111
Azulai, Haym Joseph—707
Azzaijuolo—371
Azziz, Grescion—370, 517

B

Baader, Franz von—850
Bab, Julius—621, 660
Babel, Isaak E.—569
Bacchides—723
Bach, David—401
Bach, Philipp Emanuel—403
Bache, Jules Semon—494
Bacher, R. F.—261, 262
bacillus—308
Bacon, F.—56
Bacon, Roger—3, 7
bacteriology—292, 305 ff., 338, 341, 342
Baeck, Leo—858
Baer, Yitzhak Fritz—854
Baerwald, Richard—867
Baeyer, von, Adolph—271
Baginsky, Adolf—287
Baginsky, Benno—286
Bahya ben Joseph—796
Baiz, Jacob—734
Baker, Max—20, 52, 690
Bakst, Leon—485, 518, 619
Bakunin—681
Balaam—252, 253
Balak—252, 253
Balanchine, George—520
Bales, William—521
Balfour, A. James—313
Balfour declaration — 313, 340, 682, 683, 747, 768
ballet—517, 519, 520, 522, 523
Ballin, Joel—457
Balcon, Michael—618
Bamberger, Louis—263
Bamberger, Ludwig—647, 648, 649
Bamberger, Simon—123, 816

Banach, Stefan—226
Banchieri, Adriano—371
Bandler, Heinrich—383
Banting—291, 326
Banvard, Joseph—20, 37, 38
Barber, Samuel—397
Bar Kochba—701, 726
Barany, Robert—335
Bardach—311
Barker, Evelyn—720
Barnay, Ludwig—579
Barnes, Binnie—608
Barnowsky, Victor—581, 583, 584
Barnum, P. T.—595
Baron, Salo Wittmayer—874
Barrès, Maurice—669, 670
Barrie, James M.—583
Barrios, Daniel Levide—537
Barron, Moses—326
Barrymore, John—614
Barrymores, the—609
Barsauma—420
Bartholdy, Felix Mendelssohn — 384, 386, 802
Bartholomé—478
Bartlett, Washington—800
Bartok—394
Bartolomeo, Fra—456
Baruch, Bernard—121, 122, 269, 752, 815
Baruch, Simon—324
Baruch Foundation—179
Baser, Jacob—789
Basevi, George—483
Basilea, Simone—370
Bassermann, Albert—581, 584
Bassevi, Giacomo—379

INDEX

Bernheimer, Charles Leopold—710
Bernheimer, Stephan—336
Bernshteyn, Sergey—223
Bernstamm, Leopold—476
Bernstein, A.—251, 289, 559
Bernstein, Benjamin A.—222
Bernstein, Felix—211, 229
Bernstein, Heinrich Agathon—711
Bernstein, Henri—555, 578
Bernstein, Herman—546, 700, 717
Bernstein, Julius—289
Bernstein, Leonard—385, 397
Bernstein, Ludwig B.—180
Bernstein, Natan—301
Bertali—379
Berthelot, Philippe—669
Bertholet, Alfred—67
Bertonoff, Deborah—525
Besredka, Alexander—311, 313, 314, 337, 346
Bessels, Emil—709, 710
Bethel—371
Bevan, E. R.—19, 20, 317
Bevin—790
Bewer, J. A.—4
Beyle, Henri—671
Bible—1, 2, 3, 22, 23, 27, 30, 31, 38, 39, 40, 41, 42, 43, 44, 46, 47, 49, 51, 53, 55, 56, 57, 58, 59, 68, 141, 142, 143, 163, 358, 365, 367, 396, 402, 407, 409, 411, 416, 419, 422, 433, 435, 458, 508, 525, 528 ff., 531, 532, 557, 573, 793, 794, 820, 826, 828, 829, 831, 834, 836, 844, 845, 846, 847, 848, 852, 853, 854, 859
Bible, influence of the—5 ff.
Bible of Delft—530
Bible of Queen Sophia—530
Biblical criticism—7, 69
Bibliolatry—837
Bie, Oskar—660
Bieber, Hugo—105 ff., 703 ff.
Bieberbach, L.—225
Billikopf, Jacob—180
Billroth, Theodore—390
Binder, A. W.—398
Binder, Sybille—584
Binet, Alfred—865
Bing, Richard—744
Binger, Louis Gustave—714, 715
biochemistry—304, 323
biology—341

biophysics—323
Birnbaum, Nathan—682
Biro, Lajos—618
Biro, Ludwig—570
Bishop of Fulda—436
Bismarck—647, 648, 649, 650, 651, 662, 665, 680, 687
Bjoernson, Bjoernsterne—660
Black Death—307
Black plague—281, 315
Blackman, P.—274
Blasco Ibañez—612
Blau, Joseph Leon—849
Blech, Leo—384
Blitz, Jekutiel Ben Isaac—530
Blitzstein, Marc—602
Bloch, Claude C.—751
Bloch, Darius—761
Bloch, Ernest—395, 396
Bloch, General—749
Bloch, Jean de—752, 753, 754
Bloch, Leo—490
Bloch, Marcus E.—296, 297
Bloch, Rudolph—546
Block, Jacob—863
Blondel, Charles—81
Blondell, Joan—607
Blood, Benjamin Paul—876
blood factors—339
blood transfusion—339
Bloomfield, Joseph—740
Bloomfield, Maurice—874
Blowitz, Henri Oppert de—717
Blum—671, 683, 684
Blum, Auguste—668
Blum, Isaac A.—220, 226
Blum, Léon—128, 555, 668, 669, 670
Blume, Peter—499
Blumberg, Henry—222
Blumenberg, Hermann—225
Blumenberg, Leopold—742
Blumenfeld, Ralph D.—661, 662
Blumenfeld, Simon—545
Blumenthal, Leonard M.—221
Blumenthal, Oskar—560, 588
Blumenthal, Otto—225
Boas, Franz—711, 868
Boas, Ismar—324
Boccara, Vittorio—235, 236
Bochner, Solomon—221
Bodansky, Artur—385
Bode, Wilhelm—494
Bodin, Jean—69

INDEX

Bukofzer, Manfred—400
Bullard, Arthur—548
Bülow—385
Bunsen—273
Burchardt, Hermann—716
Burckhardt, Jakob—408
Burgoyne—784
burial—445
Burney—379

Burnham—235
Burrows, Millar—35
Bush, George—739
Bush, Lewis—739
Bush, Solomon—739
Byington, E. H.—44
Byk, Alfred—275
Byron—531, 555, 603, 858

C

Cabbala—432, 451, 532, 533
Cabral—706
Caccini—373
Caceres, Simon de—731
Caedmon—54
Cahan, Abraham—546, 700
Cahen, Eugène—220
Cahen, Isidore—806
Cahen, Samuel—529
Cahina, Damia al—728
Cajori, F.—316
Calder, I. M.—46
Calderon—531
calendar—231
Calle, Alonzo della—707
calligraphy—421, 422, 458
Calvin, John—836, 837
Calvinism—836, 837, 838
Campner, S.—123
Canaan, Gilbert—542
Canaanites—819
Canon—831, 832, 847
Cantor, Eddie—604, 612
Cantor, Georg — 204, 205, 206, 207, 208, 209, 215, 220, 228, 229, 316, 862
Cantor, Moritz—212, 213, 224
Capittsa—268
Carcassone, Roger—762
Cardenel, Peire—358
Cardozo, Albert—812, 815
Cardozo, Albert Jr.—813
Cardozo, Benjamin N. — 120, 739, 797, 800, 812, 813, 814, 815, 871
Cardozo, Isaac Nunez—739
Carducci—567
Carlisle, Kitty—608
Carlitz, Leonard—222, 227
Carlyle—56, 194
Carnap, Rudolf—872
Carnovsky, Morris—608

Caro, Heinrich—272
Carol I—115
Carol, Sue—608
Carrion, Santob de—512, 513
Carter, Mrs. Leslie—596
cartographers—356
cartography—458
Caruso—596
Carvallo, Jules—806
Caspary, Adolph—788
Casseres, Benjamin de—698
Cassirer, Paul—494
Cassirer, Ernst—860
Cassius, Dion—725, 726, 727, 784
Castelnuovo, Guido—217, 218, 219
Castelnuovo-Tedesco, Mario—398
Castiglione, Camillo—494
cast medal—478
catacombs—413, 414, 415, 434
Catalan Atlas—705
Catherine II—457
Catholicism—824, 829, 830, 832, 835, 838, 847, 848, 849
Catholic Reformation—835
Cattell, J. McKeen—300
Cavour, Camillo—674
Cavour, Count—134, 674
Cayley, Arthur—213, 215
Cellini, Benvenuto—439
cemeteries—442, 444, 483, 488
ceramics—437
Cerrillo, Fanny—517
Cervetto—379, 389
Cézanne—461
Chagall, Marc—468, 469, 485
Chain, Boris—313, 314
Chain, Ernst B.—343
Chaka—786
Chaldeans, the—721
Chamberlain, Houston S. — 192, 193, 653

[885]

INDEX

INDEX

F

INDEX

H

INDEX

Hamburger, Meyer—212
Hameln, Glückl von—556
Hammerstein, Oscar—608, 609
Hammerstein II, Oscar—609
Hammond, J.—212
Hanagid, Samuel—729
Händel—389, 402, 403
Hannibal—723
Hanslick, Eduard—390
Hanuchim—730
Harby, Isaac—551
Harby, Levi Charles—734
Harby, L. G.—742
Harby, Levi Myers—740
Harden, Maximilian—686, 687, 688
Harding, Warren G.—122
Hardy, Thomas—56
Harkavy, Minna—499
Harlow, S. Ralph—340
Harly, Isaac—595
Haroun al Rashid, caliph—110
Harper, W. R.—25
Harris, David—737
Harris, Frank—610
Harris, M. J.—134
Harris, Sam H.—610
Harris, William Torrey—872
Harrison, Rex—584
Hart, Aaron—738
Hart, Joel—114, 115
Hart, Liddell—768, 776
Hart, Moss—598
Harte, Bret—740
Hartmann, Moritz—559
Hartog, Jan de—606
Hartog, Marcus—298
Hartog, Philip—276
Hartung—384
Harvard, John—22, 23
Harvard college—22, 23, 27, 28, 29, 33
Hasdai Ibn Shaprit—110
Hasenclever, Walter—587, 656
Hasidic dance—506
Hasidic movement—517
Hasidism—874
Haskala—452
"Hatikvah"—700, 701
Hauer, Joseph—393
Hauptmann, Gerhard—660
Hauschner, Auguste—559
Haussdorff, Felix—211, 872
Hauser, Mischa—382

Havdallah—163
Hawkins—731
Hayem, George—324
Hayes, Isaac Israel—709
Haymann, Julius—616
Hays, Isaac—321
Hays, Jacob—114
Hays, John—114
Hay's Journal—321
Hayya, Abraham bar—356
Hearst, William Randolph—603
Hebbel—531, 651
Hebraeus, Leo—369, 859
Hebrei, Samuel—371
Hebrew — 352, 354, 357, 358, 360, 432, 534, 557, 565, 833, 837
Hebrew language—1, 2, 3, 7, 8, 18; early popularity of—21 ff., 34, 37, 53, 54, 55, 56, 58, 59, 60, 208, 283
Hebrew prophets — 63, 64, 72, 82. (See prophets)
Hebrew proverbs—65
Hebrew spirit—36
Hebrews, the—365
Hebrew University—210, 227, 244
Hecht, Ben—549, 600, 606, 698
Hecht, Selig—304
Hecker, Julius F.—98
Hedin, Sven—713
Hegel — 70, 72, 73, 629, 633, 670, 671, 852, 853, 858, 861, 862, 870
Heidegger—72
Heidelberger, Michael—278
Heidenhain, Martin—287
Heidenhain, Rudolf P. H.—287
Heifetz, Jascha—383, 523
Heijermans, Herman—539, 590
Heilbron, I. M.—276
Heilbronner, Raoul—494
Heilprin, Angelo—710
Heilprin, Michael—734
Heimann, Moritz—564
Heine, Heinrich—386, 455, 459, 542, 545, 549, 551, 558, 566, 625, 631, 632, 633, 634, 649, 656, 692, 708, 848
Heine, Th. Th.—473
Heinemann, Isaak—874
Heins, M. H.—221
Helfman, Max—385
Hellenism—826
Hellman, George Sidney—548

[895]

INDEX

I

INDEX

M

INDEX

Massarano, Joacchino—370, 372
Massary, Fritzi—585
Massena—737, 738
Masserman, Paul—20, 52, 690, 699
Massias, Abraham A.—740
materialism—869, 870
mathematical periodicals—224
mathematical physics—242 ff.
mathematics—202 ff., 356, 862
mathematics, philosophy of—229 ff.
Mather, Cotton — 17, 18, 20, 21, 30, 33, 57
Mather, Increase—24
Mather, Richard—22
Mathieu 'le Juif' in France—358
Matisse, Henri—465
Mattos, Teixeira de—226
Maunier, Rene—82
Maurros—670
Maurois, André—555, 673, 678
Mauss, Marcel—81
Mauthner, Fritz—858, 875
Maxwell—237, 238, 747
May, Joe—616
May, Paul—135
May, Pierre—761
Mayer, August L.—493
Mayer, General—749
Mayer, Kathi—401
Mayer, Louis Burt—613
Mayer, Nathan—546
Mayer, Robert—255
Mayer, Sigmund—289
Mayflower Compact—11, 39
Mayhew, Jonathan—49, 50
Mazzini—734
McDougall—85
McKinley, William—116
McMahon—212
McReynolds, James C.—808
medal—478, 479
medal portrait—474
medallists—441
Mediaeval Jewish social thought—67 ff.
medical history—345
medical institutions—346
medicine—284, 288, 356
medicine, modern—319 ff.
Mehring, Walter—588
Meidner, Ludwig—466
Meier, Julius I.—123, 816
Meinhard, Carl—582

Meinong—865
Meis, Leon—761
Meitner, Lise—259, 260, 261, 263, 758
Meldola, Raphael—276
Meltzer, Samuel J.—303, 343, 344
Menassah ben Israel—797
Menasse, Andrea—737
Mencken, H. L.—33, 873
Mendel, Emanuel—331
Mendel, Lafayette B.—278, 327
Mendelsohn, Erich—484
Mendelssohn, Dorothea—853
Mendelssohn, Moses — 68, 386, 441, 456, 530, 541, 542, 556, 557, 558, 802, 853, 858, 859, 869
Mender, Isaac—728
Mendès, Catulle—553
Mendes, Moses—592
Mendès-France, Pierre—128, 129
Menelaus of Alexandria—207
Menhuin, Yehudi—383
Meninger, Karl A.—330
meningitis—331, 338
Menken, Ada Isaac—602, 603
menorah—413, 415, 428, 449
Merck—314
Mer, Gideon—341
Merzbacher, Gottfried—714
Merrick, Leonard—593
Messel, Alfred—484
Messiah—830
metabolism—325
metal work—438
Metcalf, James F.—776
Metchnikoff, Eliè — 308, 309, 339, 346, 875
Metchnikoff, Olga—308
meteorology—230 ff.
Metringer, Jean—470
Meyer, Arthur—673
Meyer, Eugene—122, 698
Meyer, Henry—473
Meyer, K. F.—274
Meyer, Léon—126
Meyer, Lothar—274
Meyer, Ludwig F—327
Meyer, R. J.—274
Meyer, Victor—272, 274
Meyerbeer, Giacomo—387, 388, 389
Meyerhof, Otto—290, 342
Meyerson, Emile—190, 250, 274, 280, 863

N

P

INDEX

population—175, 496, 739, 740, 741, 743, 744, 746, 748, 750, 756, 757, 759, 760, 786, 788, 790
population, Jewish, in the U. S.—168
Porges, Heinrich—384
Porsile—403
Porta, Allegro—372
Portaleone, Leone da Sommi—574
Porter, Cole—601
portrait—456
portrait art—459
positivism—75, 76, 79, 83, 865
Possart, Ernst von—579
Post, Emily—516
Postal, Bernard—787
Potter, Beatrice—166, 167
Powys, J. C.—12, 19
Poznansky, Arthur—710
Praag, Siegfried Emanuel van—540
Prager, W.—221, 227
pragmatism—855, 856
Pressburger, Arnold—618
Prince Hardenberg—732
Prince Henry—705
Prince, Thomas—17
Princeton College—27
Pringsheim, Alfred—211, 293
Pringsheim, Ernest—293

Pringsheim, Nathaniel—293
Priscus—109
Procopius—728
Prokofief—523
Prophets, the — 145, 150, 162, 821, 824, 826, 830, 831, 845. (See Hebrew prophets)
Protestantism—835, 838, 847, 848
Proust, Marcel—669
Proverbs—66
Psalms — 14, 22, 25, 28, 29, 30, 55, 59, 162, 402
psychiatry—330
psychoanalysis—332
psycho-neuroses—332
Ptolemaeus—422
public health—327, 340, 341, 346
Puccini, Giacomo—596
Pugliese, Umberto—750, 755
Puiseux—234
Pulitzer, Joseph—494, 621, 694, 695
Puritans—3, 9, 10, 11, 12, 13, 14, 15, 16, 17, 18, 21, 27, 29, 30, 34, 35, 36, 37, 38, 42, 43, 44, 48, 56, 57, 58
Purkinje—293
Pythagorean movement—819

Q

quadrant—706
Quakerism—58
Quakers—3
Queen Mary—583

Queen Louise—456
Queen Victoria—662
Querido, Israel—539
Qur'an—834

R

Rabbinowitsh, Joseph—568
Rabi, Isidore Isaac—264, 265, 758
'Rabi Zag'—358
Rabin, C.—283
Rabinovich, Ossip Aaronovich—676
Rabinovitch, Michael—756
Rabinovitch, Y. L.—223
Rabinowitz Foundation, Louis M. — 798
racial characteristics—822
Racine—531
Rack, H. Thomas—60
Radanites, the—704
Radin, Max—99
Radin, Paul—102, 711
Rádl, Emanuel—300, 317

Raffael—372
Raimund—651
Rainer, Luise—584, 613
Raisman, Abraham J.—133
Raiziss, G. W.—278
Raleigh, Walter—785
Rambert, Marie—518
Raphael—456
Rappaport, A. S.—868
Rappoport, Salomo Jehuda—852
Rashi—357, 358
Rathaus, Karol—398
Rathenau, Walther — 564, 686, 687, 688, 744, 871
Ratner, Isaac—763
Rauh, Frédéric—875

INDEX

Roosevelt, Franklin D. — 118, 119, 120, 121, 122, 124, 178, 683, 684, 697, 809
Roosevelt, Theodore—116, 172, 441, 496, 595, 743
Root, Elihu—808
Rosa, Moses Duarte Lopez—537
Rosanes, Jacob—210
Rosanoff, M. A.—278
Rosè, Arnold—383
Rose, Billy—611
Rose, Louis—801
Rose, Maurice G.—757
Rose, Maximilian—291
Rosen, Joseph—296
Rosenbach, J. B.—222
Rosenbach, Ottomar—323
Rosenberg, A. H.—789
Rosenberg, Anna—816
Rosenberg, Isaac—545
Rosenberg, Jacob—493
Rosenberg, Marc—492
Rosenberg Foundation—179
Rosenblatt, Alfred—214, 223
Rosenfeld, Morris—701
Rosengarten, Albert—482
Rosenhain, J. G.—208
Rosenman, Samuel I.—120, 816
Rosenau, Milton J.—339, 340
Rosenroth, Christian Knorr von—533
Rosenstock, Joseph—385
Rosenthal, Arthur—222
Rosenthal, Charles—476
Rosenthal, Isidor—287
Rosenthal, Jacques—495
Rosenthal, Karl August—400
Rosenthal, Moriz—383
Rosenwald, Hans—400
Rosenwald, Julius—179, 180
Rosenwald Foundation—179
Rosenzweig, Franz—530, 562, 860
Ross, Barney—757
Ross, E. A.—101
Rossi, Aasarja dei—565
Rossi, Salomone—372, 373, 374, 391

Rössler, Carl—561
Rostand—609
Roth, Cecil — 19, 183, 349 ff., 627, 628, 634, 785, 788
Roth, Joseph—563
Roth, Leon—317, 868
Rothenberg, Meyer—789
Rothenstein, John—493
Rothenstein, Sir William—463, 493
Rothschild, Lionel Nathan de—603
Rothschild, Lionel W.—298
Rothschild, Mayer A.—110
Rothschild, Nathaniel C.—298
Rothschilds—494
Rousseau—70
Rovighi, Cesare—674
Rowe, Leo S.—121
Roy, W. L.—2, 4
Royce, Josiah—799, 848
Rozental, Joseph—302
Rubensen, Robert—236
Rubinow, I. M.—180
Rubinstein, Anton—383
Rubinstein, Artur—383
Rubinstein, Harold Frederick—543
Rubinstein, Ida—518
Rubinstein, Nicholas—383
Rudolph II—108
Rudolf of Hapsburg—107
Ruedenberg, Rheinhold—241
Runes, Dagobert D.—875
Runyon, Damon—696, 697
Ruskin—56
Russell, Bertrand—205, 206
Russell Sage Foundation—170
Russia—75, 98, 118, 119, 135, 136, 173, 203, 223 ff., 277, 296, 301 ff., 675, 676, 679, 685, 733, 735, 736, 749, 750, 753, 756, 757
Ruteboeuf—358
Rutgers University—27, 314 ff.
Ruthenberg, Pinchus—787
Rutherford, Ernest—257
Ryback, Issachar—469

S

Saalschütz, Louis—211
Sabbath — 16, 36, 37, 38, 146, 836, 838
Sachs, A.—261, 758
Sachs, Curt—400, 510, 517, 520
Sachs, Julius—292, 293, 300, 342

Sachs, Michael—558
Sacks, B.—325
Sackur, O. W.—275
sacrifices—150
Saenger, Max—333
Sagher, F.—333

INDEX

INDEX

INDEX

[919]

INDEX